EDITED BY *John T. Flanagan*

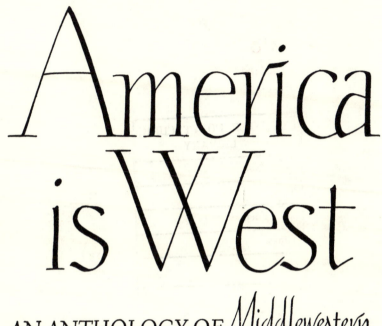

America
is West

AN ANTHOLOGY OF *Middlewestern*
Life and Literature

GREENWOOD PRESS, PUBLISHERS
WESTPORT, CONNECTICUT

From the Heartland

THE subject of this book is the heartland of America, the region loosely called the Middle West and somewhat arbitrarily defined as the twelve states of Ohio, Indiana, Illinois, Michigan, Wisconsin, Minnesota, Iowa, Missouri, Nebraska, Kansas, and the two Dakotas. Geologically this region is ancient, but its human history and consequently its literary record are comparatively recent. Probably red men from the continental interior caught fish at Mackinac Island or dug in the red pipestone quarry of southwestern Minnesota ages before De Soto first saw the Mississippi. Little more than three centuries have elapsed since Jean Nicolet donned his mandarin robe to surprise the Winnebagoes on the shores of Green Bay and even less time since La Salle descended the great river and Hennepin named a waterfall in honor of his patron saint, Anthony of Padua. It is not two centuries ago that enormous fur canoes skimmed the coast of Lake Superior and *voyageurs* gathered in their wild annual reunions at Grand Portage. Of the twelve states comprising the Middle West, only four have as yet celebrated their centenary of statehood. The first to join the Union, Ohio, was admitted in 1803; the last, North Dakota and South Dakota, entered jointly in 1889.

Over parts of the great midcontinent four flags have flown, the ensigns of France, Spain, and Great Britain all having anticipated the Stars and Stripes. Men from all corners of the world, men of mixed blood and diverse creeds, have helped to civilize the former empire of Indian and fur trader. From every European nation have poured people seeking a home west and north of the Ohio. Today the citizens of the Middle West, heterogeneous and polyglot, comprise the most multifarious population in the world.

Generations have passed since the midcentury spate of settlement, and the true pioneer has long since gone the way of the buffalo and the passenger pigeon. But the traits of character peculiar to the American frontier have persisted and dominate the literature of the region which the pioneer opened to civilization: individualism, self-reliance, a practical materialism, scepticism of custom and tradition unless rooted in common sense, political intransigence, an isolationism explained and heretofore justified by the geographical barriers and the almost antagonistic apathy of the Old World.

Nearly three hundred years have passed since what may well be called the first middlewestern book, Louis Hennepin's *Description de la Louisiane*, was written in French and published in Paris. But two centuries after the Recollect friar described his captivity on the shores of Mille Lacs Lake in northern Minnesota there were few permanent settlements along the Mississippi. A new country turns to self-expression only after the more pressing needs of food and shelter have been satisfied. Yet the Middle West has had literary spokesmen from the days of Daniel Drake, Timothy Flint, and James Hall to those of Hamlin Garland and Carl Sandburg. Among its writers have been apologists, chauvinists, critics, and always more than its share of rebels; in both self-description and self-deprecation it has been honorably vocal.

Much of the middlewestern literature of the last century was imitative and pedestrian, just as most of the American literature of the Gilded Age was undistinguished and saccharine. But the seeds of realism matured earlier in the Middle West than elsewhere in the country, particularly in the novel of the farm and the small town, and the impetus provided by Mark Twain, Edward Eggleston, Hamlin Garland, Joseph Kirkland, and E. W. Howe accelerated the naturalistic revolt against reticence, conventionality, and prudishness. After 1900 the flood of naturalism both widened and deepened. Theodore Dreiser with clumsy power told the life stories often of people born on the wrong side of the railroad tracks, the underprivileged, the weak and preyed on. Sinclair Lewis, Edgar Lee Masters, Floyd Dell, and Sherwood Anderson dissected the small town with both contempt and sympathy. The verse of Carl Sandburg reveals many facets of life, a rare appreciation of urban beauty mingled with sympathy for the underdog and an acute understanding of industrial life. For the last three decades American literature has been primarily the story of these men and their successors. Dreiser, Lewis, Anderson, Sandburg, Masters, Dell, with younger writers like Ruth Suckow and James T. Farrell, have produced the most original, the most vigorous, the most outspoken literature in the nation; their novels and short stories, their verse and autobiographies, have been the models and examples for several literary generations. Dreiser is still one of the American writers best known abroad, and Sinclair Lewis was awarded the Nobel prize—the first such award made to an American author—largely for a novel which reflected with humorous bitterness the life of an average businessman in a middlewestern city.

The ideal middlewestern writer is either one born in the north central section of the continent and by virtue of environment and education imbued with its spirit, or one who by long residence, especially in his formative years, has become an integral part of the land of his adoption and is particularly fitted to describe its people and voice its point of view. There is no better example than William Allen White, the sturdy Kansas editor who became a national figure despite a consistent loyalty to his country town daily. Conservative, friendly, forthright, vigorously independent, almost puritanical in his opposition to some of the vagaries of sophistication, White stood for the small businessman, the independent farmer, the wage earner, the housewife, the provincial minister and teacher and journalist, the American way of life. Equally far removed from big business and tenant farming, from Hollywood aesthetes and Broadway playboys, White championed individualism, a simple, unpretentious way of life which the settlers of the early Middle West had followed the sun to achieve. If his own writing lacked artistry and charm, often wanting in middlewestern literature as a whole, it possessed ample candor and strength, qualities again that typify the region for which White served as spokesman.

In this book are the writings of natives and residents alike, and also the writings of neither. The earliest men to picture what is now the Middle West were visitors from Europe or from the Atlantic seaboard, most of whom had only a cursory interest in the land of their travels. Yet we are indebted to Louis Hennepin and Jacques Marquette, to Jonathan Carver, to Alexander Henry for vivid narrative and description. The travelers who succeeded them were more closely identified with the region, remained longer, penetrated more deeply into the way of life they found. By the early nineteenth century books were being produced by men like Henry Rowe Schoolcraft who had come to settle permanently in the old Northwest Territory, and by 1850 native-born writers of the region were expressing themselves in verse and prose. The early establishment of magazines gave to these authors both a stimulus and an organ of publication. Before the Civil War Timothy Flint's *Western Monthly Review,* James Hall's *Western Monthly Magazine,* and William D. Gallagher's *Hesperian* flourished in Cincinnati and encouraged native authorship. Subsequently Francis Fisher Browne's *Lakeside Monthly* and the *Dial* brought to Chicago the leadership in periodical publication which Cincinnati had relinquished, and the *Midland Monthly* of Des Moines was a creditable attempt to foster regional self-awareness. In the twentieth century John T. Frederick's *Midland* was for eighteen years a valuable aid to promising young authors; and both Harriet Monroe's *Poetry* and Lowry C. Wimberly's *Prairie Schooner* continue to encourage middlewestern literature, although neither is limited to regional writing.

The story of the literary and artistic culture of the Middle West is happily incomplete. Much has already been achieved and the accomplishments have not been limited to verbal expression. Museums in Cleveland, Cincinnati, Detroit, Toledo, Chicago, Minneapolis, and Kansas City testify to the popular interest in the plastic arts. The original gifts of such painters as Grant Wood, John Steuart Curry, and Thomas Hart Benton, the most interesting triumvirate in modern American art, have been put to the service of an intelligent regionalism. One of the greatest living architects, Frank Lloyd Wright, has worked for years to devise a style of functional domestic architecture suitable to the Middle West. Creditable symphony orchestras in Cincinnati, Cleveland, Chicago, and Minneapolis have consistently encouraged the work of young native composers and have given their compositions a public hearing. Experimental theaters like the Cleveland Playhouse and the Goodman Memorial Theater of Chicago have done meritorious service in keeping the drama alive outside New York and in trying out the plays of obscure dramatists.

But even these achievements, like the synopsis of the early chapters of a serial story, are pointed toward the future; the best lies ahead. Lincoln Steffens once remarked that the cardinal point in his education was the realization that man's absolute successes were so few and so limited; the greatest books remained to be written, the most epochal inventions were still to be made, the vastest worlds awaited discovery. And what Steffens anticipated for the individual can equally well be predicated for the region and the nation. The cultural apogee of the United States lies in the remote beyond.

In the war-torn days of the 1940's one of the most amazing phenomena has been the unprecedented and compulsory *völkerwanderung* in Europe, a migration precipitated by the will of dictators and the inroads of conquering armies. The United States too has seen amazing populational shifts as the nation hurriedly answered the calls of industry, agriculture, and selective service. Coincident with such changes has been a concentration of artists and intellectuals in those localities where they can best continue their work and where their very presence has been a spur to the aesthetic life of the community. For such persons the Middle West has proved a special haven and, in return, it has benefited incalculably from their genius. No literature and no art could fail to be enriched by the work of gifted Europeans whose race or creed drove them into exile.

But long before such refugees and expatriates saw the Statue of Liberty gleaming in the mist, and long before directors of eastern seaboard museums began to box and crate their masterpieces for shipment to middlewestern sanctuaries, the great valley was developing a cultural life of its own. *Voyageur* and woodsman and pioneer cleared the way; farmer and immigrant and politician built the superstructure; poet and novelist and painter recorded story and scene—vigorously, freshly, memorably, and often in a new idiom. The impact of these several achievements has been felt outside the boundaries of the nation. Perhaps this anthology will help to explain why.

The task of selection has been both interesting and complex. Middle-western writers today need no apologist, but their predecessors were not always distinguished by originality and artistic excellence. For one Mark Twain or Abraham Lincoln there were numerous authors whose crudity and formlessness are memorable only because of their prox-imity to the life they represented. No modern writer can give the flavor of a camp meeting as well as Peter Cartwright, who participated in many, and no later storyteller or interpreter can be more authentic than Edward Eggleston and Mrs. Kirkland, to whom the past was con-temporary.

Inevitably the reader will find omissions. The pageant of regional life for almost four hundred years can never be confined within the pages of a single volume or perhaps even of a five-foot shelf. In general I have tried to choose complete units and to reprint material from a certain period by authors whose life span synchronized with that pe-riod. Length sometimes proved a barrier. Excerpts from novels have been used only sparingly. Failure to secure the right to reprint has caused the omission of Theodore Dreiser and John G. Neihardt.

Nor have I been guided entirely by my own prejudices and stand-ards. It is a pleasure to acknowledge many helpful suggestions from Professor R. C. Buley of Indiana University, Mr. Franklin J. Meine of Chicago, Dr. Stanley Pargellis of the Newberry Library, Professor Harry Clark of the University of Wisconsin, Dean Theodore C. Blegen of the University of Minnesota, and especially Mrs. Margaret S. Hard-ing, director of the University of Minnesota Press, whose interest and enthusiasm in large measure made possible the appearance of this vol-ume. The attractive format is due to the originality and skill of Miss Jane McCarthy of the University of Minnesota Press.

JOHN T. FLANAGAN

University of Minnesota
March 15, 1945

*This book is affectionately dedicated to
Virginia, Sheila, Moira, and Cathleen—good
middlewesterners all, and proud of it.*

Table of Contents

THE FRONTIER

THE WOODS

THE FARM

THE RIVER

THE SMALL TOWN

THE CITY

MIDDLEWESTERNERS

INTERPRETATIONS

America is West and the wind blowing

ARCHIBALD MACLEISH, *American Letter*

THE GREAT VALLEY

The Egypt of the West

by ABRAHAM LINCOLN, 1809–65. *A biographical note about Lincoln seems all but superfluous, yet a few facts about his life may prove helpful. He was born in Hardin County, Kentucky, the son of an illiterate wandering laborer. The Lincoln family moved to Indiana in 1816 and to Macon County, Illinois, in 1830. Here in the Sangamon River country Lincoln split rails, clerked in a general store, studied law, made friends, and told stories. After participating in the Black Hawk War he was elected to the Illinois legislature in 1834. After a number of years of law practice he served in the United States House of Representatives from 1847 to 1849. In 1858 he was defeated by Stephen A. Douglas in the senatorial contest after a series of memorable debates, but in 1860 he was nominated in Chicago for the presidency on the Republican ticket and triumphed in the following election. Lincoln was reelected in 1864, but only five days after Lee's surrender at Appomattox Court House he was shot and fatally wounded by Booth at Ford's Theater, Washington. Despite his scanty education Lincoln became a master of English prose. The opening selection in this book is excerpted from his second annual address to Congress.*

THE great interior region, bounded east by the Alleghanies, north by the British dominions, west by the Rocky Mountains, and south by the line along which the culture of corn and cotton meets, and which includes part of Virginia, part of Tennessee, all of Kentucky, Ohio, Indiana, Michigan, Wisconsin, Illinois, Missouri, Kansas, Iowa, Minnesota, and the Territories of Dakota, Nebraska, and part of Colorado, already has above ten millions of people, and will have fifty millions within fifty years if not prevented by any political folly or mistake. It contains more than one third of the country owned by the United States—certainly more than one million of square miles. Once half as populous as Massachusetts already is, it would have more than seventy-five millions of people. A glance at the map shows that, territorially speaking, it is the great body of the republic. The other parts are but marginal borders to it, the magnificent region sloping west from the Rocky Mountains to the Pacific being the deepest and also the richest in undeveloped resources. In the production of provisions, grains, grasses, and all which proceed from them, this great interior region is naturally one of the most important in the world. Ascertain from the statistics the small proportion of the region which has, as yet, been brought into cultivation, and also the large and rapidly increasing amount of its products, and we shall be overwhelmed with the magnitude of the prospect presented; and yet this region has no sea-coast, touches no ocean anywhere. As part of one nation, its people now find, and may forever find, their way to Europe by New York, to South America and Africa by New Orleans, and to Asia by San Francisco. But separate our common country into two nations, as designed by the present rebellion, and every man of this great interior region is thereby cut off from some one or more of these outlets—not, perhaps, by a physical barrier, but by embarrassing and onerous trade regulations.

And this is true wherever a dividing or boundary line may be fixed. Place it between the now free and slave country, or place it south of Kentucky or north of Ohio, and still the truth remains that none south of it can trade to any port or place north of it, and none north of it can trade to any port or place south of it, except upon terms dictated by a government foreign to them. These outlets, east, west, and south, are indispensable to the well-being of the people inhabiting, and to inhabit, this vast interior region. Which of the three may be the best, is no proper question. All are better than either; and all of right belong to that people and to their successors forever. True to themselves, they will not ask where a line of separation shall be, but will vow rather that there shall be no such line. Nor are the marginal regions less interested in these communications to and through them to the great outside world. They, too, and each of them, must have access to this Egypt of the West without paying toll at the crossing of any national boundary.

Our national strife springs not from our permanent part, not from the land we inhabit, not from our national homestead. There is no possible severing of this but would multiply, and not mitigate, evils among us. In all its adaptations and aptitudes it demands union and abhors separation. In fact, it would ere long force reunion, however much of blood and treasure the separation might have cost.

Our strife pertains to ourselves—to the passing generations of men; and it can without convulsion be hushed forever with the passing of one generation.

The Middle West

by FREDERICK JACKSON TURNER, 1861–1932. *Turner, one of the greatest of modern American historians, won wide fame by his advocacy of the influence of the frontier upon American history. He was born in Portage, Wisconsin, and was educated at the University of Wisconsin, B.A., 1884, and Johns Hopkins University, Ph.D., 1890. For twenty-five years he taught history at the University of Wisconsin and then from 1910 to 1924 served as professor of history at Harvard University. In 1910 he was chosen president of the American Historical Association. Turner was a prolific writer of articles and books on historical themes. Among his major works are his* Rise of the New West *(1906),* The Frontier in American History *(1920), and* The Significance of Sections in American History *(1932), which was awarded a Pulitzer prize. "The Middle West," one of the essays in* The Frontier in American History, *is an admirable statement of the geographical and economic makeup of the Upper Mississippi Valley.*

AMERICAN sectional nomenclature is still confused. Once "the West" described the whole region beyond the Alleghanies; but the term has hopelessly lost its definiteness. The rapidity of the spread of settlement has broken down old usage, and as yet no substitute has been generally accepted. The "Middle West" is a term variously used by the public, but for the purpose of the present paper, it will be applied to that region of the United States included in the census reports under the name of the North Central division, comprising the States of Ohio, Indiana, Illinois, Michigan, and Wisconsin (the old "Territory Northwest of the River Ohio"), and their trans-Mississippi sisters of the Louisiana Purchase,—Missouri, Iowa, Minnesota, Kansas, Nebraska, North Dakota, and South Dakota. It is an imperial domain. If the greater countries of Central Europe,—France, Germany, Italy, and

Austro-Hungary,—were laid down upon this area, the Middle West would still show a margin of spare territory. Pittsburgh, Cleveland, and Buffalo constitute its gateways to the Eastern States; Kansas City, Omaha, St. Paul-Minneapolis, and Duluth-Superior dominate its western areas; Cincinnati and St. Louis stand on its southern borders; and Chicago reigns at the center. What Boston, New York, Philadelphia, and Baltimore are to the Atlantic seaboard these cities are to the Middle West. The Great Lakes and the Mississippi, with the Ohio and the Missouri as laterals, constitute the vast water system that binds the Middle West together. It is the economic and political center of the Republic. At one edge is the Populism of the prairies; at the other, the capitalism that is typified in Pittsburgh. Great as are the local differences within the Middle West, it possesses, . . . in the history of its settlement, and in its economic and social life, a unity and interdependence which warrant a study of the area as an entity. . . .

The ideals of the Middle West began in the log huts set in the midst of the forest a century ago. While his horizon was still bounded by the clearing that his ax had made, the pioneer dreamed of continental conquests. The vastness of the wilderness kindled his imagination. His vision saw beyond the dank swamp at the edge of the great lake to the lofty buildings and the jostling multitudes of a mighty city; beyond the rank, grass-clad prairie to the seas of golden grain; beyond the harsh life of the log hut and the sod house to the home of his children, where should dwell comfort and the higher things of life, though they might not be for him. The men and women who made the Middle West were idealists, and they had the power of will to make their dreams come true. Here, also, were the pioneer's traits,—individual activity, inventiveness, and competition for the prizes of the rich province that awaited exploitation under freedom and equality of opportunity. He honored the man whose eye was the quickest and whose grasp was the strongest in this contest: it was "every one for himself."

The early society of the Middle West was not a complex, highly differentiated and organized society. Almost every family was a self-sufficing unit, and liberty and equality flourished in the frontier periods of the Middle West as perhaps never before in history. American democracy came from the forest, and its destiny drove it to material conquests; but the materialism of the pioneer was not the dull contented materialism of an old and fixed society. Both native settler and European immigrant saw in this free and competitive movement of the frontier the chance to break the bondage of social rank, and to rise to a higher plane of existence. The pioneer was passionately desirous to secure for himself and for his family a favorable place in the midst of these large and free but vanishing opportunities. It took a century for

4

this society to fit itself into the conditions of the whole province. Little by little, nature pressed into her mold the plastic pioneer life. The Middle West, yesterday a pioneer province, is to-day the field of industrial resources and systematization so vast that Europe, alarmed for her industries in competition with this new power, is discussing the policy of forming protective alliances among the nations of the continent. Into this region flowed the great forces of modern capitalism. Indeed, the region itself furnished favorable conditions for the creation of these forces, and trained many of the famous American industrial leaders. The Prairies, the Great Plains, and the Great Lakes furnished new standards of industrial measurement. From this society, seated amidst a wealth of material advantages, and breeding individualism, energetic competition, inventiveness, and spaciousness of design, came the triumph of the strongest. The captains of industry arose and seized on nature's gifts. Struggling with one another, increasing the scope of their ambitions as the largeness of the resources and the extent of the fields of activity revealed themselves, they were forced to accept the natural conditions of a province vast in area but simple in structure. Competition grew into consolidation. On the Pittsburgh border of the Middle West the completion of the process is most clearly seen. On the prairies of Kansas stands the Populist, a survival of the pioneer, striving to adjust present conditions to his old ideals.

The ideals of equality, freedom of opportunity, faith in the common man are deep rooted in all the Middle West. The frontier stage, through which each portion passed, left abiding traces on the older, as well as on the newer, areas of the province. Nor were these ideals limited to the native American settlers: Germans and Scandinavians who poured into the Middle West sought the country with like hopes and like faith. These facts must be remembered in estimating the effects of the economic transformation of the province upon its democracy. The peculiar democracy of the frontier has passed away with the conditions that produced it; but the democratic aspirations remain. They are held with passionate determination.

The task of the Middle West is that of adapting democracy to the vast economic organization of the present. This region which has so often needed the reminder that bigness is not greatness, may yet show that its training has produced the power to reconcile popular government and culture with the huge industrial society of the modern world. The democracies of the past have been small communities, under simple and primitive economic conditions. At bottom the problem is how to reconcile real greatness with bigness.

It is important that the Middle West should accomplish this; the future of the Republic is with her. Politically she is dominant, as is illustrated by the fact that six out of seven of the Presidents elected since 1860 have come from her borders. Twenty-six million people live in the Middle West as against twenty-one million in New England and the Middle States together, and the Middle West has indefinite capacity for growth. The educational forces are more democratic than in the East, and the Middle West has twice as many students (if we count together the common school, secondary, and collegiate attendance), as have New England and the Middle States combined. Nor is this educational system, as a whole, inferior to that of the Eastern States. State universities crown the public school system in every one of these States of the Middle West, and rank with the universities of the seaboard, while private munificence has furnished others on an unexampled scale. The public and private art collections of Pittsburgh, Chicago, St. Paul, and other cities rival those of the seaboard. . . . There is throughout the Middle West a vigor and a mental activity among the common people that bode well for its future. If the task of reducing the Province of the Lake and Prairie Plains to the uses of civilization should for a time overweigh art and literature, and even high political and social ideals, it would not be surprising. But if the ideals of the pioneers shall survive the inundation of material success, we may expect to see in the Middle West the rise of a highly intelligent society where culture shall be reconciled with democracy in the large.

FOLKLORE AND LEGEND

Addik Kum Maig

by HENRY ROWE SCHOOLCRAFT, 1793–1864. No one in his day knew more about the traditions, history, and culture of the Indians of the Great Lakes region than Henry Rowe Schoolcraft, and no one did more to preserve and record this knowledge. Schoolcraft was born in what is now Guilderland, New York, and studied chemistry and mineralogy at Union College. For some years he studied the manufacture of glass and later traveled extensively in Missouri observing the lead mines. In 1820 he accompanied General Lewis Cass's expedition to the Upper Mississippi region in the capacity of geologist, and in 1832 he led his own expedition to Lake Itasca, the true source of the Mississippi River. For a number of years Schoolcraft was Indian agent at the Sault Ste. Marie and Mackinac Island, in which capacity he became the friend as well as the advisor of the Chippewa. His wife, Jane Johnston Schoolcraft, was the daughter of a famous trader and the granddaughter of the Chippewa chief Waub-o-jeeb. Schoolcraft wrote extensively on various subjects: his Indian poem Alhalla (1843) is in trochaic tetrameter couplets, anticipating the meter of Hiawatha; his Narrative of an Expedition through the Upper Mississippi to Itasca Lake (1834) is a vivid account of a famous journey; his Algic Researches (1839) is one of the first attempts to record the folklore of the Indians; and his History, Conditions and Prospects of the Indian Tribes of the United States (1851–57) is an elaborate ethnological treatise. In addition to his interest in the Indian tribes Schoolcraft was instrumental in promoting the development of education, good government, and historical societies in Michigan. "Addik Kum Maig" is a moral tale reprinted from The Myth of Hiawatha (1856), a later version of Algic Researches.

7

A LONG time ago, there lived a famous hunter in a remote part of the north. He had a handsome wife and two sons, who were left in the lodge every day, while he went out in quest of the animals, upon whose flesh they subsisted. Game was very abundant in those days, and his exertions in the chase were well rewarded. The skins of animals furnished them with clothing, and their flesh with food. They lived a long distance from any other lodge, and very seldom saw any one. The two sons were still too young to follow their father to the chase, and usually diverted themselves within a short distance of the lodge. They noticed that a young man visited the lodge during their father's absence, and these visits were frequently repeated. At length the elder of the two said to his mother:

"My mother, who is this tall young man that comes here so often during our father's absence? Does he wish to see him? Shall I tell him when he comes back this evening?" "Bad boy," said the mother, pettishly, "mind your bow and arrows, and do not be afraid to enter the forest in search of birds and squirrels, with your little brother. It is not manly to be ever about the lodge. Nor will you become a warrior if you tell all the little things you see and hear to your father. Say not a word to him on the subject." The boys obeyed, but as they grew older, and still saw the visits of this mysterious stranger, they resolved to speak again to their mother, and told her that they meant to inform their father of all they had observed, for they frequently saw this young man passing through the woods, and he did not walk in the path, nor did he carry anything to eat. If he had any message to deliver, they had observed that messages were always addressed to the men, and not to the women. At this, the mother flew into a rage. "I will kill you," said she, "if you speak of it." They were again intimidated to hold their peace. But observing the continuance of an improper intercourse, kept up by stealth, as it were, they resolved at last to disclose the whole matter to their father. They did so. The result was such as might have been anticipated. The father, being satisfied of the infidelity of his wife, watched a suitable occasion, when she was separated from the children, that they might not have their feelings excited, and with a single blow of his war-club dispatched her. He then buried her under the ashes of his fire, took down the lodge, and removed, with his two sons, to a distant position.

But the spirit of the woman haunted the children, who were now grown up to the estate of young men. She appeared to them as they returned from hunting in the evening. They were also terrified in their dreams, which they attributed to her. She harassed their imaginations wherever they went. Life became a scene of perpetual terrors. They resolved, together with their father, to leave the country, and com-

8

menced a journey toward the south. After travelling many days along the shores of Lake Superior, they passed around a high promontory of rock where a large river issued out of the lake, and soon after came to a place called PAUWATEEG [Sault Ste. Marie].

They had no sooner come in sight of these falls, than they beheld the skull of the woman rolling along the beach. They were in the utmost fear, and knew not how to elude her. At this moment one of them looked out, and saw a stately crane sitting on a rock in the middle of the rapids. They called out to the bird, "See, grandfather, we are persecuted by a spirit. Come and take us across the falls, so that we may escape her."

This crane was a bird of extraordinary size and great age. When first descried by the two sons, he sat in a state of stupor, in the midst of the most violent eddies. When he heard himself addressed, he stretched forth his neck with great deliberation, and lifting himself by his wings, flew across to their assistance. "Be careful," said the crane, "that you do not touch the back part of my head. It is sore, and should you press against it, I shall not be able to avoid throwing you both into the rapids." They were, however, attentive on this point, and were safely landed on the south shore of the river.

The crane then resumed his former position in the rapids. But the skull now cried out, "Come, my grandfather, and carry me over, for I have lost my children, and am sorely distressed." The aged bird flew to her assistance. He carefully repeated the injunction that she must by no means touch the back part of his head, which had been hurt, and was not yet healed. She promised to obey, but soon felt a curiosity to know where the head of her carrier had been hurt, and how so aged a bird could have received so bad a wound. She thought it strange, and before they were half way over the rapids, could not resist the inclination she felt to touch the affected part. Instantly the crane threw her into the rapids. "There," said he, "you have been of no use during your life, you shall now be changed into something for the benefit of your people, and it shall be called Addik Kum Maig." As the skull floated from rock to rock, the brains were strewed in the water, in a form resembling roes, which soon assumed the shape of a new species of fish, possessing a whiteness of color, and peculiar flavor, which have caused it, ever since, to be in great repute with the Indians.

The family of this man, in gratitude for their deliverance, adopted the crane as their totem, or ancestral mark; and this continues to be the distinguishing tribal sign of the band to this day.

Mon-Daw-Min

by HENRY ROWE SCHOOLCRAFT. The Indian *tales* which Schoolcraft so carefully transcribed frequently resemble the apologue in form and
often explain, at least to the satisfaction of the red men who heard them, the
origin of familiar plants and animals and birds. Typical of these stories is the
explanation of the beginning of Indian corn, reprinted from The Myth of
Hiawatha (1856).

IN TIMES past, a poor Indian was living with his wife and children in a
beautiful part of the country. He was not only poor, but inexpert in
procuring food for his family, and his children were all too young to
give him assistance. Although poor, he was a man of a kind and contented disposition. He was always thankful to the Great Spirit for everything he received. The same disposition was inherited by his eldest
son, who had now arrived at the proper age to undertake the ceremony
of the Ke-ig-uish-im-o-win, or fast, to see what kind of a spirit would
be his guide and guardian through life. Wunzh, for this was his name,
had been an obedient boy from his infancy, and was of a pensive,
thoughtful, and mild disposition, so that he was beloved by the whole
family. As soon as the first indications of spring appeared, they built
him the customary little lodge at a retired spot, some distance from
their own, where he would not be disturbed during this solemn rite.
In the mean time he prepared himself, and immediately went into it, and
commenced his fast. The first few days, he amused himself, in the
mornings, by walking in the woods and over the mountains, examining
the early plants and flowers, and in this way prepared himself to enjoy
his sleep, and, at the same time, stored his mind with pleasant ideas for
his dreams. While he rambled through the woods, he felt a strong desire
to know how the plants, herbs, and berries grew, without any aid from
man, and why it was that some species were good to eat, and others
possessed medicinal or poisonous juices. He recalled these thoughts to
mind after he became too languid to walk about, and had confined himself strictly to the lodge; he wished he could dream of something that
would prove a benefit to his father and family, and to all others. "True!"
he thought, "the Great Spirit made all things, and it is to him that we
owe our lives. But could he not make it easier for us to get our food,
than by hunting animals and taking fish? I must try to find out this in
my visions."

On the third day he became weak and faint, and kept his bed. He
fancied, while thus lying, that he saw a handsome young man coming
down from the sky and advancing towards him. He was richly and

gayly dressed, having on a great many garments of green and yellow colors, but differing in their deeper or lighter shades. He had a plume of waving feathers on his head, and all his motions were graceful.

"I am sent to you, my friend," said the celestial visitor, "by that Great Spirit who made all things in the sky and on the earth. He has seen and knows your motives in fasting. He sees that it is from a kind and benevolent wish to do good to your people, and to procure a benefit for them, and that you do not seek for strength in war or the praise of warriors. I am sent to instruct you, and show you how you can do your kindred good." He then told the young man to arise, and prepare to wrestle with him, as it was only by this means that he could hope to succeed in his wishes. Wunzh knew he was weak from fasting, but he felt his courage rising in his heart, and immediately got up, determined to die rather than fail. He commenced the trial, and after a protracted effort, was almost exhausted, when the beautiful stranger said, "My friend, it is enough for once; I will come again to try you"; and, smiling on him, he ascended in the air in the same direction from which he came. The next day the celestial visitor reappeared at the same hour and renewed the trial. Wunzh felt that his strength was even less than the day before, but the courage of his mind seemed to increase in proportion as his body became weaker. Seeing this, the stranger again spoke to him in the same words he used before, adding, "Tomorrow will be your last trial. Be strong, my friend, for this is the only way you can overcome me, and obtain the boon you seek." On the third day he again appeared at the same time and renewed the struggle. The poor youth was very faint in body, but grew stronger in mind at every contest, and was determined to prevail or perish in the attempt. He exerted his utmost powers, and after the contest had been continued the usual time, the stranger ceased his efforts and declared himself conquered. For the first time he entered the lodge, and sitting down beside the youth, he began to deliver his instructions to him, telling him in what manner he should proceed to take advantage of his victory.

"You have won your desires of the Great Spirit," said the stranger. "You have wrestled manfully. Tomorrow will be the seventh day of your fasting. Your father will give you food to strengthen you, and as it is the last day of trial, you will prevail. I know this, and now tell you what you must do to benefit your family and your tribe. Tomorrow," he repeated, "I shall meet you and wrestle with you for the last time; and, as soon as you have prevailed against me, you will strip off my garments and throw me down, clean the earth of roots and weeds, make it soft, and bury me in the spot. When you have done this, leave my body in the earth, and do not disturb it, but come occasionally to visit the place, to see whether I have come to life, and be careful never to let the grass or weeds grow on my grave. Once a month cover me with fresh earth. If you follow my instructions, you will accomplish your object of doing good to your fellow-creatures by teaching them the knowledge I now teach you." He then shook him by the hand and disappeared.

In the morning the youth's father came with some slight refreshments, saying, "My son, you have fasted long enough. If the Great Spirit will favor you, he will do it now. It is seven days since you have tasted food, and you must not sacrifice your life. The Master of Life does not require that." "My father," replied the youth, "wait till the sun goes down. I have a particular reason for extending my fast to that hour." "Very well," said the old man, "I shall wait till the hour arrives, and you feel inclined to eat."

At the usual hour of the day the sky-visitor returned, and the trial of strength was renewed. Although the youth had not availed himself of his father's offer of food, he felt that new strength had been given to him, and that exertion had renewed his strength and fortified his courage. He grasped his angelic antagonist with supernatural strength, threw him down, took from him his beautiful garments and plume, and finding him dead, immediately buried him on the spot, taking all the precautions he had been told of, and being very confident, at the same time, that his friend would again come to life. He then returned to his father's lodge, and partook sparingly of the meal that had been prepared for him. But he never for a moment forgot the grave of his friend. He carefully visited it throughout the spring, and weeded out the grass, and kept the ground in a soft and pliant state. Very soon he saw the tops of the green plumes coming through the ground; and the more careful he was to obey his instructions in keeping the ground in order, the faster they grew. He was, however, careful to conceal the exploit from his father. Days and weeks had passed in this way. The summer was now drawing towards a close, when one day, after a long absence in hunting, Wunzh invited his father to follow him to the quiet and lonesome spot of his former fast. The lodge had been removed, and the weeds kept from growing on the circle where it stood, but in its place stood a tall and graceful plant, with bright-colored silken hair, surmounted with nodding plumes and stately leaves, and golden clusters on each side. "It is my friend," shouted the lad; "it is the friend of all mankind. It is *Mondawmin*. We need no longer rely on hunting alone; for, as long as this gift is cherished and taken care of, the ground itself will give us a living." He then pulled an ear. "See, my father," said he, "this is what I fasted for. The Great Spirit has listened to my voice, and sent us something new, and henceforth our people will not alone depend upon the chase or upon the waters."

He then communicated to his father the instructions given him by the stranger. He told him that the broad husks must be torn away, as he had pulled off the garments in his wrestling; and having done this, directed him how the ear must be held before the fire till the outer skin became brown, while all the milk was retained in the grain. The whole family then united in a feast on the newly-grown ears, expressing gratitude to the Merciful Spirit who gave it. So corn came into the world.

Christian-County Mosquitoes

by EUGENE FIELD, 1850–95. *Field was born of Vermont parentage in St. Louis and because of the early death of his mother was brought up in the East by a cousin. He attended Williams College, Knox College, and the University of Missouri but cut his college education short when at the age of twenty-one he came into a patrimony of about $8000. An expensive and strenuous tour of Europe followed. In 1873 he returned to the United States and began a long journalistic career that took him from St. Louis to Kansas City to Denver. In 1883 Melville E. Stone of the Chicago Daily News lured him to Chicago and he contributed his famous "Sharps and Flats" column to that newspaper until his death. Field became nationally known for his poetry of childhood and domesticity, his bibliomania, and his Horatian imitations. His satirical powers are suggested in Culture's Garland (1887), with its flings at the Chicago parvenus. His lyrics and stories are to be found in such volumes as A Little Book of Western Verse (1889), A Little Book of Profitable Tales (1890), and With Trumpet and Drum (1892). "Christian-County Mosquitoes," collected in Culture's Garland, shows Field's fondness for hoaxes and exaggeration.*

D R. CYRUS THOMAS, formerly of Carbondale, but now connected with the national entomological department at Washington, is temporarily in Illinois, investigating the habits of the mosquitoes that infest that magnificent Christian-county waterway, Flat Branch. By a judicious system of bear-traps exposed along the banks of Flat Branch, Dr. Thomas has possessed himself of a number of handsome specimens of Christian-county mosquitoes, and he is enabled therefore to pursue his researches with uncommon accuracy and ease. His investigations have not progressed to that extent, however, that he is able to declare positively that the Christian-county mosquito is an insect, and not a bird: in fact, there are numerous reasons for believing that these curious and

13

ravenous creatures are a species of reptile, provided, by an inscrutable dispensation of nature, with wings. But his researches have developed many interesting and hitherto unknown facts about these remarkable and remorseless nondescripts. In the first place, the Flat-Branch mosquitoes are carnivorous mammals: they nurse their young, and they are provided with incisor and molar teeth for the tearing and masticating of flesh. There is something almost human in the way they wear their beards and mustaches, yet they resemble the equine species in the particular of the spiked shoes with which they are invariably shod when they arrive at maturity, viz., the twenty-first year. In the matter of rearing their young, their habits seem to be like those of the ordinary prairie-chicken, for they retire in the early spring to quiet burrows or corn-fields along Flat Branch, and raise their broods, which have been known to number six hundred souls to one family; in July they become gregarious, and congregate in the timber, roosting in the high trees, and laying waste the human population of the surrounding country. Christian-county huntsmen—notably the Taylorville Sportsman's Association—employ different methods of capturing these destructive creatures. One way is by means of quail-nets: another is the old way of hunting them with pointer-dogs and gun; in the latter case, buckshot is used, and the heaviest kind of fowling-piece is preferred. But the most popular method of capture is the pitfall—the same employed to entrap elephants in India. A deep pit is dug, a light covering is thrown over the opening, and on this covering is placed a hindquarter of beef. Attracted thither by the fumes of the meat, the mosquito unsuspectingly steps upon the deceitful pitfall, the slight fabric yields under the leviathan's weight, and with a sickening groan the winged monster is precipitated into his gloomy prison, from which he is not hoisted by his captors till he is enfeebled by captivity and starvation. In this way thousands of mosquitoes are taken annually by the people of Christian County, who derive a handsome profit from the pelts of the mosquitoes, which are tanned into shoe-leather, and the tusks, which are utilized for those varied purposes to which ivory is usually put. Considering the importance of this industry, it is not strange that the result of Dr. Thomas's explorations and researches are [sic] awaited with a solicitude bordering upon suspense.

The Blue Duck

by LEW SARETT, 1888–   . *Poet, lecturer, woodsman, and forest ranger, Sarett was born in Chicago. He was educated at the University of Michigan, Beloit College, B.A., 1911, Harvard University, and the University of Illinois, LL.B., 1916. Much of his life has been spent as a teacher, at the University of Illinois and since 1921 as professor of argumentation and speech at Northwestern University, but for a long time he annually spent several months as a guide and forest ranger in the northern woods. This interest in and love of the out-of-doors is clearly reflected in his poetry, which deals for the most part with wild animal and bird life, natural scenery, and the reservation Indian. He has taken particular care to interpret, rather than to translate, the chants and traditions of the Chippewas. His books of poetry include Many Many Moons (1920), The Box of God (1922), and Slow Smoke (1925). In 1921 he was awarded the Helen Haire Levinson prize for poetry. The Collected Poems of Lew Sarett appeared in 1941. "The Blue Duck," reprinted from Many Many Moons, is a poetic interpretation of an American Indian medicine dance.*

Híi! Hi! Híi! Hi!
Híi! Hi! Híi! Hi!
Kéetch-ie Má-ni-dó, Má-ni-dó,
The hunter-moon is chipping,
Chipping at his flints,
At his dripping bloody flints.
He is rising for the hunt,
And his face is red with blood
From the spears of many spruces,
And his blood is on the leaves
That flutter down.
The Winter-Maker, white Bee-bóan,
Is walking in the sky,
And his windy blanket
Rustles in the trees.
He is blazing out the trail
Through the fields of nodding rice
For the swift and whistling wings
Of his She-shé-be
For the worn and weary wings
Of many duck—
Ho! Plenty duck! Plenty duck!
Ho! Plenty, plenty duck!

Hí! Hi! Hí! Hi!
Hí! Hi! Hí! Hi!
Kéetch-ie Má-ni-dó, Má-ni-dó,
The seasons have been barren.
In the Moon-of-Sugar-Making,
And the Moon-of-Flowers-and-Grass,
From the blighted berry patches
And the maple-sugar bush,
The hands of all my children
Came home empty, came home clean.
The big rain of Nee-bín, the Summer-Maker,
Washed away the many little partridge.
And good Ad-ík-kum-áig, sweet whitefish,
Went sulking all the summer-moons,
Hiding in the deepest waters,
Silver belly in the mud,
And he would not walk into my nets! Ugh!
Thus the skin-sacks and the mó-kuks
Hang within my wéeg-i-wam empty.

Soon the winter moon will come,
Slipping through the silent timber,
Walking on the silent snow,
Stalking on the frozen lake.
Lean-bellied,
Squatting with his rump upon the ice,
The phantom wolf will fling
His wailings to the stars.
Then Wéen-di-gó, the Devil-Spirit,
Whining through the lodge-poles,
Will clutch and shake my teepee,
Calling,
Calling,
Calling as he sifts into my lodge;
And ghostly little shadow-arms
Will float out through
The smoke-hole in the night—
Leaping, tossing shadow-arms,
Little arms of little children,
Hungry hands of shadow-arms,
Clutching,
Clutching,
Clutching at the breast that is not there . . .
Shadow-arms and shadow breasts . . .

Twisting,
Twisting,
Twisting in and twisting out
On the ghostly clouds of smoke . . .
Riding on the whistling wind . . .
Riding on the whistling wind . . .
Riding on the whistling wind . . .
Starward! . . .
Blow, blow, blow Kee-wáy-din, North Wind,
Warm and gentle on my children,
Cold and swift upon the wild She-shé-be,
Ha-a-ah-ee-ooo! . . . Plenty duck . . .
Ha-a-a-ah-eeee-ooooo! . . . Plenty duck. . . .

Hí! Hi! Hí! Hi!
Hí! Hi! Hí! Hi!
Kéetch-ie Má-ni-dó, Má-ni-dó,
Blow on Áh-bi-tóo-bi many wings;
Wings of teal and wings of mallard,
Wings of green and blue.
My little lake lies waiting,
Singing for her blustery lover;
Dancing on the golden-stranded shore
With many little moccasins,
Pretty little moccasins,
Beaded with her silver sands,
And with her golden pebbles.
And upon her gentle bosom
Lies mah-nó-min, sweetest wild rice,
Green and yellow,
Rustling blade and rippling blossom—
Hi-yee! Hi-yee! Blow on Áh-bi-tóo-bi plenty duck!
Ho! Plenty, plenty duck!
Ho! Plenty duck, plenty duck!
Ho! Ho!

Hí! Hi! Hí! Hi!
Hí! Hi! Hí! Hi!
Kéetch-ie Má-ni-dó, Má-ni-dó,
I place this pretty duck upon your hand;
Upon its sunny palm and in its windy fingers.
Hi-yeee! Blue and beautiful
Is he, beautifully blue!
Carved from sleeping cedar

When the stars like silver fishes
Were aquiver in the rivers of the sky;
Carved from dripping cedar
When the Kóo-koo-kóo dashed hooting
At the furtive feet
That rustle in the leaves—
Hi! And seasoned many moons, many moons,
Ho! Seasoned many, many, many sleeps!
Hi-yeee! Blue and beautiful
Is he, beautifully blue!
Though his throat is choked with wood,
And he honks not on his pole,
And his wings are weak with hunger,
Yet his heart is plenty good.
Hi-yee! His heart is plenty good!
Hi-yee! Plenty good, plenty good!
Hi-yee! Hi-yee! Hi-yee! His heart is good!

My heart like his is good!

Ugh! My tongue talks straight!

Ho!

The Black Duck Dinner

by JAMES FLOYD STEVENS, 1892— . *Stevens is best known to-day for his work in compiling and recording the Paul Bunyan tales, which he began to contribute to the American Mercury in 1924. His interest in lumber-jack life and his own experience in logging camps gave him a special aptitude for this kind of writing. Lately he has been connected with the West Coast Lumbermen's Association with headquarters at Seattle. Among Stevens's books are Paul Bunyan (1925) and Saginaw Paul Bunyan (1932). "The Black Duck Dinner," originally published in the American Mercury, June 1924, was suggested by an anecdote told in the author's hearing by a lumber-jack from Blackduck, Minnesota.*

I

I FIRST got news of Paul Bunyan when I went to work in an Oregon logging-camp. In the East he seems to be almost unheard of; even in the West, when one enters the cities, the mighty epic of his herculean deeds sinks to the whisper of a whisper. But in the logging-camps, even today, he remains as real as the trees themselves. Every logger in the Northwestern woods knows all about him—his Gargantuan stature and strength, his ear-splitting roar, his colossal deeds. Paul Bunyan is the traditional hero of the lumberjacks; he is the greatest of their contributions to American folklore; in him they see all their own robustious qualities, exaggerated almost to sublimity. Times have changed in the woods, and the rough-hewn loggers of tradition have begun to disappear, but even their well-barbered and regimented successors of today know Paul Bunyan. He is as much a part of the story of the winning of the West as Brigham Young or Buffalo Bill.

I first heard of him on sharp Autumn nights, sitting with my fellow "savages" around the bunkhouse stove, listening to Old Time Sandy. Sandy was the camp bard, and as his astounding tales of Bunyan's vast exploits poured out in the rich vernacular of the woodsman it seemed to me that no sagas of the olden days could be more exhilarating. When these tales originated, and where, I do not know. The oldest graybeards among the loggers knew nothing of their hero's beginnings; he was already a hero when they were striplings. Perhaps his creator borrowed a hint or two from "The Inestimable Life of the Great Gargantua"; perhaps not. As he stands today Bunyan is absolutely American from head to foot. He visualizes perfectly the American love of tall talk and tall doings, the true American exuberance and extravagance. He is really the creation not of one man, but of whole generations of men. Thousands of narrators by far-flung campfires have contributed their mites to the classical picture of him.

There are no stories about Paul Bunyan as a child; he is supposed to have sprung into life full-grown. There are various estimates of his size, and always they are given in the logger fashion of measuring a log in ax-handle lengths. The favorite estimate is that ninety-seven ax-handles would scarcely span him from hip to hip. His beard was as long as it was wide, and as wide as it was long. He combed it and his curly black hair with a young pine tree. He spoke commonly in gentle tones, but his voice, when he loosed it, was like the rumbling of thunder, and if by chance he bellowed from rage or pain acres of trees crashed to the ground, bunkhouses were flattened and common folk were stunned. Fortunately, though he was without sentimental geniality, he had a tolerant and considerate soul. But he was not a humanitarian; his ruling passion was the passion of toil, which catches its fire from exulting muscular energy. He thought it a privilege to perform the grand and thrilling labor of the woods, and when his loggers failed to work with his own exuberant pride, as would happen once or twice a season, he would banish them to camp and with a joyous exertion of his prodigious powers himself accomplish all their tasks.

His subordinates were much grander persons than ordinary men, but in size they were all dwarfed by their chief. The Big Swede, his aide de camp, was a stolid, amiable, faithful Nordic blond who excused his incessant and magnificent blunders with a monosyllable and a grin. As Paul Bunyan himself personally directed all operations, the Big Swede's title of foreman was only honorary; his main duty was to care for the blue ox. Johnny Inkslinger, the scribe, had all the virtues the modern camp clerk is thought to lack. There was never a shortage of pay when he was in camp, and never an overcharge, although he alone had to keep the records of thousands of men. Nor was there ever an error in his accounts of millions of feet of logs. As he used two barrels of ink a month you can imagine what figuring he had to do! Beside, he was the camp dentist and surgeon, and in this capacity he made innumerable and incredible cures—cases which even a chiropractor would flee from.

The only creature in camp equal in size to Bunyan was Babe, the blue ox. Nothing is known of Babe's ancestry, but he was certainly of noble and august parentage. All that is certain is that he was born the Winter of the blue snow, hence his unique color, and that Bunyan reared him from infancy with solicitous care. Babe repaid this care with an extravagance of affection that was ofttimes embarrassing. The great logger's only weakness was ticklishness, particularly about the neck, and the blue ox had a perverse passion for caressing that region with his tongue. Paul Bunyan never resented this attempt on his dignity, but he avoided it whenever possible. The blue ox was unfailingly obedient, tireless and patient. It was his task to skid the felled and trimmed trees from the stumps to the rollways by the rivers, where they were stored for the drives. The timber of nineteen States, save a few scant sections, so the old loggers declare, was skidded from the stumps by the all-powerful Babe.

In Paul Bunyan's camp there was a great cookhouse with a kitchen like another Mammoth Cave, and a dining hall wherein, under huge and lofty beams, the tables were ranged like the ranks of an army corps drawn up for parade on a plain. Here were served huge and incomparable Sunday dinners and the simpler week-day meals, of which the breakfasts of ham and eggs, hot cakes and coffee are most highly praised. Paul Bunyan invented a machine for the mixing of the hot cake batter, so perfectly devised that paving contractors now employ small models of it for mixing cement. The range on which a battalion of cooks fried the hot cakes was greased by a ski champion fom Norway who skiied to and fro with sides of bacon strapped to his feet. And that the men in the far end of the cookhouse might be served before the hot cakes cooled, the flunkies speeded on roller skates. It required a crew of eleven teamsters with teams and scrapers to keep the yard back of the cookhouse cleared of coffee grounds and egg shells.

But do not imagine that because Paul Bunyan's camp was a logger's dream of paradise there was any luxurious leisure in it. He worked his men twelve hours a day, and they would have been astounded by any idea of working less. And they would have been perplexed by any other scheme to ease their lot. If there were not to be great exertions, they would have asked, why their sturdy frames, their eager muscular force? If they were not meant to face hazards, why was daring in their hearts? A noble breed, those loggers of Paul Bunyan's, greatly worthy of their captain! He himself told them in a speech he made at the finishing of the Onion River drive that they were "a good band of bullies, a fine bunch of savages." I should like to quote this speech in its entirety for it celebrated the accomplishment of a historical logging enterprise, and it was a master oration which showed the full range and force of Paul Bunyan's intellectual powers. But as nine days and eight nights were required for its delivery, it is obvious that no publication save the *Congressional Record* could print it. It was at this time that Paul Bunyan served his great black duck dinner.

II

The speech ended on a Tuesday, and until the following Saturday morning there were no sounds save the snores of weary men and the scratching of the sleepless Johnny Inkslinger's pen. By Saturday noon he had a time-check and a written copy of the oration for every man in camp. The loggers then prepared for a blow-in down the river, while Paul Bunyan and the Big Swede moved the camp. After dinner the industrious Swede, using a fire hose, a ton of soap, and a tank of hair tonic, began to give the blue ox his Spring cleaning, and Johnny Inkslinger turned in for the three hours of sleep which he required each week. Paul Bunyan was arranging his personal belongings for the move and musing on his recent accomplishment. He had never driven logs down a rougher or more treacherous stream than Onion River. And the hills over which the timber had been skidded were so rocky and steep that they tried even the strength of the blue ox. Worst of all was the rank growth of wild onions that had covered the ground. They baffled all attempts to fell the trees at first, for they brought blinding floods of tears to the loggers' eyes and made their efforts not only futile but dangerous. When the Big Swede was standing on a hillside one day, dreaming of the old country, he failed to observe a blinded logger come staggering up the slope, and he did not hear him mumble, "This looks like a good stick." Not until the logger had chopped an undercut in the leg of his boot had the Big Swede realized his peril. Paul Bunyan, baffled by such incidents, was about to abandon the whole operation when the alert Johnny Inkslinger heard of the failure of the Italian garlic crop. He quickly made a contract with the Italian government, which sent over shiploads of laborers to dig up the wild onions and take them home as a substitute for the national relish. When this had been accomplished it was possible to log off the country.

There had been other difficulties to overcome, too, and as Paul Bunyan spread a tarpaulin and prepared to roll up his boots and work-clothes, he remembered them and praised the saints that they were ended. The next job offered the best promise of simple and easy logging that he had encountered since he logged off the level lands of Kansas. For miles the land rose in gentle slopes from a wide and smoothly flowing river; there was no brush or noxious vegetation among the clean, straight trees; and, best of all, the timber was of a species now extinct, the Leaning Pine. The trees of this variety all leaned in the same direction, and it was thus possible to fell them accurately without the use of wedges. Paul Bunyan was sure of a season's record on this new job. He thought of the fresh brilliancy it would give his fame, and like a row of snowy peaks glimpsed through the spaces of a forest, his teeth glittered through his beard in a magnificent smile. But another thought quickly sobered his countenance. "Those good bullies of mine!" The words came in a gusty murmur. He dropped the tarpaulin and strode over to the cookhouse. Hot Biscuit Slim, his kitchen chief, came forth to meet him. There was a knowing look in the cook's eyes.

"It's to be a great Sunday dinner tomorrer?" he asked, before Paul Bunyan could speak.

"The greatest Sunday dinner ever heard of," said Paul Bunyan. "I want this to be remembered as the noblest meal ever served in a logging camp. My loggers shall feast like the victorious soldiers of old time. It is a natural privilege of heroes to revel after conquest. Remember, as you prepare this feast, that you may also be making immortal glory for yourself."

"You jest leave it to me, Mr. Bunyan!" answered Slim. "If the baker'll do his part with the cream puffs, cakes and pies, I promise you I'll make 'em a meal to remember. First, oyscher stew, an' then for vegytables, cream' cabbage, of course, mash' potatoes an' potato cakes, lettuce an' onions—"

"No onions!" thundered Paul Bunyan. There was a terrific crash in the kitchen as hundreds of pans and skillets were shaken to the floor.

"Uh—I forgot," stammered Slim. "Well, anyway, they'll be oyscher soup, vegytables, sauces, puddin's, hot biscuits, an' meat in dumplin' stew an' mulligan stew, an' they'll be drippin' roasts, all tender an' rich seasoned—oh, the meat that I'll give 'em! the meat—" he paused sharply, shivered as though from a physical shock, and misery glistened in his eyes—"only—uh—only—"

"Only you have no meat," said Paul Bunyan gently.

"I'm admittin' it," said Slim wretchedly. "Honest, Mr. Bunyan, no matter how I try I jest *can't* remember to order meat, 'specially for Sunday dinner. I can remember vegytables, fruit an' greens easy as pie, but, by doggy, I always forget meat. I ain't pertendin' a cook's worth keepin' who can't remember meat, no matter how good he is at a fixin' it. I wouldn't blame you if you fired me right off, Mr. Bunyan."

Slim leaned against the toe of the hero's boot and wept.

"That means that I must rustle deer and bear," said Paul Bunyan patiently. "Well, bear meat and venison will make a royal feast when they have passed through your kettles and ovens. Light the fires, go ahead with your plans; you may yet make history tomorrow!"

He turned away, and Hot Biscuit Slim watched him worshipfully until he was a dim figure on distant hills.

"I'd do anything for a boss like that," he said resolutely. "I'll learn to remember meat, by doggy, I will!"

Rumors of the marvelous dinner that was being planned reached the bunkhouses, and thoughts of their coming blow-in were abandoned by the loggers as they indulged in greedy imaginings of the promised delights. The day went slowly; the sun seemed to labor down the western sky. Before it sank soft clouds obscured its light, bringing showers and early shadows.

At the approach of darkness Paul Bunyan began his return march to the camp. He was vastly disappointed by the meager results of his hunt. Although he had gone as far as the Turtle River country, he had snared but three deer and two small bears. These only filled a corner of one pocket of his mackinaw, and they would provide but a mere shred of meat apiece for his men. Paul Bunyan did not feel that he had done his best; he was not one to rest on feeble consolations. As he journeyed on he was devising other means to carry out his plan for a memorable and stupendous feast. And ere he was within an hour of the camp the Big Swede was unconsciously outlining the solution of the problem for him.

III

The Swede went to the stable some time after supper to see that Babe was at ease for the night. The clouds were thinning now, and when he opened the stable door soft light poured in on the blue ox, making lustrous spots and streaks on his sleek sides. He turned his head, his bulging blue eyes shining with gentleness and goodwill, and his tongue covered the foreman's face in a luscious caress.

"Har, now," remonstrated the Big Swede.

As he solemnly wiped his face he sniffed the fragrance of Babe's breath and stared with a feeling of envy at the clean, glowing hair. When he had finished his inspection and left the stable, it was evident that he was wrestling with some laborious problem. His whole face was tense with a terrific frown; he scratched his sides vigorously and breathed deeply of the air, sweet with the odors of washed earth. The purity of the Spring weather, the fresh cleanliness it gave the world, and the aroma and sleekness of the blue ox had brought the Big Swede to face his own sore need of a washing. He dreaded it as an ordeal, and for that reason he wished he might accomplish it immediately. He wandered aimlessly on, tormented by an unaccustomed conflict of the soul and the flesh, and at last he came to the edge of a cliff. He stared in surprise at the appearance of a lake below. He could not remember that large a body of water near the camp. But the Big Swede had no room for more than one emotion at a time, and a violent resolve now smothered his surprise.

"Yah, aye do him now," he muttered.

He disrobed swiftly and ran to a rock that jutted from the cliff. Swinging his fists, he leaped twice into the air; the second time he flung himself outward in a magnificent dive, his body made a great curve, and then, head first, he plunged downward. But there was no tumultuous surge and splash of waters as a climax to this splendid dive. Instead, the Big Swede's head struck white canvas with a dull, rending impact—for he had mistaken Paul Bunyan's tarpaulin for a lake! The force of his plunge drove him through the canvas and half-buried him in the soft earth underneath. His arms were imprisoned, but his legs waved wildly, and his muffled bellows shook the earth. A prowling logger saw what seemed to be shining marble columns dancing in the moonlight and felt the ground trembling under his feet.

"It can't be," he thought bravely.

Just then the Big Swede made another heroic effort to yell for help, and the logger was shaken from his feet. He jumped up and ran to Johnny Inkslinger with an alarming tale of dancing ghosts that shook the earth. The timekeeper, after sharpening twenty-seven pencils to use in case it was necessary to make a report on the spot, started with his medicine case for the place where the logger had directed him. When nearly there he remembered that he had failed to bring his ten-gallon carboy of alcohol, which, next to Epsom salts, he considered the most important medicine in his chest. He ran back for it, and by the time he finally reached the Big Swede, that unfortunate's bellows had diminished to groans, and his legs waved with less and less gusto. After thoroughly examining and measuring the legs Johnny deemed the proof positive that they belonged to the Big Swede. Then he got busy with paper and pencil and figured for half an hour. "According to the strictest mathematical calculations," he announced, "the Big Swede cannot continue to exist in his present position; consequently, he must be extricated. I have considered all known means by which this may be accomplished, and I have arrived at a scientific conclusion. I direct that the blue ox and a cable be brought here at once."

When the loggers had obeyed this command, Johnny made a half-hitch with the cable around the Big Swede's legs, which were waving very feebly now, and in two seconds, amid a monstrous upheaval of dirt and a further rending of the canvas, the Big Swede was dragged out. For a few moments he spat mud like a river dredge; then Johnny proffered him the ten-gallon carboy of alcohol. It was drained at a gulp, and then, with aid from the timekeeper, he was able to stagger to his shanty. When Paul Bunyan reached the camp the Big Swede was lying on his bunk, bundled in bandages from head to foot. Johnny Inkslinger was still busily attending him; bottles of medicine, boxes of pills, a keg of Epsom salts, rolls of bandages, and surgical implements were heaped about the room. The timekeeper gave a detailed account of what had happened, and then Paul Bunyan questioned the victim, who answered briefly, "Aye yoomped, an' aye yoomped, an'—*yeeminy!*"

Johnny Inkslinger gave his chief a voluminous report of the Big Swede's fractures, sprains and contusions.

"He is also suffering from melancholia because he is still unwashed," said Johnny. "But I think I'll restore him. I've dosed him with all my medicines and smeared him with all my salves. I'd have manipulated his spine, but confound him, he strained his back and he threatens violence when I touch it. But I have many formulae and systems. He shall live."

"Surely," said Paul Bunyan. "A man is the hardest animal to kill there is."

Saying this, he arose from before the shanty door and thought again of his unrealized plan. He remembered the wordless dejection of Hot Biscuit Slim on receiving the scanty supply of deer and bear meat. He determined that the Sunday dinner should yet be as he had planned it; otherwise it would be a bad augury for great achievements in his new enterprise. He walked slowly towards his headquarters, pondering various schemes that came to mind.

When he reached the white sheet of canvas he was astonished by its deceptive appearance. It had a silvery glitter in the moonlight, for its surface still held the moisture of the showers. Small wonder, thought Paul Bunyan, that the Big Swede had dived into it; never was a lake more temptingly beautiful or seemingly more deep. He was gazing at the torn canvas and the huge cavity made in the ground by the Big Swede, when he heard a great chorus of shrill and doleful voices in the sky. He looked up and saw an enormous flock of black ducks in swerving flight. They had lost their way in the low-hanging clouds at dusk, and now they were seeking a resting place.

Here, thought Paul Bunyan at once, is a noble offering of chance. Was a black duck more acute than the Big Swede, that the bright, moist canvas would not deceive him also? And once deceived, would not the ensuing dive be fatal? Wasn't a black duck's neck of more delicate structure than the Big Swede's, and wouldn't it surely break when it struck the tarpaulin? This variety of black duck grew as big as a buzzard, and here they were so numerous that clouds of them darkened the moon. Now to deceive them. Paul could mimic the voices of all the birds of the air and all the beasts of the fields and woods, save only that of the blue ox, who always replied with a jocular wink when his master attempted to simulate his mellow moo. In his moments of humor Paul Bunyan declared that he could mimic fish, and one Sunday when he imitated a mother whale bawling for her calf the loggers roared with merriment for seventeen hours, and were only sobered then by exhaustion. His voice had such power that he could not counterfeit the cry of a single small creature, but only the united cries of flocks or droves. So he now mimicked perfectly the chorus that rang mournfully in the sky, and at the same time he grasped the edge of the tarpaulin and fluttered it gently.

The effect was marvelous. Now indeed was the canvas a perfect imitation of water. Had you been standing by the sole of Paul Bunyan's boot and seen the gentle flutter you would have been sure that you were watching a breeze make pleasant ripples on the surface of a lake. Ere long the black ducks were enchanted by the sight and sound, and Paul Bunyan heard a violent rush of air above him as of a hurricane sweeping a forest. Another instant and the canvas was black with feathered forms. Paul Bunyan grasped the four corners of the tarpaulin, swung the bundle over his shoulder and strode home to the cookhouse. Hot Biscuit Slim was called forth, and when he saw the mountainous pile of black ducks that filled the kitchen yard he became hysterical with delight. He called out the assistant cooks, the flunkies and dishwashers, and, led by Cream Puff Fatty, the baker, the white-clad underlings streamed for eleven minutes from the kitchen door. The chief cook then made a short but inspiring speech and fired them with his own fierce purpose to make culinary history.

Paul Bunyan listened for a moment, and then sought repose, with peace in his benevolent heart.

All night fires roared in the ranges as preparations went on for the great dinner. Vegetables were brought from the storehouse, potatoes were pared and washed, utensils and roasting pans were made ready, and sauces and dressings were devised. The black ducks were cleaned, scalded and plucked in the kitchen yard.

Next morning most of the loggers stayed in their bunks, and those who did come to breakfast ate sparingly, saving their appetites. Time passed quietly in the camp. The loggers washed and mended their clothes and greased their boots; they shaved and bathed and then stretched out on their blankets and smoked. They were silent and pre-occupied, but now and again a breeze blowing from the direction of the cookhouse would cause them to sigh. What enchantment was in the air, so redolent with the aroma of roasting duck and stewing cabbages, so sharply sweet with the fragrance of hot ginger and cinnamon from the bakery where Cream Puff Fatty fashioned his creations! A logger who was shaving would take a deep breath of this incense, and the blood would trickle unnoticed from a slash in his cheek; another, in his bunk would let his pipe slip from his hand and enjoy ardent inhalations, bliss-fully unaware of his burning shirt; yet another, engaged in greasing his boots, would halt his task and sit in motionless beatitude, his head thrown back, his eyes closed, quite unconscious of the grease that poured from a tilted can into a prized boot.

At half past eleven the hungriest of the loggers began to mass before the cookhouse door, and as the minutes passed the throng swiftly in-creased. At five minutes to noon all the bunkhouses were empty and the furthest fringe of the crowd was far up Onion River Valley. The ground shook under a restless trampling, and the faces of the loggers were glowing and eager as they hearkened to the clatter and rumble in-side the cookhouse, where the flunkies, led by the Galloping Kid on his white horse, were rushing the platters and bowls of food to the tables. Tantalizing smells wafted forth from the steaming dishes. The loggers grew more restless and eager; they surged to and fro in a tidal move-ment; jests and glad oaths made a joyous clamor over the throng. This was softened into a universal sigh as the doors swung open at last and Hot Biscuit Slim, in spotless cap and apron, appeared wearing the im-pressive mien of a conquering general. He lifted an iron bar with a majestic gesture, paused for dramatic effect amid a breathless hush, and then struck a resounding note from the steel triangle that hung from the wall. At the sound a heaving torrent of men began to pour through the doors in a rush that was like the roaring plunge of water when the gate of a dam is lifted. The chief cook continued to pound out clang-ing rhythms until the last impatient logger was inside.

When Hot Biscuit Slim reentered the cookhouse he was reminded of a forested plain veiled in thin fog as he surveyed the assemblage of darkly clad figures, wreathed with white and fragrant blooms of steam. His impression was made the more vivid when the loggers plunged their spoons into the deep bowls of oyster soup, for the ensuing sounds seemed like the soughing of winds in the woods. The chief cook marched to the kitchen with dignity and pride, glancing to right and left at the tables that held his masterwork. He asked for no praise or acclaim; the ecstasy that now transfigured the plainest face was a sufficient light of glory for him.

The soup bowls pushed aside, the loggers began to fill their plates, which were of such circumference that even a long-armed man could hardly reach across one. The black ducks, of course, received first attention. And great as the plates were, by the time one was heaped with a brown fried drumstick, a ladle of duck dumplings, several large fragments of duck fricassee, a slab of duck baked gumbo style, a rich portion of stewed duck, and a mound of crisp brown dressing, all immersed in golden duck gravy, a formidable space was covered. Yet there was room for tender leaves of odorous cabbage beaded and streaked with creamy sauce; for mashed potatoes which seemed like fluffs of snow beside the darkness of duck and gravy; for brittle and savory potato cakes, marvelously bright as to texture and thickness; for stewed tomatoes of a sultry ruddiness, pungent and ticklish with mysterious spices; for baked beans, plump peas, sunny apple sauce and buttered lettuce, not to mention various condiments. Squares of cornbread and hot biscuits were buttered and leaned against the plate; a pot-bellied coffee-pot was tilted over a gaping cup, into which it gushed an aromatic beverage of drowsy charm; a kingly pleasure was prepared. More than one logger swooned with delight this day when his plate was filled and he bent over it for the first mouthful with the joy of a lover claiming a first embrace.

In the kitchen the chief cook, the baker and their helpers watched and listened. At first the volume of sounds that filled the vast room was like the roar and crash of an avalanche, as dishes were rattled and banged about. Then the duck bones crackled like the limbs of falling trees. At last came a steady sound of eating, a sound of seventy threshing machines devouring bundles of wheat. It persisted far beyond the usual length of time, and Hot Biscuit Slim brought out his field glasses and surveyed the tables. The loggers were still bent tensely over their plates, and their elbows rose and fell with an energetic movement as they scooped up the food with undiminished vigor.

"Still eatin' duck," marveled Hot Biscuit Slim.

"They won't be more'n able to *smell* my cream puffs," said the baker enviously.

The loggers ate on. They had now spent twice their usual length of time at the table.

"Still eatin' duck," reported Hot Biscuit Slim.

That no one might see his grief Cream Puff Fatty moved to a dark corner. He was now certain that none of the loggers could have room for his pastries. They ate on. They had now spent three times their usual length of time at the table. The baker was sweating and weeping; he was soaked with despair. Then, suddenly:

"They're eatin' cream puffs!" cried Hot Biscuit Slim.

Cream Puff Fatty could not believe it, but a thrill of hope urged him to see for himself. True enough, the loggers were tackling the pastries at last! On each plate cream puffs lay in golden mounds. As the spoons struck them their creamy contents oozed forth from breaks and crevices. Stimulated by their rich flavor, the loggers ate on with renewed gusto. They had now stayed four times as long as usual at the table. Other enchantments still kept them in their seats: lemon pies with airy frostings, glittering cakes of many colors, slabs of gingerbread, soft cinnamon rolls, doughnuts as large as saucers, and so soft and toothsome that a morsel from one melted on the tongue like cream. So endearing were the flavors of these pastries that the loggers consumed them all.

Cream Puff Fatty and Hot Biscuit Slim solemnly shook hands. Then there was glory enough for both of them.

V

At last there were no sounds at the tables save those of heavy breathing. The loggers arose in a body and moved sluggishly and wordlessly from the cookhouse. They labored over the ground towards the bunkhouses as wearily as though they had just finished a day of deadening toil. Soon Onion River Valley resounded with their snores and groans. . . .

At supper time, when Hot Biscuit Slim rang the gong, Cream Puff Fatty stood by his side. This was to be the supreme test of their achievement. For five minutes the chief cook beat the triangle, and then a solitary logger appeared in the door of a bunkhouse. He stared at them dully for a moment and then staggered back into the darkness. This was indeed a triumph! Great as other feasts in the cookhouse had been, never before had *all* of the loggers been unable to appear for supper. This was a historic day. Cream Puff Fatty and Hot Biscuit Slim embraced and mingled rapturous tears. . . . They had intimations of immortality. . . .

For five weeks the loggers lay in a delicious torpor, and then Johnny Inkslinger brought them from their bunks with doses of alcohol and Epsom salts. By this time the Big Swede had recovered from his injuries, and Paul Bunyan waited no longer to move his camp. The buildings, which rested on skids, were connected by cables, and the blue ox hauled them over the hills to the new job.

Nothing marred the beauty of that Summer; stirring breezes blew all the days over the loggers as they felled the Leaning Pine trees in perfect lines on the grassy slopes. The blue ox waxed fat with the ease of his labor. Weeks passed without the Big Swede having a serious accident. Dust gathered on Johnny Inkslinger's medicine case. Hot Biscuit Slim never once failed to remember meat. And a record number of logs were piled above the rollways. Paul Bunyan planned a great drive with prideful confidence that it would be the glorious climax of a historic season. But here fortune deserted him, for after driving the logs for nine days, and seeing an exact repetition of scenery three times, he surveyed the placid river and found it to be round; he had been driving the logs in a circle!

Nothing daunted, he thereupon determined to saw the logs and transport the lumber overland, and he erected his famed sawmill, which was nineteen stories high, with each bandsaw running through all the floors. A description of the original machines and devices used in this mill would fill the pages of a mail order catalogue. It is needless to say that it operated perfectly. The only great difficulty Paul Bunyan had to overcome originated from the smokestacks. He was compelled to equip them with hinges and drawbridge machinery so that they could be lowered to let the clouds go by.

How To Tell Corn Fairies
if you see 'em

by CARL SANDBURG, 1878–   . *No writer is more indigenous and more typical of the Middle West than Carl Sandburg. Born in Galesburg, Illinois, of uneducated immigrant stock, Sandburg was trained chiefly in the school of experience. He was at various times a porter, a milk-wagon driver, a dish-washer, a harvest hand, and a member of the fire department, and his travels took him to many parts of the country. After service in the Spanish-American War he returned to Galesburg and attended Lombard College. For a time he was a district organizer for the Social-Democratic party of Wiscon-*

sin and later secretary to the Socialist mayor of Milwaukee. A period of news-paper work followed during most of which Sandburg was associated with the Chicago Daily News. In 1914 Harriet Monroe printed his poem "Chicago" in Poetry and two years later his Chicago Poems appeared. Since then Sandburg has been recognized as one of the major American poets of the twentieth century. Subsequent volumes of verse include Cornhuskers (1918), Smoke and Steel (1920), Slabs of the Sunburnt West (1922), and The People, Yes (1936). But Sandburg has not limited himself to poetry. He has collected and sung old ballads and has written such books for children as Rootabaga Stories (1922). Moreover, he devoted fifteen years or more to the preparation of a monumental biography of Abraham Lincoln, which appeared in six volumes as Abraham Lincoln: The Prairie Years (1926) and Abraham Lincoln: The War Years (1939). His whimsical tale "How To Tell Corn Fairies If You See 'Em" is taken from Rootabaga Stories.

IF YOU have ever watched the little corn begin to march across the black lands and then slowly change to big corn and go marching on from the little corn moon of summer to the big corn harvest moon of autumn, then you must have guessed who it is that helps the corn come along. It is the corn fairies. Leave out the corn fairies and there wouldn't be any corn.

All children know this. All boys and girls know that corn is no good unless there are corn fairies.

Have you ever stood in Illinois or Iowa and watched the late sum-mer wind or the early fall wind running across a big cornfield? It looks as if a big, long blanket were being spread out for dancers to come and dance on. If you look close and if you listen close you can see the corn fairies come dancing and singing—sometimes. If it is a wild day and a hot sun is pouring down while a cool north wind blows—and this happens sometimes—then you will be sure to see thousands of corn fairies marching and countermarching in mocking grand marches over the big, long blanket of green and silver. Then too they sing, only you must listen with your littlest and newest ears if you wish to hear their singing. They sing soft songs that go pla-sizzy pla-sizzy-sizzy, and each song is softer than an eye wink, softer than a Nebraska baby's thumb.

And Spink, who is a little girl living in the same house with the man writing this story, and Skabootch, who is another little girl in the same house—both Spink and Skabootch are asking the question, "How can we tell corn fairies if we see 'em? If we meet a corn fairy how will we know it?" And this is the explanation the man gave to Spink who is older than Skabootch, and to Skabootch who is younger than Spink:—

All corn fairies wear overalls. They work hard, the corn fairies, and they are proud. The reason they are proud is because they work so hard. And the reason they work so hard is because they are proud.

31

But understand this. The overalls are corn gold cloth, woven from leaves of ripe corn mixed with ripe October corn silk. In the first week of the harvest moon coming up red and changing to yellow and silver the corn fairies sit by thousands between the corn rows weaving and stitching the clothes they have to wear next winter, next spring, next summer.

They sit cross-legged when they sew. And it is a law among them each one must point the big toe at the moon while sewing the harvest moon clothes. When the moon comes up red as blood early in the evening they point their big toes slanting toward the east. Then towards midnight when the moon is yellow and half way up the sky their big toes are only half slanted as they sit cross-legged sewing. And after midnight when the moon sails its silver disk high overhead and toward the west, then the corn fairies sit sewing with their big toes pointed nearly straight up.

If it is a cool night and looks like frost, then the laughter of the corn fairies is something worth seeing. All the time they sit sewing their next year clothes they are laughing. It is not a law they have to laugh. They laugh because they are half-tickled and glad because it is a good corn year.

And whenever the corn fairies laugh then the laugh comes out of the mouth like a thin gold frost. If you should be lucky enough to see a thousand corn fairies sitting between the corn rows and all of them laughing, you would laugh with wonder yourself to see the gold frost coming from their mouths while they laughed.

Travelers who have traveled far, and seen many things, say that if you know the corn fairies with a real knowledge you can always tell by the stitches in their clothes what state they are from.

In Illinois the corn fairies stitch fifteen stitches of ripe corn silk across the woven corn leaf cloth. In Iowa they stitch sixteen stitches, in Nebraska seventeen, and the farther west you go the more corn silk stitches the corn fairies have in the corn cloth clothes they wear.

In Minnesota one year there were fairies with a blue sash of cornflowers across the breast. In the Dakotas the same year all the fairies wore pumpkin-flower neckties, yellow four-in-hands and yellow ascots. And in one strange year it happened in both the states of Ohio and Texas the corn fairies wore little wristlets of white morning glories.

The traveler who heard about this asked many questions and found out the reason why that year the corn fairies wore little wristlets of white morning glories. He said, "Whenever fairies are sad they wear white. And this year, which was long ago, was the year men were tearing down all the old zigzag rail fences. Now these old zigzag rail fences were beautiful for the fairies because a hundred fairies could sit on one rail and thousands and thousands of them could sit on the zigzags and sing pla-sizzy pla-sizzy, softer than an eye wink, softer than a baby's thumb, all on a moonlight summer night. And they found out that year was going to be the last year of the zigzag rail fences. It made them sorry and sad, and when they are sorry and sad they wear white. So they picked the wonderful white morning glories running along the zigzag rail fences and made them into little wristlets and wore those wristlets the next year to show they were sorry and sad."

Of course, all this helps you to know how the corn fairies look in the evening, the night time and the moonlight. Now we shall see how they look in the day time.

In the day time the corn fairies have their overalls of corn gold cloth on. And they walk among the corn rows and climb the corn stalks and fix things in the leaves and stalks and ears of the corn. They help it to grow.

Each one carries on the left shoulder a mouse brush to brush away the field mice. And over the right shoulder each one has a cricket broom to sweep away the crickets. The brush is a whisk brush to brush away mice that get foolish. And the broom is to sweep away crickets that get foolish.

Around the middle of each corn fairy is a yellow-belly belt. And stuck in this belt is a purple moon shaft hammer. Whenever the wind blows strong and nearly blows the corn down, then the fairies run out and take their purple moon shaft hammers out of their yellow-belly belts and nail down nails to keep the corn from blowing down. When a rain storm is blowing up terrible and driving all kinds of terribles across the cornfield, then you can be sure of one thing. Running like the wind among the corn rows are the fairies, jerking their purple moon shaft hammers out of their belts and nailing nails down to keep the corn standing up so it will grow and be ripe and beautiful when the harvest moon comes again in the fall.

Spink and Skabootch ask where the corn fairies get the nails. The answer to Spink and Skabootch is, "Next week you will learn all about where the corn fairies get the nails to nail down the corn if you will keep your faces washed and your ears washed till next week."

And the next time you stand watching a big cornfield in late summer or early fall, when the wind is running across the green and silver, listen with your littlest and newest ears. Maybe you will hear the corn fairies going pla-sizzy pla-sizzy-sizzy, softer than an eye wink, softer than a Nebraska baby's thumb.

Shanty-Boy on the Big Eau Claire

FRANZ RICKABY, COMPILER, 1889–1925. *An early death put an untimely end to Rickaby's career as a teacher of dramatics and a collector of lumberjack ballads. He was born at Rogers, Arkansas, and was educated at Knox College, B.A., 1916, and at Harvard University, M.A., 1917. For six years, from 1917 to 1923, he was instructor and assistant professor of English at the University of North Dakota, where he also directed the Dakota Playmakers and taught dramatic writing. The last two years of his life he spent in California as a member of the English department of Pomona College. Rickaby was long interested in collecting and transcribing the songs of the lumber camps. His search for the ballads of the lumberjacks, usually anonymous and in their subject matter and breezy style very unlike the traditional English and Scottish ballads, led him into the pineries of Michigan, Wisconsin, and Minnesota, where he heard such tales in verse as "Shanty-Boy on the Big Eau Claire" and "The Banks of the Little Eau Pleine." Rickaby's collection of lumberjack verse appeared posthumously in 1926 as Ballads and Songs of the Shanty-Boy.*

EVERY girl she has her troubles; each man likewise has his.
But few can match the agony of the following story, viz.
It relates about the affection of a damsel young and fair
Who dearly loved a shanty-boy up on the Big Eau Claire.

This young and artless maiden was of noble pedigree.
Her mother kept a milliner shop in the town of Mosinee.
She sold waterfalls and ribbons and bonnets trimmed with lace
To all the gay young ladies that lived around that place.

Her shanty-boy was handsome, a husky lad was he.
In summer time he tail-sawed in a mill at Mosinee.
And when the early winter blew its cold and biting breeze,
He worked upon the Big Eau Claire a-chopping down pine trees.

The milliner swore the shanty-boy her daughter ne'er should wed.
But Sally did not seem to care for what her mother said.
So the milliner packed her ribbons and bonnets by the stack
And started another milliner shop 'way down in Fondulac.

Now Sall was broken-hearted and weary of her life.
She dearly loved the shanty-boy and wished to be his wife.
And when brown autumn came along and ripened all the crops,
She went 'way out to Baraboo and went to picking hops.

But in that occupation she found but little joy,
For her thoughts were still reverting to her dear shanty-boy.
She caught the scarlet fever and lay a week or two
In a suburban pest-house in the town of Baraboo.

And often in her ravings she would tear her raven hair
And talk about her shanty-boy upon the Big Eau Claire.
The doctors tried, but all in vain, her hapless life to save;
And millions of young hop-lice are dancing over her grave.

When the shanty-boy heard these sad news, his business he did leave.
His emotional insanity was fearful to perceive.
He hid his saw in a hollow log and traded off his axe,
And hired out for a sucker on a fleet of Sailor Jack's.

But still no peace or comfort he anywhere could find,
That milliner's daughter's funeral came so frequent to his mind.
He often wished that death would come and end his woe and grief,
And grim death took him at his word and came to his relief.

For he fell off a rapids piece on the falls at Mosinee,
And ended thus his faithful love and all his misery.
The bold Wisconsin River is now roaring o'er his bones.
His companions are the catfish, and his grave a pile of stones.

The milliner is a bankrupt now; her shop's all gone to wrack,
And she talks of moving some fine day away from Fondulac.
Her pillow is often haunted by her daughter's auburn hair
And the ghost of that young shanty-boy from up the Big Eau Claire.

And often in her slumbers she sees a dreadful sight
Which puts the worthy milliner into an awful fright.
She sees horrid ghosts and phantoms, which makes her blood run cool.
By her bedside in his glory stands the ghost of Little Bull.

Now let this be a warning to other maidens fair,
To take no stock in shanty-boys up on the Big Eau Claire;
For shanty-boys are rowdies, as everybody knows.
They dwell in the dense forest where the mighty pine tree grows.

And stealing logs and shingle-bolts, and telling awful lies,
And playing cards and swearing, is all their exercise.
But seek the solid comfort and bliss without alloy,
And play their cards according for some one-horse farmer's boy.

The Banks of the Little Eau Pleine

FRANZ RICKABY, COMPILER

ONE evening last June as I rambled
　The green woods and valleys among,
The mosquito's notes were melodious,
　And so was the whip-poor-will's song.
The frogs in the marshes were croaking,
　The tree-toads were whistling for rain,
And partridges round me were drumming,
　On the banks of the Little Eau Pleine.

The sun in the west was declining
　And tinging the tree-tops with red.
My wandering feet bore me onward,
　Not caring whither they led.
I happened to see a young school-ma'am.
　She mourned in a sorrowful strain,
She mourned for a jolly young raftsman
　On the banks of the Little Eau Pleine.

Saying, "Alas, my dear Johnny has left me.
　I'm afraid I shall see him no more,
He's down on the lower Wisconsin,
　He's pulling a fifty-foot oar.
He went off on a fleet with Ross Gamble
　And has left me in sorrow and pain;
And 't is over two months since he started
　From the banks of the Little Eau Pleine."

I stepped up beside this young school-ma'am,
　And thus unto her I did say,
"Why is it you're mourning so sadly
　While all nature is smiling and gay?"
She said, "It is for a young raftsman
　For whom I so sadly complain.
He has left me alone here to wander
　On the banks of the Little Eau Pleine."

"Will you please tell me what kind of clothing
　Your jolly young raftsman did wear?
For I also belong to the river,

And perhaps I have seen him somewhere.
If to me you will plainly describe him,
    And tell me your young raftsman's name,
Perhaps I can tell you the reason
    He's not back to the Little Eau Pleine."

"His pants were made out of two meal-sacks,
    With a patch a foot square on each knee.
His shirt and his jacket were dyed with
    The bark of a butternut tree.
He wore a large open-faced ticker
    With almost a yard of steel chain,
When he went away with Ross Gamble
    From the banks of the Little Eau Pleine.

"He wore a red sash round his middle,
    With an end hanging down at each side.
His shoes number ten were, of cowhide,
    With heels about four inches wide.
His name it was Honest John Murphy,
    And on it there ne'er was a stain,
And he was as jolly a raftsman
    As was e'er on the Little Eau Pleine.

"He was stout and broad-shouldered and manly.
    His height was about six feet one.
His hair was inclined to be sandy,
    And his whiskers as red as the sun.
His age was somewhere about thirty,
    He neither was foolish nor vain.
He loved the bold Wisconsin River
    Was the reason he left the Eau Pleine."

"If John Murphy's the name of your raftsman,
    I used to know him very well.
But sad is the tale I must tell you:
    Your Johnny was drowned in the Dells.
They buried him 'neath a scrub Norway,
    You will never behold him again.
No stone marks the spot where your raftsman
    Sleeps far from the Little Eau Pleine."

When the school-ma'am heard this information,
    She fainted and fell as if dead.
I scooped up a hat-full of water

And poured it on top of her head.
She opened her eyes and looked wildly,
    As if she was nearly insane,
And I was afraid she would perish
    On the banks of the Little Eau Pleine.

"My curses attend you, Wisconsin!
    May your rapids and falls cease to roar.
May every tow-head and sand-bar
    Be as dry as a log schoolhouse floor.
May the willows upon all your islands
    Lie down like a field of ripe grain,
For taking my jolly young raftsman
    Away from the Little Eau Pleine.

"My curses light on you, Ross Gamble,
    For taking my Johnny away.
I hope that the ague will seize you,
    And shake you down into the clay.
May your lumber go down to the bottom,
    And never rise to the surface again.
You had no business taking John Murphy
    Away from the Little Eau Pleine.

"Now I will desert my vocation,
    I won't teach district school any more.
I will go to some place where I'll never
    Hear the squeak of a fifty-foot oar.
I will go to some far foreign country,
    To England, to France, or to Spain;
But I'll never forget Johnny Murphy
    Nor the banks of the Little Eau Pleine."

The Return of Johnny Appleseed

by CHARLES ALLEN SMART, 1904–   . *A man who happily combines the vocations of writer and farmer, Smart was born in Cleveland and
was educated at Harvard, B.A., 1926. In the next few years he was a free
lance writer, a publisher's reader and editorial assistant, and a teacher of English at the Choate School, Wallingford, Connecticut. Since 1934 he and his*

wife have lived on a farm near Chillicothe, Ohio, where they raise vegetables, flowers, and sheep. In World War II Smart served in the United States Navy. He is the author of several novels and also of R.F.D. (1938), a charming and philosophical account of the adjustments which a city-bred man must make in residing in a rural community. "The Return of Johnny Appleseed" originally appeared in Harper's Magazine, August 1939.

I

IF YOU should mention the name "Johnny Appleseed" to any farmer in Ross County, Ohio, he would look at you quizzically, wondering how much you know, and then he would withdraw silently into his own memories and reflections. Just what those reflections are, and whether they have resulted in any decisions, I don't know, but I suspect they are very important indeed, simply because they may suggest the future of American agriculture and democracy.

The familiar response to the name would be there of course. Most of us know better than any schoolchild the story of the gaunt, bearded, long-haired man who wandered alone through the Middle West during its settlement, carrying a Bible, a staff, and a sack, dressed in burlap, with a rope around his waist and his cook-pan for a hat. We know that he befriended both the white people and the Indians, preached the Gospel, and set out and cared for the first nurseries and apple orchards in that savage and beautiful wilderness. We know that there was a man who did all that, and that his name was Jonathan Chapman, but the facts are less important to us than the legend. I know I am not alone here in liking Johnny Appleseed because he represents the America that has never been interested in money or public opinion, that has been friendly, sensible, and brave instead of aggressive and bloody, that has nurtured life instead of destroying it, and that has been sensitive to the beauty of this continent, and done something to create here a civilization. Johnny Appleseed stands for ourselves at our best, and that's why we all felt so keenly what happened.

The question of our being represented at all first came up at one of the monthly meetings, at our co-operative grain elevator, of the board of directors of the Ross County Farm Bureau. There is a complicated network of farm organizations, enterprises, and government services; but the sad fact is that, even taken all together, they are not actually representative. Yet it was natural and just that when a countywide activity was under way the approach was made to the directors of the Farm Bureau, and that we co-operated on equal terms with the Grange in acting for the farmers of the county as such.

I served on the Farm Bureau board for a year. Significantly and hopefully, I felt, many of us who served that year, including myself, were not re-elected. I should like to describe those meetings but will content myself with saying that in my opinion we talked too much and did too little. I can say this because no member was longer on talk and shorter on action than myself. (I am too much a writer and too little a farmer to have been on that board at all.) We were usually very tired, we didn't listen enough to the women, we were unused to collective action, and we were rightly very tender toward minority opinion, very unwilling to boss or be bossed. All of this came out very clearly in the tragi-comedy of Johnny Appleseed.

At the meeting of which I speak, the President said: "Now about this Sesquicentennial Celebration. The Committee wants us to have a float in the parade. Now what do all you folks think about that?"

We stiffened a little in our seats. The celebration was obviously going to be a big thing, and as farmers we obviously had to be represented. All of us had had enough to do with floats to know that they are not produced by people sitting in their seats. During two hours of discussion we nerved ourselves to vote twenty-five dollars and a committee of three, to get together if possible with an equal fund and committee from the Grange and produce a float. I had talked too much, and found myself on the committee. Still I went home that night feeling less guilty about my dollar for attendance and twenty-five cents for mileage.

The celebration was of the founding of the Northwest Territory. Chillicothe was an early capital of this territory and the first capital of the State of Ohio. Some of the ultimately most important political activity in American history had taken place in vanished seats within a few hundred yards of our own. Memories of profitable fairs and celebrations elsewhere stirred in the minds of our merchants. Our slightly older rival town, Marietta, was making great preparations to celebrate, and the sly rascals had got the Postmaster-General to issue a special stamp showing the Territory with Marietta but not Chillicothe. Town organizations had appointed committees to organize the whole celebration. There were going to be a costume ball, an enormous pageant by schoolchildren, a great historical parade, and the next day after the parade an appropriate reception of the ox-drawn covered wagon that was coming all the way from Massachusetts via Marietta, darn them. There were to be street decorations, and each merchant was ransacking his attic and cellar to find old tools of his trade for display in his windows. The whole thing was being financed successfully, chiefly through the sale of "wooden nickels," which all of us were sure would soon be worthy fifty dollars apiece, especially those with "sesquicentennial" spelled wrong.

Congenitally, or perhaps because of the climate, which is vitiating in its irregularities and extremes, we are not apt to act hastily or vigorously about anything; but after several weeks the whole county, with all its remote towns, hamlets, and crossroads, became aroused. We had not approached a community of interest and action like this since the War.

One rainy Saturday afternoon in April, while our wives were up on Paint Street, shopping, the six members of our joint farm committee on a float met in a smoky little office at the co-operative. With the exception of myself, they were probably as reliable and competent a committee as could have been named from all the men in the Farm Bureau and the Grange. No women had been appointed, ostensibly because the work would be fairly heavy and mechanical, and actually because we had decided that for once in our lives we were going to do something well without our women. My neighbor Mr. Oak, the master of the Grange, intelligent, reticent, and very tired, and Joe Copper, for the Farm Bureau, a stout, slow, genial, gray-haired farmer who was running for County Commissioner, were the joint chairmen. Actually, since Joe Copper was less busy than Mr. Oak, he undertook to run the show. First he tried to unload the ultimate responsibility on to me because I was supposed to be less busy than any of them, but I declined to accept it, quite definitely.

Knowing that we should have to decide on the subject of our float, I had brought along an old Ohio history with a few paragraphs on Johnny Appleseed, illustrated with an imaginary sketch. To my surprise and pleasure, several of the others had thought of the same subject. Some thought it might be fun to play Indians in some historical episode, but it was reported that the Order of Red Men and several other organizations were going to provide swarms of these. After some discussion of Johnny Appleseed, not by me, the feeling for him grew and he was unanimously selected to represent us.

Then we talked about the possible ways of presenting our hero and agreed to mount a large apple tree on a wagon, on which Johnny would ride. Each of us volunteered to do one or more special jobs of preparation, and Joe Copper correlated these quite expertly. He and Ed Raven, a lean, bright-eyed Granger who lived near him, were going to find a tree that could be spared, dig it up the week before the parade, and water it in the interval, so that it would have time to wilt and revive. They would also find a low wagon on which the big tree could be mounted, and transport both to the County Garage, where the work of assembling would be done. Harry Schermerhorn, a quiet, ingenious, and reliable little man, had some good ideas about decoration and would provide the materials and his own skill in working with them when the time came. He would be assisted in this difficult job by Mr. Oak. I said that I would get more information about Johnny Appleseed, weave a fence such as he used to protect his seedlings, and provide costume and make-up for the actor of the part. They wanted me to play the part of Johnny, but when I declined firmly, Joe Copper said he had in mind an old man with a beard who lived out his way. We had a long discussion of Johnny's age, and finally decided not to be too finicky about that. To our great delight, Elmer Graves, a powerful, good-natured fellow, said that he could get two yoke of oxen to pull the whole float when the great day arrived. We arranged to have another meeting soon and broke up cheerful and confident. By golly, it wasn't only the business men who could do things in Ross County!

II

In the following weeks we had several good meetings to report progress, check up on details, and integrate our efforts. Evidently everything was going very nicely. One afternoon I stopped at Joe Copper's house and he drove me some miles to the place where he and Ed Raven and others had dug up a large old wild apple tree, complete with a huge ball of earth, and were watering it daily. At home in odd moments I busied myself with cutting pliant willow wands and weaving a section of fence to be put on the back of the float. With the eager assistance of the Librarian of Cincinnati and a scholar at the State university, I managed to get together a few books over which the other committeemen pored with an interest that astonished me. Before we were through we were debating about historical details like a group of scholars, and I may say that these farmers showed more ability to find the wheat in the chaff than some Ph.D.'s I have known. Like the other five, I was finding the job more difficult and interesting than I had expected that it would be.

The parade was to take place on a Friday afternoon in May, and the morning before, the six of us assembled at the County Garage with most of the materials. Tree, wagon, lumber, and tools for a special bed, green and yellow cheese-cloth, sawdust to simulate earth, apple seedlings for the nursery, costume and properties for Johnny, and plenty of other little things were all soon assembled, and we set cheerfully to work. When I admired the tree, which was at least twelve feet tall and equally wide, with a good shape, and still green, Joe Copper reported nonchalantly that the first tree had withered a second time, and they had had to find and dig up another.

It appeared that the old man with the beard had demanded five dollars for his services, and had been told what he could do with his beard. Then Joe had secured Mr. Amos Locksley, a good farmer and fine old

Granger who, everyone assured me, would do very well. Soon Mr. Locksley appeared, and I saw at once that they were quite right. He was a tall, dignified, clean-shaven, very handsome old man with brown skin, white hair, and wonderful dark eyes. He was also very intelligent and willing, had read up on Johnny, and came supplied with costume and properties to supplement what I had gathered together. What delighted me most was that Mr. Locksley, it appeared, was the man who had a huge tract of woodland, full of wildflowers, and who every spring could and did open it to the public, to cut and dig and transplant as much as they chose. Except for Mr. Locksley's very neat appearance, which he didn't mind altering, it was almost a case of typecasting.

The weather was clear and warm, but there was a slaughter-house in the next lot, and I was pleased to note that I wasn't the only sissy who found the odor extreme. No one did any bossing at all, and everyone consulted everyone else almost before driving each nail, and yet for a significant wonder, the job went right along, and when in the late afternoon we had the tree mounted, the apples wired on, the nursery and fence arranged, and the float decorated with apples and practically finished, the whole thing had design and charm. With that beautiful tree, no advertising at all, and everything done with meticulous care, that was no ordinary float, I assure you. Some of our wives were working on a Garden Club float in a neighboring garage, and when they came over to fetch us home to our chores but first to inspect our work very critically, they had to admit that we had done a real job without any help from them. We attached a hose and watered the tree and seedlings for the last time that evening.

Then the problem arose of how to protect the apples from theft by small boys that night. The County Garage, with road-scrapers and so on, is big, but our float was much bigger, and couldn't possibly be put back in and locked up. We finally agreed to hire a watchman for the night, if we could, for two dollars and a half. City people on comfortable and regular salaries cannot possibly appreciate the difficulty of that decision. We were all tired and had work to do at home, and yet to net two dollars and a half you have to produce and sell a surprising number of eggs, for instance. Finally it was agreed that I'd get my hired man for the job if I could, and that Mr. Locksley would guard the tree until he came. My wife, Peggy, and I hurried home, and I propositioned my Leo James, assuring him that if he sat up all night on this job he could have the next day off. He accepted gladly and hurried to town in my truck.

Much later that night my wife and I and an old friend of ours named Helen Clive, who was visiting us, went to the costume ball and had a wonderful time. Helen made such an impression on all the local gentry that the first thing we knew we were mixed up with a lot of politicians, and the sheriff was telling me he wanted me to meet the Governor the next day. "You needn't be afraid of him, Allen," he assured me; "he's just a farm boy like you and me." I have been flattered in my time, but never more grossly and yet effectively. And I was certainly put on a spot, because our Governor at that time . . . well, I wouldn't have touched him with a ten-foot pole. One reason I had such a good time that night was that as I caroused with my luckier town acquaintances, I could keep thinking: "There aren't any farmers here, for several reasons, good and bad, and you may think they aren't up to this celebration, and can't get together and do something. Ha, ha, ha!"

And while we were there . . . The next morning James appeared as usual and reported that Mr. Locksley had not let him take over the job of watching the tree, because he, James, had had no proof that he had authority to do so. Thanks to my thoughtlessness, Mr. Locksley, who was not young, who had a cold, and who was about to take a long ride clad in almost nothing but a burlap sack, had sat up alone all night in his car, watching that float.

I hurried down to the job. Everyone else was there, already at work, and Mr. Locksley was fit and cheerful. We watered everything again, and made sure that every apple and every bit of decoration was secure. Then Mr. Locksley and I set to work on his costume and make-up, which included a long white beard to be put on almost hair by hair with gum arabic. I am far from an expert in these things, but I knew more than the others, and went ahead trusting to luck. While I worked on him we discussed his performance on the float, and agreed to make it very simple. I knew that we could trust the man's instincts. When we were through I must say he looked right and quite worthy of the legend and the float. Even in that outrageous costume, with a tin pan squashed to fit his head, he had superlative dignity. I had supplied an old leather-bound book as a Bible for him to carry, but at his suggestion we substituted a less valuable book that he had brought along for the purpose, and that looked quite as much like a Bible. I don't know why, but I was delighted when I noticed that Mr. Locksley's book was a school edition of Virgil's *Aeneid*.

It was getting on toward noon, and feeling very happy about the whole thing, we began to drift home to dinner. The parade was to assemble uptown at 2:30, and Elmer Graves said that the two yoke of oxen would appear by truck at 12:30, or 12:45 at the latest, and he would show up at the same time. Joe Copper, the Chairman, said that he would wait around with Mr. Locksley until the oxen came. With

much discussion everything had been arranged to yoke the oxen properly to the float and to take them by a good back route to their appointed place uptown. We were all very proud about those oxen. Most
of the floats were going to be drawn by teams, and a few organizations
were going to have one yoke of oxen. Well, we were going to have two
yoke. I was the last to leave. I wished Mr. Locksley luck, waved to
Joe Copper, and hurried home to lunch. Still, somehow, at that moment, I didn't feel very good. I might stay and . . . No, it was none
of my damned business. It is in moments like that that men are made
and broken and history is altered.

III

When I got home, Peggy told me that the sheriff had called up
twice—a disconcerting phrase to a farmer *or* a writer—but only about
the Governor. She had said quite truthfully that I was working on the
Farm Bureau float and, rather less truthfully, that I could not be
reached by telephone.

Immediately after lunch we hurried into town—that is, to the edge
of town, where we had to leave our car. The three of us had been invited by our old friend Miss Mary Bell to see the parade from the front
steps of her house, which is down near the center of town. The outer
streets of Chillicothe were crowded with floats, horses, oxen, and
people in costume, so that one got an impression that someone had
been working on the place with a Wellsian time-machine, slightly out
of order. Emerging from an alley, we would make our way through a
nonchalant group of pioneers in buckskins and beards, with long rifles,
or past an almost naked Indian in war paint and bonnet lighting the
cigarette of a girl in crinolines. Ohio is where all the good bands come
from: there must have been twenty different ones, in all kinds of costumes, tuning up on street corners. It was all so bizarre and exciting
that I almost succeeded in forgetting that I hadn't seen our great apple
tree anywhere, and couldn't remember the street corner where it certainly was waiting by this time.

We found Miss Mary in holiday mood on her front steps, equipped
with all kinds of robes and pillows. Hardly to our surprise, because,
like everyone else, we were feeling very superior and smug about our
celebration by this time, the parade started almost on time, and moved
along regularly, exactly as numbered and explained, with historical
notes, in the program. Every single one of the forty or fifty floats was
historical, and as near as any of us could tell, authentic, down to small
details. Most of the properties were originals, not reproductions. Each
float bore a simple placard but there was no advertising. There was
almost no one in that parade without an historical costume, and there

45

was not one single motor vehicle. Acting through nearly all of its too many organizations, with imagination, energy, and loving care, most of the people in the county had created a living record of our history from the prehistoric mound-builders to the Civil War and a little later. It was by all odds the most moving and interesting parade I have ever seen. An Armistice Day parade by the French Army and Navy, at the Arc de Triomphe—and the French know how to put on a parade—now took its place as a poor second.

Early in the parade there appeared a remarkable old rig of some kind, drawn by a handsome horse and driven by one of our best farmers, costumed as General St. Clair, the first Governor of the Northwest Territory, who had been chased out of Chillicothe a century and a half before. He was now received with cheers. There were other great pioneers and territorial and State governors. Then there came another handsome horse, drawing an interesting old rig with a liveried groom up in the back. This was driven by one of our most powerful local political bosses, who calls himself a Democrat and is the attorney for our electric company. His passenger, according to the placard, which was hardly necessary considering the multitude of his photographs on posters and public works, was "The Present Governor of Ohio." His Excellency kept bravely smiling and removing his hat to right and left, although he was recognized and his progress was accompanied with a unanimous and almost audible silence. We heard afterward that he cut several engagements and went right back to Columbus in a rage.

But no mere reminder of the quality of American politics could spoil that parade. There was every conceivable kind of a horse-drawn vehicle and several surprising early bicycles, all produced from old barns here and there. Four of our horsier and younger landowners, in costume, were driven by in a victoria. "That's charming," I thought, "but wait till you see what the real farmers have done." There were accurate reproductions of an early schoolroom, with teacher and pupils, of an early printing and newspaper office in action, and of several early churches, one Negro, with an excellent choir. The Conservation League produced some early hunters with hounds baying at two live raccoons in a dead tree. One of the best exhibits was that of a small outlying community: they produced a whole company of pioneers moving west—men, boys, and hounds walking ahead, a fine prairie schooner with women and children, a cow in tow, and even chickens, and another armed guard bringing up the rear. There were old gardens (kept fresh at what labor Peggy and I could appreciate), early firemen with equipment, and many notable old buildings now gone. There were mound-builders, hundreds of Indians, French-Canadian priests and voyageurs, all kinds of soldiers of the French and Indian Wars, the Revolution, and the War of 1812. There was, in fact, every kind of a living and dramatic historical exhibit of that period and place that one could well imagine.

As the parade went by, in perfect order, with everyone clapping and cheering, and the bands blaring gaily along at regular intervals, I began to think that maybe our Johnny Appleseed wouldn't be so outstanding after all. But then I remembered that tree—much bigger, finer, and fresher than anything of the kind that had come along, and Mr. Locksley, who somehow was more real than anyone we had seen yet. In the program, "Johnny Appleseed: Farm Bureau and Grange," with historical note, was placed towards the end, say No. 33. As the twenties went slowly by I felt my heart pounding heavily and I didn't dare to run out to the curb to look down the street and see that great tree coming. "Almost now: that must be it!" exclaimed Helen. I managed to look, and saw some little shrub in some other float. "No, not that," I said. No. 31, No. 32 . . .

And then No. 34, some damned thing or other, No. 35, and No. 36.

"It must be later, certainly," said Miss Mary.

"Yes, they may have had to calm down the oxen or something," said Helen.

Peggy said nothing, and I didn't dare to look at her.

And although I could now hardly see it, the parade went inexorably along, to the very end, which was marked by a couple of State troopers on motor cycles, followed by a crowd of small boys.

Miss Mary was touching my arm and saying: "Come on inside, Allen. It's grown quite chilly. I think you all need a glass of sherry."

"Thank you, I think we do," I said.

We drank Miss Mary's sherry and nibbled her biscuits almost in silence and hurried away. Miss Mary always understands things.

It was raining now, and I ran almost all the way to get the car. On the way I passed some farm friends sitting rather pointlessly in their car.

"Hey, Allen!"

"By God, don't ask me!" I yelled and ran on.

I got the car, picked up the girls, and drove grimly, madly, to the County Garage.

There was our float, exactly where it had been, dripping gently in the rain. Joe Copper was just standing there, looking at it and through it, with raindrops falling from his hat-brim. Without looking at me, he said: "The oxen never showed up." I asked some rather violent questions and made some rather violent comments, and he just said it again: "The oxen never showed up."

Mr. Locksley was there, still in costume, still with that tin pan on his head. He had pulled off his beard, but there were still tufts of it sticking to his face. He was up on the float, jerking the apples off the tree and throwing them to a gang of ragged children who had gathered there from nowhere. I went up to him but I couldn't say a word.

"These things happen," he said. "These things happen and there isn't any use getting sore about them."

"Thank you, Mr. Locksley," I said, and turned away.

Helen, watching Mr. Locksley with the apples and the children, was weeping unashamed. I couldn't have said whether Peggy was going to burst into tears or kick someone in the shins. Cars began to drive into the lot round the float. Some of the men jumped out, exploding as I had, but they fell silent quickly enough too, and then just stood there looking at that tree and at Mr. Locksley. Elmer Graves wasn't there.

"Let's get out of here," I said, and we did.

IV

I am not really sure just what the three of us did that night. It may have been the night when we went to the big pageant, and I helped Peggy and her Girl Scouts hawk programs and W.P.A. *Guides*, and we all nearly froze. I don't like pageants myself, but this was a good one. Or perhaps this wasn't that night. Perhaps we just stayed at home and got quietly pickled. Or perhaps we did both. I do remember that we thought people would keep calling up, and that no one did. Of course not: there wasn't anything to say. We didn't talk about it much ourselves. The unanswerable questions, the painful implications: there were more and more, the more we thought about it, and each seemed worse than the last.

The next morning we got up horribly late and James and the girl were already at work. When I got downstairs I found Fred Keeler, our County Agent, in the library with three professors of agriculture or something from the State university. I never did find out what that impressive call was all about. While I was shaking hands with them the 'phone rang and I dashed to it. It was Joe Copper, down at the County Garage. He said the *Gazette* had called up and wanted to know why we didn't get our float into the second parade, smaller and less important, that was going to greet the oxen and the covered wagon from Massachusetts via Marietta. They were going to arrive about noon. Joe wanted to know whether I thought that was a good idea, or maybe an anticlimax, and worse than not being in any parade. "Hell no, let's get it in," I said. I didn't even go back and apologize to Fred and the professors in the library. Fred always understands things too. I beat it out the back door and into the car. Peggy appeared and hopped in too, and I didn't tell her it was a stag party either. When we got to the float we found that there were at least five other wives there working on it too. And there wasn't a nasty remark out of one of them. Elmer Graves was there too, this time working like mad, and so was his wife, and her face was wet.

We didn't do any unnecessary talking: there wasn't any time for that for one thing. We got some more bright red apples, and everyone wired them on that tree again, and into the festoons along the side. It was a big job, and all our fingers weren't working their best. We restored the nursery and gave the whole thing another good soaking with the hose. The leaves were still fresh. Someone called up a neighbor of mine who had a handsome team, and he was a good egg and took them right out of the harness when they were plowing. Mr. Locksley, quietly cheerful as ever, got into his burlap sack and tin hat and found his staff and Virgil Bible. I had brought along the remnants of beard and make-up and went to work on him. I didn't have enough artificial hair left to make his own hair long in the back, but I made him a beard and he looked almost as good as he had the day before. We had arranged to hook the float on behind my truck and meet the team at an appointed place uptown. Peggy had got a big silver watch from someone and was standing over Joe Copper saying: "Only ten minutes left now, Mr. Copper," and then: "Only five minutes now, Mr. Copper." Everyone else heard her too, and as we were hooking up the float to the truck, the excitement, or the smell of the slaughter-house, or something, made me come near to emptying my stomach.

I drove my truck, and everyone piled into cars and made a little parade behind the float. I drove as slowly as I could, I thought, with that truck, but the next big boner was pulled by me, personally. Going over the railroad spur to the paper mill, I gave the whole thing such a shaking that most of the apples fell off. I stopped and got out and the street was full of our people who had climbed out of their cars and were picking up apples and wiring them on to that tree and float for the third time. We were all a little hysterical by that time, but we did it quickly and started moving again. I drove on very slowly but I didn't stop for stop-signs, or red lights, or a State trooper, or anything else. We met the team and their owner all right. His hired man, who drove them from then on, was a very sad Negro with a peg leg, and something in his face made me know there wasn't any use getting so excited: it would turn out all right, one way or another.

Then we had a long wait for the covered wagon and oxen from Massachusetts via Marietta. We all spent the time tinkering with the float and I did some more work on Mr. Locksley's beard. While we were busy at this another old man came up to me and said: "That's just what the world needs to-day."

"What's that?" I asked. "Beards?"

"Religion," he said.

"It's all right with me," I said, plying the scissors.

Finally the celebrated covered wagon and oxen appeared, and they didn't look like much to us, after all. Perhaps we just didn't like the oxen. They took the lead, and they were followed by an oxdrawn float of the Seal of Ohio, which was followed by a couple of stupid floats of the ordinary kind, with cuties, tissue paper, and advertising. Johnny Appleseed brought up the rear.

V

When the little parade finally started I got a hammer and some pliers and nails out of my truck for emergencies and followed along the sidewalk with Joe Copper. It was a good thing I did, because one yoke of oxen ran away and smashed a car, which in turn smashed the Seal of Ohio, but not beyond a few hasty repairs. I also had to grab a State trooper to help me because our tree had to go way round the traffic lights instead of under them, and at the street corners people were crowded far into the street and had to be pushed back. When I took up farming I didn't know it was going to involve handling people at parades, but then I didn't know much about it.

And it was worth it, all right. It was all worth it. A few hasty glances back at our float proved that. At the end of that silly little parade our great tree, with its leaves and apples shining in the sunlight, was really something. And Mr. Locksley wasn't there any more. Standing there before the tree in the little nursery leaning on his staff, with his Bible in his hand, looking out remotely in his incomparable dignity and beauty at the clapping crowd and staring, awe-struck children, was Johnny Appleseed himself. It sent a shiver down more spines than mine.

When we reached the end I was in a bit of a daze, but I remembered that someone had said Johnny could be got on the radio in front of the courthouse. This seemed a bit out of key, but I remembered that farm organizations, like all others, can use good publicity, and I knew that Mr. Locksley could dominate any situation. The old Negro with the peg leg knew where to take the team and float, and I got Mr. Locksley off the float and we hurried silently through the crowd. When we got near the courthouse the crowd was so thick that we couldn't make any headway. An old newspaper editor I know, who has a bad heart at that, saw our plight and jammed his way through ahead of us like a trooper. The announcer saw us and made a few remarks, and then Johnny Appleseed was standing there before a microphone. Once again that strange thing happened, and quiet spread out a little way.

"My name is Johnny Appleseed," he said. "I lived in this part of the country a long time ago, when it had hardly been touched. I liked the Indians and I liked the white people and I liked the animals, and I didn't hurt any of them. I planted seeds and set out apple trees for the settlers, and I took care of them. I told the people about God, and I tried to be a good man myself. I tried to be a good American, on this land we had found. Maybe I was, a little. Maybe I'm not dead yet."

With that he turned away, and after a minute there was a kind of exclamation from the crowd, mixed with clapping. Then he got down from the platform and gave the seedlings he had left to the children in the crowd, until they were all gone.

Then I found Mr. Locksley, and we smiled at each other a little wearily and shook hands and found our cars and went home.

This all happened a year ago, and Peggy and I have seen all these people again and again since then, and we haven't heard one word said about it. I feel sure that there has been little or no talk about it of any kind. I feel equally sure that there has been some tall thinking about it. To what effect, I don't know. But in another hundred and fifty years we may not miss the big parade, and in another hundred and fifty years we may still be producing the real thing.

THE INDIAN

Biography of Blackbird

by ALPHONSO WETMORE, 1793–1849. A veteran of the War of 1812, in which he lost an arm, Wetmore was later paymaster of the Sixth Regiment in Missouri. After practicing law in various places he settled in St. Louis, where he died of cholera. Wetmore contributed articles and sketches to St. Louis newspapers, wrote a play called The Pedlar, produced and published in 1821, and compiled the Gazetteer of the State of Missouri (1837). Appended to the Gazetteer are six short narratives of frontier life which are unusual in their realistic dialogue and background. One of these is the account of the Omaha chief Blackbird.

THE principal chief of the Omaha tribe of Indians, the location of whose village is sixty miles above Council Bluffs, and on the same side the right bank of the river, died A.D. 1802. He was a brave of iron nerves and unlimited ambition. The authority which an Indian exercises is at first obtained by winning the approbation of the people of the tribe, in the same manner that a white politician obtains the suffrages of his countrymen. There is a small difference in the moral qualities which distinguish the white and red man. The former, it is believed, could never recommend himself by horse-stealing; whereas the red aspirant is esteemed honourable in proportion to the grand larcenies he may be able to perpetrate; and this engaging quality of horse-stealing is esteemed a virtue next in grade to that of taking scalps. An Indian, therefore, has a table on his war-club, with two columns, in which he enters, in hieroglyphics, the number of these transactions of each class that are to render him illustrious. Although the government of Indian tribes is generally of a democratic character, yet there are many instances where the popularity of a chief enables him to encroach on the freedom of his countrymen extensively; and there are occasions where great achievements in war and in horse-stealing enable a chief to attain absolute authority. This despotism is, however, generally fixed by the united exertions of the chief and prophet, or big medicine-man. The instances of Tecumseh and his prophet, and Black Hawk and his prophet, show that the ambitious red man, like a white prince, unites church and state in his strides to absolute power. The subject of this biography had likewise the efficient aid of a cunning medicine-man, who furnished mental prescriptions for the people of his nation, and imposed on the superstitious magic incantations.

Blackbird had distinguished himself in the usual manner, and was acknowledged principal chief. The usual authority was conceded with cheerfulness. But Blackbird was not content with the executive duties and patriarchal authority of a democracy, and the honours attending such distinguished trust. In order to effect his purposes, he had tried in vain all the force of military achievement, the influence of grand larceny, and the power of eloquence. He had called in to his aid the juggling cunning of his medicine-man, with no better success. There existed in the nation a party of stern warriors, who valued freedom as highly as white patriots. They were unyielding in their opposition to the usurpations of Blackbird. He denominated this party a faction, or a "bad moccasin band"; but his reproaches were disregarded. The ambitious aspirant meditated their destruction. Blackbird desired the trader, who supplied his nation with merchandise, to bring him from St. Louis some "strong medicine" which he believed the whites possessed, that he might destroy the wolves of the prairies. The trader subsequently supplied a quantity of crude arsenic. Soon after the chief had tried his experiments, to test the force of the poison, the disaffected

53

braves were invited to a dog-feast at the lodge of the chief. Blackbird professed to them a disposition to heal all party dissensions, and sixty of the factious warriors sat down with him to the dog-soup, which is esteemed a great delicacy. When all had done ample justice to the hospitality of the entertainer, the pipe was passed; and when this dessert was lending its happy influence to the circle of warriors, Blackbird arose to speak. He reminded his children of their factious course in opposing his authority—authority that he claimed to derive from the "Master of Life"; and for confirmation of this suggestion he appealed to his medicine-man near him; "and," continued he, "that Omahas may for ever remember that Blackbird has the entire control of their destinies, every factious dog of you shall die before the sun rises again! I have said it, and Blackbird never lies!" The whole party, on hearing this unsparing denunciation, in wild affright ran howling out of the lodge of their chief. Sixty warriors expired that night. During the life of the chief, his authority was never again opposed in the slightest particular.

It was his practice, when the trader arrived with the annual supply of merchandise in the Omaha village, to inquire of him how great an amount of furs and peltries he required for his entire stock. The chief then selected from the assortment as great a variety and amount as he would need for his own use, and for his numerous family. When this had been arranged, and an account had been opened with the nation by the trader, the warriors were required to furnish the number of beaver-skins, robes, and buffalo-tongues that the trader desired to obtain in exchange for his goods. In this off-hand manner the chief drew his revenues, and the trader realized his profits, during all the subsequent reign of the despot. This rude dignitary was becoming inactive; and when his braves and hunters were toiling to sustain the reputation of the Omahas in war, or to subsist the people with the products of the chase, the chief and his prime minister, the medicine-man, were reposing in the village. It was the custom of the chief to indulge, in warm weather, in the *siesta despues comer*, or sleep after dinner. While in the enjoyment of this luxury, he took occasion to make it the more perfect by the polite attentions of his wives. He had six of these, and they formed three relieves. Two were employed while he slept, one scratching his back, and the other fanning his highness with the tail of a turkey! If it was ever important to ask his instructions in the affairs of the nation when he chanced to be sleeping, there was only one person in the village who would venture to awaken the chief. This was the medicine-man; and his manner of approaching him was on his hands and feet, with the utmost humility and circumspection. When awakened with a feather cautiously drawn over the soles of his feet, if he made a discouraging motion with the hand, the application was abandoned. But if he beckoned the applicant to approach, the chief was respectfully invited to attend "a dog-feast which has been provided for my father."

Blackbird was a respectable warrior, and had attained his early popularity by conquest; but the distinction he most coveted was unlimited power in his own nation. When he had attained this he became pacific towards the neighbouring nations. But a partisan leader had taken a Pawnee girl, who was, by command of the medicine-man, to be sacrificed at the stake. The son of Blackbird had seen her, and interposed in council to save her life. He laid down all the moveable property he possessed, and urged the purchase of the girl from her captor. The medicine-man was inflexible, and persisted in his vow to sacrifice her to the Great Spirit. The council approved the vow, for Blackbird had permitted it. When, on the day appointed, the captive was led out to execution, young Split Cloud, son of the chief, was seen leading his buffalo-horse, not far from the head of the column where the victim was marching. After the medicine-man, with the captive and a few old warriors, had crossed a ravine in the route, and were rising to the plain, the place appointed for the sacrifice, the young warrior cut asunder the cords that confined the arms of the girl, lifted her to his saddle, and with his bow lashed his horse to full speed before his countrymen could comprehend the meaning of his movements. He was half across the plain before pursuit was determined on; and then there were no horses at hand. He had concealed one in the next ravine, and the fugitives escaped the ill-arranged and worse-conducted pursuit of the Omahas. A solitary runner came within arrow-shot of Split Cloud, but his race terminated there—he was shot to the heart. The fugitives retired to the recesses of the Black Mountains, and took up their abode there, until home affairs should present a more inviting prospect. Their wedding was thinly attended; but the blush of affection glowed as vividly on the cheek of the bride as that which mantles over the neck more tastefully adorned, in civilized circles, on like occasions. The self-married pair passed a year in the solitude to which they had retired, content with the society each was able to afford the other, when Split Cloud deemed it advisable to revisit his nation. In this lone retreat he left his spouse, with the purpose of retracing his steps in the brief space of a few weeks. A sufficient supply of dried meat was left in the cave with its tenant, for the period of his intended absence. "The interesting state of her health" was no bar to the departure of her husband, for red women rarely trouble the neighbouring matrons at the nativity of their children. When a tribe of Indians happen to be on the march on such an occasion, the sufferer halts for an hour or two near a stream, and, after the birth of her infant, mounts with it on her horse, and overtakes the column generally the same evening.

When Split Cloud reached his native village, he found the whole tribe chanting the death-song over an infinite number of the dead inhabitants of the nation. The smallpox had reached the Omahas, and many had already been swept off: very few recovered. The medicine-man claimed to have power over the disease, but his practice hitherto had been unsuccessful. He looked grave, and was evidently suffering with great alarm. The most common treatment of the patients, when afflicted with the inflammatory action of the disease, was immersion in cold water. This usually afforded speedy relief, and terminated all the ills of life—with extinction of life itself. At last, after many new and imposing tricks, death itself played the last masterly act on the impostor—and old Medicine himself departed. Blackbird had lived moodily apart from the tribe, and his dignity was likely to secure him against the infection. But when his high-priest died he attended his funeral obsequies. This happened a few days before the return of his son. Blackbird was considering what disposition should be made of the prodigal when he was taken ill. From the moment the first symptoms were felt by the chief, he yielded to despair, and made his arrangements for the hunting-grounds beyond the grave. He desired that he might be buried with suitable variety of arms and ammunition, that his enemies might get no advantage of him. He probably anticipated meeting with the poisoned warriors on the banks of the river Phlegethon. As he himself had apprehended, Blackbird was a victim to the disease. The funeral was grand and imposing. The warrior was placed erect on his hunting-horse, and thus, followed by the whole nation, he was conveyed into the grave that had been previously prepared, on the highest point of land, near to the Missouri river. The horse, alive, was forced into the grave with the dead rider, and thus covered over. A small parcel of corn was placed before the animal; and Blackbird was supplied with dried meat, his kettle, his pipe and kinakanick, gun with ammunition, bow and full quiver of arrows, and paints suitable for ornamenting his person, both in peace and war.

When the funeral was at an end, the trader arrived. His knowledge of the smallpox enabled him to save from its ravages the remainder of the tribe. All eyes were naturally turned on the son of Blackbird, as successor to the deceased chief. Young Split Cloud deemed himself so fortunate in the altered position he now occupied, having shifted the character of fugitive and culprit for the appointment of hereditary and popular chieftain, that he relaxed much of the despotism of his predecessor. Having settled the affairs of the nation and reduced the tariff, he found leisure to depart in search of his Pawnee wife. Autumn was far advanced when he left the Omaha towns, and, as he approached the mountains, winter, with its utmost rigor, set in. The emotions with which his savage and sensitive mind was agitated had not the refinement of poetry, chastened with rhetorical arrangement, cadence, and measure, to soften his suffering. He was not able to murmur, as he approached the place where he had deposited his treasure—

> 'T is sweet to hear the watch-dog's honest bark
>   Bay deep-mouthed welcome as we draw near home,
> 'T is sweet to know there is an eye will mark
>   Our coming, and grow brighter when we come.

But he had the elements of poetry rudely commingled with the romance of his reckless life, and his singular domestic arrangements. He found the partner of his life's vicissitudes in the cave where he had left her. She was sitting near the expiring coals of her last fagot of fuel, bending over a pair of babes, who were unconscious of the manifold evils of the world they had just entered, but sensibly aware of the pain of extreme hunger, which their mother was sharing with them. The holy fountain whence they had drawn supplies had been drained; and the famished mother sat in the picture of patience and despair. Hope had hitherto pictured in her imagination a sunny spot, such as that which was about to break upon her in the arrival of her preserver. But gnawing necessity had carried her to that maddened point which fixed the cannibal purpose of eating one of her infants, to preserve herself and the other one, until the long-wished-for relief should be realized. At the precise point of time when the person of her husband darkened the entrance of the cave, she held the knife in her hand, and was fondly lingering, in the debate of her own mind, which should be made the victim—which dear object should be preserved at such countless cost. The keen perceptions, the fine-drawn threads of affection, the result of protracted privation, lent unearthly vigour to her mind, when her final resolve was fixed, to perish with her offspring, and by the same innocent cause. She hurled the instrument of her bloody purpose far away into the dark recesses of the cavern, and placed the hungry babes upon her bosom as she sunk back in despair, unmitigated with a single ray of hope. At this critical instant the young warrior, in the full vigour of manhood, animated with virtuous purposes, sprang forward and gave utterance to a scream of joy, imparting a like sensation to the suffering object of his solicitude. The interchange of sentiment was full of sadly pleasing emotions, as the long fast of the wife and mother was broken over a kettle, amply provided by the skill of the hunter.

Sixty suns had risen and set after the thrilling events just described, when the Omaha nation was made joyous with the appearance of Split

57

Cloud. He was followed by his foreign wife, whom he had twice snatched from destruction, and who now repaid him with the smiles of two young braves, peering over each of her shoulders from beneath the ample folds of—*a new scarlet blanket.*

Payton Skah

by WILLIAM JOSEPH SNELLING, 1804–48. Snelling was born in Boston, the son of Colonel Josiah Snelling, a veteran of the War of 1812. After two years at West Point, from which he was dismissed for an infraction of discipline, Snelling went to Minnesota in 1821, his father then being commandant at Fort Snelling. The next half dozen years the young man spent as a hunter, scout, interpreter, and friend of the Sioux. In 1823 he accompanied Major Stephen Long's expedition to Pembina. When his father was transferred from Fort Snelling to St. Louis, Snelling returned to Boston, where he spent the rest of his life as a journalist and contributor to magazines. In 1830 Snelling published anonymously his Tales of the Northwest, the first attempt to use the Sioux country as a background for short fiction. Snelling's tales, despite stiffness and prolixity, are remarkable for their faithful use of details and their realistic treatment of the Indian. In addition to magazine articles and hackwork under the pseudonym of Solomon Bell, Snelling wrote a caustic verse satire directed against the poetasters of his day, Truth: A New Year's Gift for Scribblers (1831). "Payton Skah" illustrates Snelling's adroit use of legendary material against a realistic background.

> His hopes destroyed, his heart strings broke,
> No words of wo the warrior spoke,
> His bosom heav'd no sigh.
> 'Thine be the fair,' the hero said;
> Then proudly rear'd his lofty head,
> And turn'd away—to die.

WE HAVE before intimated that we cannot pretend to much accuracy with regard to dates. So we are not certain that the events we are about to relate did not happen five centuries ago, perhaps more; but it is probable that the time was not so remote. Be that as it may, we shall give the facts in the same order in which tradition hands them down.

The Dahcotahs were at war with the Mandans. Many were the onslaughts they made on each other, and long were they remembered. Among the Sioux warriors who struck the post, and took the war path, none was more conspicuous than Payton Skah, or The White Otter. He belonged to the Yankton band. When he returned from the field with his head crowned with laurels, or more properly with his bridle rein adorned with Mandan scalps, the seniors of the tribe pointed to him and exhorted their sons to ride, to draw the bow, and to strike the enemy like Payton Skah.

Payton Skah was a husband and a father. As soon as he was reckoned a man, and able to support a family, he had taken to his bosom the young and graceful Tahtokah, (The Antelope) thought to be the best hand at skinning the buffalo, making moccasins, whitening leather, and preparing marrow fat, in the tribe. She was not, as is common among the Dahcotahs, carried an unwilling or indifferent bride to her husband's lodge. No, he had lighted his match in her father's tent, and held it before her eyes, and she had blown it out, as instigated by love to do. And when he had espoused her in form, her affection did not diminish. She never grumbled at pulling off his leggins and moccasins when he returned from the chase, nor at drying and rubbing them till they became soft and pliant. A greater proof of her regard was, that she was strictly obedient to her mother in law. And Payton Skah's attachment, though his endearments were reserved for their private hours, was not less than hers. No woman in the camp could show more wampum and other ornaments, than the wife of the young warrior. He was even several times known, when she had been to bring home the meat procured by his arrows, to relieve her of a part of the burthen by taking it upon his own manly shoulders. In due time, she gave him a son; a sure token that however many more wives he might see proper to take, he would never put her away. The boy was the idol of his old grandmother, who could never suffer him out of her sight a moment, and used constantly to prophecy, that he would become a brave warrior and an expert horse stealer; a prediction that his manhood abundantly verified.

In little more than a year the youngster was able to walk erect. About this time the band began to feel the approach of famine. Buffaloes were supposed to abound on the river Des Moines, and thither Payton Skah resolved to go. His mother had cut her foot while chopping wood and was unable to travel; but she would not part with her grandchild. Tahtokah unwillingly consented to leave her boy behind, at the request of her husband, which indeed she never thought of disputing. One other family accompanied them. They soon reached the Des Moines, and encamped on its banks. Many wild cattle were killed, and much of their flesh was cured. The young wife now reminded her spouse that his mother must by this time be able to walk, and that she longed to see her child. In compliance with her wishes he mounted his horse and departed, resolved to bring the rest of the band to the land of plenty.

At his arrival his compatriots, on his representations, packed up their baggage and threw down their lodges. A few days brought them to where he had left his wife and her companions. But the place was desolate. No voice hailed their approach; no welcome greeted their arrival. The lodges were cut to ribbons, and a bloody trail marked where the bodies of their inmates had been dragged into the river. Following the course of the stream, the corpses of all but Tahtokah were found on the shores and sand-bars. Hers was missing, but this gave her husband no consolation. He knew that neither Sioux nor Mandans spared sex or age, and supposed it to be sunk in some eddy of the river. And Mandans the marks the spoilers had left behind them, proved them to be.

Now Payton Skah was, for an Indian, a kind and affectionate husband. The Sioux mothers wished their daughters might obtain partners like him; and it was proverbial to say of a fond couple, that they loved like Payton Skah and Tahtokah. Yet on this occasion, whatever his feelings might have been, he uttered no sigh, he shed no tear. But he gave what was, in the eyes of his co-mates, a more honorable proof of his grief. He vowed that he would not take another wife, nor cut his hair, till he had killed and scalped five Mandans. And he filled his quiver, saddled his horse, and raised the war song immediately. He found followers, and departed incontinently. At his return but three obstacles to his second marriage remained to be overcome.

In the course of the year he fulfilled the conditions of his vow. The five scalps were hanging in the smoke of his lodge, but he evinced no inclination towards matrimony. On the contrary, his countenance was sorrowful, he pined away, and every one thought he was in a consumption. His mother knew his disposition better. Thinking, not unwisely, that the best way to drive the old love out of his head was to provide him a new one, she with true female perseverance, compelled him by teazing and clamor to do as she wished.

So the old woman selected Chuntay Washtay (The Good Heart) for her son, and demanded her of her parents, who were not sorry to form such a connexion. The bride elect herself showed no alacrity in the matter; but this was too common a thing to excite any surprise or comment. She was formally made over to Payton Skah, and duly installed in his lodge.

He was not formed by nature to be alone. Notwithstanding the contempt an Indian education inculcates for the fair sex, he was as sensible to female blandishments as a man could be. Though his new wife was by no means so kind as the old one, yet as she fulfilled the duties of her station with all apparent decorum, he began to be attached to her. His health improved, he was again heard to laugh, and he hunted the buffalo with as much vigor as ever. Yet when Chuntay Washtay, as she sometimes would, raised her voice higher than was consistent with conjugal affection, he would think of his lost Tahtokah and struggle to keep down the rising sigh.

A young Yankton who had asked Chuntay Washtay of her parents previous to her marriage, and who had been rejected by them, now became a constant visiter in her husband's lodge. He came early, and staid and smoked late. But as Payton Skah saw no appearance of regard for the youth in his wife, he felt no uneasiness. If he had seen what was passing in her mind, he would have scorned to exhibit any jealousy. He would have proved by his demeanor 'that his heart was strong.' He was destined ere long to be more enlightened on this point.

His mother was gone with his child, on a visit to a neighboring camp, and he was left alone with his wife. It was reported that buffaloes were to be found at a little oasis in the prairie, at about the distance of a day's journey, and Chuntay Washtay desired him to go and kill one, and hang its flesh up in a tree out of the reach of the wolves. 'You cannot get back to night,' she said, 'but you can make a fire and sleep by it, and return tomorrow. If fat cows are to be found there we will take down our lodge and move.'

The White Otter did as he was desired. His wife brought his beautiful black horse, which he had selected and stolen from a drove near the Mandan village, to the door of the lodge. He threw himself on its back, and having listened to her entreaties that he would be back soon, rode away.

His gallant steed carried him to the place of his destination with the speed of the wind. The buffaloes were plenty, and in the space of two hours he had killed and cut up two of them. Having hung the meat upon the branches, he concluded that as he had got some hours of daylight, he would return to his wife. He applied the lash, and arrived at the camp at midnight.

He picketed his horse carefully, and bent his way to his own lodge. All was silent within, and the dogs, scenting their master, gave no alarm. He took up a handful of dry twigs outside the door and entered. Raking open the coals in the centre of the lodge he laid on the fuel, which presently blazed and gave a bright light. By its aid he discovered a spectacle that drove the blood from his heart into his face. There lay Chuntay Washtay, fast asleep by the side of her quondam lover. Payton Skah unsheathed his knife and stood for a moment irresolute; but his better feelings prevailing, he returned it to its place in his belt, and

61

left the lodge without awakening them. Going to another place he laid himself down, but not to sleep.

But when the east began to be streaked with grey, he brought his horse, his favorite steed, to the door of the tent. Just as he reached it those within awoke, and the paramour of Chuntay Washtay came forth and stood before him. He stood still. Fear of the famous hunter and renowned warrior kept him silent. Payton Skah, in a stern voice commanded him to re-enter; and when he had obeyed followed him in. The guilty wife spoke not, but covered her face with her hands, till her husband directed her to light a fire and prepare food. She then rose and hung the earthen utensil over the fire, and the repast was soon ready. At the command of Payton Skah she placed a wooden platter or bowl before him, and another for his unwilling guest. This last had now arrived at the conclusion that he was to die, and had screwed up his courage to meet his fate with the unshrinking fortitude of an Indian warrior. He ate therefore, in silence, but without any sign of concern. When the repast was ended Payton Skah produced his pipe, filled the bowl with tobacco mixed with the inner bark of the red willow, and after smoking a few whiffs himself, gave it to the culprit. Having passed from one to the other till it was finished, the aggrieved husband ordered his wife to produce her clothing and effects, and pack them up in a bundle. This done he rose to speak.

'Another in my place,' he said to the young man, 'had he detected you as I did last night, would have driven an arrow through you before you awoke. But my heart is strong, and I have hold of the heart of Chuntay Washtay. You sought her before I did, and I see she would rather be your companion than mine. She is yours; and that you may be able to support her, take my horse, and my bow and arrows also. Take her and depart, and let peace be between us.'

At this speech the wife, who had been trembling lest her nose should be cut off, and her lover, who had expected nothing less than death, recovered their assurance and left the lodge. Payton Skah remained; and while the whole band was singing his generosity, brooded over his misfortunes in sadness and silence.

Notwithstanding his boast of the firmness of his resolution, his mind was nearly unsettled by the shock. He had set his whole heart upon Tahtokah, and when the wound occasioned by her loss was healed, he had loved Chuntay Washtay with all his might. He could vaunt of his indifference to any ill that woman could inflict to the warriors of his tribe, but the boast that they could have truly made, was not true coming from him.

Though one of the bravest of men his heart was as soft as a woman's, in spite of precept and example. At this second blight of his affections, he fell into a settled melancholy, and one or two unsuccessful hunts convinced him that he was a doomed man; an object of the displeasure of God; and that he need never more look for any good fortune. A post dance, at which the performers alternately sung their exploits, brought this morbid state of feeling to a crisis. Like the rest, he recounted the deeds he had done, and declared that to expiate the involuntary offence he had committed against the Great Spirit, he would go to the Mandan village and throw away his body. All expostulation was vain; and the next morning he started on foot and alone to put his purpose in execution.

He travelled onward with a heavy heart, and the eighth evening found him on the bank of the Missouri, opposite the Mandan village. He swam the river, and saw the lights shine through the crevices, and heard the dogs bark at his approach. Nothing dismayed, he entered the village, and promenaded through it two or three times. He saw no man abroad, and impatient of delay, entered the principal lodge. Within he found two women, who spoke to him, but he did not answer. He drew his robe over his face, and sat down in a dark corner, intending to await the entrance of some warrior, by whose hands he might honorably die. The women addressed him repeatedly, but could not draw from him any reply. Finding him impenetrable, they took no further notice, but continued their conversation as if no one had been present. Had they known to what tribe he belonged they would have fled in terror; but they supposed him to be a Mandan. He gathered from it that the men of the village were all gone to the buffalo hunt, and would not return till morning. Most of the females were with them. Here then, was an opportunity to wreak his vengeance on the tribe such as had never before occurred, and would probably never occur again. But he refrained in spite of his Indian nature. He had not come to kill any one as on former occasions, but to lay down his own life; and he remained constant in his resolution.

If it be asked why the Mandans left their village in this defenceless condition, we answer, that Indian camps are frequently left in the same manner. Perhaps they relied on the broad and rapid river, to keep off any roving band of Dahcotahs that might come thither. Payton Skah sat in the lodge of his enemies till the tramp of a horse on the frozen earth, and the jingling of the little bells round his neck, announced that a warrior had returned from the hunt. Then The White Otter prepared to go to whatever lodge the Mandan might enter, and die by his arrows or tomahawk. But he had no occasion to stir. The horseman rode straight to the lodge in which he sat, dismounted, threw his bridle to a squaw, and entered. The women pointed to their silent guest, and related how unaccountably he had behaved. The new comer turned to Payton Skah and asked who and what he was. Then the Yankton, like Caius Marcius within the walls of Corioli, rose, threw off his robe, and drawing himself up with great dignity, bared his breast and spoke. 'I am a man. Of that, Mandan, be assured. Nay, more: I am a Dahcotah, and my name is Payton Skah. You have heard it before. I have lost friends and kin by the arrows of your people, and well have I revenged them. See, on my head I wear ten feathers of the war eagle. Now it is the will of the Master of life that I should die, and to that purpose came I hither. Strike therefore, and rid your tribe of the greatest enemy it ever had.'

Courage, among the aborigines as charity among Christians, covereth a multitude of sins. The Mandan Warrior cast on his undaunted foe a look in which respect, delight, and admiration were blended. He raised his war club as if about to strike, but the Siou blenched not; not a nerve trembled—his eyelids did not quiver. The weapon dropped from the hand that held it. The Mandan tore open his own vestment, and said, 'No, I will not kill so brave a man. But I will prove that my people are men also. I will not be outdone in generosity. Strike thou; then take my horse and fly.'

The Siou declined the offer, and insisted upon being himself the victim. The Mandan was equally pertinacious; and this singular dispute lasted till the latter at last held out his hand in token of amity. He commanded the women to prepare a feast, and the two generous foes sat down and smoked together. The brave of the Missouri accounted for speaking the Dahcotah tongue by saying that he was himself half a Siou. His mother had belonged to that tribe and so did his wife, having both been made prisoners. In the morning Payton Skah should see and converse with them. And the Yankton proffered, since it did not appear to be the will of the Great Spirit that he should die, to become the instrument to bring about a firm and lasting peace between the two nations.

In the morning the rest of the band arrived, and were informed what visitor was in the village. The women screamed with rage and cried for revenge. The men grasped their weapons and rushed tumultuously to the lodge to obtain it. A great clamor ensued. The Mandan stood before the door, declaring that he would guarantee the rights of hospitality with his life. His resolute demeanor, as well as the bow and war club he held ready to make his words good made the impression he desired. The Mandans recoiled, consulted, and the elders decided that Payton Skah must be carried as a prisoner to the council lodge, there to abide the result of their deliberations.

Payton Skah, indifferent to whatever might befall him, walked proudly to the place appointed in the midst of a guard of Mandans, and accompanied by the taunts and execrations of the squaws. The preliminary of smoking over, the consultation did not last long. His new friend related how the prisoner had entered the village, alone and unarmed save with his knife; how he had magnanimously spared the women and children when at his mercy; and how he had offered to negotiate a peace between the two tribes. Admiration of his valor overcame the hostility of the Mandans. Their hatred vanished like snow before the sun, and it was carried by acclamation, that he should be treated as became an Indian brave, and dismissed in safety and with honor.

At this stage of proceedings a woman rushed into the lodge, broke through the circle of stern and armed warriors, and threw herself into the arms of the Dahcotah hero. It was Tahtokah, his first, his best beloved! He did not return her caresses, that would have derogated from his dignity; but he asked her how she had escaped from the general slaughter at the Des Moines, and who was her present husband.

She pointed to the Mandan to whom he had offered his breast. He it was she said, who had spared her, and subsequently taken her to wife. He now advanced and proposed to Payton Skah to become his *kodah*, or comrade, and to receive his wife back again, two propositions to which the latter gladly assented. For according to the customs of the Dahcotahs, a wife may be lent to one's kodah without any impropriety.

The Mandans devoted five days to feasting the gallant Yankton. At the end of that time he departed with his recovered wife, taking with him three horses laden with robes and other gifts bestowed on him by his late enemies. His kodah accompanied him half way on his return, with a numerous retinue, and at parting received his promise that he would soon return. We leave our readers to imagine the joy of Tahtokah at seeing her child again on her arrival among the Sioux, as well as the satisfaction of the tribe at hearing that its best man had returned from his perilous excursion alive and unhurt. In less than two months Payton Skah was again among the Mandans with six followers, who were hospitably received and entertained. An equal number of Mandans accompanied them on their return home, where they experienced the like treatment. As the intercourse between the tribes became more frequent hostilities were discontinued, and the feelings that prompted them were in time forgotten. The peace brought about as above related has continued without interruption to this day. As to Payton Skah, he recovered his health and spirits, was successful in war and the chase, and was finally convinced that the curse of the Almighty had departed from him.

Pontiac's Siege

by ARTHUR POUND, 1884–   . *Born at Pontiac, Michigan, Pound was educated at the University of Michigan, B.A., 1907, and then entered journalism. After serving on various newspapers in Akron, Ohio, Grand Rapids, Michigan, and New York City, Pound became state historian and director of archives for New York State. His books include biographies, verse, fiction, and history. Perhaps best known are two novels, Once a Wilderness (1934) and Hawk of Detroit (1939), the last an account of Cadillac's founding of the city. Detroit: Dynamic City (1940) is an industrial history of the motor city; the description of Pontiac's historic siege appears in this volume.*

THE conspiracy of 1761 failed through a fortuitous leak; the one matured later by Pontiac broke furiously but somewhat haphazardly. I use the word "conspiracy" only in the sense of secret preparations, and not to imply treachery. Actually, the struggle was the best conceived and managed war the American Indians ever waged against their conquerors to recover their homeland. There had been many such conflicts, and would be many more, usually without advance declaration of intention. Congress seldom bothered to declare an Indian war, although bestowing medals for heroism in those wars. Why, then, should Indians be criticized for doing likewise? Their neglect of formalities, plus habits of torture and failure to distinguish between combatants and non-combatants, worked ill against isolated settlements; but, after all, it should be remembered that they were trying to preserve the remnant of an invaded native land.

No doubt the rising of '63 had been prepared in advance, but not with the thoroughness that white planners, under similar circumstances, would have developed. Perhaps the effort at synchronization was the best the Indians could make, when their lack of political unity and the difficulties of communication are considered. Theoretically, all the posts should have been attacked on the same day; actually six weeks elapsed between the initial outbreak of Detroit on May 7th and the opening of hostilities at Venango on June 18th, with the other attacks strung along between those dates. Nearly a month separates the rising at Detroit from that at Mackinac.

Here Pontiac had done his most effective propaganda. The Detroit tribes, according to Johnson's estimate, could count a thousand fighting men and of these only part of the Hurons, under Teata, failed to join the rising. These were the "good Indians" of the Pontiac manuscript, written by a French resident sympathetic to the British. Not all French residents felt that way; part of them leaned in the other direction. The majority seem to have been as nearly neutral as men could be with a desperately cruel war proceeding just outside their doors, and the possibility that whichever way it went they might be its victims.

More by sheer vehemence of character than by any sort of formally constituted authority, Pontiac commanded the Detroit Indians. But it would be an error to deduce from Parkman's title, *The Conspiracy of Pontiac*, that the Detroit chief directed the operations of all the warriors from Fort Pitt to Mackinac. No doubt there were 10,000 braves on the warpath, with perhaps a tenth of them under Pontiac at Detroit, and the rest under Indian leaders of equal or greater ability in other sectors. Whatever his qualities as an agitator, Pontiac did not shine in the field, either as a leader or strategist. His forces never came so close to taking the post at Detroit, through nearly a year of action, as the Shawnees and Delawares came to taking Fort Pitt in eleven days of extremely active siege warfare, in which they demonstrated remarkable ability to apply white tactics against a fortified position. No less than eight minor British posts were captured, but Detroit, Niagara, and Pitt—the chief positions—were saved. Once those major strongholds were relieved, the Indian cause was lost. The whites outlasted, rather than outfought, their red antagonists.

The situation of Detroit, of course, was precarious from the outset. A month, at the very least, was required to bring reinforcements from the East to the mouth of the Straits, and between Lake Erie and Detroit the islands offered every opportunity for ambush against relief parties in small boats. The French throughout all Canada had been encouraged to assist, at least to the extent of egging on the Indians with talk of Spanish aid to France, a rumored French naval demonstration in Canadian waters and promise of help from French forces in the Illinois country, sustained through Louisiana. No doubt the Indians on the Lakes received ammunition from that source. Major Gladwin, in command at Detroit, believed that large supplies of powder and lead also came into the Lakes area from the French in Eastern Canada, over the Ottawa River route followed by Cadillac in 1701. The British were powerless to shut off munitions traffic from either west or east.

Detroit sustained the first shock of this savage war designed to sweep the whole frontier clear of British troops and settlers, and which terrorized old settlements as far east as the Hudson, Delaware, and Lehigh watersheds. At a council of Ottawas, Pottawattomies, and Hurons at the Ecorse village, Pontiac convinced his hearers that it was time to strike. Gladwin was told of this meeting, but seems to have doubted its seriousness, because he twice had the ringleader in his hand during the next fortnight and permitted him to escape. Perhaps Gladwin doubted the correctness of the information; perhaps he preferred to have the enemy commit itself before retreat, while demonstrating that the garrison was ready for all emergencies. However, he took precautions, so that the informer's effort was not wasted. Who the informer was remains unproved; one romantic tale places that role in an Ojibway girl who loved Major Gladwin and sought to save him; a more realistic view is that the warning came from one of the "good Hurons" who formed a substantial minority of that tribe. Another account names Mohigan, an Ottawa, as the informer. In one of his illuminating footnotes to the Askin Papers, Dr. Quaife indicates a possibility that Angélique Cuillerier, a niece of the last French commandant, the admired "Mademoiselle Curie" of Johnson's visit, may have informed the Scots-Irish trader, James Sterling, whom she married two years later.

At any rate Gladwin was on his guard by May 1st, when Pontiac visited the fort with forty of his warriors, ostensibly for a peaceful ceremonious visit. Denied entrance in full numbers, the leader was finally admitted with a dozen followers who saw the place prepared for defense and departed to arrange another stratagem. This was done in council at the Pottawattomie village on May 5th, women being excluded. Gladwin's informer also reported on this meeting, so that the military were ready for the elaborate deception that had been concocted. The Indians planned to gain admission on pretext of a council to reaffirm peace, draw hidden weapons from their blankets at a given signal, and attack the unprepared defenders.

First came fifteen Ottawas to spy out the location of stores. When Pontiac arrived an hour later he found both the garrison and the fur traders under arms. He must have known then that his ruse had failed, yet he had no recourse but to enter into council, because his followers had been freely admitted and to withdraw now would be to show the white feather before them. It is declared that he actually held in hand the wampum which ostensibly was to cement peace but was actually the signal for attack, when Gladwin stopped him, exposed the hidden Indian weapons and revealed his men ready to fire at the first hostile move. Apparently the Commandant thought this exposure sufficient, for he permitted his guests to leave after assuring them of continued British friendship but promising vengeance if this truce were broken.

This dramatic scene occurred on May 7th, and was followed by as muddled a set of circumstances as ever started any war. Pontiac appeared the next day, declaring himself ready to smoke the peace-pipe, whether honestly or dishonestly this time none can say. This overture was rebuffed. The next day six other chiefs arrived to announce the same purpose. No doubt they were merely testing the preparations. Soon afterward some four hundred braves were seen paddling over from the war camp across the river. When confronted by closed gates and interpreters who told them that no more than sixty chiefs would be admitted, Pontiac sent back what amounted to a declaration of war. Unless all were admitted to the fort, which he considered as much Indian as British, none would enter. The English could keep the fort and the Indians would keep the country.

Immediately long pent-up savagery burst loose on those unfortunate English who had not sought the safety of the post. Some were saved by French neighbors; others perished miserably, both on the Common and on Hog Island, now Belle Isle, where the Indians overwhelmed a small guard of soldiers sent to protect the post's meat supply and its caretakers, the Fisher family. Then the war camp was moved back to the Detroit side of the river and Pontiac began in earnest the siege of the fort.

From the shelter of near-by buildings the Indians banged away at the fort and the two vessels, the *Michigan* and *Huron*, at the near-by wharf. The defenders banged back to more purpose with their cannon, setting fire to the Indians' shelter. Astonishingly, Gladwin even yet believed this was a tempest in a teapot, soon to pass. A few lives had been lost, but Indians soon grew tired of their designs and could be easily bought off. British officers on frontier duty were notoriously slow to feel grave concern when confronted only by undisciplined savages. If his storehouses had been full, Gladwin would have let the red men fire until they were weary, but needing supplies he sent three Frenchmen—the interpreter, La Butte, and two citizens, Messieurs Chapoton and Godfroy—over to the enemy for a parley. These gentlemen, also, considered the foe could be bought off with presents. Pontiac said he would listen, asking that Captain Campbell, Lieutenant McDougall and others come over for a council. Good M'sieu Gouin, grown suspicious, advised against their going. Upon arrival all were seized and shut up in the Meloche house, home of a worthy French family. From this point on, Pontiac, forgetting whatever he might have learned of the conventions of war in serving under Montcalm, became the complete savage as regards Englishmen although remaining well-disposed toward Frenchmen.

From the fort, parties went out on sorties to burn the surrounding buildings, in order to clear the ground for combat. Preparing for the worst, Gladwin moved baggage down to the vessels and kept them ready for instant sailing. On the 21st he sent the *Huron* off to Niagara for aid, having had gruesome proof that reinforcements by small boat could not come safely through the islands. Lieutenant Cuyler and a hundred men from Niagara had been ambushed within twenty-five miles of Detroit. In that desperate water fight, some fifty men were lost, and a few captured for torture at fires within sight of the Detroit garrison. The survivors escaped back to Niagara, giving the East its first real alarm over Detroit. As long as the element of surprise held good, the Indians succeeded in defending the water gate. Sailing vessels came through without serious losses, though always in danger when becalmed.

It was only by indirection, via the imprisoned Campbell, that the garrison of Detroit learned that the Peace of St. Germain (more commonly called the Treaty of Paris) had been signed with France, a letter to that effect having been captured in the river ambush of May 20th. This treaty ended New France at one stroke. Not only was the capitulation of Canada accepted, but Louisiana was legally transferred to Spain in return for her help, Spain becoming obligated to give up Florida to the British in exchange. It is one of the ironies of history that Indians sympathetic to France and assisted by Frenchmen should have started war on the British at Detroit after France had ceded all Canada to the foe and all Louisiana to an ally. Pontiac's later furies are sometimes attributed to this disappointment. In expectation of French aid, he had put himself in rebellion, only to find that the peace treaty shut off further assistance.

During June the garrison often went hungry, and would have been hungrier except for supplies run in under cover of night by Teata's loyal Hurons and various French citizens. As long as the garrison could keep the foreshore open, a complete Indian blockade was impossible. First substantial relief from Niagara came on June 30th; sixty men, provisions, and ammunition. Barely had they escaped capture off Presque Isle, which had been taken by Pontiac's raiders two weeks earlier. Sending some of his Ottawas East for this purpose was one of Pontiac's sagacious moves, indicating that he was more than merely a local leader. Those far-ranging Ottawas even appeared before Fort Pitt, which was being pressed with more ardor and chance of success than the siege of Detroit. Apparently these far raiders were picked warriors; accounts of the terror on the Pittsburgh frontier mention those dread Westerners in their huge black headdress. From the ramparts of Detroit this frightening spectacle was an everyday occurrence.

On July 2nd, while Pontiac was haranguing French residents to join forces with him, Lieutenant (now Captain) McDougall escaped from confinement with three other whites and gained the fort. Indian pressure on the French failed; and when the definitive terms of the peace treaty were read, the more substantial part of the French community went over to the British side, forming a company of militia. That same day, July 4th, a sortie, out to recover a cache of ammunition from a

French house, killed and scalped a young Ojibway, Pontiac's nephew. Infuriated, the chief rushed to Campbell's quarters, tied the captain to a fence and killed him with arrows, cut off his head, tore out and ate his heart. In Indian tradition, this last attention was not desecration, but recognition of a foe's courage. There is credible testimony to the effect that Pontiac considered Campbell a most courageous man and, up to the time his nephew was killed, intended merely to keep his prisoner as hostage.

In spite of his increasing ferocity, the siege was going against Pontiac. The French people turned against him more and more, and the Wyandots and Pottawattomies, whose riverside villages were open to bombardment by Gladwin's sloops, were ready to welcome peace. Realizing that they could not win unless those pestilent vessels were destroyed, the Indians tried on July 10th, to burn them by means of a fire raft, at the same time trying to ignite the fort with blazing arrows. Both designs failed, and the sloops survived to batter the Wyandots and Pottawattomies to such purpose that both villages made peace, returning their captives.

With the arrival of heavy reinforcements—300 men under Captain Dalyell on July 29th—it began to look as if the war was well over on the Detroit front. The barracks were overcrowded, and the time seemed ripe for a bold, decisive stroke. Overconfidence led to disaster. Dalyell led 250 men up the river road into an ambush at Bloody Run. Our old acquaintance, Robert Rogers, appears again in Detroit history at this point, being present with twenty newly arrived Rangers, a much reduced force. In fact, Major Rogers was himself now somewhat reduced and grateful for any sort of command. But with his usual cool daring, the enemy having every advantage of position, Rogers in retreat took possession of the Campau house and held out there until reinforcements arrived. The engagement brought heavy losses—eighteen killed, including Dalyell; thirty-eight wounded; three captured, to burn anon. Morale was not helped by the discovery that some one inside the fort had given the enemy advance knowledge of the march. Apparently not all the French had been converted by news of the peace treaty. This was Pontiac's most successful action in the widespread war to which his name has been attached by history. On this occasion his tribesmen whipped as good soldiers as there were in America.

Gladwin now determined to wait it out, risking no more offensives until he possessed overwhelming strength, even if he had to wait until another spring. His chief concern, for supplies, lessened with the arrival of several cargoes. The situation at Niagara had cleared and Major Wilkins would soon be on his way with a strong force to lift the siege of Detroit in earnest. Wilkins started with 600 men, but failed to get through. However, the knowledge that he was on the water brought a week's truce to Detroit, which the garrison used with energy to round up winter provisions, ending a period of short rations.

Hardly was the truce over when Pontiac received the message which finally convinced him that his war was lost. M. Dequindre, a messenger altogether to be trusted, handed the chieftain a letter from M. Neyon, commandant at Fort Chartres on the Mississippi, saying that no help could be expected from him. In their flagging moments, Pontiac had held out to his followers this promise of western aid, now completely dashed. Now he could no longer retain even his Ottawas and Ojibways in line. The warriors began to drift quietly away. Presently there were no combatant Indians left in the area. For five years Pontiac would wander through the forest before making his final peace with the British at Oswego, but his influence departed when he stole away from Detroit, a beaten leader, leaving the stubborn Gladwin in uncontested possession of the scene of battle.

What Gladwin did then is characteristic. Obviously, the man was no dashing military leader; it is not in evidence that at any point in the five months' siege he ever set foot outside his battlements. A wise but uninspired commander, he conceived his problem to be that of holding fast, letting time, deprivations, and lack of discipline destroy the foe. If risks had to be taken, he bade others take them while he did the thinking and the husbanding of resources. Intuitively he knew, as Braddock and others did not, that he could not conquer the foe on their own ground. Therefore he let them depart without pursuit. But Gladwin was so sure they knew they were beaten that the enemy were scarcely out of sight before he reduced his garrison to 212 men and sent the rest back to Niagara, where they could be better fed over the winter. This was sound sense, but it took cold courage for the commander to reduce his effectives so soon to the number he could feed comfortably, relying solely upon his judgment that the enemy would not return.

Little by little the Detroit Indians crept back, wondering what punishments awaited them. The conqueror was disposed to be gracious. A royal proclamation of October, 1763, forbade land warrants to be issued beyond the headwaters of rivers emptying into the Atlantic. The rebellion accomplished that much for the Indians, although the measure could not be enforced. More meaningful for Indian welfare were Johnson's trade reforms and regulations, which he now had more opportunity to apply. But, by way of punishment, Croghan was sent into the Illinois country to bring its tribes into the British net and, in council at Detroit, the Ottawa confederacy was declared dissolved.

Two expeditions were started west to restore posts, recover prisoners, punish outstanding culprits and pave the way for new treaties. One, under Colonel Bouquet, who had raised the siege of Fort Pitt, penetrated the Ohio country in workman-like manner, doing all that was asked of it and no more. The other, under Major General John Bradstreet, proceeded through Niagara and along the shore of Lake Erie toward Detroit. Bradstreet, unversed in Indian lore, moved slowly, committed diplomatic indiscretions in Ohio from which Bouquet had to rescue him, and did not reach Detroit until August 26, 1764, ten months after hostilities ceased. However, when he arrived, the size of his army was convincing evidence of Britain's might.

Unaware that a storm was brewing against him in the East, Bradstreet proceeded to make new treaties with the six chief belligerent Detroit tribes. In them he perpetrated the blunder which had drawn upon him the wrath of Johnson and General Gage in relation to his Ohio negotiations. Bradstreet had no power to make treaties; that was the business of Johnson as Indian superintendent, who was jealous of his prerogatives. Worse yet, in Bradstreet's treaties he described the Indians as "King's subjects," not allies. On this ground, Bradstreet's Ohio treaties were withdrawn; those made in Detroit held, merely because they were never protested. The fact is that Bradstreet, a notoriously choleric man, scared the Indians out of their moccasins by chopping a wampum belt into bits and otherwise bulldozing them with his grand army. But the more diplomatic Johnson realized the Detroit tribes had been duped, and, to avoid disputes, ordered his agents not to insist on the letter of Bradstreet's "subject" treaties. Bradstreet also bore down severely on those Frenchmen who had aided the Indians.

When this grim general sailed away, leaving seven companies of troops and ample stores behind him, Detroit red-men knew Britain had a hard and heavy hand. As long as the Union Jack flew over Detroit—another thirty years and more—the disaffected might mutter but they never struck. Bradstreet's reputation—he had been one of the popular heroes of the Seven Years' War—did not survive ordeal by the West; but his unauthorized severity in treaty-making simplified the situation for the next generation. When the United States finally took over the area, their legal claim to sovereignty could not be challenged in the name of legal Indian rights, and the red subjects of the British Crown automatically became subject to the young Republic.

The Windigo

by MARY HARTWELL CATHERWOOD, 1847–1902. Born in Luray, Ohio, Mrs. Catherwood was taken to Illinois as a child. The death of her parents gave the responsibility of educating her to relatives, but she eventually worked her way through Granville Female Seminary and qualified as a teacher. Writing, however, proved to be her major interest. She published her first novel, A Woman in Armor, in 1875, and this volume was followed by a stream of stories, sketches, and criticisms most of which were quite undistinguished. Some years later she read the historian Francis Parkman and through him became interested in the old French settlements of the Middle West. The result was a series of short stories and novels which not only introduced new themes and characters to the public but presented them with knowledge and sympathy. Mrs. Catherwood's personal observation of the Great Lakes area and her summer visits to Mackinac Island further contributed to the success of her fiction. Among her books are such novels as The Romance of Dollard (1889), The Story of Tonty (1890), Old Kaskaskia (1893), and Lazarre (1901). Possibly her best work was done in the short story, as illustrated by such collections as The Chase of Saint Castin and Other Stories of the French in the New World (1894) and Mackinac and Lake Stories (1899). "The Windigo," an unusual tale of superstition among the French and Indians of the St. Mary's River region, appeared in the former volume.

THE cry of those rapids in Sainte Marie's River called the Sault could be heard at all hours through the settlement on the rising shore and into the forest beyond. Three quarters of a mile of frothing billows, like some colossal instrument, never ceased playing music down an inclined channel until the trance of winter locked it up. At August dusk, when all that shaggy world was sinking to darkness, the gushing monotone became very distinct.

Louizon Cadotte and his father's young seignior, Jacques de Repentigny, stepped from a birch canoe on the bank near the fort, two Chippewa Indians following with their game. Hunting furnished no small addition to the food-supply of the settlement, for the English conquest had brought about scarcity at this as well as other Western posts. Peace was declared in Europe; but soldiers on the frontier, waiting orders to march out at any time, were not abundantly supplied with stores, and they let season after season go by, reluctant to put in harvests which might be reaped by their successors.

Jacques was barely nineteen, and Louizon was considerably older. But the Repentignys had gone back to France after the fall of Quebec;

and five years of European life had matured the young seignior as decades of border experience would never mature his half-breed tenant. Yet Louizon was a fine dark-skinned fellow, well made for one of short stature. He trod close by his tall superior with visible fondness; enjoying this spectacle of a man the like of whom he had not seen on the frontier.

Jacques looked back, as he walked, at the long zigzag shadows on the river. Forest fire in the distance showed a leaning column, black at base, pearl-colored in the primrose air, like smoke from some gigantic altar. He had seen islands in the lake under which the sky seemed to slip, throwing them above the horizon in mirage, and trees standing like detached bushes on a world rim of water. The Sainte Marie River was a beautiful light green in color, and sunset and twilight played upon it all the miracles of change.

"I wish my father had never left this country," said young Repentigny, feeling that spell cast by the wilderness. "Here is his place. He should have withdrawn to the Sault, and accommodated himself to the English, instead of returning to France. The service in other parts of the world does not suit him. Plenty of good men have held to Canada and their honor also."

"Yes, yes," assented Louizon. "The English cannot be got rid of. For my part, I shall be glad when this post changes hands. I am sick of our officers."

He scowled with open resentment. The seigniory house faced the parade ground, and they could see against its large low mass, lounging on the gallery, one each side of a window, the white uniforms of two French soldiers. The window sashes, screened by small curtains across the middle, were swung into the room; and Louizon's wife leaned on her elbows across the sill, the rosy atmosphere of his own fire projecting to view every ring of her bewitching hair, and even her long eyelashes as she turned her gaze from side to side.

It was so dark, and the object of their regard was so bright, that these buzzing bees of Frenchmen did not see her husband until he ran up the steps facing them. Both of them greeted him heartily. He felt it a peculiar indignity that his wife's danglers forever passed their goodwill on to him; and he left them in the common hall, with his father and the young seignior, and the two or three Indians who congregated there every evening to ask for presents or to smoke.

Louizon's wife met him in the middle of the broad low apartment where he had been so proud to introduce her as a bride, and turned her cheek to be kissed. She was not fond of having her lips touched. Her hazel-colored hair was perfumed. She was so supple and exquisite, so dimpled and aggravating, that the Chippewa in him longed to take

75

her by the scalp-lock of her light head; but the Frenchman bestowed the salute. Louizon had married the prettiest woman in the settlement. Life overflowed in her, so that her presence spread animation. Both men and women paid homage to her. Her very mother-in-law was her slave. And this was the stranger spectacle because Madame Cadotte the senior, though born a Chippewa, did not easily make herself subservient to anybody.

The time had been when Louizon was proud of any notice this siren conferred on him. But so exacting and tyrannical is the nature of man that when he got her he wanted to keep her entirely to himself. From his Chippewa mother, who, though treated with deference, had never dared to disobey his father, he inherited a fond and jealous nature; and his beautiful wife chafed it. Young Repentigny saw that she was like a Parisian. But Louizon felt that she was a spirit too fine and tantalizing for him to grasp, and she had him in her power.

He hung his powder-horn behind the door, and stepped upon a stool to put his gun on its rack above the fireplace. The fire showed his round figure, short but well muscled, and the boyish petulance of his shaven lip. The sun shone hot upon the Sault of an August noon, but morning and night were cool, and a blaze was usually kept in the chimney.

"You found plenty of game?" said his wife; and it was one of this woman's wickedest charms that she could be so interested in her companion of the moment.

"Yes," he answered, scowling more, and thinking of the brace on the gallery whom he had not shot, but wished to.

She laughed at him.

"Archange Cadotte," said Louizon, turning around on the stool before he descended; and she spread out her skirts, taking two dancing steps to indicate that she heard him. "How long am I to be mortified by your conduct to Monsieur de Repentigny?"

"Oh—Monsieur de Repentigny. It is now that boy from France, at whom I have never looked."

"The man I would have you look at, madame, you scarcely notice."

"Why should I notice him? He pays little attention to me."

"Ah, he is not one of your danglers, madame. He would not look at another man's wife. He has had trouble himself."

"So will you have if you scorch the backs of your legs," observed Archange.

Louizon stood obstinately on the stool and ignored the heat. He was in the act of stepping down, but he checked it as she spoke.

"Monsieur de Repentigny came back to this country to marry a young English lady of Quebec. He thinks of her, not of you."

"I am sure he is welcome," murmured Archange. "But it seems the young English lady prefers to stay in Quebec."

"She never looked at any other man, madame. She is dead."

"No wonder. I should be dead, too, if I had looked at one stupid man all my life."

Louizon's eyes sparkled. "Madame, I will have you know that the seignior of Sault Sainte Marie is entitled to your homage."

"Monsieur, I will have you know that I do not pay homage to any man."

"You, Archange Cadotte? You are in love with a new man every day."

"Not in the least, monsieur. I only desire to have a new man in love with me every day."

Her mischievous mouth was a scarlet button in her face, and Louizon leaped to the floor, and kicked the stool across the room.

"The devil himself is no match at all for you!"

"But I married him before I knew that," returned Archange; and Louizon grinned in his wrath.

"I don't like such women."

"Oh, yes, you do. Men always like women whom they cannot chain."

"I have never tried to chain you." Her husband approached, shaking his finger at her. "There is not another woman in the settlement who has her way as you have. And see how you treat me!"

"How do I treat you?" inquired Archange, sitting down and resigning herself to statistics.

"Sainte Marie! Saint Joseph!" shouted the Frenchman. "How does she treat me! And every man in the seigniory dangling at her apron string!"

"You are mistaken. There is the young seignior; and there is the new English commandant, who must be now within the seigniory, for they expect him at the post tomorrow morning. It is all the same: if I look at a man you are furious, and if I refuse to look at him you are more furious still."

Louizon felt that inward breaking up which proved to him that he could not stand before the tongue of this woman. Groping for expression, he declared:

"If thou wert sickly or blind, I would be just as good to thee as when thou wert a bride. I am not the kind that changes if a woman loses her fine looks."

"No doubt you would like to see me with the smallpox," suggested Archange. "But it is never best to try a man too far."

"You try me too far—let me tell you that. But you shall try me no further."

The Indian appeared distinctly on his softer French features, as one picture may be stamped over another.

"Smoke a pipe, Louizon," urged the thorn in his flesh. "You are always so much more agreeable when your mouth is stopped."

But he left the room without looking at her again. Archange remarked to herself that he would be better-natured when his mother had given him his supper; and she yawned, smiling at the maladroit creatures whom she made her sport. Her husband was the best young man in the settlement. She was entirely satisfied with him, and grateful to him for taking the orphan niece of a poor post commandant, without prospects since the conquest, and giving her sumptuous quarters and comparative wealth; but she could not forbear amusing herself with his masculine weaknesses.

Archange was by no means a slave in the frontier household. She did not spin, or draw water, or tend the oven. Her mother-in-law, Madame Cadotte, had a hold on perennially destitute Chippewa women who could be made to work for longer or shorter periods in a Frenchman's kitchen or loom-house instead of with savage implements. Archange's bed had ruffled curtains, and her pretty dresses, carefully folded, filled a large chest.

She returned to the high window-sill, and watched the purple distances growing black. She could smell the tobacco the men were smoking in the open hall, and hear their voices. Archange knew what her mother-in-law was giving the young seignior and Louizon for their supper. She could fancy the officers laying down their pipes to draw to the board, also, for the Cadottes kept open house all the year round.

The thump of the Indian drum was added to the deep melody of the rapids. There were always a few lodges of Chippewas about the Sault. When the trapping season and the maple-sugar-making were over and his profits drunk up, time was the largest possession of an Indian. He spent it around the door of his French brother, ready to fish or to drink whenever invited. If no one cared to go on the river, he turned to his hereditary amusements. Every night that the rapids were void of torches showing where the canoes of white fishers darted, the thump of the Indian drum and the yell of Indian dancers could be heard.

Archange's mind was running on the new English garrison who were said to be so near taking possession of the picketed fort, when she saw something red on the parade ground. The figure stood erect and motionless, gathering all the remaining light on its indistinct coloring, and Archange's heart gave a leap at the hint of a military man in a red uniform. She was all alive, like a whitefisher casting the net or a hunter sighting game. It was Archange's nature, without even taking thought, to turn her head on her round neck so that the illuminated curls would show against a background of wall, and wreathe her half-bare arms across the sill. To be looked at, to lure and tantalize, was more than pastime. It was a woman's chief privilege. Archange held the secret conviction that the priest himself could be made to give her lighter penances by an angelic expression she could assume. It is convenient to have large brown eyes and the trick of casting them sidewise in sweet distress.

But the Chippewa widow came in earlier than usual that evening, being anxious to go back to the lodges to watch the dancing. Archange pushed the sashes shut, ready for other diversion, and Michel Pensonneau never failed to furnish her that. The little boy was at the widow's heels. Michel was an orphan.

"If Archange had children," Madame Cadotte had said to Louizon, "she would not seek other amusement. Take the little Pensonneau lad that his grandmother can hardly feed. He will give Archange something to do."

So Louizon brought home the little Pensonneau lad. Archange looked at him, and considered that here was another person to wait on her. As to keeping him clean and making clothes for him, they might as well have expected her to train the sledge dogs. She made him serve her, but for mothering he had to go to Madame Cadotte. Yet Archange far outweighed Madame Cadotte with him. The labors put upon him by the autocrat of the house were sweeter than mococks full of maple sugar from the hand of the Chippewa housekeeper. At first Archange would not let him come into her room. She dictated to him through door or window. But when he grew fat with good food and was decently clad under Madame Cadotte's hand, the great promotion of entering that sacred apartment was allowed him. Michel came in whenever he could. It was his nightly habit to follow the Chippewa widow there after supper, and watch her brush Archange's hair.

Michel stood at the end of the hearth with a roll of pagessanung, or plum-leather, in his fist. His cheeks had a hard garnered redness like polished apples. The Chippewa widow set her husband carefully against the wall. The husband was a bundle about two feet long, containing her best clothes tied up in her dead warrior's sashes and rolled in a piece of cloth. His arm-bands and his necklace of bear's-claws appeared at the top as a grotesque head. This bundle the widow was obliged to carry with her everywhere. To be seen without it was a disgrace, until that time when her husband's nearest relations should take it away from her and give her new clothes, thus signifying that she had mourned long enough to satisfy them. As the husband's relations were unable to cover themselves, the prospect of her release seemed distant. For her food she was glad to depend on her labor in the Cadotte household. There was no hunter to supply her lodge now.

The widow let down Archange's hair and began to brush it. The long mass was too much for its owner to handle. It spread around her like a garment, as she sat on her chair, and its ends touched the floor. Michel thought there was nothing more wonderful in the world than this glory of hair, its rings and ripples shining in the firelight. The widow's jaws worked in unobtrusive rumination on a piece of pleasantly bitter fungus, the Indian substitute for quinine, which the Chippewas called waubudone. As she consoled herself much with this medicine, and her many-syllabled name was hard to pronounce, Archange called her Waubudone, an offense against her dignity which the widow might not have endured from anybody else, though she bore it without a word from this soft-haired magnate.

As she carefully carded the mass of hair lock by lock, thinking it an unnecessary nightly labor, the restless head under her hands was turned towards the portable husband. Archange had not much imagination, but to her the thing was uncanny. She repeated what she said every night:

"Do stand him in the hall and let him smell the smoke, Waubudone."

"No," refused the widow.

"But I don't want him in my bedroom. You are not obliged to keep that thing in your sight all the time."

"Yes," said the widow.

A dialect of mingled French and Chippewa was what they spoke, and Michel knew enough of both tongues to follow the talk.

"Are they never going to take him from you? If they don't take him from you soon, I shall go to the lodges and speak to his people about it myself."

The Chippewa widow usually passed over this threat in silence; but, threading a lock with the comb, she now said:

"Best not go to the lodges awhile."

"Why?" inquired Archange. "Have the English already arrived? Is the tribe dissatisfied?"

"Don't know that."

"Then why should I not go to the lodges?"

"Windigo at the Sault now."

Archange wheeled to look at her face. The widow was unmoved. She was little older than Archange, but her features showed a stoical harshness in the firelight. Michel, who often went to the lodges, widened his mouth and forgot to fill it with plum-leather. There was no sweet which Michel loved as he did this confection of wild plums and maple sugar boiled down and spread on sheets of birch bark. Madame Cadotte made the best pagessanung at the Sault.

"Look at the boy," laughed Archange. "He will not want to go to the lodges any more after dark."

The widow remarked, noting Michel's fat legs and arms:

"Windigo like to eat him."

"I would kill a windigo," declared Michel, in full revolt.

"Not so easy to kill a windigo. Bad spirits help windigos. If man kill windigo and not tear him to pieces, he come to life again."

Archange herself shuddered at such a tenacious creature. She was less superstitious than the Chippewa woman, but the Northwest had its human terrors as dark as the shadow of witchcraft.

Though a Chippewa was bound to dip his hand in the war kettle and taste the flesh of enemies after victory, there was nothing he considered more horrible than a confirmed cannibal. He believed that a person who had eaten human flesh to satisfy hunger was never afterwards contented with any other kind, and, being deranged and possessed by the spirit of a beast, he had to be killed for the safety of the community. The cannibal usually became what he was by stress of starvation: in the winter when hunting failed and he was far from help, or on a journey when provisions gave out, and his only choice was to eat a companion or die. But this did not excuse him. As soon as he was detected, the name of "windigo" was given him, and if he did not betake himself again to solitude he was shot or knocked on the head at the first convenient opportunity. Archange remembered one such wretched creature who had haunted the settlement awhile, and then disappeared. His canoe was known, and when it hovered even distantly on the river every child ran to its mother. The priest was less successful with this kind of outcast than with any other barbarian on the frontier.

"Have you seen him, Waubudone?" inquired Archange. "I wonder if it is the same man who used to frighten us."

"This windigo a woman. Porcupine in her. She lie down and roll up and hide her head when you drive her off."

"Did you drive her off?"

"No. She only come past my lodge in the night."

"Did you see her?"

"No, I smell her."

Archange had heard of the atmosphere which windigos far gone in cannibalism carried around them. She desired to know nothing more about the poor creature, or the class to which the poor creature belonged, if such isolated beings may be classed. The Chippewa widow talked without being questioned, however, preparing to reduce Archange's mass of hair to the compass of a nightcap.

"My grandmother told me there was a man dreamed he had to eat seven persons. He sat by the fire and shivered. If his squaw wanted meat, he quarreled with her. 'Squaw, take care. Thou wilt drive me so far that I shall turn windigo.' "

People who did not give Archange the keen interest of fascinating them were a great weariness to her. Humble or wretched human life filled her with disgust. She could dance all night at the weekly dances, laughing in her sleeve at girls from whom she took the best partners. But she never helped nurse a sick child, and it made her sleepy to hear of windigos and misery. Michel wanted to squat by the chimney and listen until Louizon came in; but she drove him out early. Louizon was kind to the orphan, who had been in some respects a failure, and occasionally let him sleep on blankets or skins by the hearth instead of groping to the dark attic. And if Michel ever wanted to escape the attic, it was to-night, when a windigo was abroad. But Louizon did not come.

It must have been midnight when Archange sat up in bed, startled out of sleep by her mother-in-law, who held a candle between the curtains. Madame Cadotte's features were of a mild Chippewa type, yet the restless aboriginal eye made Archange uncomfortable with its anxiety.

"Louizon is still away," said his mother.

"Perhaps he went whitefishing after he had his supper." The young wife yawned and rubbed her eyes, beginning to notice that her husband might be doing something unusual.

"He did not come to his supper."

"Yes, mama. He came in with Monsieur de Repentigny."

"I did not see him. The seignior ate alone."

Archange stared, fully awake. "Where does the seignior say he is?"

"The seignior does not know. They parted at the door."

"Oh, he has gone to the lodges to watch the dancing."

"I have been there. No one has seen him since he set out to hunt this morning."

"Where are Louizon's canoemen?"

"Jean Boucher and his son are at the dancing. They say he came into this house."

Archange could not adjust her mind to anxiety without the suspicion that her mother-in-law might be acting as the instrument of Louizon's resentment. The huge feather bed was a tangible comfort interposed betwixt herself and calamity.

"He was sulky to-night," she declared. "He has gone up to sleep in Michel's attic to frighten me."

"I have been there. I have searched the house."

"But are you sure it was Michel in the bed?"

"There was no one. Michel is here."

Archange snatched the curtain aside, and leaned out to see the orphan sprawled on a bearskin in front of the collapsing logs. He had pushed the sashes inward from the gallery and hoisted himself over the high sill after the bed drapery was closed for the night, for the window yet stood open. Madame Cadotte sheltered the candle she carried, but the wind blew it out. There was a rich glow from the fireplace upon Michel's stuffed legs and arms, his cheeks, and the full parted lips through which his breath audibly flowed. The other end of the room, lacking the candle, was in shadow. The thump of the Indian drum could still be heard, and distinctly and more distinctly, as if they were approaching the house, the rapids.

Both women heard more. They had not noticed any voice at the window when they were speaking themselves, but some offensive thing scented the wind, and they heard, hoarsely spoken in Chippewa from the gallery:

"How fat he is!"

Archange, with a gasp, threw herself upon her mother-in-law for safety, and Madame Cadotte put both arms and the smoking candle around her. A feeble yet dexterous scramble on the sill resulted in something dropping into the room. It moved toward the hearth glow, a gaunt vertebrate body scarcely expanded by ribs, but covered by a red blanket, and a head with deathlike features overhung by strips of hair. This vision of famine leaned forward and indented Michel with one finger, croaking again:

"How fat he is!"

The boy roused himself, and, for one instant stupid and apologetic, was going to sit up and whine. He saw what bent over him, and, bristling with unimaginable revolutions of arms and legs, he yelled a yell which seemed to sweep the thing back through the window.

Next day no one thought of dancing or fishing or of the coming English. Frenchmen and Indians turned out together to search for Louizon Cadotte. Though he never in his life had set foot to any expedition without first notifying his household, and it was not the custom to hunt alone in the woods, his disappearance would not have roused the settlement in so short a time had there been no windigo hanging about the Sault. It was told that the windigo, who entered his house again in the night, must have made way with him.

Jacques Repentigny heard this with some amusement. Of windigos he had no experience, but he had hunted and camped much of the summer with Louizon.

"I do not think he would let himself be knocked on the head by a woman," said Jacques.

"White chief doesn't know what helps a windigo," explained a Chippewa; and the canoeman Jean Boucher interpreted him. "Bad spirit makes a windigo strong as a bear. I saw this one. She stole my whitefish and ate them raw."

"Why didn't you give her cooked food when you saw her?" demanded Jacques.

"She would not eat that now. She likes offal better."

"Yes, she was going to eat me," declared Michel Pensonneau. "After she finished Monsieur Louizon, she got through the window to carry me off."

Michel enjoyed the windigo. Though he strummed on his lip and mourned aloud whenever Madame Cadotte was by, he felt so comfortably full of food and horror, and so important with his story, that life threatened him with nothing worse than satiety.

While parties went up the river and down the river, and talked about the chutes in the rapids where a victim could be sucked down to death in an instant, or about tracing the windigo's secret camp, Archange hid herself in the attic. She lay upon Michel's bed and wept, or walked the plank floor. It was no place for her. At noon the bark roof heated her almost to fever. The dormer windows gave her little air, and there was dust as well as something like an individual sediment of the poverty from which the boy had come. Yet she could endure the loft dungeon better than the face of the Chippewa mother who blamed her, or the bluff excitement of Monsieur Cadotte. She could hear his voice from time to time, as he ran in for spirits or provisions for parties of searchers. And Archange had aversion, like the instinct of a maid, to betraying fondness for her husband. She was furious with him, also, for causing her pain. When she thought of the windigo, of the rapids, of any peril which might be working his limitless absence, she set clenched hands in her loosened hair and trembled with hysterical anguish. But the enormity of his behavior if he were alive made her hiss at the rafters. "Good, monsieur! Next time I will have four officers. I will have the entire garrison sitting along the gallery! Yes, and they shall be English, too. And there is one thing you will never know, besides." She laughed through her weeping. "You will never know I made eyes at a windigo."

The preenings and posings of a creature whose perfections he once thought were the result of a happy chance had made Louizon roar. She remembered all their life together, and moaned, "I will say this: he

84

was the best husband that any girl ever had. We scarcely had a disagreement. But to be the widow of a man who is eaten up—O Sainte Marie!"

In the clear August weather the wide river seemed to bring its opposite shores nearer. Islands within a stone's throw of the settlement, rocky drops in a boiling current, vividly showed their rich foliage of pines. On one of these islands Father Dablon and Father Marquette had built their first mission chapel; and though they afterwards removed it to the mainland, the old tracery of foundation stones could still be seen. The mountains of Lake Superior showed like a cloud. On the ridge above fort and houses the Chippewa lodges were pleasant in the sunlight, sending ribbons of smoke from their camp-fires far above the serrated edge of the woods. Naked Indian children and their playmates of the settlement shouted to one another, as they ran along the river margin, threats of instant seizure by the windigo. The Chippewa widow, holding her husband in her arms, for she was not permitted to hang him on her back, stood and talked with her red-skinned intimates of the lodges. The Frenchwomen collected at the seigniory house. As for the men of the garrison, they were obliged to stay and receive the English then on the way from Detour. But they came out to see the boats off with the concern of brothers, and Archange's uncle, the post commandant, embraced Monsieur Cadotte.

The priest and Jacques Repentigny did not speak to each other about that wretched creature whose hoverings around the Sault were connected with Louizon Cadotte's disappearance. But the priest went with Louizon's father down the river, and Jacques led the party which took the opposite direction. Though so many years had passed since Father Dablon and Father Marquette built the first bark chapel, their successor found his work very little easier than theirs had been.

A canoe was missing from the little fleet usually tied alongshore, but it was not the one belonging to Louizon. The young seignior took that one, having Jean Boucher and Jean's son to paddle for him. No other man of Sault Sainte Marie could pole up the rapids or paddle down them as this expert Chippewa could. He had been baptized with a French name, and his son after him, but no Chippewa of pure blood and name looked habitually as he did into those whirlpools called the chutes, where the slip of a paddle meant death. Yet nobody feared the rapids. It was common for boys and girls to flit around near shore in birch canoes, balancing themselves and expertly dipping up whitefish.

Jean Boucher thrust out his boat from behind an island, and, turning it as a fish glides, moved over thin sheets of water spraying upon rocks. The fall of the Sainte Marie is gradual, but even at its upper end there is a little hill to climb. Jean set his pole into the stone floor of the river, and lifted the vessel length by length from crest to crest of foam. His paddles lay behind him, and his arms were bare to the elbows, showing their strong red sinews. He had let his hair grow like a Frenchman's, and it hung forward shading his hatless brows. A skin apron was girded in front of him to meet waves which frothed up over the canoe's high prow. Blacksmith of the waters, he beat a path between juts of rock; struggling to hold a point with the pole, calling a quick word to his helper, and laughing as he forged his way. Other voyagers who did not care to tax themselves with this labor made a portage with their canoes alongshore, and started above the glassy curve where the river bends down to its leap.

Gros Cap rose in the sky, revealing its peak in bolder lines as the searchers pushed up the Sainte Marie, exploring mile after mile of pine and white birch and fantastic rock. The shaggy bank stooped to them, the illimitable glory of the wilderness witnessing a little procession of boats like chips floating by.

It was almost sunset when they came back, the tired paddlers keeping near that shore on which they intended to land. No trace of Louizon Cadotte could be found; and those who had not seen the windigo were ready to declare that there was no such thing about the Sault, when, just above the rapids, she appeared from the dense up-slope of forest.

Jacques Repentigny's canoe had kept the lead, but a dozen light-bodied Chippewas sprung on shore and rushed past him into the bushes.

The woman had disappeared in underbrush, but, surrounded by hunters in full chase, she came running out, and fell on her hands, making a hoarse noise in her throat. As she looked up, all the marks in her aged aboriginal face were distinct to Jacques Repentigny. The sutures in her temples were parted. She rolled herself around in a ball, and hid her head in her dirty red blanket. Any wild beast was in harmony with the wilderness, but this sick human being was a blot upon it. Jacques felt the compassion of a god for her. Her pursuers were after her, and the thud of stones they threw made him heartsick, as if the thing were done to the woman he loved.

"Let her alone!" he commanded fiercely.

"Kill her!" shouted the hunters. "Hit the windigo on the head!"

All that world of Northern air could not sweeten her, but Jacques picked her up without a thought of her offensiveness and ran to his canoe. The bones resisted him; the claws scratched at him through her blanket. Jean Boucher lifted a paddle to hit the creature as soon as she was down.

"If you strike her, I will kill you!" warned Jacques, and he sprung into the boat.

The superstitious Chippewas threw themselves madly into their canoes to follow. It would go hard, but they would get the windigo and take the young seignior out of her spell. The Frenchmen, with man's instinct for the chase, were in full cry with them.

Jean Boucher laid down his paddle sulkily, and his son did the same. Jacques took a long pistol from his belt and pointed it at the old Indian.

"If you don't paddle for life, I will shoot you." And his eyes were eyes which Jean respected as he never had respected anything before. The young man was a beautiful fellow. If he wanted to save a windigo, why, the saints let him. The priest might say a good word about it when you came to think, also.

"Where shall I paddle to?" inquired Jean Boucher, drawing in his breath. The canoe leaped ahead, grazing hands stretching out to seize it.

"To the other side of the river."

"Down the rapids?"

"Yes."

"Go down rough or go down smooth?"

"Rough—rough—where they cannot catch you."

The old canoeman snorted. He would like to see any of them catch him. They were straining after him, and half a dozen canoes shot down that glassy slide which leads to the rocks.

It takes three minutes for a skillful paddler to run that dangerous race of three quarters of a mile. Jean Boucher stood at the prow, and the waves boiled as high as his waist. Jacques dreaded only that the windigo might move and destroy the delicate poise of the boat; but she lay very still. The little craft quivered from rock to rock without grazing one, rearing itself over a great breaker or sinking under a crest of foam. Now a billow towered up, and Jean broke it with his paddle, shouting his joy. Showers fell on the woman coiled in the bottom of the boat. They were going down very rough indeed. Yells from the other canoes grew less distinct. Jacques turned his head, keeping a true balance, and saw that their pursuers were skirting toward the shore. They must make a long detour to catch him after he reached the foot of the fall.

The roar of awful waters met him as he looked ahead. Jean Boucher drove the paddle down and spoke to his son. The canoe leaned sidewise, sucked by the first chute, a caldron in the river bed where all Sainte Marie's current seemed to go down, and whirl, and rise, and froth, and roar.

"Ha!" shouted Jean Boucher. His face glistened with beads of water and the glory of mastering Nature.

Scarcely were they past the first pit when the canoe plunged on the verge of another. This sight was a moment of madness. The great chute, lined with moving water walls and floored with whirling foam, bellowed as if it were submerging the world. Columns of green water sheeted in white rose above it and fell forward on the current. As the canoemen held on with their paddles and shot by through spume and rain, every soul in the boat exulted except the woman who lay flat on its keel. The rapids gave a voyager the illusion that they were running uphill to meet him, that they were breasting and opposing him instead of carrying him forward. There was scarcely a breath between riding the edge of the bottomless pit and shooting out on clear water. The rapids were past, and they paddled for the other shore, a mile away.

On the west side the green water seemed turning to fire, but as the sunset went out, shadows sank on the broad surface. The fresh evening breath of a primitive world blew across it. Down-river the channel turned, and Jacques could see nothing of the English or of the other party. His pursuers had decided to land at the settlement.

It was twilight when Jean Boucher brought the canoe to pine woods which met them at the edge of the water. The young Repentigny had been wondering what he should do with his windigo. There was no settlement on this shore, and had there been one it would offer no hospitality to such as she was. His canoemen would hardly camp with her, and he had no provisions. To keep her from being stoned or torn to pieces he had made an inconsiderate flight. But his perplexity dissolved in a moment before the sight of Louizon Cadotte coming out of the woods towards them, having no hunting equipments and looking foolish.

"Where have you been?" called Jacques.

"Down this shore," responded Louizon.

"Did you take a canoe and come out here last night?"

"Yes, monsieur. I wished to be by myself. The canoe is below. I was coming home."

"It is time you were coming home, when all the men in the settlement are searching for you, and all the women trying to console your mother and your wife."

"My wife—she is not then talking with any one on the gallery?" Louizon's voice betrayed gratified revenge.

"I do not know. But there is a woman in this canoe who might talk on the gallery and complain to the priest against a man who has got her stoned on his account."

Louizon did not understand this, even when he looked at the heap of dirty blanket in the canoe.

"Who is it?" he inquired.

"The Chippewas call her a windigo. They were all chasing her for eating you up. But now we can take her back to the priest, and they will let her alone when they see you. Where is your canoe?"

"Down here among the bushes," answered Louizon. He went to get it, ashamed to look the young seignior in the face. He was light-headed from hunger and exposure, and what followed seemed to him afterwards a piteous dream.

"Come back!" called the young seignior, and Louizon turned back. The two men's eyes met in a solemn look.

"Jean Boucher says this woman is dead."

Jean Boucher stood on the bank, holding the canoe with one hand, and turning her unresisting face with the other. Jacques and Louizon took off their hats.

They heard the cry of the whip-poor-will. The river had lost all its green and was purple, and purple shadows lay on the distant mountains and opposite ridge. Darkness was mercifully covering this poor demented Indian woman, overcome by the burdens of her life, aged without being venerable, perhaps made hideous by want and sorrow.

When they had looked at her in silence, respecting her because she could no longer be hurt by anything in the world, Louizon whispered aside to his seignior:

"What shall we do with her?"

"Bury her," the old canoeman answered for him.

One of the party yet thought of taking her back to the priest. But she did not belong to priests and rites. Jean Boucher said they could dig in the forest mould with a paddle, and he and his son would make her a grave. The two Chippewas left the burden to the young men.

Jacques Repentigny and Louizon Cadotte took up the woman who, perhaps, had never been what they considered woman; who had missed the good, and got for her portion the ignorance and degradation of the world; yet who must be something to the Almighty, for he had sent youth and love to pity and take care of her in her death. They carried her into the woods between them.

Saukanuk

by JAMES M. PHALEN, 1872–   . *Dr. Phalen was born at Harvard, Illinois, and was educated at Northwestern University, Ph.G., 1896, and the University of Illinois, M.D., 1900. A specialist in tropical medicine, he spent some time in Manila and in 1918–19 served as medical inspector of the first* army, A.E.F. From 1927 to 1930 he was librarian of the Army Medical Library at Washington, D.C. Dr. Phalen is the author of Sinnissippi, a Valley under a Spell, a charming account of the Rock River Valley of Wisconsin and Illinois, published in 1942. "Saukanuk" is the closing chapter of the book.

For the last score of miles of its length Rock River runs roughly parallel to the Mississippi at a distance of scarcely a half dozen miles. About three miles from its junction with the greater river, it turns sharply to the right, to break through the wall of the Mississippi bluffs. The tongue of land that separates the two rivers is a continuation of the range of bluffs that limits on the east the flood-plain of the Mississippi, here comparatively narrow. The ridge ends abruptly in a sheer cliff overlooking the last miles of the Rock. The valley of the smaller river remains wide and flat, almost to the end, narrowing on its right bank as it becomes wider on the left. In this part of its course the current is divided by a score of long islands forming a labyrinth of devious channels.

One who in the summer of any year around 1780, stood at a vantage point on this narrow wooded ridge, would be able to see through breaks in the forest two Indian villages on the lands below. On a side hill to the southwest sloping down to the waters of the Rock stretches the groups of lodges that make up the principal village of the Sac nation, while on the bank of the Mississippi River, to the north, opposite a large island, stands the smaller village of the Fox tribesmen.

The beginning of these villages dates from nearly half a century before, when the vanguard of the two tribes reached the junction of the two rivers and saw in its protected location a place of settlement. In building their villages they vowed occupancy until the end of time. Other villages had been raised with similar vows in the past, but Indian memory of such events is short and uncertain. The Sacs chose their town site near the Rock and a short distance downstream from the high bluff which was to be the landmark of its location. They called their town Saukanuk. Across the tongue of land, facing the greater river the Foxes built their village, less large because their warriors were fewer in number and their women and children less. Doubtless the village was given a name but it has not come down to us.

Rome was not built in a day, nor was Saukanuk, though coming nearer to it. Captain Jonathan Carver visited a Sac village on the Wisconsin River in 1766, a village of ninety lodges, the largest and best built Indian village he had ever seen. A visitor to the site twenty years later found no signs of recent occupancy. Lieutenant Zebulon Pike in 1805 found the Sac and Fox villages at Rock Island the principal towns of the tribes. He found two smaller Sac villages on the Mississippi below Rock Island and two Fox villages in the lead country of Wisconsin. Sometime between the two dates given Saukanuk had gained primacy among Sac towns, and had reached the size and taken on a permanence rarely equalled in towns of the northern hunter tribes. After a half century of existence Saukanuk is now a town of somewhat more than a hundred lodges, with an average of three fires and six families to each lodge. Indian families of these tribes are not large, and the family at any one time will scarcely average five individuals. The population is thus something over three thousand, a metropolis as went Indian towns of that time and section. Its hundred lodges are grouped without order on the side hill. A location is chosen for each at a place where neither cut nor fill of the land is needed. The direction in which the lodge is faced is subject to the same element of chance. A fortunate grouping of saplings may well be the determining factor in the location of the lodge. It was not infrequent for Indian towns to be built as primitive fortresses with close built wigwams surrounded by palisaded walls and water-filled ditches. But Saukanuk on account of its location and the reputation of its warriors, has no use for such protection. There is ample space for expansion of the town site and no restrictions upon choice of location of new lodges. From these conditions there results a far-flung disarray of lodges, devoid of plan, deeply worn paths between the wigwams taking the place of streets. It would be a maze indeed except for the wide spacing of the buildings.

The Indian "long house" is ordinarily associated with the tribes of the Iroquois, but except for their lesser length, lodges of similar design and structure were built in every village of permanence belonging to any of the northern forest tribes. The solid structure of the Saukanuk lodges was of this plan.

The raising of new lodges is communal work, a task too difficult for the hands of the women and one of the few that are not below the dignity of a hunter-warrior. In the clear space needed, sapling poles are set in the ground to stand five paces high in two rows of ten to twelve paces length and five paces apart. The saplings are bent until their tops meet and are lashed together to form the beginning of a trellis. Along the outer sides other saplings are lashed with even spacing. The lashings are of the inner layers of bark and of twining roots. Over the frame thus prepared is fastened an outer covering of bark of the oak or the elm. Openings left at the ridge furnish some light, and provide for the escape of smoke. Doorways at each end are covered with a suspended slab of bark. At each end extensions of the roof and sides provide a space for the storage of wood for the fires and other bulky supplies. The frame completed and covered, two shelves of sapling poles are run the length of each side of the lodge. The lower one of four feet width is of a height to serve as a bed and a seat. The upper shelf, less wide, is intended primarily for the storage of the household's more prized possessions. Laterally the lodge is divided by partial partitions like the stalls in a stable.

The lodge is now ready for its occupants and soon the center line of the lodge floor is taken up with fires, one for each of the sections into which the lodge has been divided. Three fires to an ordinary lodge and six families, thirty persons perhaps, with at least one wolfish dog to each family, with a right to tenancy not to be questioned. The wooden beds are covered with the skins of bear and deer and the white man's blankets. The ground around the fires is covered with matting and the matting, by day, by family groups in lying and squatting postures. Over these fires the family meals are prepared and here on the matting they are served and eaten. In the warmer seasons the family sleeps on the shelf bed, but in the winter they are grouped, fully dressed, in huddles on the matting beside the fires, with the dogs contributing their body heat to that of the family group. The bites of fleas and their like are too familiar to these sleepers to disturb at all their slumbers or their dreams. The yellow of stripped sapling and rush matting which in the beginning colors the lodge interior is changed soon to brown and then to black with the accumulated deposits from wood smoke.

The village is made up of a hundred or more units like the one pictured. There is no building for community purposes. Public meetings are held in the open air, smaller ones in the lodges of the chieftains.

On the flat lands along Rock River above the town are the cornfields of the tribe. These cultivated fields run for a full three miles to the north with varying width, a thousand acres perhaps. Adjacent to them are the fields of the Fox village. The agriculture is of the Stone Age. The fields are the charge of the women, working with the most primitive tools. But corn needs only to be planted in the black bottomland and kept from suffocation by weeds. With a well moistened ground and a hot daily sun, the overnight growth can be measured. In the autumn the heavy ears hang ready for gathering, while between the cornhills the ground is strewn with yellow pumpkin and green squash. Patches of beans complete the farm scene. In such surroundings the shadow of famine can be kept a long way off.

On the wooded ridge north of the town and overlooking the corn lands is laid out the well-tenanted cemetery of the Sac nation. It shows the care and attention given to all their burial places by the Algonquin people. An early explorer writes thus of a burial ground of a tribe kindred to the Sacs:

"The dead are better cared for than the living. Over each grave a flat tablet of wood was supported by posts and at one end an upright tablet, carved with an intended representation of the features of the deceased. If a chief, the head was adorned by a plume, if a warrior, there were figures near it of a shield, a lance, a war club, and a bow with arrows; if a boy a small bow with one arrow, and if a woman or a girl, of a kettle, an earthen pot, a wooden spoon and a paddle. The whole was decorated with red and yellow paint and beneath slept the departed, wrapped in a robe of skins, his earthly treasures about him for use in the land of souls."

It was of the cemetery of another kindred tribe, the Chippewas, that Longfellow wrote:

> And they painted on the grave-posts
> Of the graves, yet unforgotten
> Each his own ancestral totem,
> Each the symbol of his household;
> Figures of the bear and reindeer
> Of the turtle, crane and beaver,
> Each inverted as a token
> That the owner was departed,
> That the chief who bore the symbol
> Lay beneath in dust and ashes.

Food and a campfire were kept at the new-made grave for the four-day journey of the departed to the land of the dead, which is thus no great distance away. Hunters of the village have passed it closely by, sensing its near presence, though none could say he had seen it. It is a place of continuous feasting with dancing to the sound of the rattle and drum, incident to the joyous welcome of friends newly arrived from the land of the living. Compare if you wish this savage Paradise to that of the great Franklin, where the virtuous ones from our earth had "nothing to do but to talk with one another, except now and then a little singing and drinking of *aqua vitae*."

The dwellers in Saukanuk are all of the Sac tribe, except where a man of that people has brought to his lodge a wife from the Foxes or the Winnebagos. They all speak the same Algonquin tongue. But for a seemingly primitive community it has a complex social structure. Like all northeastern tribes, this one is divided into groups which for want of a better term are called clans. Each has its emblem, the figure of a bird, beast or reptile and each is called by the name of the animal which it thus bears as its device. These groups are six to eight in number, variable in different tribes. The members of each clan are more or less related by blood, and marriage within the clan is forbidden. It thus results that in every family the husband and the wife are of different clans. All children are of the clan of their mother, on the certainty that they are of her blood. The head of the household may wear the turtle totem of his clan tattooed upon his breast, but the wife and children will give united allegiance to the clan of the otter or the beaver.

In a manner every head of a family is on an equality with every other. The tribe is a democracy in which all have a voice and all a vote. There are chiefs of varying grades and quality. The sachem or civil chief orders the general conduct of the tribe and of the town. He never sets himself against the popular will, which is the sovereign power. His province is to advise, not to dictate. There are no laws for his guidance, and no means of enforcing his will. Ancient customs and prevailing usage are the standards of conduct. The sachem's position is hereditary through the female line, but he can be easily deposed for another of his blood, for cause. War-chiefs rank high in time of conflict and in the field. They are self-made leaders, who must maintain their leadership or be set aside. They must avoid serious losses to their followers or they will soon be without them. There are minor chiefs for various functions, the medicine man probably the most important.

The most potent influence in every individual's conduct is his personal guiding spirit or *manito*, which is acquired in the years of adolescence. No act of importance will be taken without first invoking the advice and guidance of these spirits. In the midst of silent solitude their help is asked to be given directly or through the agency of dreams.

Such was the community of Saukanuk and its surroundings at the time when a son was born to the wife of Pyesa, the war-chief. Indians speak seldom of their women and more seldom still do they speak of them by name, so the mother of the child must remain nameless. There was just a day or two when her work in the field and lodge must be taken over by another or remain undone. But if the birth was regarded casually, there was no lack of warm affection for the young warrior, nor of tender care of his young body. It is not a fecund race and the little ones that come are cherished carefully. This boy is primarily his mother's child but the father in the semi-privacy of the lodge is not found lacking in the pride of paternity. The position of wife of a war-chief carries with it no dispensation from women's work. A cradle has been carried over from a previous birth or a new one is waiting the new-born. The cradle and child are slung on the back of the mother and go where she goes. The cradle is built to fix the spine of the child while it is still highly flexible, on a firm flat surface. The child is thus deprived of movement. It is bound down and its head protected by a hoop. The cradle is well calculated to give the child those lessons in endurance so necessary in its later hunter and warrior life. The cradle may be hung upon a tree trunk or from a wall-peg in the lodge. In due time the child is released from the strappings of the cradle and for a time follows his mother with uncertain steps, while she works in the fields or about the lodge.

The mind of the mother in the meantime is weighing a choice among the aged men of her kindred for one who shall be asked to put a name upon the young son. The choice is important, and the responsibility placed upon the chosen one is heavy and not to be avoided. The aged one will retire into solitude and there invoke the guidance of his *manito* in the choice of a name. When the choice is made it will have been suggested by some manifestation of nature or by the association of some animate object. The name may be the Algonquin rendering of Passing Cloud or West Wind, of Jumping Fish or Blue Heron. A family gathering is called for a feast, and a ceremonial announcement and bestowal of the name. Pyesa's son is given the name Makatawimeshekaka. It will not soon be heard again nor often repeated. A name thus bestowed is of such significance that it will never be pronounced needlessly, lest the spirits that influenced its selection be displeased. When the boy is old enough to understand, his name will be disclosed to him by his mother. In the meantime she has spoken of him and to him by a pet name, perhaps calling him "my little owlet" as did Nokomis to Hiawatha, the offspring of her daughter Wenonah and the West Wind. From this childhood name or from other circumstance he will acquire a sobriquet by which he will be called commonly through life. When asked his name he will give the one by which he is generally known. This duality of names has caused much confusion in establishing Indian identity.

Meanwhile Pyesa, the war-chief, is observing his son for the time when he will give over clinging to his mother's skirt and will join in the play of the village children. Now is come the time to take over his instruction to fit him for a man's part in the life of the town and of the tribe. He is taken for walks in the neighboring woods and told the names and the habits of the wild life and is shown his father's skill in their pursuit. He is called upon for admiring approval of exhibitions of cunning by the fox, of strength and agility by the forest cat, and of the perseverance of the hungry wolf. He is shown where he may look with hope of finding trees of purple plums and festoons of grapevines with their fruit. He is shown where grow the blackberry and the raspberry, and where nuts will be found in the autumn. There are tempting looking fruits such as the nightshade that he must shun. In walks along the river and in canoe rides along its channels he learns the ways of fishes and the manner of their capture. Swimming

95

he learns early in the Rock and soon is among the most fearless in breasting the drive of the waters toward the Mississippi and the sea.

He sees something of the making of traps for birds and small animals and of their use. He is now furnished a bow adapted to his strength, and arrows, and is encouraged to fare into the woods with others of his years. A feigned importance is given to these hunting parties by the elders. When Pyesa's son brings home the first small animal that he has taken, be it a baby rabbit, a gopher, or a robin, there is simulated excitement, but real interest, in the lodge of the chief. The boy's mother makes of the game, however small, a stew, or she mixes it into a cornmeal stirabout. The father invites a company of his close friends to the feast. There is much feigned enthusiasm for the dish and extravagant compliments for the prowess of the young hunter.

As the boy grows older he is given some small part in the building of new lodges and in the less skilled part of canoe construction. The Sacs were once builders of canoes of birchbark, but this material is not available in the Illinois country, and canoes must now be hewn out of the wood at hand. For smaller and lighter craft the trunk of the basswood is used, while for heavier and more durable ones black walnut is chosen. Trees are cut down and the trunks cut to suitable length by the use of fire and scrapers. By the same crude methods the trunk is shaped into a graceful dugout. Barring accident a dugout of walnut has a life expectancy as long as the man who makes it.

The boy is now of the years when he is expected to sit in the outer row of listeners at meetings called by the town's chiefs. With the expectancy that he will be himself one day a chief and will address the meetings of his people, he is all attention, not only to the subject matter of the discourses, but to the manner of delivery of the speaker. Oratory is a necessary accomplishment of a chief, cultivated from his youth. He acquires an accurate ear for the rhythm of his sentences, aided as he is by a language of long and stately words and of multiform inflexions. The talks follow an unvarying line. There are but few themes appropriate for the speech of chiefs and warriors. They all have to do with war, with public policy, hunting, personal strength and courage, the benefits of abstinence, and of endurance under suffering. Their thoughts and discourses are of the past and its glories. At this time there begins to appear in their speeches a foreboding awareness of encroachment by the white man's superior civilization and the appalling sense that nothing will avail against the menace. They know more of the white man's warfare than of his civil life. There are old warriors in Saukanuk who were in Montcalm's armies in his struggle with the English. There are more who were with Pontiac when in 1763 he cleared the Great Lakes country of British arms. The Sac and Fox tribes are credited with the dire vengeance that was visited upon the Illinois nation after the murder by one of its tribesmen of the great Ottawa leader in 1769 at Cahokia in the Illinois bottoms. More recently, in 1780, they joined in a British attack upon the Spanish town of St. Louis and American garrison at Cahokia. They were the principal sufferers from American retaliation when later in the same year their down-river towns were attacked and burned.

Better than the artificial language of the public address the boy likes the jovial banter that passes for conversation in the lodges. Best of all is he pleased when he finds himself on a winter's night among the lodge audience of one of the tribal story-tellers. These are men of good memory and fluent speech, speaking a language midway between that of the orators and the tribal vernacular. They preserve the oral chronicles of the tribe and collect all floating fables and tales. Metamorphosis or transformation is the background for all of their stories, in which is shown an ingenuity for the purposes of amusement and instruction that rivals the skill of Ovid himself. Similarly omnipresent is the magic canoe capable of covering its hundreds of miles in as many minutes, and moccasins that devour space like seven-league boots. There is a charm in certain words, without meaning in the language. In these stories animals are people in other forms, who reason and speak their thoughts like men. In this field they anticipate the bedtime story by centuries. Stories involving mystery and terror are circumstantially told to raise the hair of the listeners, stories of cannibalistic giants who devour men, women and children, stories of ghosts, of fairies and of mermen. Any of these may be introduced as the agent of retributive justice. Most often in these tales is heard the name of Manabozho, the king of all animal kings. Appearing most often as the Great Hare there is no limit to his transformations nor of his powers for good or evil.

Scarcely less fascinating than these stories to the boy's mind are the enactments of bold adventure by the village masters of pantomime. All Indians practice the art more or less and all are adepts in its interpretation. The chief, returned from a foray upon an enemy, will hold his audience spellbound as he depicts the incidents of the expedition. He enacts the farewell to the home village, the long tedious march, the swimming of rivers, the killing of game. Tension increases as he depicts the discovery from afar of an enemy camp. Then are enacted in turn the hasty run, the stealthy step by step approach and the crawl to a point of vantage. He signals his followers to advance and he points out the prey. He cautions patience while food is being prepared in the camp and until arms are laid aside. Then follows the rush, the despatch of the enemy and the taking of scalps. Relaxation comes to the company only when the victors are shown eating the food of the vanquished.

Always a great event in the boy's envious eyes is the feast that his father periodically gives to his fellow tribal chieftains. The main dish is invariably a mess of pounded corn, wherein are boiled without salt or other seasoning, whatever scraps of meat and fish that are at hand. Each guest, carrying his wooden dish and spoon, thrusts out his long arm to be served by the host, who sits beside his kettle and, out of courtesy, takes no share of the food himself. The dishes are returned as long as there is anything left in the kettle, and no guest may, without grave offense, refuse his full share.

The kettle empty, pipes are brought forth and filled. Tobacco is scarce and precious but there need be no self-denial in smoking. The content of kinnikinnick, the substitute, varies in different localities but here in the Rock valley it is made up of sumac leaves, gathered at the right time in autumn and the inner bark of the willow. It is the duty of the women of the lodge to light and to keep alight the fires in the pipes of their men, with coals from the lodge fires. The guests, heavy with food and soothed by smoke, are more likely to doze in sleep than to indulge in conversation. There is a certain ceremonial air to the gathering that is maintained to the leave taking.

Boyhood is merging into manhood for Pyesa's son, with a changing outlook and changing aspirations. The chief takes his son aside and tells him that the time has come for him to "talk to his heart" and then to go out and find his *manito*. The boy completes his arrangements thoughtfully. A few mornings later he steps into his father's light canoe, taking with him only his ax and his basswood bowl. He drifts down the Rock between its islands until on the left bank he comes to the foot of a bluff. Here he hauls up his canoe, fills his bowl with water and climbs to the top of the hill. He cuts brushwood for a fire which he keeps blazing day and night. He goes without food and keeps awake by singing and calling upon his *manito*. Each morning he washes himself with water from his bowl and dries himself by the fire. On the third night he falls asleep in spite of himself and his guardian spirit comes to him in his dreams. Everything is clear. He is to be a hunter and a warrior. He may have wished to be a medicine man, but that was denied to him by his guiding spirit. As to all others, this comes to him in the guise of an animal. Whether it comes to him in the form of bird, beast, or reptile, he will speak its name to nobody, not even his father. He may, however, try his skill in carving its likeness in wood and he will at once obtain a feather or bone or a wisp of hair of the animal of his dream. These contained in a small bag are thereafter his "medicine" and will be carried upon his person throughout life. He will call upon it for aid in every enterprise upon which he starts, whether in hunting, war or negotiation. It will influence every act of his life.

The war-chief's son is now fifteen and a meeting of the towns' council speaks of war. There are two principal causes of war, the killing of tribesmen and trespass upon the tribe's hunting grounds. The former may be satisfied by the payment of goods to the family of the dead man, but invasion of the hunting grounds is not so easily settled. In the scheme of Indian economy it is necessary for the tribe to have vast areas of hunting fields that can be successively hunted over and left for the multiplication of game. Trespass is a menace to the life of the tribe.

The Osages of the lower Missouri are accused on both counts. A war-chief from down the river is recruiting a band for vengeance and for protection of the tribal lands. Any warrior may volunteer to go and anyone can stay at home without question of his motives. Pyesa joins the war party and takes his son with him. In the ensuing battle the young man kills and scalps his first victim and returning to Saukanuk is permitted to put an eagle feather in his headdress and to paint the blood-red hand upon the inside of his blanket. He is the warrior son of a war-chief. At the next dance of the warriors of the tribe he takes his turn in the circle to the pride of his father and the envy of his less fortunate boyhood friends.

Following the planting of the corn the next spring he waits the feast and dance of the crane when the marriageable maidens of the village are shown in their finest dress, and the young men choose their brides. He looks with favor upon the maiden Singing Bird and so informs his mother. She speaks to the girl's mother, and the customary arrangements are made. Upon an appointed night he steals into the lodge of the girl's family. With his flint and steel he locates her where she sleeps and awakens her. He holds the light near his face that she may see him well and then he extends it close to hers. She blows out the light and he knows that he is accepted and will move with his possessions into the lodge the next morning. If the light had remained unextinguished he must try again or try elsewhere. It is well understood that the marriage can be as easily put aside as it is taken on, but this union is to be a lasting one.

The years roll over Saukanuk with a little-broken routine. Autumn and the early months of winter are the times for hunting the distant forests and gathering the skins and furs with which to buy the trader's supplies. The end of winter finds all back in the home lodges. Sugar-making will fill the days of early spring. Then follows the preparation of the corn fields by the women and the planting of the crop. The young men are now out on the spring hunt for meat to dry and cure. A band of older men with their families go to spend the warm season in the lead-workings to the north. For the hunters and warriors the summer is a time for play and for trying out their skill and luck at games and races, in which personal possessions may be doubled or lost within the hour. The women are working the fields, gathering the produce, curing meat, and preparing food, but for them, too, summer is a time of comparative ease. Hardly a year passes without the foray of a war party into the country of the Osages, Cherokees or Sioux. Pyesa can be counted on to head these bands and his son to be with him. They are adepts at the swift unheralded march, the ambush and the daybreak onslaught upon enemy villages. But one fateful day Pyesa's *manito* fails him and the lance of a Cherokee warrior cuts through the blood supply of his thigh. Dying, he hands over the "medicine" of his chieftainship to his son, who is now a man full-grown.

The young war-chief returns to Saukanuk and mourns his father for five years during which time he takes part in no war parties. He is however cherishing the idea of again humbling the Osage nation and will be satisfied with nothing short of extermination of the Cherokees. He gathers a war party of Sacs, Foxes, and Iowas and strikes quickly into the Meramec country below the Missouri River. He scatters the Osages to the four winds but finds that the Cherokees have gone from their old haunts, leaving only deserted villages. The few found are unworthy of his vengeance.

The year is 1804 when Quashquame, Pashepaho, Outchequa and Hashebarhiqua, all minor chiefs, are sent by the tribal council to see the American Father at St. Louis to bargain for the life of a tribesman who has killed an American. They are back in due time to report that negotiations for the freedom of their erring brother had proceeded favorably, but that while they were still in progress the prisoner was reported shot to death while trying to escape from his captors. They are shamefully aware, but loathe to report that during the negotiations they have in some manner sold all of the tribal lands east of the Mississippi river, including the home townsite, for a song. This they sang themselves to the accompaniment of flowing liquor between spells of maudlin self pity and of frenzied rage. There never was anything jovial about an Indian in his cups. The St. Louis governor who was later to have the highest place in the government on account of his handling of the Indians, knew well the potent influence of rum. He could well subscribe to the fictional trader McDole's formula for success.

A thousand Opportunities present
To take Advantage of their Ignorance.

But the great Engine I employ is Rum
More powerful made by certain strengthening Drugs.
This I distribute with a lib'ral hand
Urge them to drink till they grow mad and valiant;
Which makes them think me generous and just
And gives full Scope to practice all my Art.
I then begin my trade with watered Rum
The cooling draughts well suit their scorching Throats
The Fur and Peltry come in quick Return;
My scales are honest, but so well contrived
That one small Slip will turn Three Pounds to One.
Which they, poor silly Souls! ignorant of Weights
And Rules of Balancing, do not perceive.
But here they come; you'll see how I proceed.
Jack, is the Rum prepared as I commanded?

There is consternation in Saukanuk over the sale of the tribal lands and universal repudiation of the authority of its negotiators, but as years pass and there is no sign of an eviction the transaction is forgotten. But the sale is made very much of record in St. Louis and regarded as a stroke of good business.

Up to this time Saukanuk has seen few white men. At each return from the winter's hunt there are found at the village, awaiting the hunters, a small group of traders, Canadian and English, ready to exchange their guns, powder, blankets, utensils and ornaments for the skins and furs brought in. The end of the trading is marked by gifts of kegs of rum to the village and the traders depart in the midst of an alcoholic celebration. Now there are settlers moving into the tribal lands to the south and there is a report of a military post being built a short distance downstream on the great river. It is explained that the post is to be a supply point for the Indians and this is thought good news. The new settlements have each their traders who are always ready to exchange their goods, preferably rum and whiskey, for the Indian's furs. There are rumors of coming war in the air, war between the Americans and the English. In such a war the Indian must fight with the side with which he can trade and get supplies. The chiefs of the village know that they are under American rule and go down to Fort Madison to make arrangements for the supplies necessary for their winter hunt. Yes, the American Father has the goods that are needed, but he must have payment in advance, preferably in the fur of the beaver. This is an unheard-of situation, and there is despair in Saukanuk until there arrive boat-loads of British goods sent by Colonel Robert Dickson from Green Bay by his agent, La Gutrie. With them comes word that the British and Americans are really at war, and that the war-chief of the Sac and Fox nation is asked to bring his warriors to Green Bay to aid their British Father. At Green Bay the Sac war-chief is addressed as a general and placed at the head of the confederated tribes of that section. They join Tecumseh's forces before Detroit, and take part in the battles at Frenchtown and Fort Meigs. Defeat at Thames River with the death of Tecumseh sends the Sac band back to Saukanuk. For another year there is war along the Mississippi, with Prairie du Chien the center of conflict. It is different war than the inter-tribal struggles of earlier times, but nothing happens to lessen the Indian's confidence in his manner of making war.

The war ends, inconclusively for the white contestants, but not for the Indian tribes who have aided the British cause. The various tribal chieftains are summoned to St. Louis to make what peace they can with the American Fathers. The war-chief of the Sacs goes with the civil chiefs who try to explain the plight of the tribe between the two combatants. In signing a peace, they ratify, as they later discover, the sale of their homelands made a dozen years before by Quashquame.

The years of war have brought a Fox chieftain Keokuk into a position of influence in the confederated tribes. Never a warrior, he is the advocate of peace with the Americans at their own terms. A fort is built on the island in the Mississippi opposite the Fox village, and a house for an Indian agent. Settlers upon the land are coming closer to Saukanuk and its cultivated fields. Disputes and personal conflicts between settler and Indian become more common and more serious. Within the Indian villages there is a cleavage between the followers of the Sac and the Fox chiefs, not on tribal lines primarily but upon policies in relation to the pressure upon them by the settlers. The so-called "British band" of the Sac chieftain is a definite unit of opposition to the abandonment of their lands and villages. They make periodic pilgrimages over the "Sac trail" from Saukanuk to Malden in upper Canada, where the British authorities give them some supplies and some unwarranted words of encouragement. They have great faith in the word of the British Father.

In 1825 the American Father called the tribes of the upper Mississippi valley to meet at Prairie du Chien, there to settle all differences between them, and to establish boundaries between their hunting grounds. Schoolcraft, the Indian agent, came from Mackinac to lend his aid and he writes at length about the council which lasted the greater part of a month. Three tribes of the Sioux nation were there—the Dakotas, the Winnebagos and the Iowas—each hostile to the others, and the latter two allied to their Algonquin neighbors. Of these latter people, there were bands of Chippewas, Menomonies, Ottawas and Pottawattomies. No other tribe, says the Indian agent, attracted as intense an interest as did the Sacs and Foxes, who came accompanied by their allies of the Iowa tribe. He writes of them:

"These tribes were encamped on the island or opposite coast (of the Mississippi). They came to the treaty ground, armed and dressed as a war party. They were all armed with spears, clubs, guns and knives. Many of the warriors had a tuft of red horse hair tied at their elbows, and wore a necklace of grizzly bears' claws. Their head dress consisted of red dyed horse hair, tied in such a manner to the scalp lock as to present the shape of the decoration of a Roman helmet. The rest of the head was completely shaved and painted. A long iron shod lance was carried in the hand. A species of baldrick (girdle) supported part of their arms. They were, indeed, nearly nude and painted. Often the print of the hand, in white clay, marked the back or shoulders. They bore flags of feathers. They beat drums. They uttered yells at definite points. They landed in compact ranks. They looked the very spirit of defiance. Their leader stood as a prince, majestic and frowning. The wild native pride of man, in the savage state, flushed by success of war and confident of the strength of his arm, was never so fully depicted to my eyes. And the forest tribes of the continent may be challenged to have ever presented a spectacle of bold daring and martial prowess, equal to their landing. Their martial bearing and high tone and whole behavior during their stay, in and out of council, was impressive and demonstrated, in an eminent degree, to what a high pitch of physical and moral courage, bravery and success in war may lead a savage people."

This display of martial spirit would have its due effect upon neighboring Indian tribes, but upon the yet low and distant tide of adventurous settlers that was flowing up from the southern settlements, it was as powerless as King Canute's commands to the advancing sea.

The years are accumulating upon the head of the war-chief and he is no longer young. To the troubles that have come upon his town and people are added griefs of a personal nature. At about the same time his first-born son and his youngest daughter are taken by death. He mourns them by living in isolation away from his family and his friends. He spends long hours in contemplation atop the sheer bluff overlooking the Rock and in vigils beside the graves of his children. It is in relation to this sad period of his life that he says:

"With us it is a custom to visit the graves of our friends and keep them in repair for many years. The mother will go alone to weep over the grave of her child. The brave with pleasure visits the grave of his father, after he has been successful in war, and repaints the post that marks where he lies. There is no place like that where the bones of our forefathers lie to go when in grief. Here prostrate by the tombs of our fathers will the Great Spirit take pity on us."

Settlers are coming ever nearer and are casting covetous eyes upon the cultivated fields surrounding Saukanuk. Hunters returning from the winter's hunt find squatters in the fields who must be driven off. They become every day bolder and another spring finds them plowing in the village fields and doing damage to the burial-ground. The Indians threaten them violence if they persist. Thus comes about the condition desired—Indian threats upon the white settlers. An alarm is raised and the governor is called upon for protection. He calls some thousands of militia to the colors and orders them to the suppression of Indian atrocities at the mouth of the Rock. When the troops make camp south of the river, opposite Saukanuk, Keokuk and his followers have already moved across the Mississippi into Iowa. The British band with its leader remains in the village, and they try to make terms with General Gaines, the American war-chief. Even the request that they be allowed to stay long enough to harvest the crops they had planted in the spring is denied them. They must be beyond the Mississippi before another daybreak.

With nightfall the Sacs abandon their homes and begin the transport of their possessions across the river to the west. On the next day, June 26, 1831, Saukanuk, which had been built for the ages, goes up in a hundred swirls of flame and smoke.

EXPLORER AND TRAVELER

Buffalo

by LOUIS HENNEPIN, 1640?–1701. Hennepin was one of the first white men to see middle America. Born in Flanders, he became a Recollect priest, then went to Canada in 1675 and four years later accompanied La Salle's expedition across Lakes Huron and Michigan and down the Illinois River. With two Canadian companions Hennepin ascended the Mississippi River in 1680 and saw and christened the Falls of St. Anthony. Taken captive by the Sioux he spent some time in their villages in the vicinity of Mille Lacs Lake in northern Minnesota before he was released through the intercession of Dulhut. Hennepin later made his way back to Montreal and to Europe. He wrote several books about his travels, including Description de la Louisi-

ane (1683), which despite its title might be called the first book about the Middle West; Nouveau Voyage (1696); and Nouvelle Découverte d'un Très Grand Pays Situé dans L'Amérique (1697). Like Carver, Hennepin was not always accurate, nor was he averse to using accounts written by others. Nevertheless, his books remain interesting early chronicles. The description of the buffalo country is taken from the translation made by Marion E. Cross and published in 1938 by the University of Minnesota Press.

THE Seignelay River, which flows through the Illinois country, rises on this plain in a great swamp where it is almost impossible to walk. This river is only a league and a half from the Miami River. We transported all our equipment and canoes by a path which we marked for those who were to follow us. We had also left at the fork of the Miami River, as well as at the fort we constructed at its mouth, letters of instruction for the twenty-five men who were to join us, coming on the bark.

The Seignelay River is navigable for canoes a hundred paces from its source. It widens so rapidly that within a short distance it is almost as broad as, and deeper than, the Marne. Its course is through vast swamps where, in spite of its fairly strong current, it meanders to such an extent that after paddling an entire day, one has sometimes traveled only two leagues in a straight line. As far as the eye can see, there is only swamp land covered with rushes and alders. We might not have been able to find any place to camp for more than forty leagues of the way if there had not been mounds of frozen earth on which we built fires and lay down. We were short of food and even after passing this swamp, we did not find the game that we had hoped for.

The region we entered was a great open plain on which nothing grows except high grass, which, being dry at that season, had been burned by the Miami in hunting buffaloes. However hard our hunters tried to kill deer, during more than sixty leagues of our voyage they bagged only one lean stag, a little roe deer, some swans, and two geese; and there were thirty-two people to be fed. We saw the flames of the plains set afire by the Indians to facilitate the killing of buffaloes. If our canoemen had found an opportunity, they would certainly have deserted across country and joined these Indians.

That buffaloes are usually very numerous here is apparent from the bones, horns, and skulls to be seen on all sides. The Miami hunt buffaloes at the end of the autumn in the following manner:

When they see a herd the Indians assemble in great numbers. They set fire to the grass all around these animals except for one passage left on purpose. There the Indians station themselves with their bows and arrows. The buffaloes, wanting to avoid the fire, are thus forced to pass by the Indians, who at times kill as many as a hundred and twenty of them in one day. The buffaloes are distributed according to the needs of the families. These Indians, triumphant over the slaughter of so many animals, give notice to their wives, who attend to bringing in the meat. The women sometimes carry three hundred pounds on their backs, throwing their babies on top of their load, which to them does not seem more of a burden than does the sword at his side to a soldier.

Instead of hair buffaloes have very fine wool, which is longer on the female than on the male. Their horns are almost entirely black and are shorter but much thicker than those of the European oxen. They have an enormous head and an extremely short but very thick neck, sometimes six hands wide. They have a hump or small protuberance between their shoulders. Their legs are extremely thick and short and are covered with very long wool. From their heads between their horns, long black hair falls over their eyes, giving them a frightful appearance. Their meat is most succulent; they are very fat in autumn because they have been in grass up to their necks all summer long. This vast prairie region seems to be the natural habitat of the buffalo. Scattered here and there are groves where these animals retire to chew their cud and avoid the heat of the sun.

Buffaloes, or wild oxen, migrate with the changing seasons and temperatures. When they sense the approach of winter in the north, they move southward, sometimes traveling in a single file a league long. They all lie down together; the place where they have lain is often full of wild purslane, which we have sometimes eaten. The paths where they have passed are beaten like our European roads and are bare of grass. They cross streams and rivers. Buffalo cows go to islands to prevent wolves from eating their calves. When the calves are able to run, wolves would not dare to come near because the cows would kill them. In order not to drive these animals out of their country entirely, the Indians make a practice of pursuing only those that they have wounded with arrows. They refrain from further pursuit of the others, permitting them to escape so as not to frighten them unduly.

Although the Indians of this vast continent are habitually inclined to destroy animals, they have never been able to exterminate the buffalo. These animals multiply naturally, in spite of being hunted, and return in season the following years in increasing numbers.

The Indian women spin buffalo wool on a spindle and from the yarn make bags to carry the smoked or dried meat. They sometimes dry their meat in the sun. Frequently they keep meat three or four months; for although they have no salt, they cure the flesh so well that it does not spoil at all. Four months after meat has been prepared in this way, one would say on eating it that the animal was freshly killed. Instead of water, we drank broth with these Indians. This is the usual drink of all Indians of America who have had no contact with Europeans.

The average buffalo hide weighs a hundred to a hundred and twenty pounds. The Indians cut away the back and around the neck where the skin is thickest. Using only the thinnest part of the belly, they dress it very carefully with the brains of all sorts of animals, thereby making it as supple as our chamois skins dressed in oil. They paint it with various colors, trim it with red and white porcupine quills, and make it into ceremonial robes to wear at feasts. In winter, especially at night, they cover themselves with buffalo robes, which feel very comfortable on account of the curly wool.

When buffalo cows have been killed by the Indians, the little calves follow the hunters, licking their hands and fingers. The Indians sometimes take them to their children and after the children have played with them, the calves are killed with a club and eaten. The Indians keep their hoofs, dry them, and attach them to switches, which shake and rattle to accompany the changing postures and steps of the singers and dancers. This contrivance somewhat resembles a Basque tambourine.

The calves could easily be domesticated and used for tilling the soil.

In all seasons of the year, buffaloes find food as they go. When they are surprised by winter and cannot reach the warm southland before the ground is covered with snow, they are skillful at breaking through the snow and pushing it aside in order to graze on the hidden grass. Their bellowing can be heard but not as commonly as that of European oxen.

The bodies of buffaloes are much larger than those of our European oxen, especially in the fore portion. Their great bulk does not keep them from moving so fast that few Indians are able to overtake them on the run. Buffaloes often kill those who have wounded them. In season, herds of two and even four hundred are to be seen.

The Fox-Wisconsin Route

by JONATHAN CARVER, 1710–80. *France was the first nation to send its missionaries and explorers into the Great Lakes region and the northern Mississippi Valley, but early in the eighteenth century English-speaking travelers began to penetrate the transmontane country. One of the most famous of these was Jonathan Carver. He was born in Connecticut and probably began to support himself as a cobbler. Later he served under Major Robert Rogers, commandant of the celebrated Rangers, and it was at Rogers' suggestion that he began in 1766 his travels westward. Carver's route took him over the Great Lakes, across the Fox-Wisconsin portage to the Mississippi, and up the Mississippi to the Sioux country; probably he saw something of the Lake Superior region as well. In 1778 Carver published in London his much discussed Travels through the Interior Parts of North America, in the Years 1766, 1767, and 1768. Research has demonstrated that Carver was indebted to previous explorers for large sections of his book and that his respect for veracity was not consistently high, but Carver's observations on people and places remain interesting.*

ABOUT twelve miles before I reached the Carrying Place, I observed several small mountains which extended quite to it. These indeed would only be esteemed as molehills, when compared with those on the back of the colonies, but as they were the first I had seen since my leaving Niagara, a track of nearly eleven hundred miles, I could not leave them unnoticed.

The Fox River, where it enters the Winnebago Lake, is about fifty yards wide, but it gradually decreases to the Carrying Place, where it is no more than five yards over, except in a few places where it widens into small lakes, though still of a considerable depth. I cannot recollect any thing else that is remarkable in this river, except that it is so serpentine for five miles as only to gain in that place one quarter of a mile.

The Carrying Place between the Fox and Ouisconsin Rivers is in breadth not more than a mile and three quarters, though in some maps it is so delineated as to appear to be ten miles. And here I cannot help remarking, that all the maps of these parts, I have ever seen, are very erroneous. The rivers in general are described as running in different directions from what they really do; and many branches of them, particularly the Mississippi, omitted. The distances of places, likewise, are greatly misrepresented. Whether this is done by the French geographers (for the English maps are all copied from theirs) through design, or for want of a just knowledge of the country, I cannot say; but I am satisfied that travellers who depend upon them in the parts I visited, will find themselves much at a loss.

Near one half of the way, between the rivers, is a morass overgrown with a kind of long grass, the rest of it a plain with some few oak and pine trees growing thereon. I observed here a great number of rattlesnakes. Mons. Pinnisance, a French trader, told me a remarkable story concerning one of these reptiles, of which he said, he was an eye-witness. An Indian belonging to the Menomonie nation, having taken one of them, found means to tame it; and when he had done this, treated it as a Deity; calling it his Great Father, and carrying it with him in a box, wherever he went. This the Indian had done for several summers, when Mons. Pinnisance accidentally met with him at this Carrying Place, just as he was setting off for a winter's hunt. The French gentleman was surprised, one day, to see the Indian place the box which contained his god, on the ground, and opening the door, gave him his liberty; telling him whilst he did it, to be sure and return by the time he himself should come back, which was to be in the month of May following. As this was but October Monsieur told the Indian, whose simplicity astonished him, that he fancied he might wait long enough when May arrived for the arrival of his great father. The Indian was so confident of his creature's obedience, that he offered to lay the Frenchman a wager of two gallons of rum, that at the time appointed he would come and crawl into the box. This was agreed on, and the second week in May following, fixed for the determination of the wager. At that period they both met there again; when the Indian set down his box, and called for his great father. The snake heard him not; and the time being now expired, he acknowledged that he had lost. However, without seeming to be discouraged, he offered to double the bet, if his great father came not within two days more. This was further agreed on; when behold on the second day about one o'clock, the snake arrived, and of his own accord crawled in the box, which was placed ready for him. The French gentleman vouched for the truth of this story, and from the accounts I have often received of the docility of those creatures, I see no reason to doubt his veracity.

I observed that the main body of the Fox River came from the southwest, that of the Ouisconsin from the north-east; and also that some of the small branches of these two rivers, in descending into them, doubled within a few feet of each other, a little to the south of the Carrying Place. That two such rivers should take their rise so near each other, and after running such different courses, empty themselves into the sea, at a distance so amazing (for the former having passed through several great lakes, and run upwards of two thousand miles, falls into the Gulf of St. Lawrence, and the other, after joining the Mississippi, and having run an equal number of miles, disembogues itself into the Gulf of Mexico) is an instance scarcely to be met in the extensive continent of North America. I had an opportunity the year following, of making the same observations on the affinity of various head branches of the waters of the St. Lawrence and the Mississippi to each other; and now bring them as a proof, that the opinion of those geographers, who assert, that rivers taking their rise so near each other, must spring from the same source, is erroneous. For I perceived a visibly distinct separation in all of them, notwithstanding, in some places, they approached so near, that I could have stepped from one to the other.

On the 8th of October [1766] we got our canoes into the Ouisconsin River, which at this place is more than a hundred yards wide; and the next day arrived at the Great Town of the Saukies. This is the largest and best built Indian town I ever saw. It contains about ninety houses each large enough for several families. These are built of hewn plank, neatly jointed and covered with bark so compactly as to keep out the most penetrating rains. Before the doors are placed comfortable sheds, in which the inhabitants sit, when the weather will permit, and smoke their pipes. The streets are regular and spacious; so that it appears more like a civilized town, than the abode of savages. The land near the town is very good. In their plantations, which lie adjacent to their houses, and which are neatly laid out, they raise great quantities of Indian corn, beans, melons, &c. so that this place is esteemed the best market for traders to furnish themselves with provisions, of any within eight hundred miles of it.

The Saukies can raise about three hundred warriors, who are generally employed every summer in making incursions into the territories of the Illinois and Pawnee nations, from whence they return, with a great number of slaves. But those people frequently retaliate, and, in their turn, destroy many of the Saukies, which I judge to be the reason that they increase no faster.

Whilst I staid here I took a view of some mountains that lie about fifteen miles to the southward, and abound in lead ore. I ascended on one of the highest of these, and had an extensive view of the country. For many miles nothing was to be seen but lesser mountains, which appeared at distance like haycocks, they being free from trees. Only a few groves of hickory, and stunted oaks, covered some of the vallies. So plentiful is lead here, that I saw large quantities of it lying about the streets in the town belonging to the Saukies, and it seemed to be as good as the produce of other countries.

On the 10th of October we proceeded down the river, and the next day reached the first town of the Ottigaumies. This town contained about fifty houses, but we found most of them deserted, on account of an epidemical disorder that had lately raged among them, and carried off more than one half of the inhabitants. The greater part of those who survived, had retired into the woods to avoid the contagion.

On the 15th we entered that extensive river the Mississippi. The Ouisconsin, from the Carrying Place to the part where it falls into the Mississippi, flows with a smooth, but strong current; the water of it is exceedingly clear, and through it you may perceive a fine and sandy bottom, tolerably free from rocks. In it are a few islands, the soil of which appeared to be good, though somewhat woody. The land near the river also seemed to be, in general, excellent; but that at a distance is very full of mountains, where it is said there are many lead mines.

About five miles from the junction of the rivers, I observed the ruins of a large town, in a very pleasing situation. On enquiring of the neighbouring Indians, why it was thus deserted, I was informed, that about thirty years ago, the Great Spirit had appeared on the top of a pyramid of rocks, which lay at a little distance from it, towards the west, and warned them to quit their habitations; for the land on which they were built belonged to him, and he had occasion for it. As a proof that he, who gave them these orders, was really the Great Spirit, he further told them, that the grass should immediately spring up on those very rocks from whence he now addressed them, which they knew to be bare and barren. The Indians obeyed, and soon after discovered that this miraculous alteration had taken place. They shewed me the spot, but the growth of the grass appeared to be noways supernatural. I apprehend this to have been a stratagem of the French or Spaniards, to answer some selfish view; but in what manner they effected their purposes I know not.

This people, soon after their removal, built a town on the bank of the Mississippi, near the mouth of the Ouisconsin, at a place called by the French, La Prairies les Chiens [*sic*], which signifies the Dog Plains; it is a large town, and contains about three hundred families; the houses are well built after the Indian manner, and pleasantly situated on a very rich soil, from which they raise every necessary of life in great abundance. I saw here many horses of a good size and shape. This town is the great mart where all the adjacent tribes, and even those who inhabit the most remote branches of the Mississippi, annually assemble about the latter end of May, bringing with them their furs to dispose of to the traders. But it is not always that they conclude their sale here; this is determined by a general council of the chiefs, who consult whether it would be more conducive to their interest, to sell their goods at this place, or carry them on to Louisiana, or Michilimackinac. According to the decision of this council, they either proceed further, or return to their different homes.

The Mississippi, at the entrance of the Ouisconsin, near which stands a mountain of considerable height, is about half a mile over; but opposite to the last mentioned town, it appears to be more than a mile wide, and full of Islands, the soil of which is extraordinary rich, and but thinly wooded.

Indian Attack on Michilimackinac

by ALEXANDER HENRY, 1739–1824. *One of the great eighteenth-century explorers and fur traders, Alexander Henry was born in New Jersey. Little is known about his early years, but in 1760 Henry joined General Amherst's army in a commercial capacity. Not long afterward Henry determined to go west to Mackinac and there continue his trading activities. Thus he found himself in the Great Lakes region during Pontiac's famous conspiracy of 1763 and was almost a victim of savage fury in the assault on Michilimackinac. Subsequently Henry traded and journeyed in the Lake Superior country and in the Canadian Northwest. In 1776 he returned to Montreal and thence went to Europe, but Montreal was his home during the latter part of his life. Henry told his own story in a classic of the early fur trade,* Travels and Adventures in Canada and the Indian Territories between the Years 1760 and 1776 (1809). *The book was reprinted and carefully edited by James Bain in 1901. The account of the Indian attack comprises the ninth and tenth chapters of his autobiography.*

THE morning was sultry. A Chipewa came to tell me that his nation was going to play at baggatiway with the Sacs or Saakies, another Indian nation, for a high wager. He invited me to witness the sport, adding that the commandant was to be there, and would bet on the side of the Chipewa. In consequence of this information I went to the commandant and expostulated with him a little, representing that the Indians might possibly have some sinister end in view; but the commandant only smiled at my suspicions.

Baggatiway, called by the Canadians *le jeu de la crosse*, is played with a bat and ball. The bat is about four feet in length, curved, and terminating in a sort of racket. Two posts are planted in the ground at a considerable distance from each other, as a mile or more. Each party has its post, and the game consists in throwing the ball up to the post of the adversary. The ball, at the beginning, is placed in the middle of the course and each party endeavors as well to throw the ball out of the direction of its own post as into that of the adversary's.

I did not go myself to see the match which was now to be played without the fort, because there being a canoe prepared to depart on the following day for Montreal I employed myself in writing letters to my friends; and even when a fellow trader, Mr. Tracy, happened to call upon me, saying that another canoe had just arrived from Detroit, and proposing that I should go with him to the beach to inquire the news, it so happened that I still remained to finish my letters, promising to follow Mr. Tracy in the course of a few minutes. Mr. Tracy had not gone more than twenty paces from my door when I heard an Indian war cry and a noise of general confusion.

Going instantly to my window I saw a crowd of Indians within the fort furiously cutting down and scalping every Englishman they found. In particular I witnessed the fate of Lieutenant Jemette.

I had in the room in which I was a fowling piece, loaded with swan-shot. This I immediately seized and held it for a few minutes, waiting to hear the drum beat to arms. In this dreadful interval I saw several of my countrymen fall, and more than one struggling between the knees of an Indian, who, holding him in this manner, scalped him while yet living.

At length, disappointed in the hope of seeing resistance made to the enemy, and sensible, of course, that no effort of my own unassisted arm could avail against four hundred Indians, I thought only of seeking shelter. Amid the slaughter which was raging I observed many of the Canadian inhabitants of the fort calmly looking on, neither opposing the Indians, nor suffering injury; and from this circumstance I conceived a hope of finding security in their houses.

Between the yard door of my own house and that of M. Langlade, my next neighbor, there was only a low fence, over which I easily climbed. At my entrance I found the whole family at the windows, gazing at the scene of blood before them. I addressed myself immediately to M. Langlade, begging that he would put me into some place of safety until the heat of the affair should be over; an act of charity by which he might perhaps preserve me from the general massacre; but while I uttered my petition M. Langlade, who had looked for a moment at me, turned again to the window, shrugging his shoulders and intimating that he could do nothing for me:—"Que voudriez-vous que j'en ferais?"

This was a moment for despair; but the next a Pani woman, a slave of M. Langlade's, beckoned me to follow her. She brought me to a door which she opened, desiring me to enter, and telling me that it led to the garret, where I must go and conceal myself. I joyfully obeyed her directions; and she, having followed me up to the garret door, locked it after me and with great presence of mind took away the key.

This shelter obtained, if shelter I could hope to find it, I was naturally anxious to know what might still be passing without. Through an aperture which afforded me a view of the area of the fort I beheld, in shapes the foulest and most terrible, the ferocious triumphs of barbarian conquerors. The dead were scalped and mangled; the dying were writhing and shrieking under the unsatiated knife and tomahawk; and from the bodies of some, ripped open, their butchers were drinking the blood, scooped up in the hollow of joined hands and quaffed amid shouts of rage and victory. I was shaken not only with horror, but with fear. The sufferings which I witnessed I seemed on the point of experiencing. No long time elapsed before every one being destroyed who could be found, there was a general cry of "All is finished!" At the same instant I heard some of the Indians enter the house in which I was.

The garret was separated from the room below only by a layer of single boards, at once the flooring of the one and the ceiling of the other. I could therefore hear everything that passed; and the Indians no sooner came in than they inquired whether or not any Englishman were in the house. M. Langlade replied that he could not say—he did not know of any—answers in which he did not exceed the truth, for the Pani woman had not only hidden me by stealth, but kept my secret and her own. M. Langlade was therefore, as I presume, as far from a wish to destroy me as he was careless about saving me, when he added to these answers that they might examine for themselves, and would soon be satisfied as to the object of their question. Saying this, he brought them to the garret door.

The state of my mind will be imagined. Arrived at the door some delay was occasioned by the absence of the key and a few moments were thus allowed me in which to look around for a hiding place. In one corner of the garret was a heap of those vessels of birch bark used in maple sugar making as I have recently described.

The door was unlocked, and opening, and the Indians ascending the stairs, before I had completely crept into a small opening, which presented itself at one end of the heap. An instant after four Indians entered the room, all armed with tomahawks, and all besmeared with blood upon every part of their bodies.

The die appeared to be cast. I could scarcely breathe; but I thought that the throbbing of my heart occasioned a noise loud enough to betray me. The Indians walked in every direction about the garret, and one of them approached me so closely that at a particular moment, had he put forth his hand, he must have touched me. Still I remained undiscovered, a circumstance to which the dark color of my clothes and the want of light in a room which had no window, and in the corner in which I was, must have contributed. In a word, after taking several turns in the room, during which they told M. Langlade how many they had killed and how many scalps they had taken, they returned down stairs, and I with sensations not to be expressed, heard the door, which was the barrier between me and my fate, locked for the second time.

There was a feather bed on the floor, and on this, exhausted as I was by the agitation of my mind, I threw myself down and fell asleep. In this state I remained till the dusk of the evening, when I was awakened by a second opening of the door. The person that now entered was

M. Langlade's wife, who was much surprised at finding me, but advised me not to be uneasy, observing that the Indians had killed most of the English, but that she hoped I might myself escape. A shower of rain having begun to fall, she had come to stop a hole in the roof. On her going away, I begged her to send me a little water to drink, which she did.

As night was now advancing I continued to lie on the bed, ruminating on my condition, but unable to discover a resource from which I could hope for life. A flight to Detroit had no probable chance of success. The distance from Michilimackinac was four hundred miles; I was without provisions; and the whole length of the road lay through Indian countries, countries of an enemy in arms, where the first man whom I should meet would kill me. To stay where I was threatened nearly the same issue. As before, fatigue of mind, and not tranquillity, suspended my cares and procured me further sleep.

The game of baggatiway, as from the description above will have been perceived, is necessarily attended with much violence and noise. In the ardor of contest the ball, as has been suggested, if it cannot be thrown to the goal desired, is struck in any direction by which it can be diverted from that designed by the adversary. At such a moment, therefore, nothing could be less liable to excite premature alarm than that the ball should be tossed over the pickets of the fort, nor that having fallen there, it should be followed on the instant by all engaged in the game, as well the one party as the other, all eager, all struggling, all shouting, all in the unrestrained pursuit of a rude athletic exercise. Nothing could be less fitted to excite premature alarm—nothing, therefore, could be more happily devised, under the circumstances, than a stratagem like this; and this was in fact the stratagem which the Indians had employed, by which they had obtained possession of the fort, and by which they had been enabled to slaughter and subdue its garrison and such of its other inhabitants as they pleased. To be still more certain of success they had prevailed upon as many as they could by a pretext the least liable to suspicion to come voluntarily without the pickets, and particularly the commandant and garrison themselves.

The respite which sleep afforded me during the night was put an end to by the return of morning. I was again on the rack of apprehension. At sunrise I heard the family stirring, and presently after, Indian voices informing M. Langlade they had not found my hapless self among the dead, and that they supposed me to be somewhere concealed. M. Langlade appeared from what followed to be by this time acquainted with the place of my retreat, of which no doubt he had been informed by his wife. The poor woman, as soon as the Indians mentioned me, declared to her husband in the French tongue that he should no longer keep me in his house, but deliver me up to my pursuers, giving as a reason for this measure that should the Indians discover his instrumentality in my concealment, they might revenge it on her children, and that it was better that I should die than they. M. Langlade resisted at first this sentence of his wife's; but soon suffered her to prevail, informing the Indians that he had been told I was in his house, that I had come there without his knowledge, and that he would put me into their hands. This was no sooner expressed than he began to ascend the stairs, the Indians following upon his heels.

I now resigned myself to the fate with which I was menaced; and regarding every attempt at concealment as vain, I arose from the bed and presented myself full in view to the Indians who were entering the room. They were all in a state of intoxication, and entirely naked, except about the middle. One of them, named Wenniway, whom I had previously known, and who was upward of six feet in height, had his entire face and body covered with charcoal and grease, only that a white spot of two inches in diameter encircled either eye. This man, walking up to me, seized me with one hand by the collar of the coat, while in the other he held a large carving knife, as if to plunge it into my breast; his eyes, meanwhile, were fixed steadfastly on mine. At length, after some seconds of the most anxious suspense, he dropped his arm, saying, "I won't kill you!" To this he added that he had been frequently engaged in wars against the English, and had brought away many scalps; that on a certain occasion he had lost a brother whose name was Musinigon, and that I should be called after him.

A reprieve upon any terms placed me among the living, and gave me back the sustaining voice of hope; but Wenniway ordered me downstairs, and there informing me that I was to be taken to his cabin, where, and indeed everywhere else, the Indians were all mad with liquor, death again was threatened, and not as possible only, but as certain. I mentioned my fears on this subject to M. Langlade, begging him to represent the danger to my master. M. Langlade in this instance did not withhold his compassion, and Wenniway immediately consented that I should remain where I was until he found another opportunity to take me away.

Thus far secure I reascended my garret stairs in order to place myself the furthest possible out of the reach of insult from drunken Indians; but I had not remained there more than an hour, when I was called to the room below in which was an Indian who said that I must go with him out of the fort, Wenniway having sent him to fetch me. This man, as well as Wenniway himself, I had seen before. In the preceding year I had allowed him to take goods on credit, for which he was still in my debt; and some short time previous to the surprise of the fort he had said upon my upbraiding him with want of honesty that he would pay me before long. This speech now came fresh into my memory and led me to suspect that the fellow had formed a design against my life. I communicated the suspicion to M. Langlade; but he gave for answer that I was not now my own master, and must do as I was ordered.

The Indian on his part directed that before I left the house I should undress myself, declaring that my coat and shirt would become him better than they did me. His pleasure in this respect being complied with, no other alternative was left me than either to go out naked, or to put on the clothes of the Indian, which he freely gave me in exchange. His motive for thus stripping me of my own apparel was no other as I afterward learned than this, that it might not be stained with blood when he should kill me.

I was now told to proceed; and my driver followed me close until I had passed the gate of the fort, when I turned toward the spot where I knew the Indians to be encamped. This, however, did not suit the purpose of my enemy, who seized me by the arm and drew me violently in the opposite direction to the distance of fifty yards above the fort. Here, finding that I was approaching the bushes and sand hills, I determined to proceed no farther, but told the Indian that I believed he meant to murder me, and that if so he might as well strike where I was as at any greater distance. He replied with coolness that my suspicions were just, and that he meant to pay me in this manner for my goods. At the same time he produced a knife and held me in a position to receive the intended blow. Both this and that which followed were necessarily the affair of a moment. By some effort, too sudden and too little dependent on thought to be explained or remembered, I was enabled to arrest his arm and give him a sudden push by which I turned him from me and released myself from his grasp. This was no sooner done than I ran toward the fort with all the swiftness in my power, the Indian following me, and I expecting every moment to feel his knife. I succeeded in my flight; and on entering the fort I saw Wenniway standing in the midst of the area, and to him I hastened for protection. Wenniway desired the Indian to desist; but the latter pursued me round him, making several strokes at me with his knife, and foaming at the mouth with rage at the repeated failure of his purpose. At length Wenniway drew near to M. Langlade's house; and, the door being open, I ran into it. The Indian followed me; but on my entering the house he voluntarily abandoned the pursuit.

Preserved so often and so unexpectedly as it had now been my lot to be, I returned to my garret with a strong inclination to believe that through the will of an overruling power no Indian enemy could do me hurt; but new trials, as I believed, were at hand when at ten o'clock in the evening I was roused from sleep and once more desired to descend the stairs. Not less, however, to my satisfaction than surprise, I was summoned only to meet Major Etherington, Mr. Bostwick, and Lieutenant Lesslie, who were in the room below.

These gentlemen had been taken prisoners while looking at the game without the fort and immediately stripped of all their clothes. They were now sent into the fort under the charge of Canadians, because, the Indians having resolved on getting drunk, the chiefs were apprehensive that they would be murdered if they continued in the camp. Lieutenant Jemette and seventy soldiers had been killed; and but twenty Englishmen, including soldiers, were still alive. These were all within the fort, together with nearly three hundred Canadians.

These being our numbers, myself and others proposed to Major Etherington to make an effort for regaining possession of the fort and maintaining it against the Indians. The Jesuit missionary was consulted on the project; but he discouraged us by his representations, not only of the merciless treatment which we must expect from the Indians should they regain their superiority, but of the little dependence which was to be placed upon our Canadian auxiliaries. Thus the fort and prisoners remained in the hands of the Indians, though through the whole night the prisoners and whites were in actual possession, and they were without the gates.

That whole night, or the greater part of it, was passed in mutual condolence, and my fellow prisoners shared my garret. In the morning, being again called down, I found my master, Wenniway, and was desired to follow him. He led me to a small house within the fort, where in a narrow room and almost dark I found Mr. Ezekiel Solomons, an Englishman from Detroit, and a soldier, all prisoners. With these I remained in painful suspense as to the scene that was next to present itself till ten o'clock in the forenoon, when an Indian arrived, and presently marched us to the lakeside where a canoe appeared ready for departure, and in which we found that we were to embark.

Our voyage, full of doubt as it was, would have commenced immediately, but that one of the Indians who was to be of the party was absent. His arrival was to be waited for; and this occasioned a very long delay during which we were exposed to a keen northeast wind. An old shirt was all that covered me; I suffered much from the cold; and in this extremity M. Langlade coming down the beach, I asked him for a blanket, promising if I lived to pay him for it at any price he pleased; but the answer I received was this, that he could let me have no blanket unless there were some one to be security for the payment. For myself, he observed, I had no longer any property in that country. I had no more to say to M. Langlade; but presently seeing another Canadian, named John Cuchoise, I addressed to him a similar request and was not refused. Naked as I was, and rigorous as was the weather, but for the blanket I must have perished. At noon our party was all collected, the prisoners all embarked, and we steered for the Isles du Castor [Beaver Islands] in Lake Michigan.

Mamelle Prairie

by EDMUND FLAGG, 1815–90. *Flagg, journalist and traveler, was born at Wescasset, Maine, was graduated from Bowdoin College, and in 1835 accompanied his mother and sister to Louisville, Kentucky. For some time he taught in a private school for boys but later began to contribute articles to the Louisville Journal, with which paper he was intermittently connected as editorial writer or correspondent until 1861. His later years were given over to journalism, law, and diplomacy. In the summer and autumn of 1836 Flagg journeyed through Illinois and Missouri, and sent a series of letters on his travels to the Journal. In 1838 these letters were revised and republished as The Far West. Flagg later wrote both fiction and dramas but his literary reputation rests on the one volume of travels. Flagg was a whole-souled romantic and invariably saw things in high colors. But his descriptions of the prairies, the Indian mounds, St. Louis, St. Charles, the hazards of travel retain their vividness today.*

THE morning star was beaming beautifully forth from the blue eastern heavens when I mounted my horse for a visit to that celebrated spot, *Les Mamelles.* A pleasant ride of three miles through the forest-path beneath the bluffs brought me at sunrise to the spot. Every tree was wreathed with the wild rose like a rainbow; and the breeze was laden with perfumes. It is a little singular, the difficulty with which visitors usually meet in finding this place. The Duke of Sax Weimar, among other dignitaries, when on his tour of the West several years since, tells us that he lost his way in the neighboring prairie by pursuing the river road instead of that beneath the bluffs. The natural eminences which have obtained the appropriate appellation of Mamelles, from their striking resemblance to the female breast, are a pair of lofty, conical mounds, from eighty to one hundred feet altitude, swelling up perfectly naked and smooth upon the margin of that celebrated prairie which owes to them a name. So beautifully are they paired and so richly rounded, that it would hardly require a Frenchman's eye or that of an

Indian to detect the resemblance designated, remarkable though both races have shown themselves for bestowing upon objects in natural scenery significant names. Though somewhat resembling those artificial earth-heaps which form such an interesting feature of the West, these mounds are, doubtless, but a broken continuation of the Missouri bluffs, which at this point terminate from the south, while those of the Mississippi, commencing at the same point, stretch away at right angles to the west. The mounds are of an oblong, elliptical outline, parallel to each other, in immediate proximity, and united at the extremities adjoining the range of highlands by a curved elevation somewhat less in height. They are composed entirely of earth, and in their formation are exceedingly uniform and graceful. Numerous springs of water gush out from their base. But an adequate conception of these interesting objects can hardly be conveyed by the pen; at all events, without somewhat more of the quality of patience than chances to be the gift of my own wayward instrument. In brief, then, imagine a huge *spur*, in fashion somewhat like to that of a militia major, with the enormous rowel stretching off to the south, and the heel-bow rounding away to the northeast and northwest, terminated at each extremity by a vast excrescence; imagine all this spread out in the margin of an extended prairie, and a tolerably correct, though inadequate idea of the outline of the Mamelles is obtained. The semicircular area in the bow of the spur between the mounds is a deep dingle, choked up with stunted trees and tangled underbrush of hazels, sumach, and wild-berry, while the range of highlands crowned with forest goes back in the rear. This line of heights extends up the Missouri for some distance, at times rising directly from the water's edge to the height of two hundred feet, rough and ragged, but generally leaving a heavily-timbered bottom several miles in breadth in the interval, and in the rear rolling off into high, undulating prairie. The bluffs of the Mississippi extend to the westward in a similar manner, but the prairie interval is broader and more liable to inundation. The distance from the Mamelles to the confluence of the rivers is, by their meanderings, about twenty or thirty miles, and is very nearly divided into prairie and timber. The extremity of the point is liable to inundation, and its growth of forest is enormous.

The view from the summit of the Mamelles, as the morning sun was flinging over the landscape his ruddy dyes, was one of eminent, surpassing loveliness. It is celebrated, indeed, as the most beautiful prairie-scene in the Western Valley, and one of the most romantic views in the country. To the right extends the Missouri Bottom, studded with farms of the French villagers, and the river-bank margined with trees which conceal the stream from the eye. Its course is delineated, however, by the blue line of bluffs upon the opposite side, gracefully curving towards the distant Mississippi until the trace fades away at the confluence. In front is spread out the lovely Mamelle Prairie, with its waving ocean of rich flowers of every form, and scent, and hue, while green groves are beheld swelling out into its bosom, and hundreds of cattle are cropping the herbage. In one direction the view is that of a boundless plain of verdure; and at intervals in the deep emerald is caught the gleam from the glassy surface of a lake, of which there are many scattered over the peninsula. All along the northern horizon, curving away in a magnificent sweep of forty miles to the west, rise the hoary cliffs of the Mississippi, in the opposite state, like towers and castles; while the windings of the stream itself are betrayed by the heavy forest-belt skirting the prairie's edge. It is not many years since this bank of the river was perfectly naked, with not a fringe of wood. Tracing along the bold façade of cliffs on the opposite shore, enveloped in their misty mantle of azure, the eye detects the embouchure of the Illinois and of several smaller streams by the deep-cut openings. To the left extends the prairie for seventy miles with an average breadth of five from the river, along which, for most of the distance, it stretches. Here and there in the smooth surface stands out a solitary sycamore of enormous size, heaving aloft its gigantic limbs like a monarch of the scene. Upward of fifty thousand acres are here laid open to the eye at a single glance, with a soil of exhaustless fertility and of the easiest culture.

The whole plain spread out at the foot of the Mamelles bears abundant evidence of having once been submerged. The depth of the alluvion is upward of forty feet; and from that depth we are told that logs, leaves, coal, and a stratum of sand and pebbles bearing marks of the attrition of running waters, have been thrown up. Through the middle of the prairie pass several deep canals, apparently ancient channels of the rivers, and which now form the bed of a long irregular lake called *Marais Croche;* there is another lake of considerable extent called *Marais Temps Clair.* This beautiful prairie once, then, formed a portion of that immense lake which at a remote period held possession of the American Bottom; and at the base of the graceful Mamelles these giant rivers merrily mingled their waters, and then rolled onward to the gulf. That ages have since elapsed, the amazing depth of the alluvial and vegetable mould, and the ancient monuments reposing upon some portions of the surface, leave no room for doubt. By heavy and continued deposits of alluvion, the vast peninsula gradually rose up from the waters; the Missouri was forced back to the bluff *La Charbonnière,* and the rival stream to the Piasa cliffs of Illinois.

The Red Pipestone Quarry

by GEORGE CATLIN, 1796–1872. *Probably the most famous artist ever to depict the American Indian on canvas, Catlin was born in Wilkes-Barre, Pennsylvania. As a boy he loved the out-of-doors and became dexterous in hunting and fishing; he also began to collect Indian relics at an early date. Gradually his interest turned to painting and in 1828 he visited Albany where he painted a portrait of Governor DeWitt Clinton. From 1824 to 1829 he spent much of his time in Washington. But Catlin was constantly searching for some theme to which he could devote the energy of a lifetime, and he soon found it in the life and character of the American Indian. From 1829 to 1838 he roamed the West, creating more than six hundred paintings of male and female Indians, their weapons, wigwams, dances, costumes. These paintings were afterwards displayed throughout the United States and Europe and the majority of them were eventually deposited in the United States National Museum at Washington. Catlin wrote several books about his travels and his work, particularly Letters and Notes on the Manners, Customs, and Condition of the North American Indians (1841), from which the account of the red pipestone quarry is taken. The pipestone itself has since been known as catlinite in honor of the explorer.*

FROM the Fall of St. Anthony, my delightful companion (Mr. Wood . . .) and myself, with our Indian guide, whose name was O-kup-pee, tracing the beautiful shores of the St. Peters river, about eighty miles; crossing it at a place called *Traverse des Sioux*, and recrossing it at another point about thirty miles above the mouth of *Terre Bleue*, from whence we steered in a direction a little North of West for the *Côteau des Prairies*, leaving the St. Peters river, and crossing one of the most beautiful prairie countries in the world, for the distance of one hundred and twenty or thirty miles, which brought us to the base of the Côteau, where we were joined by our kind and esteemed companion Monsieur La Fromboise. . . . This tract of country as well as that along the St. Peters river, is mostly covered with the richest soil, and furnishes an abundance of good water, which flows from a thousand living springs. For many miles we had the Côteau in view in the distance before us, which looked like a blue cloud settling down in the horizon; and we were scarcely sensible of the fact, when we had arrived at its base, from the graceful and almost imperceptible swells with which it commences its elevation above the country around it. Over these swells or terraces, gently rising one above the other, we travelled for the distance of forty or fifty miles, when we at length reached the summit; and from the base of this mound, to its top, a distance of forty or fifty miles, there was not a tree or bush to be seen in any direction, and the ground everywhere was covered with a green turf of grass, about five or six inches high; and we were assured by our Indian guide, that it descended to the West, towards the Missouri, with a similar inclination, and for an equal distance, divested of every thing save the grass that grows, and the animals that walk upon it.

On the very top of this mound or ridge, we found the far-famed quarry or fountain of the Red Pipe, which is truly an anomaly of nature. The principal and most striking feature of this place, is a perpendicular wall of close-grained, compact quartz, of twenty-five and thirty feet in elevation, running nearly North and South with its face to the West, exhibiting a front of nearly two miles in length, when it disappears at both ends by running under the prairie, which becomes there a little more elevated, and probably covers it for many miles, both to the North and the South. The depression of the brow of the ridge at this place has been caused by the wash of a little stream, produced by several springs on the top, a little back from the wall; which has gradually carried away the super-incumbent earth, and having bared the wall for the distance of two miles, is now left to glide for some distance over a perfectly level surface of quartz rock; and then to leap from the top of the wall into a deep basin below, and from thence seek its course to the Missouri, forming the extreme source of a noted and powerful tributary, called the "Big Sioux."

This beautiful wall is horizontal, and stratified in several distinct layers of light grey, and rose or flesh-coloured quartz; and for most of the way, both on the front of the wall, and for acres of its horizontal surface, highly polished or glazed, as if by ignition.

At the base of this wall there is a level prairie, of half a mile in width, running parallel to it; in any and all parts of which, the Indians procure the red stone for their pipes, by digging through the soil and several slaty layers of the red stone, to the depth of four or five feet. From the very numerous marks of ancient and modern diggings or excavations, it would appear that this place has been for centuries resorted to for the red stone; and from the great number of graves and remains of ancient fortifications in its vicinity, it would seem, as well as from their actual traditions, that the Indian tribes have long held this place in high superstitious estimation; and also that it has been the resort of different tribes, who have made their regular pilgrimages here to renew their pipes.

The red pipe stone, I consider, will take its place amongst minerals, as an interesting subject of itself; and the *Côteau des Prairies* will become hereafter an important theme for geologists; not only from the fact that this is the only known locality of that mineral, but from other phenomena relating to it. The single fact of such a table of quartz, in horizontal strata, resting on this elevated plateau, is of itself (in my opinion) a very interesting subject for investigation; and one which calls upon the scientific world for a correct theory with regard to the time when, and the manner in which, this formation was produced. That it is of a secondary character, and of a sedimentary deposit, seems evident; and that it has withstood the force of the diluvial current, while the great valley of the Missouri, from this very wall of rocks to the Rocky Mountains, has been excavated, and its debris carried to the ocean, there is also not a shadow of doubt; which opinion I confidently advance on the authority of the following remarkable facts:

At the base of the wall, and within a few rods of it, and on the very ground where the Indians dig for the red stone, rests a group of five stupendous boulders of gneiss, leaning against each other; the smallest of which is twelve or fifteen feet, and the largest twenty-five feet in diameter, altogether weighing, unquestionably, several hundred tons. These blocks are composed chiefly of felspar and mica, of an exceedingly coarse grain (the felspar often occurring in crystals of an inch in diameter). The surface of these boulders is in every part covered with a grey moss, which gives them an extremely ancient and venerable appearance, and their sides and angles are rounded by attrition, to the shape and character of most other erratic stones, which are found throughout the country. It is under these blocks that the two holes, or ovens are seen, in which, according to the Indian superstition, the two old women, the guardian spirits of the place, reside. . . .

That these five immense blocks, of precisely the same character, and differing materially from all other specimens of boulders which I have seen in the great vallies of the Mississippi and Missouri, should have been hurled some hundreds of miles from their native bed, and lodged in so singular a group on this elevated ridge, is truly matter of surprise for the scientific world, as well as for the poor Indian, whose superstitious veneration of them is such, that not a spear of grass is broken or bent by his feet, within three or four rods of them, where he stops, and in humble supplication, by throwing plugs of tobacco to them, solicits permission to dig and carry away the red stone for his pipes. The surface of these boulders are [sic] in every part entire and unscratched by anything; wearing the moss everywhere unbroken, except where I applied the hammer, to obtain some small specimens, which I shall bring away with me.

The fact alone, that these blocks differ in character from all other specimens which I have seen in my travels, amongst the thousands of boulders which are strewed over the great valley of the Missouri and Mississippi, from the Yellow Stone almost to the Gulf of Mexico, raises in my mind an unanswerable question, as regards the location of their native bed, and the means by which they have reached their isolated position; like five brothers, leaning against and supporting each other, without the existence of another boulder within many miles of them. There are thousands and tens of thousands of boulders scattered over the prairies, at the base of the Côteau, on either side; and so throughout the valley of the St. Peters and the Mississippi, which are also subjects of very great interest and importance to science, inasmuch as they present to the world, a vast variety of characters; and each one, though strayed away from its original position, bears incontestible proof of the character of its native bed. The tract of country lying between the St. Peters river and the Côteau, over which we passed, presents innumerable specimens of this kind; and near the base of the Côteau they are strewed over the prairie in countless numbers, presenting almost an incredible variety of rich, and beautiful colours; and undoubtedly traceable, (if they can be traced), to separate and distinct beds.

Amongst these beautiful groups, it was sometimes a very easy matter to sit on my horse and count within my sight, some twenty or thirty different varieties, of quartz and granite, in rounded boulders, of every hue and colour, from snow white to intense red, and yellow, and blue, and almost to a jet black; each one well characterized and evidently from a distinct quarry. With the beautiful hues and almost endless characters of these blocks, I became completely surprised and charmed; and I resolved to procure specimens of every variety, which I did with success, by dismounting from my horse, and breaking small bits from them with my hammer; until I had something like an hundred different varieties, containing all the tints and colours of a painter's palette. These, I at length threw away, as I had on several former occasions, other minerals and fossils, which I had collected and lugged along from day to day, and sometimes from week to week.

Whether these varieties of quartz and granite can all be traced to their native beds, or whether they all have origins at this time exposed above the earth's surface, are equally matters of much doubt in my mind. I believe that the geologist may take the different varieties, which he may gather at the base of the Côteau in one hour, and travel the Continent of North America all over without being enabled to put them all in place; coming at last to the unavoidable conclusion, that numerous chains or beds of primitive rocks have reared their heads on this Continent, the summits of which have been swept away by the force of diluvial currents, and their fragments jostled together and strewed about, like foreigners in a strange land, over the great vallies of the Mississippi and Missouri, where they will ever remain, and be gazed upon by the traveller, as the only remaining evidence of their native beds, which have again submerged or been covered with diluvial deposits.

There seems not to be, either on the Côteau or in the great vallies on either side, so far as I have travelled, any slaty or other formation exposed above the surface on which grooves or scratches can be seen, to establish the direction of the diluvial currents in those regions; yet I think the fact is pretty clearly established by the general shapes of the vallies, and the courses of the mountain ridges which wall them in on their sides.

The *Côteau des Prairies* is the dividing ridge between the St. Peters and Missouri rivers; its southern termination or slope is about in the latitude of the Fall of St. Anthony, and it stands equi-distant between the two rivers; its general course bearing two or three degrees West of North for the distance of two or three hundred miles, when it gradually slopes again to the North, throwing out from its base the head-waters and tributaries of the St. Peters, on the East. The Red River, and other streams, which empty into Hudson's Bay, on the North; La Rivière Jaque and several other tributaries to the Missouri, on the West; and the Red Cedar, the Ioway and the Des Moines, on the South.

This wonderful feature, which is several hundred miles in length, and varying from fifty to a hundred in width, is, perhaps the noblest mound of its kind in the world; it gradually and gracefully rises on each side, by swell after swell, without tree, or bush or rock (save what are to be seen in the vicinity of the Pipe Stone Quarry), and everywhere covered with green grass, affording the traveller, from its highest elevations, the most unbounded and sublime views of—nothing at all—save the blue and boundless ocean of prairies that lie beneath and all around him, vanishing into azure in the distance without a speck or spot to break their softness.

Early River Travel

by TIMOTHY FLINT, 1780—1840. *Famous as a traveler, editor, and spokesman for the West, Flint was born near North Reading, Massachusetts, and was graduated from Harvard, B.A., 1800. He then entered the Congregational ministry and for twelve years served the parish of Lunenburg, Massachusetts. In 1815 he set out for the West, traveling down the Ohio via Cincinnati and Louisville and up the Mississippi to St. Louis and St. Charles.*

Later travels took him as far south as New Orleans and to Alexandria on the Red River. He returned to Cincinnati in 1827 and there edited for the ensuing three years the Western Monthly Review. Subsequent years were again spent in travel. Flint died in Massachusetts and was buried at Salem. A prolific writer in various fields, Flint was the author of four novels, the best of which is Francis Berrian (1826); a treatise on western geography, A Condensed Geography and History of the Western States (1828); a biography of Daniel Boone (1833); and a valuable autobiography, Recollections of the Last Ten Years (1826). Few men have drawn more realistic pictures of the young cities of the Ohio and Mississippi valleys; Flint was as specific in his observations as he was honest in his hatred of dueling and intemperance. The account of river travel is taken from his autobiography.

THE twenty-eighth of April, 1816, we came in sight of what had long been the subject of our conversations, our inquiries, and curiosity, the far-famed Mississippi. It is a view, which has left on my mind a most deep and durable impression, marking a period, from which commenced a new era in my existence. We had been looking forward to this place as the pillars of Hercules. The country on this side had still some unbroken associations with our native land. This magnificent river, almost dividing the continent, completely severed this chain. We were now, also, to experience the novelty of propelling a boat against the current of one of the mightiest and most rapid rivers in the world. The junction of the Ohio and Mississippi does not impress that idea of physical grandeur, which fills up your anticipations. But allow the fancy to range the boundless forests and prairies, through which it brings down the sweeping tribute, which it has collected from distant and nameless mountains, and from a hundred shores, and you will not contemplate this mighty stream without an intense interest. A sharp point, almost at right angles with either river, mingles their waters in the midst of deep and ancient forests, where the eye expatiates over vast and swampy woods, perhaps fifty miles in extent. Turn the point, and your eye catches the vast Mississippi, rolling down his mass of turbid waters, which seem, compared with the limpid and greenish-coloured waters of the Ohio, to be of almost a milky whiteness. They exactly resemble waters in which white ashes have been mixed and remain suspended. A speculation was got up, to form a great city at the delta, and in fact they raised a few houses upon piles of wood. The houses were inundated, and when we were there, "they kept the town," as the boatmen phrased it, in a vast flat boat, a hundred feet in length, in which there were families, liquor-shops, drunken men and women, and all the miserable appendages to such a place. To render the solitude of the pathless forest on the opposite shore more dismal, there is one gloomy-looking house there.

Having turned the point, and made our boat fast to the young willows, we reposed to give scope to our own contemplations. Our hands demanded the usual compliment, and having received it in moderation, pronounced themselves sufficiently cheered to begin their task. The margin of the stream is marked with a beautiful growth of low willows and cotton-woods, and the river, though it had overflowed the banks, and was high among the trees, was, from twenty to thirty feet from the shore, not very swift. We began to pull the boat up the stream, by a process, which, in the technics of the boatmen, is called "bush-whacking." It consists, by commencing at the bow, to seize a handful of bushes, or a single branch, and to pull upon them and walk towards the stern, as the boat ascends. The crew follow each other in this way in succession to the stern, and walk round to the bow, on the opposite side. The banks slope so rapidly, that the "setting pole" is not long enough, in the general way, for use on the opposite side, and they commonly put two hands to the oars. Whenever we come to a point, and have to encounter the full force of the current, we cross the river, in order to get into the easier current upon the opposite shore. We shall remark, elsewhere, upon the singular but almost uniform configuration of the western rivers, by which they are scooped out into points and bends. When the river is low, there is a sand-bar opposite the bend, and the current is invariably much stronger in the bend, than over the sand-bar.

We mark a very obvious difference between the aspect of the Ohio and the Mississippi. The breadth of the two rivers is nearly the same; and they present at their junction nearly the same appearances of swamp and inundation. They have much the same growth on their banks; and yet they have a character very unlike each other. The Ohio is calm and placid, and except when full, its waters are limpid to a degree. The face of the Mississippi is always turbid; the current every where sweeping and rapid; and it is full of singular boils, where the water, for a quarter of an acre, rises with a strong circular motion, and a kind of hissing noise, forming a convex mass of waters above the common level, which roll down and are incessantly renewed. The river seems always in wrath, tearing away the banks on one hand with gigantic fury, with all their woods, to deposit the spoils in another place.

To form any adequate ideas of our impressions of this new scene which I am attempting to record, you will naturally bear in remembrance what kind of family it was, that was viewing it. We were not accustomed to travelling. We had been reared in stillness and seclusion, where we had contemplated the world rather in books than in reality. The Mississippi, too, at that time was to the great proportion of the

American people, as it was to us, the "ultima Thule"—a limit almost to the range of thought. This stream, instead of being ploughed by a hundred steam boats, had seen but one. The astonishing facilities for travelling, by which it is almost changed to flying, had not been invented. The thousand travellers for mere amusement, that we now see on the roads, canals, and rivers, were then travelling only in books. The stillness of the forest had not been broken by the shouting of turnpike-makers. The Mississippi forest had seldom resounded, except with the cry of wild beasts, the echo of thunder, or the crash of undermined trees, falling into the flood. Our admiration, our unsated curiosity at that time, would be matter of surprise at the present, to the thousands of hacknied travellers on this stream, to whom all this route, and all its circumstances, are as familiar as the path from the bed to the fire.

For myself, I shall never forget my first impressions upon beginning to ascend this river, on the banks of which I have passed so many years, and suffered so many misfortunes,—and at the period of life, too, when time is most valuable, and impressions the deepest. The scene was entirely novel, and we beheld every thing, as though the water, the plants, the trees of the Mississippi, would be different from the same things elsewhere. Our first advances on the stream were well calculated to satisfy such expectations of gratified curiosity, as we had formed. The day was beautiful, the temperature soft and genial. The vegetable kingdom on the banks, had the peculiar grandeur of its empire in that region, which must be seen, and not described, in order to be felt. Even the small willows, which we grasped in our hands, as we were drawing the boat up the stream, were full of flowers, which when crushed, yielded out that fragrance which is peculiar to them; a fragrance like the odour of burning coffee, and a few other aromatics, raising the ideas of nectar and ambrosia.

On the other side, the river had only so far overflowed its banks, as to leave the tall and verdant meadow grass, and water plants of the most tender green, above the water. Innumerable multitudes and varieties of water-fowl, of different forms, and plumage, and hues, were pattering in the water among this grass; or were raising their several cries, as we frightened them from their retreat. We easily obtained as many as we wished; and when roused to the wing by our guns, they soon settled down in another place. Flocks of that species, called woodducks, were continually flying between the river and the woods, where, in the hollows of the trees, they were rearing their young. The huge sized cotton-woods, so regular and beautiful in their form, so bright in a verdure surpassing that of northern trees, were in themselves objects of curiosity. To us, under such circumstances, this novel and fresh scene revived those delightful images of youth, the spring-time of existence, which are most fondly cherished and longest remembered. . . .

No employment can be imagined more laborious, and few more dangerous, than this of propelling a boat against the current of such a river. It may not be amiss to record some of the circumstances of labour and peril; for the growing disuse of all other but steam-boats, will soon render these descriptions but little more than matter of past history. At one time you come to a place in the current, so swift that no force of oars and poles can urge the boat through it. You then have to apply, what is commonly called here a "cordelle," which is a long rope fastened at one end to the boat, thrown ashore, and seized by a sufficient number of hands to drag or track the boat up the stream. But, owing to the character of the river, and the numberless impediments in it and on its banks, this "cordelle" is continually entangling among the snags and sawyers, between the boat and the shore, and has often to be thrown over small trees, and carried round larger ones. Of course it requires great experience and dexterity to be a good leader of a cordelle. The service is extremely well adapted to the French boatmen. Sometimes you are impeded by vast masses of trees, that have lodged against sawyers. At other times, you find a considerable portion of the margin of the shore, including a surface of acres, that has fallen into the river, with all its trees upon it. Just on the edge of these trees, the current is so heavy as to be almost impassable. It is beside the question, to think of forcing the boat up against the main current any where, except with an uncommon number of hands. Therefore any impediments near the shore, must either be surmounted, or the river crossed to avoid them. It not unfrequently happens, that the boat with no small labour, and falling down the stream from the strength of the current, crosses the river to avoid such difficulties, and finds equal ones on the opposite shore.

Sometimes you are obliged to make your way among the trunks of trees, and the water boiling round your boat like that of a mill-race. Then, if the boat "swings," as the phrase is, that is, loses her direction, and exposes her side to the current, you are instantly carried back, and perhaps strike the snags below you, and your boat is snagged, or staved. We were more than once, half a day, struggling with all our own force, and all that we could raise on the banks, to force the boat through a single rapid, or by one difficult place. We were once in imminent peril, not only of our boat, but, such was the situation of the place, if we had been wrecked there, of our lives. Severer fatigue, or harder struggling to carry a point, I never saw endured, than in this case.

I would not wish to tire you, by attempting to enumerate all the difficulties and dangers of this sort, that we encountered. Should I even attempt it, my memory would not reach them; and a boatman only would be able to describe them in the proper technicals, which you of course would not understand. He would enumerate difficulties, which depend for their character upon the peculiar stage of the water, and the manner in which the sand-bars and wreck-heaps are situated. These wreck-heaps are immense piles of trees, amassed by the waters, at points, and in difficult places. Let no deluded emigrant imagine, that he can work a boat up this river, without great patience, expense, and labour, and after all, without danger. The danger and fatigue, in this kind of boating, are undoubtedly greater than those of sea navigation. Let the emigrant, then, who ascends this river, make the proper estimates of trouble, expense, and danger, in advance; and arm himself with the requisite patience and resources. Above all, let him have a full complement of faithful and experienced hands. I do not remember to have traversed this river in any considerable trip, without having heard of some fatal disaster to a boat, or having seen a dead body of some boatman, recognized by the red flannel shirt, which they generally wear. The multitudes of carcasses of boats, lying at the points, or thrown up high and dry on the wreck-heaps, demonstrate most palpably, how many boats are lost on this wild, and, as the boatmen always denominate it, "wicked river."

Travel in the Woods

by BAYNARD RUSH HALL, 1793–1863. Born in Philadelphia, Hall was left an orphan in childhood but managed to secure an education for himself by such devices as learning to set type. Following graduation at Union College and Princeton Theological Seminary he became a Presbyterian clergyman. In 1822 he migrated to Indiana, settling in the so-called New Purchase near the White River about four miles north of Gosport. The next year he was chosen as principal of the new Indiana Seminary at Bloomington, later to become the University of Indiana. Shortly after Andrew Wylie became the first president of Indiana College, however, he and Hall became involved in a controversy, following which altercation Hall resigned. In 1843 under the pseudonym of Robert Carlton, Hall published his volume The New Purchase, an account of his seven and a half years in Indiana and a book equally interesting for its frank realism and for its satirical pictures of the crudities and jealousies of frontier society. The book was reissued in 1855 with the long academic quarrel omitted. In 1916 James A. Woodburn issued a critical edition for the Princeton University Press. Hall never returned to the scenes of his early days and died in Brooklyn. The account of woodland travel is excerpted from the ninth chapter.

W HO *could* have dreamed, my dear," said Mrs. C. to her husband, "these forests so picturesque when seen from the Ohio, concealed such roads?"

Mr. C. made no reply; although the phenomenon was certainly very remarkable;—in fact, his idea about the Muses was passing in review— and he thought, maybe after all, it was something else that had echoed the flute notes. The lady's query, however, and the gentleman's silence occurred about thirty miles due north of the Ohio River, in a very new State of the far west. They were seated in a two-horse Yankee cart,— a kind of mongrel dearborne—amid what was now called their "plun-der"—with a hired driver on the front seat, and intending to find, if possible, a certain spot in a very uncertain part of the New Purchase— about one hundred and twenty honest miles in the interior, and beyond Shining River. This was the second day of practice in the elementary lessons of forest travelling; in which, however, they had been suffi-ciently fortunate as to get a taste of "buttermilk land,"—"spouty land," —and to learn the nature of "mash land"—"rooty and snaggy land"— of mud holes, ordinary and extraordinary—of quick sands—and "cor-duroys" woven single and double twill—and even fords with and with-out bottom.

The autumn is decidedly preferable for travelling on the virgin soil of native forests. One may go then mostly by land and find the roads fewer and shorter; but in the early spring, branches—(small creeks)— are brim full, and they hold a great deal; concealed fountains bubble up in a thousand places where none were supposed to lurk; creeks turn to rivers, and rivers to lakes, and lakes to bigger ones; and as if this was too little water, out come the mole rivers that have burrowed all this time under the earth, and which, when so unexpectedly found are styled out there—"lost rivers!" And every district of a dozen miles square has a lost river. Travelling by land becomes of course travelling by water, or by both: viz., mud and water. Nor is it possible if one would avoid drowning or suffocation to keep the law and follow the blazed road; but he tacks first to the right and then to the left, often making both losing tacks; and all this, not to find a road but a place where there is no road,—untouched mud thick enough to bear, or that has at least some bottom.

Genuine Hoosiers, Corn-crackers, et id omne genus—(viz. all that sort of geniuses)—lose comparatively little time in this species of navigation; for such know instinctively where it is proper to quit the submerged road of the legislature, and where they are likely to fulfill the proverb "out of the frying pan into the fire." And so we, at last, in utter despair of finding royal road to the New Purchase, did enter souse into the most-ill-looking, dark-coloured morasses, enlivened by streams of purer mud crossing at right angles, and usually much deeper than we cared to discover.

The first night we had stayed at a "public"; yet while the tavern was of brick, candour forces me to record that affairs so much resembled the hardware and crockery in their streaked and greasy state after Messrs. Brown & Co. had cleaned them, that we were rejoiced—prematurely however—when morning allowed us half-refreshed to resume our land tacking. But more than once afterwards did we sigh even for the comforts of the Brick Tavern, with its splendid sign of the sun rising and setting between two partitions of paint intended for hills; and which sun looked so much like spreading rays, that a friend soberly asked us afterward—"If we didn't put up the first night at the sign of the Fan?"

It was now after sunset on our second day, that we inquired with much anxiety at a miserable cabin, how far it was to the next tavern, and we were answered—"a smart bit yet—maybe more nor three miles by the blaze—but the most powerfullest road!" Since early morning we had, with incessant driving, done nearly twenty miles; if then we had, in a bad road, done by daylight about one and a half miles per hour, how were we likely to do three miles in the dark, and over what a native styled—the "most powerfullest road"? Hence, as the lady of the cabin seemed kind, and more than once expressed compassion for "my womin body"—(so she called Mrs. C.) and as she "allowed" we had better stop where we were, with a sudden and very respectful remembrance of the Rising or Setting Fan Tavern, we agreed to halt. And so—at long last—we were going really and actually to pass a night in a veritable, rite-dite, cabin!—in a vast forest too—and far enough from all the incumbrances of eastern civilization!

"And did you not thrill, Mr. Carlton?"

"I rather think, dear reader,—I did";—at least I felt some sort of a shiver; especially as the gloom of the frightful shades increased; and the deafening clangour of innumerable rude frogs in the mires and on the trees arose; and the whirl and hum and buzz of strange, savage insects and reptiles, and of winged and unwinged bugs, began and increased and grew still louder; and vapours damp, chilly and foetid ascended and came down; and the only field in sight was a few yards of "clearing," stuck with trunks of "deadened" trees and great stumps

134

blackened with the fires! And I think the thrill, or whatever it was, grew more and more intense on turning towards the onward road, and finding a suspicion in my mind that it only led to the endless repetition of the agreeable night scene around us—ah! ha!—maybe so—and then came retrospective visions of friends in the *far* East now—till—"what?"—I hardly know what—till something, however, like a wish came, that it were as easy to float *up* the Ohio as down. Heyho!

Nor was the cabin a fac-simile of those built in dreams and novels and magazines. Mine were of bark, and as neat as a little girl's baby house! This had, indeed, bark enough about, but still not put up right. It was in truth a barbarous rectangle of unhewed and unbarked logs, and bound together by a gigantic dove-tailing called notching. The roof was thick ricketty shingles, called clapboards; which when *clapped* on were held down by longitudinal poles kept apart by shorter pieces placed between them perpendicularly. The interstices of the log-wall were "chinked"—the "chinking" being large chips and small slabs dipping like strata of rocks in geology; and then on the chinking was the "daubing"—viz. a quant. suff. of yellow clay ferociously splashed in soft by the hand of the architect, and then left to harden at its leisure. Rain and frost had here, however, caused mud daubing to disappear; so that from without could be clearly discerned through the wall, the light of fire and candle, and from within, the light of sun, moon and stars—a very fair and harmless tit for tat.

The chimney was outside the cabin and a short distance from it. This article was built, as chaps, in raining weather, make on the kitchen hearth stick houses of light wood,—it consisted of layers of little logs reposing on one another at their corners and topped off when high enough with flag stones:—it was, moreover, daubed, and so admirably as to look like a mud stack! That, however, was, as I afterwards found inartistical—the daubing of chimneys correctly being a very *nice* task, although just as dirty as even political daubing.

The inside cabin was one room below and one loft above—to which, however, was no visible ascent.—I think the folks climbed up at the corner. The room contained principally beds, the other furniture being a table, "stick chairs" and some stools with from two to three legs apiece. Crockery and calabashes shared the mantel with two dangerous looking rifles and their powder horns. The iron ware shifted for itself about the fire place, where awkward feet feeling for the fire or to escape it, pushed kettle against pot and skillet against dutch oven.

What French cook committed suicide because something was not done "to a turn"? Ample poetic justice may be done to his wicked ghost by some smart writer, in chaining him with an iambic or two to the jamb of that cabin hearth—there for ever to be a witness of its cookery. Here came first the pettish outcries of two matron hens dangled along to a hasty execution; then notes of preparation sung out by the tea-kettle; then was jerked into position the dutch oven straddling with three short legs over the burning coals; and lastly the skillet began sputtering forth its boiling lard, or grease of some description. The instruments ready, the hostess aided by a little barefooted daughter, and whose white hair was whisped at the top of the head with a string and horn comb, the hostess put into the oven, balls of wet corn meal, and then slapped on the lid red hot and covered with coals, with a look and motion equal to this sentence—"Get out of that, till you're done." Then the two fowls, but a moment since kicking and screeching at being killed, were doused into the skillet into hot oil, where they moved around dismembered, as if indignant now at being fried.

We travellers shifted quarters repeatedly during these solemn operations, sometimes to get less heat, sometimes more, and sometimes to escape the fumes direct; but usually, to get out of the way. That, however, being impracticable, we at length sat extempore, and were kicked and jostled accordingly. In the meanwhile our landlady, in whom was much curiosity, a little reverence, and a misty idea that her guests were great folks, and towards whom as aristocrats it was republican to feel enmity, our landlady maintained at intervals a very lively talk, as for example:

"From Loo'ville, I allow!"

"No,—from Philadelphia."

A sudden pause—a turn to look at us more narrowly, while she still affectionately patted some wet meal into shape for the oven.

"Well!—now!—I wonder!—hem!—Come to enter land, 'spose—powerful bottom on the Shining—heavy timber, though. He's your old man, mam?"

Mrs. C. assented. The hostess then stopped to deposit the perfect ball, and continued:

"Our wooden country's mighty rough, I allow, for some folks—right hard to get gals here, mam—folks has to be their own niggurs, mam—what mought your name be?"

Mrs. C. told the lady, and then in a timid and piteous sort of tone inquired if girls could not be hired by the year? To this the landlady replied at first with a stare—then with a smile—and then added:

"Well! sort a allow not—most time, mam, you'll have to work your own ash-hopper"—(viz. a lie-cask, or, rather, an inverted pyramidical box to contain ashes, resembling a hopper in a mill)—"Nan"—(name of little flax head)—"Nan, sort a turn them thare chickins."

And thus the cabin lady kept on doing her small stock of English into Hoosierisms and other figures; now, with the question direct—now, with the question implied; then, with a soliloquy—then, an apostrophe; and all the time cleaning and cutting up chickens, making pones, and working and wriggling among pots, skillets and people's limbs (?) and feet, with an adroitness and grace gained by practice only; and all this, without upsetting any thing, scalding any body, or even spilling any food—excepting, maybe, a little grease, flour and salt. Nor did she lose time by dropping down curtsey fashion to inspect the progress of things baked or fried; but she bent over as if she had hinges in the hips, according to nature doubtless, but contrary to the Lady's Book; although the necessary backward motion to balance the head projected beyond the base, did render garments short by nature still shorter, as grammarians would say, by position.

Corn-bread takes its own time to bake; and therefore it was late when the good woman, having placed the "chicken fixins" on a large dinnerplate, and poured over them the last drop of unabsorbed and unevaporated oil, set all on the table, and then, giving her heated and perspiring face a last wipe with the corner of her tow-linen apron, and also giving her thumb and finger a rub on the same cleanser, she sung out the ordinary summons: "Well! come, sit up."

This sit-up we instantly performed—as well, at least, as we could—while she stood up to pour out the tea, complimenting all the time its quality, saying—" 'Tisn't nun of your spice-wood or yarb stuff, but the rele gineine *store* tea." Nanny remained near the dutch oven to keep us supplied with red-hot pones, or corn-balls—and hard enough by the way, to do execution from cannon. The teacups used held a scant pint; and to do exact justice to each cup, the mistress held the teapot in one hand and the water-pot in the other; pouring from both at once till the cup was brim full of the mixture:—an admirable system of impartiality, and if the pots had spouts of equal diameters, the very way to make precisely "half and half." But sorry am I to say, that on the present occasion, the water-pot had the best and easiest delivery.

"And *could* you eat, Mr. Carlton?"

How could we avoid it, Mr. Nice? Besides, we were most vulgarly hungry. And the consequence was, that, at the arrival of the woodman and his two sons, other corn-bread was baked, and, for want of chicken, bacon was fried.

THE FRONTIER

A Legend of Carondelet

by JAMES HALL, 1793–1868. *Hall is a good example of the versatility so often found in the early Middle West. He was soldier, lawyer, judge, prosecuting attorney, state treasurer of Illinois, editor, poet, writer of fiction, and banker; moreover, he was throughout his life a devoted publicist for the Ohio Valley and the West. Born in Philadelphia, Hall served in the War of 1812, later studied law at Pittsburgh, and in 1820 descended the Ohio River in a keelboat as far as Shawneetown, Illinois. Here he remained briefly as attorney, editor, and judge. From 1827 to 1833 Hall resided in Vandalia, then the capital of Illinois. At Vandalia he published a newspaper, a western annual, and the Illinois Monthly Magazine. In the early winter of 1833 he removed to Cincinnati, where he was consecutively lawyer, editor, and banker. Hall was a prolific writer of fiction, verse, articles, history, and statistics. Among his books are Letters from the West (1828), a valuable account of early life on the Ohio River; Legends of the West (1832) and Tales of the Border (1835), his best collections of short stories; Harpe's Head*

(1833), his sole novel; Sketches of History, Life, and Manners in the West (1835); and The Romance of Western History (1857). He also collaborated with Thomas L. McKenney in a History of the Indian Tribes of North America, sumptuously published in three folio volumes in Philadelphia (1836–44). "A Legend of Carondelet," a pleasant evocation of life in the old French settlements of the Mississippi Valley, was collected in Legends of the West.

THERE is no knowledge so valuable as a knowledge of the world. Thousands have grown gray in the acquisition of learning, without ever getting the slightest insight into the human character, while many seem to be born with an intrinsic perception of the workings of the human heart. There is a something called common sense, which books do not teach, but which, nevertheless, is worth more than all the lore of antiquity. A man may starve with his head full of Latin and Greek, while a single grain of common sense operates like the presence of the prophet of old upon the widow's cruse. The fortunate individual who is born with this desirable quality, bears a charmed existence, and glides along in the voyage of life with an ease that surprises his companions. There is a thriftiness about such persons which is almost miraculous; like those hardy plants that spring up in the crevices of the rock, they flourish in the midst of barrenness, when every thing perishes around them.

To this class belonged Timothy Eleazer Tompkinson, the hopeful heir of a worthy mariner, whose domicil was situated in a small sea-port of New England, but who, being almost constantly abroad, was obliged to leave his only son to the care of a maiden aunt and to the teaching of a public school. This amiable youth exhibited, even in childhood, some of the touches of the disposition which adhered to him through life. He liked salt water better than attic wit; and loved to steer his little boat, in the most stormy weather, around the capes and headlands of the neighbouring sea-coast, better than to trace out the labyrinths of a problem, or to wander among the shoals and quicksands of metaphysics. In his tenderest years, he launched his bark upon the ocean with the temerity of a veteran pilot; and when the gay breeze swept along, and the waves danced and sparkled in the sun, his little sail might be seen skimming over the surface like a sea-bird. Often as he strolled off in the morning might the shrill voice of his aunt, the worthy Miss Fidelity Tompkinson, be heard hailing him with, "Where are you going, Timmy dear?" "Don't go near the water, dear"; and as often would he toss his head and march on, smiling at the simplicity of his watchful guardian and marvelling at the timidity of women. In vain did the village pedagogue remind him that time flies swifter than a white squall, and that in the voyage of life there is but one departure, which, if taken wrong, can never be corrected. Tim would listen with a smile, and then placing his tarred hat on one side of his head, stroll off whistling to the beach.

At sixteen it was concluded that the years and gifts of Timothy rendered him a suitable candidate for college honours, and his name was accordingly entered upon the books of a celebrated institution. Here he was soon distinguished; not for Latin or logic, but for cleverness, ingenuity, and gymnastic feats. He never was a great talker, but, on the contrary, expressed himself with a laudable brevity, and with that idiomatic terseness of language which is common along shore, where a significant sea-phrase answers all the purpose of a long argument; and he reasoned, plausibly enough, that one who employed so few words, had little use for any other tongue than his own, which afforded a copious medium for the conveyance of his slender stock of ideas. In the mathematical sciences, he was better skilled. Few could estimate with more accuracy the number of superficial yards between his own chamber and a neighbouring orchard, or calculate with more nicety the difference of distance between these points upon a direct line, or by the meanders of a number of obtuse angles. He knew the exact height of every window in the college edifice, and the precise force required to elevate a projectile from the college green to the roof of the tutor's boarding-house. He knew precisely the angle at which an object could be presented to the retina of a professor's eye, and was acquainted with the depth of every intellect and the measure of every purse in the Senior class. In short, however deficient in Athenian polish, he had all the hardihood of a Spartan youth, and was especially gifted with that thrifty quality called common sense. He was a lucky boy, too. Though foremost in every act of mischief, he was always the last to be found out or punished; and though he never studied, he always managed to glide unnoticed through the college examinations, or to obtain praise for productions which were strongly suspected to be not his own. In difficulty or danger, he was sure to have a device to meet the exigency, and was so often successful on such occasions, that his companions compared him to the active animal, which, when thrown into the air, always lights upon its feet.

It will be readily imagined that our hero gained but few scholastic attainments; yet he was, nevertheless, a general favourite. He was blessed with the finest temper in the world. His good nature was absolutely invincible. Although the very prince of mischief, none suspected him of malice. In the midst of a bitter reproof he would smile in the professor's face; and the student who treated him with insolence was, perhaps, the first to receive some kind act from his hand. If the faculty frowned upon him, he had the *faculty* of turning the storm into sunshine, and of averting punishment by a well-timed jest or compliment. Every body loved Tim, and Tim loved every body. He hated study; but then he liked college, because the students were jolly fellows, and the professors took flattering kindly, and stood quizzing with that patience which is the result of long endurance.

How long these halcyon days would have lasted, and whether the name of Timothy Eleazer Tompkinson would have been numbered among the alumni of the college, is now beyond the reach of conjecture; for just as he had attained his twentieth year, the news came that his father had discharged the debt of nature, leaving all his other debts unpaid, his sister fortuneless, and his son a beggar. Our hero paid the tribute of a tear to the memory of his departed parent, and more than one drop attested his sympathy for the desolate condition of his kind aunt. But he soon brushed the moisture from either eye, and as the good president condoled with him in a tone of sincere affection, he acknowledged with a smile that his case might have been much more desperate.

"The worst of it is," said the reverend principal, "that you will not be able to take out a degree."

"I shall be sorry to quit college," replied the youth, "but as for the degree, that is neither here nor there."

The president shook his head and took snuff, while Tim cast a sidelong glance out of the window, gazing wistfully over the green landscape, which was now decked with the blossoms of spring, and longing to rove uncontrolled about that beautiful world, that seemed so redolent of sunshine, and flowers, and balmy breezes.

"It is a sad thing," said the president, "for a young man to be cast upon the cold charity of the wide world."

"The wider the world is the better," said Tim; "it is a fine thing to have sea-room; and as to its coldness, I don't regard that; a light heart will keep a man warm in the stiffest northeaster that ever blew."

The worthy president applied his handkerchief to his nose, then wiped his spectacles, and wondered how marvellously the wind is tempered to the shorn lamb.

"Thou hast a bold heart," said the president, "still I cannot bear to see you cast forth without a profession."

"Oh, never mind that; I'm all the better without it. To a man without a farthing in his pocket, a profession is only an incumbrance, which forces him to wear good clothes and talk like a book. I shall put out into the world as light as a feather, and float along with the breeze."

Arguments were thrown away upon the common sense of our hero, who was already panting to exercise among men the same devices which had smoothed all the asperities of college life, which had won him the affection of his fellow-students, and gained even the kindness of his superiors.

"There goes," said the president, as he gazed after him, "the shrewdest boy and the greatest dunce that ever left college—the most obstinate, yet the most conciliatory spirit."

Obstinate as he was, there was one point on which he yielded. He abandoned a long-cherished intention of going to sea, upon the earnest solicitation of his aunt. It was the only request from his sole remaining relative. She had nursed his infancy with unceasing kindness; she now leaned upon him for support, and her tears were irresistible. But in abandoning the ocean, he stipulated for free permission to roam at large over the wide expanse of his native country, and in a few days after the intelligence had arrived of his father's death, he was seen leaving his native village with an elastic step, with a staff in his hand, and a small portmanteau under his arm.

Here I must leave my hero for the present, and ask the gentle reader to accompany me to the pleasant village of Carondelet, or, as it is more commonly called, Vide Poche, on the margin of the Mississippi. Although now dwindled into an obscure and ruinous hamlet, remarkable only for its outlandish huts and lean ponies, it was then the goodly seat of a prosperous community. It is situated on the western shore of the river, in a beautiful little amphitheatre, which seemed to have been scooped out for the very purpose. The banks of the Mississippi at this place are composed of a range of hills rising abruptly from the water's edge. The town occupies a sort of cove, formed by a small plat of table land, surrounded on three sides by hills. The houses occupy the whole of this little area, including the hill-sides; and are models of primitive rudeness, carelessness and comfort. They were sometimes of stone; but usually of framed timber, with mud walls; and all the rooms being arranged on the ground floor, their circumference was often oddly disproportioned to their height. In a few of the better sort, spacious piazzas, formed by the projection of the roof, surrounded the buildings, giving to them both coolness and a remarkable air of comfort. The enormous steep roofs were often quadrangular, so as to form a point in the middle, surmounted by a ball, a weathercock, or a cross. Gardens, stocked with fruit trees and flowering shrubs, encompassed the dwellings, enclosed with rough stone walls, or stockades made by driving large stakes in the ground. The dwelling stood apart, having each its own little domain about it; and when it is added that the streets were narrow and irregular, it will be observed that the whole scene was odd and picturesque.

The inhabitants presented, as I suppose, a fair specimen of the French peasantry, as they existed in France previous to the first revolution.

They had all the levity, the kindness, and the contentment which are so well described by Sterne, with a simplicity which was perfectly childlike. Though subject at the date of our tale to a foreign king, they were as good republicans as if they had been trained up in one of our own colonies. They knew the restraints and distinctions of a monarchy only by report, practising the most rigid equality among themselves, and never troubling their heads to inquire how things were ordered elsewhere. The French commandants and priests, who ruled in their numerous colonies, had always the knack of giving a parental character to their sway, and governed with so much mildness, that the people never thought of questioning either the source or extent of their authority; while the English invariably alienate the affections of their colonists by oppression. The inhabitants of Vide Poche were all plebeians; a few who traded with the Indians had amassed some little property; the remainder were hunters and boatmen—men who traversed the great prairies of the West, and traced the largest rivers to their sources, fiddling and laughing all the way, lodging and smoking in the Indian wigwams, and never dreaming of fatigue or danger.

To return to our story. It was a sultry afternoon in June. Not a breath of air was stirring—the intense glare of the sun had driven every animal to some shelter—the parched soil glowed with heat, and even the plants drooped. There was, however, a pleasant coolness and an inviting serenity among the dwellings of the French. The trees that stood thick around them threw a dense shade, which contrasted delightfully with the glaring fierceness of the sunbeams. The broad leaf of the catalpa and the rich green of the locust afforded relief to the eye; bowers of sweetbrier and honeysuckle, mingled with luxuriant clumps of the white and red rose, gave fragrance to the air, and a romantic beauty to the scene.

In the cool veranda of one of the largest of those dwellings, sat a round-faced, laughing Frenchman. Near him sat Madame, his wife, a dark-eyed, wrinkled, sprightly old lady; and at her side was a beautiful girl of seventeen, their only daughter. The worthy couple had that mahogany tinge of complexion which belongs to this region; as to the young lady, politeness compels me to describe her hue as a brunette—and a beautiful brunette it was—fading into snow-white upon her neck, and deepening into a rich damask on her round smooth cheek. The ladies were sewing; and the gentleman was puffing his pipe with the composure of a man who feels conscious that he has a right to smoke his own tobacco in his own house, and with the deliberation of one who is master of his own time.

While thus engaged, their attention was attracted by the apparition of a man leading a jaded horse along the street. The stranger was young and slender; his dress had once been genteel, but was much worn, and showed signs of recent exposure to the weather. The traveller himself was tanned and weather-beaten, his hair tangled, and his chin unshaved; while the sorry nag, which he led by the bridle, had just life enough left in him to limp upon three legs. Worn down with fatigue, and covered with sweat and dust, the new comer halted in the street, as if unable to proceed, and looked around in search of a public house. Of a boy, who passed along, he inquired for a tavern; but the lad, unable to understand him, shook his head. He put the same question to several others, with no better success; until Monsieur Dunois, the gentleman whom we have described above, seeing his embarrassment, stepped forward and invited him into his porch.

The stranger was no other than our friend Timothy Eleazer Tompkinson, who, in the course of a few months, had made his way from New England to Louisiana. It is unnecessary to recount the various expedients by which he maintained himself upon his journey. He was a lawyer, a doctor, or a mechanic, as occasion required. At one place, he pleaded a cause before a magistrate; at another, he drew a tooth; for one man he mended a lock; for another he set a timepiece; and by these and similar devices, he not only supported himself, but procured the means to purchase a horse, saddle, and bridle. Arrived at the frontier of Kentucky, his restless spirit still urged him forward, and he determined to strike across the wilderness to the French settlements, on the Mississippi. The distance was nearly three hundred miles, and the whole region through which he had to travel was uninhabited, except by Indians. Unaccustomed to the forest, he must have perished, had he not encountered a solitary hunter, who, pleased with his free and bold spirit, voluntarily conducted him throughout a considerable part of the route, taught him how to avoid the haunts of the savages, and instructed him in some of the arts of forest life. For the last two days he had wandered without food; and both himself and his horse were nearly exhausted when he reached the Mississippi, where some friendly Indians, of the Kaskaskia tribe, had ferried him across in their canoe. The arrival of a stranger at this secluded hamlet, by land, was quite an event, and little else was talked of, this evening, at the tea-tables of Carondelet.

M. Dunois, who had traded and travelled, valued himself highly on his knowledge of the English language, which he had attempted to teach to his daughter; and he no sooner discovered that this was the vernacular tongue of the stranger, than he opened a conversation in that dialect. The cork was drawn from a bottle of excellent claret, a pitcher of limpid water from the fountain was brought, and our hero having moistened his parched lips, and seated himself in the coolest veranda of Vide Poche, felt quite refreshed. The following dialogue then ensued:

"Pray, sir," said Timothy Eleazer, with his best college bow, "can you direct me to a tavern?"

"Tavern! *vat* you call? eh? *Oh la! d'auberge*—no, *Monsieur, dere* is no tavern *en Vide Poche.*"

"That is awkward enough—what shall I do? my horse must be fed, and I am almost starved."

"*Eh bien?* you will have some *ros bif*, and somebody for eat your *cheval! n'est ce pas?*"

"I need food and lodging, and know not where to go."

"*Fude! vat* is *fude*, Marie? Ah ha! *aliment. Sacré! Monsieur* is *hongry; Loge!* here is *ver* good place, *chez moi*. You shall stay *vid* me. *Ver* good *loge* here, and plenty for eat you, *et votre cheval.*"

Timothy "hoped he didn't intrude"; but a man who has been lost in the woods is not very apt to stand on ceremony; and as he glanced at the symptoms of plenty which surrounded him, at the good-humoured hostess, and at the fair Marie, a spectator would have judged that his fears of intrusion were overbalanced by feelings of self-gratulation at having fallen into the hands of such good Samaritans. He soon found that the hospitality of this worthy family was of the most substantial kind. In a moment his tired nag was led to the stable, and our hero, so lately a wanderer, found himself an honoured and cherished guest.

The air of Vide Poche agreed well with him. The free and social habits of the French were exactly to his taste. Although their pockets, as the name of their town implied, were not lined with gold, there was plenty in their dwellings and cheerfulness in their hearts.

He was delighted with the harmony and the apparent unity, both of feeling and interest, which bound this little community together. They were like a single family; their hearts beat in unison, "as the heart of one man." There was but one circle. Though some were poorer than others, they all mingled in the same dance; and as none claimed superiority, or attempted to put others to shame by affecting a show of wealth, there was little envy or malice. All were equally illiterate, with the exception of Mons. Dunois and the priest, who had travelled, and who spoke, the one Latin, and the other, as we have seen, English. But so far from assuming any airs on account of these attainments, they were the plainest and most sociable men in the village, and were reverenced as much for their benevolence as for their superior knowledge.

All this chimed so well with the feelings of Mr. Timothy Eleazer Tompkinson, that he resolved forthwith to engraft himself upon this cheerful and vigorous stock. The next thing was to choose a profession;

but he had too much common sense to suffer so small a matter as this to cause him any embarrassment. I am not aware of the precise motive which determined him to embrace the practice of physic. It might have been benevolence, or a conviction of special vocation for the healing art; but I rather attribute it to a motive which I suspect too often allures our youth to become the disciples of Aesculapius, namely, the occult nature of the science, which enables an adroit practitioner to cover his ignorance so completely as to defy detection. Timothy had discovered that when he practiced law, any spectator could expose the fallacy of his arguments; when he mended clocks, they often refused to go; but the case was different with his patients; if, in spite of his drugs, they refused *to go*, it was well for them and for him; and if they *did go*, nobody knew whom to blame. To say the truth, he never presumed to "exhibit" any drug more active than charcoal, brickdust, or flour; and his success had heretofore been quite marvelous.

He therefore took the earliest opportunity of disclosing to his host that he was a physician, and was disposed to exercise his calling for the benefit of the good people of Carondelet.

"*Eh bien!*" exclaimed M. Dunois, "*un medecin! ver* good; *ver mosh* fine *ting* for Vide Poche; *vat* can you cure?"

"Oh, I am not particular; I can cure one thing almost as well as another."

"You can cure every *ting*, eh?—*de fevre, de break-bone, de catch-cold—dat* is fine *ting*, you shall stay *chez Vide Poche*."

So the question was settled.

Had there been a newspaper in Carondelet, the name of Doctor Timothy Eleazer Tompkinson, "from the United States," would, doubtless, have figured in its columns. But as there was no such thing, our hero resorted to other means of acquiring notoriety. In the first place, having procured a suitable cabin, the whole village was searched for vials, and gallipots, and little boxes, and big bottles, which, being filled with liquids and unguents of various hues, were "wisely set for show," at the window. But the greatest affair of all was a certain machine, for the invention of which Doctor Tompkinson ought to have had a patent. This was no other than a wheel, turning on an axis, and surrounded by an immovable rim, within which it revolved. Upon the wheel Timothy wrote the name of every disease which he could recollect, as well as every dreadful accident to which flesh is heir; and on the rim he inscribed the cures. When the remedy for any disorder was required, the wheel was set in motion, and on its stopping, the cure was found opposite the disease. The honest villagers crowded to see "the magic wheel," and vied in their courtesies to its fortunate possessor, who was rising fast into celebrity, when his prospects were clouded by an untoward event.

In the midst of the village stood the chapel—a low, oblong building, whose gable end was presented to the street, and behind which was a cemetery, where all the graves were marked by great wooden crosses, instead of tombstones. Here the good Catholics repaired every morning and evening to perform their devotions, and confess their peccadilloes to the priest. Hither one morning, at an earlier hour than usual, was seen repairing the fair Marie Dunois, with a step as light as the zephyr and a face radiant as the dawn. Kneeling beside the worthy old man, who placed his withered hand upon her raven locks, she began in a low, earnest tone to unburthen her mind. Suddenly the ecclesiastic started from his seat, exclaiming.

"Ah, the insolent! how did he dare to make such an avowal?"

"He meant no harm, I assure you, father," replied Marie.

"How do you know that?"

"He told me so, with his own mouth. He said that he valued my happiness more than his own; and that he would rather swallow all the physic in his shop, than offend me."

"Very pretty talk, truly! Do you not know that he is a heretic, and that no reliance can be placed in him?"

"Very true, Father Augustin, but then he is so agreeable."

"Besides, he is a Yankee; and does not understand your language."

"Oh, I understand him very well; and he says he will teach me to speak English. Don't you think him very handsome, Father Augustin?"

"I am afraid, my child, that this adventurer has imposed too much upon your youth and innocence."

"No, indeed, Father Augustin, I am old enough to know when a gentleman is sincere, and all that. Don't you think Doctor Tompkinson plays beautifully on the flute? and on the violin, he plays almost as well as you, father."

"Pshaw! go, go, I shall inform your parents."

"Oh, dear, I have no objections to that; they will feel highly honoured by Doctor Tompkinson's partiality for me."

Nevertheless the pretty Marie blushed and cast down her eyes when she met her father at breakfast that morning, and no sooner was that meal despatched than she hastened to her own room. Presently came Father Augustin, and after an hour's conference, Monsieur Dunois, evidently much agitated, sallied forth in search of our hero.

"*Vel, sair!*" he exclaimed as they met, "I *ave* found you out! I *ave* catch de *Yankee!*"

"How?"

"How! you *ave* court my daughter; *dat is how! sacré!* you *ave* make love *avec ma Marie, dat* is how enough, *Monsieur docteur*."

"My dear sir, pray be composed, there is some mistake."

"*Dere* is no mistake. I *vill* not be *compose*—I *will* not be *impose, too! diable!* Suppose some *gentilhomme* court *ma Marie contrair* to my *vish*, shall I sit down *compose?*"

"Really, sir, I see no reason for this passion," replied the cautious Timothy, who saw his advantage in keeping cool.

"*Sair, I ave raison*," exclaimed the enraged Frenchman; "I *ave* too *mosch raison. Vous etez traitre!* you are *de* sly *dem rogue!* You very pretty *docteur!* very *ansome* Yankee *docteur!* can you no mix *de physique*, and draw *de* blood, *vidout* make love *avec* all the *French* gal?"

"I assure you, sir, the ladies have misconstrued something that I have said merely in jest—"

"*Jest! vat* is *jest? ah ha! raillerie; fon—vat, sair,* you court *ma fille* for *fon?* very *ansome fon!* you make love *avec de French* gal for *fon, eh?* Suppose *bam bye* you marry some of *dem* for *fon! diable!* Suppose, maybe, I break all your bone, for *fon, vid* my *cane, eh,* how you like him?"

"My dear sir, if you will tell me coolly what you complain of, I will endeavour to explain."

"*Sair,* I complain for many *ting.* I sorry for you make love *avec ma fille, vidout* my leave—*dat* is *von ting;* I very *mosch incense* for you court *ma chile* for *fon—dat* is *nodder ting; den* I *ave raison* to be *fâche* for you *faire la cour* a two, *tree* lady all same *tem.*"

The last of these accusations was unjust. Timothy had not really intended to pay his devotions to more than one lady. But the females all admired him, and in their confidential conversations with the priest, who was no great connoisseur in the affairs of the heart, spoke of him in such high terms of approbation, as to induce the holy man to believe that he was actually playing the coquette. What Monsieur Dunois and the priest believed, soon became the belief of the village; and the men all condemned, while the ladies sympathized with, the ingenious stranger. The doctor, of course, changed his lodging; and ceased to have any intercourse with Mademoiselle Dunois, except by means of expressive glances and significant pressures of the hand as they met in the dances, which occurred almost every evening.

Things now looked gloomy; our friend Timothy lost his practice; and a fortunate circumstance it was for him, as well as for those who might otherwise have been his patients. He now had leisure to make hunting excursions, and expeditions upon the water; and his skill in the management of a boat, as well as his courage and address in every emergency, soon gained him friends. His vivacity, his versatility and promptness, won daily upon his comrades; he became a daring hunter, a skilful woodsman, and a favourite of all the young men of the village.

Such was the posture of affairs, and Doctor Tompkinson was sitting one evening in his lonely room, *quite out of patients*, as a punster would say, when he was called in haste to visit a young lady who had met with the misfortune of having a fish-bone stuck in her throat. The priest had exercised all his skill—the old ladies had exhausted their recipes without effect; and, as a last resort, it was determined to consult Dr. Tompkinson and the magic wheel. Our hero, with great alacrity, brushed the dust from the neglected machine, set it in motion, and waited patiently until it stopped, when opposite to the word "choking" was found "bleeding." The doctor, somewhat perplexed, repeated the experiment; but, the result being the same, resolved to obey the oracle, and trust to fortune. Having prepared his bandages and lancet, he repaired to the sufferer, who, opening her eyes and beholding the operator brandishing a bright instrument, and naturally supposing that the part affected would be the first point of attack, and that her throat would be cut from ear to ear, uttered a terrific scream, and—out flew the bone! "St. Anthony! what a miraculous cure!" exclaimed the priest.

"Ste. Genevieve! what a noble physician!" cried all the ladies.

And the whole village of Vide Poche was alive with wonder and loud in praise of the consummate sagacity of the young American! Never did a man rise so suddenly to the highest pinnacle of public favour—never did Doctor Tompkinson shake so many hard hands, or receive so many bright smiles and courtesies, as on this evening. The news soon flew to the tea-table of Monsieur Dunois, who had already begun to repent of his harshness to our hero, and whose ardent feelings, easily excited, now prompted him into the opposite extreme. Seeing the object of his solicitude passing his door, while the first gush of returning kindness was flowing through his heart, he rushed out and caught him in his arms. "*Ah, mon ami!*" exclaimed he, "I *ave* been *mistake!* I *ave* been *impose!* you are *de grand medecin!* you shall marry *avec* my *gal!*" and without waiting for any reply, he dragged him into the house.

Shortly after this event, the smartest and merriest wedding that ever was seen in Carondelet was celebrated under the hospitable roof of Monsieur Dunois, and our hero became the happy husband of the beautiful and artless Marie. On that night, every fiddle and every foot in Vide Poche did its duty; even the priest wore his best robes and kindest smile at the marriage feast of the lucky heretic. Mr. Tompkinson immediately abandoned the practice of physic; the magic wheel disappeared; and he embarked in business as an Indian trader. Here his genius found an appropriate field. With his band of adventurous boat-

men he navigated the long rivers of the West to their tributary fountains; he visited the wigwams of tribes afar off, to whom the white
man was not yet known as a scourge; he chased the buffalo over plains
until then untrodden by any human foot but that of the savage, and returned laden with honest spoil. Year after year he pursued this toil-
some traffic; until, having earned a competency, he sat down contented, and waxed as fat, as lazy, and as garrulous as any of his townsmen. He grew as swarthy as his neighbors, and as he wore a *capot* and
smoked a short pipe, no one would have suspected that he was not a
native, had it not been for his aunt, the worthy Miss Fidelity Tompkinson, who occupied the best room in his mansion, and who resolutely
refused, through life, to eat *gumbo*-soup, to speak French, or to pay
any reverence to that respectable man, the priest.

A Buffalo and Elk Hunt

by HENRY HASTINGS SIBLEY, 1811–91. *Eminent as fur trader,
soldier, and politician, Sibley was born in Detroit. After some schooling at
a local academy and several years of tutoring in the classics and studying law,
he became a clerk in the sutler's store at Fort Brady, Sault Ste. Marie. From
1829 to 1834 he was in the service of the American Fur Company at Mackinac Island and later at Cleveland. Then he became a partner of Joseph Ro-
lette and Hercules L. Dousman in the fur trade with the Sioux and he stationed himself at Mendota on the Minnesota River. There he built a
commodious stone house which he himself termed the first private dwelling
in the vicinity. The rest of his life was given over to business and politics.
After serving as territorial delegate to Congress, Sibley was elected the first
governor of Minnesota in 1858. When the Sioux uprising occurred in 1862
Sibley led a hastily assembled army to the defense of settlers in southwestern
Minnesota and later commanded several punitive expeditions against the
Sioux. He spent his remaining years in St. Paul where he was an extremely
influential figure. Sibley's Unfinished Autobiography was edited by Theodore
C. Blegen in 1932. He contributed frequently to periodicals, and the account
of a hunting trip in 1842 was written for a New York sporting periodical,
The Spirit of the Times, under the pseudonym of Hal—a Dacotah.*

IT IS a fact much to be regretted that the game on the Western Prairies
is rapidly diminishing in number. A residence of twelve years on the
West side of the Mississippi, during which time I have made very many
hunting excursions, has satisfied me that the larger animals are fast disappearing, and will soon be exterminated. Upon the plains which were

the scene of my sports in former years, where the Elk and Buffalo were to be found by hundreds and by thousands, the hunter may now roam for days together, without encountering a single herd. Nor is this surprising, when we reflect that of the Indians west of the Mississippi, at least a hundred thousand subsist entirely by the chase, and the improvidence of these people is so great, that often ten times as many cattle are killed as can be consumed by a camp, either by being driven over precipices, or by other methods. What will become of these starving thousands when buffalo shall have failed altogether, is a question which I am unable to solve. Present appearances indicate with much certainty, that ere twenty years have elapsed, but few buffalo will be found, and those only on the immense plains of New Mexico, or on the distant prairies which skirt the base of the Rocky Mountains.

In the month of October, 1842, I took with me eight horses and carts, in charge of five Canadians and one American, and with my old hunting companions, Alex. F[aribault] and Jack Frazer, wended my way towards the buffalo region. We expected to find these animals at or about the *Minday Mecoche Wakkon*, or Lake of the Spirit Land, a distance of a hundred and fifty miles. The first few days we amused ourselves with shooting grouse, ducks, and geese, of which there were a great abundance. One of the party knocked over twenty ducks at a single shot, nineteen of which were secured. Of course we did not lack for provant. As we advanced farther inland, where we hoped to find elk, a veto was put on all discharges of fire arms at small game, as the report of a gun will set the keen-eared animals in motion at the distance of miles. On the seventh day out, Jack Frazer reported that he had seen some game, but whether buffalo or elk he could not tell, as they were too far off. Our glass being put in requisition, we soon found them to be a small herd of the latter, lying down at the base of a hill about six miles off. Notwithstanding the excitement which warmed us at the prospect of a chase, the beauty of the scene which broke upon our vision from the height whereon we stood, attracted the attention of the most thoughtless of the party. A large lake, which might have been taken for the "Glimmer Glass" of Cooper, stretched itself out at right angles with our course, about a mile beyond where the elk lay. The prairie, clothed in its variegated autumn garb, appeared to rise and fall like the undulations of the ocean, and in all directions might be perceived points of woodland giving forth all the different tints and hues peculiar to an American forest. A thin belt of lofty trees encircled the lake, showing through their intervals the bright sheet of water, which lay, unruffled by a breeze, in all its glorious beauty. It seemed almost a sacrilege against Nature thus to invade her solitudes, only to carry with us dismay and death. But other, and certainly not more holy thoughts, soon dissipated in us all sense of the magnificence of the scene. Our measures were taken to circumvent the elk.

Alex., Jack Frazer, and myself, as the only experienced hunters, were to approach and fire, while the others of the party mounted their horses, and were stationed under the cover of the hill, except one man, who remained in charge of the carts and baggage. With this man I left my hunting horse, ready saddled, with instructions to mount as soon as he heard our guns, and come with all speed to my stand. These precautions taken, and having stripped ourselves of all superfluous clothing, we commenced the delicate operation of approach. A few yards brought us in full view of the herd, which, unsuspicious of danger, were lolling lazily in the sunshine. Throwing ourselves flat upon the ground, we wormed ourselves along with Indian stealthiness, under cover of the short grass. We had proceeded thus about half a mile, when we came to a marsh, which it was found we must necessarily pass. The water here was two feet deep, and the exertion of crawling through the knotted grass, and of securing, at the same time, our guns from moisture, while we kept ourselves concealed, was excessively severe. By dint of unremitting efforts we passed silently through this serious obstacle, and emerged upon dry ground within sixty yards of the game. We here examined our arms, renewed our primings, and sprang upon our feet, not wishing to fire until the elk rose. As these magnificent creatures bounded off in great confusion, our double barrels were discharged, and three elk fell dead. Jack F., who sported a single barrel, made a clean miss, as usual. In fact, he was a miserable shot. With an eye like an eagle, firm nerves, and active withal as a wild cat, it was not one of Jack's "gifts" to shoot well. Unfortunately, Alex. F. and myself had aimed our second barrels at the same large animal, which came to the ground riddled with balls and buckshot, otherwise we might have secured a fourth without doubt. As the remaining fifteen or twenty fled at full speed, we could hear the shouts of the horsemen as they discharged their pieces. They failed, however, to hit a single elk. My horse was presently at my side, and as soon as I was mounted, the noble animal entering into the spirit of the chase, set off at racing speed. The elk were now a mile ahead, and I passed successively each of the Canadians on their jaded horses, vainly struggling to keep with the chase. Wright, the American, who was well mounted, was thrown headlong from the saddle, and when I overtook the herd after a run of six miles, I perceived his horse running side by side with the elk. I had left my double barrel behind, trusting to a revolving pistol to do execution. But my hands were so benumbed by long immersion in the cold water, that I could not pull the trigger. Shifting the revolver to my left hand, I managed to discharge it at a large female elk, at a distance of not more than ten feet. The ball took effect *a posteriori*, and the animal was so much wounded that she plunged headlong into a wide boggy stream, through which, after incredible efforts, she succeeded in passing, leaving me no other alternative than to abandon the chase, the nature of the ground rendering it impossible to cross.

I succeeded in securing the runaway horse, with which I returned to my companions, who had already made preparations to encamp on the border of the lake. Here we spent one day in preserving the meat of the slain elk, which was accomplished by cutting it into thin slices, when it was spread out upon a scaffold, and a fire kindled under, which soon dried it thoroughly.

The next morning there were myriads of ducks and geese in and about the lake, and the discipline of the camp was so far relaxed as to allow a few shots to be fired among them, which afforded us an ample supply.

Continuing our course southwestwardly, we reached Lac Blanc, a fine sheet of water, which bore upon its surface swan, geese, and ducks in great numbers, which we did not disturb, as there was fresh "sign" of elk and traces of buffalo. From this point we followed a small stream which ran through very swampy ground, and which was literally covered with wild-fowl. These poor creatures were not at all shy, giving evidence of their utter ignorance of the arts of the great destroyer, man. In fact, geese, mallard, and other wild ducks, were innumerable, and I doubt not that either good shot of the party might have destroyed a thousand in a day. But we were in search of nobler game, and not a single discharge of a gun was permitted.

The day after we struck the stream, and while we were still following it, Jack Frazer was going along in the high grass at a little distance from the party, when he threw himself suddenly from his horse, and appeared to seize hold of some object at his feet, at the same time calling for assistance. There was a general roar of laughter when we reached him. He had seized two large racoons which were sleeping quietly in the grass, each one by the tail. Startled at this unexpected assault upon their nether extremities, the coons made a joint effort to nab our friend Jack, who, with tail hold fairly fixed, endeavored to evade their bite by jumping about in all directions. He was so expert with his sudden pulls and twitches, that he escaped without injury for a little time, until, encumbered with the weight of his victims, he ceased hopping, and at that moment one of them got Jack by the leg, when he incontinently gave up the battle. With a desire to see fair play, none of us would interfere while this farce was being enacted, but seeing our *compagnon* so badly treated, we revenged him by knocking the coons on the head.

The accidental discharge of a gun by one of the men caused me to lose a shot at three buffalo. They had been quietly feeding on the low grounds along the stream, when, hearing the discharge, they dashed away over the open prairie. After holding a *conseil de guerre*, we concluded not to follow them until the next morning, as the day was already far spent. Selecting a favorable spot, we encamped, and the arms of the party were put in order for the expected sport. A large buck came out of the woods at the opposite side of the stream, without perceiving us. We could not allow him to be fired at. The next morning Jack Frazer was despatched with the most active of the Canadians to reconnoitre. In a short time they returned, and reported that three buffalo were lying down in one of the low places in the prairie. Two men were then placed in charge of the carts, with directions to proceed slowly along at an angle slightly deviating from the line to the buffalo, while the rest of us, seven in number, mounted our horses and prepared for the chase.

Approaching the bulls within three hundred yards, we charged down the hill upon them at full speed. The first flight of the buffalo is comparatively slow, but when pressed by the huntsman, the rapidity with which these apparently unwieldy animals get over the ground, is amazing. Alex. F. and myself having the fleetest horses, each of us singled out a victim, leaving the third to be dealt with by the remainder. We were shortly alongside, and our double barrels told with deadly effect, the huge beasts rolling on the ground in death, within a hundred yards of each other. The other horsemen followed the remaining buffalo, discharging numberless shots at him, but notwithstanding each man swore that he had hit him, the bull got clean off, and his pursuers were brought to a sudden halt by the sight of a large herd of cattle, which they were unwilling to disturb until we joined them. Meanwhile the prairie had been set on fire by some Indian to windward of us, and as the wind blew violently, the flames came down upon us with such rapidity that we had not even time to secure the meat of the two buffalo killed. It was decided to attempt a passage through the flaming barrier, leaving the men with the carts to get to some shelter ere the fire reached them. Five times did we approach the raging element, and as many times were we repulsed, scorched and almost suffocated, until, by a desperate use of whip and spur, we leaped our horses across the line of fire, looking, as we emerged from the cloud of smoke, more like individuals from the lower regions, than inhabitants of this earth.

It took some time to recover from the exhaustion attendant upon our enterprise when, being fully prepared at all points, we went off in search of the buffalo. We shortly discovered them on the top of a hill, which was bare of grass, and to which the fire had driven them. Alex. F.

and myself made a large circle to gain the rear of the herd, and the rest placing themselves out of view, waited for our charge. When about half a mile distant, the huge mass set itself in motion, and the herd, composed of several hundreds, took to flight. We were soon among them, and the discharge of fire-arms from all the horsemen was incessant and well-sustained. Alex. F. and myself had each shot two cows, and others of the party had succeeded in bringing down an animal or two, when we all bore down en masse close to the heels of the affrighted buffalo. Jack Frazer's horse stumbled over a calf, fell, and threw his rider headlong from the saddle. Merely casting a glance to ascertain that Jack's neck was not broken, away we sped, until horse after horse gave out, and in a short time I found myself alone with the herd, the nearest of my companions being a quarter of a mile in the rear.

There was a very fine fat cow in the centre of the band, which I made several attempts to separate from the others, but without effect. She kept herself close to an old bull, who, by his enormous size, appeared to be the patriarch of the tribe. Being resolved to get rid of this encumbrance, I shot the old fellow behind the shoulder. The wound was mortal, and the bull left the herd, and went off at a slow gallop in a different direction. As soon as I had fired I slackened the speed of my horse to enable me to reload, determining to pursue the retiring mass, trusting to find the wounded animal on my return. Unfortunately I changed my mind, and rode after the bull to give him the *coup de grace*. I rode carelessly along with but one barrel of my gun loaded, when, upon getting near the buffalo, he turned as quick as lightning to charge. At this critical instant I had risen in my stirrups, and released my hold on the bridle rein. At the moment the buffalo turned, my horse, frightened out of his propriety, gave a tremendous bound sidewise, and, alas! that I shall tell it, threw Hal clear out of the saddle, and within ten feet of the enraged monster! Here was a predicament! Imagine your humble servant face to face with the brute, whose eyes glared through the long hair which garnished his frontlet like coals of fire—the blood streaming from his nostrils. In this desperate situation I made up my mind, that my only chance for escape was to look my enemy in the eye: as any attempt to run would only invite attack. Holding my gun ready cocked to fire if he attempted a rush, I stood firmly, although I must confess I was awfully frightened, and thought my last hour had come! How long he stood there pawing and roaring, I have now not the least idea, but certainly thought he was a long time making his decision what he should do. At last he turned slowly away, and I gave him a parting salute, which let out the little blood left in his body. He went a short distance and fell dead.

I did not fail to render due homage to that Almighty Being who had so wonderfully preserved my life. The frequenter of Nature's vast solitudes may be a wild and reckless, but he cannot be essentially an irreligious man. The solemn silence of forest and prairie—the unseen dangers which are incident to this mode of life, and the consciousness that Providence alone can avert them; all these have the effect to lead even the thoughtless man, occasionally, to reflection.

The only one of the party within view now came up. I was so near the buffalo when dismounted, that he thought I had struck him with the barrels of my gun. I despatched him in search of my horse, which, as is usual in such cases, had followed the herd of buffalo at full speed. I now felt much pain in one of my feet, which had received a serious blow when I fell. I had to use my hunting knife to free me from sock and moc[c]asin, and in ten minutes I was unable to walk, or even stand without support. Knowing the man who had gone after my horse to be a mere tyro in woodcraft, I feared he would not be able to find his way back to me, and being ten miles from camp, with no fuel to light a fire, and clad in scanty Indian costume, the prospect of spending a cold October night where I was, was any thing but agreeable. I had no other alternative than to load my gun heavily with powder, and discharge it in quick succession, hoping that some of my comrades would hear the reports and come to my aid. After a short time spent in this pleasant exercise, I perceived Jack Frazer, who, having recovered his horse, was looking for the rest of the party, when my gun attracted his attention. I despatched him after the missing man, and he soon returned with him and my horse. When I mounted it was with difficulty I could support myself in the saddle.

On our way to camp, we discovered a single buffalo cow feeding. Jack started off in pursuit, and I had the pleasure of witnessing a most beautiful chase, albeit unable to take part in it. The cow made for the height of land opposite, and as she reached the summit Jack overtook her, when she turned and charged him furiously. I thought it was all over with him, for the animal was within three feet when he discharged his gun. I saw her fall before the report of his gun reached my ears: the ball had broken her neck. Had it taken effect in any other part, Jack must have been seriously injured, if not killed.

When we got to the camping ground, all the party were assembled. The injury I had received was of too serious a nature to allow of rest. I passed a sleepless night, and being satisfied that it was necessary to have surgical assistance as soon as possible, I determined to return home—offering to leave four men with Alex. and Jack, if they were disposed to continue the sport. The disappointment was a serious one, but my hunting companions refused to leave me, and it was arranged that the next day should be employed in securing the meat of the buffalo killed, and the day following we should leave for home.

In the morning, while the men went in search of the meat, we rode over to get a view of *Minday Mecoche Wakkon*, or Lake of the Spirit Land, already mentioned. This beautiful sheet of water has an island in it, which the Sioux Indians never venture upon—as they believe it to be the residence of demons. Their traditions say, that in days of yore, several of that tribe landed upon the island from a canoe, when they were instantly seized and devoured. Hence the name. We saw several others disporting themselves in the Lake, apparently not much afraid of us, or of the spirits of the island.

When all was ready for our departure homewards, I told my companions that as our progress would be necessarily slow with the loaded carts, they would have time to scan the country on either side of us, and perhaps find buffalo, and they could easily rejoin us at night. This plan suited them well, and they were off bright and early, while we retraced our trail—myself on horseback, leading the procession. About noon I perceived, directly in our line of march, a large herd of elk, and I made a signal to the men to halt. I then despatched them to give the elk a volley, bidding them to be very careful in approaching, while I, with my game leg, rode to windward to endeavor to get a shot as they passed. Having ensconced myself snugly in ambush, I presently heard a rustling in the bushes, and a huge buck came bounding out close to me. I could have keeled him over with a load of No. 6, but I forbore to pull trigger on him, lest I should spoil the sport of my party, and he got safely off. In two minutes after the whole herd of elk went dashing past, but at too great a distance for me to shoot. The men, as I feared, made a bungling attempt to get near the elk, and had been discovered. There must have been a hundred or more in this band, and we watched their movements with lively pleasure as they bounded over the prairie. Alex. F. and Jack Frazer joined us in the evening, having three buffalo tails pendant at their belts—trophies of the number slain.—They had fallen in with several large droves of buffalo, and might have killed many more, but, as the meat could not be taken, they very properly abstained from useless slaughter.

We hastened homewards as fast as our trammelled condition would allow, only now and then shooting a few ducks or other wild fowl, wherewith to make a *bouillon* in the evening. On the 22d day after our departure from home, we reached our domicils, having in the interval killed 16 buffalo, 3 elk, 8 raccoons, 12 wolves, 7 geese, 244 ducks, and 80 grouse, besides sundry other small snaps not worth recording.

When I next go on a buffalo hunt, "May you be there to see."

Ball at Thram's Huddle

by MRS. CAROLINE KIRKLAND, 1801–64. *Caroline Matilda Stansbury was born in New York. After her marriage to William Kirkland she lived in Geneva, New York, and later she and her husband removed to Detroit. William Kirkland had bought an extensive tract of land in the Michigan backwoods, and it was her experience here that supplied Mrs. Kirkland with the material for her western stories. About 1843 Mrs. Kirkland returned to New York City where she edited the Union Magazine; this was later merged with Sartain's Magazine and published in Philadelphia. European travel afforded Mrs. Kirkland the material for other books, but her chief work consists of three volumes based on her Michigan residence: A New Home— Who'll Follow? (1839), written under the pseudonym of Mrs. Mary Clavers; Forest Life (1842); and Western Clearings (1845). In these books, which consist of sketches and essay-like narratives, she revealed her careful observation of the social life of the community. She excelled in what might be called domestic realism and she was particularly adept at catching the idiom of the frontier. "Ball at Thram's Huddle" is one of the tales in Western Clearings.*

IT WAS on the sultriest of all melting afternoons, when the flies were taking an unanimous siesta, and the bees, baked beyond honey or humming, swung idly on the honeysuckles, that I observed, with half-shut eye, something like activity among the human butterflies of our most peaceful of villages. If I could have persuaded myself to turn my head, I might doubtless have ascertained to what favoured point were directed the steps (hasty, considering all things,) of the Miss Liggitts, Miss Pinn, and my pretty friend, Fanny Russell; but the hour was unpropitious to research, and slumber beguiled the book from my fingers, before the thought "Where *can* they be going!" had fairly passed through my mind. Fancy had but just transported me to the focus of a circle of glass-blowers, the furnace directly in front, and the glowing fluid all round me, when I was recalled to almost equally overcoming realities, by a light tap at the door. I must have given the usual invitation mechanically, for before I was fairly awake, the pink face of one of my own hand-maidens shone before my drowsy eyes.

"If you don't want me for nothin', I'd like to go down to the store to get some notions for the ball."

"The ball! what! a red-hot ball!" I replied, for the drowsy influence was settling over me again, and I was already on the deck of a frigate, in the midst of a sharply-contested action.

"Massy no, marm! this here Independence ball up to Thram's Huddle," said Jane, with a giggle.

I was now wide awake with astonishment. "A dance, Jane, in such weather as this!"

"Why law! yes; nothin' makes a body so cool as dancin' and drinkin' hot tea."

This was beyond argument. Jane departed, and I amused myself with the flittings of gingham sun-bonnets and white aprons up and down the street, in the scorching sun.

It was waxing toward the tea-hour, when that prettiest of Fannies, Fanny Russell, her natural ringlets of shadowy gold, which a duchess might envy, looking all the richer under the melting influence of the time, came tripping into the little porch.

"If you *would* be so kind as to lend me that large feather fan; I would take such good care of it! It's for the ball."

Sweet Fanny! one must be churlish indeed, to deny thee a far greater boon!

Next came that imp, Ring Jones; but he goes slyly round to the kitchen-door, with an air of great importance. Presently, enter Jane.

"Ring Jones has brought a kind of a bill, marm, for our Mark; and Mark ain't to hum, and Ring says he can't go without an answer."

"But I cannot answer Mark's billets, you know, Jane."

"No, marm; but—this 'ere is something about the *team*, I guess."

And in the mean time Jane had, *sans cérémonie*, broken the wafer, and was spelling out the contents of Mark's note.

"I can't justly make it out; but I know it's something about the *team*; and they want an answer right off."

Thus urged, I took the note, which was after this fashion.

"The agreeable Cumpany of Mr. Mark Loring and Lady is requested to G. Nobleses Tavern to Thram's huddle Independence the 4th July."

And here followed the names of some eight or ten managers.

"But, Jane, here's nothing about the team, after all."

"Jist look o' t'other side, marm; you see they didn't want to put it right in the ticket, like."

Upon this hint, I discerned, in the extreme corner of the paper, a flourish which might be interpreted "over." Over I went accordingly, and there came the gist of the matter.

"Mark we want to hav you be ready with your Team at one o'clock percisely to escort the ladies if you can't let us know and don't forgit to Put in as many Seats as you can and All your Buffaloes."

I ventured to promise that the team, and the seats, and the buffaloes, should be at Mark's disposal at "one percisely," and Ring Jones departed, highly exalted in his own opinion, by the success of his importunity.

It was to be supposed that we had now contributed our quota of aid on this patriotic occasion; but it seemed that more was expected. The evening was far advanced, when the newly-installed proprietor of the half-finished "hotel" at Thram's Huddle alighted at our door; and, wiping his dripping brow, made known the astounding fact that he had scoured the country for dried apples, without success, and informed us that he had come, as a *dernier resort*, to beg the loan of some; "for," as he sensibly observed, "a ball without no pies, was a thing that was never heerd on, no wheres."

When this matter was settled, he mustered courage to ask, in addition, for the great favour of a gallon of vinegar, for which he declared himself ready to pay any price; "that is, any thing that was reasonable."

I could not refrain from inquiring what indispensable purpose the vinegar was to serve.

"Why, for the lettuce, you see!—and if it's pretty sharp, it'll make 'em all the spryer."

Mr. Noble departed, in a happy frame of mind, and we heard no more of the ball that night.

The next day, the eldest Miss Liggitt "jist called in," as she happened to be passing, to ask if I was "a-goin' to want that 'ere flowery white bunnet-curting" of mine.

Some time ago I might not have comprehended that this description applied to a blonde-gauze veil, which had seen its best days, and was now scarce presentable. It did not require any great stretch of feminine generosity to lend this; but when it came to "a pair of white lace gloves," I pleaded poverty, and got off.

Our Jane, who is really quite a pretty girl, though her hair be of the sandiest, and her face and neck, at this time of the year, one continuous freckle, had set her heart upon a certain blue satin ribbon, which she did not like exactly to borrow, but which she had none the less made up her mind to have, for the grand occasion. So she began, like an able tactician, by showing me one of faded scarlet, on which she requested my opinion.

"Don't you think this'll look about right?"

"That horrid thing! No, Jane, pray don't be seen in that!"

"Well! what kind o' colour *do* you think would look good with this belt?" holding up a cincture, blue as the cloudless vault above us.

"Blue, or white; certainly not scarlet."

"Ah! but I ha'n't got neither one nor t'other"; and she looked very pensive.

I was hard-hearted, but Jane was not without resource.

"If you'd a-mind to let me have that 'ere long blue one of your'n: you don't never wear it, and I'd be willin' to pay you for't."

Who could hold out? The azure streamer became Jane's, in fee simple.

Spruce and warm looked our good Mark, in his tight blue coat, with its wealth of brass buttons, his stock five fathoms—I mean inches—deep, and his exceeding square-toed boots, bought new for this very solemnity. And a proud and pleasant heart beat in his honest bosom, I doubt not, as he drove to the place of rendezvous, buffaloes and all, with cerulean Jane at his side, a full half hour before the appointed time. They need not have cautioned Mark to be "percise." For my part, I longed for "the receipt of fern-seed to walk invisible," or some of those other talismans which used in the good old times to help people into places where they had no business to be; and in this instance, the Fates seemed inclined to be propitious, in a degree at least.

The revellers had scarcely passed on the western road in long and most rapid procession—the dust they raised had certainly not subsided —when a black cloud, which had risen stealthily while all were absorbed in the outfit, began to unfold its ominous shroud. The fringes of this portentous curtain scarcely passed the zenith, when a low, distant muttering, and a few scattering but immense drops, gave token of what was coming; and long ere the gay *cortege* could have reached the Huddle, which is fully six miles distant, a heavy shower, with thunder and lightning accompaniments, must have made wet drapery of every damsel's anxiously elaborate ball-dress. Beaver and broad-cloth might survive such a deluge, but alas for white dresses, long ringlets, and blonde-gauze "bunnet-curtings!"

The shower was too violent to last, and when it had subsided, and all was

> Fresh as if Day again were born,
> Again upon the lap of Morn,

I fortunately recollected an excellent reason for a long drive, ("man is his own Fate,") which would bring us into the very sound of the violins of the Huddle. A young woman who had filled the very important place of "help" in our family, was lying very ill at her father's; and the low circumstances of her parents made it desirable that she should be frequently remembered by her friends during her tedious illness. So in a light open wagon, with a smart pony, *borrowed* for the nonce, *selon les règles*, we had a charming drive, and moreover, the much-coveted pleasure of seeing the heads of the assembled company at Mr. Noble's; some bobbing up and down, some stretched far out of the window, getting breath for the next exercise, and some, with bodies to them, promenading the hall below. I tried hard to distinguish the "belle chevelure" of my favourite Fanny Russell, or the straight back and nascent whiskers of our own Mark; but we passed too rapidly to see all that was to be seen, and in a few moments found ourselves at the bars which led to the forlorn dwelling of poor Mary Anne Simms.

The only apartment that Mr. Simms' log-hut could boast, was arranged with a degree of neatness which made a visitor forget its lack of almost all the other requisites for comfort; and one corner was ingeniously turned into a nice little room for the sick girl, by the aid of a few rough boards eked out by snow-white curtains. I raised the light screen, and what bright vision should meet my eyes, but the identical Fanny, for whom I had looked in vain among the bobbing heads at the Huddle. She was whispering kindly to Mary Anne, whose pale cheek had acquired something like a flush, and her eyes a decided moisture, from the sense of Fanny's cheering kindness.

Fanny explained very modestly: "I was so near Mary Anne and I didn't know when I should get time to come again—"

"Didn't you get wet, coming over?"

"Not so *very*: we—we had an umbrella."

I remembered having lent one to Mark.

"But you are losing the ball, Fanny; you'll not get your share of the dancing." And at this moment I heard a new step in the outer part of the room, and a very familiar voice just outside the curtain:

"Come, Miss Russell, isn't it about time to be a-goin'? There's another shower a-comin' up."

Fanny started, blushed, and took leave. Common humanity obliged us to give time for a retreat, before we followed; for we well knew that our very precise Mr. Loring would not have been brought face to face with us, just then, for the world. When we did emerge, the sky was threatening enough, and as there was evidently no room for us where we were, we had no resource but to make a rapid transit to Mr. Noble's. We gained the noisy shelter just in time. Such a shower!— and it proved much more pertinacious than its predecessor; so that I had the pleasure of sitting in "Miss Nobleses" kitchen for an hour or more. We were most politely urged to join the festivities which were now shaking the frail tenement almost to dislocation; but even if we had been ball-goers, we should have been strikingly *de trop*, where the company was composed exclusively of young folks. So we chose the kitchen.

The empress of this torrid region, a tall and somewhat doleful looking dame, was in all the agonies of preparation; and she certainly was put to her utmost stretch of invention, to obtain access to the fireplace, where some of the destined delicacies of the evening were still in process of qualification, so dense was the crowd of damp damsels, who were endeavouring in various ways to repair the cruel ravages of the shower. One "jist wanted to dry her shoes"; another was dodging after a hot iron, "jist to rub off her hankercher"; while others were taking turns in pinching with the great kitchen tongs the long locks which streamed, Ophelia-like, around their anxious faces. Poor "Miss Nobles" edged, and glided, and stooped, among her humid guests, with a patience worthy of all praise; supplying this one with a pin, that with a needle-and-thread, and the other with one of her own side-combs; though the last mentioned act of courtesy forced her to tuck behind her ear one of the black tresses which usually lay coiled upon her temple. In short, the whole affair was a sort of prelibation of the Tournament, saving that *my* Queen of Beauty and Love was more fortunate than the Lady Seymour, in that her *coiffure* is decidedly improved by wet weather, which is more than could probably be said of her ladyship's.

At length, but after a weary while, all was done that could be done toward a general beautification; and those whose array was utterly beyond remedy, scampered up stairs with the rest, wisely resolving not to lose the fun, merely because they were not fit to be seen.

The dancing now became "fast and furious," and the spirit of the hour so completely aroused that thirst for knowledge which is slanderously charged upon my sex as a foible, that I hesitated not to slip up stairs, and take advantage of one of the various knot-holes in the oak boards which formed one side of the room, in order that a glimpse of something like the realities of the thing might aid an imagination which could never boast of being "all compact." It was but a glimpse, to be sure, for three candles can do but little toward illuminating a long room, with dark brown and very rough walls; but there was a tortuous country-dance, one side quivering and fluttering in all the colours of the rainbow, the other presenting more nearly the similitude of a funeral; for our beaux, in addition to the solemn countenances which they think proper to adopt on all occasions of festivity, have imbibed the opinion that nothing but broad-cloth is sufficiently dignified wear for a dance, be the season what it may. And there were the four Miss Liggitts, Miss Mehitable in white, Miss Polly Ann in green, Miss Lucindy in pink, and Miss Olive all over black-and-blue, saving the remains of the blonde-gauze veil, which streamed after her like a meteor, as she *galoped* "down the middle." My own Jane was playing off her most *recherchées* graces at the expense of the deputy sheriff, who seemed for once caught, instead of catching; and to my great surprise, Fanny Russell, evidently in the pouts, under cover of my fan, was enacting the part of wallflower, while Mark leaned far out of the window, at the risk of taking an abrupt leave of the company.

Peeping is tiresome. I was not sorry when the dance came to an end, as even country-dances must; and when I had waited to see the ladies arranged in a strip at one end of the room, and the gentlemen in ditto at the other, and old Knapp the fiddler testing the absorbent powers of a large red cotton handkerchief upon a brow as thickly beaded as the fair neck of any one of the nymphs around him, (and some of them had necklaces which would have satisfied a belle among our neighbors, the Pottowatomies,) I ran down stairs again, to prepare for our moonlight flitting.

Mrs. Noble now renewed her entreaties that we would at least stay for supper; and in the pride of her heart, and the energy of her hospitality, she opened her oven-door, and holding a candle that I might not fail to discern all its temptations, pointed out to me two pigs, a large wild turkey, a mammoth rice-pudding, and an endless array of pies of all sizes; and these she declared were "not a beginning" of what was intended for the "refreshment" of the company. A cup-board was next displayed, where, among custards, cakes, and "saase," or preserves, of different kinds, figured great dishes of lettuce, "all ready, only jist to pour the vinegar and molasses over it," bowls of large pickled cucumbers, and huge pyramids of dough-nuts. But we continued inexorable, and were just taking our leave, when Fanny Russell, her pretty eyes overflowing and her whole aspect evincing the greatest vexation and discomposure, came running down stairs, and begged we would let her go home with us.

"What *can* be the matter, Fanny!"

"Oh, nothing! nothing at all! But—I want to go home."

It is never of much use advising young girls, when they have made up their minds to be foolish; yet I did just call my little favourite aside, and give her a friendly caution not to expose herself to the charge of being rude or touchy. But this brought only another shower of tears, and a promise that she would tell me all about it; so we took her in and drove off.

I could not but reflect, as we went saunteringly home, enjoying the splendour of the moonlight, and the delicious balminess of that "stilly hour," how much all balls are alike. Here had been all the solicitude and sacrifice in the preparation of costume; all the effort and expense in providing the refreshments; for the champagne and ices, the oysters and the perigord pies, are no more to the pampered citizen, than are the humbler cates we have attempted to enumerate, to the plain and poor backwoodsman; then here was the belle of the evening, in as pretty a paroxysm of insulted dignity, as could have been displayed on the most classically-chalked floor; and, to crown all, judging from past experience in these regions, some of the "gentlemen" at least would, like their more refined prototypes, vindicate their claims to the title, by going home vociferously drunk. We certainly are growing very elegant.

Little Preacher from Down East

by PETER CARTWRIGHT, 1785–1872. *One of the most famous Methodist circuit riders in the Middle West, Cartwright was born in Amherst County, Virginia, and spent most of his life as an itinerant preacher in Kentucky and later in Illinois. He was widely known as an exhorter and evangelist in the Sangamon country and in 1832 defeated Abraham Lincoln in a contest for a seat in the Illinois legislature. Cartwright's experiences with camp meetings, hecklers, and preaching stations were legion. There are many graphic and amusing scenes in his Autobiography (1856).*

THERE happened to be at our quarterly meeting a fresh, green, live Yankee from down east. He had regularly graduated, and had his diploma, and was regularly called, by the Home Missionary Society, to visit the far-off west—a perfect moral waste, in his view of the subject; and having been taught to believe that we were almost cannibals, and that Methodist preachers were nothing but a poor, illiterate set of ignoramuses, he longed for an opportunity to display his superior tact and talent, and throw us poor upstarts of preachers in the west, especially Methodist preachers, into the shades of everlasting darkness. He, of course, was very forward and officious. He would, if I had permitted it, have taken the lead of our meeting. At length I thought I would give him a chance to ease himself of his mighty burden, so I put him up one night to read his sermon. The frame building we were worshiping in was not plastered, and the wind blew hard; our candles flared and gave a bad light, and our ministerial hero made a very awkward out in reading his sermon. The congregation paid a heavy penance and became restive; he balked, and hemmed, and coughed at a disgusting rate. At the end of about thirty minutes the great blessing came; he closed, to the great satisfaction of all the congregation.

I rose and gave an exhortation, and had a bench prepared, to which I invited the mourners. They came in crowds; and there was a solemn power rested on the congregation. My little hot-house reader seemed to recover from his paroxysm of a total failure, as though he had done all right, and, uninvited, he turned in to talk to the mourners. He would ask them if they did not love Christ; then he would try to show them that Christ was lovely; then he would tell them it was a very easy thing to become a Christian; that they had only to resolve to be a Christian, and instantly he or she was a Christian. I listened a moment, and saw this heterodoxy would not do; that it produced jargon and confusion. I stepped up to him and said:

"Brother, you don't know how to talk to mourners. I want you to go into the congregation, and exhort sinners."

He did not appear the least disconcerted, but at my bidding he left the altar, and out he went into the crowd, and turned in to talking to sinners. There was a very large man, who stood a few steps from the mourners, who weighed about two hundred and thirty pounds; he had been a professor, but was backslidden. The power of God arrested him, and he cried out aloud for mercy, standing on his feet. My little preacher turned round, and pressed back through the crowd; and coming up to this large man, reached up, and tapped him on the shoulder, saying,

"Be composed; be composed."

Seeing, and indistinctly hearing this, I made my way to him, and cried out at the top of my voice,

"Pray on, brother; pray on, brother; there's no composure in hell or damnation."

And just as I crowded my way to this convicted man, who was still crying aloud for mercy, the little preacher tapped him again on the shoulder, saying,

"Be composed; be composed, brother."

I again responded:

"Pray on, brother; pray on, brother; there is no composure in hell."

I said to the throng that crowded the aisle that led to the altar, "Do, friends, stand back, till I get this man to the mourners' bench."

But they were so completely jammed together that it seemed almost impossible for me to get through with my mourner. I let go his arm, and stepped forward to open the way to the altar, and just as I had opened the aisle, and turned to go back, and lead him to the mourners' bench, the Lord spoke peace to his soul, standing on his feet; and he cried, "Glory to God," and in the ecstasy of his joy, he reached forward to take me in his arms; but, fortunately for me, two men were crowded into the aisle between him and myself, and he could not reach me. Missing his aim in catching me, he wheeled round and caught my little preacher in his arms, and lifted him up from the floor; and being a large, strong man, having great physical power, he jumped from bench to bench, knocking the people against one another on the right and left, front and rear, holding up in his arms the little preacher. The little fellow stretched out both arms and both feet, expecting every moment to be his last, when he would have his neck broken. O! how I desired to be near this preacher at that moment, and tap him on the shoulder, and say, "Be composed; be composed, brother!" But as solemn as the times were, I, with many others, could not command my risibilities, and for the moment, it had like to have checked the rapid flow of good feeling with those that beheld the scene; but you may depend on it, as soon as the little hot-bed parson could make his escape, he was missing.

In the fall of 1840–41 I was appointed to Jacksonville district; and on September 15, 1841, our annual conference was held in Jacksonville [Illinois]. Bishop Morris presided. The Jacksonville district embraced the following appointments, namely: Carrollton station, Carrollton circuit, Grafton, Whitehall, Winchester, Jacksonville station, Jacksonville circuit, and Manchester, eight appointments. In the course of this year we had a camp quarterly meeting, for the Winchester circuit, in what was called Egypt. We had a beautiful camp-ground, a few miles from Winchester. There was a general turn-out among the members, who tented on the ground. William D. R. Trotter was the circuit preacher.

We had been threatened by many of the baser sort, that they would break up our camp meeting; and there was a general rally from the floating population of the river, and the loose-footed, doggery-haunting, dissipated renegades of the towns and villages all round. They came and pitched their tents a few hundred yards from the camp-ground. Many also came in wagons and carriages, bringing whisky and spirits of different kinds, pies, cigars, tobacco, etc. We had many respectable tent-holders and proper officers on the ground, but I plainly saw we were to have trouble, so I summoned the tent-holders and friends of good order together, and we adopted rules to govern the meeting, and then urged them, one and all, to aid me in executing those rules for the maintenance of good order. But I thought there was a disposition in some of the friends to shrink from responsibility, and that they must be roused to action.

When we were called to the stand by the sound of the trumpet, I called the attention of the congregation to the absolute necessity of keeping good order. I stated that my father was a Revolutionary soldier, and fought for the liberties we enjoyed, and all the boon he had left me was liberty; and that, as the responsible officer of the camp meeting, if the friends of order and the sworn officers of the law would give me backing, I would maintain order at the risk of my life. My lecture roused the friends of order, and they gave me their countenance and aid; but the whisky-sellers and whisky-drinkers, nothing daunted, commenced their deeds of darkness. Some were soon drunk, and interrupted our devotions very much. I then ordered several writs, and took into custody several of those whisky-venders and drunken rowdies;

but these rowdies rose in mob force, and rescued the whisky-seller and his wagon and team from the officer of the law. The officer came running to me, and informed me of the rising of the mob, and that the whisky man was given up, and was making his escape; and it appeared to me he was very much scared. I told him to summon me and five other men that I named, and I would insure the retaking of the transgressor, in spite of any mob. He did so. We rushed upon them and stopped the team. The man that had transgressed drew a weapon, and ordered us to stand off; that he would kill the first man that touched him; and as one of the men and myself that were summoned to take him rushed on him, he made a stroke at my companion with his weapon, but missed him. I then sprang upon him and caught him by the collar, and jerked him over the wagon bed, in which he was standing, among his barrels. He fell on all-fours. I jumped on him, and told him he was my prisoner, and that if he did not surrender I should hurt him. The deputy sheriff of the county, who was with the mob, and a combatant at that, ran up to me and ordered me to let the prisoner go. I told him I should not. He said if I did not he would knock me over. I told him if he struck to make a sure lick, for the next was mine. Our officer then commanded me to take the deputy sheriff, and I did so. He scuffled a little; but finding himself in rather close quarters, he surrendered.

We then took thirteen of the mob, the whisky-seller, and the sheriff, and marched them off to the magistrate, to the tune of good order. They were fined by the justice of the peace; some paid their fine, some appealed to court. This appealing we liked well, because they then had to give security, and this secured the fine and costs, which some of them were not able to pay.

This somewhat checked them for a while, but they rallied again and gave us trouble. There was one man, a turbulent fellow, who sold whisky about a quarter of a mile off. He had often interrupted us by selling whisky at our camp meetings. He generally went armed with deadly weapons, to keep off officers. I sent the constable after him, but he had a musket, well loaded, and would not be taken. He kept a drinking party round him nearly all night; however, toward morning they left him, and went off to sleep as best they could, and he lay down in his wagon, and went to sleep, with his loaded musket by his side.

Just as the day dawned I slipped over the creek and came up to his wagon. He was fast asleep. I reached over the wagon bed and gathered his gun and ammunition; then struck the wagon bed with the muzzle of the musket, and cried out, "Wake up! wake up!" He sprang to his feet, and felt for his gun. I said, "You are my prisoner; and if you resist, you are a dead man!" He begged me not to shoot, and said that he would surrender. I told him to get out of the wagon, and march before me to the camp-ground; that I was going to have him tried for violating good order and the laws of his country. He began to beg most piteously, and said if I would only let him escape that time, he would gear up and go right away, and never do the like again. I told him to harness his team, and start. He did so. When he got ready to go I poured out his powder, and fired off his musket and gave it to him; and he left us, and troubled us no more.

On Sunday night the rowdies all collected at the Mormon camp. It was so called, because some Mormons had come and pitched a tent a quarter of a mile from our encampment, with whisky and many other things to sell. They ate and drank; and by way of mockery, and in contempt of religion, they held a camp meeting; they preached, prayed, called for mourners, shouted, and kept up a continual annoyance. They sent me word they would give me ten dollars if I would bring an officer and a company to take them; that they could whip our whole encampment. They fixed out their watchers.

I bore it, and waited till late in the night; and when most of our tent-holders were retired to rest, I rose from my bed, dressed myself in some old shabby clothing that I had provided for the purpose, and sallied forth. It was a beautiful moonlight night. Singly and alone I went up to the Mormon camp. When I got within a few rods of their encampment I stopped, and stood in the shadow of a beautiful sugar-tree. Their motley crowd were carrying on at a mighty rate. One young man sprung upon a barrel, and called them to order, saying he was going to preach to them and must and would have order, at the risk of his life. Said he, "My name is Peter Cartwright: my father fought through the old war with England, and helped to gain our independence, and all the legacy he left me was liberty. Come to order and take your seats, and hear me!"

They obeyed him and took their seats. He then sung and prayed, rose up, took his text, and harangued them about half an hour. He then told them he was going to call for mourners, and ordered a bench to be set out; and it was done. He then invited mourners to come forward and kneel down to be prayed for. A vast number of the crowd came and kneeled, more than his bench could accommodate. This self-styled preacher, or orator of the night, then called lustily for another bench; and still they crowded to it. A thought struck me that I would go and kneel with them, as this would give me a fine chance to let loose on them at a proper time; but as I had determined to rout the whole company and take their camp single-handed and alone, I declined kneeling with the mourners. So this young champion of the devil called on several to pray for these mourners; he exhorted them almost like a real preacher. Several pretended to get religion, and jumped and shouted at a fearful rate. Their preacher by this time was pretty much exhausted, and became thirsty. He ordered a pause in their exercise, and called for something to drink; he ordered the tent-holder to bring the best he had.

Just at this moment I fetched two or three loud whoops, and said, "Here! here! here, officers and men, take them! take them! every one of them, tent-holders and all!" and I rushed on them. They broke, and ran pell-mell. Fortunately, five or six little lads were close by, from our encampment, who had been watching me raise the shout, and rushed with me into their camp; but all the motley crowd fled, tent-holders and all, and the lads and myself had not only peaceable, but entire possession of all their whisky, goods, chattels, and some arms, and not a soul to dispute our right of possession. Thus you see a literal fulfillment of Scripture, "The wicked fleeth when no man pursueth"; or, "One shall chase a thousand, and two put ten thousand to flight."

The Standing Candidate

by JOHN S. ROBB,   ?   . *Little is known about Robb's life. For some years he was a practicing journalist in St. Louis and later he went to California. Under the pseudonym of Solitaire he contributed sketches and articles to the St. Louis Weekly Reveille. These and other items were afterwards collected in such books as* Streaks of Squatter Life, *and* Far West Scenes (1846). "The Standing Candidate" *is reprinted from this volume.*

At Buffalo Head, Nianga county, state of Missouri, during the canvass of 1844, there was held an extensive political *Barbecue*, and the several candidates for congress, legislature, county offices, &c., were all congregated at this southern point for the purpose of making an *immense* demonstration. Hards, softs, whigs and Tylerites were represented, and to hear their several expositions of state and general policy, a vast gathering of the Missouri sovereigns had also assembled. While the impatient candidates were awaiting the signal to mount the "stump," an odd-looking old man made his appearance at the brow of a small hill bounding the place of meeting.

"Hurrah for old *Sugar!*" shouted an hundred voices, while on, steadily, progressed the object of the cheer.

Sugar, as he was familiarly styled, was an old man, apparently about fifty years of age, and was clad in a coarse suit of brown linsey-woolsey. His pants were patched at each knee, and around the ankles they had worn off into picturesque points—his coat was not of the modern close-fitting cut, but hung in loose and easy folds upon his broad shoulders, while the total absence of buttons upon this garment, exhibited the owner's contempt for the storm and the tempest. A coarse shirt, tied at the neck with a piece of twine, completed his body covering. His head was ornamented with an old woollen cap, of divers colors, below which beamed a broad, humorous countenance, flanked by a pair of short, funny little grey whiskers. A few wrinkles marked his brow, but time could not count them as sure chronicles of his progress, for *Sugar's* hearty, sonorous laugh oft drove them from their hiding place. Across his shoulder was thrown a sack, in each end of which he was bearing to the scene of political action, a keg of *bran new whiskey*, of his own manufacture, and he strode forward on his moccasin covered feet, encumbered as he was, with all the agility of youth. *Sugar* had long been the *standing candidate* of Nianga county, for the legislature, and founded his claim to the office upon the fact of his being the first "squatter" in that county—his having killed the first *bar* there, ever killed by a white man, and, to place his right beyond cavil, he had *'stilled* the first keg of whiskey! These were strong claims, which urged in his comic rhyming manner would have swept the "diggins," but *Sugar*, when the canvass opened, always yielded his claim to some liberal purchaser of his *fluid*, and duly announced himself a candidate for the *next* term.

"Here you air, old fellar!" shouted an acquaintance, "allays on hand 'bout 'lection."

"Well, Nat," said *Sugar*, "you've jest told the truth as easy as ef you'd taken sum of my mixtur—

> 'Whar politicians congregate,
> I'm allays thar, at any rate!' "

"Set him up!—set the old fellar up somewhar, and let us take a univarsal liquor!" was the general shout.

"Hold on, boys,—keep cool and shady," said old *Sugar*, "whar's the candidates?—none of your splurgin round till I git an appropriation fur the sperits. Send em along and we'll negotiate fur the *fluid*, arter which I shall gin 'em my instructions, and they may then *per*cede to

> 'Talk away like all cre-*a*-tion,
> What they knows about the nation.' "

The candidates were accordingly summoned up to pay for *Sugar's* portable grocery, and to please the crowd and gain the good opinion of the owner, they made up a purse and gathered round him. *Sugar* had placed his two kegs upon a broad stump and seated himself astride of them, with a small tin cup in his hand and a paper containing brown sugar lying before him—each of his kegs was furnished with a *spiggot*, and as soon as the money for the whole contents was paid in, *Sugar* commenced addressing the crowd as follows:

"Boys, fellars, and candidates," said he, "I, *Sugar*, am the furst white man ever seed in these yeur diggins—I killed the furst *bar* ever a white skinned in this county, and I kalkilate I hev hurt the feelings of his relations sum sence, as the *bar-skin* linin' of my cabin will testify;—'sides that, I'm the furst manufacturer of whiskey in the range of this district, and powerful mixtur' it is, too, as the hull bilin' of fellars in this crowd will declar';—more'n that, I'm a candidate for the legislatur', and intend to gin up my claim, *this* term, to the fellar who kin talk the *pootyest;*—now, finally at the eend, boys, this mixtur' of mine will make a fellar talk as iley as goose-grease,—as sharp as lightnin', and as *per*suadin' as a young gal at a quiltin', so don't spar it while it lasts, and the candidates kin drink furst, 'cause they've got to do the talkin'!"

Having finished his charge he filled the tin cup full of whiskey, put in a handful of brown sugar, and with his forefinger stirred up the sweetening, then surveying the candidates he pulled off his cap, remarking, as he did so:

"Old age, allays, afore beauty!—your daddy furst, in course," then holding up the cup he offered a toast, as follows:

"Here is to the string that binds the states; may it never be bit apart by political *rats!*" Then holding up the cup to his head he took a hearty swig, and passed it to the next oldest looking candidate. While they were tasting it, *Sugar* kept up a fire of lingo at them:

"Pass it along lively, gentle*men*, but don't spar the *fluid*. You can't help tellin' truth arter you've swaller'd enough of my mixtur', jest fur this reason, it's been 'stilled in honesty, rectified in truth, and poured out with wisdom! Take a *leetle* drop more," said he to a fastidious candidate, whose stomach turned at thought of the way the "mixtur' " was mixed. "Why, Mister," said *Sugar*, coaxingly,

> " 'Ef you wur a babby, jest new born,
> 'Twould do you good, this juicy *corn!* "

"No more, I thank you," said the candidate, drawing back from the proffer.

Sugar winked his eye at some of his cronies, and muttered—"He's got an *a*-ristocracy stomach, and can't go the *native licker.*" Then dismissing the candidates he shouted,—"crowd up, constitoo*ents*, into a circle, and let's begin fair—your daddy furst, allays; and mind, no

changin' places in the circle to git the sugar in the bottom of the cup.
I know you're arter it, Tom Williams, but none on your yankeein'
round to git the sweetnin'—it's all syrup, fellars, cause *Sugar* made and
mixed it. The gals at the frolicks allays git me to prepar' the cordials,
'cause they say I make it mity drinkable. Who next? What *you*, old
Ben Dent!—Well, hold your hoss for a minit, and I'll strengthen the
tin with a speck more, jest because you can kalkilate the valee of the
licker, and do it jestiss!"

Thus chatted *Sugar* as he measured out and sweetened up the contents of his kegs, until all who would drink had taken their share, and
then the crowd assembled around the speakers. We need not say that
the virtues of each political party were duly set forth to the hearers—
that follows as a matter of course, candidates dwell upon the strong
points of their argument, always. One among them, however, more
than his compeers, attracted the attention of our friend *Sugar*, not because he had highly commended the contents of his kegs, but because
he painted with truth and feeling the claims of the western *pioneers!*
Among these he ranked the veteran Col. Johnson and his compatriots,
and as he rehearsed their struggles in defence of their firesides, how
they had been trained to war by conflict with the ruthless savage, their
homes oft desolated, and their children murdered,—yet still, ever foremost in the fight, and last to retreat, winning the heritage of these
broad valleys for their children, against the opposing arm of the red
man, though aided by the civilized power of mighty Britain, and her
serried cohorts of trained soldiery! We say as he dwelt upon these
themes *Sugar's* eye would fire up, and then, at some touching passage
of distress dwelt upon by the speaker, tears would course down his
rude cheek. When the speaker concluded he wiped his eyes with his
hard hand, and said to those around him:—

"That arr true as the yearth!—thar's suthing' like talk in that fellar!
—he's the right breed, and his old daddy has told him about them
times. So did mine relate 'em to me, how the ony sister I ever had,
when a babby had her brains dashed out by one of the red skinned
devils! But didn't we pepper them fur it? Didn't I help the old man,
afore he grew too weak to hold his shootin' iron, to send a few on 'em
off to rub out the account? Well, I *did!—Hey!*" and shutting his teeth
together he yelled through them the exultation of full vengeance.

The speaking being done, candidates and hearers gathered around
old *Sugar*, to hear his comments upon the speeches, and to many inquiries of how he liked them, the old man answered:—

"They were all pooty good, but that tall fellar they call Tom, from
St. Louis; *you*, I mean, *stranger*," pointing at the same time to the candidate, "you jest scart up my feelin's to the right pint—you jest made

173

me feel wolfish as when I and old dad war arter the red varmints; and now what'll *you* take? I'm goin' to publicly decline in your favor."

Pouring out a tin full of the liquor, and stirring it as before, he stood upright upon the stump, with a foot on each side of his kegs, and drawing off his cap, toasted:—

"The memory of the western *pioneers!*"

A shout responded to his toast, which echoed far away in the depths of the adjoining forest, and seemed to awaken a response from the spirits of those departed heroes.

"That's the way to sing it out, boys," responded old *Sugar*, "sich a yell as that would *scar* an inimy into ager fits, and make the United States Eagle scream 'Hail Columby.' "

"While you're up, *Sugar*," said one of the crowd, "give us a stump speech, yourself."

"Bravo!" shouted an hundred voices, "a speech from *Sugar*."

"Agreed, boys," said the old man, "I'll jest gin you a few words to wind up with, so keep quiet while your daddy's talkin'

'Sum tell it out jest like a song,
I'll gin it to you sweet and strong.'

"The ony objection ever made to me in this arr county, as a legislatur', was made by the *wimin*, 'cause I war a *bachelor*, and I never told you afore why I *re*-mained in the state of number one—no fellar stays single *pre*-meditated, and, in course, a hansum fellar like me, who all the gals declar' to be as enticin' as a jay bird, warn't goin' to stay alone, ef he could help it. I did see a creatur' once, named *Sofy Mason*, up the Cumberland, nigh onto Nashville, Tenne*see*, that I tuk an orful hankerin' arter, and I sot in to lookin' anxious fur matrimony, and gin to go reglar to meetin', and tuk to dressin' tremengeous finified, jest to see ef I could win her good opinion. She did git to lookin' at me, and one day, cumin' from meetin', she was takin' a look at me a kind of shy, jest as a hoss does at suthin' he's scart at, when arter champin' at a distance fur awhile, I sidled up to her and blarted out a few words about the sarmin'—she said yes, but cuss me ef I know whether that wur the right answer or not, and I'm a thinkin' she didn't know then, nuther! Well, we larfed and talked a leetle all the way along to her daddy's, and thar I gin her the best bend I had in me, and raised my bran new hat as peert and *per*lite as a minister, lookin' all the time so enticin' that I sot the gal tremblin'. Her old daddy had a powerful numerous lot of healthy niggers, and lived right adjinin' my place, while on tother side lived Jake Simons—a sneakin', cute varmint, who war wusser than a miser fur stinginess, and no sooner did this cussed sarpint see me sidlin'

174

up to Sofy, than he went to slickin' up, too, and sot himself to work to cut me out. That arr wur a struggle ekill to the battle of Orleans. Furst sum new fixup of Jake's would take her eye, and then I'd sport suthin' that would outshine him, until Jake at last gin in tryin' to outdress me, and sot to thinkin' of suthin' else. Our farms wur jest the same number of acres, and we both owned three niggers apiece. Jake knew that Sofy and her dad kept a sharp eye out fur the main chance, so he thort he'd clar me out by buyin' another nigger; but I jest follor'd suit, and bought one the day arter he got his, so he had no advantage thar; he then got a *cow*, and so did I, and jest about then both on our *pusses* gin out. This put Jake to his wits' eend, and I war a wunderin' what in the yearth he would try next. We stood so, hip and thigh, fur about two weeks, both on us talkin' sweet to Sofy, whenever we could git her alone. I thort I seed that Jake, the sneakin' cuss, wur gittin' a mite ahead of me, 'cause his tongue wur so iley; howsever, I didn't let on, but kep a top eye on him. One Sunday mornin' I wur a leetle mite late to meetin', and when I got thar the furst thing I seed war Jake Simons, sittin' close bang up agin Sofy, in the same pew with her daddy! I biled a spell with wrath, and then tarned sour; I could taste myself! Thar they wur, singin' *himes* out of the same book. Je-e-eminy, fellars, I war so *enormous* mad that the new silk handercher round my neck lost its color! Arter meetin' out they walked, linked arms, a smilin' and lookin' as pleased as a young couple at thar furst christenin', and Sofy tarned her 'cold shoulder' at me so orful pinted, that I wilted down, and gin up right straight—Jake had her, thar wur no disputin' it! I headed to-ward home, with my hands as fur in my trowsers pockets as I could push 'em, swarin' all the way that she wur the last one would ever git a chance to rile up my feelin's. Passin' by Jake's plantation I looked over the fence, and thar stood an explanation of the marter, right facin' the road, whar every one passin' could see it—his consarned *cow* was tied to a stake in the gardin', *with a most promisin' calf alongside of her!* That *calf* jest soured my milk, and made Sofy think, that a fellar who war allays gittin' ahead like Jake, wur a right smart chance for a lively husband!"

A shout of laughter here drowned *Sugar's* voice, and as soon as si-lence was restored he added, in a solemn tone, with one eye shut, and his forefinger pointing at his auditory:—

"What is a cussed sight wusser than his gittin' Sofy war the fact, that he *borrowed that calf the night before from Dick Harkley!* Arter the varmint got Sofy hitched, he told the joke all over the settle*ment,* and the boys never seed me arterwards that they didn't *b-a-h* at me fur lettin' a *calf* cut me out of a gal's affections. I'd a shot Jake, but I thort it was a free country, and the gal had a right to her choice without bein' made a widder, so I jest sold out and travelled! I've allays thort sence then, boys, that *wimin* wur a good deal like *licker*, ef you love 'em too hard thar sure to throw you some way:

> 'Then here's to *wimin*, then to *licker*,
> Thar's nuthin' swimmin' can be slicker!' "

Spelling Down the Master

by EDWARD EGGLESTON, 1837–1902. *Eggleston was the first of a long series of realistic middlewestern novelists and one of the first American writers to use dialect extensively in fiction. Born in Vevay, Indiana, he was a frail child who had to battle continually against ill health. His earliest ambition was to enter the church and he was for some years a Methodist minister and circuit rider, in southeastern Indiana in 1856 and on the Minnesota frontier from 1857 to 1866. After resigning his pulpit in Winona, Minnesota, he became associated with the Little Corporal, a juvenile magazine published at Evanston, Illinois. Gradually he withdrew from church work, although he later occupied a Brooklyn pastorate from 1874 to 1879, and devoted his attention to the writing of fiction and history. Among his many books are seven novels: The Hoosier Schoolmaster (1871), based not upon his own experiences but upon those of his brother George Cary Eggleston, who actually had been a rural pedagogue in Indiana, The End of the World (1872), The Mystery of Metropolisville (1873), The Circuit Rider (1874), Roxy (1878), The Graysons (1888), and The Faith Doctor (1891). Eggleston's earlier novels are heavily moralistic and are filled with caricatures rather than characters but they are valuable genre pictures of primitive middlewestern society; later books like Roxy and The Faith Doctor show a remarkable improvement in plot construction and characterization. His faithful recording of speech, manners, and attitudes made his subsequent devotion to history almost inevitable. "Spelling Down the Master" is the fourth chapter of The Hoosier Schoolmaster.*

I 'LOW," said Mrs. Means, as she stuffed the tobacco into her cob pipe after supper on that eventful Wednesday evening, "I 'low they'll appint the Squire to gin out the words to-night. They mos' always do, you see, kase he's the peartest *ole* man in this deestrick; and I 'low some of the young fellers would have to git up and dust ef they would keep up to him. And he uses sech remarkable smart words. He speaks so polite, too. But laws! don't I remember when he was poarer nor Job's turkey? Twenty year ago, when he come to these 'ere diggins, that air Squire Hawkins was a poar Yankee school-master, that said 'pail' instid of bucket, and that called a cow a 'caow,' and that couldn't tell to save his gizzard what we meant by *'low* and by *right smart*. But he's larnt our ways now, an' he's jest as civilized as the rest of us. You would-n know he'd ever been a Yankee. He didn't stay poar long. Not he. He jest married a right rich girl! He! he!" And the old woman grinned at Ralph, and then at Mirandy, and then at the rest, until Ralph shuddered. Nothing was so frightful to him as to be fawned on and grinned at by this old ogre, whose few lonesome, blackish teeth seemed ready to devour him. "He didn't stay poar, you bet a hoss!" and with this the coal was deposited on the pipe, and the lips began to crack like parchment as each puff of smoke escaped. "He married rich, you see," and here another significant look at the young master, and another fond look at Mirandy, as she puffed away reflectively. "His wife hadn't no book-larnin'. She'd been through the spellin'-book wunst, and had got as fur as 'asperity' on it a second time. But she couldn't read a word when she was married, and never could. She warn't overly smart. She hadn't hardly got the sense the law allows. But schools was skase in them air days, and, besides, book-larnin' don't do no good to a woman. Makes her stuck up. I never knowed but one gal in my life as had ciphered into fractions, and she was so dog-on stuck up that she turned up her nose one night at a apple-peelin' bekase I tuck a sheet off the bed to splice out the table-cloth, which was ruther short. And the sheet was mos' clean too. Had-n been slep on more'n wunst or twicet. But I was goin' fer to say that when Squire Hawkins married Virginny Gray he got a heap o' money, or, what's the same thing mostly, a heap o' good land. And that's better'n book-larnin', says I. Ef a gal had gone clean through all eddication, and got to the rule of three itself, that would-n buy a feather-bed. Squire Hawkins jest put eddication agin the gal's farm, and traded even, an' ef ary one of 'em got swindled, I never heerd no complaints."

And here she looked at Ralph in triumph, her hard face splintering into the hideous semblance of a smile. And Mirandy cast a blushing, gushing, all-imploring, and all-confiding look on the young master.

"I say, ole woman," broke in old Jack, "I say, wot is all this 'ere spoutin' about the Square fer?" and old Jack, having bit off an ounce of "pigtail," returned the plug to his pocket.

As for Ralph, he wanted to die. He had a guilty feeling that this speech of the old lady's had somehow committed him beyond recall to Mirandy. He did not see visions of breach-of-promise suits. But he trembled at the thought of an avenging big brother.

"Hanner, you kin come along, too, ef you're a mind, when you git the dishes washed," said Mrs. Means to the bound girl, as she shut and latched the back door. The Means family had built a new house in front of the old one, as a sort of advertisement of bettered circumstances, an eruption of shoddy feeling; but when the new building was completed, they found themselves unable to occupy it for anything else than a lumber room, and so, except a parlor which Mirandy had made an effort to furnish a little (in hope of the blissful time when somebody should "set up" with her of evenings), the new building was almost unoccupied, and the family went in and out through the back door, which, indeed, was the front door also, for, according to a curious custom, the "front" of the house was placed toward the south, though the "big road" (Hoosier for *highway*) ran along the northwest side, or, rather, past the north-west corner of it.

When the old woman had spoken thus to Hannah and had latched the door, she muttered, "That gal don't never show no gratitude fer favors"; to which Bud rejoined that he didn't think she had no great sight to be pertickler thankful for. To which Mrs. Means made no reply, thinking it best, perhaps, not to wake up her dutiful son on so interesting a theme as her treatment of Hannah. Ralph felt glad that he was this evening to go to another boarding place. He should not hear the rest of the controversy.

Ralph walked to the school-house with Bill. They were friends again. For when Hank Banta's ducking and his dogged obstinacy in sitting in his wet clothes had brought on a serious fever, Ralph had called together the big boys, and had said: "We must take care of one another, boys. Who will volunteer to take turns sitting up with Henry?" He put his own name down, and all the rest followed.

"William Means and myself will sit up to-night," said Ralph. And poor Bill had been from that moment the teacher's friend. He was chosen to be Ralph's companion. He was Puppy Means no longer! Hank could not be conquered by kindness, and the teacher was made to feel the bitterness of his resentment long after. . . . But Bill Means was for the time entirely placated, and he and Ralph went to spelling-school together.

Every family furnished a candle. There were yellow dips and white dips, burning, smoking, and flaring. There was laughing, and talking, and giggling, and simpering, and ogling, and flirting, and courting. What a dress party is to Fifth Avenue, a spelling-school is to Hoopole County [Indiana]. It is an occasion which is metaphorically inscribed with this legend: "Choose your partners." Spelling is only a blind in Hoopole County, as is dancing on Fifth Avenue. But as there are some in society who love dancing for its own sake, so in Flat Creek district there were those who loved spelling for its own sake, and who, smelling the battle from afar, had come to try their skill in this tournament, hoping to freshen the laurels they had won in their school-days.

"I 'low," said Mr. Means, speaking as the principal school trustee, "I 'low our friend the Square is jest the man to boss this 'ere consarn to-night. Ef nobody objects, I'll app'int him. Come, Square, don't be bashful. Walk up to the trough, fodder or no fodder, as the man said to his donkey."

There was a general giggle at this, and many of the young swains took occasion to nudge the girls alongside them, ostensibly for the purpose of making them see the joke, but really for the pure pleasure of nudging. The Greeks figured Cupid as naked, probably because he wears so many disguises that they could not select a costume for him.

The Squire came to the front. Ralph made an inventory of the agglomeration which bore the name of Squire Hawkins, as follows:

1. A swallow-tail coat of indefinite age, worn only on state occasions, when its owner was called to figure in his public capacity. Either the Squire had grown too large or the coat too small.

2. A pair of black gloves, the most phenomenal, abnormal, and unexpected apparition conceivable in Flat Creek district, where the preachers wore no coats in the summer, and where a black glove was never seen except on the hands of the Squire.

3. A wig of that dirty, waxen color so common to wigs. This one showed a continual inclination to slip off the owner's smooth, bald pate, and the Squire had frequently to adjust it. As his hair had been red, the wig did not accord with his face, and the hair ungrayed was doubly discordant with a countenance shrivelled by age.

4. A semicircular row of whiskers hedging the edge of the jaw and chin. These were dyed a frightful dead-black, such a color as belonged to no natural hair or beard that ever existed. At the roots there was a quarter of an inch of white, giving the whiskers the appearance of having been stuck on.

5. A pair of spectacles with tortoise-shell rim. Wont to slip off.

6. A glass eye, purchased of a peddler, and differing in color from its natural mate, perpetually getting out of focus by turning in or out.

7. A set of false teeth, badly fitted, and given to bobbing up and down.

8. The Squire proper, to whom these patches were loosely attached.

It is an old story that a boy wrote home to his father begging him to come West, because "mighty mean men get into office out here." But Ralph concluded that some Yankees had taught school in Hoopole County who would not have held a high place in the educational institutions of Massachusetts. Hawkins had some New England idioms, but they were well overlaid by a Western pronunciation.

"Ladies and gentlemen," he began, shoving up his spectacles and sucking his lips over his white teeth to keep them in place, "ladies and gentlemen, young men and maidens, raley I'm obleeged to Mr. Means fer this honor"; and the Squire took both hands and turned the top of his head round half an inch. Then he adjusted his spectacles. Whether he was obliged to Mr. Means for the honor of being compared to a donkey was not clear. "I feel in the inmost compartments of my animal spirits a most happifying sense of the success and futility of all my endeavors to sarve the people of Flat Creek deestrick and the people of Tomkins township, in my weak way and manner." This burst of eloquence was delivered with a constrained air and an apparent sense of a danger that he, Squire Hawkins, might fall to pieces in his weak way and manner. . . . For by this time the ghastly pupil of the left eye, which was black, was looking away round to the left, while the little blue one on the right twinkled cheerfully toward the front. The front teeth would drop down so that the Squire's mouth was kept nearly closed, and his words whistled through.

"I feel as if I could be grandiloquent on this interesting occasion," twisting his scalp round, "but raley I must forego any such exertions. It is spelling you want. Spelling is the corner-stone, the grand, underlying subterfuge, of a good eddication. I put the spellin'-book prepared by the great Daniel Webster alongside the Bible. I do, raley. I think I may put it ahead of the Bible. For if it wurn't for spellin'-books and sich occasions as these, where would the Bible be? I should like to know. The man who got up, who compounded this work of inextricable valoo was a benufactor to the whole human race or any other." Here the spectacles fell off. The Squire replaced them in some confusion, gave the top of his head another twist, and felt of his glass eye, while poor Shocky stared in wonder, and Betsey Short rolled from side to side in the effort to suppress her giggle. Mrs. Means and the other old ladies looked the applause they could not speak.

"I app'int Larkin Lanham and Jeems Buchanan fer captings," said the Squire. And the two young men thus named took a stick and tossed it from hand to hand to decide which should have the "first choice." One tossed the stick to the other, who held it fast just where he happened to catch it. Then the first placed his hand above the second, and [thus] the hands were alternately changed to the top. The one who held the stick last without room for the other to take hold had gained the lot. This was tried three times. As Larkin held the stick twice out of three times, he had the choice. He hesitated a moment. Everybody

180

looked toward tall Jim Phillips. But Larkin was fond of a venture on unknown seas and so he said, "I take the master," while a buzz of surprise ran round the room and the captain of the other side, as if afraid his opponent would withdraw the choice, retorted quickly, and with a little smack of exultation and defiance in his voice, "And *I* take Jeems Phillips."

And soon all present, except a few of the old folks, found themselves ranged in opposing hosts, the poor spellers lagging in, with what grace they could, at the foot of the two divisions. The Squire opened his spelling-book and began to give out the words to the two captains, who stood up and spelled against each other. It was not long till Larkin spelled "really" with one *l*, and had to sit down in confusion, while a murmur of satisfaction ran through the ranks of the opposing forces. His own side bit their lips. The slender figure of the young teacher took the place of the fallen leader, and the excitement made the house very quiet. Ralph dreaded the loss of prestige he would suffer if he should be easily spelled down. [Therefore he] listened carefully to the words which the Squire did not pronounce very distinctly, spelling them with extreme deliberation. This gave him an air of hesitation which disappointed those on his own side. They wanted him to spell with a dashing assurance. But he did not begin a word until he had mentally felt his way through it. After ten minutes of spelling hard words Jeems Buchanan, the captain on the other side, spelled "atrocious" with an *s* instead of a *c*, and subsided, his first choice, Jeems Phillips, coming up against the teacher. This brought the excitement to fever-heat. For though Ralph was chosen first, it was entirely on trust, and most of the company were disappointed. The champion who now stood up against the school-master was a famous speller.

Jim Phillips was a tall, lank, stoop-shouldered fellow who had never distinguished himself in any other pursuit than spelling. Except in this one art of spelling he was of no account. He could not catch well or bat well in ball. He could not throw well enough to make his mark in that famous Western game of bull-pen. He did not succeed well in any study but that of Webster's Elementary. But in that he was—to use the usual Flat Creek locution—in that he was "a hoss." This genius for spelling is in some people a sixth sense, a matter of intuition. Some spellers are born, and not made, and their facility reminds one of the mathematical prodigies that crop out every now and then to bewilder the world. Bud Means, foreseeing that Ralph would be pitted against Jim Phillips, had warned his friend that Jim could "spell like thunder and lightning," and that it "took a powerful smart speller" to beat him, for he knew "a heap of spelling-book." To have "spelled down the master" is next thing to having whipped the biggest bully in Hoopole County, and Jim had "spelled down" the last three masters. He divided the hero-worship of the district with Bud Means.

For half an hour the Squire gave out hard words. What a blessed thing our crooked orthography is! Without it there could be no spelling-schools. As Ralph discovered his opponent's mettle he became more and more cautious. He was now satisfied that Jim would eventually beat him. The fellow evidently knew more about the spelling-book than old Noah Webster himself. As he stood there, with his dull face and long sharp nose, his hands behind his back, and his voice spelling infallibly, it seemed to Hartsook that his superiority must lie in his nose. Ralph's cautiousness answered a double purpose: it enabled him to tread surely, and it was mistaken by Jim for weakness. Phillips was now confident that he should carry off the scalp of the fourth school-master before the evening was over. He spelled eagerly, confidently, brilliantly. Stoop-shouldered as he was, he began to straighten up. In the minds of all the company the odds were in his favor. He saw this, and became ambitious to distinguish himself by spelling without giving the matter any thought.

Ralph always believed that he would have been speedily defeated by Phillips had it not been for two thoughts which braced him. The sinister shadow of young Dr. Small sitting in the dark corner by the water-bucket nerved him. A victory over Phillips was a defeat to one who wished only ill to the young school-master. The other thought that kept his pluck alive was the recollection of Bull. He approached a word as Bull approached the raccoon. He did not take hold until he was sure of his game. When he took hold, it was with a quiet assurance of success. As Ralph spelled in this dogged way for half an hour the hardest words the Squire could find, the excitement steadily rose in all parts of the house, and Ralph's friends even ventured to whisper that "maybe Jim had cotched his match, after all!"

But Phillips never doubted of his success.

"Theodolite," said the Squire.

"T-h-e, the, o-d, od, theod, o, theodo, l-y-t-e, theodolite," spelled the champion.

"Next," said the Squire, nearly losing his teeth in his excitement. Ralph spelled the word slowly and correctly, and the conquered champion sat down in confusion. The excitement was so great for some minutes that the spelling was suspended. Everybody in the house had shown sympathy with one or the other of the combatants, except the silent shadow in the corner. It had not moved during the contest, and did not show any interest now in the result.

"Gewhilliky crickets! Thunder and lightning! Licked him all to smash!" said Bud, rubbing his hands on his knees. "That beats my time all holler!"

And Betsey Short giggled until her tuck-comb fell out, though she was on the defeated side.

Shocky got up and danced with pleasure.

But one suffocating look from the aqueous eyes of Mirandy destroyed the last spark of Ralph's pleasure in his triumph, and sent that awful below-zero feeling all through him.

"He's powerful smart, is the master," said old Jack to Mr. Pete Jones. "He'll beat the whole kit and tuck of 'em afore he's through. I know'd he was smart. That's the reason I tuck him," proceeded Mr. Means.

"Yaas, but he don't lick enough. Not nigh," answered Pete Jones. "No lickin', no larnin', says I."

It was now not so hard. The other spellers on the opposite side went down quickly under the hard words which the Squire gave out. The master had mowed down all but a few, his opponents had given up the battle, and all had lost their keen interest in a contest to which there could be but one conclusion, for there were only the poor spellers left. But Ralph Hartsook ran against a stump where he was least expecting it. It was the Squire's custom, when one of the smaller scholars or poorer spellers rose to spell against the master, to give out eight or ten easy words, that they might have some breathing-spell before being slaughtered, and then to give a poser or two which soon settled them. He let them run a little, as a cat does a doomed mouse. There was now but one person left on the opposite side, and, as she rose in her blue calico dress, Ralph recognized Hannah, the bound girl at old Jack Means's. She had not attended school in the district, and had never spelled in spelling-school before, and was chosen last as an uncertain quantity. The Squire began with easy words of two syllables, from that page of Webster, so well known to all who ever thumbed it, as "baker," from the word that stands at the top of the page. She spelled these words in an absent and uninterested manner. As everybody knew that she would have to go down as soon as this preliminary skirmishing was over, everybody began to get ready to go home, and already there was the buzz of preparation. Young men were timidly asking girls if "they could see them safe home," which was the approved formula, and were trembling in mortal fear of "the mitten." Presently the Squire, thinking it time to close the contest, pulled his scalp forward, adjusted his glass eye, which had been examining his nose long enough, and turned over the leaves of the book to the great words at the place known to spellers as "incomprehensibility," and began to give out those "words of eight syllables with the accent on the sixth." Listless scholars now turned round, and ceased to whisper, in order to be in at the master's final triumph. But to their surprise "ole Miss Meanses' white nigger," as some of them called her in allusion to her slavish life, spelled these great words with as perfect ease as the master. Still not doubting the result, the Squire turned from place to place and selected all the hard words he could find. The school became utterly quiet; the excitement was too great for the ordinary buzz. Would "Meanses' Hanner" beat the master? Beat the master that had laid out Jim Phillips? Everybody's sympathy was now turned to Hannah. Ralph noticed that even Shocky had deserted him, and that his face grew brilliant every time Hannah spelled a word. In fact, Ralph deserted himself. As he saw the fine, timid face of the girl so long oppressed flush and shine with interest, as he looked at the rather low but broad and intelligent brow and the fresh, white complexion and saw the rich, womanly nature coming to the surface under the influence of applause and sympathy—he did not want to beat. If he had not felt that a victory given would insult her, he would have missed intentionally. The bulldog, the stern, relentless setting of the will, had gone, he knew not whither. And there had come in its place, as he looked in that face, a something which he did not understand. . . .

The Squire was puzzled. He had given out all the hard words in the book. He again pulled the top of his head forward. Then he wiped his spectacles and put them on. Then out of the depths of his pocket he fished up a list of words just coming into use in those days—words not in the spelling-book. He regarded the paper attentively with his blue right eye. His black left eye meanwhile fixed itself in such a stare on Mirandy Means that she shuddered and hid her eyes in her red silk handkerchief.

"Daguerreotype?" sniffed the Squire. It was Ralph's turn.

"D-a-u, dau—"

"Next."

And Hannah spelled it right.

Such a buzz followed that Betsey Short's giggle could not be heard, but Shocky shouted: "Hanner beat! my Hanner spelled down the master!" And Ralph went over and congratulated her. . . .

And then the Squire called them to order, and said: "As our friend Hanner Thomson is the only one left on her side, she will have to spell against nearly all on t'other side. I shall therefore take the liberty of procrastinating the completion of this interesting and exacting contest until to-morrow evening. I hope our friend Hanner may again carry off the cypress crown of glory. There is nothing better for us than healthful and kindly simulation."

184

Zury Chooses a Wife

by JOSEPH KIRKLAND, 1830–94. *Kirkland came naturally by his gift of depicting pioneer social life since his mother, Mrs. Caroline Kirkland, was one of the early realistic writers about the middlewestern frontier. Born in Geneva, New York, Kirkland spent his boyhood on the Michigan frontier and his life after 1856 in Chicago and Illinois. He served three years in the Civil War, then entered the coal business at Tilton, Illinois. The Chicago fire of 1871 brought commercial disaster, and Kirkland was consecutively thereafter an employee of the Internal Revenue Service, a lawyer, and a journalist. The closing years of his life were years of busy writing during which he produced many articles and sketches published in various periodicals, a play, and three novels: Zury: The Meanest Man in Spring County (1887), The McVeys (1888), and The Captain of Company K (1891). Kirkland was at his best in describing the rural life of the mid-century. His characterization of Zury, the parsimonious, aggressive, illiterate but shrewd farmer, who is feared but also respected, is unforgettable.*

THE top of the heap was his [Zury's] accustomed place, but still he perceived that he was living under one useless disability, and, with his quick adaptation of means to ends and remedies to deficiencies, he simply—married. In doing this, he was guided by his father's shrewd words; counsel which had lain fallow in his memory for years.

Zury's marriageability had, of course, not been unobserved in the household of the three daughters. Peddicomb had remarked what a good "outin'" the Prouders had made in their purchase of swine from him, and cherished the same kind of feeling toward them that most of us experience when some other person has done better in a joint transaction than we did.

"Them Praouders, the' 'll skin outer the land all the' kin skin, 'n' then sell offen the place all 't anybody 'll buy, 'n' then feed t' the hawgs all a hawg 'll eat, 'n' then give th' rest t' th' dawg, 'n' then what th' dawg won't tech the' 'll live on theirselves."

"Yew bet," tittered Semantha, the second. "That thar ornery Zury Praouder he'd let a woman starve t' death ef he could. 'N' o' man Praouder wuz th' same way, tew. Th' o' woman she wuz near abaout skin 'n' bone when the' buried her. I seen her in her coffin, 'n' I know."

"Oh, don't *yew* be scaret, S'manthy. I hain't saw Zury a-lookin' over t' your side o' the meetin'-haouse, no gre't," kindly rejoined Flora, the youngest daughter.

"Who, me? He knows better! Not ef husbands wuz scarcer ner hen's teeth."

"Six hunderd 'n' forty acres o' good land, all fenced 'n' paid fer; 'n' a big orchard; 'n' all well stocked, tew." (He added this with a pang, remembering once more the pig-purchase, which by this time had grown to a mighty drove, spite of many sales.)

"Don't care ef he owned all ou' doors. Th' more the' 've got, th' more it shows haow stingy the' be."

Then the meek Mary ventured a remark.

"Mebbe ef Zury wuz t' marry a good gal it 'd be the makin' on him."

"Oh, Mary, *yew* hain't no call t' stan' up fer Zury! Th' o' man he 'd a ben more in yewr line."

"No, Zury would n't want *me*, ner no other man, I don't expect," she answered with a laugh—and a sigh.

One Sunday afternoon Zury rode over to Peddicomb's to get a wife. He tried to decide which girl to ask, but his mind would wander off to other subjects,—crops, live stock, bargains, investments. He did n't much think that either girl he asked would say no, but if she did, he could ask the others. When he came near the house he caught sight of one of the girls, in her Sunday clothes, picking a "posy" in the "front garding." It was Mary.

"Good day, Mary. Haow 's all the folks?"

"Good day, Zury—Mr. Praouder, I s'pose I should say. Won't ye 'light?"

"Wal, I guess not. I jes' wanted t' speak abaout a little matter."

"Wal, father he 's raoun' some 'ers. Haow 's the folks t' your 'us?"

"All peart; that is t' say th' ain't no one naow ye know, but me 'n' Jule 'n' Mac. That makes a kind of a bob-tail team, ye know, Mary. Nobody but Jule t' look out fer things. Not b't what he 's a pretty fair of a nigger as niggers go. He c'd stay raoun' 'n' help some aoutside."

"Whatever is he a-drivin' at?" thought Mary, but she said nothing.

"The's three of you gals to hum. Ye don't none of ye seem t' go off yit, tho' I sh'd a-thought Flory she 'd a-ben picked up afore this, 'n' S'manthy tew for that matter."

Neither of them saw the unintended slur this rough speech cast upon poor Mary.

"Don't ye think we 'd better git married, Mary?"

"What, *me*?"

"Wal, yes." He answered this in a tone where she might have detected the suggestion, "Or one of your sisters," if she had been keen and critical. But she was neither. She simply rested her work-worn hand upon the gate post and her chin upon her hand, and looked dreamily off over the prairie. She pondered the novel proposition for some time, but fortunately not quite long enough to cause Zury to ask if either of her sisters was at home, as he was quite capable of doing.

She looked up at him, the blood slowly mounting to her face, and considered how to say yes. He saw that she meant yes, so he helped her out a little. He wanted to have it settled and go.

"Wal, Mary, silence gives consent, they say. When shall it be?"

"Oh, yew ain't in no hurry, Zury, I don't expect."

He was about to urge prompt action, but the thought occurred to him that she must want to get her "things" ready, and the longer she waited the more "things" she would bring with her. So he said:—

"Suit yerself, Mary. I'll drop over 'n' see ye nex' Sunday, 'n' we 'll fix it all up."

Mary had no objection to urge, though possibly in her secret heart she wished there had been a little more sentiment and romance about it. No woman likes "to be cheated out of her wooing," but then this might come later. He called for her with the wagon on the appointed day, and they drove to the house of a justice of the peace who lived a good distance away. This was not for the sake of making a wedding trip, but because this particular justice owed Zury money, as Zury carefully explained.

And so Mary went to work for Zury very much as Jule did, only it was for less wages, as Jule got a dollar a month besides his board and clothes, while Mary did not.

For a year or two or three after marriage (during which two boys were born to them) Zury found that he had gained, by this investment, something more than mere profit and economy—that affection and sympathy were realities in life. But gradually the old dominant mania resumed its course, and involved in its current the weak wife as well as the strong husband. The general verdict was that both Zury and Mary were "jest 'as near 's they could stick 'n' live." "They 'd skin a flea fer its hide 'n' taller."

"He gin an acre o' graound fer the church 'n' scule-house, 'n' it raised the value of his hull farm more 'n' a dollar an acre. 'N' when he got onto the scule-board *she* 'llaowed she had n't released her daower right, 'n' put him up t' tax the deestrick fer the price of that same acre o' ground."

So Zury, claiming the proud position of "the meanest ma-an in Spring Caounty," would like to hear his claim disputed. If he had a rival he would like to have him pointed out, and would "try pootty hard but what he 'd match him."

Strange as it may seem, these grasping characteristics did not make Zury despised or even disliked among his associates. His "meanness" was not underhanded.

"Th' ain't nothin' *mean* abaout Zury, *mean* 's he is. Gimme a man as sez right aout 'look aout fer yerself,' 'n' I kin git along with him. It 's these h'yer sneakin' fellers th't 's one thing afore yer face 'n' another behind yer back th't I can't abide. Take ye by th' beard with one hand 'n' smite ye under th' fifth rib with t' other! He pays his way 'n' dooz 's he 'grees every time. When he buys 'taters o' me, I'd jest 's live 's hev him measure 'em 's measure 'em myself with him a-lookin' on. He knows haow t' trade, 'n' ef yew don't, he don't want ye t' trade with him, that 's all; ner t' grumble if ye git holt o' the hot eend o' th' poker arter he 's give ye fair notice. Better be shaved with a sharp razor than a dull one."

On an occasion when the honesty of a more pretentious citizen was compared with Zury's to the advantage of the latter, he said:—

"Honest? Me? Wal, I guess so. Fustly, I would n't be noth'n' else, nohaow; seck'ndly, I kin 'fford t' be, seein' 's haow it takes a full bag t' stand alone; thirdly, I can't 'fford t' be noth'n' else, coz honesty 's th' best policy."

He was evidently quoting, unconsciously but by direct inheritance, the aphorisms of his fellow Pennsylvanian, Dr. Franklin.

In peace as in war strong men love foemen worthy of their steel. Men liked to be with Zury and hear his gay, shrewd talk; to trade with him, and meet his frankly brutal greed. He enjoyed his popularity, and liked to do good turns to others when it cost him nothing. When elected to local posts of trust and confidence he served the public in the same efficient fashion in which he served himself, and he was therefore continually elected to school directorships and other like "thank 'ee jobs."

I Become Cow Vandemark

by HERBERT QUICK, 1861–1925. *John Herbert Quick was born on a farm in Grundy County, Iowa, of New York Dutch stock with a touch of Irish blood—in which he resembled his character Jake Vandemark. As a child he suffered an attack of infantile paralysis which left his feet and ankles permanently deformed but this affliction did not prevent him from having a successful career as lawyer and writer. After qualifying as a public school teacher he taught in various places and was at one time principal of a grade school in Mason City. Then he studied law and after passing the Iowa bar examinations in 1889 practiced his profession at Sioux City from 1890 to*

1908. His real ambition was literary, however, and he soon turned from law to fiction; The Fairview Idea (1919) is typical of a number of novels which mixed not too successfully realism, moralizing, and melodrama. About this time too he had a public career: he was appointed a member of the Federal Farm Loan Bureau from 1916 to 1919 and in 1920 was chairman of a commission to wind up the business of the American Red Cross at Vladivostok. Quick's best work came in the last few years of his life: Vandemark's Folly (1921), The Hawkeye (1923), The Invisible Woman (1924), a remarkable trilogy of novels depicting life in pioneer Iowa; and One Man's Life (1925), his autobiography. Quick also wrote a thoughtful pamphlet on rural conditions, The Real Trouble with the Farmers (1924). Mississippi Steamboatin' (1926) was completed by his son Edward Quick. "I Become Cow Vandemark" is taken from the sixth chapter of Vandemark's Folly.

I

I WAS off with the spring rush of 1855 for the new lands of the West! I kept thinking as I drove along of Lawyer Jackway's sarcastic toast, "Sold again, and got the tin, and sucked another Dutchman in!" But after all I couldn't keep myself from feeling pretty proud, as I watched the play of my horses' ears as they seemed to take in each new westward view as we went over the tops of the low hills, and as I listened to the "chuck, chuck" of the wagon wheels on their well-greased skeins. Rucker and Jackway might have given me a check on the towpath; but yet I felt hopeful that I was to make a real success of my voyage of life to a home and a place where I could be somebody. There was pleasure in looking back at my riches in the clean, hard-stuffed straw-tick, the stove, the traveling home which belonged to me.

It seems a little queer to me now to think of it as I look out of my bay-window at my great fields of corn, my pastures dotted with stock, my feedyard full of fat steers; or as I sit in the directors' room of the bank and take my part as a member of the board. But I am really not as rich now as I was then.

I was going to a country which seemed to be drawing everybody else, and must therefore be a good country—and I had a farm. I had a great farm. It was a mile square. It was almost like the estate that General Cantine had near the canal at Ithaca I thought. To my boy's mind it looked too big for me; and sometimes I wondered if I should not be able to rent it out to tenants and grow rich on my income, like the Van Rensselaers of the Manor before the Anti-Rent difficulties.

All the while I was passing outfits which were waiting by the roadside, or making bad weather of it for some reason or other; or I was passed by those who had less regard for their horse flesh than I, or did not realize that the horses had to go afoot; or those that drew lighter loads. There were some carriages which went flourishing along with shining covers; these were the aristocrats; there were other slow-going rigs drawn by oxen. Usually there would be two or more vehicles in a train. They camped by the roadside cooking their meals; they stopped at wayside taverns. They gave me all sorts of how-d'-ye-does as I passed. Girls waved their hands at me from the hind-ends of rigs and said bold things—to a boy they would not see again; but which left him blushing and thinking up retorts for the next occasion—retorts that never seemed to fit when the time came; and talkative women threw remarks at me about the roads and the weather.

Men tried half a dozen times a day to trade me out of my bay mare Fanny, or my sorrel mare Flora—they said I ought to match up with two of a color; and the crowbaits offered me would have stocked a horse-ranch. People with oxen offered me what looked like good swaps, because they were impatient to make better time; and as I went along so stylishly I began turning over in my mind the question as to whether it might not be better to get to Iowa a little later in the year with cattle for a start than to rush the season with my fine mares and pull up standing like a gentleman at my own imaginary door.

II

As I went on to the westward, I began to see Blue Mound rising like a low mountain off my starboard bow, and I stopped at a farm in the foot-hills of the Mound where, because it was rainy, I paid four shillings for putting my horses in the stable. There were two other movers stopping at the same place. They had a light wagon and a yoke of good young steers, and had been out of Madison two days longer than I had been. I noticed that they left their wagon in a clump of bushes, and that while one of them—a man of fifty or more, slept in the house, the other, a young fellow of twenty or twenty-two, lay in the wagon, and that one or the other seemed always to be on guard near the vehicle. The older man had a long beard and a hooked nose, and seemed to be a still sort of person, until some one spoke of slavery; then he broke out in a fierce speech denouncing slave-holders, and the slavocracy that had the nation in its grip.

"You talk," said the farmer, "like a black Abolitionist."

"I'm so black an Abolitionist," said he, "that I'd be willing to shoulder a gun any minute if I thought I could wipe out the curse of slavery."

The farmer was terribly scandalized at this, and when the old man walked away to his wagon, he said to the young man and me that that sort of talk would make trouble and ruin the nation; and that he didn't want any more of it around his place.

190

"Well," said the traveler, "you won't have any more of it from us. We're just pulling out." After the farmer went away, he spoke to me about it.

"What do you think of that kind of talk?" he asked.

"I don't own any niggers," said I. "I don't ever expect to own any. I don't see how slavery can do me any good; and I think the slaves are human."

I had no very clear ideas on the subject, and had done little thinking about it; but what I said seemed to be satisfactory to the young man. He told his friend about it, and after a while the old man, whose name was Dunlap, came to me and shook my hand, saying that he was glad to meet a young fellow of my age who was of the right stripe.

"Can you shoot?" he asked.

I told him I never had had much chance to learn, but I had a good gun, and had got some game with it almost every day so far.

"What kind of a gun?" he asked.

I told him it was a double-barreled shotgun, and he looked rather disappointed. Then he asked me if I had ever thought of going to Kansas. No, I told him, I thought I should rather locate in Iowa.

"We are going to Kansas," he said. "There's work for real men in Kansas—men who believe in freedom. You had better go along with Amos Thatcher and me."

I said I didn't believe I could—I had planned to locate in Iowa. He dropped the subject by saying that I would overtake him and Thatcher on the road, and we could talk it over again. When did I think of getting under way? I answered that I thought I should stay hauled up to rest my horses for a half-day anyhow, so perhaps we might camp that night together.

"A good idea," said Thatcher, smilingly, as they drove off. "Join us; we get lonesome."

I laid by that forenoon because one of my mares had limped a little the day before, and I was worrying for fear she might not be perfectly sound. I hitched up after noon and drove on, anxiously watching her to see whether I had not been sucked in on horse flesh, as well as in the general settlement of my mother's estate. She seemed to be all right, however, and we were making good headway as night drew on, and I was halted by Amos Thatcher who said he was on the lookout for me.

"We have a station off the road a mile or so," said he, "and you'll have a hearty welcome if you come with me—stable for your horses, and a bed to sleep in, and good victuals."

I couldn't think what he meant by a station; but it was about time to make camp anyhow, and so I took him into the wagon with me, and we drove across country by a plain trail, through a beautiful piece of oak openings, to a big log house in a fine grove of burr oaks, with a log barn back of it—as nice a farmstead as I had seen. There were fifteen or twenty cattle in the yards, and some sheep and hogs, and many fat hens. If this was a station, I thought, I envied the man who owned it. As we drove up I saw a little negro boy peeping at us from the back of the house, and as we halted a black woman ran out and seized the pickaninny by the ear, and dragged him back out of sight. I heard a whimper from the little boy, which seemed suddenly smothered by something like a hand clapped over his mouth. Mr. Dunlap's wagon was not in sight, but its owner came out at the front door and greeted me in a very friendly way.

"What makes you call this a station?" I asked of Thatcher.

Dunlap looked at him sternly.

"I forgot myself," said Thatcher, more to Dunlap than to me.

"Never mind," replied Dunlap. "If I can tell B from a bull's foot, it's all right."

Then turning to me he said, "The old lady inside has a meal of victuals ready for us. Come in and we'll let into it."

There was nothing said at the meal which explained the things that were so blind to me; but there was a good deal of talk about rifles. The farmer was named Preston, a middle-aged man who shaved all his beard except what grew under his chin, which hung down in a long black fringe over his breast like a window-lambrequin. His wife's father, who was an old Welshman named Evans, had worked in the lead mines over toward Dubuque, until Preston had married his daughter and taken up his farm in the oak openings. They had been shooting at a mark that afternoon, with Sharp's rifles carried by Dunlap and Thatcher, and the old-fashioned squirrel rifles owned on the farm. After supper they brought out these rifles and compared them. Preston insisted that the squirrel rifles were better.

"Not for real service," said Dunlap, throwing a cartridge into the breech of the Sharp, and ejecting it to show how fast it could be done.

"But I can roll a squirrel's eye right out of his head most every time with the old-style gun," said Preston. "This is the gun that won the Battle of New Orleans."

"It wouldn't have won against the Sharp," said Thatcher; "and you know we expect to have a larger mark than a squirrel's head, when we get to Kansas."

This was the first breech-loader I had ever seen, and I looked it over with a buying eye. It didn't seem to me that it would be much better for hunting than the old-fashioned rifle, loaded with powder and a molded bullet rammed down with a patch of oiled cloth around it; for after you have shot at your game once, you either have hit it, or it runs or flies away. If you have hit it, you can generally get it, and if it goes away, you have time to reload. Besides those big cartridges must be costly, I thought, and said so to Mr. Dunlap.

"When you're hunting Border Ruffians," said he, "a little expense don't count one way or the other; and you may be willing to pay dear for a chance to reload three or four times while the other man is ramming home a new charge. Give me the new guns, the new ideas, and the old doctrine of freedom to fight for. Don't you see?"

"Why, of course," said I, "I'm for freedom. That's why I'm going out on the prairies."

"Prairies!" said old Evans. "Prairies! What do you expect to do on the prairies?"

"Farm," I answered.

"All these folks that are rushing to the prairies," said the old man, "will starve out and come back. God makes trees grow to show men where the good land is. I read history, and there's no country that's good for anything, except where men have cut the trees, niggered off the logs, grubbed out the stumps, and made fields of it—and if there are stones, it's all the better. 'In the sweat of thy face shalt thou eat bread,' said God to Adam, and when you go to the prairies where it's all ready for the plow, you are trying to dodge God's curse on our first parents. You won't prosper. It stands to reason that any land that is good will grow trees."

"Some of this farm was prairie," put in Preston, "and I don't see but it's just as good as the rest."

"It was all openings," replied Evans. "The trees was here once, and got killed by the fires, or somehow. It was all woods once."

"You cut down trees to make land grow grass," said Thatcher. "I should think that God must have meant grass to be the sign of good ground."

"Isn't the sweat of your face just as plenty when you delve in the prairies?" asked Dunlap.

"You fly in the face of God's decree, and run against His manifest warning when you try to make a prairie into a farm," said Evans. "You'll see!"

"Sold again, and got the tin, and sucked another Dutchman in!" was the ditty that ran through my head as I heard this. Old man Evans' way of looking at the matter seemed reasonable to my cautious mind; and, anyhow, when a man has grown old he knows many things that he can give no good reason for. I have always found that the well-educated fellow with a deep-sounding and plausible philosophy that runs against the teachings of experience, is likely, especially in farming, to make a failure when he might have saved himself by doing as the old settlers do, who won't answer his arguments but make a good living just the same, while the new-fangled practises send their followers to the poorhouse. At that moment, I would have traded my Iowa farm for any good piece of land covered with trees. But Dunlap and Thatcher had something else to talk to me about. They were for the prairies, especially the prairies of Kansas.

"Kansas," said Dunlap, "will be one of the great states of the Union, one of these days. Come with us, and help make it a free state. We need a hundred thousand young farmers, who believe in liberty, and will fight for it. Come with us, take up a farm, and carry a Sharp's rifle against the Border Ruffians!"

This sounded convincing to me, but of course I couldn't make up my mind to anything of this sort without days and days of consideration; but I listened to what they said. They told me of an army of free-state emigrants that was gathering along the border to win Kansas for freedom. They, Dunlap and Thatcher, were going to Marion, Iowa, and from there by the Mormon Trail across to a place called Tabor, and from there to Lawrence, Kansas. They were New England Yankees. Thatcher had been to college, and was studying law. Dunlap had been a business man in Connecticut, and was a friend of John Brown, who was then on his way to Kansas.

"The Missouri Compromise has been repealed," said Thatcher, his eyes shining, "and the Kansas-Nebraska Bill has thrown the fertile state of Kansas into the ring to be fought for by free-state men and pro-slavery men. The Border Ruffians of Missouri are breaking the law every day by going over into Kansas, never meaning to live there only long enough to vote, and are corrupting the state government. They are corrupting it by violence and illegal voting. If slavery wins in Kansas and Nebraska, it will control the Union·forever. The greatest battle in our history is about to be fought out in Kansas, a battle to see whether this nation shall be a slave nation, in every state and every town, or free. Dunlap and I and thousands of others are going down there to take the state of Kansas into our own hands, peacefully if we can, by violence if we must. We are willing to die to make the United States a free nation. Come with us!"

"But we don't expect to die," urged Dunlap, seeing that this looked pretty serious to me. "We expect to live, and get farms, and make homes, and prosper, after we have shown the Border Ruffians the muzzles of those rifles. Thatcher, bring the passengers in!"

Thatcher went out of the room the back way.

"We call this a station," went on Dunlap, "because it's a stopping-place on the U.G. Railway."

"What's the U.G. Railway?" I asked.

"Don't you know that?" he queried.

"I'm only a canal hand," I answered, "going to a farm out on the prairie, that I was euchred into taking in settling with a scoundrel for my share of my father's property; and I'm pretty green."

Thatcher came in then, leading the little black boy by the hand, and following him was the negro woman, carrying a baby at her breast, and holding by the hand a little woolly-headed pickaninny about three years old. They were ragged and poverty-stricken, and seemed scared at everything. The woman came in bowing and scraping to me, and the two little boys hid behind her skirts and peeked around at me with big white eyes.

"Tell the gentlemen," said Thatcher, "where you're going."

"We're gwine to Canayda," said she, "'scusin' your presence."

"How are you going to get to Canada?" asked Thatcher.

"The good white folks," said she, "will keep us hid out nights till we gits thar."

"What will happen," said Thatcher, "if this young man tells any one that he's seen you?"

"The old massa," said she, "will find out, an' he'll hunt us wif houn's, an' fotch us back, and then he'll sell us down the ribber to the cotton-fiel's."

I never heard anything quite so pitiful as this speech. I had never known before what it must mean to be really hunted. The woman shrank back toward the door through which she had come, her face grew a sort of grayish color; and then ran to me and throwing herself on her knees, she took hold of my hands, and begged me for God's sake not to tell on her, not to have her carried back, not to fix it so she'd be sold down the river to work in the cotton-fields.

"I won't," I said, "I tell you I won't. I want you to get to Canada!"

"God bress yeh," she said. "I know'd yeh was a good young gem-man as soon as I set eyes on yeh! I know'd yeh was quality!"

"Who do you expect to meet in Canada?" asked Thatcher.

"God willin'," said she, "I'm gwine to find Abe Felton, the pa of dese yere chillun."

"The Underground Railway," said Dunlap, "knows where Abe is, and will send Sarah along with change of cars. You may go, Sarah. Now," he went on, as the negroes disappeared, "you have it in your power to exercise the right of an American citizen and perform the God-accursed legal duty to report these fugitives at the next town, join a posse to hunt them down under a law of the United States, get a reward for doing it, and know that you have vindicated the law— or you can stand with God and tell the law to go to hell—where it came from—and help the Underground Railway to carry these people to heaven. Which will you do?"

"I'll tell the law to go to hell," said I.

Dunlap and Thatcher looked at each other as if relieved. I have always suspected that I was taken into their secret without their ordinary precautions; and that for a while they were a little dubious for fear that they had spilt the milk of secrecy. But all my life people have told me their secrets.

They urged me hard to go with them; and talked so favorably about the soil of the prairies that I began to think well again of my Iowa farm. When I had made it plain that I had to have a longer time to think it over, they began urging me to let them have my horses on some sort of a trade; and I began to see that a part of what they had wanted all the time was a faster team as well as a free-state recruit. They urged on me the desirability of having cattle instead of horses when I reached my farm.

"Cows, yes," said I, "but not steers."

So I slept over it until morning. Then I made them the proposition that if they would arrange with Preston to trade me four cows, which I would select from his herd, and would provide for my board with Preston until I could break them to drive, and would furnish yokes and chains in place of my harness, I would let them have the team for a hundred dollars boot-money. Preston said he'd like to have me make my selection first, and when I picked out three-year-old heifers, two of which were giving milk, he said it was a whack, if it didn't take me more than a week to break them. Dunlap and Thatcher hitched up, and started off the next morning. I had become Cow Vandemark overnight, and am still Cow Vandemark in the minds of the old settlers of Vandemark Township and some who have just picked the name up.

But I did not take on my new name without a struggle, for Flora and Fanny had become dear to me since leaving Madison—my first horses. How I got my second team of horses is connected with one of the most important incidents in my life; it was a long time before I got them and it will be some time before I can tell about it. In the meantime, there were Flora and Fanny, hitched to Dunlap and Thatcher's light wagon, disappearing among the burr oaks toward the Dubuque highway. I thought of my pride as I drove away from Madison with these two steeds, and of the pretty figure I cut the morning when red-haired Alice climbed up, offered to go with me, and kissed me before she climbed down. Would she have done this if I had been driving oxen, or still worse, those animals which few thought worth anything as draught animals—cows? And then I thought of Flora's lameness the day before yesterday. Was it honest to let Dunlap and Thatcher drive off to liberate the nation with a horse that might go lame?

"Let me have a horse," said I to Preston. "I want to catch them and tell them something."

I rode up behind the Abolitionists' wagon, waving my hat and shouting. They pulled up and waited.

"What's up?" asked Dunlap. "Going with us after all? I hope so, my boy."

"No," said I, "I just wanted to say that that nigh mare was lame day before yesterday, and I—I—I didn't want you to start off with her without knowing it."

Dunlap asked about her lameness, and got out to look her over. He felt of her muscles, and carefully scrutinized her for swelling or swinney or splint or spavin or thoroughpin. Then he lifted one foot after another, and cleaned out about the frog, tapping the hoof all over for soreness. Down deep beside the frog of the foot which she had favored he found a little pebble.

"That's what it was," said he, holding the pebble up. "She'll be all right now. Thank you for telling me. It was the square thing to do."

"If you don't feel safe to go on with the team," said I, "I'll trade back."

"No," said he, "we're needed in Kansas; and," turning up an oil-cloth and showing me a dozen or so of the Sharp's rifles, "so are these. And let me tell you, boy, if I'm any judge of men, the time will come when you won't feel so bad to lose half a dozen horses, as you feel now to be traded out of Flora and Fanny, and make a hundred dollars by the trade. Get up, Flora; go long, Fanny; good-by, Jake!" And they drove off to the Border Wars. I had made my first sacrifice to the cause of the productiveness of the Vandemark Farm.

That night a wagon went away from the Preston farm with the passengers going to Canada by the U.G. Railway. The next morning I began the task of fitting yokes to my two span of heifers, and that afternoon, I gave Lily and Cherry their first lesson. I had had some experience in driving cattle on Mrs. Fogg's farm in Herkimer County, but I should have made a botch job of it if it had not been for Mr. Preston, who knew all there was to know about cattle, and while protesting that cows could not be driven, helped me to drive them. In less than a week my cows were driving as prettily as any oxen. They were light and active, and overtook team after team of laboring steers every day I drove them. Furthermore, they gave me milk. I fed them well, worked them rather lightly, and by putting the new milk in a churn I bought at Mineral Point, I found that the motion of the wagon would bring the butter as well as any churning. I had cream for my coffee, butter for my bread, milk for my mush, and lived high. A good deal of fun was poked at me about my team of cows; but people were always glad to camp with me and share my fare.

Economically, our cows ought to be made to do a good deal of the work of the farms. I have always believed this; but now a German expert has proved it. I read about it the other day in a bulletin put out by the Agricultural Department; but I proved it in Vandemark Township before the man was born that wrote the bulletin. If not pushed too hard, cows will work and give almost as much milk as if not worked at all. This statement of course won't apply to the fancy cows which are high-power milk machines, and need to be packed in cotton, and kept in satin-lined stalls; but to such cows as farmers have, and always will have, it does apply.

I was sorry to leave the Prestons, they were such whole-souled, earnest people; and before I did leave them I was a full-fledged Abolitionist so far as belief was concerned. I never did become active, however, in spiriting slaves from one station to another of the U.G. Railway.

I drove out to the highway, and turning my prow to the west, I joined again in the stream of people swarming westward. The tide had swollen in the week during which I had laid by at the Prestons'. The road was rutted, poached deep where wet and beaten hard where dry, or pulverized into dust by the stream of emigration. Here we went, oxen, cows, mules, horses; coaches, carriages, blue jeans, corduroys, rags, tatters, silks, satins, caps, tall hats, poverty, riches; speculators, missionaries, land-hunters, merchants; criminals escaping from justice; couples fleeing from the law; families seeking homes; the wrecks of homes seeking secrecy; gold-seekers bearing southwest to the Overland Trail; politicians looking for places in which to win fame and fortune; editors hunting opportunities for founding newspapers; adventurers on their way to everywhere; lawyers with a few books; Abolitionists going to the Border War; innocent-looking outfits carrying fugitive slaves; officers hunting escaped negroes; and most numerous of all, homeseekers "hunting country"—a nation on wheels, an empire in the commotion and pangs of birth. Down I went with the rest, across ferries, through Dodgeville, Mineral Point and Platteville, past a thousand vacant sites for farms toward my own farm so far from civilization, shot out of civilization by the forces of civilization itself.

I saw the old mining country from Mineral Point to Dubuque, where lead had been dug for many years, and where the men lived who dug the holes and were called Badgers, thus giving the people of Wisconsin their nickname as distinguished from the Illinois people who came up the rivers to work in the spring, and went back in the fall, and were therefore named after a migratory fish and called Suckers; and at last, I saw from its eastern bank far off to the west, the bluffy shores of Iowa, and down by the river the keen spires and brick and wood buildings of the biggest town I had seen since leaving Milwaukee, the town of Dubuque.

I camped that night in the northwestern corner of Illinois, in a regular city of movers, all waiting their turns at the ferry which crossed the Mississippi to the Land of Promise.

IV

Iowa did not look much like a prairie country from where I stood. The Iowa shore towered above the town of Dubuque, clothed with woods to the top, and looking more like York State than anything I had seen since I had taken the schooner at Buffalo to come up the Lakes. I lay that night, unable to sleep. For one thing, I needed to be wakeful, lest some of the motley crowd of movers might take a fancy to my cattle. I was learning by experience how to take care of myself and mine; besides, I wanted to be awake early so as to take passage by ferryboat "before soon" as the Hoosiers say, in the morning.

That April morning was still only a gray dawn when I drove down to the ferry, without stopping for my breakfast. A few others of those who looked forward to a rush for the boat had got there ahead of me, and we waited in line. I saw that I should have to go on the second trip rather than the first, but movers can not be impatient, and the driving of cattle cures a person of being in a hurry; so I was in no great taking because of this little delay. As I sat there in my wagon, a black-bearded, scholarly-looking man stepped up and spoke to me.

"Going across?" he asked.

"As soon as the boat will take me," I said.

"Heavy loaded?" he asked. "Have you room for a passenger?"

"I guess I can accommodate you," I answered. "Climb in."

"It isn't for myself I'm asking," he said. "There's a lady here that wants to ride in a covered wagon, and sit back where she can't see the water. It makes her dizzy—and scares her awfully; can you take her?"

"If she can ride back there on the bed," said I.

He peeped in, and said that this was the very place for her. She could lie down and cover up her head and never know she was crossing the river at all. In a minute, and while it was still twilight, just as the ferryboat came to the landing, he returned with the lady. She was dressed in some brown fabric, and wore a thick veil over her face; but as she climbed in I saw that she had yellow hair and bright eyes and lips; and that she was trembling so that her hands shook as she took hold of the wagon-bow, and her voice quivered as she thanked me, in low tones. The man with the black beard pressed her hand as he left her. He offered me a dollar for her passage; but I called his attention to the fact that it would cost only two shillings more for me to cross with her than if I went alone, and refused to take more.

"There are a good many rough fellows," said he, "at these ferries, that make it unpleasant for a lady, sometimes—"

"Not when she's with me," I said.

He looked at me sharply, as if surprised that I was not so green as I looked—though I was pretty verdant. Anyhow, he said, if I should be asked if any one was with me, it would save her from being scared if I would say that I was alone—she was the most timid woman in the world.

"I'll have to tell the ferryman," I said.

"Will you?" he asked. "Why?"

"I'd be cheating him if I didn't," I answered.

"All right," he said, as if provoked at me, "but don't tell any one else."

"I ain't very good at lying," I replied.

He said for me to do the best I could for the lady, and hurried off. In the meantime, the lady had crept back on my straw-bed, and pulled the quilts completely over her. She piled pillows on one side of her, and stirred the straw up on the other, so that when she lay down the bed was as smooth as if nobody was in it. It looked as it might if a heedless boy had crawled out of it after a night's sleep, and carelessly thrown the coverlet back over it. I could hardly believe I had a passenger. When I was asked for the ferriage, I paid for two, and the ferryman asked where the other was.

"Back in the bed," I said.

He looked back, and said, "Well, I owe you something for your honesty. I never'd have seen him. Sick?"

"Not very," said I. "Don't like the water."

"Some are that way," he returned, and went on collecting fares.

As we drove up from the landing, through the rutted streets of the old mining and Indian-trading town, the black-bearded man came to me as we stopped, held back by a jam of covered wagons—a wonderful sight, even to me—and as if talking to me, said to the woman, "You'd better ride on through town"; and then to me, "Are you going on through?"

"I've got to buy some supplies," said I; "but I've nothing to stop me but that."

"Tell me what you want," he said hurriedly, and looking about as if expecting some danger, "and I'll buy it for you and bring it on. Which way are you going?"

"West into Iowa," I answered.

"Go on," said he, "and I'll make it right with you. Camp somewhere west of town. I'll come along to-night or to-morrow. I'll make it right with you."

"I don't see through this," I said, with my usual indecision as to doing something I did not understand. "I thought I'd look around Dubuque a little."

"For God's sake," said the woman from the bed, "take me on—take me on!"

Her tones were so pleading, she seemed in such an agony of terror, that I suddenly made up my mind in her favor. Surely there would be no harm in carrying her on as she wished.

"All right," I said to her, but looking at him, "I'll take you on! You can count on me." And then to him, "I'll drive on until I find a good camping-place late this afternoon. You'll have to find us the best way you can."

He thanked me, and I gave him a list of the things I wanted. Then he went on up the street ahead of us, walking calmly, and looking about him as any stranger might have done. We stood for some time, waiting for the jam of teams to clear, and I gee-upped and whoa-hawed on along the street, until we came to a building on which was a big sign, "Post-Office." There was a queue of people waiting for their mail, extending out at the door, and far down the sidewalk. In this string of emigrants stood our friend, the black-bearded man. Just as we passed, a rather thin, stooped man, walking along on the other side of the street, rushed across, right in front of my lead team, and drawing a pistol, aimed at the black-bearded man, who in turn stepped out of line and drew his own weapon.

"I call upon you all to witness," said the black-bearded man, "that I act in self-defense."

A bystander seized the thin man's pistol hand, and yelled at him not to shoot or he might kill some one—of course he meant some one he did not aim at, but it sounded a little funny, and I laughed. Several joined in the laugh, and there was a good deal of confusion. At last I heard the black-bearded man say, "I'm here alone. He's accused his wife of being too thick with a dozen men. He's insanely jealous, gentle-men. I suppose his wife may have left him, but I'm here alone. I just crossed the river alone, and I'm going west. If he's got a warrant, he's welcome to have it served if he finds his wife with me. Come on, gentlemen—but take the fool's pistol away from him."

As I drove on I saw that the woman had thrown off the quilt, and was peeping out at the opening in the cover at the back, watching the black-bearded and the thin man moving off in a group of fellows, one of whom held the black-bearded man by the arm a good deal as a deputy sheriff might have done.

The roads leading west out of Dubuque were horrible, then, being steep stony trails coming down the hollows and washed like watercourses at every rain. Teams were stalled, sometimes three and four span of animals were used to get one load to the top, and we were a good deal delayed. I was so busy trying to keep from upsetting when I drove around stalled outfits and abandoned wagons, and so occupied in finding places where I might stop and breathe my team, that I paid little attention to my queer-acting passenger; but once when we were standing I noticed that she was covered up again, and seemed to be crying. As we topped the bluffs, and drew out into the open, she sat up and began to rearrange her hair. After a few miles, we reached a point from which I could see the Iowa prairie sweeping away as far as the eye could see. I drew out by the roadside to look at it, as a man appraises one with whom he must live—as a friend or an enemy.

I shall never forget the sight. It was like a great green sea. The old growth had been burned the fall before, and the spring grass scarcely concealed the brown sod on the uplands; but all the swales were coated thick with an emerald growth full-bite high, and in the deeper, wetter hollows grew cowslips, already showing their glossy, golden flowers. The hillsides were thick with the woolly possblummies in their furry spring coats protecting them against the frost and chill, showing purple-violet on the outside of a cup filled with golden stamens, the first fruits of the prairie flowers; on the warmer southern slopes a few of the splendid bird's-foot violets of the prairie were showing the azure color which would soon make some of the hillsides as blue as the sky; and standing higher than the peering grass rose the rough-leafed stalks of green which would soon show us the yellow puccoons and sweet-williams and scarlet lilies and shooting stars, and later the yellow rosin-weeds, Indian dye-flower and goldenrod. The keen northwest wind swept before it a flock of white clouds; and under the clouds went their shadows, walking over the lovely hills like dark ships over an emerald sea.

The wild-fowl were clamoring north for the summer's campaign of nesting. Everywhere the sky was harrowed by the wedged wild geese, their voices as sweet as organ tones; and ducks quacked, whistled and whirred overhead, a true rain of birds beating up against the wind.

Over every slew, on all sides, thousands of ducks of many kinds, and several sorts of geese hovered, settled, or burst up in eruptions of birds, their back-feathers shining like bronze as they turned so as to reflect the sunlight to my eyes; while so far up that they looked like specks, away above the wind it seemed, so quietly did they circle and sail, floated huge flocks of cranes—the sand-hill cranes in their slaty-gray, and the whooping cranes, white as snow with black heads and feet, each bird with a ten-foot spread of wing, piping their wild cries which fell down to me as if from another world.

It was sublime! Bird, flower, grass, cloud, wind, and the immense expanse of sunny prairie, swelling up into undulations like a woman's breasts turgid with milk for a hungry race. I forgot myself and my position in the world, my loneliness, my strange passenger, the problems of my life; my heart swelled, and my throat filled. I sat looking at it, with the tears trickling from my eyes, the uplift of my soul more than I could bear. It was not the thought of my mother that brought the tears to my eyes, but my happiness in finding the newest, strangest, most delightful, sternest, most wonderful thing in the world—the Iowa prairie—that made me think of my mother. If I only could have found her alive! If I only could have had her with me! And as I thought of this I realized that the woman of the ferry had climbed over the back of the spring-seat and was sitting beside me.

"I don't wonder," said she, "that you cry. Gosh! It scares me to death!"

Toward the Sunset

by OLE EDVART RÖLVAAG, 1876–1931. The greatest novelist of immigrant life in the Middle West, Rölvaag himself experienced the America fever and emigrated from his home in Norway to the United States in 1896. For a time he worked as a farm hand in South Dakota, then attended a Norwegian Lutheran academy at Canton in that state and eventually earned his B.A. degree in 1905 at St. Olaf College, Northfield, Minnesota. After a year spent in study at Oslo, Rölvaag joined the faculty at St. Olaf and taught there until his death, being especially famous for his courses in Ibsen and Norwegian immigration. But teaching was always merely a livelihood to Rölvaag; his real ambition was to write fiction, and before he died he had written in Norwegian half a dozen novels most of which dealt with the Scandinavian immigrants in Minnesota and South Dakota. Most famous is his trilogy: Giants in the Earth (1927), Peder Victorious (1929), and Their Fathers' God (1931); *the dates are those of the English translations. These books show not only the obstacles facing the Norwegian settlers, mostly fishing folk, on the western prairies but also the cultural adjustments and the linguistic barriers. Rölvaag felt strongly that the Norwegian immigrants should retain their old traditions and culture, but not even his own characters were faithful to that ideal. "Toward the Sunset," the opening pages of Giants in the Earth, pictures the land to which the Norwegians came.*

I

BRIGHT, clear sky over a plain so wide that the rim of the heavens cut down on it around the entire horizon. . . . Bright, clear sky, to-day, to-morrow, and for all time to come.

. . . And sun! And still more sun! It set the heavens afire every morning; it grew with the day to quivering golden light—then softened into all the shades of red and purple as evening fell. . . . Pure colour everywhere. A gust of wind, sweeping across the plain, threw into life waves of yellow and blue and green. Now and then a dead black wave would race over the scene . . . a cloud's gliding shadow . . . now and then. . . .

It was late afternoon. A small caravan was pushing its way through the tall grass. The track that it left behind was like the wake of a boat —except that instead of widening out astern it closed in again.

"Tish-ah!" said the grass. . . . "Tish-ah, tish-ah!" . . . Never had it said anything else—never would it say anything else. It bent resiliently under the trampling feet; it did not break, but it complained aloud every time—for nothing like this had ever happened to it before. . . . "Tish-ah, tish-ah!" it cried, and rose up in surprise to look at this rough, hard thing that had crushed it to the ground so rudely, and then moved on.

A stocky, broad-shouldered man walked at the head of the caravan. He seemed shorter than he really was, because of the tall grass around him and the broad-brimmed hat of coarse straw which he wore. A few steps behind him followed a boy of about nine years of age. The boy's blond hair was clearly marked against his brown, sunburnt neck; but the man's hair and neck were of exactly the same shade of brown. From the looks of these two, and still more from their gait, it was easy to guess that here walked father and son.

Behind them a team of oxen jogged along; the oxen were drawing a vehicle which once upon a time might have been a wagon, but which now, on account of its many and grave infirmities, ought long since to have been consigned to the scrap heap—exactly the place, in point of fact, where the man had picked it up. Over the wagon box long willow saplings had been bent, in the form of arches in a church chancel—six of them in all. On these arches, and tied down to the body on each side, were spread first of all two hand-woven blankets, that might well have adorned the walls of some manor house in the olden times; on top of the blankets were thrown two sheepskin robes, with the wool side down, which were used for bed-coverings at night. The rear of the wagon was stowed full of numberless articles, all the way up to the top. A large immigrant chest at the bottom of the pile, very long and high, devoured a big share of the space; around and above it were piled household utensils, tools, implements, and all their clothing.

Hitched to this wagon and trailing behind was another vehicle, homemade and very curious-looking, so solidly and quaintly constructed that it might easily have won a place in any museum. Indeed, it appeared strong enough to stand all the jolting from the Atlantic to the Pacific. . . . It, too, was a wagon, after a fashion; at least, it had been intended for such. The wheels were made from pieces of plank fitting roughly together; the box, considerably wider than that of the first wagon, was also loaded full of provisions and household gear, covered over with canvas and lashed down securely. Both wagons creaked and groaned loudly every time they bounced over a tussock or hove out of a hollow. . . . "Squeak, squeak!" said the one. . . . "Squeak, squeak!" answered the other. . . . The strident sound broke the silence of centuries.

A short distance behind the wagons followed a brindle cow. The caravan moved so slowly that she occasionally had time to stop and snatch a few mouthfuls, though there was never a chance for many at a time. But what little she got in this way she sorely needed. She had been jogging along all day, swinging and switching her tail, the rudder of the caravan. Soon it would be night, and then her part of the work would come—to furnish milk for the evening porridge, for all the company up ahead.

Across the front end of the box of the first wagon lay a rough piece of plank. On the right side of this plank sat a woman with a white kerchief over her head, driving the oxen. Against her thigh rested the blond head of a little girl, who was stretched out on the plank and sleeping sweetly. Now and then the hand of the mother moved across the child's face to chase away the mosquitoes, which had begun to gather as the sun lowered. On the left side of the plank, beyond the girl, sat a boy about seven years old—a well-grown lad, his skin deeply tanned, a certain clever, watchful gleam in his eyes. With hands folded over one knee, he looked straight ahead.

This was the caravan of Per Hansa, who with his family and all his earthly possessions was moving west from Fillmore County, Minnesota, to Dakota Territory. There he intended to take up land and build himself a home; he was going to do something remarkable out there, which should become known far and wide. No lack of opportunity in that country, he had been told! . . . Per Hansa himself strode ahead and laid out the course; the boy Ole, or *Olamand*, followed closely after, and explored it. Beret, the wife, drove the oxen and took care of little Anna Marie, pet-named *And-Ongen* (which means "The Duckling"), who was usually bubbling over with happiness. Hans Kristian, whose everyday name was *Store-Hans* (meaning "Big Hans," to distinguish him from his godfather, who was also named Hans, but who, of course, was three times his size), sat there on the wagon, and saw to it that everyone attended to business. . . . The cow Rosie trailed behind, swinging and switching her tail, following the caravan farther and farther yet into the endless vista of the plain.

"Tish-ah, tish-ah!" cried the grass. . . . "Tish-ah, tish-ah!" . . .

II

The caravan seemed a miserably frail and Lilliputian thing as it crept over the boundless prairie toward the sky line. Of road or trail there lay not a trace ahead; as soon as the grass had straightened up again behind, no one could have told the direction from which it had come or whither it was bound. The whole train—Per Hansa with his wife and children, the oxen, the wagons, the cow, and all—might just as well have dropped down out of the sky. Nor was it at all impossible to imagine that they were trying to get back there again; their course was always the same—straight toward the west, straight toward the sky line. . . .

Poverty-stricken, unspeakably forlorn, the caravan creaked along, advancing at a snail's pace, deeper and deeper into a bluish-green infinity—on and on, and always farther on. . . . It steered for Sunset Land! . . .

For more than three weeks now, and well into the fourth, this caravan had been crawling across the plain. . . . Early in the journey it had passed through Blue Earth; it had left Chain Lakes behind; and one fine day it had crept into Jackson, on the Des Moines River. But that seemed ages ago. . . . From Jackson, after a short lay-up, it had pushed on westward—always westward—to Worthington, then to Rock River. . . . A little west of Rock River, Per Hansa had lost the trail completely. Since then he had not been able to find it again; at this moment he literally did not know where he was, nor how to get to the place he had to reach. But Split Rock Creek must lie out there somewhere in the sun; if he could only find that landmark, he could pick his way still farther without much trouble. . . . Strange that he hadn't reached Split Rock Creek before this time! According to his directions, he should have been there two or three days ago; but he hadn't seen anything that even looked like the place. . . . Oh, my God! If something didn't turn up soon! . . . My God! . . .

The wagons creaked and groaned. Per Hansa's eyes wandered over the plain. His bearded face swung constantly from side to side as he examined every inch of ground from the northeast to the southwest. At times he gave his whole attention to that part of the plain lying between him and the western sky line; with head bent forward and eyes fixed and searching, he would sniff the air, like an animal trying to find the scent. Every now and then he glanced at an old silver watch which he carried in his left hand; but his gaze would quickly wander off again, to take up its fruitless search of the empty horizon.

It was now nearing six o'clock. Since three in the afternoon he had been certain of his course; at that time he had taken his bearings by means of his watch and the sun. . . . Out here one had to get one's cross-bearings from the very day itself—then trust to luck. . . .

For a long while the little company had been silent. Per Hansa turned halfway around, and without slackening his pace spoke to the boy walking behind.

"Go back and drive for a while now, Ola. . . . You must talk to mother, too, so that it won't be so lonesome for her. And be sure to keep as sharp a lookout as you can."

"I'm not tired yet!" said the boy, loath to leave the van.

"Go back, anyway! Maybe you're not, but I can feel it beginning to tell on me. We'll have to start cooking the porridge pretty soon. . . . You go back, and hold her on the sun for a while longer."

"Do you think we'll catch up with them to-night, Dad?" The boy was still undecided.

"Good Lord, no! They've got too long a start on us. . . . Look sharp, now! If you happen to see anything suspicious, sing out!" . . . Per Hansa glanced again at his watch, turned forward, and strode steadily onward.

Ole said no more; he stepped out of the track and stood there waiting till the train came up. Then Store-Hans jumped down nimbly, while the other climbed up and took his seat.

"Have you seen anything?" the mother asked in an anxious voice.

"Why, no . . . not yet," answered the boy, evasively.

"I wonder if we shall ever see them again," she said, as if speaking to herself, and looked down at the ground. "This seems to be taking us to the end of the world . . . beyond the end of the world!"

Store-Hans, who was still walking beside the wagon, heard what she said and looked up at her. The buoyancy of childhood shone in his brown face. . . . Too bad that mother should be so scared! . . .

"Yes, Mother, but when we're both steering for the sun, we'll both land in the same place, won't we? . . . The sun is a sure guide, you know!"

These were the very words which he had heard his father use the night before; now he repeated them. To Store-Hans the truth of them seemed as clear as the sun itself; in the first place, because dad had said it, and then because it sounded so reasonable.

He hurried up alongside his father and laid his hand in his—he always felt safer thus.

The two walked on side by side. Now and then the boy stole a glance at the face beside him, which was as stern and fixed as the prairie on which they were walking. He was anxious to talk, but couldn't find anything to say that sounded grown-up enough; and so he kept quiet. At last, however, the silence grew too heavy for him to bear. He tried to say indifferently, just like his father:

"When I'm a man and have horses, I'm going to make a road over these plains, and . . . and put up some posts for people to follow. Don't you think that'll be a good idea?"

A slight chuckle came from the bearded face set toward the sun.

"Sure thing, Store-Hans—you'll manage that all right . . . I might find time to help you an hour or two, now and then."

The boy knew by his father's voice that he was in a talkative mood. This made him so glad, that he forgot himself and did something that his mother always objected to; he began to whistle, and tried to take just as long strides as his father. But he could only make the grass say: "Swish-sh, swish-sh!"

On and on they went, farther out toward Sunset Land—farther into the deep glow of the evening.

The mother had taken little Anna up in her lap and was now leaning backward as much as she could; it gave such relief to her tired muscles. The caresses of the child and her lively chatter made her forget for a moment care and anxiety, and that vague sense of the unknown which bore in on them so strongly from all directions. . . . Ole sat there and drove like a full-grown man; by some means or other he managed to get more speed out of the oxen than the mother had done— she noticed this herself. His eyes were searching the prairie far and near.

Out on the sky line the huge plain now began to swell and rise, almost as if an abscess were forming under the skin of the earth. Although this elevation lay somewhat out of his course, Per Hansa swung over and held straight toward the highest part of it.

The afternoon breeze lulled, and finally dropped off altogether. The sun, whose golden lustre had faded imperceptibly into a reddish hue, shone now with a dull light, yet strong and clear; in a short while, deeper tones of violet began to creep across the red. The great ball grew enormous; it retreated farther and farther into the empty reaches of the western sky; then it sank suddenly. . . . The spell of evening quickly crowded in and laid hold of them all; the oxen wagged their ears; Rosie lifted her voice in a long moo, which died out slowly in the great stillness. At the moment when the sun closed his eye, the vastness of the plain seemed to rise up on every hand—and suddenly the landscape had grown desolate; something bleak and cold had come into the silence, filling it with terror. . . . Behind them, along the way they had come, the plain lay dark green and lifeless, under the gathering shadow of the dim, purple sky.

Ole sat motionless at his mother's side. The falling of evening had made such a deep impression on him that his throat felt dry; he wanted to express some of the emotions that overwhelmed him, but only choked when he tried.

"Did you ever see anything so beautiful!" he whispered at last, and gave a heavy sigh. . . . Low down in the northwest, above the little hill, a few fleecy clouds hovered, betokening fair weather; now they were fringed with shining gold, which glowed with a mellow light. As if they had no weight, they floated lightly there. . . .

The mother drew herself forward to an upright position. She still held the child in her lap. Per Hansa and Store-Hans were walking in the dusk far up ahead. For the last two days Per had kept well in advance of the caravan all the time; she thought she knew the reason why.

"Per," she called out, wearily, "aren't we going to stop soon?"

"Pretty soon." . . . He did not slacken his pace.

She shifted the child over into the other arm and began to weep silently. Ole saw it, but pretended not to notice, though he had to swallow big lumps that were forcing themselves up in his throat; he kept his eyes resolutely fixed on the scene ahead.

"Dad," he shouted after a while, "I see a wood over there to the westward!"

"You do, do you? A great fellow you are! Store-Hans and I have seen that for a long time now."

"Whereabouts is it?" whispered Store-Hans, eagerly.

"It begins down there on the slope to the left, and then goes around on the other side," said his father. "Anyway, it doesn't seem to be much of a wood."

"D'you think they are there?"

"Not on your life! But we're keeping the right course, anyhow."

"Have the others been this way?"

"Of course they have—somewhere near, at any rate. There's supposed to be a creek around here, by the name of Split Rock Creek, or whatever they call it in English."

"Are there any people here, do you think?"

"People? Good Lord, no! There isn't a soul around these parts."

The sombre blue haze was now closing rapidly in on the caravan. One sensed the night near at hand; it breathed a chill as it came.

At last Per Hansa halted. "Well, I suppose we can't drive any farther to-day. We and the animals would both drop pretty soon." With these words he faced the oxen, held his arms straight out like the horizontal beam of a cross, shouted a long-drawn "Whoa!"—and then the creaking stopped for that day.

III

The preparations for the night were soon made; each had his own task and was now well used to it. Store-Hans brought the wood; it lay strapped under the hind wagon and consisted of small logs and dry branches from the last thicket they had passed.

Ole got the fireplace ready. From the last wagon he brought out two iron rods, cleft in one end; these he drove into the ground and then went back to the wagon for a third rod, which he laid across the other two. It was also his duty to see that there was water enough in the keg, no matter where they happened to stop; for the rest of it, he was on hand to help his mother.

The father tended to the cattle. First he lifted the yoke off the oxen and turned them loose; then he milked Rosie and let her go also. After that he made up a bed for the whole family under the wagon.

While the mother waited for the pot to boil she set the table. She spread a home-woven blanket on the ground, laid a spoon for each one on it, placed a couple of bowls for the milk, and fetched the dishes for the porridge. Meanwhile she had to keep an eye on And-Ongen, who was toddling about in the grass near by. The child stumbled, laughed, lay there a moment chattering to herself, then got up, only to trip on her skirt and tumble headlong again. Her prattling laughter rang on the evening air. Now and then the voice of the mother would mingle with it, warning the child not to stray too far.

Store-Hans was the first to get through with his task; he stood around awhile, but, finding nothing more to do, he strolled off westward. He was itching to know how far it was to the hill out there; it would be great fun to see what things looked like on the other side!

. . . Now he started off in that direction. Perhaps he might come across the others? They surely must be somewhere. Just think, if he could only find them! He would yell and rush in on them like an Indian—and then they would be scared out of their senses! . . . He had gone quite far before he paused to look back. When he did so the sight sent a shiver over him; the wagons had shrunk to two small specks, away off on the floor of a huge, dusky room. . . . I'd better hurry at once, he thought; mother will surely have the porridge ready by this time! His legs had already adopted the idea of their own accord. But thoughts of his mother and the porridge didn't quite bring him all the feeling of safety he needed; he hunted through his mind for a few strains of a hymn, and sang them over and over in a high-pitched, breaking voice, until he had no more breath left to sing with. . . . He didn't feel entirely safe until the wagons had begun to assume their natural size once more.

The mother called to them that supper was ready. On the blanket stood two dishes of porridge—a large dish for the father and the two boys, a smaller one for the mother and And-Ongen. The evening milk was divided between two bowls, and set before them; Rosie, poor thing, was not giving much these days! The father said that he didn't care for milk this evening, either; it had a tangy taste, he thought; and he drank water with his porridge. But when Ole also began to complain of the tangy taste and asked for water, the father grew stern and ordered him to go ahead and get that drop of milk down as quick as he could! There was nothing else on the table but milk and porridge.

Suddenly Ole and Store-Hans flared up in a quarrel; one blamed the other for eating too close to the edge, where the porridge was coolest. The father paused in his meal, listening to them a moment, then chuckled to himself. Taking his spoon and cutting three lines through the crust of the porridge, he quickly settled the matter between them.

"There you are! Here, Store-Hans, is your land; now take it and be satisfied. Ola, who is the biggest, gets another forty. . . . Shut up your mouths, now, and eat!" Per Hansa himself got the smallest share that evening.

Aside from this outbreak it was quiet at the table. A spell of silence lay upon them and they were not able to throw it off. . . . As soon as the father had eaten he licked his spoon carefully, wiped it off on his shirt sleeve, and threw it on the blanket. The boys did likewise as they finished; but And-Ongen wanted to tuck her spoon in her dress and keep it there till morning.

They sat around in the same silence after they were done. Then she who was the smallest of them repeated in a tiny voice:

"Thanks to Thee, Our Lord and Maker. . . .

"Now I want to go to sleep in your lap!" she said, after the Amen. She climbed up into her mother's lap and threw her arms around her neck.

"Oh, how quickly it grows dark out here!" the mother murmured.

Per Hansa gave a care-free shrug of his shoulders. "Well," he said, dryly, "the sooner the day's over, the sooner the next day comes!"

But now something seemed to be brewing back there over the prairie whence they had come. Up from the horizon swelled a supernatural light—a glow of pale yellow and transparent green, mingled with strange touches of red and gold. It spread upward as they watched; the colors deepened; the glow grew stronger, like the witching light of a fen fire.

All sat silently gazing. It was And-Ongen, hanging around her mother's neck, who first found her voice.

"Oh, look! . . . She is coming up again!"

In solemn grandeur the moon swung up above the plain. She had been with them many nights now; but each time she seemed as wonderful a sight as ever. To-night a hush fell on their spirits as they watched her rise—just as the scene had hushed them the evening before, far away to the eastward somewhere on the plain. The silvery beams grew stronger; the first pale fen fire began to shimmer and spread; slowly the light mellowed into a mist of green and yellow and blue. And-Ongen exclaimed that the moon was much bigger to-night; but it had seemed bigger the night before also. Store-Hans again solemnly told her the reason for it—that the moon had to grow, just as she did! This seemed to her quite logical; she turned to her mother and asked whether the moon had milk and porridge every evening, too.

Per Hansa had been sitting on the tongue of the wagon, smoking his pipe. Now he got up, knocked out the ashes carefully, put his pipe in his pocket, and wound up his watch. These duties done, he gave the order to turn in for the night.

A little while later they all lay under the quilts, gazing off into the opalescent glow. When the mother thought that the children had gone to sleep she asked, soberly:

"Do you suppose we'll ever find the others again?"

"Oh yes—I'm sure of it . . . if they haven't sunk through the ground!"

This was all Per Hansa said. He yawned once or twice, long and heavily, as if he were very sleepy, and turned away from her.

. . . After that she said no more, either.

212

IV

Truth to tell, Per Hansa was not a bit sleepy. For a long while he lay wide awake, staring into the night. Although the evening had grown cool, sweat started out on his body from time to time, as thoughts which he could not banish persisted in his mind.

He had good reason to sweat, at all the things he was forced to lie there and remember. Nor was it only to-night that these heavy thoughts came to trouble him; it had been just the same all through the day, and last night, too, and the night before. And now, the moment he had lain down, they had seized upon him with renewed strength; he recalled keenly all the scruples and misgivings that had obsessed his wife before they had started out on this long journey—both those which had been spoken and those which had been left unsaid. The latter had been the worst; they had seemed to grow deeper and more tragic as he had kept prying into them in his clumsy way. . . . But she wasn't a bit stupid, that wife of his! As a matter of fact, she had more sense than most people. Indeed she had!

. . . No, it wasn't a pleasant situation for Per Hansa, by any means. He had not seen a happy moment, day or night, since the mishap had struck them on the second afternoon this side of Jackson. There the first wagon had got stuck in a mud hole; in pulling it out they had wrecked it so hopelessly that he had been forced to put back to Jackson for repairs. Under the circumstances, it had seemed to him utterly senseless to hold up all the rest of the company four days. He simply wouldn't listen to their waiting for him; for they had houses to build and fields to break, if they were to get anything into the ground this season. They must go on without him; he'd come along all right, in his own good time. . . . So they had given him full instructions about the course he was to follow and the halting places where he was to stop for the night; it had all seemed so simple to him at the time. Then they had started on together—Tönseten, who knew the way, and Hans Olsa, and the two Solum boys. They all had horses and strong new wagons. They travelled fast, those fellows! . . .

If he only had paid some attention to Hans Olsa, who for a long while had insisted on waiting for him. But he had overruled all their objections; it was entirely his own doing that Hans Olsa and the others had gone on, leaving him behind.

But he soon had learned that it wasn't so easy. Hadn't he lost his way altogether the other day, in the midst of a fog and drizzling rain? Until late in the afternoon that day he hadn't had the faintest idea what direction he was taking. It had been after this experience that he had formed the habit of keeping so far ahead of the caravan. He simply couldn't endure listening to her constant questions—questions which he found himself unable to answer. . . .

The only thing he felt sure of was that he wasn't on the right track; otherwise he would have come across the traces of their camps. It was getting to be a matter of life and death to him to find the trail —and find it soon. . . . A devil of a jaunt it would be to the Pacific Ocean—the wagon would never hold out *that* long! . . . Oh yes, he realized it all too well—a matter of life and death. There weren't many supplies left in the wagon. He had depended on his old comrade and Lofot-man, Hans Olsa, for everything.

Per Hansa heaved a deep sigh; it came out before he could stop it. . . . Huh!—it was an easy matter enough for Hans Olsa! He had ample means, and could start out on a big scale from the beginning; he had a wife in whose heart there wasn't a speck of fear! . . . The Lord only knew where they were now—whether they were east or west of him! And they had Tönseten, too, and his wife Kjersti, both of them used to America. Why, they could talk the language and everything. . . .

And then there were the Solum boys, who had actually been born in this country. . . . Indeed, east or west, it made no difference to them where they lay that night.

But here was he, the newcomer, who owned nothing and knew nothing, groping about with his dear ones in the endless wilderness! . . . Beret had taken such a dislike to this journey, too—although in many ways she was the more sensible of the two. . . . Well, he certainly had fixed up a nice mess for himself, and no mistake!

He wondered why he had ever left Fillmore County; as he lay there thinking it over, he couldn't understand what had prompted him to do such a thing. He could easily have found a job there and stayed until his wife got up from childbed; then he could have moved west next spring. This had been what she had wanted, though she had never said it in so many words.

The quilt had grown oppressively heavy; he threw it aside. . . . How long it took her to go to sleep to-night! Why wouldn't she try to get as much rest as possible? Surely she knew that it would be another tough day to-morrow? . . .

. . . Just so that confounded wagon didn't go to pieces again! . . .

V

The night wore on. The children slept quietly and peacefully. The mother also seemed to have found rest at last. Per Hansa thought that she was sound asleep; he began to move slowly away from her. He threw his hand over on the quilt between them as if making a motion in his sleep. . . . No, she didn't stir; he lay quiet for a while, then moved again. In so doing his hand happened to fall on that of Store-Hans; it was so chubby and round, that hand, so healthy and warm, and quite firm for the hand of only a child. Per Hansa lay still for a long time, holding the boy's hand with a desperate earnestness. . . . Slowly the troublesome thoughts seemed to lighten and lift; his courage ebbed back again; surely everything would come out all right in the end!

Little by little he slipped the quilt off, crept out of bed as quietly as a mouse, got into his trousers, and pulled on his shoes.

Outside, the misty sheen of the moonlight shimmered so brightly that it blinded him. Near at hand, the prairie was bathed in a flood of tarnished green; farther off the faint blue tones began to appear, merging gradually into the purple dimness that shrouded all the horizon.

Per Hansa looked for the North Star, found it, turned about until he had it over his right shoulder; then he glanced at his watch, took a few steps, hesitated, and looked back as if taking a bearing of the wagons and the star. The next moment he faced about resolutely, and hurried off westward.

It felt good to be moving again; he almost broke into a trot. There were the oxen, busily grazing; they needed to get their fill all right, poor devils! . . . Rosie lay closer to the wagons; his eyes had passed over her at first, a dark spot in the vague, deceptive light. The cow must have noticed the shadow gliding along so swiftly; she gave a long moo. . . . This enraged Per Hansa; he broke into a run and got out of her sight as quickly as he could, for fear she would moo again. . . . If she only hadn't waked Beret!

He set his course toward the point where he thought the crest of the ridge must lie. Now and then he stopped and looked around, to find out if he could still see the wagons. When he had lost them at last, and they were wholly swallowed up in the night, he gave an involuntary gasp—but clenched his teeth and went on.

The ridge lay farther off than he had thought. He had walked for a solid hour before he finally reached what he felt to be the highest point; he reckoned that he must be at least four miles from camp. . . . There he fell to examining the ground carefully; but first of all he looked at his watch again, and then at the North Star and the moon, trying to fix the bearings of the camp in his mind.

On the other side of the ridge the lay of the land seemed to be different; the slope was a little steeper; a thick underbrush covered it;

through the tall bushes the moonlight shimmered strangely. . . . Per Hansa felt no fear, but every sense within him was alert. First he searched the northerly slope of the hill, beyond the edge of the thicket, stooping over as he went, his eyes scanning every foot of the ground. When he had found no trace of what he was looking for, he came back to the same starting point and searched an equal distance in the opposite direction; but he discovered nothing on this tack, either.

Now he began to walk along the edge of the thicket, in and out, crisscrossing the line in every direction; he pushed his way into each little grassless opening, and kicked over the earth there, before he went on. Sweat was running off him in streams. A quarter of an hour went by; he was still searching frantically. . . . All at once, right at the edge of the woods, he struck a piece of level ground with a larger clearing on it; in the middle of this clearing lay a wide, round patch in the grass. Per Hansa threw himself down on his knees, like a miser who has found a costly treasure; he bent over and sniffed the ground. His blood throbbed; his hands shook as he dug. . . . Yes, he was right —here there had been a fire! It couldn't have been many days ago, either; the smell of the ashes was still fresh. . . . His eyes had grown so moist and dim that he had to wipe them. . . . But he wasn't crying —no, not yet! . . .

He began to crawl around on all fours, farther and farther down the slope. Suddenly he stopped, sat up on his haunches, and held something in his hand that he was examining closely. . . .

"I'll be damned if it isn't fresh horse dung!" . . . His voice rang with a great joy. He tried the stuff between his fingers—crumbled it, sniffed at it . . . there was no doubting the fact any longer.

Now he got up, walking erectly with a confident step, like a man who has just made a lucky strike, and began to search along the whole slope. . . . He might as well go ahead and find the ford to-night; then he wouldn't be delayed by hunting for it in the morning. The under-brush thickened as he made his way down the slope. . . . Here, then, was Split Rock Creek; and here they had camped, as Tönseten had said they would! . . .

Once he had reached the edge of the creek, it did not take him long to find the ford that the others had used; the ruts still stood there plainly, as fresh and deep as if they had been made that very day. For a while he paused at the edge of the water, and looked about him. . . . Had they chosen the best crossing, after all? The bank of the creek on the other side formed a bend; the brink looked pretty steep. At last he waded out into the water, with his shoes still on. . . . Oh, well, the grade wasn't so steep that the oxen couldn't easily make it; there would be a bad jolt here at the edge, but after that they would have an even slope up the bank. . . . Stepping out on the opposite shore, he stood as if rooted to the ground.

. . . "What in the devil . . . !"

Per Hansa bent over and picked up the object that lay before him; he held it out in the moonlight, turned it over and over in his hands, smelled of it . . . then took a bite.

. . . "By God! if it isn't one of Hans Olsa's dried mutton legs!"

He straightened himself up and gazed with deep thankfulness into the quivering bluish-green haze that glowed all around him. . . . "Yes, that's the way it goes, when people have more than they can take care of!" . . . He stuck the mutton leg under his arm; whistling a love ballad of Nordland, which seemed to have come into his mind unconsciously, he crossed the creek again.

On the way back he took his own time. Nothing mattered now; the night was fair and mild; his aching weariness was gone; he felt refreshed and strengthened. His wife and children were sleeping safe and sound; of food they still had supplies for a couple of weeks; and now he had found the trail again and could be certain of it all the way to Sioux Falls. . . . That wretched wagon was the only difficulty; it would have to hang together for a few days more! . . .

When he drew near enough to the wagons to make them out clearly in the moonlight, he slackened his pace, and a shiver passed over him.

Wasn't some one sitting there on the wagon tongue? Surely that was a human form?

In growing apprehension, he hurried on.

"Good Heavens, Beret! What are you doing out here in the middle of the night?" His voice was full of alarm, yet softened by his great concern for her.

"It felt so awful to lie there alone, after you had gone. . . . I could hardly breathe . . . so I got up."

The words came with difficulty; he realized that her voice was hoarse with weeping; he had to pull himself sharply together in order to keep his own tears back.

"Were you awake, Beret? . . . You shouldn't lie awake that way in the night!" he said, reproachfully.

"How can I sleep? . . . You lie there tossing back and forth, and say nothing! . . . You might have told me. I know very well what's the matter!"

Suddenly she could stand it no longer. She ran over to him, flung her arms around his neck, and leaned close against him. The dam of her pent-up tears broke in a flood of emotion; she wept long and bitterly.

"Now calm yourself, dear. . . . You *must* calm yourself, Beret-girl!" . . . He had put his arm lovingly around her, but found it hard to speak. . . . "Don't you see that I've got one of Hans Olsa's dried mutton legs under my arm?" . . .

. . . That night Per Hansa was good to his wife.

THE WOODS

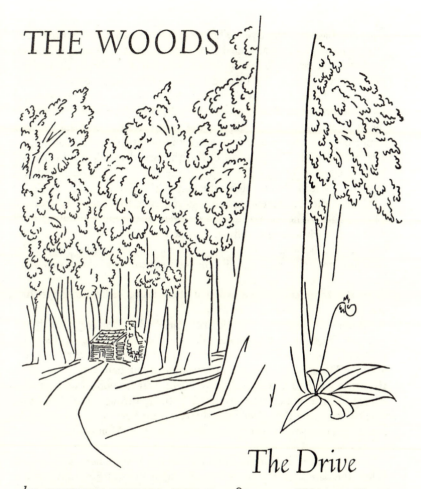

The Drive

by STEWART EDWARD WHITE, 1873– . *White was born at Grand Rapids, Michigan, where he later attended high school. He was graduated from the University of Michigan, Ph.B., 1895, and studied law for a time at Columbia University but relinquished his course when Brander Matthews persuaded him that he had a talent for writing. The many books that followed this decision are set in widely different places, the Michigan woods, the Canadian Northwest, Alaska, California, Arizona, and Africa. Among his best work are novels of Michigan lumbering, such as The Blazed Trail (1902) and The Riverman (1908); a collection of cowboy yarns, Arizona Nights (1907); and a series of sketches and essays on wilderness life entitled The Forest (1903). White is a prolific writer who has not always escaped melodrama and triteness. "The Drive" describes an exciting event in The Blazed Trail.*

At the banks of the river, Thorpe rapidly issued his directions. The affair had been all prearranged. During the week previous he and his foremen had reviewed the situation, examining the state of the ice, the heads of water in the three dams. Immediately above the first roll-ways was Dam Three with its two wide sluices through which a veritable flood could be loosened at will; then four miles farther lay the rollways of Sadler & Smith, the up-river firm; and above them tumbled over a forty-five foot ledge the beautiful Siscoe Falls; these first rollways of Thorpe's—spread in the broad marsh flat below the dam—contained about eight millions; the rest of the season's cut was scattered for thirty miles along the bed of the river.

Already the ice cementing the logs together had begun to weaken. The ice had wrenched and tugged savagely at the locked timbers until they had, with a mighty effort, snapped asunder the bonds of their hibernation. Now a narrow lane of black rushing water pierced the rollways, to boil and eddy in the consequent jam three miles below.

To the foremen Thorpe assigned their tasks, calling them to him one by one, as a general calls his aids.

"Moloney," said he to the big Irishman, "take your crew and break that jam. Then scatter your men down to within a mile of the pond at Dam Two, and see that the river runs clear. You can tent for a day or so at West Bend or some other point about half-way down; and after that you had better camp at the dam. Just as soon as you get logs enough in the pond, start to sluicing them through the dam. You won't need more than four men there, if you keep a good head. You can keep your gates open five or six hours. And Moloney!"

"Yes, sir."

"I want you to be careful not to sluice too long. There is a bar just below the dam, and if you try to sluice with the water too low, you'll centre and jam there, as sure as shooting."

Bryan Moloney turned on his heel and began to pick his way down-stream over the solidly banked logs. Without waiting the command, a dozen men followed him. The little group bobbed away irregularly into the distance, springing lightly from one timber to the other, holding their quaintly fashioned peaveys in the manner of a rope-dancer's balancing pole. At the lowermost limit of the rollways each man pried a log into the water, and standing gracefully erect on this unstable craft, floated out down the current to the scene of his dangerous labor.

"Kerlie," went on Thorpe, "your crew can break rollways with the rest until we get the river fairly filled, and then you can move on down-stream as fast as you are needed. Scotty, you will have the rear. Tim and I will boss the river."

At once the signal was given to Ellis, the dam watcher. Ellis and his assistants thereupon began to pry with long iron bars at the ratchets of the heavy gates. The chore-boy bent attentively over the ratchet-pin, lifting it delicately to permit another inch of raise; dropping it accurately to enable the men at the bars to seize a fresh purchase. The river's roar deepened. Through the wide sluiceways a torrent foamed and tumbled. Immediately it spread through the brush on either side to the limits of the freshet banks, and then gathered for its leap against the uneasy rollways. Along the edge of the dark channel the face of the logs seemed to crumble away. Farther in toward the banks where the weight of timber still outbalanced the weight of the flood, the tiers grumbled and stirred, restless with the stream's calling. Far down the river, where Bryan Moloney and his crew were picking at the jam, the water in eager streamlets sought the interstices between the logs, gurgling excitedly like a mountain brook.

The jam creaked and groaned in response to the pressure. From its face a hundred jets of water spurted into the lower stream. Logs up-ended here and there, rising from the bristling surface slowly, like so many arms from lower depths. Above, the water eddied back foaming; logs shot down from the rollways, paused at the slackwater, and finally hit with a hollow and resounding *boom!* against the tail of the jam. A moment later they too up-ended, so becoming an integral part of the *chevaux de frise.*

The crew were working desperately. Down in the heap somewhere, two logs were crossed in such a manner as to lock the whole. They sought those logs.

Thirty feet above the bed of the river six men clamped their peaveys into the soft pine; jerking, pulling, lifting, sliding the great logs from their places. Thirty feet below, under the threatening face, six other men coolly picked out and set adrift, one by one, the timbers not inextricably imbedded. From time to time the mass creaked, settled, perhaps even moved a foot or two; but always the practised rivermen, after a glance, bent more eagerly to their work.

Outlined against the sky, big Bryan Moloney stood directing the work. He had gone at the job on the bias of indirection, picking out a passage at either side that the centre might the more easily "pull." He knew by the tenseness of the log he stood on that, behind the jam, power had gathered sufficient to push the whole tangle down-stream. Now he was offering it the chance.

Suddenly the six men below the jam scattered. Four of them, holding their peaveys across their bodies, jumped lightly from one floating log to another in the zigzag to shore. When they stepped on a small log they re-leaped immediately, leaving a swirl of foam where the little timber had sunk under them; when they encountered one larger, they hesitated for a barely perceptible instant. Thus their progression was of fascinating and graceful irregularity. The other two ran the length of their footing, and, overleaping an open of water, landed heavily and firmly on the very ends of two small floating logs. In this manner the force of the jump rushed the little timbers end-on through the water. The two men, maintaining marvellously their balance, were thus ferried to within leaping distance of the other shore.

In the meantime a barely perceptible motion was communicating itself from one particle to another through the centre of the jam. A cool and observant spectator might have imagined that the broad timber carpet was changing a little its pattern, just as the earth near the windows of an arrested railroad train seems for a moment to retrogress. The crew redoubled its exertions, clamping its peaveys here and there, apparently at random, but in reality with the most definite of purposes. A sharp *crack* exploded immediately underneath. There could no longer exist any doubt as to the motion, although it was as yet sluggish, glacial. Then in silence a log shifted—in silence and slowly—but with irresistible force. Jimmy Powers quietly stepped over it, just as it menaced his leg. Other logs in all directions up-ended. The jam crew were forced continually to alter their positions, riding the changing timbers bent-kneed, as a circus rider treads his four galloping horses.

Then all at once down by the face something crashed. The entire stream became alive. It hissed and roared, it shrieked, groaned and grumbled. At first slowly, then more rapidly, the very forefront of the centre melted inward and forward and downward until it caught the fierce rush of the freshet and shot out from under the jam. Far up-stream, bristling and formidable, the tons of logs, grinding savagely together, swept forward.

The six men and Bryan Moloney—who, it will be remembered, were on top—worked until the last moment. When the logs began to cave under them so rapidly that even the expert rivermen found difficulty in "staying on top," the foreman set the example of hunting safety.

"She 'pulls,' boys," he yelled.

Then in a manner wonderful to behold, through the smother of foam and spray, through the crash and yell of timbers protesting the flood's hurrying, through the leap of destruction, the drivers zigzagged calmly and surely to the shore.

All but Jimmy Powers. He poised tense and eager on the crumbling face of the jam. Almost immediately he saw what he wanted, and

without pause sprang boldly and confidently ten feet straight downward, to alight with accuracy on a single log floating free in the
current. And then in the very glory and chaos of the jam itself he
was swept down-stream.

After a moment the constant acceleration in speed checked, then
commenced perceptibly to slacken. At once the rest of the crew began to ride down-stream. Each struck the caulks of his river boots
strongly into a log, and on such unstable vehicles floated miles with
the current. From time to time, as Bryan Moloney indicated, one of
them went ashore. There, usually at a bend of the stream where the
likelihood of jamming was great, they took their stands. When necessary, they ran out over the face of the river to separate a congestion
likely to cause trouble. The rest of the time they smoked their pipes.

At noon they ate from little canvas bags which had been filled that
morning by the cookee. At sunset they rode other logs down the river
to where their camp had been made for them. There they ate hugely,
hung their ice-wet garments over a tall framework constructed around
a monster fire, and turned in on hemlock branches.

All night long the logs slipped down the moonlit current, silently,
swiftly, yet without haste. The porcupines invaded the sleeping camp.
From the whole length of the river rang the hollow *boom, boom,
boom,* of timbers striking one against the other.

The drive was on.

The Peshtigo Fire

by STEWART HALL HOLBROOK, 1893– . *Born in Newport, Vermont, Holbrook was educated in the Vermont elementary schools and attended high school at Colebrook, New Hampshire. After serving as a first-
sergeant in the field artillery during World War I Holbrook worked as a
newspaperman for some years and was a feature writer for the Portland-
Oregonian from 1930 to 1937. Holbrook has contributed frequently to various magazines and his special interest in lumbering and the forest has led
him to write such books as* Holy Old Mackinaw, A Natural History of the
American Lumberjack *(1938) and* Burning an Empire *(1943). The account of the Peshtigo fire originally appeared in the* American Scholar, *Spring
1944.*

IN A logging camp where I worked twenty-odd years ago was a remarkably fine chronicler of the woods named John Cameron. In his

half century in timber from Maine to Oregon he had seen a good many things, among them events of the first importance in America's oldest industry—lumber—the effects of some of which are being felt today by Americans who know nothing of the causes.

John Cameron was a veritable Nestor of the woods, almost immemorially old and grizzled, but durable, a *lignum vitae* man. He was squat and solid, and his face and neck were tanned and seamed by the sun and by winds that had blown upon him all the way from the Penobscot to the Columbia. He wore a beard like General Grant's. Moreover, John was a man of intellectual probity, as careful of his facts as he was of the figures of logs which he set down on his scale sheets. I came to have great faith in his memory of past events, a memory which both time and no little research have proved to have been honest and accurate.

I

Sitting on the deacon seat in camp, while winds howled through the towering Douglas fir and the rain came down like bullets, I used to look into the fire of the barrel-stove and do my best to keep John telling of his life in the timber. The fact that he was a marked man sat lightly on his shoulders, although he was conscious of the distinction. For you must know that John Cameron was a survivor of the Great Peshtigo Disaster, words that are spoken with capitals by those who know the significance of Peshtigo. Veterans of Waterloo and Gettysburg have had no greater distinction.

This disaster, one of the greatest in American history, occurred in October seventy-three years ago, and through a fate so ironic that perverse gods must have arranged it, is known hardly to one American in ten thousand.

The time was 1871. The scene was Peshtigo, a booming lumber town in northeast Wisconsin which stood on both sides of the swift Peshtigo River that flowed southeast to enter Lake Michigan's Green Bay, six miles distant. A narrow-gauge railroad connected the town with its port, called Peshtigo Harbor, whence lumber and woodenware products were shipped to Chicago at the far southern end of the big lake. The town of close to two thousand people had been built up quickly around the sawmill and factory of the Peshtigo Company, a wealthy concern headed by the eminent William B. Ogden of Chicago, with Isaac Stephenson of Marinette second in command.

Every working day the company's factory turned out 600 common pails, 170 tubs, 250 fish kits, 5,000 broom handles, 50 boxes of clothes pins, 45,000 shingles, 8 dozen barrel heads, 260 paint pails, 200 tobacco pails, 200 keelers, and 200 kannakins. (Keelers were small oval tubs often used as bathtubs for babies. A kannakin was a special sort of wooden bucket.) And every working day the company's sawmills—one at Peshtigo, one at the Harbor—made a lot of lumber. The company employed, in camps and mills, no fewer than 800 men.

Remote as Peshtigo was from the rest of the world in 1871, it was soon to have direct rail connection with Chicago. The Chicago & North Western was building through from Fort Howard (now West Green Bay) to Menominee, Michigan. Large gangs of men were slashing through the woods, clearing the right-of-way, and incidentally planting the means of destruction, not only of Peshtigo and all it contained, but also of a vast empire of timber. For the railroad builders at that time made the slash (the debris of their clearing operations) into long piles and set them on fire, leaving them unattended to burn as they would.

The town was lively with transient labor, with newly arrived settlers, and with drummers for everything from saws and axes to Dr. Perry Davis' Painkiller, "Friend of Man & Beast." They were cared for at the roomy Peshtigo House and three other hotels, and were entertained at four sizable saloons. The forest began right at Peshtigo's village limits and ran west and north—how far, no man knew except timber cruisers and Indians—broken by several natural clearings in a hardwood area a few miles from Peshtigo. These clearings, where farmers already had taken root, were known as the Upper, the Middle, and the Lower Sugar Bush.

Romantic novelists to the contrary, social life in the United States has always kept close to the frontier. In this so-called raw lumber settlement of the big woods a Congregational meeting house reared its spire on the east side of town. On the west side Catholics had almost completed a church and parish house. A small Episcopalian society met in Good Templars Hall. The Good Templars themselves were rehearsing, in October of '71, a "side-splitting farce, The Vermont Wool Grower," to be followed by "the great moral spectacle, Ten Nights in a Bar Room." The village had a roomy schoolhouse. There were a number of stores, including one of a druggist who read many books and would lend them to literates. Thus the village was taking on a permanent form, with a likely future. And to top its civic pride and dignity, Luther B. Noyes had just started the *Marinette and Peshtigo Eagle*, a weekly paper as large as a small blanket. True, the *Eagle* was printed in nearby Marinette; but the paper carried much news of Peshtigo, and Peshtigo folks read it intently.

Editor Noyes started publication in June of 1871, just in time to cover the biggest story the paper was ever to know. But there were a few preliminary items ahead of the Big Story, many of them having a direct bearing on it. On September 9 the *Eagle* noted that "Mulligan's brigade of choppers, axes in hand, armed and equipped as the railroad authorities direct, 32 strong, rank and file, passed this place on Saturday en route for the north side of the river, to clear for the railroad." On the 16th the paper noted ". . . heavy fires northeast of the village [Peshtigo] in the woods." Mulligan's brigade was doing its work. On the 30th the *Eagle* reported that ". . . last Sunday all hands turned out to fight fire in the woods near the Peshtigo factory."

The woods around Peshtigo, and indeed much of the woods of Wisconsin and Michigan as well, were ready for fire. A drought lay on the land from early May through September, with only one rain, "a smart shower" on July 8, to break it. A contemporary said that the very atmosphere seemed to pant, and everything along Green Bay was parched and cracked. The swamps of tamarack and the marshes of cedar were "black, dry and cheerless." Continuous small forest fires throughout hot September had destroyed the one telegraph line into the region. But in those days, and for many years after, little or no heed was paid to fires in the woods unless and until they actually threatened personal property, like houses and barns. Such were the weather conditions at the end of September.

II

On the 8th of October, Peshtigo awoke to find a copper sun in the sky, and a village that lay baked and sultry in an autumn heat such as no man, red or white, could remember. The air was deathly still. Flocks of birds were seen to form and fly away, but not one made a sound of any kind. By noon the sun disappeared entirely, and a strange yellow half-light, coming from no visible source and ghastly in its effect on men and things, lighted the sawdust streets and plank sidewalks and made the swift, silent waters of the Peshtigo River look bilious.

Up from the Harbor that morning came 200 new laborers fresh from Chicago, who were going to lay rails. They lurched up and down West Front Street, shouting, "emitting horrible blasphemies," and performing generally in the manner of mass drunks. As for the solid villagers, they attended church services, then sat down to heavy Sunday dinners. The unmarried employees of the Peshtigo Company had an extra-good meal in the company's rambling big boarding house.

The afternoon wore on, hot and silent—and smoky enough to make eyes run. Suppertime saw black and white ashes drifting through screenless windows and getting into the food. When night closed down over the village in the forest, folks could plainly see a sullen red over the treetops to the southwest. The smoke thickened. John Cameron, in from a cruise of timber, sat on the steps of the company's boarding house and at about nine o'clock thought he could hear a new noise in the night, a low moaning, soft, deep, far-off, that gradually changed to a sullen roar. Cameron had heard big winds in his time, and big cataracts, too, but nothing like this sound that was now welling up, back there in the big timber.

The wind rose for a few moments, rustling the trees that still stood in the village. Then it fell, and there was silence again, except for that deep, steady roar, far off to the southwest. Or, Cameron began to wonder, *was* it far off?

As he peered into the night that seemed to be growing lighter by the minute, John Cameron saw a whirling slab of fire come hurtling out of nowhere and drop fair into the sawdust street. He brushed his streaming eyes, but this slab of fire was no illusion. It was followed by another and another. Cameron yelled a long incoherent cry. More fire rained down.

In a flash, it seemed, the splintered pine sidewalks of Peshtigo were blazing. Startled men and women crowded onto doorsteps. The top of a house leaped with sudden flame. There came a crashing and deep booming from the surrounding forest, while underneath all was a steady roar that was greater than Niagara's. Now a deer, wide-eyed and shaking, flitted out of the forest and stood stock still in the midst of town dogs who whimpered and sniffed but made no attempt to attack the wild creature. Down the street trotted a legion of housecats, pausing to look at what was behind them.

City folk are given to thinking that things happen in a leisurely way in the back country, where life all but stands still. City folk should have stood on the smoldering streets of Peshtigo that night. In less than five minutes all hell rode into town on the back of a rising hurricane.

It was a seething, searing hell, and the hurricane it was riding traveled almost as fast as light itself. It swept in so suddenly that no man could say for certain what happened in the next few moments. What is assuredly and horribly known is that some forty men, their senses blown away in that first blast of flame, rushed into the company's boarding house and then and there were burned to cinders.

Others ran to the bridge that crossed the river, and there ran headlong into people from the other side of town. Human beings, horses, cows, wagons, met in the middle of the bridge. Now the structure itself began to burn. Here was tragic confusion, a frantic, struggling mass. Some were trampled, others went overboard in the crush, to fall into the river where they must swim, or drown. Now the big sawmill, by the east end of the bridge, started burning like a vast furnace. The very logs in the mill pond began to smoke, then to light up with flame.

John Cameron and many others were fleeing down the east bank of the river below the dam, where many drowned and others lived it out. On the way they saw things they never forgot. Never. They saw horses and cattle, and men and women, stagger a brief moment over the smoking sawdust streets, then go down to burn brightly like so many flares of pitch-pine. Forty years afterward an ancient man's voice choked when he told of watching pretty Helga Rockstad as she ran down a blazing sidewalk, her blond hair streaming out behind and of seeing the long blond hair leap into a flame that stopped Helga in her tracks. Looking at the spot next morning, he related, he had found two nickel garter buckles and a little mound of white-gray ash.

The river was truly the safest place in Peshtigo that night, and even the river wasn't too safe. Clinging to a log in the water young Amelia Slaughter, aged nine, watched while Peshtigo burned on both banks and the river filled with human beings and animals, wallowing, swimming, rearing, bellowing, shouting. She saw Mrs. Heidenworth struggling and apparently drowning; then, grasping the long horn of a passing cow, towed out of sight and to safety.

Down past the refugees in the river a burning log floated swiftly; presently came more logs, all afire and hissing as they moved—a swift, steady procession of danger and often of death, for the plunging logs knocked people off their legs and into the water, stunned them, then went on, flaming and hissing like some special engines of destruction turned loose by the fire devils who seemed to have taken charge of Peshtigo. A bit later, little Amelia heard a roar, and felt a concussion of air that nearly stunned her. It was the factory going up in a tremendous explosion. Out of the factory came a torrent of fire in the shape of thousands of blazing buckets and tubs and shingles which tore through the night like small meteors and fell everywhere like rain. . . . Between nine and ten o'clock the entire town of Peshtigo was wiped clean.

III

Peshtigo was merely the fire-center that night. The flames had taken a ghastly toll there, but fire had also devastated the Sugar Bush districts, and swept on north, leaping the broad Menominee River and rushing on into Michigan, destroying the settlement of Birch Creek. Nor was this all. New Franken and Robinsonville, on the long lean Peninsula formed of Brown, Kewanee, and Door counties, had been destroyed. The same fire roared into New Brussels and Little Sturgeon, while the religious Belgian settlers shouted that the Last Days were here. And so they were for many.

Three months later a sort of official death list was made up. Six hundred had died in Peshtigo; one hundred and twenty died in the Lower Sugar Bush, seventy-five in the Middle, sixty in the Upper. The total dead on the Peninsula was seventy-five; and at Birch Creek, Michigan, twenty-two. The toll on isolated homesteads, and at logging camps and trappers' cabins was set at two hundred. All of these were not "probable" but certain deaths, a minimum figure which totalled up to 1,152. It was the greatest toll taken by a single forest fire in the United States. Of forest land, the flames swept 1,280,000 acres, a veritable empire of timber.

Rain began falling on October 9—just twenty-four hours too late to be of much help. On the 14th the *Eagle* came out with a Fire Extra. It was a single sheet, about one quarter the size of the usual blanket-size format, printed on both sides. Editor Noyes apologized for this tabloid, saying it was due to the fact that his paper supply had not arrived from Chicago; Chicago, so he had heard rumored by a man on a passing steamboat, had had a fire of its own.

Editor Noyes' "rumor" about Chicago, of course, was fact. At approximately the same time that fire swept into Peshtigo on the night of the eighth, the notorious cow kicked over the celebrated lantern of the immortal Mrs. O'Leary in the big city at the foot of the lake. While John Cameron and other citizens were fleeing to the Peshtigo River, residents of Chicago's South Side were fighting to cross the bridges to the north side of its river. The Chicago Fire went directly into history, and ultimately into the movies.

Chicago got virtually all the publicity. Yet only about two hundred lives were lost in Chicago. And I doubt gravely that the destruction of property in the city was so great a loss to the United States as was the laying waste of more than one and a quarter million acres of timber land; in more ways than one Wisconsin is still paying for the Peshtigo Fire. The world immediately heard of Chicago's loss. Troops came to keep order. Relief trains rolled in. Queen Victoria, Charles Darwin, Alfred Lord Tennyson, and thousands of less eminent Britons contributed books to found a new library in Chicago. Everything came to the blackened city as quickly and as bountifully as is the custom of America in disasters.

It was six weeks, however, before even *Harper's Weekly*, the news-magazine of the time, learned of the horror that had swept through the Wisconsin backwoods; then it devoted many pages of text and wood-cuts to depicting the disaster. But the big city held the spotlight, for Americans apparently cannot get excited over more than one disaster at a time. When I talked with six survivors of Peshtigo, in 1942, all were bitter about Chicago. "Nobody in the United States," vowed one old lady, who had clung to a log in the river that night, "ever heard of the Peshtigo Fire." That is not quite true, but it is almost true. Even in Wisconsin few school children or college men and women seem yet to have heard of it.

IV

On November 18, five weeks after the fire, Editor Noyes was moved to note that winter had struck hard on the heels of the disaster. "As the blasts of winter howl a requiem over the ruins of Peshtigo," he wrote in the *Eagle*, "the survivors will hear in imagination the hissing, crackling flames, the roar of the tornado like that of an earthquake, and mingled with the terrific din will come shuddering on the fiery blast the helpless wail of the innocents who yielded up their lives as the storm went howling and shrieking by."

The tragedy of it was that the innocents had died in vain. Not then, nor for many years, were the American people, either in Wisconsin or elsewhere, ready to do anything to prevent disasters like that at Peshtigo. Peshtigo, indeed, was simply Wisconsin's *first* great forest fire. It was the greatest in loss of life, but in the area damaged cannot be compared with the 3,000,000-acre fire which swept the state one day and night in 1894. In that year, too, the Hinckley fire in Minnesota took 418 lives in the timber. In 1910, forest fires in Minnesota, Montana, and Idaho killed more than one hundred fire fighters and forty-two civilians, and removed an immense forest. The Moose Lake and Cloquet forest fires, also in Minnesota, took close to 600 lives one night in 1918.

It was as a result of the fires of 1910—forty years after Peshtigo—that the United States really began to give serious consideration to the protection of her forests. That the protection is still far from adequate is to be seen in these national statistics: forest fires in the United States today average 172,000 yearly, and they burn up the better part of 36,000,000 acres of forest each year. That more lives have not been lost in recent years is due chiefly to better roads and transportation, and to an immense amount of good luck. As late as 1936 I saw a forest fire in Oregon that took an even dozen lives; and another in 1933 that took but one life yet destroyed twelve billion feet of timber—enough to have supplied the lumber needs of the entire United States in that year.

This ghastly waste goes on year after year, in spite of the finest forest fire control agencies in the world—those of the federal forest service, the various state forestry departments, and many private associations and patrols. These agencies are doing fine work in the quick detection of fires and in their suppression. What we need, what we must have, is more prevention.

A Boyhood in the Bush

by THOMAS J. LEBLANC, 1894–   . *Born in Cheboygan, Michigan, Dr. LeBlanc was educated at the University of Michigan, B.A., 1916, and Johns Hopkins University, D.Sc., 1923. After serving as a field scientist for the Rockefeller Foundation and as statistician in the United States Public Health Service, he joined the faculty of the University of Cincinnati, where since 1935 he has been professor and head of the department of preventive medicine in the College of Medicine. Dr. LeBlanc has also won a reputation as a writer and has contributed to various magazines sketches of lumberjack life in Michigan logging communities. One of the most vivid of these, "A Boyhood in the Bush," appeared in the American Mercury, September 1924.*

I

My BOYHOOD was spent in a small northern lumbering town in the heart of the pine forests that cluster along the Canadian border, and my earliest memories are of the whine of the great whirling disk saws in the mills, the crunch of the logs as they crowded the river that ran through the center of the town, the slap of the boards as they fell into place on the decks of the waiting schooners, and the call of the scalers and tally-men. At night the village was bathed in the radiance of the burners that stood against the dark sky like huge torches, each giving off its own flaming feather of sparks. Always there was the closeness of the bush that jostled the edges of the town and made inroads at some of the weaker spots. Over all was the clean fragrant smell of the pines.

Children were not numerous in such wild settlements and I had few playmates. To the few of us living there winter was a time of dog teams and, if we were lucky, an occasional visit to a lumber-camp. In this respect I was fortunate in having Billy. Billy was a friend of the family whose business I never knew. It was sufficient for me that he would call at our house with his sleigh, load me into the box, buried in bearskins, and whisk me away behind his jangling bells for a two- or three-day visit to a camp. For miles we rode, enveloped in a cloud of vapor from the horses, the bobs of the sleigh ringing on the surface of the snow. Finally we would turn on to the glistening surface of a tote road and I would cautiously raise myself and expose my face to the biting cold. We would be gliding down an icy lane, shining like a mirror, and with the tall snow-shrouded pines rising on either side. I used to liken it to riding down the aisle of a cathedral, a giant cathedral with a polished floor. I had once been in one at Christmas time, when the columns were hung with evergreens. Soon we would swing into the camp, a cluster of long, low log buildings huddled in a small clearing and completely buried in snow. Here we received a boisterous and profane greeting from the cook and cookee, and whoever else happened to be in camp.

At noon I sat proudly on the front seat of the stew sleigh, which was loaded with the noon meal for the men•at the cutting. Upon our arrival at some central point the cook beat upon a dishpan with a large spoon and roared at the top of his voice, "Yow! 'S goin' to waste!" The ring of axes would then suddenly cease and answering calls would come from the white depths of the woods. Woolen-clad figures came tumbling in from all directions and soon the sleigh was surrounded by a noisy crowd of cutters, and they were served their noon meal of stew, bread, beans and tea by the cookee, who by the way, was the butt of most lumber-camp humor. The meal finished, the men engaged in various diversions: jacking blue jays, wrestling, or throwing things at the cookee. The noon hour over, they returned their various ways and soon the woods rang with the clear resonant notes of their biting axes, with now and then a call of "Comin' down!" followed by the crash of some old forest giant that shook the great folds of snow from the near-by trees as though a shiver had run through them.

At night the lumberjacks came riding in on loads of logs if the tote road passed near the camp, and it usually did. Supper was served at a long low table in one of the buildings and was a roaring and swashbuckling feast presided over by the foreman. The foreman held his position for the same reason that a leader-dog in a team holds his. If the occasion arose he could lick any one in camp, or at least his side could lick the other. All disputes were settled in this manner, promptly forgotten, and no grudge held. Immediately after supper the men gathered in the bunkhouse, a low cabin heated by a huge cylindrical baseburner stove that glowed cherry red in the dim light of the kerosene lamps. The walls were lined by a layer of double- or triple-decked bunks. There was no ventilation and when twenty or thirty lumberjacks gathered about the stove, all smoking cut plug tobacco, and with the place draped with steaming socks, mittens and mackinaws, the atmosphere was almost tangible. Add to this the melancholy whine of some inspired genius of the Jew's harp and the whole took on the air of a witch's cavern. Truly it was a sinister place.

Here as a boy, I sat silently drinking in every word of the tales that flew back and forth: epic tales of battles against thaws, floods, and log jams; tales of record cuttings, of how Black Bill beat Joe into the water with his logs, of the intense rivalry that existed between camps; tales of smallpox, the only disease that these men knew; of the legendary Paul Bunyan and his famous ox that was sixty feet between the eyes; of how Jean Frechette picked up a three hundred pound cask of chain and loaded it into the box of a sleigh; of Georges St. Pierre, who, upon hearing of this, snorted, and, placing his arms around a small horse that stood near by, lifted it clear off the ground and held it struggling; and, lastly, tales of great fights and great fighters . . . tales of men.

During the night a teamster with a sprinkling sleigh flooded the tote road with water and by morning it was a smooth, unbroken sheet of ice. Getting out at two in the morning in weather that was always ten to twenty below zero required considerable enthusiasm, but one who did venture forth was magnificently repaid. These teamsters, and especially the night men, were the most picturesquely profane fellows that I have ever heard, and I have heard many. They were no ordinary blasphemers, but virtuosi. Their horses were full of spirit, and sprinkling the road at night was always attended by unlooked for contingencies. On these occasions, if you were fortunate enough to be present, you were afforded the treat of hearing an artist perform. There was no ordinary disconnected and unrelated flow of vulgarities, but a symphony of rational and harmonious phrases. Let us suppose that it was the off horse that offended. The teamster began his picture by addressing the horse in a low restrained voice. The main theme was genealogical and concerned the horse's ancestors. This was then amplified by a counterpoint that dealt with the horse's present status. The teamster had a fine feeling for the climax, and as he progressed his voice grew louder and louder, and his harmonies more full and round, finally ending in one completely summarizing and devastating phrase. One unconsciously listened for the rumble of the tympani and the crash of the cymbals. I have heard some of the older artists lecture to a horse on some of its major deficiencies for a full five minutes without once repeating the same phrase. Needless to say, their bark was worse than their bite, and sometimes I suspected that the horses appreciated that fact.

II

Such visits to the camps were the high lights in the winter season and served to hasten the coming of spring. With spring came the drive and with the drive came the lumberjacks, and with their coming the boys of the town looked forward to days and days of riotous entertainment. When the ice melted, the logs that had been piled along the headwaters of the river and on the shores of the lakes were tumbled into the water and their journey to the mills began. The crews followed the drive along the lakes and slower reaches of the river until the current was fast enough to swing the logs along, with the occasional untangling of a jam. Booms of logs fastened together by chains were thrown across the mouth of the river, and soon the bay was a heaving carpet of pine logs, each branded on the end with the mark of its owner. As the drive neared completion and the last fleet of logs swung into view around the upper bend of the river, the lumberjacks began to appear, at first singly and then in groups. Each rode a log easily and gracefully, his calked boots sunk into the soft bark, and leaning on his pike-pole or peavy. I remember how the sight used to thrill me. These fellows, superb in their disdain for danger, with such an air of complete poise, apparently gliding down the surface of a boiling river, seemed more like gods than mere men. I thought that if the gods ever actually visited the earth they would travel like this.

Across the river, some distance from the mouth and connecting the two halves of the town, was a bridge. During the drive the water level was high enough for the bridge to be reached by a leap from the logs that swirled beneath. This made a natural terminal for the lumberjacks. As each one approached the bridge on his log he let out a howl that would have sent the shivers up and down the spine of a lone wolf. This was to notify the town that it was about to be honored by his presence; it also called his friends to the bridge ends. At the proper time he gave forth another howl, a howl of warning to the passers-by as he hurled his pike-pole up on the floor of the bridge. Then, crouching on his log and measuring his distance accurately, at just the proper instant he leaped, caught the lower stringer of the bridge and like a cat swung himself up over the rail. A third howl, answered by his friends, denoted that he had officially arrived. Sometimes, but only rarely, he misjudged the distance and missed the lower stringer, in which case he never gave the third howl. His friends stood for a few minutes gazing mutely down stream at the pounding logs and then hurried off to tell the town bartenders that so-and-so had missed the bridge. Telling the bartenders was in the nature of a published obituary.

When the drive was finished and the last man in, down to the cook and cookee, the men were paid off. This pay amounted to a considerable sum, since they received three to five dollars a day all winter and had no expenses. Upon receipt of his money each jack hurried to his favorite boarding-house and purchased a ticket which assured him board, room, tobacco and laundry all summer. The last item was merely a concession to gentility. Purchase of his ticket left him a considerable balance and with this thrust in the breast pocket of his shirt he swaggered forth . . . and the fun began.

First came the burling contests. Burling consisted of standing on a log with calked boots and, by running or walking at right angles to the axis of the log, imparting a spinning motion to it, somewhat in the manner of a treadmill. Two men on the same log constituted a burling contest. The river near the bridge was dotted with logs, each supporting a pair of burlers. One man won as soon as the other missed his footing and fell into the water. After this elimination the contest narrowed down to the two most skilful burlers. This ended the first day and the final spin was held over until the next. In the meantime the jacks were usually about evenly divided in opinion as to which was the better man of the two final contestants. Betting went on furiously and it was nothing for a whole camp crew to bet their last cent on one of the burlers if he happened to be from their camp. It made no practical difference whether they won or lost, for the money was spent in any case, the winners spending lavishly because they had won, and the losers accepting their hospitality for the equally good reason that they had lost.

All this occurred late in June. After the burling contest was decided, together with the score of fights that always attended such a public show, the next great social event, as it were, was the series of Fourth of July dances. They were so designated because they began on the Fourth, but they lasted until men and maidens, and especially the last, had been exhausted. They were held in places called boweries erected on vacant lots by the lumberjacks themselves. A bowery consisted of a large square floor, roofed over and buried in fragrant cedar and balsam boughs; it resembled somewhat a band stand or pavilion but it was built of clear, knotless white-pine boards, most of them two feet in width. At one end was a platform for the orchestra and the caller. The music was provided by an organ and a fiddler, not a violinist. The distinction is very real. A violinist clamps a violin between the lower border of his mandible and the prominence of his clavicle. With half-closed eyes he sways with the music, while his fingers flutter up and down the length of the fingerboard as he coaxes out the velvet tones. A fiddler, and especially a lumberjack fiddler, lays a fiddle carelessly against his chest, thumps loudly with one foot, and uses only the middle six inches of the bow and a single position on the keyboard to tear out a melody that sets the calked boots to chewing up the new pine floor. While he plays he stares defiantly at his audience and only lowers his eyes at intervals to expectorate over the edge of the platform with sufficient accuracy to avoid harsh criticism from the dancers.

The dances in favor were the so-called square ones, and the party was continuous. There were halts only at the end of the different sets of figures to change partners or to allow fresh couples to replace jaded ones. The whole thing was full of gaudy color, with the lumberjacks in their brilliant woolens, the girls in their calicoes, and the cedar boughs and festoons of bunting over all. The girls were the town's finest and many were the romances that began to the tune of "Swing Yer Partner" or "All Join Hands." I hope I am not divulging any secret when I observe that some of these same girls, thrilled in those far-off days by a whirl in the arms of a perspiring jack, are now matrons of society in the North. A lumberjack, when he went to a dance, was fascinating in direct proportion to the vigor with which he whirled his partner, while the girls were classified as charming or not according to whether their skirts stood out gracefully when they were whirled through the figures. Undoubtedly some of the matrons that I have mentioned will be furious when I whisper that the girls resorted to the unfair device of sewing buckshot into the lower hems of their skirts. I know this to be a fact because once, in my childish absorption of what was going on at one end of the hall, I was struck over the eye by three whirling shot. The dances stopped when all the girls in town were so exhausted that they had to go home. By this time the bowery had spent its usefulness; the floor was chewed paper-thin by the grinding and stamping of calked boots.

III

The social activity of the town now moved to the saloons. Four stood at each end of the bridge, and as a boy I posted myself every night to command a view of all eight doors. When a fight started, I could be at the scene of battle in an instant. I never had long to wait. The show began with the sudden bursting open of the swinging doors by the rocketing rush of the two contestants, followed more leisurely by the crowd from within. Sometimes the fighters stopped their mauling upon reaching the road, and then each would regain the proper state of frenzy by reciting in a loud, vivid and profane manner what he intended to do to the other. These announced plans were usually very extravagant and gruesome, such as complete removal of the heart, plucking out an eye, or tearing off a leg to be used as a club. The audience listened attentively, if a little bored, but never interrupted the recital. When the proper pitch of battle fury had been reached the two jacks hurled themselves upon each other, and in an instant became a gyrating, cursing mass of thrashing fists and flying feet. They cursed and clawed, sometimes, for an hour at a time, and ended a half mile from their starting point. Sometimes the oratorical preliminaries were dispensed with and the two jacks set immediately to the task of doing each other bodily harm.

These man-like animals, with the hearts and minds of children, set simple rules to govern their encounters. They operated on the rather logical premise that when one fights one does it in order to mutilate or maim the other fellow. There was no code. The task in hand was to beat the other fellow thoroughly, and the quickest and most efficient method was the best. Therefore, nothing was barred. Clawing, gouging, biting, butting, choking, kneeing and kicking were among the better known maneuvers, and not the least of the finer points of the game was to flop your adversary to the ground, and, just as he landed, to plant your calked boot accurately on his face. Many a jack had intricate if not beautiful designs tattooed on his cheeks by this method. They asked no quarter and gave none. The fight was continuous and ended only when one man could no longer resist. He was then officially out. Usually his opponent was the first to assist him to his feet and it was no uncommon sight to see two such fighters a half hour later arm in arm at the bar, singing each other's praises. A grudge never existed and the difference that caused a fight was considered permanently settled when the fight was concluded.

The favorite refreshment was a quart bottle of rot-gut whisky into which had been stuffed a handful of fine-cut chewing tobacco. The whole was shaken vigorously and was then ready for consumption. A treat on the street consisted in hauling out one's bottle, giving it a shake, drawing the cork with the teeth, running a thumb around the neck (a mark of good breeding, as the ruder members of the guild neglected this charming office) and extending it with the remark, "Have a smile, Jack." A refusal on any grounds constituted an insult, which in turn meant a fight. Very few ever refused.

But life for Jack was not all laughter, dancing and fighting. Sometimes there was a tear in his eye, for underneath his hard surface was a soft sentiment and a heart that could swell. I have seen a whole barroom, including the bartender, sad and tearful when some husky, whisky baritone sang, "The Little Boy in Green" or recited "Father, Dear Father, Come Home With Me Now." When the Widow Monahan's cottage at the edge of town burned early one morning, the whole saloon population swarmed to the scene, and by nightfall, after numerous fights and much profanity, the widow gazed through her tears over a flashing new picket fence at a handsome new cottage, complete even to the chicken-coop full of chickens. On another occasion Smoky Paquette, one of the hardest fighters of the North, was told that Father de Vere, the parish priest, had been pining for years for a stained-glass window for his little church. Though none of the jacks had ever seen the inside of a church, least of all Smoky, he, after a proper mellowing with rot-gut, elected himself collector for the worthy pastor. He mounted a table in the Deerhead Saloon and in a bellow that made the flames of the kerosene lamps quiver announced, "I jest heerd that le bon père d'Vere wants a picture windy fer his church, an' I'm 'nouncing that you lousy log rollers is about to tally in fer it." Then with his round felt bush-hat in a fist like a Smithfield ham, he made the rounds of the eight saloons. His method was simple and to the point. He approached each jack, thrust the hat under the victim's nose with his left hand, cocked back his right, and in a voice like a peevish bear, announced that he was collecting for a picture windy for the church. Since Smoky had proven his ferocity on a hundred occasions, his method brought results, and soon one of the cookees, properly lickered up, was wobbling on his way to the priest's house with the money for a picture windy stuffed in the front of his shirt.

So day followed day, each jammed with action and excitement, until all the cash of the men was spent and the town settled down into its summer doze. Then Jack sat in front of his boarding-house and whittled miniature cant-hooks and peavies for the kids. Or he and his friends strolled along in pairs, and where they walked their calked boots gouged the sidewalk into two parallel troughs. After a summer shower these troughs filled with water, and when the sun reappeared I sat fascinated, watching the men swaggering along the little silvery lanes, their heavy boots throwing out sprays of diamonds at every step. Or sometimes I crouched near the basement window of a saloon in the cool, moist draft that came from the beer coils, and listened to tales by my favorite old jack, Pop Gardner. Once I said to him, "Pop, you're getting old. Some day a tree will get you, or you'll die in a barroom. Why don't you quit?" Pop bristled up in his red arm-chair and, glaring down at me, replied, "Sure thing, bucko, a tree will get me, er I'll turn in my check in a barroom; but what of it? Ain't I pickin' my own way of goin', eh? An' won't I be cashin' in among frien's? 'N that's a hell of a lot mor' 'n some of these soft bellies can say. God a-mighty, kid, think o' peterin' out in a hoss-pee-tal among strangers!"

Jack had no thought of the hereafter. His religion was chance, and chances existed only to be taken. If you were lucky certain things happened to you, and if you were unlucky other things happened. In either case you could do nothing about it. His life was hard. He worked hard, played hard, and fought hard. His liquor was hard, his muscles were hard and so was his voice. Everything about him was hard except his heart, and that was soft, full of rough sentiment, and a capacity for loyalty, friendship and generosity that knew no bounds. Clean, hard and vital, Jack was an honest man.

The river that formerly writhed with logs is now lined with summer cottages. The lake shore where Jack stacked his logs is strewn with he-fairies, in life-guard bathing suits, and with grease on their hair. The bridge at either end is flanked by filling stations that pump gasoline into the digestive tracts of thirsty Fords. The vacant lots

where the boweries once stood now swarm with tea-rooms, and instead
of the buxom damsels of the buckshot skirts, we have their hollow-
chested daughters, faces daubed like clowns, smoking cigarettes over
plates of cinnamon toast. The kindly, tolerant Father de Vere has given
place to a half dozen pulpit-pounders who hurl politics at dull and
stupid congregations. All of them, chips . . . chips and edgings from
what once was a noble stand of timber.

Five Peas on a Barrel-Head

by LEW SARETT. *Although most of Sarett's poetry deals with nature and
Indian themes, he occasionally writes about the lumberjack and life in the
pineries. "Five Peas on a Barrel-Head" is a sympathetic portrait of a woodsman doomed by a violent crime to imprisonment.*

THE warden spoke of him as "Ninety-four,
The Mystery," and swore no man could plumb
His murky depths, his thinking. The prisoners,
Shunning him always for his sullenness,
Dubbed him "the loco Finn," and they would mutter
Stark tales of Waino's brawls in logging-camp—
Of the autumn night when Waino, swaggering,
Reeling with rot-gut gin, gone berserker,
Lifted his ax and split three heads wide open
As pretty as a knife could cleave three apples.
That drunken hour forever shut from him
The bounding sweep of Lake Superior's blue,
The surge and lapse of breakers on her crags,
The dulcet talk of rambling brooks and pines
Marching upon her shores.

               Little enough
There was about the Finnish lumberjack
To show the hot black lava in his breast.
Power he radiated, from his fists,
Iron and gnarled, his huge gorilla arms,
The granite of his block of head set square
And squat upon his bulging granite shoulders;

But power unfired, stagnant as a ditch.
Never a gleam lit up his slate-gray eyes.
His broad flat face was as shallow as a plate,
As empty of emotion. And when one dusk
He crept away and clambered to the roof
Of the heating-plant, catapulted himself
Flat on the air like any flying-squirrel,
Clutched at a cable and scrambled down its length
Hand over hand till he crossed the prison-wall
And there dropped twenty feet to earth, to dash
For the freedom of the hills—only to crumple
Under the slugs that whistled from the towers—
The desperado took our breath away.

"To think the stolid Finn," cried Hobbs, the warden,
"Could hold a hunger terrible enough
To breed such recklessness!" He shrugged his arms.
"And yet a black bear sleeping in his den
Seems droll enough and harmless; but who can say
When bears will run amuck and gut a township."
For this they clamped the logger in solitary,
And later in the warehouse, in cellar-gloom.
Here, where the stone walls dripped with chilly slime
And melancholy, month on month the Finn
Shifted his bales and boxes, rolled his barrels;
Burrowing underground like a sightless mole
Month upon month, he brooded and fell to bone
And pallid flesh.

Regiments of mice
Began to levy on his sacks of barley,
His prunes, his corn and peas. MacDonald flung
A dozen traps before the blinking Finn
And told him to make an end of all the rodents.
Furtively Waino tucked the string of traps
Under his cot and never set a spring.
Something he liked about the squealing mice,
Something about their merrymaking, their sharp
And gusty delight in the high affairs of mice;
Something—somehow they brought him lively news
Of the pregnant earth six feet beyond the walls
They tunneled under: news of the clover roots
Swollen with April rains; of bugs and birds
Stirring with bright new life; of dandelions

240

Spreading their buttered crowns to the green and gold
Of soft spring showers—somehow they brought him news.

One morning a slim wan finger of the sun
That wriggled through the single grated window
High in the cellar, scrawled upon the floor
A slow gold syllable and fell aslant
A sack of parched green peas. A rill of peas
Dribbled from one torn corner, where mice,
Prowling at night, had gnawed the gunny-bag.
The stoic Waino held his empty eyes
An hour upon the peas; then, moved by a whim,
He rolled a keg of pickled fish, salt herring,
Into the sunlight and set it on an end.
He scraped his fingers on a barrel that held,
Thick on one broken hoop, a crust of mud
Scooped from the rain-soaked soil of the prison-yard
When it had fallen in loading; by patient clawing
He gathered handful on handful of the soil
And piled it on the floor. From a shattered box
He salvaged a scanty pound of fine-ground cork,
And from a bale a fistful of excelsior.
Puddling the whole with water in a pail,
He poured the synthetic earth upon the keg
Of pickled fish and formed a plot of soil
Bound by the jutting staves and a strip of tin
He lashed around the barrel-head to form a wall.

He gathered from the dribbling sack five peas;
Stabbing his thumb upon the dirt, he drew
The pattern of a cross, and solemnly
Into the form he poked his five parched peas,
Covered them firmly, and went about his work.
Each morning he drenched the rounded plot of earth
And scrutinized it eagerly for life.
One day he marked upon the black a cloud
Of thick soft green no larger than his palm.
He bent on it and knew the cloud of frail
Green spears at once as grass, a catch from beyond
The walls. He speculated on the passing bird
Whose bill had taken up the seeds, whose droppings
Had yielded him this gift of swelling life.
And when the blades of green were tall and thick
As fur on a gopher's back, he broke the clump

And patiently transplanted spear on spear
Over his barrel-garden to form a sod
Around his seeds.

              Another morning his eyes
Gleamed suddenly and wetly when they fell
On five white succulent stems that pierced the soil
And hungrily stretched for the wisp of passing sun.
Eagerly, day on day, he marked their growth:
The first faint lancing green that stabbed the soil,
The slow unfurling patch of velvet leaf,
The pea-vines eager to climb a little sky—
These glinted his eyes with the luster of a dream
And put in Waino's throat a quiet laughter
Like bubbles in the bottom of a well.

One Sunday morning Waino, loath to go
To hear the bellowing of the prison chaplain,
Sulked in his cellar and worshipped at his shrine
Of blossoming peas; bent on his barrel-plot,
He found delight in pruning the roving stems,
In sniffing at the new-blown crinkled petals,
And training the vines on tiny trellises.
The clatter of the cellar door, the creak
Of coming footsteps, brought him up alert.
He shambled out to meet a dim black figure
Groping among the bales—the half-breed, Fillion,
The bluffest voyageur on Lac la Croix,
Whose hot French blood had driven him to sink
A thirsty dagger to the fickle heart
Of Rose Labrie, the village courtesan;
His Indian strain of philosophic calm
And taciturnity had won for him
The freedom of a trusty.

              "Those cook, La Plante,"
The Frenchman mumbled, "she's want one keg from herring.
M'sieu, you got one keg from fish in here?
Some place in cellar—yes?"

              The eyes of Waino
Fluttered a moment; he drew his gnarled red hand
Dully across his forehead.

              "No," he rasped,
"That fish—that keg of fish ain't here in warehouse."

"Bah Gar!" the Frenchman muttered, as the Finn
Shuffling, retreated to a dusky corner,
"Those cook M'sieu La Plante, she's got-it down
On inventory barrel from herring-fish
It's deliver-it last fall. I look around—
Me—I am look around; I find it—maybe."

Fumbling among the boxes, methodically
The mixed-blood penetrated every corner.
Furtively Waino stepped across the floor,
Planted his burly frame before the keg
To shelter it, and waited. Fillion came
At last and faced him, puzzled.

        "Sacré! That's funny"—
Scratching his head—"those fish she ain't in here."

He turned to go, but as he wheeled, his eyes
Fell on a splash of green, a spray of leaves
That peeped around the elbow of the Finn.

"Ho-ho!" he laughed, "you got-it posies here?
She's pretty—yes?"

        The white-faced Finn dropped back,
Trembling from crown to toe. The voyageur
Stepped forward to survey the patch of green
And sniff the blossoms.

        "Mon Calvary!" he cried,
"That's keg from fish!—those keg she's growing on!"

Gorilla-like the Finn crouched sullenly
Beside the barrel and tensed the huge bunched hands
That dangled at his sides.

        "That's fish all right
La Plante she's got-it on those inventory!
Almost I'm thinking—me—she's lost, those fish!"
Cried Fillion as he stooped to tilt the keg
And roll it to a truck.

        The Finn crouched down;
Sharp fury flickered from his squinting eyes
Raggedly, hotly as the darting tongue
Of any badgered snake; his raw red throat
Rattled with stony syllables:

243

"Don't!—
Don't touch that fish! You take that keg, by Christ,
I break—I break your goddam back in two!"

Fillion glanced up an instant at the Finn,
Snorted, and wrapped his arms about the staves.
With a desperate roar the Finn flung up his head
And shattered the cold gray granite of his posture;
Lifting his groping hands above his head,
He clutched from on a shelf a syrup-jug
And crashed its huge black bulk on Fillion's skull.

The voyageur collapsed and sank to earth
Like an ox that drops beneath a butcher's sledge.
Minute on minute he sprawled upon the floor,
Stone-cold and stunned; a steaming crimson river
Spurted and dribbled from his severed scalp—
A ragged wound from his cow-lick to his ear.
Slowly his eyelids fluttered open; he gasped,
Rose to his knees and tottered to his feet—
Only to crumple like a hamstrung doe.
He struggled to his knees again and crawled
Blindly and dizzily across the floor
And up the steps to safety—while Waino huddled
Over his keg and shook with guttural sobs
That racked his ribs and rocked his huge broad back.

The warden, flanked by Clancy and Moran,
Came on him thus a dozen minutes later.
Hobbs fixed his cold gray eyes upon the Finn,
Slowly remarked his quivering shoulders, his head
Shaggy and wet with sweat, and driven deep
Into the vines upon the keg of fish.
Grimly he turned his interest to the plot—
The pulsing green of stem, the satin-white
Of petal, the rich cool pungence of the earth.
Slowly the iron of his jaw relaxed;
Gently and dubiously he wagged his head.
With something of a smile, a quizzical grin,
He muttered to Moran:

"Go tell La Plante
There is no keg of herring in the warehouse;

He must have been mistaken. And tell him, too,
To strike the item from the inventory."

Clancy, amazed, let down his lantern jaw
And stared; the warden was too much for him.

My Winter in the Woods

by GLANVILLE SMITH, 1901— . *Born at St. Cloud, Minnesota,
Smith was educated at the University of Minnesota, B.A., 1924. During a
period of travel he visited the Hawaiian Archipelago, the South Pacific, and
various islands in the Caribbean Sea. Essays and stories based on his travels
appeared in such magazines as the National Geographic and the Atlantic
Monthly. In 1936 he was awarded a Guggenheim fellowship to do a book on
the West Indies, Many a Green Isle (1941). Since 1930 he has been the
memorial designer for the Cold Spring, Minnesota, Granite Company. "My
Winter in the Woods" was originally published in the Atlantic Monthly,
April 1934.*

I

THERE are ten thousand lakes in Minnesota, and at each of them in
the winter of 1932–1933 was an author, driven from his usual job by
the depression, but determined, now that he could not earn any money
respectably, to see what he could do with his pen. I was one of these
authors and my lake was Burntside, near Ely and the Border.

At first I supposed I was unique, living alone in a cedar cabin in
that lonesome country, and intending to write. But presently I learned
that at Crab Lake, the next one to the west, there was an author who
was going to write a book. Later I saw something of this author. He
was a young fellow of considerable egotism, who never reread what
he wrote, but just sent it in, and so it would be published. This made
me very envious, for as a rule I am the only person who ever reads
what I write.

Shortly after, I learned of another author, at Lake Shagawa, which
was the next lake to the east. I never met this author. An occasion was
arranged when we were supposed to meet, but just before it, startled
by a rap on her cabin door, she backed into her stove while drying
after a bath in the washtub: this made it impossible for her to sit down,

and so she could not think of going to a party. However, I got a note from her in a handwriting so bold and sweeping that I realized at once that she must certainly be a real author.

After learning, thus, that each of the nearer lakes boasted its own author, I saw that I was not unique at all, but merely a symptom of a great general movement which somehow had escaped notice in the papers. This was discouraging. It was only too easy to imagine how ten thousand manuscripts would be sent simultaneously to the *Atlantic* in the spring, all entitled 'My Winter in the Woods,' and each from a different lake. I thought some of organizing a Ten Thousand Authors of Minnesota League, so that the financial return on the one essay that was accepted could be distributed justly among us all. But the Crab Lake member was not interested, for he got everything published anyhow; and the Lake Shagawa member was too busy applying Unguentine to her blisters to think about committees or by-laws. Thus the scheme fell through.

The astonishing thing to consider, however, is that many months have elapsed and still no essay entitled 'My Winter in the Woods' has been published in the *Atlantic!* Can it be that all of the ten thousand authors grew as lazy as I did, and never wrote their essays? For the comfort of their several souls I hope they were sidetracked as I was, thanks to being too busy enjoying their winter in the woods to write about it. Love poems, so I rationalized, are not composed while the lovers are in the rapture of an embrace, but when they are parted. The literary expression of their rapture would seem a tasteless impertinence at the time; and for a like reason, or so I rationalized, my essay did not get written.

Besides, to reënforce my excuse with more practical considerations, there was so much else to do.

II

Authors are notoriously a soft lot. When the faucets in their apartments for some reason yield no water, or the lights do not turn on, they are likely to lose faith in providence, and to take to a desperate kind of writing to express the trouble that haunts their lives. But I had not been at Burntside ten minutes before I knew that I was destined to be the sole creator of my own comfort.

For water I had either to walk a quarter of a mile to a spring, or to chop a hole in the lake ice, or to melt snow on the stove. Anybody who has tried melting snow for water knows that many many bushels of the former are required to produce a very very few pints of the latter, and it takes all day. I tried it once. Chopping a hole in the ice sounds easy, but actually it is a labor, especially when the wind is blowing and the temperature is twenty below. But to climb drifts to get to a spring is really not a bad chore, and the water you bring back a quarter of a mile over hill and dale takes on a value and deliciousness unknown to that which flows at a touch glibly from a faucet.

The light of a kerosene lamp, too, has a value that mere electricity cannot equal. It is more elemental. The oil for which you have already paid is, before your very eyes, turned into the radiance that makes night cheerful. There is a pleasure in this not to be found in turning switches and paying a bill at the end of the month to some impersonal corporation.

My warmth, too, I owed to my own efforts. I was not only fireman, but wood sawyer. And the wood was cut down across the bay, and hauled back over the ice by this same person, all of which made me value very highly the warmth my fire gave me. Radiators, moreover, are certainly deficient in soul, whereas a good air-tight stove that you can open up and pop corn in, and that provides space on top for a broad-bottomed teakettle, is a friend and a companion.

As for food, I had to cook it or go hungry. There was nobody to do the washing but me, nor the mending, nor the sweeping, nor the dishwashing, nor the bed making. And all of these things, as I soon learned, require to be done very often. It was all good experience for an author, though it kept him from his writing.

Then there was a great deal of talking to do. You will perhaps wonder at this, when I lived in such a lonesome country. But I hope you will not think the romantic isolation of my winter in the woods spoiled entirely when I tell you how many friends I had. The Crab Lake author was not one of them. He was too successful for me to enjoy very much, and after two or three visits he saw his welcome was not very hearty, and so he stopped coming.

Of course I had a dog all the time, named Terry, who was a great comfort. But my chief friend was the Captain, who came after a while and lived with me. Though he was not an author, he did not mind sharing a cabin with one, and we certainly got along very well together. The Crab Lake author he cared for no more than I did, and when this visitor said our dog looked like 'an overgrown wildcat' he threatened to brain him with the pancake griddle. I have sometimes thought that this was perhaps why the Crab Lake author never came back. No, the Captain was not an author and did not intend to try to be one, but the depression was making life tiresome for him in what he called the Mazda Canyons, and so he came to live with me in the woods. We certainly got along very well together, and there was always a great deal to talk about. And then we spent a good deal of time laughing at things and at one another. In the woods you can lead a very regular life and be very healthy, and never have a cold, and this was how we lived, and so we were very healthy and never had colds, and this led naturally to our doing a great deal of laughing.

Then next door lived a timber cruiser who was very picturesque and handsome, and with him lived his wife, and both of them were great talkers. They did not care for cards, and between housework and talking they always chose the latter. Thus their cabin was a maze of newspapers, jelly glasses not put away, and laundry bundles burst open, but they always had plenty of time for talking. Even if Mrs. Harris was upstairs she would join in the talk, and through the ceiling would come 'Not five miles, Van, *nearly seven*,' or 'His father was an alderman,' like a voice from heaven. With these people lived a nephew who went to school and a mother-in-law who was very old and pretty and wore little lace caps, but, though they were pleasant, they did not talk much.

III

The timber cruiser, our landlord, was a grand man, and he had a certain chair in our cabin where he would sit and talk for hours at a stretch. This was hard on an author who itched to do some writing, but since he never repeated his stories, except by request, we gradually learned a great deal.

We learned from him the character of the moose and the brush wolf, and the tracks the fisher made, and the scandals of the lumbering business. Then he was very eloquent talking about the geology of that lonesome country, and would tell us that the hills about us were the oldest mountains in America and that they were already old and mossy when the Appalachians were young and jagged and the Rockies were still under water. He was very proud of this. Then he would talk about the glaciers, and tell how the shores of Lake Superior were tipping, the north shore tipping up, which makes it precipitous and full of waterfalls, and the south shore tipping down, which makes it a series of estuaries where the lake water is gradually creeping back into the river valleys. This was all very interesting. Then he told many stories of the early days.

One of the stories he told was about the jamboree to which the Hudson Bay fur traders used to treat the Indians on a certain island in the lake. It was an annual event, and came in blueberry time. A large cask was filled with blueberries, and over the blueberries whiskey was poured until the cask was too full to hold a drop more, when the refreshments were ready. The squaws, when they saw these preparations being made, as a measure of prudence would steal their braves' guns and hide them in the woods, for by the time the braves came to after the jamboree, and realized at what prices they had sold their furs to the traders, the traders were gone. At such a time it is a salve to outraged vanity to shoot some neighbor or kinsman as if he were to blame, and until the danger of this was over the squaws did not return the guns. The island on which the traders entertained the braves is known as Blueberry Island to this day.

Then he had many stories about the early days on the Range to the south of us. One of these stories was about One-eyed Pete, who exchanged a piece of hill property he had for a cedar swamp, for he saw a good chance to make some money selling ties to the railroad, which was surveyed to come that way. And he did make some money at it, but on the hill property iron ore was discovered in great abundance,—in fact, one of the great Eveleth mines was dug there,—and so he missed having a fortune. The rest of his life he spent in the saloons, telling his story, and crying out of his one eye.

Then our timber cruiser had a very good story about opening the mine at Biwabik. Biwabik was in the woods, and there was no road to it; it was just a tract of ground being stripped by hand labor to open up a mine. There were plenty of men there, however, who had come through the woods looking for work. And there was work for them, all right, and they were paid for it and were ready to spend their money, and still the road builders were nowhere near Biwabik. So some enterprising merchant sent up a carload of barrel beer to a bridge on the Ely line, and there the beer was unloaded and rolled into the river; and a crew of log drivers floated it down to Wynne Lake, which is very large, and rafted it across, and down the river to Biwabik. And so it got to the mining camp before the road did and sold at a glorious profit, for the men were ready to spend their money and thought beer a first-class investment at any price.

These are some of the stories of the early days that our timber cruiser told us, sitting behind our stove with his hat on and snapping his suspenders.

He was also the good friend of Chief Boshay, who lived on an island in the lake and was a great medicine man and prophet. From this noble Chippewa he brought us translated prophecies which gave our life a kind of Old Testament splendor. A warning came from him one day to prepare for a plague of eagles. It was an unusual problem to know how to prepare for a thing of this kind, but we kept Terry in, for he seemed the likeliest victim among us. However, no eagles came, though we heard tales of the Lac la Croix papooses being carried off; we saw no birds larger than the ruffed grouse that flocked nightly in the birch boughs over our cabin, or the Arctic golden-eyed ducks that swam all winter in the open rapids of the Kawishiwi River.

249

The old chief's wife fell sick one day, and powerful Indian medicine was tried to keep the evil spirits off the island. For one thing, a gun was shot off every ten minutes; I heard these shots at night, standing in the dark on a hill that looked toward the island, and it was very sad and awful. Nor was this medicine successful, for his wife died soon after. She was a very old Chippewa woman, and, having lived long enough to see her people ruined, probably did not much mind dying. Though I met their daughter, Mrs. Columbus, and another daughter and some grandchildren, I never saw the old chief, who was an inaccessible demigod strangely left behind by a grander age; but our timber cruiser told us a good deal about him, for he much admired him. Indeed, they had this in common, that they both had that large and durable character that makes men isolated, memorable, and mythological even while they are still alive.

You see there was a great deal to talk about without ever stirring from camp.

IV

As if this were not enough to keep us busy talking, there was a farm a half mile away where lived a family of Finns named Knuutti. The younger generation had dropped one u from this odd-looking name, and I told them that by and by they would get it down to plain 'Nutty,' which struck them as very droll. Indeed, I early got among them the reputation of being witty, and, as everybody knows, it is very easy to be witty when the reputation has once been established. So there was a great deal of talking and laughing at the Knuuttis'.

Either the Captain or I would go there every night for the milk, and the Knuutti milk was most unusually rich and good, for the Finns are the one people who know how to farm the narrow, marshy, winding valleys of that cold, rocky, lonesome country; somehow they convert muskeg into milk. But of course the country north of the Range is much like Finland, so they have ages of experience behind them to help them to live in comfort and prosperity in it, though most farmers would starve there.

The walk over for the milk was always a treat, through the deep pine woods where there was no wind. And for a destination there was the Knuutti kitchen, unmercifully scrubbed, with the butcher knives and popcorn ears hung on the wall, and a great cookstove with three teakettles steaming on it, and a line overhead of wool socks drying. Sometimes this brightly lit room was empty and quiet; even if it was full of people it was sometimes still, when the soft breathy voices of two of the grandchildren could be heard singing 'Jingle Bells' while they wiped the dishes. There was always a box of books in the corner from the state loan library, and the *National Geographic*, which was a favorite, and several tattered detective-story magazines; and these were a contributing factor in the quiet. But more often the room was full of talk and laughter, for everybody was good-humored, and natural politeness and sociability were the law of that household.

Though it was in the woods, the farm was a kind of crossroads in the life of a large family. The old mother, who was very strong and quiet, wore a red bandanna tied over her hair, and when the weather was coldest she put her feet in the oven to show her authority. The sons and daughters, if they lived elsewhere, came home often, and several of them were married. There were a great many grandchildren, who lived on skis outdoors, and indoors committed poetry to memory for the Christmas programme.

You will not believe me when I tell you that instead of being 'buffaloed,' wheedled, or lambasted into taking part in a Christmas programme, as children are in the best society, the young Finns and Indians of that lonesome country got up the programme themselves, with some help from their elders. I felt that the world had rolled absolutely upside down when I heard them energetically but peacefully choosing among themselves what poetry they'd learn, and which part each would play. Young Reino, as blond as a snowdrift, would be a redskin chief, and so on. And when somebody asked what part should be given *me*, the whole crowd, as if touched off by a button, shrilled, 'Santy Claus!'—and I nearly suffocated with surprise, pride, and pleasure.

Among those children everybody was good-humored and polite, and thus in the Knuutti kitchen there was always plenty of talking and laughing.

V

The great occasion was bath night, on Saturday of each week, when the whole family assembled, together with many of their friends. The bathhouse was new and fine, tightly built of logs, and in it the boys bathed first; then some friends who came several miles and had the privileges of the place; and then the women got their bath. Afterward everybody went back to the kitchen to 'play whist and the fiddle,' when sometimes hot lemonade or even something stronger would be served, with glasses for the guests and preserve bottles with screw tops for the relatives, especially the younger ones. This was never a quiet time in that kitchen; there was always a great deal of talking and laughing, all mixed up together in one big jovial family noise, until the whist game got really serious, when things would be quieter.

As for the bath itself, it deserves a description.

Architecturally the Knuuttis' log bathhouse had very little in common with the Baths of Caracalla in Rome, but what went on inside the two of them had a good deal in common. In both of them a bath was treated as a social affair, and not as some shameful thing calling for solitary confinement. The bathhouse was divided in two. The first room was a dressing room, and there we stripped and hung our clothes on pegs on the log walls, and then we went into the hot room. In the hot room was a furnace which had been stoked with pitchy pine for several hours, over which, and between two low brick walls, were piled a great many stones of egg size. On the level top of this pile of hot stones were laid wet white-cedar switches, to heat, made of twigs chosen for their softness. Connected with the furnace was a tank, and, since the water in it was boiling, it emitted ominous banging noises. Beside the tank was a tub of icy well water. Along the wall was an ascending rack of three tiers, each tier a plank wide enough to sit or lie on. Now you have a description of a Finnish bathhouse.

We climbed on the rack to the topmost tier, for there the heat was greatest, and somebody would begin to pour boiling water by dippersful slowly on the hot stones. The room was already at a temperature too high to allow the steam which then rose from the stones to condense enough to be seen, but we could feel it coming. If, for a prank, somebody flung a dipperful of water at the base of the chimney, where the rocks were hottest, the effect was indescribable, and drove all but the toughest from the top tier down to one less scalding. During such an ordeal you seem to melt into water. It is hard to believe that the yellow moisture which drains away from your fingertips is your own sweat, or that you will live to tell the tale.

Then commenced the switching, with cedar switches plunged into buckets of hot water, when the room filled with a spicy evergreen perfume. Each man switched himself roundly from head to toe, for this seems to drive the heat in, which the Finns think very healthful. They live in a cold, lonesome country, and believe in getting together and heating themselves through and through.

The weaker members of the party then would retire awhile to the dressing room, sitting silently on the benches till their heads whirled back to stability on their shoulders. Then back to the hot room for a soaping, which was generally coöperative: You soap me and I'll soap you. Then a rinsing in warm water mixed from the hot and the cold. And then, if you could stand it, a bucketful of ice water poured over your head.

After such a bath, and even if the cold water was poured over you breathtakingly at last, there was need of cooling down many degrees before you could dress. But it was easy to manage this: we ran out naked into the night, when January and forty below felt like balmy June; and under the hot weight of our bodies the soft snow in which we rolled grew hard and granular.

Then there came a very peaceful time in the dressing room, everybody with all his joints softened and relaxed; smoking, and talking, and laughing, and feeling very peaceful together. And presently the fresh long-legged underwear would be unfolded, and legs thrust into it lazily, and so to the wool socks, the pacs, and all the comfortable catalogue of clothes proper to winter in the woods; and this is the end of my description of a Finnish bath. It makes a man very limber, and God knows he is clean after it.

VI

I was very regular in my Saturday baths with the Knuutti boys, and grateful to them for taking me in, who was no Finn at all, for I deeply enjoyed the talking and laughing, and the soaping and the rinsing and rolling in the snow and the peaceful loose-in-the-joints feeling afterward. But the Captain, who is careful of his health, never would go, for he said such changes in temperature were fatal, and he could not understand at all why they did not kill me. So, in spite of a great deal of talking about it, he never went, but took his bath alone in a washtub, over the rim of which his long legs folded comically. He enjoyed his baths well enough, however, and would sing songs while he drew the washcloth across his chest so as not to splash too much; and Terry the dog, who kept him company, would look on with a solemn expression.

His first bath, by the way, he did not enjoy as much as the others, because after he had heated his water and poured it in the tub, and undressed, the water was too hot and he had no cold in the house with which to temper it. It did not make him feel any better to notice that he had smoked up the dishpans and buckets, heating all this fine bath water. But the question was: Should he dress again and go to the spring for cold water, or should he wait for the hot water to cool of itself? He decided to wait, and he was still waiting, wandering around with not a stitch on like a lost spirit, when I got home from my bath at the Knuuttis'. So I got him his cold water, and then went skiing in the moonlight, for the cabin was full of steam, and one steam bath in an evening was enough for me. After that he was more careful, for it had been a legitimate, not to say perfectly splendid, occasion for laughter at his expense, and we avoid this if we can.

Just the same, we did a great deal of laughing at one another all the time, and there were always things that demanded talking to be done about them, so there was always a great deal of laughing and talking.

For instance, there was a cabin to be talked about that we were planning to build on an island the timber cruiser owned and would sell us for two hundred dollars. Now of course we couldn't buy the island, and we never bought it. Still, two hundred dollars is a very reasonable price for an island, and, since the bargain was so great, our dreams for a cabin we should like to build on our island were very vivid. We lay awake nights quarreling over what sort of mattress we should use in our bunks; and then we would start to laugh, and cuff one another, and then we would feel very affectionate and not care what kind of mattress we'd have, and go to sleep. In such ways as this we got plenty of talking and laughing done without my ever doing any writing.

Then there was always the housework. Even with the two of us to divide the duties, they took a great deal of time. Neither of us ever, I think, will take for granted the housework that goes on about us, for we have learned that it takes both thought and time.

We cooked alternately, the Captain one day and I the next. He was fond of eating, but was not much interested in cooking; thus at noon or six o'clock on his days he would start up with a jerk and fry something. On the other hand, I liked both eating and cooking, and had learned early that frying is an elementary part of the art, and that most of the fun and triumph lies beyond. So I baked things, with cheese. Even on his days I would find myself making custards or Scotch oatcake. This was fun, but took a great deal of time.

Dishwashing was easy. We put on our hats and did it in the little glazed porch our cabin had, and the steam from the hot water made frost flowers a half inch deep on the windows, till the porch looked like a greenhouse of colorless plants. Still, it took some time, though it was easy enough.

The mending was more of a problem. The Captain had a sailmaker's needle which he used for all purposes, and the sight of the two of us bent up over our mending never failed to amuse our visitors.

Wash day was the week's chief tussle, for there were always a suit of woolen underwear and a heavy flannel shirt apiece, not to mention other problems, such as fetching the water from the spring and heating it in dishpans, and wringing out our clothes without a wringer, and then living in their moist company while they dried. And after the washing, which invariably took a full morning, came the sweeping and the mopping and cleaning the stove. It was a strenuous day.

And while speaking of household problems let me mention one that was uncommon: the Captain's sweetheart was a grocer's daughter, and since she was very fond of him, and could not believe that he lived anything but a life of hardship in that lonesome country, she very often sent very large boxes full of things to eat. In many ways this was an excellent arrangement, and when I spend another winter in the woods I shall certainly have a sweetheart who is a grocer's daughter, or take along a friend who has one. However, her rich boxes kept us very busy eating things up, which, together with the laughing and the talking and all the housework, kept me from writing my essay.

VII

You will say that a winter in the woods would be a perfect time for reading, and this was my thought, too, so I took with me Taine's *History of English Literature*, which would be proper meat for an author to chew on, and a great many other good things such as Shakespeare, Xenophon, *The Oregon Trail*, Spenser, Sir Philip Sidney, *Mutiny on the Bounty*, and as many of the Chinese poets as I could get in one suitcase. And indeed I did get some of these read. But an old battered schoolbook that the Captain brought was our chief cultural prop, for it contained all the dear old poems that you never really get sick of. The Captain would snatch it out of my hand and glue his eyes rapturously on the much-loved pages, and read out 'Wee sleekit, cowrin', tim'rous beastie' or 'In Xanadu did Kubla Khan,' in a happy loud voice. But Taine, in four very bulky volumes crammed full of thought suitable to the inspiration of an author, never did get finished.

And then, most important distraction of all, there were the woods themselves. Obviously, it would be as foolish to spend a winter in the woods without really enjoying them as to spend a winter in the city without going to any concerts or prize fights, and since we saw this truth plainly we went hiking very often.

It was a rugged, rocky country of ups and downs, raggedly grown up in birch and pine, with cedar or spruce swamps or cranberry bogs in the hollows, and all very lonesome. The lake was large and sprawled out, with a hundred islands in it richly wooded, including the island we were going to buy for two hundred dollars, and the famous Blueberry Island, and the one on which Chief Boshay lived, as well as a great many that were beautiful in spite of being nameless or unhistoric. With skis, travel over the snowy ice was easy for me; I am short-legged. The Captain, who has long legs, preferred snowshoes. Since we had only one pair of each, these dissimilar preferences were very fortunate. We went many miles on our skis and snowshoes, while sundogs and bewilderingly complicated haloes followed the sun across the sky; and looked at our two-hundred-dollar island, and ate our lunch in corners out of the wind. Then there were trips to Ely, six and a half miles away, for the provisions the Captain's sweetheart had not thought to send. All this was great fun and very healthful, and we learned a great deal. For one thing, we learned to love that big, rough, lonesome country very deeply, and on moonlight nights, when we would stop and look about us, it seemed that our hearts must break with the deep joy that came pouring into them.

However, all these fine excursions, together with the poetry we read, and the eating we had to do to keep up with the generosity of the Captain's sweetheart, and the cooking and dishwashing and mending and laundry work, and the Finnish baths, not to mention some hunting (even a little poaching) and fishing through the ice, and chopping wood, and feeding the chickadees, and taking pictures, and packing greens for Christmas presents, and repairing the snowshoes, and thanking the grocer's daughter in many letters for the many boxes she sent, and especially all the talking and laughing we did, filled up the time from morning to night, and for this reason the Burntside member of the Ten Thousand Authors of Minnesota League never got around to writing his essay on 'My Winter in the Woods.'

But things are better now. I have a job, which is a blessing. I work as many hours a day as the code will let me, at somebody else's business. I am in a world again where faucets and electric switches make providence seem near and real. My baths I take privately in a bathtub. I scan the papers avidly for the details of the latest cure for colds. And often when I am called away from the table for a long time by some kind friend on the telephone, or listen silently while Ed Wynn on the radio does both my talking and laughing for me when I am out to call, I think how wonderful it is that we are on the road of recovery, and leaving the depression behind. And one of the minor delights of the new day is that now I have time again to do a little writing.

THE FARM

Mrs. Hill and Mrs. Troost

by ALICE CARY, 1820–71. *Alice Cary and Phoebe Cary were well-known sentimental and domestic poets in the middle nineteeth century. Alice Cary was born and spent her girlhood at Mount Healthy just outside Cincinnati. Later the sisters removed to New York City where, for a time, they were under the patronage of Rufus Griswold and Horace Greeley and were deemed important literary figures. Together they published in 1849 Poems; another joint volume, Last Poems, was published posthumously in 1873. Alice Cary was also the author of a volume of prose sketches dealing with the rural life of her youth, Clovernook (1852). Although there is a core of realism in the book the atmosphere is one of pathos and sentimentality. "Mrs. Hill and Mrs. Troost" illustrates the didacticism as well as the homely detail with which Clovernook abounds.*

It was just two o'clock of one of the warmest of the July afternoons. Mrs. Hill had her dinner all over, had put on her clean cap and apron, and was sitting on the north porch, making an unbleached cotton shirt for Mr. Peter Hill, who always wore unbleached shirts at harvest time. Mrs. Hill was a thrifty housewife. She had been pursuing this economical avocation for some little time, interrupting herself only at times to "*shu!*" away the flocks of half-grown chickens that came noisily about the door for the crumbs from the table-cloth, when the sudden shutting down of a great blue cotton umbrella caused her to drop her work, and exclaim—

"Well, now, Mrs. Troost! who would have thought you ever *would* come to see me!"

"Why, I have thought a great many times I would come," said the visitor, stamping her little feet—for she was a little woman—briskly on the blue flag stones, and then dusting them nicely with her white cambric handkerchief, before venturing on the snowy floor of Mrs. Hill. And, shaking hands, she added, "It *has* been a good while, for I remember when I was here last I had my Jane with me—quite a baby then, if you mind—and she is three years old now."

"Is it possible?" said Mrs. Hill, untying the bonnet strings of her neighbor, who sighed, as she continued, "Yes, she was three along in February"; and she sighed again, more heavily than before, though there was no earthly reason that I know of why she should sigh, unless perhaps the flight of time, thus brought to mind, suggested the transitory nature of human things.

Mrs. Hill laid the bonnet of Mrs. Troost on her "spare bed," and covered it with a little, pale-blue crape shawl, kept especially for like occasions; and, taking from the drawer of the bureau a large fan of turkey feathers, she presented it to her guest, saying, "A very warm day, isn't it?"

"Oh, dreadful, dreadful; it seems as hot as a bake oven; and I suffer with the heat all summer, more or less. But it's a world of suffering"; and Mrs. Troost half closed her eyes, as if to shut out the terrible reality.

"Hay-making requires sunshiny weather, you know; so we must put up with it," said Mrs. Hill; "besides, I can mostly find some cool place about the house; I keep my sewing here on the porch, and, as I bake my bread or cook my dinner, manage to catch it up sometimes, and so keep from getting overheated; and then, too, I get a good many stitches taken in the course of the day."

"This *is* a nice, cool place—completely curtained with vines," said Mrs. Troost; and she sighed again; "they must have cost you a great deal of pains."

"Oh, no—no trouble at all; morning-glories grow themselves; they only require to be planted. I will save seed for you this fall, and next summer you can have your porch as shady as mine."

"And if I do, it would not signify," said Mrs. Troost; "I never get time to sit down from one week's end to another; besides, I never had any luck with vines; some folks haven't, you know."

Mrs. Hill was a woman of a short, plethoric habit; one that might be supposed to move about with little agility, and to find excessive warmth rather inconvenient; but she was of a happy, cheerful temperament; and when it rained she tucked up her skirts, put on thick shoes, and waddled about the same as ever, saying to herself, "This will make the grass grow," or "it will bring on the radishes," or something else equally consolatory.

Mrs. Troost, on the contrary, was a little thin woman, who looked as though she might move about nimbly at any season; but, as she herself often said, she was a poor unfortunate creature, and pitied herself a great deal, as she was in justice bound to do, for nobody else cared, she said, how much she had to bear.

They were near neighbors—these good women—but their social interchanges of tea-drinking were not of very frequent occurrence, for sometimes Mrs. Troost had nothing to wear like other folks; sometimes it was too hot, and sometimes it was too cold; and then again, nobody wanted to see her, and she was sure she didn't want to go where she wasn't wanted. Moreover, she had such a great barn of a house as no other woman ever had to take care of. But in all the neighborhood it was called the big house, so Mrs. Troost was in some measure compensated for the pains it cost her. It was, however, as she said, a barn of a place, with half the rooms unfurnished, partly because they had no use for them, and partly because they were unable to get furniture. So it stood right in the sun, with no shutters, and no trees about it, and Mrs. Troost said she didn't suppose it ever would have. She was always opposed to building it, but she never had her way about anything. Nevertheless, some people said Mr. Troost had taken the dimensions of his house with his wife's apron strings—but that may have been slander.

While Mrs. Troost sat sighing over things in general, Mrs. Hill sewed on the last button, and shaking the loose threads from the completed garment, held it up a moment to take a satisfactory view, as it were, and folded it [a]way.

"Well, did you ever!" said Mrs. Troost; "you have made half a shirt, and I have got nothing at all done. My hands sweat so I can't use the needle, and it's no use to try."

"Lay down your work for a little while, and we will walk in the garden."

So Mrs. Hill threw a towel over her head, and taking a little tin basin in her hand, the two went to the garden—Mrs. Troost under the shelter of the blue umbrella, which she said was so heavy that it was worse than nothing. Beans, radishes, raspberries, and currants, besides many other things, were there in profusion, and Mrs. Troost said

259

everything flourished for Mrs. Hill, while her garden was all choked up with weeds. "And you have bees, too—don't they sting the children, and give you a great deal of trouble? Along in May, I guess it was, Troost (Mrs. Troost always called her husband so) bought a hive, or rather he traded a calf for one—a nice, likely calf, too, it was—and they never did us one bit of good"—and the unhappy woman sighed.

"They *do* say," said Mrs. Hill, sympathizingly, "that bees won't work for some folks; in case their king dies they are very likely to quarrel, and not do well; but we have never had any ill luck with ours; and we last year sold forty dollars worth of honey, besides having all we wanted for our own use. Did yours die off, or what, Mrs. Troost?"

"Why," said the ill-natured visitor, "my oldest boy got stung one day, and, being angry, upset the hive, and I never found it out for two or three days; and, sending Troost to put it up in its place, there was not a bee to be found, high or low."

"You don't tell! the obstinate little creatures! but they must be treated kindly, and I have heard of their going off for less things."

The basin was by this time filled with currants, and they returned to the house. Mrs. Hill, seating herself on the sill of the kitchen door, began to prepare her fruit for tea, while Mrs. Troost drew her chair near, saying, "Did you ever hear about William McMicken's bees?"

Mrs. Hill had never heard, and expressing an anxiety to do so was told the following story:

"His wife, you know, was she that was Sally May, and it's an old saying—

    'To change the name, and not the letter,
    You marry for worse, and not for better.'

"Sally was a dressy, extravagant girl; she had her bonnet 'done up' twice a year always, and there was no end to her frocks and ribbons and fine things. Her mother indulged her in everything; she used to say Sally deserved all she got; that she was worth her weight in gold. She used to go everywhere, Sally did. There was no big meeting that she was not at, and no quilting that she didn't help to get up. All the girls went to her for the fashions, for she was a good deal in town at her Aunt Hanner's, and always brought out the new patterns. She used to have her sleeves a little bigger than anybody else, you remember, and then she wore great stiffners in them—la, me! there was no end to her extravagance.

"She had a changeable silk, yellow and blue, made with a surplus front; and when she wore that, the ground wasn't good enough for her to walk on, so some folks used to say; but I never thought Sally was a bit proud or lifted up; and if anybody was sick, there was no better-hearted creature than she; and then, she was always good-na-

260

tured as the day was long, and would sing all the time at her work. I remember, along before she was married, she used to sing one song a great deal, beginning

'I've got a sweetheart with bright black eyes';

and they said she meant William McMicken by that, and that she might not get him after all—for a good many thought they would never make a match, their dispositions were so contrary. William was of a dreadful quiet turn, and a great home body; and as for being rich, he had nothing to brag of, though he was high larnt, and followed the river as clark sometimes."

Mrs. Hill had by this time prepared her currants, and Mrs. Troost paused from her story while she filled the kettle, and attached the towel to the end of the well-sweep, where it waved as a signal for Peter to come to supper.

"Now, just move your chair a leetle nearer the kitchen door, if you please," said Mrs. Hill, "and I can make up my biscuit, and hear you, too."

Meantime, coming to the door with some bread-crumbs in her hand, she began scattering them on the ground, and calling, "Biddy, biddy, biddy—chicky, chicky, chicky"—hearing which, a whole flock of poultry was about her in a minute; and stooping down, she secured one of the fattest, which, an hour afterwards, was broiled for supper.

"Dear me, how easily you do get along!" said Mrs. Troost.

And it was some time before she could compose herself sufficiently to take up the thread of her story. At length, however, she began with—

"Well, as I was saying, nobody thought William McMicken would marry Sally May. Poor man, they say he is not like himself any more. He may get a dozen wives, but he'll never get another Sally. A good wife she made him, for all she was such a wild girl.

"The old man May was opposed to the marriage, and threatened to turn Sally, his own daughter, out of house and home; but she was headstrong, and would marry whom she pleased; and so she did, though she never got a stitch of new clothes, nor one thing to keep house with. No; not one single thing did her father give her, when she went away, but a hive of bees. He was right down ugly, and called her Mrs. McMicken whenever he spoke to her after she was married; but Sally didn't seem to mind it, and took just as good care of the bees as though they were worth a thousand dollars. Every day in winter she used to feed them—maple-sugar, if she had it; and if not, a little Muscovade in a saucer or some old broken dish.

"But it happened one day that a bee stung her on the hand—the right one, I think it was,—and Sally said right away that it was a bad sign; and that very night she dreamed that she went out to feed her bees, and a piece of black crape was tied on the hive. She felt that it was a token of death, and told her husband so, and she told me and Mrs. Hanks. No, I won't be sure she told Mrs. Hanks, but Mrs. Hanks got to hear it some way."

"Well," said Mrs. Hill, wiping the tears away with her apron, "I really didn't know, till now, that poor Mrs. McMicken was dead."

"Oh, she is not dead," answered Mrs. Troost, "but as well as she ever was, only she feels that she is not long for this world." The painful interest of her story, however, had kept her from work, so the afternoon passed without her having accomplished much—she never could work when she went visiting.

Meantime Mrs. Hill had prepared a delightful supper, without seeming to give herself the least trouble. Peter came precisely at the right moment, and, as he drew a pail of water, removed the towel, from the well-sweep, easily and naturally, thus saving his wife the trouble.

"Troost would never have thought of it," said his wife; and she finished with an "Ah, well!" as though all her tribulations would be over before long.

As she partook of the delicious honey, she was reminded of her own upset hive, and the crisp-red radishes brought thoughts of the weedy gardens at home; so that, on the whole, her visit, she said, made her perfectly wretched, and she should have no heart for a week; nor did the little basket of extra nice fruit, which Mrs. Hill presented her as she was about to take leave, heighten her spirits in the least. Her great heavy umbrella, she said, was burden enough for her.

"But Peter will take you in the carriage," insisted Mrs. Hill.

"No," said Mrs. Troost, as though charity were offered her; "it will be more trouble to get in and out than to walk"—and so she trudged home, saying, "Some folks are born to be lucky."

Growing Up with the Country

by STANLEY WATERLOO, 1846–1913. *Born in St. Clair County, Michigan, Waterloo spent his youth in the backwoods and became skillful in hunting, fishing, and trapping. He attended the University of Michigan for a time but failed to graduate. In 1870 he went to Chicago to study law but* soon drifted into journalism. After the great fire of 1871 Waterloo went to St. Louis where for a dozen years he worked as a reporter and editor. Subsequent newspaper work took him to St. Paul and back to Chicago. In later years he spent most of his time writing fiction. Among his novels are A Man and a Woman (1892); The Story of Ab (1897), a successful tale of prehistoric man; The Cassowary (1906); and A Son of the Ages (1914). "Growing Up with the Country," a sketch of life in rural Michigan, is an excerpt from A Man and a Woman.

Have you ever seen a buckwheat field in bloom? Have you stood at its margin and gazed over those acres of soft eider-down? Have your nostrils inhaled the perfume of it all, the heavy sweetness toned keenly with the whiff of pine from the adjacent wood? Have you noted the wild bees in countless myriads working upon its surface and gathering from each tiny flower's heart that which makes the clearest and purest and most wine-like of all honey? Have you stood at the forest's edge, perched high upon a fence, maybe of trees felled into a huge windrow when first the field was cleared, or else of rails of oak or ash, both black and white—the black ash lasts the longer, for worms invade the white—and looked upon a field of growing Indian corn, the green spread of it deep and heaving, and noted the traces of the forest's tax-collectors left about its margins: the squirrel's dainty work and the broken stalks and stripped ears upon the ground, leavings of the old raccoon, the small bear of the forest, knowing enough to become a friend of man when caught and tamed, and almost human in his ways, as curious as a scandal-monger and selfish as a money-lender?

Have you gone into the hard maple wood, the sugar bush, in the early spring, the time of frosty nights and sunny days, and driven home the gouge and spile, and gathered the flowing sap and boiled it in such pots and kettles as later pioneers have owned, and gained such wildwood-scented product as no confectioner of the town may ever hope to equal? Have you lain beside some pond, a broadening of the creek above an ancient beaver-dam, at night, in mellowest midsummer, and watched the muskrats at their frays and feeding? Have you hunted the common wildcat, short-bodied demon, whose tracks upon the snow are discernible each winter morning, but who is so crafty, so gifted with some great art of slyness, that you may grow to manhood with him all about you, yet never see him in the sinewy flesh unless with dog and gun, and food and determination, you seek his trail, and follow it unreasoningly until you terminate the stolid quest with a discovery of the quarry lying close along the body of some sloping, stunted tree, and with a lively episode in immediate prospect? Did you ever chase a wolverine, last of his kind in a clearing-overflowed region, strange combination in character and form of bear and lynx, gluttonous and voracious, and strong and fearless, a beast descended almost unchanged from the time of the earliest cave-men, the horror of the bravest dog, and end his too uncivilized career with a rifleshot at thoughtful distance?

Have you seen the wild pigeons, before pot-hunters invaded their southern roosts and breeding-grounds and slaughtered them by millions, exterminating one of the most wonderful of American game birds, sweep over in such dense clouds that the sun would be obscured, and at times so close to earth that a long pole thrust aloft from tree or hillock would stun such numbers as would make a gallant pot-pie? Have you followed the deer in the dense forest, clinging doggedly to his track upon the fresh snow from the dusk of early morning, startling him again and again from covert, and shooting whenever you caught even so much as a glimpse of his gray body through distant interstices of tree and brush, until, late in the afternoon, human endurance, which always surpasses that of the wild beast, overcame him, and he leaped less strongly with each new alarm and grew more reckless before twilight, and came within easy range and fed his enemies on the morrow? Have you watched for him beside the brackish waters of the lick, where, perched upon a rude, high scaffold built beside a tree, mosquito-bitten and uneasy, you waited and suffered, preserving an absolute silence and immobility until came ghost-like flitting figures from the forest to the shallow's edge, when the great gun, carrying the superstitious number of buckshot, just thirteen, roared out, awakening a thousand echoes of the night, and, clambering down, found a great antlered thing in its death agony?

Have you wandered through new clearings neglected for a season and waded ankle-deep in strawberry blooms, and, later, fed there upon such scarlet fruit, so fragrant and with such a flavor of its own that the scientific horticulturist owns to-day his weakness? Have you looked out upon the flats some bright spring morning and found them transformed into a shallow lake by the creek's first flood, and seen one great expanse of shining gold as the sun smote the thin ice made in the night but to disappear long before mid-day and leave a surface all ripples and shifting lights and shadows, upon which would come an occasional splash and great out-extending circles, as some huge mating pickerel leaped in his glee? Have you stood sometime, in sheer delight of it, and drawn into distended lungs the air clarified by hundreds of miles of sweep over an inland sea, the nearest shore not a score of miles away, and filtered through aromatic forests to your senses, an invisible elixir, exhilarating, without a headache as the price? Have you seen the tiger-lilies and crimson Indian-tobacco blossoms flashing in the lowlands? Have you trapped the mink and, visiting his haunts, noticed there the old blue crane flitting ever ahead of you through dusky corridors, uncanny, but a friend? Have you—but there are a thousand things!

If you have not seen or known or felt all these fair things—so jumbled together in the allusion here, without a natural sequence or thought or reason or any art—if you have not owned them all and so many others that may not here be mentioned, then you have missed something of the gifts and glories of growth in a new land. Such experience comes but to one generation. But one generation grows with the conquest, and it is a great thing. It is man-making.

Under the Lion's Paw

by HAMLIN GARLAND, 1860–1940. *The first dirt farmer in American literature and one of the important early realists, Garland was born at West Salem, Wisconsin. He was graduated from the Cedar Valley Seminary in Osage, Iowa, in 1881, and spent much of his early life in farm work. After a short period of homesteading in McPherson County, South Dakota, Garland became a backtrailer and went to Boston where he devoted himself to study, lecturing, and writing. He was prominent throughout the 1890's as an agrarian and devotee of Henry George's single tax plan, and he established himself firmly in literature with such books as Main-Travelled Roads (1891), Crumbling Idols (1894), a series of essays in which he expressed his faith in veritism and regionalism, and Rose of Dutcher's Coolly (1895). A number of popular, romantic stories followed, typified by such a novel as The Captain of the Gray Horse Troop (1902). Subsequently Garland returned to the scenes and episodes of his youth in autobiographical volumes like A Son of the Middle Border (1917) and A Daughter of the Middle Border (1921), which was awarded a Pulitzer prize. Although much of Garland's work is mediocre, he has an assured place in the development of American realistic rural fiction. "Under the Lion's Paw," a moving picture of the mortgage-harried farmer, is one of the most dramatic tales in Main-Travelled Roads.*

I

It was the last of autumn and first day of winter coming together. All day long the plowmen on their prairie farms had moved to and fro in their wide level fields through the falling snow, which melted as it fell, wetting them to the skin—all day, notwithstanding the frequent squalls of snow, the dripping, desolate clouds, and the muck of the furrows, black and tenacious as tar.

Under their dripping harness the horses swung to and fro silently, with that marvelous uncomplaining patience which marks the horse. All day the wild geese, honking wildly, as they sprawled sidewise down the wind, seemed to be fleeing from an enemy behind, and with neck outthrust and wings extended, sailed down the wind, soon lost to sight.

Yet the plowman behind his plow, though the snow lay on his ragged great-coat, and the cold clinging mud rose on his heavy boots, fettering him like gyves, whistled in the very beard of the gale. As day passed, the snow, ceasing to melt, lay along the plowed land, and lodged in the depth of the stubble, till on each slow round the last furrow stood out black and shining as jet between the plowed land and the gray stubble.

When night began to fall, and the geese, flying low, began to alight invisibly in the near corn-field, Stephen Council was still at work "finishing a land." He rode on his sulky plow when going with the wind, but walked when facing it. Sitting bent and cold but cheery under his slouch hat, he talked encouragingly to his four-in-hand.

"Come round there, boys!—Round agin! We got t' finish this land. Come in there, Dan! *Stiddy*, Kate,—stiddy! None o' y'r tantrums, Kittie. It's purty tuff, but got a be did. *Tchk! tchk!* Step along, Pete! Don't let Kate git y'r single-tree on the wheel. *Once* more!"

They seemed to know what he meant, and that this was the last round, for they worked with greater vigor than before.

"Once more, boys, an' then, sez I, oats an' a nice warm stall, an' sleep f'r all."

By the time the last furrow was turned on the land it was too dark to see the house, and the snow was changing to rain again. The tired and hungry man could see the light from the kitchen shining through the leafless hedge, and he lifted a great shout, "Supper f'r a half a dozen!"

It was nearly eight o'clock by the time he had finished his chores and started for supper. He was picking his way carefully through the mud, when the tall form of a man loomed up before him with a premonitory cough.

"Waddy ye want?" was the rather startled question of the farmer.

"Well, ye see," began the stranger, in a deprecating tone, "we'd like t' git in f'r the night. We've tried every house f'r the last two miles, but they hadn't any room f'r us. My wife's jest about sick, 'n' the children are cold and hungry—"

"Oh, y' want 'o stay all night, eh?"

"Yes, sir; it 'ud be a great accom—"

"Waal, I don't make it a practice t' turn anybuddy way hungry, not on sech nights as this. Drive right in. We ain't got much, but sech as it is—"

But the stranger had disappeared. And soon his steaming, weary team, with drooping heads and swinging single-trees, moved past the well to the block beside the path. Council stood at the side of the "schooner" and helped the children out—two little half-sleeping children—and then a small woman with a babe in her arms.

"There ye go!" he shouted jovially, to the children. "*Now* we're all right! Run right along to the house there, an' tell Mam' Council you wants sumpthin' t' eat. Right this way, Mis'—keep right off t' the right there. I'll go an' git a lantern. Come," he said to the dazed and silent group at his side.

"Mother," he shouted, as he neared the fragrant and warmly lighted kitchen, "here are some wayfarers an' folks who need sumpthin' t' eat an' a place t' snooze." He ended by pushing them all in.

Mrs. Council, a large, jolly, rather coarse-looking woman, took the children in her arms. "Come right in, you little rabbits. 'Most asleep, hey? Now here's a drink of milk f'r each o' ye. I'll have s'm tea in a minute. Take off y'r things and set up t' the fire."

While she set the children to drinking milk, Council got out his lantern and went out to the barn to help the stranger about his team, where his loud, hearty voice could be heard as it came and went between the haymow and the stalls.

The woman came to light as a small, timid, and discouraged-looking woman, but still pretty, in a thin and sorrowful way.

"Land sakes! An' you've traveled all the way from Clear Lake t'-day in this mud! Waal! waal! No wonder you're all tired out. Don't wait f'r the men, Mis'—" She hesitated, waiting for the name.

"Haskins."

"Mis' Haskins, set right up to the table an' take a good swig o' tea whilst I make y' s'm toast. It's green tea, an' it's good. I tell Council as I git older I don't seem to enjoy Young Hyson n'r Gunpowder. I want the reel green tea, jest as it comes off'n the vines. Seems t' have more heart in it, some way. Don't s'pose it has. Council says it's all in m' eye."

Going on in this easy way, she soon had the children filled with bread and milk and the woman thoroughly at home, eating some toast and sweet-melon pickles, and sipping the tea.

"See the little rats!" she laughed at the children. "They're full as they can stick now, and they want to go to bed. Now, don't git up,

Mis' Haskins; set right where you are an' let me look after 'em. I know all about young ones, though I'm all alone now. Jane went an' married last fall. But, as I tell Council, it's lucky we keep our health. Set right there, Mis' Haskins; I won't have you stir a finger."

It was an unmeasured pleasure to sit there in the warm, homely kitchen, the jovial chatter of the housewife driving out and holding at bay the growl of the impotent, cheated wind.

The little woman's eyes filled with tears which fell down upon the sleeping baby in her arms. The world was not so desolate and cold and hopeless, after all.

"Now I hope Council won't stop out there and talk politics all night. He's the greatest man to talk politics and read the *Tribune*—How old is it?"

She broke off and peered down at the face of the babe.

"Two months 'n' five days," said the mother, with a mother's exactness.

"Ye don't say! I want 'o know! The dear little pudzy-wudzy!" she went on, stirring it up in the neighborhood of the ribs with her fat forefinger.

"Pooty tough on 'oo to go gallivant'n' 'cross lots this way—"

"Yes, that's so; a man can't lift a mountain," said Council, entering the door. "Mother, this is Mr. Haskins, from Kansas. He's been eat up 'n' drove out by grasshoppers."

"Glad t' see yeh!—Pa, empty that wash-basin 'n' give him a chance t' wash."

Haskins was a tall man, with a thin, gloomy face. His hair was a reddish brown, like his coat, and seemed equally faded by the wind and sun, and his sallow face, though hard and set, was pathetic somehow. You would have felt that he had suffered much by the line of his mouth showing under his thin, yellow mustache.

"Hain't Ike got home yet, Sairy?"

"Hain't seen 'im."

"W-a-a-l, set right up, Mr. Haskins; wade right into what we've got; 'tain't much, but we manage to live on it—she gits fat on it," laughed Council, pointing his thumb at his wife.

After supper, while the women put the children to bed, Haskins and Council talked on, seated near the huge cooking-stove, the steam rising from their wet clothing. In the Western fashion Council told as much of his own life as he drew from his guest. He asked but few questions, but by and by the story of Haskins' struggles and defeat came out. The story was a terrible one, but he told it quietly, seated with his elbows on his knees, gazing most of the time at the hearth.

"I didn't like the looks of the country, anyhow," Haskins said, partly rising and glancing at his wife. "I was ust t' northern Ingyannie, where we have lots o' timber 'n' lots o' rain, 'n' I didn't like the looks o' that dry prairie. What galled me the worst was goin' s' far away acrosst so much fine land layin' all through here vacant."

"And the 'hoppers eat ye four years, hand runnin', did they?"

"Eat! They wiped us out. They chawed everything that was green. They jest set around waitin' f'r us to die t' eat us, too. My God! I ust t' dream of 'em sittin' 'round on the bedpost, six feet long, workin' their jaws. They eet the fork-handles. They got worse 'n' worse till they jest rolled on one another, piled up like snow in winter. Well, it ain't no use. If I was t' talk all winter I couldn't tell nawthin'. But all the while I couldn't help thinkin' of all that land back here that nobuddy was usin' that I ought 'o had 'stead o' bein' out there in that cussed country."

"Waal, why didn't ye stop an' settle here?" asked Ike, who had come in and was eating his supper.

"Fer the simple reason that you fellers wantid ten 'r fifteen dollars an acre fer the bare land, and I hadn't no money fer that kind o' thing."

"Yes, I do my own work," Mrs. Council was heard to say in the pause which followed. "I'm a gettin' purty heavy t' be on m' laigs all day, but we can't afford t' hire, so I keep rackin' around somehow, like a foundered horse. S' lame—I tell Council he can't tell how lame I am, f'r I'm jest as lame in one laig as t' other." And the good soul laughed at the joke on herself as she took a handful of flour and dusted the biscuit-board to keep the dough from sticking.

"Well, I hain't *never* been very strong," said Mrs. Haskins. "Our folks was Canadians an' small-boned, and then since my last child I hain't got up again fairly. I don't like t' complain. Tim has about all he can bear now—but they was days this week when I jes wanted to lay right down an' die."

"Waal, now, I'll tell ye," said Council, from his side of the stove, silencing everybody with his good-natured roar, "I'd go down and *see* Butler, *anyway*, if I was you. I guess he'd let you have his place purty cheap; the farm's all run down. He's ben anxious t' let t' somebuddy next year. It 'ud be a good chance fer you. Anyhow, you go to bed and sleep like a babe. I've got some plowin' t' do, anyhow, an' we'll see if somethin' can't be done about your case. Ike, you go out an' see if the horses is all right, an' I'll show the folks t' bed."

When the tired husband and wife were lying under the generous quilts of the spare bed, Haskins listened a moment to the wind in the eaves, and then said, with a slow and solemn tone,

"There are people in this world who are good enough t' be angels, an' only haff t' die to *be* angels."

Jim Butler was one of those men called in the West "land poor." Early in the history of Rock River he had come into the town and started in the grocery business in a small way, occupying a small building in a mean part of the town. At this period of his life he earned all he got, and was up early and late sorting beans, working over butter, and carting his goods to and from the station. But a change came over him at the end of the second year, when he sold a lot of land for four times what he paid for it. From that time forward he believed in land speculation as the surest way of getting rich. Every cent he could save or spare from his trade he put into land at forced sale, or mortages on land, which were "just as good as the wheat," he was accustomed to say.

Farm after farm fell into his hands, until he was recognized as one of the leading landowners of the county. His mortgages were scattered all over Cedar County, and as they slowly but surely fell in he sought usually to retain the former owner as tenant.

He was not ready to foreclose; indeed, he had the name of being one of the "easiest" men in the town. He let the debtor off again and again, extending the time whenever possible.

"I don't want y'r land," he said. "All I'm after is the int'rest on my money—that's all. Now, if y' want 'o stay on the farm, why, I'll give y' a good chance. I can't have the land layin' vacant." And in many cases the owner remained as tenant.

In the meantime he had sold his store; he couldn't spend time in it; he was mainly occupied now with sitting around town on rainy days smoking and "gassin' with the boys," or in riding to and from his farms. In fishing-time he fished a good deal. Doc Grimes, Ben Ashley, and Cal Cheatham were his cronies on these fishing excursions or hunting trips in the time of chickens or partridges. In winter they went to Northern Wisconsin to shoot deer.

In spite of all these signs of easy life Butler persisted in saying he "hadn't enough money to pay taxes on his land," and was careful to convey the impression that he was poor in spite of his twenty farms. At one time he was said to be worth fifty thousand dollars, but land had been a little slow of sale of late, so that he was not worth so much.

A fine farm, known as the Higley place, had fallen into his hands in the usual way the previous year, and he had not been able to find a tenant for it. Poor Higley, after working himself nearly to death on it in the attempt to lift the mortgage, had gone off to Dakota, leaving the farm and his curse to Butler.

This was the farm which Council advised Haskins to apply for; and the next day Council hitched up his team and drove down town to see Butler.

"You jest let *me* do the talkin'," he said. "We'll find him wearin' out his pants on some salt barrel somew'ers; and if he thought you *wanted* a place he'd sock it to you hot and heavy. You jest keep quiet; I'll fix 'im."

Butler was seated in Ben Ashley's store telling fish yarns when Council sauntered in casually.

"Hello, But; lyin' agin, hey!"

"Hello, Steve! how goes it?"

"Oh, so-so. Too dang much rain these days. I thought it was goin' t' freeze up f'r good last night. Tight squeak if I get m' plowin' done. How's farmin' with *you* these days?"

"Bad. Plowin' ain't half done."

"It 'ud be a religious idee f'r you t' go out an' take a hand y'rself."

"I don't haff to," said Butler, with a wink.

"Got anybody on the Higley place?"

"No. Know of anybody?"

"Waal, no; not eggsackly. I've got a relation back t' Michigan who's ben hot an' cold on the idee o' comin' West f'r some time. *Might* come if he could get a good layout. What do you talk on the farm?"

"Well, I d'know. I'll rent it on shares or I'll rent it money rent."

"Waal, how much money, say?"

"Well, say ten per cent, on the price—two-fifty."

"Waal, that ain't bad. Wait on 'im till 'e thrashes?"

Haskins listened eagerly to his important question, but Council was coolly eating a dried apple which he had speared out of a barrel with his knife. Butler studied him carefully.

"Well, knocks me out of twenty-five dollars interest."

"My relation'll need all he's got t' git his crops in," said Council, in the safe, indifferent way.

"Well, all right; *say* wait," concluded Butler.

"All right; this is the man. Haskins, this is Mr. Butler—no relation to Ben—the hardest-working man in Cedar County."

On the way home Haskins said: "I ain't much better off. I'd like that farm; it's a good farm, but it's all run down, an' so'm I. I could make a good farm of it if I had half a show. But I can't stock it n'r seed it."

"Waal, now, don't you worry," roared Council in his ear. "We'll pull y' through somehow till next harvest. He's agreed t' hire it plowed, an' you can earn a hundred dollars plowin' an' y' c'n git the seed o' me, an' pay me back when y' can."

Haskins was silent with emotion, but at last he said, "I ain't got nothin' t' live on."

"Now, don't you worry 'bout that. You jest make your headquarters at ol' Steve Council's. Mother'll take a pile o' comfort in havin' y'r wife an' children 'round. Y' see, Jane's married off lately, an' Ike's away a good 'eal, so we'll be darn glad t' have y' stop with us this winter. Nex' spring we'll see if y' can't git a start again." And he chirruped to the team, which sprang forward with the rumbling, clattering wagon.

"Say, looky here, Council, you can't do this. I never saw—" shouted Haskins in his neighbor's ear.

Council moved about uneasily in his seat and stopped his stammering gratitude by saying: "Hold on, now: don't make such a fuss over a little thing. When I see a man down, an' things all on top of 'm, I jest like t' kick 'em off an' help 'm up. That's the kind of religion I got, an' it's about the *only* kind."

They rode the rest of the way home in silence. And when the red light of the lamp shone out into the darkness of the cold and windy night, and he thought of this refuge for his children and wife, Haskins could have put his arm around the neck of his burly companion and squeezed him like a lover. But he contented himself with saying, "Steve Council, you'll git y'r pay f'r this some day."

"Don't want any pay. My religion ain't run on such business principles."

The wind was growing colder, and the ground was covered with a white frost, as they turned into the gate of the Council farm, and the children came rushing out, shouting, "Papa's come!" They hardly looked like the same children who had sat at the table the night before. Their torpidity, under the influence of sunshine and Mother Council, had given way to a sort of spasmodic cheerfulness, as insects in winter revive when laid on the hearth.

III

Haskins worked like a fiend, and his wife, like the heroic woman that she was, bore also uncomplainingly the most terrible burdens. They rose early and toiled without intermission till the darkness fell on the plain, then tumbled into bed, every bone and muscle aching with fatigue, to rise with the sun next morning to the same round of the same ferocity of labor.

The eldest boy drove a team all through the spring, plowing and seeding, milked the cows, and did chores innumerable, in most ways taking the place of a man.

An infinitely pathetic but common figure, this boy on the American farm, where there is no law against child labor. To see him in his coarse clothing, his huge boots, and his ragged cap, as he staggered with a pail of water from the well, or trudged in the cold and cheerless dawn out into the frosty field behind his team, gave the city-bred visitor a sharp pang of sympathetic pain. Yet Haskins loved his boy, and would have saved him from this if he could, but he could not.

By June the first year the result of such Herculean toil began to show on the farm. The yard was cleaned up and sown to grass, the garden plowed and planted, and the house mended.

Council had given them four of his cows.

"Take 'em an' run 'em on shares. I don't want 'o milk s' many. Ike's away s' much now, Sat'd'ys an' Sund'ys, I can't stand the bother anyhow."

Other men, seeing the confidence of Council in the newcomer, had sold him tools on time; and as he was really an able farmer, he soon had round him many evidences of his care and thrift. At the advice of Council he had taken the farm for three years, with the privilege of re-renting or buying at the end of the term.

"It's a good bargain, an' y' want 'o nail it," said Council. "If you have any kind ov a crop, you c'n pay y'r debts, an' keep seed an' bread."

The new hope which now sprang up in the heart of Haskins and his wife grew great almost as a pain by the time the wide field of wheat began to wave and swirl in the winds of July. Day after day he would snatch a few moments after supper to go and look at it.

"Have ye seen the wheat t'-day, Nettie?" he asked one night as he rose from supper.

"No, Tim, I ain't had time."

"Well, take time now. Le's go look at it."

She threw an old hat on her head—Tommy's hat—and looking almost pretty in her thin, sad way, went out with her husband to the hedge.

"Ain't it grand, Nettie? Just look at it."

It was grand. Level, russet here and there, heavy-headed, wide as a lake, and full of multitudinous whispers and gleams of wealth, it stretched away before the gazers like the fabled field of the cloth of gold.

"Oh, I think—I *hope* we'll have a good crop, Tim; and oh, how good the people have been to us!"

"Yes; I don't know where we'd be t'-day if it hadn't ben f'r Council and his wife."

"They're the best people in the world," said the little woman, with a great sob of gratitude.

"We'll be in the field on Monday, sure," said Haskins, gripping the rail on the fence as if already at the work of the harvest.

The harvest came, bounteous, glorious, but the winds came and blew it into tangles, and the rain matted it here and there close to the ground, increasing the work of gathering it threefold.

Oh, how they toiled in those glorious days! Clothing dripping with sweat, arms aching, filled with briers, fingers raw and bleeding, backs broken with the weight of heavy bundles, Haskins and his man toiled on. Tommy drove the harvester, while his father and a hired man bound on the machine. In this way they cut ten acres every day, and almost every night after supper, when the hand went to bed, Haskins returned to the field shocking the bound grain in the light of the moon. Many a night he worked till his anxious wife came out at ten o'clock to call him in to rest and lunch.

At the same time she cooked for the men, took care of the children, washed and ironed, milked the cows at night, made the butter, and sometimes fed the horses and watered them while her husband kept at the shocking.

No slave in the Roman galleys could have toiled so frightfully and lived, for this man thought himself a free man, and that he was working for his wife and babes.

When he sank into his bed with a deep groan of relief, too tired to change his grimy, dripping clothing, he felt that he was getting nearer and nearer to a home of his own, and pushing the wolf of want a little farther from his door.

There is no despair so deep as the despair of a homeless man or woman. To roam the roads of the country or the streets of the city, to feel there is no rood of ground on which the feet can rest, to halt weary and hungry outside lighted windows and hear laughter and song within,—these are the hungers and rebellions that drive men to crime and women to shame.

It was the memory of this homelessness, and the fear of its coming again, that spurred Timothy Haskins and Nettie, his wife, to such ferocious labor during that first year.

IV

" 'M, yes; 'm, yes; first-rate," said Butler, as his eye took in the neat garden, the pigpen, and the well-filled barnyard. "You're gitt'n quite a stock around yeh. Done well, eh?"

Haskins was showing Butler around the place. He had not seen it for a year, having spent the year in Washington and Boston with Ashley, his brother-in-law, who had been elected to Congress.

"Yes, I've laid out a good deal of money durin' the last three years. I've paid out three hundred dollars f'r fencin'."

"Um—h'm! I see, I see," said Butler while Haskins went on:

"The kitchen there cost two hundred; the barn ain't cost much in money, but I've put a lot o' time on it. I've dug a new well, and I—"

"Yes, yes, I see. You've done well. Stock worth a thousand dollars," said Butler, picking his teeth with a straw.

"About that," said Haskins, modestly. "We begin to feel 's if we was gitt'n a home f'r ourselves; but we've worked hard. I tell you we begin to feel it, Mr. Butler, and we're goin' t' begin to ease up purty soon. We've been kind o' plannin' a trip back t' *her* folks after the fall plowin's done."

"*Eggs*-actly!" said Butler, who was evidently thinking of something else. "I suppose you've kind o' calc'lated on stayin' here three years more?"

"Well, yes. Fact is, I think I c'n buy the farm this fall, if you'll give me a reasonable show."

"Um-m! What do you call a reasonable show?"

"Well, say a quarter down and three years time."

Butler looked at the huge stacks of wheat, which filled the yard, over which the chickens were fluttering and crawling, catching grasshoppers, and out of which the crickets were singing innumerably. He smiled in a peculiar way as he said, "Oh, I won't be hard on yeh. But what did you expect to pay f'r the place?"

"Why, about what you offered it for before, two thousand five hundred, or *possibly* three thousand dollars," he added quickly as he saw the owner shake his head.

"This farm is worth five thousand and five hundred dollars," said Butler, in a careless and decided voice.

"*What!*" almost shrieked the astounded Haskins. "What's that? Five thousand? Why, that's double what you offered it for three years ago."

"Of course, and it's worth it. It was all run down then; now it's in good shape. You've laid out fifteen hundred dollars in improvements, according to your own story."

"But *you* had nothin' t' do about that. It's my work an' my money."

"You bet it was; but it's my land."

"But what's to pay me for all my—"

"Ain't you had the use of 'em?" replied Butler, smiling calmly into his face.

Haskins was like a man struck on the head with a sandbag; he couldn't think; he stammered as he tried to say: "But—I never'd git the use— You'd rob me! More'n that: you agreed—you promised that I could buy or rent at the end of three years at—"

"That's all right. But I didn't say I'd let you carry off the improvements, nor that I'd go on renting the farm at two-fifty. The land is doubled in value, it don't matter how; it don't enter into the question; an' now you can pay me five hundred dollars a year rent, or take it on your own terms at fifty-five hundred, or—git out."

He was turning away when Haskins, the sweat pouring from his face, fronted him, saying again:

"But *you've* done nothing to make it so. You hain't added a cent. I put it all there myself, expectin' to buy. I worked an' sweat to improve it. I was workin' for myself an' babes—"

"Well, why didn't you buy when I offered to sell? What y' kickin' about?"

"I'm kickin' about payin' you twice f'r my own things,—my own fences, my own kitchen, my own garden."

Butler laughed. "You're too green t'eat, young feller. *Your* improvements! The law will sing another tune."

"But I trusted your word."

"Never trust anybody, my friend. Besides, I didn't promise not to do this thing. Why, man, don't look at me like that. Don't take me for a thief. It's the law. The reg'lar thing. Everybody does it."

"I don't care if they do. It's stealin' jest the same. You take three thousand dollars of my money—the work o' my hands and my wife's." He broke down at this point. He was not a strong man mentally. He could face hardship, ceaseless toil, but he could not face the cold and sneering face of Butler.

"But I don't take it," said Butler, coolly. "All you've got to do is to go on jest as you've been a-doin', or give me a thousand dollars down, and a mortgage at ten per cent on the rest."

Haskins sat down blindly on a bundle of oats near by, and with staring eyes and drooping head went over the situation. He was under the lion's paw. He felt a horrible numbness in his heart and limbs. He was hid in a mist, and there was no path out.

Butler walked about, looking at the huge stacks of grain, and pulling now and again a few handfuls out, shelling the heads in his hands and blowing the chaff away. He hummed a little tune as he did so. He had an accommodating air of waiting.

Haskins was in the midst of the terrible toil of the last year. He was walking again in the rain and the mud behind his plow; he felt the dust and dirt of the threshing. The ferocious husking-time, with its cutting wind and biting, clinging snows, lay hard upon him. Then he thought of his wife, how she had cheerfully cooked and baked, without holiday and without rest.

"Well, what do you think of it?" inquired the cool, mocking, insinuating voice of Butler.

"I think you're a thief and a liar!" shouted Haskins, leaping up. "A black-hearted houn'!" Butler's smile maddened him; with a sudden leap he caught a fork in his hands, and whirled it in the air. "You'll never rob another man, damn ye!" he grated through his teeth, a look of pitiless ferocity in his accusing eyes.

Butler shrank and quivered, expecting the blow; stood, held hypnotized by the eyes of the man he had a moment before despised—a man transformed into an avenging demon. But in the deadly hush between the lift of the weapon and its fall there came a gush of faint, childish laughter and then across the range of his vision, far away and dim, he saw the sun-bright head of his baby girl, as, with the pretty, tottering run of a two-year-old, she moved across the grass of the dooryard. His hands relaxed; the fork fell to the ground; his head lowered.

"Make out y'r deed an' mor'gage, an' git off'n my land, an' don't ye never cross my line agin; if y' do, I'll kill ye."

Butler backed away from the man in wild haste, and climbing into his buggy with trembling limbs drove off down the road, leaving Haskins seated dumbly on the sunny piles of sheaves, his head sunk into his hands.

A Start in Life

by RUTH SUCKOW, 1892– . *No writer has presented more quietly truthful pictures of middlewestern farm life than Ruth Suckow. Born in Hawarden, Iowa, of German ancestry, she lived in various small communities because her father was a Congregational minister who frequently changed parishes. She was educated at Grinnell College and the University of Denver, B.A., 1917. After a short interval of teaching she managed an apiary at Earlville, Iowa, for six years. In 1929 she married Ferner Nuhn. Her first stories appeared in the Midland, the Smart Set, and H. L. Mencken's American Mercury; they were afterwards collected in such volumes as Iowa Interiors (1926) and Carry-Over (1936). Her novels include Country People (1924), The Bonney Family (1928), and her most ambitious story, The Folks (1934). In all her work she has been consistently· faithful to the Iowa scene,* and her characters are usually farmers or small-town residents portrayed realistically and unsatirically against a background she knows well. "A Start in Life," with its pathetic picture of a young girl beginning work as a domestic in a farm home, is reprinted from Carry-Over.

I

The Switzers were scurrying around to get Daisy ready by the time that Elmer Kruse should get through in town. They had known all week that Elmer might be in for her any day. But they hadn't done a thing until he appeared. "Oh, it was so rainy to-day, the roads were so muddy, they hadn't thought that he'd get in until maybe next week." It would have been the same any other day.

Mrs. Switzer was trying now at the last moment to get all of Daisy's things into the battered telescope that lay open on the bed. The bed had not "got made"; and just as soon as Daisy was gone, Mrs. Switzer would have to hurry off to the Woodworth's where she was to wash to-day. Daisy's things were scattered over the dark brown quilt and the rumpled sheet that were dingy and clammy in this damp weather. So was the whole bedroom, with its sloping ceiling and old-fashioned square-paned windows, the commode that they used for a dresser, littered with pin tray, curlers, broken comb, ribbons, smoky lamp, all mixed up together; the door of the closet open, showing the confusion of clothes and shabby shoes. . . . They all slept in this room—Mrs. Switzer and Dwight in the bed, the two girls in the cot against the wall.

"Mamma, I can't find the belt to that plaid dress."

"Oh, ain't it somewheres around? Well, I guess you'll have to let it go. If I come across it I can send it out to you. Someone'll be going past there."

She had meant to get Daisy all mended and "fixed up" before she went out to the country. But somehow . . . oh, there was always so much to see to when she came home. Gone all day, washing and cleaning for other people; it didn't leave her much time for her own house.

She was late now. The Woodworths liked to have her get the washing out early so that she could do some cleaning too before she left. But she couldn't help it. She would have to get Daisy off first. She had already had on her wraps ready to go, when Elmer came—her cleaning cap, of a blue faded almost into grey, and the ancient black coat with gathered sleeves that she wore over her work dress when she went out to wash.

"What's become of all your underclothes? They ain't all dirty, are they?"

"They are, too. You didn't wash for us last week, mamma."

"Well, you'll just have to take along what you've got. Maybe there'll be some way of getting the rest to you."

"Elmers come in every week, don't they?" Daisy demanded.

"Yes, but maybe they won't always be bringing you in."

She jammed what she could into the telescope, thinking with her helpless, anxious fatalism that it would have to do somehow.

"Daisy, you get yourself ready now."

"I am ready. Mamma, I want to put on my other ribbon."

"Oh, that's way down in the telescope somewhere. You needn't be so anxious to fix yourself up. This ain't like going visiting."

Daisy stood at the little mirror preening herself—such a homely child, "all Switzer," skinny, with pale sharp eyes set close together and thin, stringy, reddish hair. But she had never really learned yet how homely she was. She was the oldest, and she got the pick of what clothes were given to the Switzers. Goldie and Dwight envied her. She was important in her small world. She was proud of her blue coat that had belonged to Alice Brooker, the town lawyer's daughter. It hung unevenly about her bony little knees, and the buttons came down too far. Her mother had tried to make it over for her.

Mrs. Switzer looked at her, troubled, but not knowing how she could tell her all the things she ought to be told. Daisy had never been away before except to go to her Uncle Fred's at Lehigh. She seemed to think this would be the same. She had so many things to learn. Well, she would find them out soon enough—only too soon. Working for other people—she would learn what that meant. Elmer and Edna Kruse were nice young people. They would mean well enough by Daisy. It was a good chance for her to start in. But it wasn't the same.

Daisy was so proud. She thought it was quite a thing to be "starting in to earn." She thought she could buy herself so much with that dollar and a half a week. The other children stood back watching her, round-eyed and impressed. They wished that they were going away, like Daisy.

They heard a car come splashing through the mud on low.

"There he is back! Have you got your things on? Goldie—go out and tell him she's coming."

"No, me tell him, me!" Dwight shouted jealously.

"Well—both of you tell him. Land! . . ."

She tried hastily to put on the cover of the bulging telescope and to fasten the straps. One of them broke.

"Well, you'll have to take it the way it is."

It was an old thing, hadn't been used since her husband, Mert, had "left off canvassing" before he died. And he had worn it all to pieces.

"Well, I guess you'll have to go now. He won't want to wait. I'll try and send you out what you ain't got with you." She turned to Daisy. Her face was working. There was nothing else to do, as everyone said. Daisy would have to help, and she might as well learn it now. Only, she hated to see Daisy go off, to have her starting in. She knew what it meant. "Well—you try and work good this summer, so they'll want you to stay. I hope they'll bring you in sometimes."

Daisy's homely little face grew pale with awe, suddenly, at the sight of her mother crying, at something that she dimly sensed in the pressure of her mother's thin strong arms. Her vanity in her new importance was somehow shamed and dampened.

Elmer's big new Buick, mud-splashed but imposing, stood tilted on the uneven road. Mud was thick on the wheels. It was a bad day for driving, with the roads a yellow mass, water lying in all the wheel ruts. This little road that led past these few houses on the outskirts of town, and up over the hill, had a cold rainy loneliness. Elmer sat in the front seat of the Buick, and in the back was a big box of groceries.

"Got room to sit in there?" he asked genially. "I didn't get out, it's so muddy here."

"No, don't get out," Mrs. Switzer said hastily. "She can put this right on the floor there in the back." She added, with a timid attempt at courtesy, "Ain't the roads pretty bad out that way?"

"Yes, but farmers get so they don't think so much about the roads."

"I s'pose that's so."

He saw the signs of tears on Mrs. Switzer's face, and they made him anxious to get away. She embraced Daisy hastily again. Daisy climbed over the grocery box and scrunched herself into the seat.

"I guess you'll bring her in with you some time when you're coming," Mrs. Switzer hinted.

"Sure. We'll bring her."

He started the engine. It roared, half died down as the wheels of the car spun in the thick wet mud.

In that moment, Daisy had a startled view of home—the small house standing on a rough rise of land, weathered to a dim colour that showed dark streaks from the rain; the narrow sloping front porch whose edge had a soaked gnawed look; the chickens, greyish-black, pecking at the wet ground; their playthings, stones, a wagon, some old pail covers littered about; a soaked, discoloured piece of underwear hanging on the line in the back yard. The yard was tussocky and overhung the road with shaggy long grass where the yellow bank was caved in under it. Goldie and Dwight were gazing at her solemnly. She saw her mother's face—a thin, weak, loving face, drawn with neglected weeping, with its reddened eyes and poor teeth . . . in the old coat and heavy shoes and cleaning-cap, her work-worn hand with its big knuckles clutching at her coat. She saw the playthings they had used yesterday, and the old swing that hung from one of the trees, the ropes sodden, the seat in crooked. . . .

The car went off, slipping on the wet clay. She waved frantically, suddenly understanding that she was leaving them. They waved at her. Mrs. Switzer stood there a little while. Then came the harsh rasp of the old black iron pump that stood out under the box-elder tree. She was pumping water to leave for the children before she went off to work.

II

Daisy held on as the car skidded going down the short clay hill. Elmer didn't bother with chains. He was too used to the roads. But her eyes brightened with scared excitement. When they were down, and Elmer slowed up going along the tracks in the deep wet grass that led to the main road, she looked back, holding on her hat with her small scrawny hand.

Just down this little hill—and home was gone. The big car, the feel of her telescope under her feet, the fact that she was going out to the country, changed the looks of everything. She saw it all now.

Dunkels' house stood on one side of the road. A closed-up white house. The windows stared blank and cold between the old shutters. There was a chair with a broken straw seat under the fruit trees. The Dunkels were old Catholic people who seldom went anywhere. In the front yard was a clump of tall pines, the rough brown trunks wet, the green branches, dark and shining, heavy with rain, the ground underneath mournfully sodden and black.

The pasture on the other side. The green grass, lush, wet and cold, and the outcroppings of limestone that held little pools of rain-water in all the tiny holes. Beyond, the low hills gloomy with timber against the lowering sky.

They slid out on to the main road. They bumped over the small wooden bridge above the swollen creek that came from the pasture. Daisy looked down. She saw the little swirls of foam, the long grass that swished with the water, the old rusted tin cans lodged between the rocks.

She sat up straight and important, her thin, homely little face strained with excitement, her sharp eyes taking in everything. The watery mud-holes in the road, the little thickets of plum-trees, low and wet, in dark interlacings. She held on fiercely, but made no sound when the car skidded.

She felt the grandeur of having a ride. One wet Sunday, Mr. Brooker had driven them all home from church, she and Goldie and Dwight packed tightly into the back seat of the car, shut in by the side curtains against which the rain lashed, catching the muddy scent of the roads. Sometimes they could plan to go to town just when Mr. Pattey was going to work in his Ford. Then they would run out and shout eagerly, "Mr. Pattey! Are you going through town?" Sometimes he didn't hear them. Sometimes he said, with curt good nature, "Well, pile in"; and they all hopped into the truck back. "He says we can go along with him."

She looked at the black wet fields through which little leaves of bright green corn grew in rows, at showery bushes of sumach along the roadside. A gasolene engine pumping water made a loud desolate sound. There were somber-looking cattle in the wet grass, and lonely, thick-foliaged trees growing here and there in the pastures. She felt her telescope on the floor of the car, the box of groceries beside her. She eyed these with sharp curiosity. There was a fresh pine-apple— something the Switzers didn't often get at home. She wondered if Edna would have it for dinner. Maybe she could hint a little to Edna.

She was out in the country. She could no longer see her house even if she wanted to—standing dingy, streaked with rain, in its rough grass on the little hill. A lump came into her throat. She had looked forward to playing with Edna's children. But Goldie and Dwight would play all morning without her. She was still proud of her being the oldest, of going out with Elmer and Edna; but now there was a forlornness in the pride.

She wished she were in the front seat with Elmer. She didn't see why he hadn't put her there. She would have liked to know who all the people were who lived on these farms; how old Elmer's babies were; and if he and Edna always went to the movies when they went into town on Saturday nights. Elmer must have lots of money to buy a car like this. He had a new house on his farm, too, and Mrs. Metzinger had said that it had plumbing. Maybe they would take her to the movies, too. She might hint about that.

When she had gone to visit Uncle Fred, she had had to go on the train. She liked this better. She hoped they had a long way to go. She called out to Elmer:

"Say, how much farther is your place?"

"What's that?" He turned around. "Oh, just down the road a ways. Scared to drive in the mud?"

"No, I ain't scared. I like to drive most any way."

She looked at Elmer's back, the old felt hat crammed down carelessly on his head, the back of his neck with the golden hair on the sunburned skin above the blue of his shirt collar. Strong and easy and slouched a little over the steering-wheel that he handled so masterfully. Elmer and Edna were just young folks; but Mrs. Metzinger said that they had more to start with than most young farmers did, and that they were hustlers. Daisy felt that the pride of this belonged to her too, now.

"Here we are!"

"Oh, is this where you folks live?" Daisy cried eagerly.

The house stood back from the road beyond a space of bare yard with a little scattering of grass just starting—small, modern, painted a bright new white and yellow. The barn was new too, a big splendid barn of frescoed brick, with a silo of the same. There were no trees. A raw desolate wind blew across the back yard as they drove up beside the back door.

Edna had come out on the step. Elmer grinned at her as he took out the box of groceries, and she slightly raised her eyebrows. She said kindly enough:

"Well, you brought Daisy. Hello, Daisy, are you going to stay with us this summer?"

"I guess so," Daisy said importantly. But she suddenly felt a little shy and forlorn as she got out of the car and stood on the bare ground in the chilly wind.

"Yes, I brought her along," Elmer said.

"Are the roads very bad?"

"Kind of bad. Why?"

"Well, I'd like to get over to mamma's some time to-day."

"Oh, I guess they aren't too bad for that."

Daisy pricked up her sharp little ears. Another ride. That cheered her.

"Look in the door," Edna said in a low fond voice, motioning with her head.

Two little round, blond heads were pressed tightly against the screen door. There was a clamour of "Daddy, daddy!" Elmer grinned with a half bashful pride as he stood with the box of groceries, raising his eyebrows with mock surprise and demanding: "Who's this? What you shoutin' 'daddy' for? You don't think daddy's got anything for you, do you?" He and Edna were going into the kitchen together, until Edna remembered and called back hastily:

"Oh, come in, Daisy!"

Daisy stood, a little left out and solitary, there in the kitchen, as Billy, the older of the babies, climbed frantically over Elmer, demanding candy, and the little one toddled smilingly about. Her eyes took in all of it. She was impressed by the shining blue-and-white linoleum, the range with its nickel and enamel, the bright new woodwork. Edna

283

was laughing and scolding at Elmer and the baby. Billy had made his father produce the candy. Daisy's sharp little eyes looked hungrily at the lemon drops until Edna remembered her.

"Give Daisy a piece of your candy," she said.

He would not go up to Daisy. She had to come forward and take one of the lemon drops herself. She saw where Edna put the sack, in a dish high in the cupboard. She hoped they would get some more before long.

"My telescope's out there in the car," she reminded them.

"Oh! Elmer, you go and get it and take it up for her," Edna said.

"What?"

"Her valise—or whatever it is—out in the car."

"Oh, sure," Elmer said with a cheerful grin.

"It's kind of an old telescope," Daisy said conversationally. "I guess it's been used a lot. My papa used to have it. The strap broke when mamma was fastening it this morning. We ain't got any suit-case. I had to take this because it was all there was in the house, and mamma didn't want to get me a new one."

Edna raised her eyebrows politely. She leaned over and pretended to pat the baby as he came toddling up to her, then rubbed her cheek against his round head with its funny fuzz of hair.

Daisy watched solemnly. "I didn't know both of your children was boys. I thought one of 'em was a girl. That's what there is at home now—one boy and one girl."

"Um-hm," Edna replied absently. "You can go up with Elmer and take off your things, Daisy," she said. "You can stop and unpack your valise now, I guess, if you'd like to. Then you can come down and help me in the kitchen. You know we got you to help me," she reminded.

Daisy, subdued, followed Elmer up the bright new stairs. In the upper hall, two strips of very clean rag rug were laid over the shining yellow of the floor. Elmer had put her telescope in one of the bedrooms.

"There you are!"

She heard him go clattering down the stairs, and then a kind of murmuring and laughing in the kitchen. The back door slammed. She hurried to the window in time to see Elmer go striding off toward the barn.

She looked about her room with intense curiosity. It too had a bright varnished floor. She had a bed all of her own—a small, old-fashioned bed, left from some old furnishings, that had been put in this room that had the pipes and the hot-water tank. She had to see everything, but she had a stealthy look as she tiptoed about, started to open the drawers of the dresser, looked out of her window. She put her coat and hat on the bed. She would rather be down in the kitchen with Edna than unpack her telescope now.

She guessed she would go down where the rest of them were.

III

Elmer came into the house for dinner. He brought in a cold, muddy, outdoor breath with him. The range was going, but the bright little kitchen seemed chilly, with the white oilcloth on the table, the baby's varnished high chair and his little fat, mottled hands.

Edna made a significant little face at Elmer. Daisy did not see. She was standing back from the stove, where Edna was at work, looking at the baby.

"He can talk pretty good, can't he? Dwight couldn't say anything but 'mamma' when he was that little."

Edna's back was turned. She said meaningly:

"Now, Elmer's come in to dinner, Daisy, we'll have to hurry. You must help me get on the dinner. You can cut bread and get things on the table. You must help, you know. That's what you are supposed to do."

Daisy looked startled, a little scared and resentful. "Well, I don't know where you keep your bread."

"Don't you remember where I told you to put it this morning? Right over in the cabinet, in that big box. You must watch, Daisy, and learn where things are."

Elmer, a little embarrassed at the look that Edna gave him, whistled as he began to wash his hands at the sink.

"How's daddy's old boy?" he said loudly, giving a poke at the baby's chin.

As Edna passed him, she shook her head, and her lips just formed: "Been like that all morning!"

He grinned comprehendingly. Then both their faces became expressionless.

Daisy had not exactly heard, but she looked from one to the other, silent and dimly wondering. The queer ache that had kept starting all through the morning, under her interest in Edna's things and doings, came over her again. She sensed something different in the atmosphere than she had ever known before—some queer difference between the position of herself and of the two babies, a faint notion of what mamma had meant when she had said that this would not be visiting.

"I guess I'm going to have the toothache again," she said faintly.

No one seemed to hear her.

Edna whisked off the potatoes, drained the water. . . .

285

"You might bring me a dish, Daisy." Daisy searched a long time while Edna turned impatiently and pointed. Edna put the rest of the things on the table herself. Her young, fresh, capable mouth was tightly closed, and she was making certain resolutions.

Daisy stood hesitating in the middle of the room, a scrawny, unappealing little figure. Billy—fat, blond, in funny, dark blue union-alls—was trotting busily about the kitchen. Daisy swooped down upon him and tried to bring him to the table. He set up a howl. Edna turned, looked astonished, severe.

"I was trying to make him come to the table," Daisy explained weakly.

"You scared him. He isn't used to you. He doesn't like it. Don't cry, Billy. The girl didn't mean anything."

"Here, daddy'll put him in his place," Elmer said hastily.

Billy looked over his father's shoulder at Daisy with suffused, resentful blue eyes. She did not understand it, and felt strangely at a loss. She had been left with Goldie and Dwight so often. She had always made Dwight go to the table. She had been the boss.

Edna said in a cool, held-in voice, "Put these things on the table, Daisy."

They sat down. Daisy and the other children had always felt it a great treat to eat away from home instead of at their own scanty, hastily set table. They had hung around Mrs. Metzinger's house at noon, hoping to be asked to stay, not offended when told that "it was time for them to run off now." Her pinched little face had a hungry look as she stared at the potatoes and fried ham and pie. But they did not watch and urge her to have more, as Mrs. Metzinger did, and Mrs. Brooker when she took pity on the Switzers and had them there. Daisy wanted more pie. But none of them seemed to be taking more, and so she said nothing. She remembered what her mother had said, with now a faint comprehension: "You must remember you're out working for other folks, and it won't be like it is at home."

After dinner, Edna said: "Now you can wash the dishes, Daisy." She went into the next room with the children. Daisy, as she went hesitatingly about the kitchen alone, could hear Edna's low contented humming as she sat in there rocking, the baby in her lap. The bright kitchen was empty and lonely now. Through the window, Daisy could see the great barn looming up against the rainy sky. She hoped that they would drive to Edna's mother's soon.

She finished as soon as she could, and went into the dining-room, where Edna was sewing on the baby's rompers. Edna went on sewing. Daisy sat down disconsolately. That queer low ache went all through her. She said in a small dismal voice:

"I guess I got the toothache again."

Edna bit off a thread.

"I had it awful hard a while ago. Mamma come pretty near taking me to the dentist."

"That's too bad," Edna murmured politely. But she offered no other condolence. She gave a secret little smile at the baby asleep on a blanket and a pillow in one corner of the shiny leather davenport.

"Is Elmer going to drive into town to-morrow?"

"To-morrow? I don't suppose so."

"Mamma couldn't find the belt of my plaid dress and I thought if he was, maybe I could go along and get it. I'd like to have it."

Daisy's homely mouth drooped at the corners. Her toothache did not seem to matter to anyone. Edna did not seem to want to see that anything was wrong with her. She had expected Edna to be concerned, to mention remedies. But it wasn't toothache, that strange lonesome ache all over her. Maybe she was going to be terribly sick. Mamma wouldn't come home for supper to be told about it.

She saw mamma's face as in that last glimpse of it—drawn with crying, and yet trying to smile, under the old cleaning-cap, her hand holding her coat together. . . .

Edna glanced quickly at her. The child was so mortally unattractive, unappealing even in her forlornness. Edna frowned a little, but said kindly:

"Now you might take Billy into the kitchen out of my way, Daisy, and amuse him."

"Well, he cries when I pick him up," Daisy said faintly.

"He won't cry this time. Take him out and help him play with his blocks. You must help me with the children, you know."

"Well, if he'll go with me."

"He'll go with you, won't he, Billy boy? Won't you go with Daisy, sweetheart?"

Billy stared and then nodded. Daisy felt a thrill of comfort as Billy put his little fat hand in hers and trotted into the kitchen beside her. He had the fattest hands, she thought. Edna brought the blocks and put the box down on the floor beside Daisy.

"Now, see if you can amuse him so that I can get my sewing done."

"Shall you and me play blocks, Billy?" Daisy murmured.

He nodded. Then he got hold of the box with one hand, tipped out all the blocks on the floor with a bang and a rattle, and looked at her with a pleased proud smile.

"Oh, no, Billy. You mustn't spill out the blocks. Look, you're too little to play with them. No, now-now wait! Let Daisy show you. Daisy'll build something real nice—shall she?"

He gave a solemn nod of consent.

Daisy set out the blocks on the bright linoleum. She had never had such blocks as these to handle before. Dwight's were only a few old, unmatched, broken ones. Her spirit of leadership came back, and she firmly put away that fat hand of Billy's whenever he meddled with her building. She could make something really wonderful with these blocks.

"No, Billy, you mustn't. See, when Daisy's got it all done, then you can see what the lovely building is."

She put the blocks together with great interest. She knew what she was going to make—it was going to be a new house; no, a new church. Just as she got the walls up, in came that little hand again, and then with a delighted grunt Billy swept the blocks pell-mell about the floor. At the clatter, he sat back, pursing up his mouth to give an ecstatic "Ooh!"

"Oh, Billy—you mustn't, the building wasn't done! Look, you've spoiled it. Now you've got to sit 'way off here while I try to build it over again."

Billy's look of triumph turned to surprise and then to vociferous protest as Daisy picked him up and firmly transplanted him to another corner of the room. He set up a tremendous howl. He had never been set aside like that before. Edna came hurrying out. Daisy looked at Edna for justification, but instinctively on the defensive.

"Billy knocked over the blocks. He spoiled the building."

"Wah! Wah!" Billy gave loud heart-broken sobs. The tears ran down his fat cheeks and he held out his arms piteously toward his mother.

"I didn't hurt him," Daisy said, scared.

"Never mind, lover," Edna said crooning. "Of course he can play with his blocks. They're Billy's blocks, Daisy," she said. "He doesn't like to sit and see you put up buildings. He wants to play, too. See, you've made him cry now."

"Do' wanna stay here," Billy wailed.

"Well, come in with mother then." She picked him up, wiping his tears.

"I didn't hurt him," Daisy protested.

"Well, never mind now. You can pick up the blocks and then sweep the floor, Daisy. You didn't do that when you finished the dishes. Never mind," she was saying to Billy. "Pretty soon daddy'll come in and we'll have a nice ride."

Daisy soberly picked up the blocks and got the broom. What had she done to Billy? He had tried to spoil her building. Of course it was Daisy, the oldest, who should lead and manage. There had been no one to hear her side. Everything was different. She winked back tears as she swept, poorly and carelessly.

Then she brightened up as Elmer came tramping up on the back porch and then through the kitchen.

"Edna!"

"She's in there," Daisy offered.

"Want to go now? What! Is the baby asleep?" he asked blankly. Edna gave him a warning look and the door was closed.

Daisy listened hard. She swept very softly. She could catch only a little of what they said—"Kind of hate to go off . . . what we got her for . . ." She had no real comprehension of it. She hurried and put away the broom. She wanted to be sure and be ready to go.

Elmer tramped out, straight past her. She saw from the window that he was backing the car out from the shed. She could hear Edna and Billy upstairs, could hear the baby cry a little as he was wakened. Maybe she ought to go out and get on her wraps, too.

Elmer honked the horn. A moment later Edna came hurrying downstairs, in her hat and coat, and Billy in a knitted cap and red sweater crammed over his union-alls, so that he looked like a little Brownie. The baby had his little coat, too.

Edna called out: "Come in and get this boy, daddy." She did not look at Daisy, but said hurriedly: "We're going for a little ride, Daisy. Have you finished the sweeping? Well, then, you can pick up those pieces in the dining-room. We won't be gone so very long. When it's a quarter past five, you start the fire, like I showed you this noon, and slice the potatoes that were left, and the meat. And set the table."

The horn was honked again.

"Yes! Well, we'll be back, Daisy. Come, lover, daddy's in a hurry."

Daisy stood looking at them. Billy clamoured to sit beside his daddy. Edna took the baby from Elmer and put him beside her on the back seat. There was room—half of the big back seat. There wasn't anything, really, to be done at home. That was the worst of it. They just didn't want to take her. They all belonged together. They didn't want to take anyone else along. She was an outsider. They all—even the baby—had a freshened look of expectancy.

The engine roared—they had started; slipping on the mud of the drive, then forging straight ahead, around the turn, out of sight.

IV

She went forlornly into the dining-room. The light from the windows was dim now in the rainy, late afternoon. The pink pieces from the baby's rompers were scattered over the gay rug. She got down on her hands and knees, slowly picking them up, sniffing a little. She heard the Big Ben clock in the kitchen ticking loudly.

That dreadful ache submerged her. No one would ask about it, no one would try to comfort her. Before, there had always been mamma coming home, anxious, scolding sometimes, but worried over them if they didn't feel right, caring about them. Mamma and Goldie and Dwight cared about her—but she was away out in the country, and they were at home. She didn't want to stay here, where she didn't belong. But mamma had told her that she must begin helping this summer.

Her ugly little mouth contorted into a grimace of weeping. But silent weeping, without any tears; because she already had the cold knowledge that no one would notice or comfort it.

Color in the Wheat

by HAMLIN GARLAND. *Garland's reputation is largely based on his grim sketches of middle border farm life. But he also had a sincere feeling for the natural beauty and the vitality of the prairies. "Color in the Wheat," one of the lyrics of* Prairie Songs (1893), *illustrates this appreciation of the rural landscape.*

LIKE liquid gold the wheat field lies,
A marvel of yellow and green,
That ripples and runs, that floats and flies,
With the subtle shadows, the change—the sheen
That plays in the golden hair of a girl.
A cloud flies there—
A ripple of amber—a flare
Of light follows after. A swirl
In the hollows like the twinkling feet
Of a fairy waltzer, the colors run
To the western sun,
Through the deeps of the ripening wheat.

I hear the reapers' far-off hum,
So faint and far, it seems the drone
Of bee or beetle; seems to come
From far-off, fragrant, fruity zone,

A land of plenty, where,
Toward the sun, as hasting there,
The colors run before the wind's feet
In the wheat.

The wild hawk swoops
To his prey in the deeps;
The sun-flower droops
To the lazy wave; the wind sleeps—
Then running in dazzling links and loops
A marvel of shadow and shine,
A glory of olive and amber and wine
Runs the color in the wheat.

Buck in the Bottoms

by AUGUST DERLETH, 1909–   . *Derleth is the most prolific of the younger American writers. A native of Sauk City, Wisconsin, he was educated at the University of Wisconsin, B.A., 1930, and has spent nearly all his life in the region of his birth. Among the more than thirty-five volumes of fiction, verse, and autobiography that have already poured from his pen are* Country Growth (1940), *a collection of short stories; historical novels of the Wisconsin River Valley such as* Wind over Wisconsin (1938), Restless Is the River (1939), *and* Bright Journey (1940); *a biography of Zona Gale,* Still Small Voice (1940); Village Year: A Sac Prairie Chronicle (1941); *and* Selected Poems (1944). *It is Derleth's ambition to produce a Sac Prairie saga in a number of volumes, several of which have already appeared. His best work illustrates an intelligent regionalism and reveals an intimate knowledge of his chosen locale. "Buck in the Bottoms" is one of the stories in* Country Growth.

THE kitchen door swung suddenly open, and a swirl of soft snowflakes billowed in. Gus Elker came after, himself almost white with snow, his sad eyes looking lugubriously from the dark shadow of his cap, his half-moon of mustard-color mustache hung with snow.

"My soul and body! if it ain't Gus Elker," exclaimed my great-aunt Lou, looking at him over her spectacles, her patching forgotten in her lap. "Ain't lost, are you, Gus?"

"No, ma'am. I come for Joe." His voice had a hollow, breathless sound, as if he had been running.

From the back porch came briefly, sharply, the barking of a fox.

My great-uncle Joe eyed the door quickly, flashed a glance at his wife, and peered at Gus, narrowing his eyes and pursing his lips to hide the grin that lay behind them. "What's up, Gus? Sheriff after you?"

"Come in and set," Great-aunt invited, not without an edge of suspicion in her voice.

"Thanks, ma'am, but I ain't the time. I got work t' do." He turned to Great-uncle and began to speak swiftly, urgently, words chasing each other from his lips, his doleful features working as if some inner torment strove to make itself manifest there. "It's that deer we seen month ago, that buck I showed you in the bottoms. You know that buck we seen, you and I, purty as a pitcher, astandin' there jest this side o' Ferry Bluff. Philander Hewitt's after him, him and his dogs. I like t' die if he ain't! I come home the Mill Road, and there sure enough I seen him start out. I don't figger he seen me, but I heard his boys callin' t' each other and talkin' about that deer. I figger he counts on the weather t' keep the warden off."

Great-uncle brought the front feet of his chair down with a bang, and his heavy face clouded up with anger. "That ornery skunk!" he exclaimed. "He knows damn' well there ain't no season in this county. We got t' do something, Gus."

My great-aunt's lips began to twitch, half in mirth, half in scorn. "Why don't you call up the warden?"

"I reckon we c'n handle this, Woman," said Great-uncle stiffly.

"Hoh!" she snorted.

Gus Elker broke in eagerly. "I got me my fox outside. You heard him. Them hounds o' Hewitt's is foxhounds. They ain't no business runnin' deer. Now, I never seen a foxhound that wasn' a foxhound first and any other kind o' hound second. I don't figger them dogs o' Hewitt's is a bit different. I figger we c'n cut into the hills and head 'em off—that deer'll run the Fair Valley way, sure—and lay fox trail across that deer's track. They'll take after the fox, and the deer'll be safe, safe leastwise till the snow comes heavy enough t' cover his tracks."

By the way my great-uncle grinned, I knew he was taken with the idea. He bent away from the lamp on the table as if to escape its small heat and asked, " 'Tain't cold, is it?"

Gus shook his head. "Snowin', is all."

"Joe Stoll, you ain't goin' out on a night like this!" said Great-aunt.

My great-uncle looked a picture of injury. "Don't reckon I'll sit here and let that skunk Hewitt run down that deer, do you, Woman?" He got up and added, without turning, "Come on, Old Timer."

There was a moment's ominous quiet. Then Great-aunt said, "If that boy takes cold, Joe Stoll, you'll answer for it!"

Gus Elker began to look distressed; he kept glancing from her to the clock and presently said, "C'mon, c'mon—they'll git too head a start on us. Be dog if I'm goin' t' let that Philander Hewitt shoot that deer."

Great-uncle turned to me and said, "Git on your mackinaw."

I put on my mackinaw and followed them out to the porch, glancing once, quickly, towards my great-aunt, who sat without further protest, though her tight lips and snapping eyes spoke eloquently enough. Gus Elker's pet fox was sitting doglike in his awkward cage, and Gus looked at him affectionately, bending over the cage solicitously to see if he was still all right. The snow was coming thinly down, large flakes, but not heavy; a slight wind was blowing, and the earth was so far only partly covered. Great-uncle loomed large between me and the dark beyond, craning his neck and looking around. Presently he said, "It's aimin' t' snow some. Old Timer, you git your overshoes on."

I went back into the house for my overshoes.

"Aimin' to make quite a trip?" asked Great-aunt with mock pleasantry.

"I don't know," I said.

"See to it that uncle o' yourn don't stop any bullets. He's big enough to get in the way, and I don't reckon I want to see him shot—not just yet, anyhow." She put her patching aside suddenly and got up to peer out of the window. " 'Tis a nice night to be in the snow," she said irrelevantly. "Joe and I used to like it first we was married."

Her eyes were filled with grave concern, the half-anger of the previous moment gone, when I met them as I went out the door.

"Mind you keep your feet dry," she called after me.

Gus and Great-uncle Joe had left the porch and were already cutting across the barnyard towards the bottoms, two spectral figures in the strange half-light of the snow-filled night. Gus was talking animatedly, burdened by the fox in its wicker cage. I ran and caught up with them.

"I figger that buck'll head direc'ly for the Ferry Bluff, keep in along the ridge there, and hit out for the Fair Valley woodlots by way o' his run, circle around them hills, and come back to about here. I seen that buck time and again along them hills, and I don't misdoubt he'll do it. Good cover in them hills, too, and not too many fences—not that he'd be the one t' stop for a fence or two if they come in his way."

My great-uncle said something unintelligible in reply.

"If the snow'd come thicker, we wouldn't have t' fuss about it," said Gus. "Cover his tracks in no time. You reckon the dogs has hit the deer's trail by this time?"

There was only one answer to that, and my great-uncle made it. We had come across the road and stood on a slight rise facing into the dark south, where lay the bottoms and the Ferry Bluff to southwest. At that place we could hear the yelping and barking of dogs, the shouting of voices, clear as a bell in the winter night. They were coming from southeastward, working towards the Ferry Bluff. Just then the train crossed the bridge at Arena, seven miles away, and whistled, as if to cinch the direction of the dogs' barking; the whistle came from due south, and the barking was off to the left.

"Headin' for the Ferry Bluff, all right," murmured Great-uncle. "I reckon we better cut in behind the Fair Valley store, follerin' the hills this side o' the bottoms. We c'n keep out o' the bottoms and have better going. That way we'll be down wind, too; won't scare that buck off to the side."

He reached over and took the cage from Gus, and began to walk, quickly as his bulk would allow, towards the west. Gus came after, and I brought up the rear. The dogs gave tongue again, one of them especially musical, and Gus said, "That's his bitch, Lady; I know her voice anywhere."

Great-uncle made for a trail he knew, and, coming upon it, began to quicken his pace, glancing from time to time into the impenetrable, snow-clouded dark towards the south, as if to reassure himself that the hounds would not get to the Fair Valley woodland before us. Trees bordered and arbored the little-used trail, pressing ghostlike all around, first snow clinging to their old trunks and gnarled limbs, and the last tenacious leaves rattling and rustling in the occasional wind. From all sides rose the sibilant whispering of snow sifting down, the soft susurrus of flakes against leaves and twigs and grass, though by this time most of the grass was covered; the whiteness of snow lay upon everything, and the night became almost imperceptibly lighter, as if a moon were behind the wind-blown clouds and a faint light filtered through. An owl called once from an upland pasture behind us, but, apart from this and the barks of the dogs and the ceaseless sifting of snowflakes, there was no sound, no voice from the dark December night.

Great-uncle steadily increased his gait, until at last Gus Elker, to keep up, had to make odd, comic spurts, running awkwardly and with a peculiar rolling manner, and was left breathless each time. In this way we crossed behind the Fair Valley store and cut into the woods there. My great-uncle paused to listen once or twice, and, apparently satisfied, went on. The dogs were still in the Ferry Bluff range to the south.

"His run," said Gus breathlessly, "his run jest ahead a piece. Down the side hill, Joe."

"Reckon I c'n see it," replied Great-uncle. "What'll happen to that fox?"

"Don't you worry about Alec. He's a cute one. That fox knows where he gits fed; don't you worry. He'll head straight for home, lickety split, see if he don't."

Great-uncle drew up sharply near a clump of cedars, whose pungent fragrance rose aromatically all around. "That's his run, all right. Reckon we better jest wait a bit. If he comes this way."

"He'll come," said Gus. "I know that deer."

In the silence we heard the sound of his coming, the whisper of broken snow—for it was no more than that—and the faint jarring of earth when his hoofs struck. I held my breath, and he burst out of undergrowth to the south, mounted the rise, and came down towards us, a pale ghost, fleet as a bird, and almost soundless as a whippoorwill on wing. Upwind, he caught no scent of us, came on, and passed along the side hill towards the wooded hollow northeast of us, his head erect, his antlers proud.

"Purty a sight 's a man could wish t' see," whispered Gus.

The old buck was beautiful. He passed and faded into the night as if he had no body. From behind him came the dogs' baying, rising and falling, approaching the underbrush south of the Fair Valley woods.

Great-uncle moved swiftly; he crossed the deer run, opened the fox cage, and Alec came out. The fox paused a brief moment uncertainly; then he was off, crossing and recrossing the deer run, and crossing again before he melted into the shadows and vanished in a beeline towards Gus Elker's place beyond Stone's Pocket and my great-uncle's farm.

"That'll fetch 'em," said Great-uncle, coming back to where we stood. "Reckon we c'n wait t' see the fun."

In a few minutes, Hewitt's dogs came up, led by the long black and white foxhound bitch, Lady. They came down the hill, loping easily, voiceless now, intent upon the trail, now somewhat more difficult to follow because of the increasing heaviness of the snowfall. Lady was the first of them to hit the fox trail; she stopped short, ran back and forth, whining eagerly, and paused to give fierce, exultant tongue. Then she was off on the fox path.

My great-uncle turned to look inquiringly at Gus, and Gus reassured him. "Alec's got a safe place—he'll be snug as a bug. They won't git him, don't you worry."

Dog after dog followed Lady.

"It's workin', Gus," said Great-uncle.

But my great-uncle had spoken too soon. For after the foxhounds came three of Tim Leveritt's Irish deerhounds; they started down the fox trail, came back, found the deer track, and were away towards the hollow down which the buck had fled.

Gus Elker leaned forward, his mouth twitching. "Aw, now—aw, now," he said sorrowfully, as if somehow Hewitt had played a trick on him. "I didn't know he had them deerhounds along."

Great-uncle muttered something unintelligible to conceal his disappointment.

"What'll we do now, Joe?"

"For one thing—git outa here before Hewitt comes up. Guess then we might 's well go home and pray they don't git that buck—if you ain't forgot how t' pray."

"I like t' had him eatin' outa my hand, too," mourned Gus. "He got so he was used t' man smell, almost."

Great-uncle said nothing. He turned and led the way back, and the silence was made doubly profound by the deep baying of the hounds, now in two groups, but apparently converging. Gus dropped behind, pausing every little while to listen, his lugubrious eyes intent, his mouth working and worrying at his snow-hung mustache.

"He's swingin' 'round," he said once. "Reckon he'll come down my orchard through your corn stubble and head 'round back t' the bottoms again. That's what he's like t' do."

My great-uncle said, "I c'n hear my old woman settin' to me now," and turned to look briefly behind him. "You all right, Old Timer? No wet feet or nothin', hey?"

I shook my head.

Gus went on, talking more to himself than to us. "It should aworked, it had ought t' aworked. Didn't know he was aimin' t' git Tim Leveritt's Irish deerhounds, too. I bet me Tim don't know Hewitt's usin' 'em like this, by Jukas! no. Tim, he obeys the law. That Philander—he's always huntin' outa season. Time somebody put the warden onto him. Time he was nicked for fifty or a hundred dollars; that'd fetch him.—Now them dogs is like as not t' cross the fox track headin' towards my place and the whole pack take after that buck again. And the snow near blindin', too."

The snow was coming more thickly now; it had become heavier and wetter, and clung more tightly to trees and bushes, bending the slighter limbs and branches with its weight. The wind had gone down, and the clouds closed down, and snow came earthward with less sound, flakes larger, and so many more of them that it was difficult to see my great-uncle as anything but a great, moving blur up ahead.

296

"But it'll hol' back them dogs, too," resumed Gus. "Seems like I c'n hear 'em now, barkin' puzzled-like."

I ran into Great-uncle, who had stopped on the path. Looking around, I saw the familiar markings of the rise just south of the farm. Gus Elker came up, brushing vaguely at the snow before his eyes.

"What is it, Joe? What you seein'?"

"Ain't seein' nothin'," replied my great-uncle shortly. "Cast your ear northwards."

Amid much excited barking of dogs rose the sound of voices, coming unmistakably from the region of my great-uncle's place.

"That there's no dog," said Gus, singling out a familiar sound. "That's your wife, Joe."

My great-uncle descended the rise, crossed the road, and went hurriedly towards the outbuildings beyond the house. . . .

Great-aunt Lou stood at the pasture end of a disused runway to a long-abandoned barn, an amazing figure clad in an old horsehide overcoat of my great-uncle's; there was a shotgun held in the crook of one arm. All around her were dogs, and beyond them, Philander Hewitt and his two grown sons trying to check the clamor of the animals. In her free hand my great-aunt held a lantern, the yellow glow of which kept them all in a magic circle, a world set apart from the darkness of night and the falling snow.

Great-uncle Joe stepped ponderously into the light. "You aimin' t' run my cows, Philander?" he asked ominously.

"Pah!" said Philander Hewitt, his red face glistening with melted snow, his small eyes snapping. "Know 's well 's you, you ain't used this old barn for years."

My great-uncle went over to the rail fence, brushed the snow away, and hoisted himself leisurely up. "What I want t' know is what in hell you're doin' with them dogs. Tim Leveritt's, too. Breakin' the law again, Philander?"

"We went after fox."

"Hoh! sounds likely. You don't see no fox this close t' my buildings."

"We lost the track hereabouts—your woman was standin' in it, best we could make out."

"Don't seem my wife could take up the whole track," said Great-uncle with exasperating stolidity.

With a gruff "Good night to you all," Philander Hewitt turned angrily to his sons and said, "Heel the dogs for home."

Great-uncle and Gus watched them out of sight with stolid satisfaction. The expression on Great-aunt Lou's face was of withheld amusement, her cheeks sucked in and her mouth faintly curved. Her eyes were laughing.

"They didn't get that deer," said Gus. "And Philander sure had a mad on. He had his heart set on that deer, heart or stummick."

Great-uncle turned towards my great-aunt, his heavy brows far down upon his eyes. "What in Kingdom Come are you doin' in that get-up, Woman?" he asked. "And that gun o' mine?"

"Best coat in the house to keep the snow off," she said. "I brought the gun for protection, hearin' noises." She turned from him. "I'm goin' in. Are you comin'?"

She led us up the lane, into the barnyard and to the house, where the yellow lamplight shone bright as her lantern. She blew out the lantern and hung it on a peg driven into the wall of the back porch.

"What I can't figger out," said Gus abruptly, edging towards the old woodstove in the kitchen and stretching his hands to be warmed, "is what become o' that buck. Like 's not, snow covered his tracks; it's sure thick enough. But he went mighty fast."

"Well, Hewitt didn't get him; so you needn't to worry," said Great-aunt. " 'Pears to me that deer didn't take to either one of you very much; seemed anxious to get away from you just as fast as from Philander Hewitt."

"That deer all but knows my name," said Gus in mild protest.

"Hoh!" snorted my great-aunt, and began to smile. "I heard him comin'," she said, "and the dogs after; so I figured that fox hadn't put them off long. I put on Joe's coat and took his gun—no tellin' what I might run into—and went out, and my conscience! if there wasn't that deer come right smack into that old runway, the fence too high on either side, and the snow blindin' him. But he got my wind, and he went —but he went the wrong way, and got into the old barn. Quick as a flash, I seen what to do. I run down there and closed that door, and then I went over his tracks and covered 'em up. By the time the dogs got there, the snow was deep enough, and time Hewitt and you all came up, they couldn't asmelled that deer more 'n if 'twas over in the next county."

Great-uncle looked at her with profound skepticism. "You tellin' us that deer's locked in that old barn building?"

"I reckon it's the same one Gus calls by his first name," replied my great-aunt tartly.

My great-uncle began to blow himself up, but Gus said only, "I don't care where he is, long 's he's safe."

"Might be we ought t' go out and take a look at him," proposed Great-uncle.

Great-aunt Lou looked meaningly at him over her spectacles. "I'd think you'd scared that deer good plenty already, Joe Stoll. To my way of thinkin', it's time he was let out. You, boy. Just swing that door back. Reckon you two better set a spell."

I went out into the close-pressing winter night, across the barnyard to the old, abandoned barn, daring a brief glance within before I opened the door; so I saw his dark shadow, and the antlers' danger, and the luminous soft eyes with the pale light in them. I crouched down behind the door when I opened it, and in a moment he was gone: only an instant of hesitation, then the proud, magnificent body bounded down the runway and was lost in the thick wall of snowflakes drifting steadily from the black December sky.

The Proud Farmer

by VACHEL LINDSAY, 1879–1931. *Of all modern poets Nicholas Vachel Lindsay is the closest approximation to the traditional wandering bard. Born in Springfield, Illinois, Lindsay was educated at Hiram College, Hiram, Ohio, the Chicago Art Institute, and the New York School of Art, his mother having directed him toward a career of Christian cartooning. Lindsay's own interests included drawing, poetry, and a passion for reform. After several years of lecturing for the Y.M.C.A. and the Anti-Saloon League, Lindsay set out in 1912 on a long tour of the West, preaching the gospel of beauty and reciting his original verses in return for meals and lodging. This was the beginning of a career as reader and bard; Lindsay himself claimed that he had recited the famous "Congo" five thousand times. His earliest poems to achieve prominence were published in Harriet Monroe's Poetry magazine. Among his better known volumes of verse are General William Booth Enters into Heaven, and Other Poems (1913), The Congo and Other Poems (1914), and The Chinese Nightingale and Other Poems (1917). Lindsay's Collected Poems appeared in 1923 and in subsequent revised editions. Despite his national celebrity Lindsay never found poetry very profitable; disillusioned and harassed by ill health, he committed suicide by drinking lysol. His most famous verse such as "The Congo" is distinguished by its heavily cadenced, booming lines, but Lindsay wrote more frequently and often more effectively in quieter mediums. "The Proud Farmer" is a sincere tribute to the poet's grandfather, Ephraim Samuel Frazee, a pioneer farmer-preacher.*

INTO the acres of the newborn state
He poured his strength, and plowed his ancient name,
And, when the traders followed him, he stood
Towering above their furtive souls and tame.

That brow without a stain, that fearless eye
Oft left the passing stranger wondering
To find such knighthood in the sprawling land,
To see a democrat well-nigh a king.

He lived with liberal hand, with guests from far,
With talk and joke and fellowship to spare,—
Watching the wide world's life from sun to sun,
Lining his walls with books from everywhere.

He read by night, he built his world by day.
The farm and house of God to him were one.
For forty years he preached and plowed and wrought—
A statesman in the fields, who bent to none.

His plowmen-neighbors were as lords to him.
His was an ironside, democratic pride.
He served a rigid Christ, but served him well—
And, for a lifetime, saved the countryside.

Here lie the dead, who gave the church their best
Under his fiery preaching of the word.
They sleep with him beneath the ragged grass . . .
The village withers, by his voice unstirred.

And tho' his tribe be scattered to the wind
From the Atlantic to the China Sea,
Yet do they think of that bright lamp he burned
Of family worth and proud integrity.

And many a sturdy grandchild hears his name
In reverence spoken, till he feels akin
To all the lion-eyed who build the world—
And lion-dreams begin to burn within.

The Judas Goose

by WINIFRED VAN ETTEN, 1902—   . *Born in Emmetsburg, Iowa,
Mrs. Van Etten was educated at Cornell College, B.A., 1925, and Columbia
University, M.A., 1928. After teaching Latin and English at the Emmets-
burg High School she served as instructor of English at Cornell College,*

1928–34. *Her stories have appeared in the* Atlantic Monthly *and other magazines. She is the author of a novel entitled* I Am the Fox *(1936).* "The Judas Goose" *is reprinted from the* Atlantic Monthly, *February 1938.*

I

IT WAS old Joe Diemouth who told me the story of the goose Judas, and it was a story I always remembered, chiefly at first because it was so different from most of Joe's stories—no adventures or dangers or heroism on his part, none of the atmosphere of mighty hunter that first made me, a lad in the gun-worshiping stage, the old man's satellite. And in later years I have remembered it because of its own peculiar quality of somehow epitomizing a kind of life that has disappeared forever. As I look back now, I realize that my own boyhood days bore the last imprints of that disappearing life, and there is in me still a sense of continuity with it strong enough to turn me homesick when I visit the little town now with all its brisk and colorless modernity.

Joe was a very old man when I first knew him, but still a hunter. He lived just behind us, and sometimes I would rouse vaguely out of sleep and hear a rattletrap buggy leaving Joe's yard and would know that he was up in the cold and dark of three o'clock to go hunting. He would stand for hours in ice water above his knees to get a shot at a wild duck. He nearly drove his daughter and his granddaughters crazy, and of course he did finally get himself pneumonia and they all thought he'd die. He fooled them, though, but after that he had to take his hunting out in talk. He showed me how to build traps and told me stories of the great dogs he'd owned and his adventures with them, explained every trophy that decorated his walls—the mounted fish, and the buffalo and moose horns and antlers that hung on every wall of his cottage home.

His wife, passionately neat, had anti-macassars—two or three or half a dozen of them—on every piece of her gold plush furniture. Old Joe couldn't do anything with her when it came to tidies. He himself seemed almost as incongruous in that stuffed and dusted little place. Even with his infirmities, Joe belonged outside, with the marshes and wild things, not in with the tidies and canaries. How Joe despised those canaries! He would tell me about his goose Judas, his voice raised over the inconsequential twitterings of those contemptibly tame and useless canaries—caged things, content to be caged.

At the time he had Judas, when he was a young man with a young family, Joe lived on a farm about ten miles from town. Ten miles were ten miles in those days, and a farmer had to be a self-sufficient person. There could be no running into town to buy a loaf of bread if the wife

301

found she was out just ten minutes before dinner. Joe was a hunter not only because he liked to hunt but because he had to. Ducks and wild geese were plentiful and furnished about the only fresh meat the family got. About thirty rods from the farmhouse was a slough. You can drive all over northwest Iowa now without seeing a slough,—all the water has been drained off,—but in those days farmers simply farmed around the sloughs, and there were acres and acres that were too swampy to cultivate at all. The wild ducks and geese loved Joe's slough and they hadn't learned yet to be wary. His little girls loved the slough, too, and so did Joe, who spent a lot of time prowling around there. One day he found a wild goose's nest and brought the eggs home with him to put under a hen. Out of three goslings hatched, two were ganders, and as soon as they were large enough they were killed and eaten. But the one was a goose, and Joe made up his mind to raise it for a decoy.

At first the wild goose was just another fowl around the barnyard. It was months before anyone gave her a name, and then it wasn't a very nice name the goose got for herself. "Judas" they called her, and it didn't seem right, both because she was a lady and because by that time they were all fond of her, and you don't call any creature you are fond of "Judas." But Judas it was, because she had earned her title and it was all too appropriate.

By the time she had acquired her name she had also become a great pet of all the family, but particularly of Joe. She used to follow him about wherever he went, coaxing for extra food and for attention. She loved to be petted, and if she caught Joe sitting down anywhere she'd come up to him and nuzzle him like a dog wanting caresses. She was a pretty thing, and it gave her endless pleasure to have her long dark throat stroked gently. She'd bend her head down and make little singing sounds of satisfaction just as long as anyone would keep on petting her. The children loved her. Joe's littlest girl used to take Judas's dark head in her hand and softly stroke the pretty arrangements of feathers on neck and body, fingering the white muffler around the throat and ruffling the plumage to see it fall once more into its delicate design.

They clipped her wings so that she couldn't fly away, but it would scarcely have been necessary, for Judas showed no inclination to leave her home. She was far tamer than any of the domestic flock, lovely to look at, and so intelligent that it seemed impolite to refer to her as a goose.

II

The thing that got Judas her name was her extraordinary attitude toward her duties as a decoy. She seemed to know what it was all about, to realize what her function was, and to take an unnatural kind of pleasure in it. There was nothing of the ignorant cat's-paw about Judas. She knew she was supposed to call down other wild geese out of the sky in order that Joe could shoot them. She did it knowingly and deliberately. It was fantastic to see her. She and Joe worked together like a couple of sportsmen, or a sportsman and his best-loved dog, and the slough was their hunting ground. It was a favorite resort for Judas at all times, and the brush that surrounded it made excellent cover for Joe and his gun.

In the spring and fall, when the wild geese were honking overhead, Judas played her siren part to perfection. Paddling around on the pond, she sent her lonesome call skyward and lured her tribesmen down to doom. She seemed to exult in her powers and liked to show them off under less favorable conditions than the pond provided her. Often and often she would stand in the farmyard, only a few feet from the door of the house, and call down a gander for Joe, lurking in the doorway, to shoot.

You might have thought she was just lonesome, calling for a companion, and too stupid to realize what was going to happen to any bird she brought down to join her. But her conduct when Joe's gun had done its work left no room for such a charitable supposition. Judas clearly enjoyed seeing other geese shot. When a gander crumpled into a soft heap beside her she jumped up and down in her joy. She did a victory dance about the body, and when Joe approached to pick it up she stretched out her neck to him and discussed the kill in low, well-pleased tones of voice. She definitely knew what that gun meant, for whenever Joe appeared with it on his arm she followed, noisy with excitement and anticipating the sport with all the eagerness of a hunting dog.

There was something a little dreadful about Judas, a little preposterous—something chilling. She was, really, a detestable fowl if one considered her from the aspect of her relationship to her own kindred. But, considered from a human point of view, she was a pet and a loyal helper. Perhaps there was something a little touching about her preference of her human friends to her own kind—a betrayer appears noble if he has done his betraying out of loyalty to you.

Judas was about three years old when she began to show a change of heart toward her own race. It was early spring, and the wild geese were thick in the swamp. Joe got all he wanted and Judas exhibited her usual interest in all the proceedings, calling ganders down in the barnyard to be slaughtered, doing her dance and singing her song when they were killed. It was astonishing that Joe was able to get close enough to kill so many of them, but the gander is a gallant fellow, waiting always for the goose to fly first. And Judas, of course, never flew.

Then, gradually, Joe became aware that Judas was not around the barnyard as much as she used to be. The children reported seeing her on the pond, and with her always a young gander. Judas had taken a mate. He never came around the farm buildings at all, and Judas never tried to bring him there. She seemed to realize that that was no place for her beloved. She made her nest in an old strawstack several fields beyond the house, where the children discovered her devotedly tending her eggs.

The gander wasn't around much in the daytime, now, but every morning he came to the pond and called until Judas left her nest and went to the water for a swim with him. He seemed to be trying to get her to go away. Often he flew a short distance and anxiously called and Judas as anxiously answered. But she couldn't fly far on account of her clipped wings, and besides she had her eggs to tend. So she stayed, and the gander stayed with her.

They were pretty to see together as they took their morning swim, often side by side like a well-married pair talking over domestic affairs. Then again they would have one of their worried discussions of going away, the gander flying and calling and Judas explaining and explaining why it was that she couldn't go. He never seemed to understand that Judas couldn't fly. He put on many a demonstration for her and then she would try, but was able, of course, to rise only a few feet in the air. Her lover never gave up. He seemed to feel that in due time he would be able to teach this strange bride of his all she needed to know for the long, strong flight his heart demanded for him and for her.

Joe got worried about this love affair of Judas. Sooner or later, he thought, the mate would win. Judas's wings would grow, and she was getting shyer and shyer of human beings. The gander must have been telling her with masculine positiveness that no good could come of her association with them, for it was almost impossible now to catch her.

Joe decided he would have to kill the gander. He couldn't allow such a valuable decoy as Judas to be wooed away from him, and that he was sure was going to happen. The little girls cried when he said he was going to shoot the gander—they kept hoping that he would become tame, too, and they liked the idea of having the pair of them around. They liked the idea of Judas's being happy with a mate. Joe was sure it wouldn't work. The gander wouldn't tame in the first place, and even if he did he doubted if Judas would be useful as a decoy as long as he was about. So Joe made up his mind to kill him.

Joe Diemouth forgot all about what a glorious sport hunting was when he came to this part of his tale. I don't know how many times I heard the story of Judas, but every time when Joe told how he had made up his mind to kill the gander he almost cried. His weather-beaten little face crinkled up and his bright old eyes grew misty. He couldn't see now how he'd ever had the heart to do it. A wild goose was a pretty, graceful thing, a gallant thing ready to give its life for its mate. It was a treat, now, merely to get a look at one. Old Joe would willingly sit up to his neck in a slough just to see one zooming toward him. He wouldn't ask for a shot at it. He wouldn't even want to shoot it. But in those days wild fowl of all descriptions were so plentiful that it never occurred to Joe to think of them except in terms of something to be shot if possible. Still, when he came to tell me of the actual shooting of Judas's mate, he always looked guilty, and he didn't like the telling of that part of his story.

It was a late spring that year, a tantalizing, procrastinating spring. Just as it began to look as if winter were actually routed, just as the sun began to have some real warmth in it and the green blush on the rolling prairies was more than a hallucination caused by wishing for green in a gray world, there'd come a hard freeze and discourage everything for another two weeks. The family got up one morning as cold as they had been any time that winter, it seemed, and found everything frozen up. The little pond had half an inch of ice.

Joe was in a bad temper over this setback, and when he saw Judas's mate come down to the pond he decided it was a good time to do away with him. Besides, Judas wasn't around, and Joe, in spite of her antics with other geese, didn't quite like the idea of killing her mate while she looked on. He went back to the house and got his gun. Then he attempted to creep close enough to the pond to shoot the visitor. But the gander was cautious. A dozen times Joe tried for a shot at him, but each time he made off. Joe was getting irritated. Finally he chanced a shot, which went wild and left the gander flying overhead in circles and making it perfectly apparent that he knew exactly where Joe was ambushed.

Joe was crouched in the brush, cursing, mad enough by this time to kill the bird with a good heart. And then he saw Judas. She was coming down to the pond in a tearing hurry. It seemed almost as if, having heard that one shot and knowing well what a shot was likely to mean, she'd left her nest and come rushing to investigate. Joe kept very quiet. All right, let her bring her mate down as she'd brought so many others. He was determined by this time to get that gander.

Judas came out on the ice and called anxiously. She marched about, peering and plaintively inquiring. And her lover answered that cry. Down he came. He lit beside her on the ice and pushed her about a bit with his body and neck. It seemed almost as if he were trying to get between her and Joe. She, glad to see him, stretched out her neck to him and talked. He kept nudging her about, in great anxiety, but he couldn't make it clear to her what he wanted. He flew a little, coaxing, and Judas this time did her best to follow, but her wings weren't equal yet to flight in spite of the fact that Joe hadn't been able for some time to catch her and clip them. So the gander came back to the ice beside her. He stood in front of her and turned his head in the direction of Joe's cover. Joe took aim and just as he pulled the trigger it seemed to him that the gander raised his head up haughtily, disdaining or defying death. The next instant he was a heap of wind-ruffled feathers on the ice.

"I never felt so low-down in my life," old Joe told me. He felt so terrible the instant he had pulled that trigger that he stayed in the cover for a long time afterwards. He had a feeling that he didn't want Judas to see him.

It was like the time he'd had to kill his favorite hound because he'd got so old and sick and deaf. He had to be killed, for pity's sake, and Joe couldn't bear to turn him over to someone else, perhaps clumsy, to kill. It was up to him to do it himself. The hound was so deaf he figured he could sneak up on him when he was asleep and get it over and the old dog would never know what hit him. And he did find the old fellow snoozing in the sun in a position where he could get a sure shot at him. He crept up close and there wasn't a movement from the hound. He put his gun to his shoulder, took careful aim, and then, just as he fired, the dog looked up—looked directly at his master training a gun on him. And in that last instant of life there was a look in his eyes that haunted old Joe for years. He used to wake up in the night in a cold sweat, seeing the grieved eyes of old War-Dance, the best dog he'd ever had.

It was like that when he'd killed Judas's mate, except, in a way, he felt worse—meaner. He'd killed War-Dance to keep him from suffering, but he'd killed the gander just because it appealed to him as convenient. Someway he'd half expected to see Judas jump up and down and express her usual glee when a bird was shot beside her. But she did nothing of the kind. She stayed around the pond for quite a while, looking at her fallen mate, seeming not to understand that he was dead. Then she left the pond reluctantly and went back to her nest.

Joe took the body of the gander and buried it. It didn't seem decent to eat a creature that had stood up and defied death for his mate the way that gander had. Joe could see him, lifting his head haughtily, contemptuously, as he took aim. Old Joe used to mutter something at this point about a soul. He was rather incoherent about it. Joe was never one to deal in abstractions, and he had no churchly phrases in which to express his meaning, but it seemed to me that he was trying to say that Judas's mate had a soul and you couldn't eat a creature that had a soul. Soul, to old Joe, apparently meant personality. Any living thing that impressed itself on him as having personality, as being an individual, he thought of as having a soul.

I know he believed his hunting dogs went to some kind of special heaven. And for all I know they did. At least, there is something in dogs, and in wild creatures, that seems to express the soul of a place. There's something gone from that country now that it used to have, clearly when old Joe was a young man, faintly but still perceptibly when I was a boy. And I don't believe it's just that intimations of immortality have fled from me because I'm no longer young. It's really gone—something that used to be there. The great prairies have to express themselves to-day in terms of scraggly villages full of radios and oil-burning furnaces. And what have those things to say of the spirit of the place? The little wild things, driven away now, forever, said it better because they were in themselves the soul of the marching land and the brooding water. They're gone, now, and the land has lost its voice and lies inarticulate, though the noise of an alien life fills it.

Judas didn't show up again after the death of her mate. Old Joe went to look for her. He found her on her nest, dead. The eggs were cold.

No, she didn't die of a broken heart. Old Joe examined her and found a shot in her. Evidently it had glanced off the ice and struck her, not hard enough to kill her outright, but enough to cause her death. So, said old Joe, he lost his decoy anyway, and he might as well have allowed Judas's mate to live. And, mighty huntsman though I fancied myself to be, I thought so too.

The Movers

by JAMES HEARST, 1900–   . *In the twentieth century Iowa has produced a number of gifted writers of fiction, drama, and verse; among the most promising of the poets is James Hearst. Born of Scotch-Irish ancestry near Cedar Falls, Iowa, Hearst attended a rural school and later the Iowa State Teachers College at Cedar Falls. An accident suffered while swimming* prevented him from continuing the study of medicine and made a sedentary life mandatory. For some years he has divided his time between writing and managing a farm jointly owned by himself and his brother. He has lectured on poetry and taught creative writing at Iowa State Teachers College. Hearst's poetry has appeared in two slim volumes, Country Men (1937), and The Sun at Noon (1943). It is remarkable for its fresh rural imagery and its reflective insight.

THE east wind whips the skirts of the snow
with a passing shower,
and over Iowa on the first of March
wheels churn hub deep in the mud
or grit their teeth across the icy roads.

Home is only a shadow
flying down the wind in a
twisted swirl of snowflakes,
traveling down the road in an old lumber wagon
drawn by two shaggy horses
whose bones are too big for their flesh.

Even the wild goose
is not so homeless as these movers.
Peering ahead through the sliding curtain
of March rain they pass
with the furniture of home packed in a wagon.
Past corner, past grove, to the hilltop they go
until only chairlegs point from the skyline
like roots of trees torn from the earth.
And they are gone. . . .

This, the parade of the landless, the tenants,
the dispossessed,
out of their Canaan they march
with Moses asleep in the Bible.

Who will call them back, who will ask:
are you the chosen people, do you inherit
only a backward glance and a cry and a heartbreak?
are you the meek?

But the early twilight
drops like a shawl on their shoulders
and sullen water
slowly fills the wagon ruts and the hoof prints.

Inquiry

by JAMES HEARST

Now catch your breath and hear the softly rounded
Shoot thundering into the yielding air.
These are crocus blooms the root has hounded
Day after day to grow, to develop and bear.
Even though snow, now lying in strips defeated
Under the lilac bush, might strike like a snake
At the open ground, the sky has been plucked and depleted
The cloth has been shaken—see the last twisting flake
Grope for a twig and miss and dissolve in the air!
Beat up the blood in your heart and bleed like a tree
For the scars you receive, O winter-bound sleeper—prepare
For the thrust of a leaf, for a glimpse of a sky like the sea!
I retreat from a room grown too small, and the indifferent page,
And listen to the voice of the creek now angry and swollen,
And see the sun arch his back like a bee in a rage
As he sparkles the air with clouds of his yellow pollen.
And I wonder if people are given the promise and bloom
That is given the root and all this slow-rolling land
As they come from their houses. Is there escape from the tomb?
Do people forget their mortality saying, The spring is at hand?

One Book—The Almanac

by DELLA LUTES, 18?—1942. *Della Thompson was born in Jackson,
Michigan, and was educated in the public schools. She later married Louis
Irving Lutes. After a period of service as a district school teacher and as a
teacher in the Detroit public schools she entered magazine work, and subsequently devoted most of her time to writing. Such books as Home Grown
(1937), Millbrook (1938), and Gabriel's Search (1940), are full of details
about life in early Michigan, about homesteading, schooling, cooking, hunting, and social gatherings. Mrs. Lutes wrote nostalgically about the past and
somehow convinced her reader that she told the truth. Her interest in food
and recipes stimulated her to write The Country Kitchen (1936). "One Book
—The Almanac" appeared originally in the Saturday Review of Literature,
August 12, 1939.*

WHEN I was a little girl living in southern Michigan—yes, and after I got to be a big girl and taught a deestrick school, the almanac was (as it had been for two hundred—and perhaps more—years) as definitely valued a factor in the amenities of living as a clock. In fact, the almanac and the clock companioned one another, both in the disposal of time and in their location in the home. The clock stood on a shelf in the kitchen, and the almanac hung (by a string punched through its binding) on a nail driven in the shelf.

The almanac, however, held the whip hand, for a farmer could get up with the sun, go to dinner by the feel of his stomach, and to bed when it was dark; neither could the clock tell how many eclipses there would be during the year, nor could it foretell the weather. The clock was a convenience, but the almanac was a necessity. By it the farmer planted his crops, mowed his hay, reaped his grain, and arranged his social affairs such as going visiting in the winter when an unexpected snow storm might seriously interfere with travel, or in planning the church sociables.

Not all the almanacs that were familiar in the homes of our midwestern locality performed this service of prognostication, being either too cautious or less familiar with those activities of planets which aided the astrologer in his forecasts. Jayne's *Medical Almanac and Guide to Health*, for instance, conservatively offered only "conjectures of the weather," but then Jayne's was one of those we could get along without and was not treasured from year to year as were some of the others, notably—of our acquaintance—Hostetter's, Ayer's, and Landreth's *Rural Register and Almanac*. Of these, my father, being what was known as a "small farmer," which meant that he raised more "truck" than "crops," most highly regarded Landreth's, a veritable—and reliable—guide to the farmer. Landreth's Warranted Seeds bore the test of time, and the *Rural Register* (first published in 1847) told you how to use them and gave volumes of agrarian advice. This almanac had its own special nail at the opposite end of the shelf from the others and was held sacred to my father's use. When the year was ended, a new *Register* took its place, but the old one was carefully stored in the huge top drawer of his own bureau along with packages of seeds, fishing tackle, a "wallet" containing deeds, notes, and a faded yellow sheet of foolscap paper which testified that somewhere prior to the Revolution three brothers named, respectively, John, James, and William Thompson, had sailed from England and landed on the Massachusetts coast. The almanac was treasured for the sake of comparison, not only of astrological and climatic conditions, but as reference in husbandry. When the time approached for Rosy, the red cow, to calve, he looked back to the date when the year before he had written on the margin, "Took Rosy to bull."

Landreth's *Rural Register and Almanac* held little interest for anyone in our family except my father, but the strings of the other two, with which we were familiar, had frequently to be renewed. Of these two my father had some preference for Ayer's, not because of any great value placed on the apparently panaceaic qualities of Sarsaparilla or Dr. Ayer's Pills, but because of the faith (and pleasure) he had in the lyric measures with which weather conditions were foretold. If Ayer's almanac said "Cold—and—blustering" (in a sort of "Gobelins —'ll—git—you" style slithering down the page) from February the seventeenth to the twenty-first, he brought in an extra quantity of corn to shell for the hens and piled the wood behind the kitchen stove after the box was filled. If it said, "Look—out—for—frosts" on the first of June, he looked out for frost, lowered the top of the cold frame where his early cabbage plants were growing, and anxiously sniffed the air as the sun went down.

Hostetter's *Illustrated United States Almanac* was especially popular with the lighter-minded members of the family, for it had a precious disposition toward humor and made up in wit what it lacked in prognostication. This almanac was also, outside of *Godey's Ladies' Book, Frank Leslie's* and *Peterson's Magazines*, the only piece of illustrated literature that came to our midwestern hands. Ayer's (with mustard-colored cover) had, to be sure, a few scattered exemplifications of the artist's skill, such as the bandaged head of a distressed individual suffering with neuralgic pains, a gouty foot (both relieved by the magic of Dr. Ayer's Pills), and a woman with a phenomenal growth of hair (Ayer's Hair Vigor).

Dr. Jayne's *Medical Almanac and Guide to Health* showed the sharply relieved profile of a woman's head with a huge goiter, also a realistic section of tapeworm, all reasonably interesting to a morbid nature, but hardly worth mentioning on the same day with Hostetter's memorable half page (lifted bodily, one would judge, from some English book) delineating an artist's interpretation of contemporary wit.

On the cover (a sort of distempered green which yellowed with age) we made the acquaintance, first, of St. George at everlasting odds with the Dragon—and, secondly, the brazen gentleman who apparently had had a run-in with Taurus the Bull or Leo the Lion, to the obvious disadvantage of his inner works; but the real meat of the nut came to view when you opened the book upon Miss Soprano seated on a piano stool with her back to the instrument, smugly inquiring of the "cousin from rural districts" whether she had "dropped a note"; or upon the indignant diner who, with a napkin tied under his chin, is exhibiting a singular-looking object on the soup spoon. "Waiter," he says, "do you know what that is?"

"That, sir," replies the grinning waiter, "looks like a mouse. We often find them in the soup, sir. No extra charge, sir."

Full half a dozen such happy interpretations of that day's humor lightened the more depressing recital of human ills—one a month for half the year, conned zealously for twice that time.

Both Ayer's and Hostetter's believed in relieving the humdrum existence of the farmer's life with merry quip and jest, and were triply cherished therefore. And—a jaded eye and ear, judging by the weary round of so-called waggery over radio and on comic strip, calls them fair. Take this, for instance: A young man accused of laziness was asked if he took it from his father. "I think not," said the impertinent youth; "Father's got all the laziness he ever had." Or what the milkman said when he found a fish in the milk: "Good heavens! The brindle cow's been swimming again." Or, worthy, it seems to us, of the more sophisticated journals of today:

Young lady: "Bub, won't you give me your baby sister? I love little babies." Young hopeful: "No—ma'am—I tant." Young lady: "Why won't you give your baby to me?" Hopeful (indignantly): "'Cause she'd tarve to death. Your dress opens behime."

Of course, in the present day of enlightenment toward an infant's needs, this joke would fail of point, but in 1877 it carried weight.

Both Hostetter's and Ayer's almanacs endeared themselves to the midwestern heart by offering an opportunity to laugh. God knows there was little enough occasion. But they also offered more substantial meat for the mental tooth: "How to clean marble"—for marble was a familiar medium in the furnishings of that time; how to make a pumpkin poultice; to cure a sty on the eye; receipts for sour cream cake and Queen of All Puddings (good enough to try today—if anybody still made puddings); how to cure warts with spirits of turpentine, or a sore throat with roasted lemon.

Adages, puns, conundrums, adorned the pages of these almanacs, some of them of a quality that makes one wonder how they have escaped the radio's eye: An Indian said that, when he first heard of it, he was much surprised that the white men had killed their Savior, but, when he knew them better, he wondered that they didn't steal his clothes.

"When was Adam married? On his wedding Eve."

"On which side of a mule would you look for the most hair? The outside."

"As you cannot avoid your own company, make it as agreeable as you can."

"In an alphabetical race, which letter would be first in starting? S."

"If you want to keep your boy at home, make it pleasanter for him than the street."

Certain almanacs were treasured beyond years of other usefulness by annotations on the margin: "Picked the first strawberries today." Or, on the interspersed blank pages, records of reference were made: "Sowed Early Rose potatoes." I have an old copy of *Herrick's Almanac* of the eighties in which are recorded births, deaths, visits, "Vandoos," illnesses, weddings, and the birth of a litter of thirteen pigs. "The mother laid on two and killed them. Then she ate them."

There was a *Michigan Almanac* which cost fifteen cents. Some of our neighbors occasionally bought one. My father never did. He could get all he needed out of those that were free. The *Michigan Almanac* was almost as good as a course at the agricultural college or a reading of Blackstone in a country lawyer's office. It was crammed from cover to cover with informative paragraphs and statistics: Courts—open, circuit, supreme; names of all the states (twenty-two) with date of admission to the Union; Post offices and railroad stations; Lake commerce; location of land offices, saleable lands, and so forth. It was sponsored by the Detroit *Weekly Tribune* and stood for no nonsense. It posted you on when the sun entered Aries and spring began; on when the sun entered Cancer and summer began, when the sun entered Libra, autumn began. But we needed no such high-sounding gong to advise us on the change of seasons. Spring began when the pussy willows came out and the peepers sang; summer began when the clover was ready to cut; and you knew when fall threatened by the turning leaves.

There was also a small almanac published in Cooperstown, New York, during the seventies and eighties, called *Phinney's Calendar or Western Almanac*. For a little book it contained a surprising amount of information and a still more amazing amount of advertising—mostly schoolbooks, tracts, and Sunday-school books, and insurance. It also carried, in certain issues at least, advertisements of the ubiquitous Mr. Beadle's dime novels, handbooks, and songbooks, of which there were astonishing numbers. In the year 1870 he named 176 volumes of novels, songbook collections numbering from one to twenty-three, and various schoolbooks, books of games, etc. I do not know how much distribution the almanac had, but in both volume and value of material it ranked high and should be worthy of a considerable place in the roll of American almanacs.

Poor Richard's Almanac was probably the earliest of the almanacs published in this country (1687), and its fame, particularly because of the maxims and aphorisms for which it was noted, will doubtless stand forever at the top of the roster of this type of American literature.

The Old Farmer's Almanac (which did not, in general, reach our midwestern country but which, to the more sober and literate East, offered equal unquestioned informative material) also carried a side line of weather prognostications, but in a far less spirited style. Where, for instance, The Old Farmer for the last of July, 1874, pessimistically prophesied "uncomfortable weather with frequent showers," Dr. Ayer's admitted "scorching heat," but supplemented the statement with the more heartening "Fine hay weather."

This Old Farmer's Almanac, sedate, informative, dependable, and convincing as one might expect from its source, was then, as it is today after 136 years of consecutive publishing, a substantial volume of miscellaneous but well-directed information. The man who fain would study the skies (and, amazingly, many an humble farmer did) could use the Old Farmer's Almanac as a textbook with confidence. My own father, with only the lesser ordinary almanacs to go by, sat with me on many a starlit night and traced for my childish pleasure the Milky Way, the Great and the Little Dipper, and read for me a tale written by the stars far more fascinating than any the millions of books of today provided for my children seem to do. His translation was doubtless crude, perhaps often wrong, but at least it taught me that there *was* a sky, showed me its sustaining and comforting beauty, and instilled a habit of looking *up*. (One of the first things I ever bought for him after I began earning money was a simple book of astronomy.)

The Old Farmer's Almanac (which sold then and still does for fifteen cents), in common with others, also announced the eclipses of the year but added considerable other information, such as names and characters of the aspects, names and characters of the signs of the zodiac (from which my cousin Cory and I once contrived ourselves a secret alphabetical code which resembled a cross between Achibbiddi and Glagoutic), chronological cycles, movable feasts and fasts, and a table of tides, a feature that I regret being denied. Any mention of the mysterious, seemingly mythical sea was a prick to the imagination of the inland child.

Almost all almanacs were moral in tone, and the older ones definitely religious. They were, therefore, a marked influence on character. Even the stanzas of verse which decorated the calendar pages of many were spiritual in tone, or, at least, inspirational.

In a perusal of old almanacs (dating back of a hundred years) one is impressed by their changing character as other reading matter found its way to the scattered and often isolated homes. In the 1700's the almanac was a compendium of serious information, unleavened by wit

314

or humor. Of these the *Vermont Register and Almanac* was most voluminous. It apparently had no sponsor except the house publishing it at Montpelier, and it was (at least those I have examined were) over one hundred pages in length. There is no indication on the volumes I have been able to study (1818–1821) that it was sold for a price, but it must have been. It carried indispensable information—lists of post offices and postmasters and of practicing attorneys throughout the state, town clerks, jurors (with fees), literary institutes, together with aphorisms, short fables inciting charity and economy, and always the marginal notes: "March 7th—Joseph's heifer calved"; "Dec. 1, 1819—Turned ram to sheep."

The North American Almanac and Gentleman's and Lady's Diary for the year of our Lord Jesus Christ, 1776 (calculated—like *The Old Farmer's*—"for the medium of Boston and New England") contained, besides all the features of other almanacs, including a list of Friends' meeting places, occasional bits of verse, the credit for which it would seem should go somewhere other than just to the good judgment of the compiler; for example, the "Bacchanal on the Earth's Drinking Habits," whose author was not a poor disciple of the famed maker of tents:

> The thirsty Earth soaks up the rain
> And drinks and gapes for rain again;
> The planets suck in the earth and are,
> With constant drinking, fresh and fair;
> The sea itself, which one would think
> Should have but little need of drink,
> Yet drinks ten thousand rivers up
> So fill'd that they o'erflow the cup:
> The busy sun—and one would guess
> By's drunken fiery face no less—
> Drinks up the sea, and when he's done,
> The moon and stars drink up the sea.
> They drink and dance by their own light;
> They drink and revel all the night:
> Nothing in nature's sober found.
> But an eternal health goes round:
> Fill up the bowl then! fill it high!
> Fill all the glasses there; for why
> Should every creature drink but I?
> Why? Man of Morals—tell me why!

The almanac and the Bible were without doubt the two greatest mediums for influence upon the lives of people from earliest days of settlement in this country—as well as others—to the time when, in the nineteenth century, a book ceased to be little less than a miracle. An almanac was not only a source of entertainment—which it decidedly was—through its paragraphs of wit and wisdom, but the only volume of reference to which the common people had access. Whether the Bible or the almanac wielded the greater power is perhaps a debatable matter. The Bible was a threat held over the head and a rainbow before the eye. But the almanac took a man by the hand on the first of January year in and year out and led him through vicissitudes of wind and weather. In the progression of time and opportunity for news gathering its scope of usefulness widened, and one almanac vied with another in assembling and disseminating information. In the seventies and eighties it told when and where court would convene; served as a road map; acquainted the reader with national affairs; gave statistics regarding army, navy, development of railroads, canals, and the opportunities for commerce. Through its fun and humor it sharpened the wits; by proverb and adage it aroused thought, provoked judgment. It gave some good medical advice and much that was worthless. In this particular some almanacs were worse than others. Those sponsored by patent medicine could ruin the best of health by consistent and imaginative reading, let alone application.

Mr. Clarence S. Brigham, director of the National Antiquarian Society at Worcester, Massachusetts (where is a collection of 35,000 almanacs, the largest in the world) in his bulletin, *An Account of American Almanacs*, quotes a paragraph from Moses Coit Tyler's *History of American Literature* in which the case of the almanac is so clearly faced that it seems to me I can do no better, in closing, than to requote the same:

"No one who would penetrate to the core of early American literature, and would read in it the secret history of the people in whose minds it took root and from whose mind it grew, may by any means turn away, in lofty literary scorn, from the almanac—most despised, most prolific, most indispensable of books, which every man uses, and no man praises; the very quack, clown, pack horse, and pariah of modern literature, yet the one universal book of modern literature; the supreme and only literary necessity even in households where the Bible and the newspaper are still undesired or unattainable luxuries."

Belling a Fox

by CHARLES D. STEWART, 1868–   . *Born in Zanesville, Ohio, Stewart was educated in the public schools of Milwaukee and for some years has made his home in Hartford, Wisconsin. He has contributed fiction, verse, essays, and nature sketches to the Atlantic Monthly and other magazines. At present he is vice-president of the Society of Midland Authors. Among his books are an amusing picaresque novel* The Fugitive Blacksmith *(1905), a study of the textual difficulties of Shakespeare (1914), a novel entitled* Buck *(1919), and* Fellow Creatures *(1935), a collection of essays and sketches. While he does not precisely belong in the tradition of nature writers, Stewart is at his best in describing and interpreting the life of the fields and the woods. He is both an acute observer and a charming stylist. This account of a Wisconsin fox hunt is taken from* Fellow Creatures.

THE fox is so wary of approach, and has such uncanny knowledge of a trap, that the problem of getting his pelt usually reduces itself to a matter of mere brute force. A special breed of hound, having superior strength and endurance, is used to wear him out, and, finally, run him down. The foxhound, compounded of the greyhound, the bloodhound, and—as some think—the bulldog, for the combined qualities of fleetness, fineness of scent, and tireless tenacity, is a substantial reminder, not to say a loud advertisement, of the qualities of the fox. For the foxhound, aside from the growl and bark of a dog, has a voice like a town crier; and this large part of him has its practical uses in the chase. It enables his master to keep track of him in the distance, to read his mind and emotions, and, by this knowledge of what is going on, to head him off in his work, and get the fox away from him before he has torn it to pieces.

Some writers hold the hound in such high esteem as to pronounce him the most sagacious of the dog tribe; but I could never see a hound in that way. He gets his impressive countenance from the bloodhound; and a bloodhound is not as wise as he looks. He is a dog of one idea, and that idea simply has him by the nose. When he is being led on by a fresh trail, he will run till his feet leave bloody tracks in the snow; and, like all monomaniacs, he lacks the initiative to quit. He is, in short, a hound.

I can see, however, that the proprietor of a hound, or of a kennel of thirty or forty hounds, being influenced by live memories of the hunt, might conceive the same enthusiasm toward a hound that the average man has toward a dog. George Washington, who was a devoted fox hunter, usually hunting three times a week, had a well-trained pack and a fine stable of horses at Mount Vernon. With his usual attention to detail, he had intimate knowledge of each of his horses, and knew every hound by name and according to his particular merits. Among the hounds were Vulcan, Ringwood, Singer, Truelove, Music, Forester, Rockwood, and Sweetlips. When I reflect upon certain of these names, I begin to suspect that Washington would hardly have shared my sentiments toward the ever-bellowing hound.

Here in Wisconsin we do it differently. We have a method of hunting the fox which employs nothing of this mere conquering force, but moves purely along lines of fox nature and human nature. It is known as belling the fox, and consists in following his trail in the snow and ringing a good-sized dinner bell. For this work an old man is best adapted, the reason being not merely that he has had years of experience and is hard for a fox to throw off the trail, but that his weight of years will keep him from getting in a hurry. Youth, becoming wrought up and interested in the chase, unconsciously walks faster and faster. Age and philosophy is willing to save its strength and to keep trudging along. There is plenty of time to catch a fox. This form of the hunt has regard for the Shakespearean adage that what you haven't got in your head you have got to take out of your heels. Grandpa, who is playing the part of the hound, with the assistance of the dinner bell, is fully as wise as he looks; and it is an axiom of the chase that haste is not required. He keeps in mind that other old adage—the more haste, the less speed.

Of all the methods of circumventing the fox, this is the one that is the surest of success. It is, therefore, the method of the professional fox hunter, and has been since before the time when Wisconsin became a state. There are several generations of experience behind it.

The art of belling the fox first came to my attention twenty-eight years ago, when I took up my residence in the country; and it has been of constant interest to me, for the reason that it is such an infallible clue to the fox's habits. And not only to his habits, but to the workings of his mind. By this trail in the snow, Reynard becomes his own biographer. Every act of his life is written down and made manifest. Here he halted and poked his nose into a burrow, in the hope of getting a rabbit or a mouse; there he crossed over to the swamp in search of better hunting; then he looked into the end of a hollow log and seemed to be curious about a woodchuck's winter quarters. Finally, after much casting about, he caught a rabbit and feasted on it; and having thus made a night of it, and got his stomach comfortably filled, he curled up in the snow to spend the day.

To the man who follows him day after day, winter after winter, it is the true history of the fox written down on the white page of nature. Not a detail is omitted. Every doing of the night is put on record; and the snowy bed whereon he slept bears witness for itself.

If the reader is disposed to follow him through a sample night and day, we will start at the beginning, early in the morning, with Grandpa Wellington Dewey to bear the bell and Charlie Carpenter to operate the gun. I might explain before we start out that not for a moment are we going to see the fox—that is, not till the final moment when we have out-manoeuvred him and stretched him on the snow. The fox is a natural scout and spy. He has senses that are wonderfully acute, and a nature that is all suspicion. He believes in being neither seen nor heard; and he has every art of precaution that the most accomplished spy could ever think of.

In spite of his superior equipment in the way of ears and nose, the two hunters will deliberately undertake to out-scout him and out-spy him. The sport has a deep and peculiar fascination, entirely aside from the fifteen or twenty dollars at stake. We are coping with the animal sight-unseen, relying upon our knowledge of how a fox will play the game. He is being hunted in the abstract; and the work combines with this purely mental interest a feature that is generally considered the better element of sport—a square deal for the animal that is hunted. It is a contest of wits, never descending to mere brute force; and it has none of the cruelty of trapping. When the fox is beaten at his own game, his end will be quick and sure.

Having with us an accomplished bellman, and a more active man who will know how to come in opportunely with the gun, we strike out into the country and begin casting about upon the face of nature. During the night a light snow has fallen on what was already a substantial crust; and this is the board on which we are going to play.

Presently we have the luck to discover what we think must surely be the trail of a fox, and we sing out the news to Grandpa Dewey. He comes to pass upon it, and very soon informs us that it is the track of Farmer Brown's young collie. We had been told to look for tracks that were all in a line, as if they had been made by an animal hopping along on one foot; and, so far as we can see, this trail fits the description exactly. A collie trotting in the snow does make a trail that is remarkably straight; and he steps in his own tracks with such precision as to give little clue to the number of his legs. But it is not quite the trail of the fox.

Again we spread out over the territory and continue our search. Finally Grandpa Dewey proves himself the true fox finder; and he lets it be known with a laconic "Hyar we are." Whereupon we all hurry over to the point that is to be the beginning of our travels.

Desirous of learning the secrets of a bellman, we stoop over and bend our mind upon one of these intaglios in the snow. The fox and the dog belong to the same large family, the Canidae; and the more closely we look at this track, the more the fact seems evident to us. There are the same little cushions, the toes arranged around the heel, and the same straight line leading off toward the hills. If the other was a dog, we should be willing to swear that this was a dog, too. Not until Grandpa Dewey and Charlie Carpenter have united in the statement that the two are quite different do we get our attention down to the matter; and then we begin to see. The difference is like that between two signatures—at first very similar, and then distinguishable at a glance. Reynard differs from the dog in having a pad that expresses slenderness, the toes being more elongated in their arrangement round the heel. His paw is more ladylike and "spirituelle," and the line of his footfall is, if anything, straighter and more precise than that of the collie. On the paw of every animal Nature has set the family seal; and this is the Fox, his mark.

The experienced fox hunter, however, would be able to recognize the trail by its general record, independent of any such assistance from canine palmistry. He notes the wide, light leap as Reynard clears an obstruction, and reads the nature of his quick decisions as he changes his course to this side or that. He knows the fox's handwriting in general; and, by a knowledge of the swamps and ridges and runways that the fox is likely to have in mind, he makes a guess at the nature of the message.

I have said that there was a fresh fall of snow during the night. By this means we know that the trail is a fresh one. It is not the record of a fox's wanderings two or three nights ago. But while this fresh fall of snow is very welcome to a hunter, as giving him a clean slate, he does not need any such adventitious happenings to tell him whether a trail is old or new. A footprint that has stood long in the cold has its interior covered with fine "spiculae"—a mat, frosted appearance. The bellman knows it at a glance, as a jeweler would judge a diamond or a cameo.

Now that we have Mr. Wily on the line, our interest in him goes up several degrees; and we naturally expect, as we walk along in the direction in which his toes are pointing, that there will be some signs of an intention to hunt the fox. All this while Grandpa Dewey has been carrying the bell by the clapper; and he still continues to do so. It has been about as much use to him as any other dead weight would be—a mere dumb-bell; and he is in as little of a hurry as he was before.

But we readily agree with him that there is no great call for hurry, when he reminds us that, as this is daytime, the fox is sleeping. The fox has elliptical pupils like those of a cat; and being that variety of animal, he hunts all night and does his sleeping by day. Somewhere ahead of us he is comfortably curled up, taking his nap and digesting the rabbit; and as he has no idea that we are after him, he may be depended upon to wait till we come. His bed may be fifteen minutes ahead of us, or it may be an hour; but anyway we have him on the line, and he cannot very well break the connection. We just keep trudging along, and sooner or later we shall find where he put up for the day.

"In his den?" we inquire. It has suddenly occurred to us that we should like to see a fox's den. This alone would make the trip worth while. But it is evident that this query has no meaning to either Grandpa Dewey or Charlie Carpenter. When we repeat the word, emphasizing it, we see that it has no place in the consciousness of the fox hunter, or of his cousins or his uncles or his aunts. Whereupon we say what we mean—his burrow, his hole in the ground, the place where he lives. But this elicits no look of understanding. It would be impossible to find a fox in such a place. A fox sleeps in the open, even in the coldest weather. He simply curls up and drops down in his tracks; but he always sleeps with his nose pointing back on the trail; for he knows that if he has callers they are likely to come by that route. He may make his bed on the lee side of a juniper bush, or, if it is very cold, among the undergrowth of a tamarack swamp; but he is fond of a slope facing south. He has even been known to make his bed on top of a pile of field stone, possibly because it afforded him a good lookout. A fox finds safety by knowing what is going on around him, not by hiding in a hole, where he can neither hear nor see, and where he would surely be cornered and caught. Grandpa Dewey knew a man who, several years ago, followed a trail that led to a burrow. It was a woodchuck burrow, which some fox had enlarged the year before to put her cubs in. But this fox that hid in it was wounded.

As this seems contrary to Æsop and the Bible, and even the Encyclopedia itself, it is not welcome news. We do not like to see the authority put in the wrong. It is even contrary to the expression, a "fox's den." But Grandpa settles the whole matter by telling us that the best way is to wait and see. We shall find that this fox has been sleeping in the snow somewhere ahead of us. And so we decide that, as he has been following these records since the early sixties, and the fox has no way of erasing any of the facts by night or day, we had better hold our opinions in abeyance.

When we have come to the place where the fox is now resting, as we surely shall, we shall see his empty bed in the snow; but there will be no fox in sight. And as we should never be able to overtake him, even though we had the swiftest horse in the country, that is another reason for not being in a hurry.

It is a beautiful winter day, sparkling and crisp. The sun shines across the white fields; it illumines the armfuls of snow that the trees have caught in their crotches, and makes the distant tamarack seem all the darker by contrast. And as the fox will know that we are coming, by the rustle of our coats or the squeak of our boots in the snow, quite as well as if we were making what "we" should call a noise; and as he would be likely to smell us if we made no noise whatever, there is no restraint upon us. We are free to admire the scenery and talk things over.

After much trudging up hill and down dale, Grandpa suddenly does get in a hurry. He sees the fox's bed ahead of him—a round place in the snow; whereupon he breaks into a running walk like that of an Indian. The moment he reaches it, he stoops over and passes his hand round its interior, and then straightens up, with his hurry all gone. Instead of being soft and spongy, as it would be if the fox had just left it, this bed has had time to freeze and form a crust. A touch of Grandpa's finger has been enough to tell the story.

A fox settles down with the intention of spending the day; but he does not always remain of one mind. Something disturbs him; he becomes restless and suspicious, and finally moves on to another locality. This is what has happened here. And lest we should have conveyed a wrong impression by the word "bed," let us explain that it is nothing that the fox makes. He simply curls up and lies down on the surface of the snow as lightly and daintily as he does everything else; but the warmth of his body gradually settles the snow and melts it, and lets him down into it. Now we know that the fox is not very far away. As we shall presently come upon the bed that finally suited him, we follow along with rising expectations.

Meanwhile we seem to have lost Charlie Carpenter. He wandered off with the gun on his shoulder, to one side of our route and a considerable distance in advance. Now he is nowhere in sight, and we wonder what has become of him. He does not seem to care whether we start the fox or not; and Grandpa Dewey, still carrying the bell by the clapper, does nothing but trudge along.

Again he breaks into his jog trot and makes for the summit of a little knoll. This time he has started the fox. The inside of this bed is spongy and damp. The fox is only two or three minutes away. Immediately the bell comes into action. Grandpa sets it going at a great rate, clanging away as if it were three or four dinner bells, and all the dinners in a hurry. He explains that this is to let Charlie Carpenter know that the fox has been started. Charlie is ahead somewhere, a mile or more away. And then, having made so much ado about it, Grandpa settles into his former state of calm deliberation and follows along the trail, ringing the bell as he goes. Instead of hastening, now that he has the fox at hand, he becomes even more leisurely; and the bell settles down to a steady, monotonous "clangety-clang," swinging with every step and giving forth its note with the uninspired regularity of a scissors grinder going his daily rounds. It may be a long walk that we have before us, and there is no use in wearing ourselves out. And besides, the slower we go, the sooner we are likely to get the fox. This, it seems, is about all we have to do. Meanwhile, we have learned the art of starting the fox, which is the first step in belling him. And we have learned fact number one, upon which these hunters always depend: which is, that a fox does not live in a den.

Charlie Carpenter, a mile or so ahead, has got to his present position by describing a big circle. And now his business is to keep well ahead and strictly out of that fox's sight and out of his hearing and powers of smell. He must keep moving on in order to do it. He has not seen the fox; because, if he had, the fox would have seen him.

As for ourselves, we need observe no precautions. The fox is perfectly aware that we are behind him. He knew it before we reached his bed, and it took no bell to apprise him of the fact. If we had seen him at the moment he left his bed, we should have seen little more than a streak of reddish color flashing across the snow. Once in a great while you might catch a fox napping. If, for instance, he had his bed on a hillside, and you came up the opposite side of the hill, with the wind blowing your scent away from him, and such snow underfoot that your boots did not crunch in the least, you might catch a fox in bed. But you would hardly be aware of his presence before he was aware of yours; and then it would be too late to take action. A hunter near Pike Lake came across a fox in such favoring circumstances a few years ago. He had his shotgun in hand, but could not get it to his shoulder in time. It was, he said, "just as if a puff of wind came along at that instant and blew the fox out of sight like a leaf." This was a very good description of the fox's lightness and speed. His coloring, too, is that of the autumn leaf. One instant he flashed upon the sight, then he was gone.

The three parties to the present transaction, Grandpa Dewey, the fox, and Charlie Carpenter, are now moving along out of sight of one another. Charlie Carpenter, far in the lead, is listening to the bell and trying to strike a position where it will come steadily toward him. By taking a stand and listening closely, he is able to tell whether it is coming straight on or veering to this side or that; and he manoeuvres about accordingly. But when he corrects his course and takes up a new experimental position, he must also move on, and keep well in advance. By the sound of the bell, the fox's route is being projected ahead of him. Charlie is very deliberately dealing with the fox's future, surveying it by sound. The fox is free to go where he will; and if, after he has come straight on for a while, he suddenly strikes off, at an angle, the hunter has got to circle about and strike up another position. Sooner or later the fox will come straight on; and when he does, the hunter will be there to meet him.

All this sounds very well in theory. But it strikes us as being altogether too deliberate a way of working with a fox. So here we begin to ask questions. If Charlie Carpenter has not *seen* the fox, how does he know that the fox is somewhere between him and the bell?

This brings us to fact number two in fox psychology. A fox will run no faster than he is chased. This is a fact which may be stated without any reservations. It is no exaggeration to say that there is no limit to the slowness with which a fox will travel in suiting his pace to that of his pursuer. He will stop and look back, curiously. The veriest cripple, a man on crutches, could keep up with a fox as well as the average horse or hound. He will go fast or slow according as it is necessary to keep out of harm's way; but in neither case is he a fugitive. If you were to see a fox at the moment he discovered your approach, you would no doubt think that the panic-stricken animal would keep on running till his fright wore off. But not so. He goes like a streak until he has put his established distance between you and him; and then he does not run at all. How fast he goes after that depends entirely upon yourself. A wolf will not act like this. When he is surprised by the human presence, he simply "lights out"; he makes tracks for distant parts, with the idea of leaving all trouble behind. He becomes a fugitive at once. But the fox would rather skulk than run. As I have said, he is a natural scout and spy.

A man who hunts the fox with hounds is not in a position to learn this fact; at least, not to its full extent. To see a hound running hour after hour behind a fox who manages to keep just so far ahead, you would be likely to think it was a race. You would say that the dog was almost as fast as the fox. If the dog could only go a little faster! It is nip and tuck! And the owner of the hound, with that justifiable pride which every man feels in his dog, would be inclined to see it in the same way. But this is not the truth in the case. An experienced beller of the fox, understanding the whole psychology of the animal, sees it from a quite different point of view. There is no race going on. The fox will run slow before a slow hound and fast before a fast one. And, by the same token, he will walk if you do. The fox is simply keeping his distance; and whether he does it by going fast or slow does not alter the essential fact. This difference in point of view is important; for it is by knowing the inner facts rather than by mere appearances that the man with the bell is able to go out after a fox and deliberately cope with him.

A fox, surprised by a hound in a small patch of woods, will take out across the open at a speed that is surprising. Then, not only will he slow up, but he may sit down on some convenient elevation and look back. He keeps his wits, or rather his cunning, about him; he wants to see what is going on. When the hound has struck his pace, the fox will soon gauge it and lead him a chase accordingly. The spectator of such a chase, knowing that the hound is a slow one, turns admirer of the witty Reynard, and says that the fox is doing this just to "tease" the dog. Many entertaining writers upon the fox have said this. A veteran bellman would not see it in that way. He knows very well that, when the fox gets half a mile or so ahead of him and skulks along at a set distance and out of sight, the fox is not doing it to tease *him*. This is to humanize the fox without warrant. The plain fact is that the fox will not retreat before you any faster than he is driven. And this because it is his nature to be cunning and to depend on strategy. And the bellman has, to use a current expression, psychoanalyzed him.

Of all the hunters of the fox, the rider behind a pack of thoroughbred English foxhounds is furthest from any opportunity to learn the whole inner nature of the fox. Some generations ago the English foxhound was a much slower animal; he could wear out a fox in time, but the contest was likely to be long. For the sport of riding to hounds, this was impracticable; the chase dragged out unconscionably. Consequently, the hound was bred up for speed, until a good pack can now overtake a fox in the space of thirty minutes. Such hounds can push a fox from the start, and wear him down so quickly that the fox is doing his best to keep away from them. A hunter who never follows the fox except under such circumstances would hardly become fully acquainted with him. He would be likely to conceive of the fox as an animal that gets away from you in a panic, and keeps up his best gait to the end. But here the fox cannot very well do anything else. A writer in an English encyclopedia, having seen an American red fox before a hound, put on record his opinion that the American fox was much slower than the fox in England. I think the American fox had him very much fooled.

The art of belling the fox is just the opposite of this. It takes the fox according to his nature, and meets him on his own ground. The hunt becomes pure strategy, scout against scout, spy against spy, and trick for trick. The fox, having taken his distance, will go no faster than he is driven. But, to get within that set distance, you have to cope with an animal whose every sense is bent upon keeping you from doing it. It is practically impossible to approach within gunshot of a fox.

How then, we ask, does Charlie expect to do it?

This brings us to fact number three—and the one that gets the fox. The eye of an animal, or of a man for that matter, is not caught by color or form so quickly as it is by motion. Charlie Carpenter is not going to approach the fox. He is going to let the fox approach him. He is going to be a tree, a log of wood, a bump on the face of nature, anything but a man that moves. And he must be careful to have no smell; for which reason, he will place himself down the wind from the prospective path of the fox.

But we must get back to our belling. While we have been talking, the trail has led us across a wide field in the direction of a range of hills. Suddenly, in the very middle of the field, the trail comes to an end. It stops as abruptly as if the fox had taken wing and flown. Evidently the age of miracles is not past. We had been supposing that a fox, earth-bound like ourselves, could not travel without leaving footprints in the snow. The fox has back-tracked. He has turned carefully about and come toward us, following his own trail. But we have noticed no trail leading off from this one. It must have escaped our eye. The reason is that the fox, before striking out in a new direction, has leaped wide of the present trail, breaking the connection. Moreover, he has been at pains to let every footstep fall accurately into the tracks he made before. The result is that there is no double trail to show where he leaped off.

That a fox will double on his trail has been known to fox hunters since before the time of Shakespeare. A pack of hounds, hunting by scent and coming to this abrupt end of things, would be said to be "at fault," or, to use an expression that Shakespeare was fond of, they would be "at a check." But the hunter who depends upon hounds, following the trail on the bare ground, is not in a position to observe all this fine attention to detail, which the bellman becomes so familiar with. The hounds in such a case as this would have to spread out in all directions, and scour the surrounding territory, in the effort to pick up the new trail. If they did not succeed, the huntsman might "lift them," trying some place of his own purely by guess.

Grandpa Dewey, being his own hound, turns back at once, keeping his eyes about him. The fox has thrown him off the main track and run him into a blind switch; but he understands all this sort of work. Presently he has found where the fox leaped off. The new trail leads off from the other like the branch line of a railroad, which falls short of connecting up with the main system. So now we are on our way again, "clangety-clang, clangety-clang," the bell heralding our advance like the bell of a locomotive.

This, of course, is not the only little trouble a fox can make for a bellman. It sometimes happens that his route lies across a ploughed field, where the snow has all blown into the furrows, leaving the clods standing bare. In crossing such a field the fox will keep to the bare places, carefully picking his way and stepping from clod to clod. This puts the hunter out and delays him in his work. Whether the fox does this purposely or not, we shall not presume to say; but the hunter, thus impeded, puts it down to the rascality of the fox.

Again, the fox's preference for the south side of a hill as a place to spend the day helps him in breaking his trail. The prevailing winds being from the north in winter, the tracks on the opposite side of the hill, where he came up and over, are in a position where they will soon drift full of snow. If there is any wind moving, that important part of his trail will be obliterated. Such things so frequently happen just at the point where the fox is casting about and getting ready to go to bed that the hunter becomes convinced of their deliberate purpose.

There is no question, however, that the fox has an instinct for breaking his trail. Closely pressed, he will run up the trunk of a half-fallen tree, for the sake of making a wide jump and putting a bigger hiatus in his line of scent, and he seems to be quite as conscious of the visibility of his trail as of its tell-tale odor. A farmer of my acquaintance related to me, with some surprise, the following experience. He was standing in his woods, thinking of some work to be done, when a fox came along, hotly pursued by a hound. Suddenly that fox ran "right plump at a big tree, quicker'n scat." He struck the tree a considerable distance from the ground; and at the moment of striking he gave another spring and shot off to one side, making a wide break in his trail. Considering what a fox will do with a tree that is half-fallen, I see no reason to doubt this. It would be but a step further in his practice to make use of a vertical surface in an emergency, especially as the rough bark would make the trick quite practicable. It is in line with his known instincts.

Many things happen on the trail of a fox, some of them the most evident artifice and some of a nature that might be accounted for as mere chance, but are yet open to doubt. Usually the fox is considered the guilty party, the hunter knowing that he is quite capable of such things. As it is with a man's reputation, so it is with that of the fox. If he is known as a rascal, everything he does comes under suspicion. If he has a reputation for business or political acumen, his most accidental success is imputed to him for surpassing wisdom.

From a few such experiences on the trail, we begin to see that Grandpa Dewey has to be a man of parts. There is more to do than follow a plain track and ring a dinner bell. He is the detective in the case, the shrewd solver of mysteries, who knows the workings of the fox's mind and cannot be thrown off the trail. Charlie Carpenter, on the other hand, is the scout and spy, the master of stealth and camouflage. While the fox tries to fool Grandpa Dewey, Charlie undertakes to fool the fox.

About this time, things ought to be growing interesting on the other end; so we will leave the bellman to his own devices while we circle round and watch the outcome.

Charlie Carpenter is still scouting about warily with his gun, keeping well ahead, taking a stand, and bending his ear to determine whether the bell is coming straight on. The bell grows plainer and plainer, neither to the left nor to the right. Several times he has done this; then had to make a large, circuitous forward movement as the fox changed his course. In no case must the fox be allowed to come in sight. The sound of the bell serves to gauge the distance of the fox.

This time he seems to have struck it right. The bell advances steadily in his direction. Charlie goes a little farther down the wind, making a final correction in his position. The bell comes steadily on. He is coming to close quarters with the fox; pretty soon the wary animal will appear on the scene. And now is the time for decisive action.

Charlie Carpenter has had his eye on a tree that might serve as a screen to shoot from; but this is no longer available. Not far along the route, he sees a small decayed log with a fringe of weeds and brush. He drops down flat behind this, pointing his gun over the top. From now on there must be no movement, no sign of life. The barrel of the gun must not move and wobble about in getting the prospective aim. Anything like that would certainly be noticed. The prospective aim must already be taken. Charlie's cap is of a dull russet color, blending with the weeds and the bark of the log. A red plaid would hardly be advisable. Next to motion, color is the quickest to attract attention. The two together would be fatal. Form is not so important. Even the whole form of a man, if he remains quite motionless, is not readily picked out from the surroundings.

Charlie has hardly got himself into position when the fox comes in sight, picking his way along. Sometimes he pauses and looks back, as if to make sure that he is well ahead of this strange sound that keeps haunting his trail. But there is no dog in the case,—the fox is well aware of that,—and hence no occasion for hurry. So he pursues his wary way and keeps straight on.

Meanwhile Charlie Carpenter, peering over the log, is as motionless as death. The cap does not bob up and down; he does not become nervous with the gun. It is plain that he has a firm grip on fact number three. He waits till the fox crosses the path of his gun before he takes finer aim and fires. And the next instant it is all over. A beautiful specimen of the red male fox, with his fur at its prime.

Nor need we shed any tears over his fate, thus dishonestly dealt with and craftily waylaid. If he had conducted himself like a wolf, running from evil and giving it a wide berth, instead of flirting with it and placing such cheeky reliance on his trickery, he would not have come to this sad end. Moral: in any situation in life, the simple and straightforward method is the best. Be sure that your cunning will find you out.

Summing up our knowledge, we find that this most effective way of hunting the fox divides itself under three heads—starting the fox from his bed, following him with the bell, and waylaying him. And the uniform success of the method is based upon three facts, which might be set down formally as follows. First, a fox does not live in a den. Second, a fox will not run any faster than he is chased. Third, you cannot easily approach within gunshot of a fox; but you may make arrangements to have him approach you.

Anyone at all familiar with the methods of the English fox hunt, or who has read any one of thirty or forty books in the average public library, will find difficulty in accepting these facts as good natural history. Fact number one will be especially bothersome. The first move in an English fox hunt is based upon the fact that the fox resorts to a den, not only in spring, when it has cubs to care for, but at all times. The English fox hunt is a sport usually followed in late fall and winter. Of the various functionaries of a fox-hunting establishment, the one known as the "earth-stopper" goes forth to prepare for the hunt. As the fox is an animal that hunts by night, the earth-stopper goes forth at night, and stops up the fox's burrow in the covert (a patch of gorse or undergrowth). This has to be done in the fox's absence, for the reason that, when the fox comes home in the morning, he takes to his den; or, if he is lying near it, he will immediately run to it when the hounds are turned into the covert, and will refuse to come forth. To stop his burrow is the only way to get him started. The earth-stopper at the same time visits all other burrows in a large territory, and stops them up, together with any drains or other holes that the fox could get into. For the fox, shut out of his own home, will put out his best speed to reach some other burrow, which he has in mind or can find by the way. His whole instinct is toward a burrow. That this is the fox's habit in England we cannot question. The English fox-hunter knows a fox.

I must admit that, twenty-eight years ago, when I moved into a fox neighborhood, I doubted the word of every old hunter who told me about his habits. I thought that these hunters were faulty observers, like those neighbors who still plant their gardens by the phases of the moon. But the time is long past when I doubted the American hunter's knowledge of the fox. This was one of the disadvantages of a literary knowledge of a subject, without practical experience.

When I had become thoroughly convinced that the fox had no instinct for a den in winter, and would hardly be caught dead in such a place, I began to look narrowly into the fox's habits in spring and summer. The fox, like other wild animals, has got to have a place to shelter and hide her young; and the place has to be visited because the cubs need to be fed. But that is about all you can say about a fox's den in spring. The old foxes do not sleep in it, or betray any instincts toward the burrow as a place of habitation. And never is it a place to hide in. They hunt by night; and by day they give the den a wide berth, sleeping at a distance, but in a location that commands a full view of the hiding-place of the young and of the surrounding territory. If you approach a fox's den, you will hear a peculiar yelping in the distance—a warning to the young to lie low. Very often the burrow is in a location that seems recklessly open to observation. Several years ago, a pair of foxes had their young hidden near my place, on a hill opposite a ploughed field belonging to my nearest neighbor. Whenever the farmer came too near that place, he would hear the warning in the distance. It has been asked (Burroughs puts this query) why it is that a fox will make her den in such an open place. I think the answer is to be found in the fact that the fox finds his safety in knowing what is going on, not in mere hiding.

A fox will not take refuge in a den unless it is wounded or utterly exhausted and unable to go farther. The instances are so rare when a fox has been cornered in a burrow that old hunters refer to them as the work of "fool foxes," the theory being that Nature occasionally produces an idiot, even among foxes. Considering that a fox's trail can be followed, either by scent or by the tracks in the snow, a fox would be a fool to spend much time in such a place. The oldest hunter I ever knew—he began hunting foxes in 1846—remembered but three such cases in over seventy years. And usually these cases are accounted for by the fact that the fox was young; and having been raised in that burrow, dropped into it in passing, by way of a visit.

The English fox resorts to a burrow at all times, regardless of having

330

cubs to care for; and there is no object in such a practice except that of hiding itself away. The American fox sleeps out in the open in the severest weather, showing no instinct toward a den; and in spring and summer, the male fox gives the burrow a wide berth, remaining on watch, while the female makes visits to it. The English fox clings to a den; the other stays away, when the whole call of his nature would be toward it. Thus my inquiry into the history of the red fox served but to accentuate the difference between the English and the American fox in this regard.

And now, as to harmonizing these facts, I have been able to arrive at but one conclusion. It is that the fox in England is not living in a state of nature.

A wider knowledge of animals in general, and the study of instinct as inherited experience, tends to strengthen this view. Wild animals accommodate themselves to the way of man more than we are likely to think. We pride ourselves upon our study of animals, forgetting that the animals also study us.

But setting aside any theory of instinct and getting down to the fox's own problems, a study of the English fox hunt brings the whole matter to a point.

In England, the fox is sacred to the chase. To kill a fox except in fair pursuit with horse and hound is vulpicide,—fox murder,—a social crime. An Englishman seldom sinks so low in the social scale as to trap or shoot a fox. The hunt is surrounded by laws, some statutory, some social and traditional. The fox was originally "vermin," and was hunted as such. Though now he is the very opposite of vermin, being carefully preserved, the old view of him is still kept up for legal purposes; for thus the riders get their right to chase him over the farmers' land and tramp down fields that are in crop.

But, aside from the statutes, there are other laws,—gentlemen's laws, —as strong as those of the Medes and Persians. It is not usual, for instance, to dig a fox out of a burrow into which he has escaped after giving the field a good run. It is sometimes done, as when young dogs are being given a practice run, and it is necessary to give them their first taste of blood. Here the little fox terrier comes into play, his business being to hold the fox in a particular branch of his tunnel while the spade is being used. But this is exceptional; it is not a recognized part of the sport. So, also, if a fox got into a burrow, in his own covert, which the earth-stopper had missed, the assembled field of riders would not dig him forth and compel him to start out for a run. They would rather go home, however disappointed, and call the day a "blank." It is not part of the game.

Consider then the red fox in full flight across an English moor, with a pack of thirty or forty hounds after him and a field of swift riders on his trail. The hounds have been bred for speed, with the object of beating the fox in about thirty minutes. What are his chances for escape? He may, if he should get far enough away and have time, try some of his tricks for delay; but these will hardly avail him with such a regiment of hounds. His one great resource will be to take advantage of law—gentlemen's law. If he has some distant burrow in mind, and his wind holds out till he can get to it, he is safe. A fox in a burrow has escaped. In view of this fact, and a long racial experience, would it not be a "fool fox" that did not hunt a burrow? Naturally, such a fox would have a burrow to which he religiously came home in the morning, and a complete repertoire of holes in the surrounding country, which he had discovered in his nightly hunts. Would he not be an idiot if he had not? To apply the American language to the case, "I'll say he would." There can be no doubt that an Englishman knows a fox; also that a fox knows an Englishman.

I must confess that, when I finally evolved this theory, after much bafflement over the fox in public libraries, it was a great relief to me. A large part of our standard literature on the fox seems to have been taken from English tradition. It is rather disconcerting to read dozens of books and articles on the red fox, every one of which is at variance with your own positive knowledge of the animal.

This brings harmony into a set of facts that were very much at outs with each other. In short, the conduct of a fox in the midst of a fox-hunting aristocracy is no indication of what a fox will do which gets back to nature in a free country. And this is good zoology.

THE RIVER

The Last of the Boatmen

by MORGAN NEVILLE, 1783–1840. *Neville, born in Pittsburgh, was the son of Colonel Presley Neville and the grandson of General John Neville, both Revolutionary soldiers. After his school years at the Pittsburgh Academy, Neville entered journalism and was for a time editor of the Pittsburgh Gazette. In 1824 Neville left Pittsburgh for Cincinnati, where he spent the rest of his life. Little of Neville's work, beyond a few poems and sketches, has survived, but he is famous for his story."The Last of the Boatmen," which appeared in James Hall's pioneer western annual, The Western Souvenir, a Christmas and New Year's Gift for 1829. Posterity is indebted to Morgan Neville for placing firmly in American letters the character and exploits of Mike Fink.*

I EMBARKED a few years since, at Pittsburg, for Cincinnati, on board of a steam boat—more with a view of realising the possibility of a speedy return against the current, than in obedience to the call of either business or pleasure. It was a voyage of speculation. I was born on the banks of the Ohio, and the only vessels associated with my early recollections were the canoes of the Indians, which brought to Fort Pitt their annual cargoes of skins and bear's oil. The Flat boat of Kentucky, destined only to float with the current, next appeared; and after many years of interval, the Keel boat of the Ohio, and the Barge of the Mississippi were introduced for the convenience of the infant commerce of the West.

At the period, at which I have dated my trip to Cincinnati, the steam boat had made but few voyages back to Pittsburg. We were generally skeptics as to its practicability. The mind was not prepared for the change that was about to take place in the West. It is now consummated; and we yet look back with astonishment at the result.

The rudest inhabitant of our forests;—the man whose mind is least of all imbued with a relish for the picturesque—who would gaze with vacant stare at the finest painting—listen with apathy to the softest melody, and turn with indifference from a mere display of ingenious mechanism, is struck with the sublime power and self-moving majesty of a steam boat;—lingers on the shore where it passes—and follows its rapid, and almost magic course with silent admiration. The steam engine in five years has enabled us to anticipate a state of things, which, in the ordinary course of events, it would have required a century to have produced. The art of printing scarcely surpassed it in its beneficial consequences.

In the old world, the places of the greatest interest to the philosophic traveller are ruins, and monuments, that speak of faded splendour, and departed glory. The broken columns of Tadmor—the shapeless ruins of Babylon, are rich in matter for almost endless speculation. Far different is the case in the western regions of America. The stranger views here, with wonder, the rapidity with which cities spring up in forests; and with which barbarism retreats before the approach of art and civilization. The reflection possessing the most intense interest is—not what has been the character of the country, but what shall be her future destiny.

As we coasted along this cheerful scene, one reflection crossed my mind to diminish the pleasure it excited. This was caused by the sight of the ruins of the once splendid mansion of Blennerhasset. I had spent some happy hours here, when it was the favorite residence of taste and hospitality. I had seen it when a lovely and accomplished woman presided—shedding a charm around, which made it as inviting, though not so dangerous, as the island of Calypso;—when its liberal and polished owner made it the resort of every stranger, who had any pretensions to literature or science.—I had beheld it again under more inauspicious circumstances:—when its proprietor, in a moment of visionary speculation, had abandoned this earthly paradise to follow an adventurer—himself the dupe of others. A military banditti held possession, acting "by authority." The embellishments of art and taste disappeared beneath the touch of a band of Vandals: and the beautiful domain which presented the imposing appearance of a palace, and which had cost a fortune in the erection, was changed in one night, into a scene of devastation. The chimneys of the house remained for some years—the insulated monument of the folly of their owner, and pointed out to the stranger the place where once stood the temples of hospitality. Drift wood covered the pleasure grounds; and the massive, cut stone, that formed the columns of the gateway, were scattered more widely than the fragments of the Egyptian Memnon.

When we left Pittsburg, the season was not far advanced in vegetation. But as we proceeded the change was more rapid than the difference of latitude justified. I had frequently observed this in former voyages: but it never was so striking, as on the present occasion. The old mode of traveling, in the sluggish flat boat seemed to give time for the change of season; but now a few hours carried us into a different climate. We met spring with all her laughing train of flowers and verdure, rapidly advancing from the south. The buck-eye, cottonwood, and maple, had already assumed, in this region, the rich livery of summer. The thousand varieties of the floral kingdom spread a gay carpet over the luxuriant bottoms on each side of the river. The thick woods resounded with the notes of the feathered tribe—each striving to outdo his neighbor in noise, if not in melody. We had not yet reached the region of paroquets; but the clear toned whistle of the cardinal was heard in every bush; and the cat-bird was endeavouring, with its usual zeal, to rival the powers of the more gifted mockingbird.

A few hours brought us to one of those stopping points, known by the name of "wooding places." It was situated immediately above Letart's Falls. The boat, obedient to the wheel of the pilot, made a graceful sweep towards the island above the chute, and rounding to, approached the wood pile. As the boat drew near the shore, the escape steam reverberated through the forest and hills, like the chafed bellowing of the caged tiger. The root of a tree, concealed beneath the water, prevented the boat from getting sufficiently near the bank, and it became necessary to use the paddles to take a different position.

"Back out! Mannee! and try it again!" exclaimed a voice from the shore. "Throw your pole wide—and brace off!—or you'll run against a snag!"

This was a kind of language long familiar to us on the Ohio. It was a sample of the slang of the keel-boatmen.

The speaker was immediately cheered by a dozen of voices from the deck; and I recognised in him the person of an old acquaintance, familiarly known to me from my boyhood. He was leaning carelessly against a large beech; and, as his left arm negligently pressed a rifle to his side, presented a figure, that Salvator would have chosen from a million, as a model for his wild and gloomy pencil. His stature was upwards of six feet, his proportions perfectly symmetrical, and exhibiting the evidence of Herculean powers. To a stranger, he would have seemed a complete mulatto. Long exposure to the sun and weather on the lower Ohio and Mississippi had changed his skin; and, but for the fine European cast of his countenance, he might have passed for the principal warrior of some powerful tribe. Although at least fifty years of age, his hair was as black as the wing of the raven. Next to his skin he wore a red flannel shirt, covered by a blue capot, ornamented with white fringe. On his feet were moccasins, and a broad leathern belt, from which hung, suspended in a sheath, a large knife, encircled his waist.

As soon as the steam boat became stationary, the cabin passengers jumped on shore. On ascending the bank, the figure I have just described advanced to offer me his hand.

"How are you, Mike?" said I.

"How goes it?" replied the boatman—grasping my hand with a squeeze, that I can compare to nothing, but that of a blacksmith's vise.

"I am glad to see you, Mannee!"—continued he in his abrupt manner. "I am going to shoot at the tin cup for a quart—off hand—and you must be judge."

I understood Mike at once, and on any other occasion, should have remonstrated, and prevented the daring trial of skill. But I was accompanied by a couple of English tourists, who had scarcely ever been beyond the sound of Bow Bells; and who were travelling post over the United States to make up a book of observation, on our manners and customs. There were, also, among the passengers, a few bloods from Philadelphia and Baltimore, who could conceive of nothing equal to Chestnut or Howard streets; and who expressed great disappointment, at not being able to find terrapins and oysters at every village—marvellously lauding the comforts of Rubicum's. My tramontane pride was aroused; and I resolved to give them an opportunity of seeing a Western Lion—for such Mike undoubtedly was—in all his glory. The philanthropist may start, and accuse me of want of humanity. I deny the charge, and refer for apology to one of the best understood principles of human nature.

Mike, followed by several of his crew, led the way to a beech grove, some little distance from the landing. I invited my fellow passengers to witness the scene.—On arriving at the spot, a stout, bull-headed boatman, dressed in a hunting shirt—but bare-footed—in whom I recognised a younger brother of Mike, drew a line with his toe; and stepping off thirty yards—turned round fronting his brother—took a tin cup, which hung from his belt, and placed it on his head. Although I had seen this feat performed before, I acknowledge, I felt uneasy, whilst this silent preparation was going on. But I had not much time for reflection; for this second Albert exclaimed—

"Blaze away, Mike! and let's have the quart."

My "compagnons de voyage," as soon as they recovered from the first effect of their astonishment, exhibited a disposition to interfere. But Mike, throwing back his left leg, levelled his rifle at the head of his brother. In this horizontal position the weapon remained for some seconds as immovable, as if the arm which held it, was affected by no pulsation.

"Elevate your piece a little lower, Mike! or you will pay the corn," cried the imperturbable brother.

I know not if the advice was obeyed or not; but the sharp crack of the rifle immediately followed, and the cup flew off thirty or forty yards—rendered unfit for future service. There was a cry of admiration from the strangers, who pressed forward to see if the foolhardy boatman was really safe. He remained as immoveable, as if he had been a figure hewn out of stone. He had not even winked, when the ball struck the cup within two inches of his skull.

"Mike has won!" I exclaimed; and my decision was the signal which, according to their rules, permitted him of the target to move from his position. No more sensation was exhibited among the boatmen, than if a common wager had been won. The bet being decided, they hurried back to their boat, giving me and my friends an invitation to partake of "the treat." We declined, and took leave of the thoughtless creatures. In a few minutes afterwards, we observed their "Keel" wheeling into the current,—the gigantic form of Mike, bestriding the large steering oar, and the others arranging themselves in their places in front of the cabin, that extended nearly the whole length of the boat, covering merchandize of immense value. As they left the shore, they gave the Indian yell; and broke out into a sort of unconnected chorus—commencing with—

"Hard upon the beech oar!—
She moves too slow!
All the way to Shawneetown,
Long while ago."

In a few minutes the boat "took the chute" of Letart's Falls, and disappeared behind the point, with the rapidity of an Arabian courser.

Our travellers returned to the boat, lost in speculation on the scene, and the beings they had just beheld; and, no doubt, the circumstance has been related a thousand times with all the necessary amplifications of finished tourists.

Mike Fink may be viewed, as the correct representative of a class of men now extinct; but who once possessed as marked a character, as that of the Gypsies of England, or the Lazaroni of Naples. The period of their existence was not more than a third of a century. The character was created by the introduction of trade on the Western waters; and ceased with the successful establishment of the steam boat.

There is something inexplicable in the fact, that there could be men found, for ordinary wages, who would abandon the systematic, but not laborious pursuits of agriculture, to follow a life, of all others, except that of the soldier, distinguished by the greatest exposure and privation. The occupation of a boatman was more calculated to destroy the constitution and to shorten life, than any other business. In ascending the river, it was a continued series of toil, rendered more irksome by the snail like rate, at which they moved. The boat was propelled by poles, against which the shoulder was placed; and the whole strength, and skill of the individual were applied in this manner. As the boatmen moved along the running board, with their heads nearly touching the plank on which they walked, the effect produced on the mind of an observer was similar to that on beholding the ox, rocking before an overloaded cart. Their bodies, naked to their waist for the purpose of moving with greater ease, and of enjoying the breeze of the river, were exposed to the burning suns of summer, and to the rains of autumn. After a hard day's push, they would take their "fillee," or ration of whiskey, and having swallowed a miserable supper of meat half burnt, and of bread half baked, stretch themselves without covering, on the deck, and slumber till the steersman's call invited them to the morning "fillee." Notwithstanding this, the boatman's life had charms as irresistible, as those presented by the splendid illusions of the stage. Sons abandoned the comfortable farms of their fathers, and apprentices fled from the service of their masters. There was a captivation in the idea of "going down the river"; and the youthful boatman who had "pushed a keel" from New Orleans, felt all the pride of a young merchant, after his first voyage to an English sea port. From an exclusive association together, they had formed a kind of slang peculiar to themselves; and from the constant exercise of wit, with "the squatters" on shore, and crews of other boats, they acquired a quickness, and smartness of vulgar retort, that was quite amusing. The frequent battles they were engaged in with the boatmen of different parts of the river, and with the less civilized inhabitants of the lower Ohio, and Mississippi, invested them with that ferocious reputation, which has made them spoken of throughout Europe.

On board of the boats thus navigated, our merchants entrusted valuable cargoes, without insurance, and with no other guarantee than the receipt of the steersman, who possessed no property but his boat; and the confidence so reposed was seldom abused.

Among these men, Mike Fink stood an acknowledged leader for many years. Endowed by nature with those qualities of intellect, that give the possessor influence, he would have been a conspicuous member of any society, in which his lot might have been cast. An acute observer of human nature has said—"Opportunity alone makes the hero. Change but their situations, and Caesar would have been but the best wrestler on the green." With a figure cast in a mould that added much of the symmetry of an Apollo to the limbs of a Hercules, he possessed gigantic strength; and accustomed from an early period of life to brave the dangers of a frontier life, his character was noted for the most daring intrepidity. At the court of Charlemagne, he might have been a Roland; with the Crusaders, he would have been the favourite of the Knight of the Lion-heart; and in our revolution, he would have ranked with the Morgans and Putnams of the day. He was the hero of a hundred fights, and the leader in a thousand daring adventures. From Pittsburg to St. Louis, and New Orleans, his fame was established. Every farmer on the shore kept on good terms with Mike—otherwise, there was no safety for his property. Wherever he was an enemy, like his great prototype, Rob Roy, he levied the contribution of Black Mail for the use of his boat. Often at night, when his tired companions slept, he would take an excursion of five or six miles, and return before morning, rich in spoil. On the Ohio, he was known among his companions by the appellation of the "Snapping Turtle"; and on the Mississippi, he was called "The Snag."

At the early age of seventeen, Mike's character was displayed, by enlisting himself in a corps of Scouts—a body of irregular rangers, which was employed on the North-western frontiers of Pennsylvania, to watch the Indians, and to give notice of any threatened inroad.

At that time, Pittsburg was on the extreme verge of white population, and the spies, who were constantly employed, generally extended their explorations forty or fifty miles to the west of this post.

They went out, singly, lived as did the Indian, and in every respect, became perfectly assimilated in habits, taste, and feeling, with the red men of the desert. A kind of border warfare was kept up, and the scout thought it as praiseworthy to bring in the scalp of a Shawnee, as the skin of a panther. He would remain in the woods for weeks together, using parched corn for bread, and depending on his rifle for his meat—and slept at night in perfect comfort, rolled in his blanket.

In this corps, whilst yet a stripling, Mike acquired a reputation for boldness, and cunning, far beyond his companions. A thousand legends illustrate the fearlessness of his character. There was one, which he told himself, with much pride, and which made an indelible impression on my boyish memory. He had been out on the hills of Mahoning, when, to use his own words, "he saw signs of Indians being about." —He had discovered the recent print of the moccasin on the grass; and found drops of fresh blood of a deer on the green bush. He became cautious, skulked for some time in the deepest thickets of hazel and briar; and, for several days, did not discharge his rifle. He subsisted patiently on parched corn and jerk, which he had dried on his first coming into the woods. He gave no alarm to the settlements, because he discovered with perfect certainty, that the enemy consisted of a small hunting party, who were receding from the Alleghany.

As he was creeping along one morning, with the stealthy tread of a cat, his eye fell upon a beautiful buck, browsing on the edge of a barren spot, three hundred yards distant. The temptation was too strong for the woodsman, and he resolved to have a shot at every hazard. Re-priming his gun, and picking his flint, he made his approaches in the usual noiseless manner. At the moment he reached the spot, from which he meant to take his aim, he observed a large savage, intent upon the same object, advancing from a direction a little different from his own. Mike shrunk behind a tree, with a quickness of thought, and keeping his eye fixed on the hunter, waited the result with patience. In a few moments, the Indian halted within fifty paces, and levelled his piece at the deer. In the meanwhile, Mike presented his rifle at the body of the savage; and at the moment the smoke issued from the gun of the latter, the bullet of Fink passed through the red man's breast. He uttered a yell, and fell dead at the same instant with the deer. Mike re-loaded his rifle, and remained in his covert for some minutes, to ascertain whether there were more enemies at hand. He then stepped up to the prostrate savage, and having satisfied himself, that life was extinguished, turned his attention to the buck, and took from the carcass those pieces, suited to the process of jerking.

In the meantime, the country was filling up with a white population; and in a few years the red men, with the exception of a few fractions

340

of tribes, gradually receded to the Lakes and beyond the Mississippi. The corps of Scouts was abolished, after having acquired habits, which unfitted them for the pursuits of civilized society. Some incorporated themselves with the Indians; and others, from a strong attachment to their erratic mode of life, joined the boatmen, then just becoming a distinct class. Among these was our hero, Mike Fink, whose talents were soon developed; and for many years, he was as celebrated on the rivers of the West, as he had been in the woods.

I gave to my fellow travellers the substance of the foregoing narrative, as we sat on deck by moonlight and cut swiftly through the magnificent sheet of water between Letart and the Great Kanhawa. It was one of those beautiful nights, which permitted every thing to be seen with sufficient distinctness to avoid danger;—yet created a certain degree of illusion, that gave reins to the imagination. The outline of the river hills lost all its harshness; and the occasional bark of the house dog from the shore, and the distant scream of the solitary loon, gave increased effect to the scene. It was altogether so delightful, that the hours till morning flew swiftly by, whilst our travellers dwelt with rapture on the surrounding scenery, which shifted every moment like the capricious changes of the kaleidoscope—and listening to the tales of border warfare, as they were brought to mind, by passing the places where they happened. The celebrated Hunter's Leap, and the bloody battle of Kanhawa, were not forgotten.

The afternoon of the next day brought us to the beautiful city of Cincinnati, which, in the course of thirty years, has risen from a village of soldiers' huts to a town,—giving promise of future splendour, equal to any on the sea-board.

Some years after the period, at which I have dated my visit to Cincinnati, business called me to New Orleans. On board of the steam boat, on which I had embarked, at Louisville, I recognised, in the person of the pilot, one of those men, who had formerly been a patroon, or keel boat captain. I entered into conversation with him on the subject of his former associates.

"They are scattered in all directions," said he. "A few, who had capacity, have become pilots of steam boats. Many have joined the trading parties that cross the Rocky mountains; and a few have settled down as farmers."

"What has become," I asked, "of my old acquaintance, Mike Fink?"

"Mike was killed in a skrimmage," replied the pilot. "He had refused several good offers on steam boats. He said he could not bear the hissing of steam, and he wanted room to throw his pole. He went to the Missouri, and about a year since was shooting the tin cup, when he had corned too heavy. He elevated too low, and shot his companion

341

through the head. A friend of the deceased, who was present, suspecting foul play, shot Mike through the heart, before he had time to reload his rifle."

With Mike Fink expired the spirit of the Boatmen.

Putting a Black-Leg on Shore

by BENJAMIN DRAKE, 1795–1841. *A younger brother of the celebrated Dr. Daniel Drake, Benjamin Drake was born at Mays Lick, Kentucky. After a rudimentary education he clerked in his brother's drug store at Cincinnati, spent a short time in business, and studied and practiced law until ill health forced him to stop. He early began to contribute to Cincinnati periodicals and from 1826 to 1834 he edited the Cincinnati Chronicle. He collaborated with E. D. Mansfield in publishing Cincinnati in 1826 (1827), a useful gazetteer, and subsequently he published lives of Black Hawk (1838), William Henry Harrison (1840), and Tecumseh (1841). Probably his best known work today is Tales and Sketches from the Queen City (1838), a volume picturing many aspects of frontier life with close fidelity. "Putting a Black-Leg on Shore" is one of these stories.*

A NUMEROUS and peculiar race of *modern* gentlemen, may be found in the valley of the Mississippi. A naturalist would probably describe them as a genus of bipeds, gregarious, amphibious and migratory. They seldom travel "solitary and alone"; are equally at home on land or water; and like certain vultures, spend most of their winters in Mississippi and Louisiana; their summers in the higher latitudes of Kentucky and Ohio. They dress with taste and elegance; carry gold chronometers in their pockets; and swear with the most genteel precision. They are supposed to entertain an especial abhorrence of the prevailing *temperance* fanaticism; and, as a matter of conscience, enter a daily protest against it, by sipping "mint-julaps" before breakfast, "hail-storms" at dinner, and "old Monongahela" at night. These gentlemen, moreover, are strong advocates of the race-path and the cock-pit; and, with a benevolence, which they hold to be truly commendable, patronise modest merit, by playing *chaperon* to those wealthy young men, who set out on the pilgrimage of life, before they have been fully initiated into its pleasures. Every where throughout the valley, these mistletoe gentry are called by the original, if not altogether classic, cognomen of "Black-legs." The history of this euphonious epithet, or the reason of its application to so distinguished a variety of humanity, is unknown. The subject is one of considerable interest, and worthy the early attention of the Historical Society, to which it is respectfully commended.

It was the fortune of the steam-boat Sea Serpent of Cincinnati, commanded by Captain Snake, on her return from New Orleans in the spring of 1837, to number among her cabin passengers, several highly respectable Black-Legs. One of them, Major Marshall Montgomery, a native of the "Old Dominion," belonged to the "Paul Clifford" school; and indeed, had, for some years past, borne testimony, to the merit of Mr. Bulwer's romances, by making the hero of one of them, his great prototype. In stature, the Major was over six feet, muscular, and finely proportioned. His taste in dress, was only surpassed by the courtliness of his manners, and the ready flow of his conversation. In what campaign he had won the laurels that gave him his military title, is unknown. It has been conjectured that the warlike prefix to his name, may have resulted from the luxuriant brace of black whiskers, which garnished his cheeks.

On a certain day, after dinner, the ladies having retired to their cabin for a *siesta*, the gentlemen, as usual, sat down to cards, chess and back-gammon. The boat had just "wooded," and was nobly breasting the current of the river at the rate of eight knots an hour. Captain Snake, having nothing else to do, was fain to join in a rubber of whist; and it so happened that he and the Major were seated at the same table. This game, at the suggestion of Major Montgomery, was soon changed to "loo"; and, played with varying success until at length, a pool of considerable magnitude had accumulated. As the contest for the increasing stake, advanced, much interest was excited among the by-standers, and still more in the players, with the exception of the Major, whose staid expression of countenance was a subject of general remark. He seemed careless about the run of the cards, and threw them, as if quite regardless of the tempting spoil that lay before him. At length the game was terminated. The fickle goddess disclosed her preference for the Major, by permitting him to win the "pool," amounting to near three hundred dollars. His success produced no outward signs of joy; he seemed, indeed, almost sorry to be compelled to take the money of his friends; and with much composure of manner, proposed to continue the play; making, at the same time, a very polite tender of his purse, to any gentleman at the table, who might need a temporary loan.

In the group of spectators, there was a tall, spindle-legged young fellow from the Western Reserve, in Ohio, who had been to the South with a lot of cheese, for the-manufacture of which, that thriving New England colony, is becoming quite famous. This cheese-monger had been watching the game from the beginning, and at last, fixing his eyes upon the winning Major, said, in a low, solemn tone of voice, suited to a more lugubrious subject,

"Well, now, that's right down slick, any how."

The Major, looking up, found the gaze of the company turned upon him. Knitting his brows he said, sternly, in reply,

"Let's have no more of your Yankee impertinence."

"Now, Mister," continued Jonathan in his drawling tone and with provoking coolness of manner, "you hadn't ought to let them there little speckled paste-boards, play hide and go seek in your coat sleeve."

This remark, accompanied with a knowing wink of the speaker's eye, instantly transformed the Major into a young earthquake. Springing upon his feet, as if bent on blood and carnage, he bawled out at the top of his voice,

"Do you mean to insinuate, you Yankee pedlar—you infernal wooden-nutmeg, that I have cheated?"

The young cheese merchant, leisurely rolling a huge cud of tobacco, from one cheek to the other, and looking the Major steadfastly in the eye, replied with imperturbable gravity,

"Why your the beatomest shakes, I ever seed: who insinevated that you cheated? I didn't, no how: but if you don't behave a little genteeler, I conclude I'll tell as how I seed you slip a card under your sleeve, when you won that everlasting big pond of money."

"You are a liar," thundered the Major, in a perfect whirlwind, at the same time attempting to bring his bamboo in contact with the shoulders of his antagonist; but Jonathan caught the descending cane in his left hand; and, in turn, planted his dexter fist, with considerable impulse, on the lower end of the Major's breast bone, remarking,

"I say Mister, make yourself skerse there, or you'll run right against the end of my arm."

Unfortunately for the reputation of Major Montgomery, at this moment, a card fell from his coat sleeve; and, with it, fell his courage, for he turned suddenly round to the table to secure the spoils of victory. The Captain however, had saved him the trouble, having himself taken up the money, for the purpose of returning it to those to whom it rightfully belonged. The Major finding that his winnings and his reputation were both departing, became once more, highly excited, and uttered direful anathemas against those, who might dare to question his honour.

It is, perhaps, generally known to the reader, that the captain of a steam boat on the western waters, is of necessity, almost as despotic as the Grand Turk. The safety of his boat, and the comfort of his passengers, in performing a long and perilous trip, require, indeed, that such should be the case. Between port and port, he is sometimes called to act in the triple capacity of legislator, judge and executioner. It is rumored, perhaps without any foundation, that in cases of great emergency, more than one of these commanders, have seriously threatened a resort to the salutory influence of the "second section." Be this as it may, travellers on our western boats will consult their comfort and safety, by deporting themselves according to the gentlemanly principle. We throw out this hint for the public generally; and, in the fulness of our benevolence, commend it to the especial notice of tourists from the "fast anchored Isle."

Captain Snake made no reply to the imprecations of the Major, having far too much respect for his official station, to permit himself to be drawn into a personal conflict with one of his passengers. Stepping to the cabin door, his clear shrill voice was heard above the din of the Major's volcanic burst of passion and the loud whiz of the Sea Serpent. Instantly the tinkle of the pilot's bell responded to the order of his commander, and the boat lay-to, near the lee shore. Again the Captain's voice was heard,

"Jack! man the yawl; Major Montgomery wishes to go on shore."

"Aye, aye, Sir."

The Major looked round in utter astonishment.—The Captain again called out,

"Steward! put Major Montgomery's trunk in the yawl; he wishes to go on shore!"

"Aye, aye, Sir!"

The Major turned towards the Captain with a face indicating a mingled feeling of anger and dismay.—He had seen too much of life in the West, not to understand the fate that awaited him. Before he could make up his mind as to the best mode of warding off the impending catastrophe, Jack bawled out, "the yawl is ready, sir," and, the steward cried, "the trunk is on board, sir."

Captain Snake, bowed formally, and with a courteous, but singularly emphatic manner, said:

"Major Montgomery, the yawl waits."

The Major, however, retained his position near the card-table, and began to remonstrate against such very exceptionable treatment of a Virginia gentleman, whose character had never been questioned. He concluded by a broad intimation, that on their arrival at Cincinnati, he should hold the captain personally responsible under the laws of honor.

In reply, the captain of the Sea Serpent, bowed again most profoundly, and turning toward the door of the cabin, said, calmly,

"Steward, call the Fireman to assist Major Montgomery into the yawl; he wishes to go on shore."

The redoubtable Major, in the vain hope that the passengers would sustain him in the contest, now threw himself on his reserved rights, ran up the flag of nullification, and ferociously brandished his Bowie knife: at this moment the Fireman made his appearance. He was a full grown Kentuckian, born on the cedar knobs of the Blue Licks, and raised on sulphur water, pone and 'possum fat.—Like many of his countrymen, he was an aspiring fellow, for he stood six-feet-four in his moccasins, and exhibited corresponding developments of bone and muscle. Hatless and coatless, with naked arms, and a face blackened with smoke and ashes, he might have passed for one of old Vulcan's journeymen, who had been forging thunderbolts for Jupiter, in some *regio-infernalis*. He stalked carelessly up to the bellicose Major, and before the latter was aware of it, seized the hand that held the upraised knife, and wrenched it from him. The next instant the Major found himself fairly within the brawny arms of his antagonist. He struggled stoutly to extricate his elegant person from such an unwelcome embrace, but in vain. The fireman, displeased with the restless disposition of his captive, gave him one of those warm fraternal hugs, which an old bear is wont to bestow upon an unmannerly dog, that may venture to annoy his retreat from a farmer's hog-pen. This loving squeeze so completely mollified the rebellious feelings of the Major, that he suffered himself to be passively led into the yawl. The Captain's shrill voice was again heard,

"Pull away, my boys, Major Montgomery wishes to go on shore."

The oars dipped into the water and the yawl glided quickly to the beach. The afternoon was cloudy and dark; a drizzling rain was falling; the cotton-wood trees wore a funeral aspect; no vestige of a human habitation could be seen upon either shore, and the turbid waters of the Mississippi, were hastening onwards, as if to escape from such a gloomy place.

Many of the passengers supposed that after the Major had been disgraced by being set on shore, he would be suffered to return; but those who entertained this opinion knew very little of the character of Captain Snake. That Major Montgomery should be a black-leg, was in his estimation, no very heinous affair; for he held that in this republican country, and this democratic age, every man has a natural and inalienable right to choose his own occupation: But after having been permitted to play "loo" with the Captain of the fast running Sea Serpent, that the Major should slip a card, and then, lubberly rascal, be caught at it,—this was too bad,—absolutely unpardonable: There was something so vulgar, so very unprofessional in such conduct, that it was not to be tolerated.

The yawl touched the shore and was hastily disburthened of its trunk. The Major, however, after rising on his feet, looked wistfully back upon the Sea Serpent, and manifested no disposition to take refuge in a cane-brake: Whereupon, the Capt. becoming impatient, cried out,

"Fireman, lend a hand to assist Major Montgomery on shore."

The huge Kentuckian now began to approach the Major, who, having no particular relish for another fraternal hug, sprung to the beach, and sunk to his knees in mud. Thinking forbearance no longer a virtue, he poured out on the Captain, a torrent of abuse: and, with wrathful oaths, threatened to publish him and his ugly, snail creeping steamer, from Olean Point to the alligator swamps of the Balize. The Captain made no reply, but the fireman, roused by hearing such opprobrious terms applied to his beloved Sea Serpent, called out in a voice, that was echoed from shore to shore,

"I say, Mr. Jack-of-knaves, it looks rather wolfy in these parts."

"Shut your black mouth, you scoundrel," retorted the Major, boiling over with rage.

"I say stranger," continued the fireman with provoking good humor, "would you swap them buffalo robes on your cheeks for a pair of 'coon-skins'?"

The Major stooped down for a stone to hurl at his annoying foe, but alas, he stood in a bed of mortar, and had no resource but that of firing another volley of curses.

"Halloo! my hearty," rejoined the fireman, "When you want to be rowed up 'salt river' again just tip me the wink; and remember Mr. King-of-Clubs, don't holler till you get out of the woods, or you'll frighten all the varmints."

During this colloquy, the young cheese-merchant, stood on the guards of the boat, a silent spectator; but at length, as if suddenly shocked by the dreadful profanity of the Major, he raised his voice and bawled out,

"I say Mister, if you was away down east, I guess 'squire Dagget would fine you ever so much, for swearing so wicked;—that's the how."

The pilot's bell tinkled, the wheels resumed their gyrations, and again the majestic Sea Serpent,

"Walked the waters like a thing of life."

Jonathan, with a look in which the solemn and comic were curiously blended, turned his eyes first towards the Captain, then upon the Major, and exclaimed,

"Well now the way these ere steam captains do things, is nothing to no body, no how."

And thus terminated one of those little episodes in the drama of life, not uncommon on the western Waters.

Keelboat Life

by SAMUEL LANGHORNE CLEMENS, 1835–1910. More famous as "Mark Twain," Clemens was born in Florida, Missouri. Four years after his birth the Clemens family removed to Hannibal, a sleepy river town which was to figure largely in Twain's writing. The boy's education was gained chiefly via the printing office, and when Twain left Hannibal in 1853 to see the world he followed his printer's craft in Keokuk, Philadelphia, and Cincinnati. In 1857 he boarded an Ohio River steamboat with the intention of going to South America; instead he became an apprentice to the famous pilot Horace Bixby, and until the Civil War closed the Mississippi Twain was connected with various river craft. After a farcical army experience Twain crossed the plains to Nevada and spent the next few years doing reporting, editing, and prospecting for gold in that state and in California. The publication of his jumping frog story in 1865 brought him his first writing fame. After the publication of Innocents Abroad (1869) and Roughing It (1872) his literary position was assured. In the next decade he published his best known works, Tom Sawyer (1876), Life on the Mississippi (1883), and Huckleberry Finn (1885). The closing years of his life found him as celebrated for his travels and his lecture appearances as he was for his books. His autobiography was published posthumously in 1924. "Keelboat Life," a selection from Life on the Mississippi, illustrates the idiom and character of the early river boatmen. It also reveals the exaggerations implicit in the tall tale.

BY WAY of illustrating keelboat talk and manners, and that now departed and hardly remembered raft-life, I will throw in, in this place, a chapter from a book which I have been working at, by fits and starts, during the past five or six years, and may possibly finish in the course of five or six more. The book is a story which details some passages in the life of an ignorant village boy, Huck Finn, son of the town drunkard of my time out West, there. He has run away from his persecuting father, and from a persecuting good widow who wishes to make a nice, truth-telling, respectable boy of him; and with him a slave of the widow's has also escaped. They have found a fragment of a lumber raft (it is high water and dead summer time), and are floating down the river by night, and hiding in the willows by day—bound for Cairo, whence the negro will seek freedom in the heart of the free States. But, in a fog, they pass Cairo without knowing it. By and by they begin to suspect the truth, and Huck Finn is persuaded to end the dismal suspense by swimming down to a huge raft which they have seen in the distance ahead of them, creeping aboard under cover of the darkness, and gathering the needed information by eavesdropping:

But you know a young person can't wait very well when he is impatient to find a thing out. We talked it over, and by and by Jim said it was such a black night, now, that it wouldn't be no risk to swim down to the big raft and crawl aboard and listen—they would talk about Cairo, because they would be calculating to go ashore there for a spree, maybe; or any way they would send boats ashore to buy whiskey or fresh meat or something. Jim had a wonderful level head, for a nigger; he could most always start a good plan when you wanted one.

I stood up and shook my rags off and jumped into the river, and struck out for the raft's light. By and by, when I got down nearly to her, I eased up and went slow and cautious. But every thing was all right—nobody at the sweeps. So I swum down along the raft till I was most abreast the camp fire in the middle, then I crawled aboard and inched along and got in among some bundles of shingles on the weather side of the fire. There was thirteen men there—they was the watch on deck of course. And a mighty rough-looking lot, too. They had a jug, and tin cups, and they kept the jug moving. One man was singing—roaring, you may say; and it wasn't a nice song—for a parlor, any way. He roared through his nose, and strung out the last word of every line very long. When he was done they all fetched a kind of Injun war-whoop, and then another was sung. It begun:

> "There was a woman in our towdn,
>> In our towdn did dwed'l [dwell],
> She loved her husband dear-i-lee,
>> But another man twyste as wed'l.

> "Singing too, riloo, riloo, riloo,
>> Ri-too, riloo, rilay—e,
> She loved her husband dear-i-lee,
>> But another man twyste as wed'l."

And so on—fourteen verses. It was kind of poor, and when he was going to start on the next verse one of them said it was the tune the old cow died on; and another one said, "Oh, give us a rest!" And another one told him to take a walk. They made fun of him till he got mad and jumped up and begun to cuss the crowd, and said he could lam any thief in the lot.

They was all about to make a break for him, but the biggest man there jumped up and says:

"Set whar you are, gentlemen. Leave him to me; he's my meat."

Then he jumped up in the air three times and cracked his heels together every time. He flung off a buckskin coat that was all hung with fringes, and says, "You lay thar tell the chawin-up's done"; and flung his hat down, which was all over ribbons, and says, "You lay thar tell his sufferin's is over."

Then he jumped up in the air and cracked his heels together again and shouted out:

"Whoo-oop! I'm the old original iron-jawed, brass-mounted, copper-bellied corpse-maker from the wilds of Arkansaw! Look at me! I'm the man they call Sudden Death and General Desolation! Sired by a hurricane, dam'd by an earthquake, half-brother to the cholera, nearly related to the small-pox on the mother's side! Look at me! I take nineteen alligators and a bar'l of whiskey for breakfast when I'm in robust health, and a bushel of rattle-snakes and a dead body when I'm ailing! I split the everlasting rocks with my glance, and I squench the thunder when I speak! Whoo-oop! Stand back and give me room according to my strength! Blood's my natural drink, and the wails of the dying is music to my ear! Cast your eye on me, gentlemen! and lay low and hold your breath, for I'm 'bout to turn myself loose!"

All the time he was getting this off, he was shaking his head and looking fierce, and kind of swelling around in a little circle, tucking up his wrist-bands, and now and then straightening up and beating his breast with his fist, saying, "Look at me, gentlemen!" When he got through, he jumped up and cracked his heels together three times, and let off a roaring "Whoo-oop! I'm the bloodiest son of a wildcat that lives!"

Then the man that had started the row tilted his old slouch hat down over his right eye; then he bent stooping forward, with his back sagged and his south end sticking out far, and his fists a-shoving out and drawing in in front of him, and so went around in a little circle about three times, swelling himself up and breathing hard. Then he straightened, and jumped up and cracked his heels together three times before he lit again (that made them cheer), and he begun to shout like this:

"Whoo-oop! bow your neck and spread, for the kingdom of sorrow's a-coming! Hold me down to the earth, for I feel my powers a-working! whoo-oop! I'm a child of sin, *don't* let me get a start! Smoked glass, here, for all! Don't attempt to look at me with the naked eye, gentlemen! When I'm playful I use the meridians of longitude and parallels of latitude for a seine, and drag the Atlantic Ocean for whales! I scratch my head with the lightning and purr myself to sleep with the thunder! When I'm cold, I bile the Gulf of Mexico and bathe in it; when I'm hot I fan myself with an equinoctial storm; when I'm thirsty I reach up and suck a cloud dry like a sponge; when I range the earth hungry, famine follows in my tracks! Whoo-oop! Bow your neck and spread! I put my hand on the sun's face and make it night in the earth; I bite a piece out of the moon and hurry the seasons; I shake myself and crumble the mountains! Contemplate me through leather—*don't* use the naked eye! I'm the man with a petrified heart and biler-iron bowels! The massacre of isolated communities is the pastime of my idle moments, the destruction of nationalities the serious business of my life! The boundless vastness of the great American desert is my enclosed property, and I bury my dead on my own premises!" He jumped up and cracked his heels together three times before he lit (they cheered him again), and as he come down he shouted out: "Whoo-oop! bow your neck and spread, for the Pet Child of Calamity's a-coming!"

Then the other one went to swelling around and blowing again—the first one—the one they called Bob; next, the Child of Calamity chipped in again, bigger than ever; then they both got at it at the same time, swelling round and round each other and punching their fists most into each other's faces, and whooping and jawing like Injuns; then Bob called the Child names, and the Child called him names back again; next, Bob called him a heap rougher names, and the Child come back at him with the very worst kind of language; next, Bob knocked the Child's hat off, and the Child picked it up and kicked Bob's ribbony hat about six foot; Bob went and got it and said never mind, this warn't going to be the last of this thing, because he was a man that never forgot and never forgive, and so the Child better look out, for there was a time a-coming, just as sure as he was a living man, that he would have to answer to him with the best blood in his body. The Child said no man was willinger than he for that time to come, and he would give Bob fair warning, *now*, never to cross his path again, for he could never rest till he had waded in his blood, for such was his nature, though he was sparing him now on account of his family, if he had one.

Both of them was edging away in different directions, growling and shaking their heads and going on about what they was going to do; but a little black-whiskered chap skipped up and says:

"Come back here, you couple of chicken-livered cowards, and I'll thrash the two of ye!"

351

And he done it, too. He snatched them, he jerked them this way and that, he booted them around, he knocked them sprawling faster than they could get up. Why, it warn't two minutes till they begged like dogs—and how the other lot did yell and laugh and clap their hands all the way through, and shout "Sail in, Corpse-Maker!" "Hi! at him again, Child of Calamity!" "Bully for you, little Davy!" Well, it was a perfect pow-wow for a while. Bob and the Child had red noses and black eyes when they got through. Little Davy made them own up that they was sneaks and cowards and not fit to eat with a dog or drink with a nigger; then Bob and the Child shook hands with each other, very solemn, and said they had always respected each other and was willing to let bygones be bygones. So then they washed their faces in the river; and just then there was a loud order to stand by for a crossing, and some of them went forward to man the sweeps there, and the rest went aft to handle the after sweeps.

I lay still and waited for fifteen minutes, and had a smoke out of a pipe that one of them left in reach; then the crossing was finished, and they stumped back and had a drink around and went to talking and singing again. Next they got out an old fiddle, and one played, and another patted juba, and the rest turned themselves loose on a regular old-fashioned keelboat break-down. They couldn't keep that up very long without getting winded, so by and by they settled around the jug again.

They sung "Jolly, Jolly Raftsman's the Life for Me," with a rousing chorus, and then they got to talking about differences betwixt hogs, and their different kind of habits; and next about women and their different ways; and next about the best ways to put out houses that was afire; and next about what ought to be done with the Injuns; and next about what a king had to do, and how much he got; and next about how to make cats fight; and next about what to do when a man has fits; and next about differences betwixt clear-water rivers and muddy-water ones. The man they called Ed said the muddy Mississippi water was wholesomer to drink than the clear water of the Ohio; he said if you let a pint of this yaller Mississippi water settle, you would have about a half to three-quarters of an inch of mud in the bottom, according to the stage of the river, and then it warn't no better than Ohio water—what you wanted to do was to keep it stirred up—and when the river was low, keep mud on hand to put in and thicken the water up the way it ought to be.

The Child of Calamity said that was so; he said there was nutritiousness in the mud, and a man that drunk Mississippi water could grow corn in his stomach if he wanted to. He says:

"You look at the graveyards; that tells the tale. Trees won't grow worth shucks in a Cincinnati graveyard, but in a Sent Louis graveyard they grow upwards of eight hundred foot high. It's all on account of the water the people drunk before they laid up. A Cincinnati corpse don't richen a soil any."

And they talked about how Ohio water didn't like to mix with Mississippi water. Ed said if you take the Mississippi on a rise when the Ohio is low, you'll find a wide band of clear water all the way down the east side of the Mississippi for a hundred mile or more, and the minute you get out a quarter of a mile from shore and pass the line, it is all thick and yaller the rest of the way across. Then they talked about how to keep tobacco from getting mouldy, and from that they went into ghosts and told about a lot that other folks had seen; but Ed says:

"Why don't you tell something that you've seen yourselves? Now let me have a say. Five years ago I was on a raft as big as this, and right along here it was a bright moonshiny night, and I was on watch and boss of the stabboard oar forrard, and one of my pards was a man named Dick Allbright, and he come along to where I was sitting, forrard—gaping and stretching, he was—and stooped down on the edge of the raft and washed his face in the river, and come and set down by me and got out his pipe, and had just got it filled, when he looks up and says:

" 'Why looky-here,' he says, 'ain't that Buck Miller's place, over yander in the bend?'

" 'Yes,' says I, 'it is—why?' He laid his pipe down and leant his head on his hand, and says:

" 'I thought we'd be furder down.' I says:

" 'I thought it too, when I went off watch'—we was standing six hours on and six off—'but the boys told me,' I says, 'that the raft didn't seem to hardly move, for the last hour,' says I, 'though she's a-slipping along all right, now,' says I. He give a kind of a groan, and says:

" 'I've seed a raft act so before, along here,' he says, ' 'pears to me the current has most quit above the head of this bend durin' the last two years,' he says.

"Well, he raised up two or three times, and looked away off and around on the water. That started me at it too. A body is always doing what he sees somebody else doing, though there mayn't be no sense in it. Pretty soon I see a black something floating on the water away off to stabboard and quartering behind us. I see he was looking at it, too. I says:

" 'What's that?' He says, sort of pettish:

" 'Tain't nothing but an old empty bar'l.'

" 'An empty bar'l!' says I, 'why,' says I, 'a spy-glass is a fool to *your* eyes. How can you tell it's an empty bar'l?' He says:

353

" 'I don't know; I reckon it ain't a bar'l, but I thought it might be,' says he.

" 'Yes,' I says, 'so it might be, and it might be any thing else, too; a body can't tell nothing about it, such a distance as that,' I says.

"We hadn't nothing else to do, so we kept on watching it. By-and-by I says:

" 'Why looky-here, Dick Allbright, that thing's a-gaining on us, I believe.'

"He never said nothing. The thing gained and gained, and I judged it must be a dog that was about tired out. Well, we swung down into the crossing, and the thing floated across the bright streak of the moonshine, and, by George, it *was* a bar'l. Says I:

" 'Dick Allbright, what made you think that thing was a bar'l, when it was half a mile off?' says I. Says he:

" 'I don't know.' Says I:

" 'You tell me, Dick Allbright.' He says:

" 'Well, I knowed it was a bar'l; I've seen it before; lots has seen it; they says it's a ha'nted bar'l.'

"I called the rest of the watch, and they come and stood there, and I told them what Dick said. It floated right along abreast, now, and didn't gain any more. It was about twenty foot off. Some was for having it aboard, but the rest didn't want to. Dick Allbright said rafts that had fooled with it had got bad luck by it. The captain of the watch said he didn't believe in it. He said he reckoned the bar'l gained on us because it was in a little better current than what we was. He said it would leave by-and-by.

"So then we went to talking about other things, and we had a song, and then a break-down; and after that the captain of the watch called for another song; but it was clouding up, now, and the bar'l stuck right thar in the same place, and the song didn't seem to have much warm-up to it, somehow, and so they didn't finish it, and there warn't any cheers, but it sort of dropped flat, and nobody said any thing for a minute. Then everybody tried to talk at once, and one chap got off a joke, but it warn't no use, they didn't laugh, and even the chap that made the joke didn't laugh at it, which ain't usual. We all just settled down glum, and watched the bar'l, and was oneasy and oncomfortable. Well, sir, it shut down black and still, and then the wind began to moan around, and next the lightning began to play and the thunder to grumble. And pretty soon there was a regular storm, and in the middle of it a man that was running aft stumbled and fell and sprained his ankle so that he had to lay up. This made the boys shake their heads. And every time the lightning come, there was that bar'l with the blue lights winking around it. We was always on the look-out for it. But by-and-by, toward dawn, she was gone. When the day come we couldn't see her anywhere, and we warn't sorry, neither.

"But the next night about half past nine, when there was songs and high jinks going on, here she comes again, and took her old roost on the stabboard side. There warn't no more high jinks. Every-body got solemn; nobody talked; you couldn't get any body to do anything but set around moody and look at the bar'l. It begun to cloud up again. When the watch changed, the off watch stayed up, 'stead of turning in. The storm ripped and roared around all night, and in the middle of it another man tripped and sprained his ankle, and had to knock off. The bar'l left toward day, and nobody see it go.

"Every-body was sober and down in the mouth all day. I don't mean the kind of sober that comes of leaving liquor alone—not that. They was quiet, but they all drunk more than usual—not together, but each man sidled off and took it private, by himself.

"After dark the off watch didn't turn in; nobody sung, nobody talked; the boys didn't scatter around, neither; they sort of huddled together, forrard; and for two hours they set there, perfectly still, looking steady in the one direction, and heaving a sigh once in a while. And then, here comes the bar'l again. She took up her old place. She stayed there all night; nobody turned in. The storm come on again, after midnight. It got awful dark; the rain poured down; hail, too; the thunder boomed and roared and bellowed; the wind blowed a hurricane; and the lightning spread over every thing in big sheets of glare, and showed the whole raft as plain as day; and the river lashed up white as milk as far as you could see for miles, and there was that bar'l jiggering along, same as ever. The captain ordered the watch to man the after sweeps for a crossing, and nobody would go—no more sprained ankles for them, they said. They wouldn't even *walk* aft. Well then, just then the sky split wide open, with a crash, and the lightning killed two men of the after watch, and crippled two more. Crippled them how, say you? Why, *sprained their ankles!*

"The bar'l left in the dark betwixt lightnings, toward dawn. Well, not a body eat a bite at breakfast that morning. After that the men loafed around, in twos and threes, and talked low together. But none of them herded with Dick Allbright. They all give him the cold shake. If he come around where any of the men was, they split up and sidled away. They wouldn't man the sweeps with him. The captain had all the skiffs hauled up on the raft, alongside of his wigwam, and wouldn't let the dead men be took ashore to be planted; he didn't believe a man that got ashore would come back; and he was right.

"After night come, you could see pretty plain that there was going to be trouble if that bar'l come again; there was such a muttering going on. A good many wanted to kill Dick Allbright, because he'd seen the bar'l on other trips, and that had an ugly look. Some wanted to put him ashore. Some said, 'Let's all go ashore in a pile, if the bar'l comes again.'

"This kind of whispers was still going on, the men being bunched together forrard watching for the bar'l, when lo and behold you! here she comes again. Down she comes, slow and steady, and settles into her old tracks. You could 'a' heard a pin drop. Then up comes the captain, and says:

" 'Boys, don't be a pack of children and fools; I don't want this bar'l to be dogging us all the way to Orleans, and *you* don't; well, then, how's the best way to stop it? Burn it up—that's the way. I'm going to fetch it aboard,' he says. And before any body could say a word, in he went.

"He swum to it, and as he come pushing it to the raft, the men spread to one side. But the old man got it aboard and busted in the head, and there was a baby in it! Yes, sir; a stark-naked baby. It was Dick Allbright's baby; he owned up and said so.

" 'Yes,' he says, a-leaning over it, 'yes, it is my own lamented darling, my poor lost Charles William Allbright deceased,' says he—for he could curl his tongue around the bulliest words in the language when he was a mind to, and lay them before you without a jint started, anywheres. Yes, he said, he used to live up at the head of this bend, and one night he choked his child, which was crying, not intending to kill it,—which was prob'ly a lie,—and then he was scared, and buried it in a bar'l, before his wife got home, and off he went, and struck the northern trail and went to rafting; and this was the third year that the bar'l had chased him. He said the bad luck always begun light, and lasted till four men was killed, and then the bar'l didn't come any more, after that. He said if the men would stand it one more night,—and was a-going on like that,—but the men had got enough. They started to get out a boat to take him ashore and lynch him, but he grabbed the little child all of a sudden and jumped overboard with it hugged up to his breast and shedding tears, and we never see him again in this life, poor old suffering soul, nor Charles William neither."

"*Who* was shedding tears?" says Bob; "was it Allbright or the baby?"

"Why, Allbright, of course; didn't I tell you the baby was dead? Been dead three years—how could it cry?"

"Well, never mind how it could cry—how could it *keep* all that time?" says Davy. "You answer me that."

"I don't know how it done it," says Ed. "It done it though—that's all I know about it."

"Say—what did they do with the bar'l?" says the Child of Calamity.

"Why, they hove it overboard, and it sunk like a chunk of lead."

356

"Edward, did the child look like it was choked?" says one.

"Did it have its hair parted?" says another.

"What was the brand on that bar'l, Eddy?" says a fellow they called Bill.

"Have you got the papers for them statistics, Edmund?" says Jimmy.

"Say, Edwin, was you one of the men that was killed by the lightning?" says Davy.

"Him? Oh, no! he was both of 'em," says Bob. Then they all hawhawed.

"Say, Edward, don't you reckon you'd better take a pill? You look bad—don't you feel pale?" says the Child of Calamity.

"Oh, come, now, Eddy," says Jimmy, "show up; you must 'a' kept part of that bar'l to prove the thing by. Show us the bunghole—*do*—and we'll all believe you."

"Say boys," says Bill, "Less divide it up. Thar's thirteen of us. I can swaller a thirteenth of the yarn, if you can worry down the rest."

Ed got up mad and said they could all go to some place which he ripped out pretty savage, and then walked off aft, cussing to himself, and they yelling and jeering at him, and roaring and laughing so you could hear them a mile.

"Boys, we'll split a watermelon on that," says the Child of Calamity; and he came rummaging around in the dark amongst the shingle bundles where I was, and put his hand on me. I was warm and soft and naked; so he says "Ouch!" and jumped back.

"Fetch a lantern or a chunk of fire here, boys—there's a snake here as big as a cow!"

So they run there with a lantern and crowded up and looked in on me.

"Come out of that, you beggar!" says one.

"Who are you?" says another.

"What are you after here? Speak up prompt, or overboard you go."

"Snake him out, boys. Snatch him out by the heels."

I began to beg, and crept out amongst them trembling. They looked me over, wondering, and the Child of Calamity says:

"A cussed thief! Lend a hand and less heave him overboard!"

"No," says Big Bob, "less get out the paint-pot and paint him a skyblue all over from head to heel, and *then* heave him over!"

"Good! that's it. Go for the paint, Jimmy."

When the paint come, and Bob took the brush and was just going to begin, the others laughing and rubbing their hands, I begun to cry, and that sort of worked on Davy, and he says:

" 'Vast there! He's nothing but a cub. I'll paint the man that teches him!"

357

So I looked around on them, and some of them grumbled and growled, and Bob put down the paint, and the others didn't take it up.

"Come here to the fire, and less see what you're up to here," says Davy. "Now set down there and give an account of yourself. How long have you been aboard here?"

"Not over a quarter of a minute, sir," says I.

"How did you get dry so quick?"

"I don't know, sir. I'm always that way, mostly."

"Oh, you are, are you? What's your name?"

I warn't going to tell my name. I didn't know what to say, so I just says:

"Charles William Allbright, sir."

Then they roared—the whole crowd, and I was mighty glad I said that, because, maybe, laughing would get them in a better humor.

When they got done laughing, Davy says:

"It won't hardly do, Charles William. You couldn't have growed this much in five year, and you was a baby when you come out of the bar'l, you know, and dead at that. Come, now, tell a straight story, and nobody'll hurt you, if you ain't up to any thing wrong. What *is* your name?"

"Aleck Hopkins, sir. Aleck James Hopkins."

"Well, Aleck, where did you come from, here?"

"From a trading scow. She lays up the bend yonder. I was born on her. Pap has traded up and down here all his life; and he told me to swim off here, because when you went by he said he would like to get some of you to speak to a Mr. Jonas Turner, in Cairo, and tell him—"

"Oh, come!"

"Yes, sir, it's as true as the world. Pap he says—"

"Oh, your grandmother!"

They all laughed, and I tried again to talk, but they broke in on me and stopped me.

"Now, looky-here," says Davy; "you're scared, and so you talk wild. Honest, now, do you live in a scow, or is it a lie?"

"Yes, sir, in a trading scow. She lays up at the head of the bend. But I warn't born in her. It's our first trip."

"Now you're talking! What did you come aboard here for? To steal?"

"No, sir, I didn't. It was only to get a ride on the raft. All boys does that."

"Well, I know that. But what did you hide for?"

"Sometimes they drive the boys off."

"So they do. They might steal. Looky-here; if we let you off this time, will you keep out of these kind of scrapes hereafter?"

358

" 'Deed I will, boss. You try me."

"All right, then. You ain't but little ways from shore. Overboard with you, and don't you make a fool of yourself another time this way. Blast it, boy, some raftsmen would rawhide you till you were black and blue!"

I didn't wait to kiss good-by, but went overboard and broke for shore. When Jim come along by and by, the big raft was away out of sight around the point. I swum out and got aboard, and was mighty glad to see home again.

The boy did not get the information he was after, but his adventure has furnished the glimpse of the departed raftsman and keelboatman which I desire to offer in this place.

Jim Bludso, of the Prairie Belle

by JOHN HAY, 1838–1905. Born in Salem, Indiana, Hay grew up in Warsaw, Illinois, and was graduated from Brown University, B.A., 1858. He then began the study of law in Springfield, Illinois, next door to Lincoln's office. From 1861 to Lincoln's death Hay served as his secretary and later collaborated with John Nicolay in a life of the president (1890). Hay's closing years were devoted to journalism and diplomacy; after work on the New York Tribune he was ambassador to Great Britain in 1897, and from 1898 to his death was Secretary of State. Besides his life of Lincoln, Hay wrote a book of Spanish travel, Castilian Days (1871), and a realistic economic novel, The Breadwinners (1884). But he is probably best remembered as the author of such Pike County ballads as "Jim Bludso" and "Little Breeches."

> WALL, no! I can't tell whar he lives,
>   Becase he don't live, you see;
> Leastways, he's got out of the habit
>   Of livin' like you and me.
> Whar have you been for the last three year
>   That you haven't heard folks tell
> How Jimmy Bludso passed in his checks
>   The night of the Prairie Belle?

He weren't no saint,—them engineers
  Is all pretty much alike,—
One wife in Natchez-under-the-Hill
  And another one here, in Pike;
A keerless man in his talk was Jim,
  And an awkward hand in a row,
But he never flunked, and he never lied,—
  I reckon he never knowed how.

And this was all the religion he had,—
  To treat his engine well;
Never be passed on the river;
  To mind the pilot's bell;
And if ever the Prairie Belle took fire,—
  A thousand times he swore,
He'd hold her nozzle agin the bank
  Till the last soul got ashore.

All boats has their day on the Mississip,
  And her day come at last,—
The Movastar was a better boat,
  But the Belle she *wouldn't* be passed.
And so she come tearin' along that night—
  The oldest craft on the line—
With a nigger squat on her safety-valve,
  And her furnace crammed, rosin and pine.

The fire bust out as she clared the bar,
  And burnt a hole in the night,
And quick as a flash she turned, and made
  For that willer-bank on the right.
There was runnin' and cursin', but Jim yelled out,
  Over all the infernal roar,
"I'll hold her nozzle agin the bank
  Till the last galoot's ashore."

Through the hot, black breath of the burnin' boat
  Jim Bludso's voice was heard,
And they all had trust in his cussedness,
  And knowed he would keep his word.
And, sure's you're born, they all got off
  Afore the smokestacks fell,—
And Bludso's ghost went up alone
  In the smoke of the Prairie Belle.

360

He weren't no saint,—but at jedgment
I'd run my chance with Jim,
'Longside of some pious gentlemen
That wouldn't shook hands with him.
He seen his duty, a dead-sure thing,—
And went for it thar and then;
And Christ ain't a going to be too hard
On a man that died for men.

The "Fashionable Tour" on the Upper Mississippi

by THEODORE C. BLEGEN, 1891.— . *Born in Minneapolis and educated at the University of Minnesota, B.A., 1912, Ph.D., 1925, Dr. Blegen has taught history at Hamline University and the University of Minnesota. From 1922 to 1939 he was assistant superintendent and later superintendent of the Minnesota Historical Society, and since 1940 he has been dean of the Graduate School of the University of Minnesota. A Guggenheim fellowship enabled him to do work in Norway on Norwegian immigration to the United States, a subject on which he has published two definitive volumes: Norwegian Migration to America, 1825–1860 (1931), and Norwegian Migration to America: The American Transition (1940). Among his numerous other articles and books are an edition of Henry Hastings Sibley's autobiography (1932), and Building Minnesota (1938). The account of fashionable travel on the Mississippi River, which appeared in Minnesota History, December 1939, illustrates the rare combination of careful research and popular appeal.*

From the days of trail blazer and trader to those of lumberman, farmer, and town builder, rivers have been of great importance to the Northwest; and one in particular captured the imagination of the pioneers—the Mississippi. It was the path of explorer and voyageur, the line of steamboat pageantry, the route of incoming settlers, the link of frontier with civilization. To all it was dignified by the term "the river"; and it is still "the river"—great in its sweep from Itasca to the sea, great in its span of the nation's history, great, too, in its role in American life. The very magnitude of "the river," geographically, historically, and in many-sided interest, perhaps explains why no historian has yet succeeded in writing the book of the Mississippi—a

361

magnum opus that tells the story in its full range and interprets it in all its varied aspects. One must turn to Mark Twain, to the poets and singers, to the narratives of old steamboat men, and a hundred other sources to understand the meaning of the Mississippi and to know the glamor of the "War Eagle," the "Northern Belle," "Time and Tide," and other steamboats that churned its waters. The historians are doing their part, however, for they are piecing together this chapter and that in the story, hunting out and preserving the old records, and gradually building up materials for a broad history of the Mississippi.[1]

That history should include some account of the beginnings of the Northwest tourist trade, which has become, we are told, a major industry. It was the Mississippi and its steamboats that inaugurated the trade and spread the fame of Minnesota as a vacation land, promising to the enterprising tourist the adventure of a journey to a remote frontier coupled with the enjoyment of picturesque scenery and of good fishing and hunting.

Giacomo Beltrami, a passenger on the "Virginia" when that first steamboat on the upper river made its maiden journey in 1823, may perhaps be called the first modern tourist of Minnesota. The mercurial Italian was bent on a voyage of exploration, but he traveled up the Mississippi as a tourist who compared the wonders of its towering bluffs and wooded hillsides with the scenery of the Rhine. Beltrami recorded the astonishment of the Indians when they viewed the boat on which he was traveling. "I know not what impression the first sight of the Phœnician vessels might make on the inhabitants of the coast of Greece; or the Triremi of the Romans on the wild natives of Iberia, Gaul, or Britain," he wrote, "but I am sure it could not be stronger than that which I saw on the countenances of these savages at the arrival of our steam-boat." Some "thought it a monster vomiting fire, others the dwelling of the Manitous, but all approached it with reverence or fear."[2]

To another traveler goes the distinction of calling attention to the vacation possibilities of an upper Mississippi journey and also of giving it a slogan-like name. George Catlin, the well-known artist of American Indian life, made a trip by steamboat up the Mississippi from St. Louis to Fort Snelling and the Falls of St. Anthony in 1835. "The majestic river from the Balize to the Fall of St. Anthony, I have just passed

[1] Two recent publications of much interest and value are William J. Petersen, *Steamboating on the Upper Mississippi* (Iowa City, Iowa, 1937), and Mildred L. Hartsough, *From Canoe to Steel Barge on the Upper Mississippi* (Minneapolis, 1934).

[2] Giacomo C. Beltrami, *A Pilgrimage in Europe and America*, 2:199, 200 (London, 1828).

over; with a high-wrought mind filled with amazement and wonder," he wrote.

"All that can be seen on the Mississippi below St. Louis, or for several hundred miles above it, gives no hint or clue to the magnificence of the scenes which are continually opening to the eye of the traveller, and riveting him to the deck of the steamer, through sunshine, lightning or rain, from the mouth of the Ouisconsin to the Fall of St. Anthony."

After describing the scenery above Prairie du Chien he said, "I leave it for the world to come and gaze upon for themselves." He proposed a "Fashionable Tour"—a trip "by steamer to Rock Island, Galena, Dubuque, Prairie du Chien, Lake Pepin, St. Peters, Fall of St. Anthony," and he expressed the opinion that

"This Tour would comprehend but a small part of the great 'Far West'; but it will furnish to the traveller a fair sample, and being a part of it which is now made so easily accessible to the world, and the only part of it to which *ladies* can have access, I would recommend to all who have time and inclination to devote to the enjoyment of so splendid a Tour, to wait not, but make it while the subject is new, and capable of producing the greatest degree of pleasure." [3]

One wonders why the modern boosters of Minnesota and the Northwest have not built a monument to George Catlin.

The idea of a "Fashionable Tour" up the Mississippi quickly spread. Each year saw increasing numbers of sight-seers who took Catlin's advice. Most of them in the earlier years were men, but there were a few women who were willing to hazard the dangers of a journey to the outposts of America. One of these, a vivacious lady of eighty years, was none other than Elizabeth Schuyler Hamilton, the widow of Alexander Hamilton. She had gone west to visit her son William in Wisconsin in the summer of 1837 and decided "to ascend the Mississippi to the St. Peter's." She journeyed to Fort Snelling on the new steamboat "Burlington," saw the Falls of St. Anthony and Minnehaha, and, as befitted a queen of fashion, was accorded a royal reception by the officers of the fort. "A carpet had been spread," wrote a friend of Mrs. Hamilton, "an armchair [was] ready to receive her, the troops were under arms, we passed between two double rows of soldiers, and a very fine band was playing." [4]

The "Fashionable Tour" was stamped with the approval of this distinguished lady, who was delighted with the Minnesota country and

[3] George Catlin, *Letters and Notes on the Manners, Customs, and Condition of the North American Indians*, 2:590–592 (Philadelphia, 1857).
[4] Joseph Schafer, "High Society in Pioneer Wisconsin," in *Wisconsin Magazine of History*, 20:449 (June, 1937).

her experiences. The next year, in 1838, Captain Frederick Marryat, the author of *Mr. Midshipman Easy,* traveled up the river, saw the sights, witnessed a game of la crosse, which curiously he said was "somewhat similar to the game of golf in Scotland," and studied "the Indians in their primitive state." [5] His *Diary in America,* published in England in 1839, recorded the entire experience—and his was but one of many narratives putting before the world the story of travel on the upper Mississippi. Something more was needed, however, to establish the popularity of the "Fashionable Tour." The impetus came from the motion pictures of our grandfathers, the panoramas, great unwinding rolls of painted canvas which artists exhibited in America and Europe to the accompaniment of lectures. As early as 1839 John Rowson Smith and John Risley presented a panorama of the upper valley. About a decade later John Banvard showed to the world a vast panorama of the Mississippi. His canvas, with its many scenes, was three miles long, but unhappily it portrayed only the river below St. Louis. By 1849, however, three more Mississippi panoramas were giving the public a demonstration of the potential delights of the "Fashionable Tour." Henry Lewis had spent the summer of 1848 making a leisurely tour of the river between St. Louis and Fort Snelling and the next year began to exhibit his famous panorama, a canvas twelve hundred yards long and twelve feet high. Leon Pomarede and S. B. Stockwell, both associates of Lewis, soon had competing panoramas on display, and by the end of the 1850's there were eight or ten panoramas of the upper Mississippi touring the show halls of the nation.[6]

The panoramists tried to picture in faithful detail not only the river but also the life alongside it—the native Indians and their villages and the American towns and cities. In their attempts at realistic effects they used ingenious devices. Pomarede, for example, somehow managed to make real smoke and steam roll from the steamboats in his pictures.[7] And yet the artists felt the inadequacy of their efforts. Lewis wrote in his diary one day, "As I looked I felt how hopeless art was to convay the *soul* of such a scene as this and as the poet wishes for the pencil of the artist so did I for the power of descript[i]on to tell of the thousand thoughts fast crowding each other from my mind." [8]

Crowds of people went to see these travel movies of the 1840's and

[5] Frederick Marryat, *A Diary in America, with Remarks on Its Institutions,* 2:78–124 (London, 1839). This section of Captain Marryat's narrative is reprinted in *Minnesota History,* 6:168–184.

[6] Bertha L. Heilbron, ed., *Making a Motion Picture in 1848: Henry Lewis' Journal of a Canoe Voyage from the Falls of St. Anthony to St. Louis,* 3–11 (St. Paul, 1936).

[7] Heilbron, ed., *Making a Motion Picture in 1848,* 7.

[8] Heilbron, ed., *Making a Motion Picture in 1848,* 35. The scene that provoked this comment was that from Trempealeau Mountain, looking north.

1850's and thus toured the great river vicariously. The throngs that wished to view Banvard's panorama were so great when it was displayed in Boston and New York that railroads ran special excursions to accommodate them. In these two cities alone more than four hundred thousand people saw the exhibition. "The river comes to me instead of my going to the river," wrote Longfellow. Whittier, after seeing a panorama, sang of the "new Canaan of our Israel," and Thoreau, who not only viewed a panorama but also made the tour itself, envisaged a coming heroic age in which simple and obscure men, the real heroes of history, would build the foundations of new castles in the West and throw bridges across a "Rhine stream of a different kind." Risley's canvas, unwound before audiences in Oslo in 1852, touched the imagination of the Norwegian poet Vinje, who came away from the exhibition convinced that America was destined to conquer the world. Banvard had a run of twenty months in London, with admissions exceeding six hundred thousand.[9]

Meanwhile, people were coming singly, in honeymoon couples, in small groups, and sometimes in parties of hundreds to make the tour portrayed in the panoramas. Sometimes they chartered boats to carry them up the river and back, and often the steamboat companies, with an eye to increasing business, organized excursions of their own, advertising their plans far in advance through newspaper announcements and offering low rates. Such excursions were conducted from places as far away as New Orleans and Pittsburgh. Ordinarily the fare from St. Louis to St. Paul was $12.00. From Galena it was $6.00, though rate wars brought it at times as low as $1.00. The tours were made expeditiously. In 1850, for example, the "Dr. Franklin" left Galena on Thursday, spent one day in St. Paul, and was back to Galena on Tuesday. The round trip from St. Louis normally took eight or nine days, but might be made in six or seven on speedy boats. The idea of excursion boats reserved for patrons of the "Fashionable Tour" captured the fancy of travelers, and by the late 1830's such outings were not uncommon on the upper Mississippi.[10] The tourists could view the scenery, see Indians at first hand, and enjoy their vacations without the hubbub and the annoyances encountered on vessels heavily loaded with freight for the frontier forts or fur-trading stations.

As the fame of the upper Mississippi Valley spread, travelers from

[9] Dorothy Dondore, "Banvard's Panorama and the Flowering of New England," in *New England Quarterly*, 11:821–826 (December, 1938); Theodore C. Blegen, *Norwegian Migration to America, 1825–1860*, 342, 343n. (Northfield, 1931); Heilbron, ed., *Making a Motion Picture in 1848*, 4.

[10] Hartsough, *From Canoe to Steel Barge*, 163, 164; *Minnesota Chronicle and Register* (St. Paul), August 12, 1850; Petersen, *Steamboating on the Upper Mississippi*, 256, 260, 261.

365

the far South and the East increased in number. By the middle 1840's tourists from New York, Washington, Pittsburgh, and Cincinnati, as well as from New Orleans, St. Louis, and Galena were making the trip. Each traveler helped to spread the story of what was to be seen from the decks of a steamboat pushing upstream to old Fort Snelling.

The time came when one could go all the way from the East to the Mississippi by rail. The "Fashionable Tour" was thus brought more easily within the range of possibility for thousands of people. When the Rock Island Railroad was completed from Chicago to the Mississippi River in 1854, a special celebration was arranged which included a voyage in chartered steamboats up the river from Rock Island to St. Paul.[11] Twelve hundred persons in a flotilla of seven steamboats made the tour commemorating this union of steel and water. The party included ex-President Millard Fillmore, the historian George Bancroft, Professor Benjamin Silliman of Yale, and a regiment of journalists. Charles A. Dana of the *New York Tribune*, Samuel Bowles of the *Springfield Republican*, Thurlow Weed of the *Albany Evening Journal*, and Epes Sargent of the *Boston Transcript* were among the writers whose detailed reports advertised Minnesota not only to prospective settlers but also to those interested in an unusual kind of pleasure jaunt.[12] The journey upstream was enlivened by music, dancing, popular lectures, mock trials, and promenades from boat to boat. Four of the steamboats, for example, were lashed together as they plowed their way up through Lake Pepin. At the river towns there were gala receptions, with addresses of welcome by local citizens and responses by the visiting dignitaries. Everyone talked about the marvels of the Mississippi scenery and the coming greatness of the West, and everyone accepted the view of Catherine Sedgwick that the "fashionable tour will be in the track" of this excursion.[13] St. Paul was out in force to welcome the visitors, to listen to the praises of Fillmore and Bancroft, and to provide vehicles for a trip to the Falls of St. Anthony and Minnehaha. Dana, writing to the *New York Tribune*, described the infant town of St. Paul. There were, he wrote,

"Brick dwellings and stone warehouses, a brick capitol with stout, white pillars, a county court-house, a jail, several churches, a market, schoolhouses, a billiard-room, a ten-pin alley, dry goods' stores, gro-

[11] The best account of this event is William J. Petersen, "The Rock Island Railroad Excursion of 1854," *Minnesota History*, 15:405–420.
[12] The Minnesota Historical Society has had typewritten copies made of the letters about the excursion printed in the *Boston Evening Transcript* and various other eastern newspapers.
[13] Catherine M. Sedgwick, "The Great Excursion to the Falls of St. Anthony," in *Putnam's Monthly Magazine*, 4:323 (September, 1854).

366

ceries, confectioners and ice-creamers, a numerous array of those establishments to which the Maine law is especially hostile, and a glorious, boundless country behind." [14]

There were a few discordant notes in the general hymn of praise, however. One journalist wrote:

"As the Upper Mississippi must now become a route for fashionable Summer travel, it is only proper to say that those who resort here must not yet expect to find all the conveniences and comforts which abound on our North River steamers. Everything is very plain; the staterooms are imperfectly furnished, but the berths are roomy; the table is abundant, but butter-knives and sugar-tongs are not among its luxuries." [15]

In due time these and many other luxuries appeared. Companies, competing sharply for traffic, vied with one another in bettering accommodations, providing well-furnished staterooms, improving steamboat architecture, serving good food, rigging up bars where, as Mark Twain says, "everybody drank, and everybody treated everybody else," employing bands and orchestras, and in other ways adding to the attractions of the "Fashionable Tour." And when large and luxurious river boats docked at the St. Paul levee, their captains liked to invite local citizens on board to see the wonders of the ships and to join in "grand balls," as was done, for example, when in 1857 the "Henry Clay" brought up an excursion party from St. Louis. The captains and pilots, the envied monarchs of the river, took unbounded pride in their boats. One pilot in after years recalled the "Grey Eagle" as "long, lean, and as graceful as a grey-hound"—the "sweetest thing in the way of a steamboat that a man ever looked at." Steamboats, he believed, had souls; and his idea of heaven was the "Grey Eagle" plying "celestial waters, carrying angels on their daily visits, with their harps," Daniel Harris, captain, and himself the pilot. [16]

The general picture of beautiful boats, luxury, and gala entertainment must not close one's eyes to another side of river traffic—the vast throngs, on most of the boats, of immigrants who crowded the lower decks while the tourists occupied cabins and balconies on top of the decks. Coming in ever-increasing swarms, the immigrants accounted for great profits to the steamboat companies, and, with the expansion of freighting, they help to explain why, in the 1850's, the number of

[14] *New York Tribune*, June 20, 1854, quoted in Petersen, *Steamboating on the Upper Mississippi*, 279.
[15] *New York Tribune*, June 20, 1854, quoted in Petersen, *Steamboating on the Upper Mississippi*, 284.
[16] Mark Twain, *Life on the Mississippi*, 370 (Boston, 1883); Petersen, *Steamboating on the Upper Mississippi*, 265; George B. Merrick, "Steamboats and Steamboatmen of the Upper Mississippi," in *Saturday Evening Post* (Burlington, Iowa), November 6, 1915.

steamboat arrivals at St. Paul sometimes ran to more than a thousand in a single season. Bound for the Promised Land, the immigrants faced, as Dr. William J. Petersen says, the hazards of "runners, blacklegs, and gamblers, explosions, tornadoes, and devastating fires, snags and sandbars, poor food and wretched accommodations, sickness, suffering, and death." When cholera and other diseases broke out on board ship, they were likely to spread with appalling rapidity. On one occasion a traveler complained because the towel in the washroom was filthy. "Wal now," said the purser, "I reckon there's fifty passengers on board this boat, and they've all used that towel, and you're the first on 'em that's complained of it." [17]

What did the people who made the "Fashionable Tour" in early days see? For most, the magnificence of the scenery made up for torment by mosquitoes and the inconvenience of crowded quarters. Indeed, many were so delighted that they accepted philosophically the hazards of explosions and collisions. The scenery held them spellbound upon the decks of the steamboats through the days, and often far into the nights. Said one traveler:

"I had taken my impressions of the Mississippi scenery from the descriptions of the river below St. Louis, where the banks are generally depressed and monotonous. But nothing can surpass the grandeur of the Upper Mississippi. Is it then strange that I was fascinated while floating through these Western paradises, over which the moon shed her soft, shadowy light, and where the notes of the whippo[or]will rose and died far away, as I had heard them in my boyhood's home?" [18]

Another tourist wrote:

"We came . . . on the Steamer Yankee, and a delightful trip we had. The scenery of the Upper Mississippi, for wilderness, beauty and grandeur, is unequaled and perfectly indescribable.

"We had grand moonlight scenes on this glorious river, that were perfectly enchanting. It seemed as though I could gaze all night; that my eyes would never tire or be satisfied, in beholding the beauty and grandeur of its ever-varying banks and lofty hills." [19]

And Fredrika Bremer, the kindly and observant visitor to America from Sweden, wrote:

"I have . . . seen the scenery on the upper Mississippi, its high bluffs crowned with autumn-golden oaks, and rocks like ruined walls

[17] Petersen, *Steamboating on the Upper Mississippi*, 353, 357.
[18] Luther W. Peck, "The Upper Mississippi," in *National Magazine*, 9:483 (December, 1856).
[19] H. W. Hamilton, *Rural Sketches of Minnesota, the El Dorado of the Northwest*, 8 (Milan, Ohio, 1850).

and towers, ruins from the times when the Megatherium and mastodons walked the earth,—and how I did enjoy it!" [20]

Sometimes a traveler, vexed by the slow progress of his boat, annoyed by its unscheduled stops on sand bars, or wearied alike by travel and by travelers, failed to join the usual chorus. Ida Pfeiffer, an Austrian lady of wealth, had sober second thoughts. "This is a grand thing to think of at first," she wrote, "but after a few days one gets tired of the perpetual monotony of the scenery." Even she relented, however, when her boat entered Lake Pepin, for the sight of it, she said, "almost made me amends for my long and tedious voyage up the river." George T. Borrett, an English visitor, made the journey during a period of extremely low water. He chronicles his impressions with solemn detail:

"A broad expanse of extremely shallow water; a number of oddly-shaped marshy-looking islands, a tortuous channel in and out amongst them, very difficult of navigation, and intersected by frequent sandbanks, on the top of which the keel of our boat grated at every other bend in the stream, with a dull sound that brought home to the passengers the uncomfortable apprehension of the possibility of sticking fast on one of these banks and seeing much more of the Mississippi than we had bargained for; a low vegetation on most of these islands, very much like that which may be seen on any of the alluvial deposits on the Thames; a range of steep bluffs on either bank rising abruptly from the water's edge, sparsely wooded and bare alternately, but bold in outline and precipitous. Such was my first impression of the Mississippi scenery, and such it is now, for there was little or no variety."

The "Father of Waters" appeared to him "very much in the light of an imposter." "I think it extremely doubtful," he said, "whether, in his then state of aqueous insolvency, proud little Father Thames himself would have owned him even for a poor relation." Borrett's boat was crowded, the accommodations were inadequate, and he found the company intolerable. Ida Pfeiffer shared his scornful attitude toward the fellow passengers and was especially indignant at the impudence of two young ladies who patted her on the shoulder and genially called her "grandma." She also thought that the manners displayed at the dinner table were somewhat less than perfect, particularly the strange custom of certain people of pelting "each other with the gnawed cobs of Indian corn." In the evening, she says, the ladies took possession of the ten available rocking chairs, "placed them in a circle, threw them-

[20] Adolf B. Benson, ed., "Fredrika Bremer's Unpublished Letters to the Downings," in *Scandinavian Studies*, 11:192 (May, 1931).

selves back in them, many even held their hands over their heads, stuck their feet far out, and then away they went full swing." [21]

Let us draw the distressed Ida away from this shocking spectacle and introduce her to a fellow sufferer, Anthony Trollope, the English novelist, who made the "Fashionable Tour" in Civil War days. The author of *Barchester Towers* also had many melancholy reflections to record. "Nine-tenths of the travellers," he exclaimed, "carry children with them. . . . I must protest that American babies are an unhappy race." The parents seemed to Trollope as untalkative as their babies were discontented and dyspeptic. "I found no aptitude, no wish for conversation," he said; "nay, even a disinclination to converse." And poor Trollope's cabin was too hot. This circumstance led him to generalize about the effects upon Americans of their taste for living in the "atmosphere of a hot oven." To that taste he attributed their thin faces, pale skins, unenergetic temperament, and early old age.[22]

When Catlin made his tour in 1835, there was only a lonely frontier outpost at the junction of the Minnesota and Mississippi rivers and a rough trading post close by to signalize white civilization at the northern terminus of the "Fashionable Tour." The characteristic note of the region was Indian life. Catlin, like Marryat a few years later, was entertained by a Sioux game of la crosse and by a variety of Indian dances. From Fort Snelling south into Iowa, the wilderness was broken only by an occasional Indian village or trader's post. Charles Lanman in 1846 felt that at St. Peter's, at the mouth of the Minnesota River, he was "on the extreme verge of the civilized world, and that all beyond, to the ordinary traveller," was "mysterious wilderness." In 1852 Mrs. Elizabeth Ellet thought it "curious to see the primitive undergrowth of the woods, and even trees, left" in portions of St. Paul "not yet improved by buildings." In walking from her hotel to the home of Governor Ramsey, she "passed through quite a little forest . . . and saw a bear's cub at play—an incident in keeping with the scene." She was attracted by the "curious blending of savage and civilized life. . . . The lodges of the Dakotas had vanished from the opposite shore . . . but their canoes yet glided over the waters of the Mississippi, and we met them whenever we stepped outside the door." [23]

[21] Ida Pfeiffer, *A Lady's Second Journey Round the World*, 431, 432, 433 (New York, 1856); George T. Borrett, *Letters from Canada and the United States*, 135–144 (London, 1865). Sections of Borrett's book that relate to his journey up the Mississippi and his visit to Minnesota have been reprinted in *Minnesota History*, 9:270–284, 379–388.

[22] Anthony Trollope, *North America*, 1:206–209 (London, 1862).

[23] Charles Lanman, *A Summer in the Wilderness, Embracing a Canoe Voyage up the Mississippi and around Lake Superior*, 56 (New York, 1847); Mrs. Elizabeth Ellet, *Summer Rambles in the West*, 77, 78, 81 (New York, 1853).

Mrs. Ellet found "excellent quarters" in the Rice Hotel in St. Paul. St. Anthony, she reported, "has but recently emerged from a wilderness into the dignity of a village."

"In the summer months the town is much resorted to by visitors, especially from the southwestern States. These have come in such numbers that no accommodations could be found for them, and they were obliged to return with but a glance at the curiosities they had come to view. Now the state of things is more favorable to the lovers of fine scenery; an excellent hotel—the St. Charles—having recently passed into the proprietorship of Mr. J. C. Clark, and under his excellent management, already obtained a reputation as one of the best in the northwestern country." [24]

Mrs. Ellet boarded one of Willoughby and Powers' stagecoaches for what was called the "grand tour." It consisted of a drive from St. Paul to St. Anthony, then out to Lakes Harriet and Calhoun, "thence to the Minnehaha Falls and Fort Snelling, and by the Spring Cave to St. Paul, arriving in time for the visitors, if in haste, to return with the boat down the river." Shortly before Mrs. Ellet's arrival, the beauties of the Lake Minnetonka region began to be appreciated, and during her stay in St. Paul she took advantage of an opportunity to visit what in due time was to become one of the most popular summer resorts in the Northwest.[25] Frontenac, White Bear, the St. Croix country, and many other places became widely known as ideal for tourists and vacation seekers.

When Charles Francis Adams, Jr., went up the Mississippi in 1860, he did so not for the sake of the "Fashionable Tour" but as a minor figure in a political excursion. This excursion was headed by William H. Seward and the elder Charles Francis Adams, whose purpose was to win the Northwest for Lincoln and the Republican party. To the observant and sensitive Charles Francis, Jr., however, it was a sightseeing tour of the wild and wooly West, and in his diary he gives us vivid pictures of the changing scenes, describes steamboat races, and reveals an eye for the picturesque. After the speeches and cheers at Prairie du Chien, he found himself on the deck of a Mississippi steamboat proceeding upstream at night. Of this experience, he wrote:

"To me it all seemed strange and unreal, almost weird,—the broad river bottom, deep in shadow, with the high bluffs rising dim in the starlight. Presently I saw them wood-up while in motion, and the bright lights and deep shadows were wonderfully picturesque. A large flat-boat, piled up with wood, was lashed alongside, and, as the steamer pushed steadily up stream, the logs were thrown on board. As the

[24] Ellet, *Summer Rambles*, 92.   [25] Ellet, *Summer Rambles*, 89, 126.

hands, dressed in their red flannel shirts, hurried backward and forward, shipping the wood, the lurid flickerings from the steamer's
'beacon lights' cast a strong glare over their forms and faces, lighting
up steamer, flat-boat and river, and bringing every feature and garment out in strong relief." [26]

The early pioneers were not so absorbed with the task of building
cities, towns, and farms that they closed their eyes to the recreational
attractions of Minnesota. They were, in fact, belligerent boosters.
Every newspaper was a tourist bureau; but James M. Goodhue, the
editor of the *Minnesota Pioneer*, was perhaps the leading promoter of
them all. He intoxicated himself with his own superlatives. In 1852 he
invited the world, and more especially the people of the South, to
make the "Fashionable Tour," to breathe the marvelous air of Minnesota and be healed of earthly ailments. In true Goodhuean style, he
asked:

"Who that is idle would be caged up between walls of burning brick
and mortar, in dog-days, down the river, if at less daily expense, he
could be hurried along through the valley of the Mississippi, its shores
studded with towns, and farms, flying by islands, prairies, woodlands,
bluffs—an ever varied scene of beauty, away up into the land of the
wild Dakota, and of cascades and pine forests, and cooling breezes?—
Why it is an exhilarating luxury, compared with which, all the fashion
and tinsel and parade of your Newports and Saratogas, are utterly
insiped."

He pictured the miserable life of a southern planter and of his "de-
bilitated wife and pale children, almost gasping for breath." "What is
such a life to him and those he loves, but death prolonged?" he asked.

"A month in Minnesota, in dog-days, is worth a whole year anywhere else; and, we confidently look to see the time, when all families
of leisure down South, from the Gulf of Mexico along up, will make
their regular summer hegira to our Territory; and when hundreds of
the opulent from those regions, will build delightful cottages on the
borders of our ten thousand lakes and ornament their grounds with
all that is tasteful in shrubbery and horticulture, for a summer retreat." [27]

In this, as in many other fields, Goodhue the booster was Goodhue
the prophet. Even before the Civil War large numbers of people from
the South flocked to Minnesota as a summer resort; and the habit was
resumed not long after Appomattox. Folk from east and west joined

[26] Theodore C. Blegen, ed., "Campaigning with Seward in 1860," *Minnesota
History*, 8:167. The journal of the younger Adams is there published from a typewritten copy in the possession of the Minnesota Historical Society.

[27] *Minnesota Pioneer*, July 22, 1852.

in exploiting the vacation and tourist attractions of Minnesota. The day of the "Fashionable Tour" on the upper Mississippi passed when steamboating declined in the face of railroad competition. Local excursions continued to be popular, but the gala period of the steamboats and the great excursions was over. The fame of Minnesota as a summer resort had been established, however, and the railroads made the lakes and rivers of the north country even more accessible than they had been when sleek and picturesque vessels graced the river in its golden age.

Old Times on the Missouri

by CHARLES D. STEWART. *In his youth Stewart roamed over a good deal of the Mississippi Valley. These experiences he afterwards put to good use in his fiction and essays. The description of steamboating on the Missouri is reprinted from* Fellow Creatures.

THE Missouri River as you see it on the map is the picture of a stream that has been forever dissatisfied with its channel, and, like a man who chafes under the conditions of his lot, it has a crooked career. It is always traveling sideways by the operation of eating away one of its banks, and thus on one shore or the other it has leveled the landscape as far as eye can see. There is not a season in which it does not succeed in calling the map a liar and teaching a pilot to swear. It takes away a man's farm, and adds what it pleases to the possessions of the man on the opposite shore, and in a general way does as it pleases—that is, until it comes to one of Missouri's rock-ribbed hills in its sideward journey. It bares the hill to the bone, and when it can go no farther it impatiently doubles its speed and hurries along to the end of obstruction. Then it strikes off and builds prairie until it comes to a range of rock on the other side. It cleans the rocky wall as bare as a Thanksgiving turkey, and leaves it as flat as the side of a skyscraper, but often much taller. Thus the lower river is shored with toppling walls and alluvial prairie facing one another, the scene alternating to opposite shores many times in a day's journey. And every foot of this prairie has at some time been in succession shore and channel of the river. On the down trip the steamer hugs the hills and makes good time as it shoots along in dangerous proximity to the rocky wall, where the channel is

373

deep as well as swift, and where there are no sand bars. But what with crossing and recrossing to hug the hills alternately the pilot has to know much of the shifty bottom. On the up trip it does not pay to face the swift current next to the rocky wall, so you keep nearer the middle and trust to Providence for a channel. Sometime you will strike a sand bar and stop with a swash and a grind on bottom like "a rusty nail in monumental mockery." The black roustabouts put out the spar in front with rope and tackle, and start up the "doctor" engine in the bows, and you crawl back foot by foot and work the boat sideways after the manner of pulling the same rusty nail. For half a day the boat is loaded to the hogway with impatience and profanity. I have blushed in my day to know that a country preacher was a passenger on the "General Meade."

Few craft now navigate this muddy drain except for short trips between the small towns. When the Pacific railways were built, the long cigar-shaped craft that used to make the twelve-hundred-mile trip were thrown out of employment, and sank one by one in the service on the lower river. In '86 the "General Meade" had long been the last of the race, and the only true Missouri boat afloat, plying from St. Louis in vast superiority to the little boats of the river towns, and so old that she had become a burlesque on Fate and insurance companies, for the companies had refused to take risks in those waters. Few passengers now know the lower Missouri. In '86 the steward had occasion to make a few extra bunks in the long line of unused staterooms, and at the old bar over the boilers the captain kept one jug of peach brandy which could be partaken of without cost. If you had taken this route out of St. Louis, I could have assured you of being a distinguished guest. While you were aboard, the steward and Aunt Mary would have pie,—prune pie and mock-apple pie, of dry bread and vinegar,—a marvelous imitation. Thus you would have an insight of the old days of Indians, and risky woodpiles, and the long Fort Benton trip, of which Aunt Mary was a sole survivor. And while the roustabouts sat along the hogways with tin pans of delicious peach cobbler, the steward would get out his package of cornstarch, preserved for special occasions, and he would prepare for a season of custard pie "kase dey is a passengah abo'hd."

The Missouri fleet of long, lithe craft was built during the War of the Rebellion, and especially designed to encounter the dangers of navigation between St. Louis and Fort Benton in Montana. They were built extra long so that the bows could run high on a sand bar, and yet leave the stern in deep water with a chance to get off immediately by means of the wheel. There was no fancy flummery of storied cabins and jig-sawed woodwork. The boats were intended to carry freight

374

and passengers who were to be pioneers; to take necessities of life to the men at the fort and bring back booty of the plains.

Long before '85 all the fleet had succumbed to snag and sawyer and the dangers of fire and water. The long trips were a thing of the romantic past. In reaching the Northwest it was first the Oregon trail, then the Missouri fleet, and then the Pacific railways. But for a quarter of a century the "General Meade" kept on regardless of the proprieties of history or of the fact that she ought to sink or burn or blow up. She took farm machinery upriver, and on the way down stopped for the piles of wheat sacks wherever a farmer displayed a red shirt on a pole. Whenever she sank it was in medium water, and she was soon at it again in victorious competition with the locomotives that whirled along the banks.

I used to wonder how she kept afloat twenty-five years on these most dangerous of waters, but now I only marvel how a boat could go through a single summer after the manner of the "Meade." But I did not worry about the summer at the time. One need not worry on a boat that has run twenty-five years. When you figure on her sinking, there is only one chance in twenty-six for her to go down. And when a boat has gone through all sorts of perils unscathed, one need not worry about taking dangerous chances. So life aboard the "Meade" went on in a careless and happy manner.

I recall several instances. It was considered dangerous for a boat to turn into the Osage River. One boat had met her fate by turning out of the muddy Missouri and taking into her pumps the clear aguish water of the Osage. The mixture caused the boilers to foam and sent boat and crew to the four winds. The "General" turned into the Osage every week.

And there was the St. Charles Bridge, which, according to all logic, should have sent us to the bottom. The current was swift there, and the piers obstructing the channel made it swifter still. Our only competitor—a high-cabin Mississippi boat—managed to make the passage and so did we. A train of freight cars ran off between the outer piers, still more obstructing the channel and increasing the current of the middle piers. As a result our competitor was "stalled" at a critical moment; the rudder failed to control her as she stood motionless with a full head of steam on; she swung against the masonry and sank.

This obstructed the channel still more. But the "General Meade" kept on running, and each trip managed to pull past the piers with extra firing. Sometimes when we were almost stalled between those piers, when the "niggers" were shoving the cordwood under the boilers, and we were running with forced speed and yet hardly moving, I would ramble astern and covertly take a look at the axle of the wheel.

375

This piece of mechanism—an immense octagonal shaft of wrought iron—had been broken in the old days, and was mended with a ponderous casting clamped on with bolts. The blacksmith at St. Louis used to come down with big wrenches and screw it up whenever it had worked loose during a trip. Sometimes the axle sagged, and as it hung down continuously while the wheel went round, I felt with mechanical insight the grind and wrench in that place that *meant* something, especially between the piers. But the sweating backs managed to shove in the wood that sent us ahead foot by foot as though we were running a race—which in fact we were. And in every race with that stone wall the "General Meade" won.

It was against the laws of our country to steam down the Missouri at nighttime, but the "General Meade" always ran nights on the down trip. It was by this means that she broke her own record and was presented with a locomotive headlight by the wheat-loving men of the St. Louis elevators. Not only did we ply the Osage, but on one trip with much close steering in the bends we went up to where the trees brushed the smokestacks on both sides, and we came across a farmer who had never heard a steam whistle. Consider for a moment that only one who knows steam power has ever heard this loudest voice of all, and imagine if you can how the noise would inspire an aguish human soul of the quiet woods to its first sensation of boundless power.

And suppose that you who lived in the backwoods with your sallow Lize, and who had never heard Barnum's calliope or seen an elephant or a locomotive, should have this wondrous creation come round the bend and stop all on account of *you*, and raise its voice to hail you and your pile of wheat sacks—what would you think about it? The farmer jumped up and down and yelled, "Toot her agin, boys; toot her agin. My wife Lize is sick up to the house, and kain't come down to see, but if ye'll toot her agin fer Lize I'll give ye a pair o' deer horns." Oh, deceitful humanity! The captain knew that John only wanted to hear it again himself. He turned her open on the loudest blast, and added the deer horns to the headlight.

Not only did she end the last of her race, but with a part of the old crew in the person of Aunt Mary, the aged darky who helped the steward and baked the jar full of cookies for the spoiled captain whom she "brung up" in her slave days. And to him of a later generation than those who ran the "Meade" to Montana she used to tell the story of the time when the "Meade" came down from the fort with the smallpox aboard and Indians along the shore, and how she got into St. Louis with most of the crew buried along the Missouri.

Many river boats burn up. There was the queen of the rivers, the beautiful "Natchez"—her immaculate white engine room a triumph of mechanism.

How she used to walk up the current with seemingly no more slip to her paddles than if she were wheeling on land. Yet she (watched and tended like a queen) burned up with her gay passengers.

Not so the "Meade." Her sheet-iron stove smoked up the cabin every morning when I made the fire, and the lids were so warped that you could always see without lifting them when to put in more wood. The cook often remarked, as he threw a handful of salt from the pantry into the kitchen so that the exact amount always fell into the soup pot, that he would not trade it for any stove he ever saw.

The "Meade" did not burn, neither did she blow up. The corroded bell wire that ran all the length from the towering pilot house to the engines in the stern, and went around divers corners into unseen places, never broke at a critical moment in all those years. When a roughening wind came, her long hull would bend lithely on the waters; she seemed to be getting better as time passed. Whenever she sank it was always in shallow water—merely a sort of delay.

The insurance companies declared those waters unnavigable, in spite of the government snag boats and the government lights on the white-washed posts at the bends. Certainly they did not get their statistics from such boats as the "General Meade." However, when I left her in '85 I had a secret idea that her time would soon come. Coming back after a couple of years in the South, I lost track of her. But she had not sunk or come to a violent end; she had simply disappeared. Lately I made it my business to ascertain what had become of her. She is not only afloat, but bearing on her back much of the cargo that goes down the Mississippi. She has been dismantled of engines and upper works and turned into a wharf boat at St. Louis.

She now bears as much freight as dozens of other boats—momentarily wheeled across her immortal buoyancy. During her life many a man who thought he had a fixed home on land has seen his farm eaten away and his house tumbled into the river. But the dangerous abode of the captain on the Missouri stuck like a mortgage on the waters.

The only conclusion I can draw is that it is dangerous to be safe.

River Town

by MARQUIS W. CHILDS, 1903–   . *A native of Clinton, Iowa, Childs was educated at the University of Wisconsin, B.A., 1923, and the University of Iowa, M.A., 1925. After serving for some time as a member of the United Press staff, Childs joined the St. Louis Post-Dispatch in 1926. He is the author of various magazine articles and books and is today a widely read feature writer and syndicated columnist. He has written Sweden—the Middle Way (1936), This Is Democracy (1938), and I Write from Washington (1942). "River Town," published in Harper's Magazine, November 1932, is an interpretation of Clinton, Iowa.*

I

THERE is a special province which belongs to the Mississippi, carved out of the States through which it flows. It can be cut in two at St. Louis to form two distinct domains, one of the upper river, the other of the lower. The latter is well known and frequently celebrated; it has certain picturesque advantages and two great books to its credit; although Hannibal is geographically above St. Louis, Mark Twain in *Tom Sawyer* and *Huckleberry Finn* was writing about the lower river where his interest was.

The province of the upper river does not deserve its obscurity. The life along its reaches was the life of the Mississippi with a special quality of the Northwest added, a defiant, reckless courage and arrogance that the stream in the south lacked. Even to-day a river town is a special kind of town. It is only technically in Wisconsin, Minnesota, Illinois, or Iowa. By virtue of the Mississippi, the extravagant commerce that flowed for so many years on its broad surface and the incorrigible human cargo that came along with this commerce, the river towns escaped the blighting respectability of the mid-western Main Street.

Many of the upper river towns that flourished in the days of the great lumber boom have disappeared altogether; visible now only as moldering ghost towns. Others are dying, shrinking slowly into a pale semblance of the past. Galena, in Illinois, is shut off from the Mississippi, its tributary Fever River choked with sand. Bad Axe in Wisconsin has become the hamlet Genoa. Dubuque, Iowa, dwindles, and so do Clinton, Burlington, Muscatine. Beef Slough, in Wisconsin, once the center of tempestuous life, with a hundred raft crews charging in and out of saloon and brothel, has disappeared. So has West Newton, across the river in Minnesota.

378

II

Winslow is a town such as Clinton or Dubuque. It is in Iowa but it has no more to do with that rural State than has Tombstone, Arizona. In the beginning Joshua Winslow, a hard-bitten Yankee from northern New York, came with his ailing wife and built on a rise of ground where the river was open, free from sand bars and towheads—the small islands which clog the stream. That was in 1836. Considerably before the Civil War Joshua and his wife had died of ague and chills and fever and the other miserable diseases that attended pioneer settlement in the valley.

By 1865 Winslow was a thriving town of more than three thousand population. It had eighty-six saloons and a subscription library. The Winslow Young Men's Association, which fostered the library, organized in 1865 a lecture series and brought to the town Emerson, Horace Greeley, P. T. Barnum, the freed slave, Douglass, and two or three others of almost equal note. The Association also gave a Promenade Festival at which the sum of three hundred and forty-two dollars was raised to buy books; one of the local wits offered a humorous monologue in the person of "Professor A-gassick" of "Cambrick University," discoursing on Adam and Eve and the revised story of the Garden.

Already there were half a dozen sawmills at Winslow. In that year old Rizen Abbott paid a war tax to the government on ten thousand dollars of his income, and J. L. Westbrook is shown in the published lists with almost as much. But they were pikers still, buying the logs they sawed in their mills from timber contractors in the pineries to the north or from chance raftsmen who came drifting down the stream to barter logs. As the West came to demand lumber and more lumber, Abbott, Westbrook, and the Devines began to realize that God had been indeed very good to them. To the north were the incredibly fine stands of pine, so large that man could never exhaust them; to the west was the treeless prairie, with the railroad beginning to push in; and the river was at their door, a free highway for the northern lumber.

Scarcely a town on the upper river between St. Paul and St. Louis but had its mills. They were called sawdust towns. In the spring when the river opened and the first rafts came down the muddied, drift-laden flood to Winslow, the great circular saws set up their familiar shrieking whine again—the sawmill sound that carried so far on still hot days in the summer. The shift was twelve to fourteen hours a day, the pay eighty-five cents to a dollar and a quarter. There were numerous accidents. Often men were ripped in two; the saws stopped for a few minutes, and the undertaker had a difficult job. There were many Germans and Irish in the mills. On Saturday pay night no good woman stirred out of the house without a strong man at her side. Two constables were required to keep the drunks on Main Street from falling under the buggy wheels. There were sixty-three saloons in the six blocks between the levee and the Randall House at the corner of Sixth Street. Iowa's prohibition law came early, but to Winslow and the other river towns it made no difference. The proprietors of the saloons were brought into court once a month to pay a fine of ten dollars and costs, which was the equivalent of a license fee.

But it took a raft crew to make the town really lively. In the early days they were all from the northwest: Wisconsin woodsmen who turned to rafting during the summer, French Canadians many of them. Later on boys from along the river took to rafting, and there were Winslow men on almost every raft. And there were the bums who came back each season, starved, ragged, eager to get a berth for a single trip, enough money for a drunk. They were known to captains up and down the river by their nicknames, "St. Louis Blackie," "Sliver," "The Tomcat." They had no other names. A captain would walk along the levee and prod one sleeping bundle of rags after another. "Here you, Bat-Eye, and you, Mugs, go on aboard the *Fanny Harris* and report to the mate." When the season ended in the late fall they migrated by some circuitous and difficult route to the deep south where they worked on the sugar plantations. All raftsmen had in common a proud, willful independence. They took the town when they turned to pleasure.

The floating brothels, rigged on small barges, knew them. Often these pleasure craft would follow a raft, or two or three rafts, to the mills at Winslow, sure of patronage when the crew were paid off. The roosters, which was the name the raftsmen acquired because of necessity they roosted anywhere they could during the strenuous downriver trip, loved a brawl. They went often to the German beer garden, the Schützen park, on the edge of town. Sometimes they were admitted, sometimes not, depending upon the state of the Schützen Verein's treasury. But always they fought, and the Germans almost invariably lost and swore never again to traffic with such brutes. After a particularly violent battle, Heinrich Schenk, lawyer for the Schützen Verein, had twenty raftsmen haled up in the justice of peace court. The small room would just accommodate the hulking defendants and two or three constables. The complaining witnesses had to wait outside. At intervals Heinrich would lean out of the window to call, "Send up another black eye," or, "Another one with teeth out, if you please."

Certain of these roosters acquired highly colored reputations in

Winslow. Big Jack Manville had been a Winslow boy, but no one was so feared. Once he smashed a dozen windows on Main Street before the constabulary could control him. He appeared in court the next day, sober and subdued, tall and dignified, looking like a kindly colossus. Two or three merchants had come to see that he was at last put in jail, but they lost their courage when they saw Big Jack in the flesh. After waiting a while, he said, "If there's not going to be any action here I'm going home," and went out.

You could tell when a neighbor had come off the river: his clothes would be decorating the back fence in order that they might be deloused by the sun and air. Men were compelled to shed their river clothes in the barn or woodshed before conscientious wives would allow them to step into the house. Sometimes raftsmen bound down river to a mill below Winslow would steal an hour or two at home. A ribald story passed around that Shady Ashcraft kept his little boy on the river bank watching for his return. At the approach of Shady's raft, the youngster was required to run like hell and bear this warning to his mother, "Go on to bed, ma, because pa's just about to step on shore." Many raftsmen spent the winter at home in pleasant idleness, slept late, danced, played cards, called on the girls, bought a Stetson hat and a pair of box-toed shoes. There were boat yards at Winslow, busy through the winter, employing skilled caulkers and woodworkers who made good wages and spent freely. In the spring there were two or three launchings that called for all the rancid butter from the country round about to grease the ways.

Respectable mothers in Winslow despaired of their children. Little girls who wore white aprons to school came home in tears. Some big girl or loutish boy had pulled their braids. In summer, despite the furious vigilance of the raftsmen, most boys lived on and along the big rafts that were tied up by the mills, waiting to approach the log chute. It was a wonderful place to swim and dive, but dangerous; slip under that unbroken carpet of brown logs, and it was ten to one that you would never come up alive again. The roosters were heroes who sometimes accepted the tribute of youthful awe. Two huskies were bathing on the edge of the raft. "C'mere, bub," called the one, "and I'll show you something." On his chest was tattooed a full-rigged ship; dangling over his shoulder and trailing down his spinal column went a very realistic rope that disappeared below the small of his back. He bent over to let the boys read the legend that was tattooed along the rope. It said, "More rope where this came from." The two men roared with laughter.

The sawdust piles had become small mountains. Rizen Abbott—called Goat Abbott for obscure reasons—was already a rich man. On

381

Abbott's slough he had three great mills topped by three tall stacks, and the square piles of sweet-smelling lumber covered acres of ground in his yards. He was a broad, thick man. When there was good sleighing, he often gathered all the children of his neighborhood into his big sleigh, took them for a swift ride, and then bought them boots with red tops and copper toes and a box of candy all around. Each day at six o'clock he was all but stationary. He would take more whiskey, but it would not stay down. He was full of whiskey; he carried in four or five pockets half-pint flasks which contained what was for him a single drink. But his vigorous mind was apparently never dimmed. Mrs. Abbott was a proud woman. She had few friends and even they said that she was distant, cold. She wanted their one son, Will, to be a gentleman and go to Harvard College. Goat Abbott wanted him to go into the lumber business.

III

Abbott and Westbrook and the Devines were all in the pool, the combine of lumbermen which dominated the entire upper river and a good share of Wisconsin and Minnesota. It was common talk in Winslow that they stole as much of the forest as they bought. J. L. Westbrook was a hard man. He was godfearing, and he wore a little fringe of whiskers, like a half moon around his face. The stern tenets of his Methodism would not permit him to work his men on Sundays. On Saturday at midnight it was his custom to order his steamboats which were to return north for rafts restocked with provisions. The Westbrook foreman turned over to the grocer a long, long list of supplies, and the grocer and his two brothers and his wife toiled until midnight Sunday to fill the orders and get the supplies aboard. Westbrook was obviously not responsible for the souls of the grocer and his family.

It was in this custom that the hatred between the grocer's family, the Sewells, and the Westbrooks originated; it is the most distinguished hatred in Winslow, having come down intact to the present day. Once when J. L.'s younger son, Philomen, was eighteen, J. L. became enraged at something the boy said and there in the street he thrashed him with an axe handle until he broke his arm. It was late at night, and only a few men gathered. When J. L. strode away, the onlookers picked up Philomen, carried him into a saloon, and went for a doctor. It was in this way, they say, that the old man broke Philomen's spirit. But J. L. had an older son, Horatio, who was just as mean as his father.

The Devines were milder. They were French-Irish and they liked to live in pleasant, easy style. Old man Devine came to Winslow with only his shirt on his back, but as soon as he began to make money he let his family spend it. They built a house on Fifth Avenue, young

Bernadotte and Paris went away to a military school, and Antoinette, Louisa, and Fanny were sent to Ferry Hall in Lake Forest.

There were others whose fortunes were mounting upward as the logs flowed in a ceaseless brown web down the broad stream. There were the Tollivers and the Bradleys and the Gardiners. But Goat Abbott, Westbrook, and the Devines ruled the roost. Sometimes their mills and their lumber piles burned—burned for days—and all the town was black and reeked with smoke and all the women made sandwiches and coffee for the fire-fighters. They built up the mills again and spurned the insurance which cautious underwriters held at fabulous rates.

These three families were expanding rapidly. They were making money in undreamed-of sums. They were not the biggest on the upper river; they were under the domination of old man Weyerhaeuser. But they had long since become the richest men in Winslow, outstripping pompous Peter Van Hewitt Smith who came west with six hundred thousand dollars and a number of grand ideas, which he slowly and painfully relinquished. The pace on the river had become faster, harder. During the open season Abbott and the others lived on their boats between Winslow and Beef Slough at the mouth of the Chippewa River. For three weeks, during the big fight over the Beef Slough boom, Goat never took off his clothes. The rafting crews worked fourteen, eighteen, twenty hours a day. The rafts crowded one on the other so fast at the rafting booms that time and again men slipped beneath the treacherous, shifting surface of the logs, and there was no thought for them, because a man was so cheap. For one entire week the river before Winslow was covered with logs for seven miles, and people came from round the whole county on a Sunday in mid June to see the spectacle.

Goat Abbott, when at last he wearied of his wife's nagging, built a huge house, all turrets and towers and porches and three upstairs balconies and a stained-glass window on the stairway twenty feet high. Goat had them panel one room in white pine with a low polish. He said he liked the smell of the wood and, after all, it was the way he'd made his money.

A little later Louisa Devine married Philomen Westbrook. The two families built for them a handsome house on the bluff back of the town. From the wide windows of their drawing-room (Louisa, who had lived in New York, said it was not a parlor) you could look over the hills and the flat roofs of the town to the shining river. There were separate quarters for the servants in the stable. No one had ever called them servants before, to say nothing of having special quarters for them. Later on, old man Devine built another big house for Antoinette and Billy Rickard on the bluff and another one for himself; so that the three houses dominated all of Winslow.

The Devines were living high. It was Bernadotte Devine who built the first houseboat. It was called *The Princess*, for his sister, Fanny. That had been Fanny's name since she was a child with long, carefully curled golden hair. The Little Princess. And the towboat that pushed *The Princess* was called *The Duchess*. Those first boats introduced a grand, lazy, blissful sort of life. The logging business was almost at an end; they were all rich, they could take time. Or at any rate the Devines could. *The Princess* was fitted out by Marshall Field's, eight bedrooms, five baths, a main saloon, a dining saloon, the master's library, and a verandah deck that ran the whole length of the boat, tricked out with blooming plants along the rail and with hanging baskets of fern. There were no cares, no worries, no smoke, no vibration—just drifting along on *The Princess*, scarcely aware of the puffing *Duchess* which pushed behind. It was a great life while it lasted.

The best of the Devine crews, the crack pilots, were always assigned to *The Duchess*. And the colored stewards on *The Princess* were chosen for their musical ability, as much as for anything else. Toward the late afternoon *The Princess* and *The Duchess* would head into some quiet slough, and the whole party would go swimming along a sandbar, then picnic there, and in the moonlight listen to the niggers singing on the deck and the strumming of the banjos. On the verandah deck there were hammocks that held two, a hammock for each couple, and the official chaperon was not too watchful. The Devines had friends all up and down the river, and before each trip hampers of the finest imported champagne and claret and liqueurs and whiskies were carried on board. Stop at Burlington and have a party; it was there that the new Brussels carpet in the main saloon was initiated with spilled champagne; that was the trip on which they made the distillery towns, from Peoria to Louisville, up the Ohio. Nothing to do, nothing in the wide world to do, through long lazy afternoons; the green, mysterious shore slipping gently past the rail.

Soon there were other houseboats. The Tollivers built and equipped *The Chaperon* and *The Summer Girl*, and old Westbrook was at last pried loose from the cash for *The Eva* and *The Uncle Tom*. But the Devines managed to lead. They initiated the Outing Club. Paris advanced the money to built the big gabled clubhouse on a point of land at Weehasket, five miles below Winslow, where the river makes a great bend, sweeps by in all its swelling might and majesty. The *Winslow Gazette* said, with considerable justice, that no verandah in the Middlewest could boast a finer view. There were twenty suites, bedroom, bath, and small sitting room; card rooms, three dining rooms. The ladies spent long, carefree weeks there; husbands drove down in the afternoon in smart turnouts, with a groom up behind. Visitors from Minneapolis and Chicago liked to stop at the Outing Club.

How they dominated the town, the Devines and the Westbrooks. Goat Abbot was away most of the time; he had branched out into railroads and timber on the West Coast, with his son, Will, who had gone to Harvard and was a gentleman but good at business, too. Mrs. Abbott had shut herself away entirely; she lived with an old servant in the big house and sometimes you saw her sallow, withered face at the window. She refused to meet her oldest friends; they said it was because she was so unhappy with Goat. The Devines and the Westbrooks had it all to themselves. They were like the ruling families of some small middle-European principality.

Each detail of their life was discussed. When Paris Devine was drowned off *The Princess*, three thousand people packed the levee to see them bring his body ashore. The town knew that Antoinette didn't get along with Billy Rickard; the report of a separation hovered in the air for years. The very appearance of their children, riding in a high-wheeled wicker pony cart, with a watchful, British-looking governess, was enough to set every curtain along the street to fluttering. Other children stopped their play to stare with awe that was not unmixed with envy at sight of the smart Shetland pony and the smart little cart and the youngster who held the reins with such casual pride. On their second trip to London Louisa and Philo bought a Daimler and brought it back to Winslow; it was the first car the town had seen near by. Billy Rickard drank too much and ran with women; that was established. Louisa and Philo and their children traveled between California, New York, and Europe, with brief stopovers in Winslow. Old man Westbrook was dying of a cancer; he got scant sympathy from the town; everyone knew that Horatio would get the money and conserve it as meanly as his father had.

All the mills were closed now except one that Goat Abbott kept open to saw the few logs which still came down from the north. The sawdust mountains were brown and discolored; they had begun to settle into the river. There were great mines of rotting lath and waste lumber where the yards had been. The tempo of the town was slower. A number of the best pilots had gone to the Yukon; a few found berths in the government service; others settled down to loaf away their lives or they took to modest farming. Iowa was dry in earnest, but Fairview, across the Mississippi in Illinois, was dripping wet, and a stream of thirsty Iowans poured through Winslow and over the high bridge.

Returning very drunk, they gave to Main Street a semblance of the wild and bloody past. The high bridge had never paid before; it now became as the mines of Ophir; liquor was smuggled across in wheelbarrows and baby-buggies and push carts, anything on wheels.

The old-timers were dropping away. Jumbo Bradley committed suicide. Goat Abbott had a stroke in Seattle; but not before he had made sure of a proper entry into heaven. "They may be right; you can't tell," he was often heard to say as age crept upon him. "These Christians, these church folks, may be right. Anyway I can't afford to take such a big chance as that." He gave to the Episcopal church handsome carved choir stalls, an altar, and a communion service of handwrought gold; a new organ, a new roof, and an endowment. He left an estate of $17,000,000 and when his son, Will, died six years later, it had appreciated to $33,000,000. Mrs. Abbott lives on, more withered and yellow, seldom venturing from the house, never from the big yard and the protection of the high cedar hedges around it; intruders are turned away by Anna who has been with the Abbotts for thirty-eight years. The Westbrook fortune went, when the old man died after incredible months of torture, to Horatio, who was to administer it for Philo, the two sisters, Ella and Jennie, and himself.

It was strange how quickly it ended. Horatio Westbrook, closed away in his massive, fortresslike house on the little park off Fifth Avenue, occupied himself solely with preserving the great fortune he had inherited from his father; administering the income to his family with all the niggardliness the law would allow; dominating the town by the cold threat of his personality. The Devines, upon the death of the head of the family, ventured into Southern pine and high finance. Within a few years they took such severe losses that their way of living had to be curtailed in drastic fashion. Louisa and Philo and their children came back for a month or two in the summer, but the rest of the year they were at Pasadena. Antoinette divorced Rickard, supporting him in a sanitarium for alcoholics until his death. Fanny terminated a romance long frustrated and married Captain Henry Robaire of her father's fleet; he had one-eighth Chippewa Indian blood. As Mrs. Robaire she developed a giddy streak and was given to becoming tipsy, a foolish smile on her foolish face, beneath the absurd crown of graying yellow curls.

IV

Although an air of quiescence and decay hangs increasingly over Winslow, its character persists, stubborn and unregenerate. For many of the figures of the great past live on; like figures from some heroic frieze buried under wind-blown sand and lost to time; difficult and ununderstandable. Big Jack Manville, Captain Cameron, Mr. Jabez, and many more survive. They are not unlike certain houses which a pretentious generation has covered with a thin coating of stucco, a meager surface that does not conceal their sharp, uncompromising angularity. Big Jack lives alone in a small yellow cottage; he can see the river from his front door; his mate's license hangs in a gilt frame over the radio. Mr. Jabez sits on the rotting remains of a shiere boom and talks of the past in his fine Irish speech. Captain Cameron is eighty-six but he looks as though he were carved out of hickory, as tough and as limber, with the fringe of stiff-looking whiskers that encircles his face.

Winslow bears a resemblance to the dying New England coastal towns of a generation ago. There are many spinsters, odd crustacea cast upon the beach by the receding wave of energy. Some of them are so old that they were brought to the West by their fathers as little girls, from Boston and Gloucester and New Bedford. The river attracted these New Englanders. Winslow was destined to be a great town, one to rival Chicago. Wilda Cranch's father came west to start an insurance company in Winslow. It failed swiftly, and Mr. Cranch died of the galloping consumption. That happened in 1857; Wilda was four years old; but when she speaks of it to-day there is the shadow of forgotten emotion in the parchment of her face. The Monday girls must be seventy—yes, seventy-five—but to Winslow they are still the Monday girls. Olive Read lives alone in the big, shuttered house at the end of Chestnut Street; children play in the tangled undergrowth and shrubbery of the lawn until she comes out to drive them off; the neighbors leave custards and small loaves of newly baked bread on her doorstep. Effie Law was with her father, the Captain, when he was killed in the explosion of the *Silver Wave* near Bellevue. She has lived on the charity of the neighbors since that time, repaying their generosity with the mild humors of her imbecility. Until a recent date a whole tribe of idiots lived and bred in a cluster of squalid huts along the river bank, beside the deserted button factory; one family's reputed ignorance of the laws pertaining to incest was the source of three or four of the more furtive jokes in the town; the kind told in a shocked whisper at the Winslow Ladies' Literary Society and to the accompaniment of guffaws of laughter in Frankie Jonas' pool hall.

The young have gone away. It is a confession of failure to remain in Winslow; an occasion for apology to return for more than a week-end or a few days. Winslow's younger generation lives in Chicago and New York, St. Louis and Minneapolis. When they meet afar they agree that Winslow is dead; they speak with pity of Fred Caddock and Georgia Hensley and others who are caught there. Returning for a brief visit, they are depressed by the very absence of change; by the fact that houses and people seem quite the same. It is only after a longer interval that the processes of withering decay are apparent. Certain faces have disappeared; here a house has fallen into ruin, gaping and black; and age is seen like a thick film upon all familiar things. Even those industries that grew out of the lumber boom are passing. They are dismantling the sash-and-door factory and selling it for junk.

The only new life has no real relation to the town. The Pershing Memorial Highway runs along Main Street, and in summer there is a constant flow of cars. Winslow happens, too, to be a distributing center for one of the large alcohol rings. Alcohol for Iowa, Nebraska, a part of Minnesota, and the Dakotas crosses the river at this point and comes within the jurisdiction of an Italian with a soft voice and soft yellow-white face. This young gentleman, dressed expensively, slouched down in the seat of a long low car, waves his hand to police and townsfolk along Main Street with a fine impartiality. It is not difficult to identify at least ten members of the ring stationed in Winslow. They make the Dew Drop Inn their headquarters, coming and going in an indifferent, easy way or pausing for a whispered consultation. Nick, the local head of the syndicate, sometimes boasts, pays off his drivers with a flourish from a showy roll of bills for the benefit of hangers-on in Jonas' place. Two or three Winslow young men have gone to work for Nicholas. It is a great temptation, as he pays $25 a trip to Des Moines, $60 to Lincoln, and furnishes a big car with a built-in, concealed eighty-gallon tank. There is a mild risk from hijackers, less from the law, but the poorest driver makes $50 a week, others as high as $100.

The alcohol is not taken across the high bridge. The trucks from Chicago stop at the Illinois shore, arriving there always at night. The ten-gallon containers are transferred to flat-bottomed skiffs and ferried over the river. Sitting on his porch through long summer evenings, Mr. Jabez has learned to identify the brief, flashing signals of the truck drivers across the river. He counts the skiff loads that come over on dark nights. "Well, by Jesus Christ," he says with a sudden flare of indignation, "you can't beat a country like this one." But his anger subsides to philosophic contemplation of the spectacle of lawlessness at his doorstep, and he reflects that Winslow has never in its history been law-abiding. "It's a river town, and you know what they are," he adds.

The death of the Little Princess the other day gave the righteous in Winslow the opportunity to write a very moral epitaph to a whole long period of history. Fanny was found drowned in her bathtub, whether accidentally or not will never be known. Captain Robaire had departed three weeks before with the contents of their joint safety deposit box. It had not contained much, the town said, but at least it would have given Fanny a decent burial. As it was, Horatio Westbrook and four others put in a hundred dollars each for a modest funeral. Fanny had quarreled long before her death with those members of her own family who had retained any part of the original Devine fortune. They telegraphed to Louisa, but no one was certain of her address, and no answer came. Antoinette Rickard, living obscure and forgotten in the south of France, cabled an appeal to Horatio. That was all.

Because so much has gone on there, the town is full of tales. Not one person who walks down the street but has a history that the rest of the town can furnish on demand. People seem to live more and more in the past, feeding upon reminiscences of the great days. There are times when Mr. Jabez dwells completely in a world that has long since disappeared, speaks of friends long dead as though they might come round the corner to question his story, and refers to landmarks obliterated years ago as though they stood shining and new to the gaze of the smallest child. Beneath the present weariness, the film of decay and age, lies the memory of this stirring past. Winslow is a river town if only in the dim reflection of ancient glory.

THE SMALL TOWN

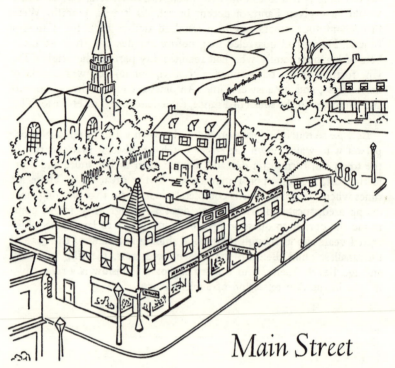

Main Street

by SINCLAIR LEWIS, 1885–   . The first American writer to win the
Nobel prize for literature, Lewis was born in Sauk Center, Minnesota, and
was educated at Yale, B.A., 1907. After a long period of journalistic and editorial activity during which he worked in New Haven, New York, and San
Francisco, Lewis turned his attention to fiction and since 1915 has produced
some twenty novels. Main Street (1920) first brought him fame through its
scathing indictment of a small middlewestern community. Babbitt (1922), a
satirical picture of an American businessman; Arrowsmith (1925), the
chronicle of a devoted bacteriologist; and Elmer Gantry (1927), a burlesque
of evangelical religion, were similarly successful. His later novels deal with
such widely divergent themes as hotel-keeping, prison life, and fascism. Perhaps the best of them are Dodsworth (1929) and It Can't Happen Here
(1935). Lewis has had considerable experience in writing for and acting in
the theater, and in recent years he has lectured on creative writing both at the
University of Wisconsin and at the University of Minnesota. Arrowsmith has
been called by a jury of critics the best American novel of the last twenty
years. This selection is, of course, an excerpt from Main Street.

WHEN Carol had walked for thirty-two minutes she had completely covered the town, east and west, north and south; and she stood at the corner of Main Street and Washington Avenue and despaired.

Main Street with its two-story brick shops, its story-and-a-half wooden residences, its muddy expanse from concrete walk to walk, its huddle of Fords and lumber-wagons, was too small to absorb her. The broad, straight, unenticing gashes of the streets let in the grasping prairie on every side. She realized the vastness and the emptiness of the land. The skeleton iron windmill on the farm a few blocks away, at the north end of Main Street, was like the ribs of a dead cow. She thought of the coming of the Northern winter, when the unprotected houses would crouch together in terror of storms galloping out of that wild waste. They were so small and weak, the little brown houses. They were shelters for sparrows, not homes for warm laughing people.

She told herself that down the street the leaves were a splendor. The maples were orange; the oaks a solid tint of raspberry. And the lawns had been nursed with love. But the thought would not hold. At best the trees resembled a thinned woodlot. There was no park to rest the eyes. And since not Gopher Prairie but Wakamin was the county-seat, there was no court-house with its grounds.

She glanced through the fly-specked windows of the most pretentious building in sight, the one place which welcomed strangers and determined their opinion of the charm and luxury of Gopher Prairie— the Minniemashie House. It was a tall lean shabby structure, three stories of yellow-streaked wood, the corners covered with sanded pine slabs purporting to symbolize stone. In the hotel office she could see a stretch of bare unclean floor, a line of rickety chairs with brass cuspidors between, a writing-desk with advertisements in mother-of-pearl letters upon the glass-covered back. The dining-room beyond was a jungle of stained table-cloths and catsup bottles.

She looked no more at the Minniemashie House.

A man in cuffless shirt-sleeves with pink arm-garters, wearing a linen collar but no tie, yawned his way from Dyer's Drug Store across to the hotel. He leaned against the wall, scratched a while, sighed, and in a bored way gossiped with a man tilted back in a chair. A lumber-wagon, its long green box filled with large spools of barbed-wire fencing, creaked down the block. A Ford, in reverse, sounded as though it were shaking to pieces, then recovered and rattled away. In the Greek candy-store was the whine of a peanut-roaster, and the oily smell of nuts.

There was no other sound nor sign of life.

She wanted to run, fleeing from the encroaching prairie, demanding the security of a great city. Her dreams of creating a beautiful town were ludicrous. Oozing out from every drab wall, she felt a forbidding spirit which she could never conquer.

She trailed down the street on one side, back on the other, glancing into the cross streets. It was a private Seeing Main Street tour. She was within ten minutes beholding not only the heart of a place called Gopher Prairie, but ten thousand towns from Albany to San Diego:

Dyer's Drug Store, a corner building of regular and unreal blocks of artificial stone. Inside the store, a greasy marble soda-fountain with an electric lamp of red and green and curdled-yellow mosaic shade. Pawed-over heaps of toothbrushes and combs and packages of shaving-soap. Shelves of soap-cartons, teething-rings, garden-seeds, and patent medicines in yellow packages—nostrums for consumption, for "women's diseases"—notorious mixtures of opium and alcohol, in the very shop to which her husband sent patients for the filling of prescriptions.

From a second-story window the sign "W. P. Kennicott, Phys. & Surgeon," gilt on black sand.

A small wooden motion-picture theater called "The Rosebud Movie Palace." Lithographs announcing a film called "Fatty in Love."

Howland & Gould's Grocery. In the display window, black, overripe bananas and lettuce on which a cat was sleeping. Shelves lined with red crêpe paper which was now faded and torn and concentrically spotted. Flat against the wall of the second story the signs of lodges— the Knights of Pythias, the Maccabees, the Woodmen, the Masons.

Dahl & Oleson's Meat Market—a reek of blood.

A jewelry shop with tinny-looking wrist-watches for women. In front of it, at the curb, a huge wooden clock which did not go.

A fly-buzzing saloon with a brilliant gold and enamel whisky sign across the front. Other saloons down the block. From them a stink of stale beer, and thick voices bellowing pidgin German or trolling out dirty songs—vice gone feeble and unenterprising and dull—the delicacy of a mining-camp minus its vigor. In front of the saloons, farmwives sitting on the seats of wagons, waiting for their husbands to become drunk and ready to start home.

A tobacco shop called "The Smoke House," filled with young men shaking dice for cigarettes. Racks of magazines, and pictures of coy fat prostitutes in striped bathing-suits.

A clothing store with a display of "ox-blood-shade Oxfords, with bull-dog toes." Suits which looked worn and glossless while they were still new, flabbily draped on dummies like corpses with painted cheeks.

The Bon Ton Store—Haydock & Simons'—the largest shop in town.

392

The first-story front of clear glass, the plates cleverly bound at the edges with brass. The second story of pleasant tapestry brick. One window of excellent clothes for men, interspersed with collars of floral piqué which showed mauve daisies on a saffron ground. Newness and an obvious notion of neatness and service. Haydock & Simons. Haydock. She had met a Haydock at the station; Harry Haydock; an active person of thirty-five. He seemed great to her, now, and very like a saint. His shop was clean!

Axel Egge's General Store, frequented by Scandinavian farmers. In the shallow dark window-space heaps of sleazy sateens, badly woven galateas, canvas shoes designed for women with bulging ankles, steel and red glass buttons upon cards with broken edges, a cottony blanket, a granite-ware frying-pan reposing on a sun-faded crêpe blouse.

Sam Clark's Hardware Store. An air of frankly metallic enterprise. Guns and churns and barrels of nails and beautiful shiny butcher knives.

Chester Dashaway's House Furnishing Emporium. A vista of heavy oak rockers with leather seats, asleep in a dismal row.

Billy's Lunch. Thick handleless cups on the wet oilcloth-covered counter. An odor of onions and the smoke of hot lard. In the doorway a young man audibly sucking a toothpick.

The warehouse of the buyer of cream and potatoes. The sour smell of a dairy.

The Ford Garage and the Buick Garage, competent one-story brick and cement buildings opposite each other. Old and new cars on grease-blackened concrete floors. Tire advertisements. The roaring of a tested motor; a racket which beat at the nerves. Surly young men in khaki union-overalls. The most energetic and vital places in town.

A large warehouse for agricultural implements. An impressive barricade of green and gold wheels, of shafts and sulky seats, belonging to machinery of which Carol knew nothing—potato-planters, manure-spreaders, silage-cutters, disk-harrows, breaking-plows.

A feed store, its windows opaque with the dust of bran, a patent medicine advertisement painted on its roof.

Ye Art Shoppe, Prop. Mrs. Mary Ellen Wilks, Christian Science Library open daily free. A touching fumble at beauty. A one-room shanty of boards recently covered with rough stucco. A show-window delicately rich in error: vases starting out to imitate tree-trunks but running off into blobs of gilt—an aluminum ash-tray labeled "Greetings from Gopher Prairie"—a Christian Science magazine—a stamped sofa-cushion portraying a large ribbon tied to a small poppy, the correct skeins of embroidery-silk lying on the pillow. Inside the shop, a glimpse of bad carbon prints of bad and famous pictures, shelves of phonograph records and camera films, wooden toys, and in the midst an anxious small woman sitting in a padded rocking chair.

A barber shop and pool room. A man in shirt sleeves, presumably Del Snafflin the proprietor, shaving a man who had a large Adam's apple.

Nat Hicks's Tailor Shop, on a side street off Main. A one-story building. A fashion-plate showing human pitchforks in garments which looked as hard as steel plate.

On another side street a raw red-brick Catholic Church with a varnished yellow door.

The post-office—merely a partition of glass and brass shutting off the rear of a mildewed room which must once have been a shop. A tilted writing-shelf against a wall rubbed black and scattered with official notices and army recruiting-posters.

The damp, yellow-brick schoolbuilding in its cindery grounds.

The State Bank, stucco masking wood.

The Farmers' National Bank. An Ionic temple of marble. Pure, exquisite, solitary. A brass plate with "Ezra Stowbody, Pres't."

A score of similar shops and establishments.

Behind them and mixed with them, the houses, meek cottages or large, comfortable, soundly uninteresting symbols of prosperity.

In all the town not one building save the Ionic bank which gave pleasure to Carol's eyes; not a dozen buildings which suggested that, in the fifty years of Gopher Prairie's existence, the citizens had realized that it was either desirable or possible to make this, their common home, amusing or attractive.

It was not only the unsparing unapologetic ugliness and the rigid straightness which overwhelmed her. It was the planlessness, the flimsy temporariness of the buildings, their faded unpleasant colors. The street was cluttered with electric-light poles, telephone poles, gasoline pumps for motor cars, boxes of goods. Each man had built with the most valiant disregard of all the others. Between a large new "block" of two-story brick shops on one side, and the fire-brick Overland garage on the other side, was a one-story cottage turned into a millinery shop. The white temple of the Farmers' Bank was elbowed back by a grocery of glaring yellow brick. One store-building had a patchy galvanized iron cornice; the building beside it was crowned with battlements and pyramids of brick capped with blocks of red sandstone.

She escaped from Main Street, fled home.

She wouldn't have cared, she insisted, if the people had been comely. She had noted a young man loafing before a shop, one unwashed hand holding the cord of an awning; a middle-aged man who had a way of staring at women as though he had been married too long and too prosaically; an old farmer, solid, wholesome, but not clean—his face like a potato fresh from the earth. None of them had shaved for three days.

"If they can't build shrines, out here on the prairie, surely there's nothing to prevent their buying safety-razors!" she raged.

She fought herself: "I must be wrong. People do live here. It *can't* be as ugly as—as I know it is! I must be wrong. But I can't do it. I can't go through with it."

She came home too seriously worried for hysteria; and when she found Kennicott waiting for her, and exulting, "Have a walk? Well, like the town? Great lawns and trees, eh?" she was able to say, with a self-protective maturity new to her, "It's very interesting."

Death in the Woods

by SHERWOOD ANDERSON, 1876–1941. *Born in Camden, Ohio, Anderson grew up in small Ohio communities and received a desultory education. He served in the Spanish-American War and afterwards engaged in the manufacture of paint at Elyria, Ohio, and in the advertising business in Chicago. He published his first book, Windy McPherson's Son, in 1916 when he was forty. Anderson frequently tried his hand at the novel but lacked a firm sense of plot and character development; the best of his longer fiction is Dark Laughter (1925). His short stories, at which he excelled, have been collected in such volumes as Winesburg, Ohio (1919), The Triumph of the Egg (1921), and Horses and Men (1923). He also wrote several revealing autobiographical volumes such as A Story Teller's Story (1924) and Tar (1926). Anderson dealt frequently with the frustrations and disillusionment of small-town characters but he also had a streak of poetry in his makeup. Harry Hansen has called him a corn-fed mystic. "Death in the Woods," a story remarkable for its restrained treatment of an unpleasant theme, originally appeared in the American Mercury, September 1926.*

I

SHE was an old woman and lived on a farm near the town in which I lived. All country and small town people have seen such old women, but no one knows much about them. Such an old woman comes into town driving an old worn-out horse or she comes afoot carrying a basket. She may own a few hens and have eggs to sell. She brings them in a basket and takes them to a grocer. There she trades them in. She gets some salt pork and some beans. Then she gets a pound or two of sugar and some flour.

Afterwards she goes to the butcher's and asks for some dog-meat. She may spend ten or fifteen cents, but when she does she asks for something. In my day the butchers gave liver to anyone who wanted to carry it away. In our family we were always having it. Once one of my brothers got a whole cow's liver at the slaughter-house near the fair-grounds. We had it until we were sick of it. It never cost a cent. I have hated the thought of it ever since.

The old farm woman got some liver and a soup-bone. She never visited with anyone and as soon as she got what she wanted she lit out for home. It made quite a load for such an old body. No one gave her a lift. People drive right down a road and never notice an old woman like that.

There was such an old woman used to come into town past our house one Summer and Fall when I was sick with what was called in-flammatory rheumatism. She went home later carrying a heavy pack on her back. Two or three large gaunt-looking dogs followed at her heels.

The old woman was nothing special. She was one of the nameless ones that hardly anyone knows, but she got into my thoughts. I have just suddenly now, after all these years, remembered her and what happened. It is a story. Her name was, I think, Grimes, and she lived with her husband and son in a small unpainted house on the bank of a small creek four miles from town.

The husband and son were a tough lot. Although the son was but twenty-one, he had already served a term in jail. It was whispered about that the woman's husband stole horses and ran them off to some other county. Now and then, when a horse turned up missing, the man had also disappeared. No one ever caught him. Once, when I was loafing at Tom Whitehead's livery-barn, the man came there and sat on the bench in front. Two or three other men were there, but no one spoke to him. He sat for a few minutes and then got up and went away. When he was leaving he turned around and stared at the men. There was a look of defiance in his eyes. "Well, I have tried to be friendly. You don't want to talk to me. It has been so wherever I have gone in this town. If, some day, one of your fine horses turns up missing, well, then what?" He did not say anything actually. "I'd like to bust one of you on the jaw," was about what his eyes said. I remember how the look in his eyes made me shiver.

The old man belonged to a family that had had money once. His name was Grimes, Jake Grimes. It all comes back clearly now. His father, John Grimes, had owned a sawmill when the country was new and had made money. Then he got to drinking and running after women. When he died there wasn't much left.

Jake blew in the rest. Pretty soon there wasn't any more lumber to cut and his land was nearly all gone.

He got his wife off a German farmer, for whom he went to work one June day in the wheat harvest. She was a young thing then and scared to death. You see, the farmer was up to something with the girl—she was, I think, a bound girl and his wife had her suspicions. She took it out on the girl when the man wasn't around. Then, when the wife had to go off to town for supplies, the farmer got after her. She told young Jake that nothing really ever happened, but he didn't know whether to believe it or not.

He got her pretty easy himself, the first time he was out with her. He wouldn't have married her if the German farmer hadn't tried to tell him where to get off. He got her to go riding with him in his buggy one night when he was threshing on the place, and then he came for her the next Sunday night.

She managed to get out of the house without her employer's seeing, but when she was getting into the buggy he showed up. It was almost dark, and he just popped up suddenly at the horse's head. He grabbed the horse by the bridle and Jake got out his buggy-whip.

They had it out all right! The German was a tough one. Maybe he didn't care whether his wife knew or not. Jake hit him over the face and shoulders with the buggy-whip, but the horse got to acting up and he had to get out.

Then the two men went for it. The girl didn't see it. The horse started to run away and went nearly a mile down the road before the girl got him stopped. Then she managed to tie him to a tree beside the road. (I wonder how I know all this. It must have stuck in my mind from small town tales when I was a boy.) Jake found her there after he got through with the German. She was huddled up in the buggy seat, crying, scared to death. She told Jake a lot of stuff, how the German had tried to get her, how he chased her once into the barn, how another time, when they happened to be alone in the barn together, he tore her dress open clear down the front. The German, she said, might have got her that time if he hadn't heard his old woman drive in at the gate. She had been off to town for supplies. Well, she would be putting the horse in the barn. The German managed to sneak off to the fields without his wife seeing. He told the girl he would kill her if she told. What could she do? She told a lie about ripping her dress in the barn when she was feeding the stock. I remember now that she was a bound girl and did not know where her father and mother were. Maybe she did not have any father. You know what I mean.

She married Jake and had a son and daughter but the daughter died.

Then she settled down to feed stock. That was her job. At the German's place she had cooked the food for the German and his wife. The wife was a strong woman with big hips and worked most of the time in the fields with her husband. She fed them and fed the cows in the barn, fed the pigs, the horses and the chickens. Every moment of every day as a young girl was spent feeding something.

Then she married Jake Grimes and he had to be fed. She was a slight thing and when she had been married for three or four years, and after the two children were born, her slender shoulders became stooped.

Jake always had a lot of big dogs around the house, that stood near the unused sawmill near the creek. He was always trading horses when he wasn't stealing something and had a lot of poor bony ones about. Also he kept three or four pigs and a cow. They were all pastured in the few acres left of the Grimes place and Jake did little.

He went into debt for a threshing outfit and ran it for several years, but it did not pay. People did not trust him. They were afraid he would steal the grain at night. He had to go a long way off to get work and it cost too much to get there. In the Winter he hunted and cut a little firewood, to be sold in some nearby town. When the boy grew up he was just like his father. They got drunk together. If there wasn't anything to eat in the house when they came home the old man gave his old woman a cut over the head. She had a few chickens of her own and had to kill one of them in a hurry. When they were all killed she wouldn't have any eggs to sell when she went to town, and then what would she do?

She had to scheme all her life about getting things fed, getting the pigs fed so they would grow fat and could be butchered in the Fall. When they were butchered her husband took most of the meat off to town and sold it. If he did not do it first the boy did. They fought sometimes and when they fought the old woman stood aside trembling.

She had got the habit of silence anyway—that was fixed. Sometimes, when she began to look old—she wasn't forty yet—and when the husband and son were both off, trading horses or drinking or hunting or stealing, she went around the house and the barnyard muttering to herself.

How was she going to get everything fed?—that was her problem.

398

The dogs had to be fed. There wasn't enough hay in the barn for the horses and the cow. If she didn't feed the chickens how could they lay eggs? Without eggs to sell how could she get things in town, things she had to have to keep the life of the farm going? Thank heaven, she did not have to feed her husband—in a certain way. That hadn't lasted long after their marriage and after the babies came. Where he went on his long trips she did not know. Sometimes he was gone from home for weeks and after the boy grew up they went off together.

They left everything at home for her to manage and she had no money. She knew no one. No one ever talked to her in town. When it was Winter she had to gather sticks of wood for her fire, had to try to keep the stock fed with very little grain.

The stock in the barn cried to her hungrily, the dogs followed her about. In the Winter the hens laid few enough eggs. They huddled in the corners of the barn and she kept watching them. If a hen lays an egg in the barn in the Winter and you do not find it, it freezes and breaks.

One day in Winter the old woman went off to town with a few eggs and the dogs followed her. She did not get started until nearly three o'clock and the snow was heavy. She hadn't been feeling very well for several days and so she went muttering along, scantily clad, her shoulders stooped. She had an old grain bag in which she carried her eggs, tucked away down in the bottom. There weren't many of them, but in Winter the price of eggs is up. She would get a little meat for the eggs, some salt pork, a little sugar, and some coffee perhaps. It might be the butcher would give her a piece of liver.

When she had got to town and was trading in her eggs the dogs lay by the door outside. She did pretty well, got the things she needed, more than she had hoped. Then she went to the butcher and he gave her some liver and some dog-meat.

It was the first time anyone had spoken to her in a friendly way for a long time. The butcher was alone in his shop when she went in and was annoyed by the thought of such a sick-looking old woman out on such a day. It was bitter cold and the snow, that had let up during the afternoon, was falling again. The butcher said something about her husband and her son, swore at them, and the old woman stared at him, a look of mild surprise in her eyes as he talked. He said that if either the husband or the son were going to get any of the liver or the heavy bones with scraps of meat hanging to them that he had put into the grain bag, he'd see him starve first.

Starve, eh? Well things had to be fed. Men had to be fed, and the horses that weren't any good but maybe could be traded off, and the poor thin cow that hadn't given any milk for three months.

Horses, cows, pigs, dogs, men.

The old woman had to get back before darkness came if she could. The dogs followed at her heels, sniffing at the heavy grain bag she had fastened on her back. When she got to the edge of town she stopped by a fence and tied the bag on her back with a piece of rope she had carried in her dress-pocket for just that purpose. That was an easier way to carry it. Her arms ached. It was hard when she had to crawl over fences and once she fell over and landed in the snow. The dogs went frisking about. She had to struggle to get to her feet again but she made it. The point of climbing over the fences was that there was a short cut over a hill and through a wood. She might have gone around by the road, but it was a mile further that way. She was afraid she couldn't make it. And then, besides, the stock had to be fed. There was a little hay left, a little corn. Perhaps her husband and son would bring some home when they came. They had driven off in the only buggy the Grimes family had, a rickety thing, a rickety horse hitched to the buggy, two other rickety horses led by halters. They were going to trade horses, get a little money if they could. They might come home drunk. It would be well to have something in the house when they came back.

The son had an affair on with a woman at the county seat, fifteen miles away. She was a bad woman, a tough one. Once, in the Summer, the son had brought her to the house. Both she and the son had been drinking. Jake Grimes was away and the son and his woman ordered the old woman about like a servant. She didn't mind much; she was used to it. Whatever happened she never said anything. That was her way of getting along. She had managed that way when she was a young girl at the German's and ever since she had married Jake. That time her son brought his woman to the house they stayed all night, sleeping together just as though they were married. It hadn't shocked the old woman, not much. She had got past being shocked early in life.

With the pack on her back she went painfully along across an open field, wading in the deep snow, and got into the woods.

There was a path, but it was hard to follow. Just beyond the top of the hill, where the wood was thickest, there was a small clearing. Had someone once thought of building a house there? The clearing was as large as a building lot in town, large enough for a house and a garden. The path ran along the side of the clearing and when she got there the old woman sat down to rest at the foot of a tree.

It was a foolish thing to do. When she got herself placed, the pack against the tree's trunk, it was nice, but what about getting up again? She worried about that for a moment and then quietly closed her eyes.

She must have slept for a time. When you are about so cold you can't get any colder. The afternoon grew a little warmer and the snow came thicker than ever. Then after a time the weather cleared. The moon even came out.

There were four Grimes dogs that had followed Mrs. Grimes into town, all tall gaunt fellows. Such men as Jake Grimes and his son always keep just such dogs. They kick and abuse them, but they stay. The Grimes dogs, in order to keep from starving, had to do a lot of foraging for themselves, and they had been at it while the old woman slept with her back to the tree at the side of the clearing. They had been chasing rabbits in the woods and in adjoining fields and in their ranging had picked up three other farm dogs.

After a time all the dogs came back to the clearing. They were excited about something. Such nights, cold and clear and with a moon, do things to dogs. It may be that some old instinct, come down from the time when they were wolves and ranged the woods in packs on Winter nights, comes back into them.

The dogs in the clearing, before the old woman, had caught two or three rabbits and their immediate hunger had been satisfied. They began to play, running in circles in the clearing. Round and round they ran, each dog's nose at the tail of the next dog. In the clearing, under the snow-laden trees and under the wintry moon they made a strange picture, running thus silently, in a circle their running had beaten in the soft snow. The dogs made no sound. They ran around and around in the circle.

It may have been that the old woman saw them doing that before she died. She may have awakened once or twice and looked at the strange sight with dim old eyes.

She wouldn't be very cold now, just drowsy. Life hangs on a long time. Perhaps the old woman was out of her head. She may have dreamed of her girlhood, at the German's, and before that, when she was a child and before her mother lit out and left her.

Her dreams couldn't have been very pleasant. Not many pleasant things had happened to her. Now and then one of the Grimes dogs left the running circle and came to stand before her. The dog thrust his face close to her face. His red tongue was hanging out.

The running of the dogs may have been a kind of death ceremony. It may have been that the primitive instinct of the wolf, having been aroused in the dogs by the night and the running, made them somehow afraid.

"Now we are no longer wolves. We are dogs, the servants of men. Keep alive, man! When man dies we become wolves again."

When one of the dogs came to where the old woman sat with her back against the tree and thrust his nose close to her face he seemed satisfied and went back to run with the pack. All the Grimes dogs did it at some time during the evening, before she died. I knew all about it afterward, when I grew to be a man, because once in a wood on another Winter night I saw a pack of dogs act just like that. The dogs were waiting for me to die as they had waited for the old woman that night when I was a child, but when it happened to me I was a young man and had no intention whatever of dying.

The old woman died softly and quietly. When she was dead and when one of the Grimes dogs had come to her and had found her dead all the dogs stopped running.

They gathered about her.

Well, she was dead now. She had fed the Grimes dogs when she was alive, what about now?

There was the pack on her back, the grain bag containing the piece of salt pork, the liver the butcher had given her, the dog-meat, the soup bones. The butcher in town, having been suddenly overcome with a feeling of pity, had loaded her grain bag heavily. It had been a big haul for the old woman.

A big haul for the dogs now.

IV

One of the Grimes dogs sprang suddenly out from the others and began worrying the pack on the old woman's back. Had the dogs really been wolves that one would have been the leader of the pack. What he did, all the others did.

All of them sank their teeth into the grain bag the old woman had fastened with ropes to her back.

They dragged the old woman's body out into the open clearing. The worn-out dress was quickly torn from her shoulders. When she was found, a day or two later, the dress had been torn from her body clear to the hips but the dogs had not touched her body. They had got the meat out of the grain bag, that was all. Her body was frozen stiff when it was found and the shoulders were so narrow and the body so slight that in death it looked like the body of some charming young girl.

Such things happened in towns of the Middle West, on farms near town, when I was a boy. A hunter out after rabbits found the old woman's body and did not touch it. Something, the beaten round path in the little snow-covered clearing, the silence of the place, the place where the dogs had worried the body trying to pull the grain bag away or tear it open—something startled the man and he hurried off to town.

I was in Main street with one of my brothers who was taking the afternoon papers to the stores. It was almost night.

The hunter came into a grocery and told his story. Then he went to a hardware-shop and into a drug-store. Men began to gather on the sidewalks. Then they started out along the road to the place in the wood.

My brother should have gone on about his business of distributing papers but he didn't. Everyone was going to the woods. The undertaker went and the town marshal. Several men got on a dray and rode out to where the path left the road and went into the woods, but the horses weren't very sharply shod and slid about on the slippery roads. They made no better time than those of us who walked.

The town marshal was a large man whose leg had been injured in the Civil War. He carried a heavy cane and limped rapidly along the road. My brother and I followed at his heels and as we went other men and boys joined the crowd.

It had grown dark by the time we got to where the old woman had left the road but the moon had come out. The marshal was thinking there might have been a murder. He kept asking the hunter questions. The hunter went along with his gun across his shoulders, a dog following at his heels. It isn't often a rabbit hunter has a chance to be so conspicuous. He was taking full advantage of it, leading the procession with the town marshal. "I didn't see any wounds. She was a beautiful young girl. Her face was buried in the snow. No, I didn't know her." As a matter of fact, the hunter had not looked closely at the body. He had been frightened. She might have been murdered and someone might spring out from behind a tree and murder him too. In a woods, in the late afternoon, when the trees are all bare and there is white snow on the ground, when all is silent, something creepy steals over the mind and body. If something strange or uncanny has happened in the neighborhood all you think about is getting away from there as fast as you can.

The crowd of men and boys had got to where the old woman crossed the field and went, following the marshal and the hunter up the slight incline and into the woods.

My brother and I were silent. He had his bundle of papers in a bag slung across his shoulder. When he got back to town he would have to go on distributing his papers before he went home to supper. If I went along, as he had no doubt already determined I should, we would both be late. Either mother or our younger sister would have to warm our supper.

Well, we would have something to tell. A boy did not get such a chance very often. It was lucky we just happened to go into the grocery when the hunter came in. The hunter was a country fellow. Neither of us had ever seen him before.

Now the crowd of men and boys had got to the clearing. Darkness comes quickly on such Winter nights but the full moon made everything clear. My brother and I stood near the trees, beneath which the old woman had died.

She did not look old, lying there frozen in that light. One of the men turned her over in the snow and I saw everything. My body trembled with some strange mystical feeling and so did my brother's. It might have been the cold.

Neither of us had ever seen a woman's body before. It may have been the snow, clinging to the frozen flesh, that made it look so white and lovely, so like marble. No woman had come with the party from town, but one of the men, he was the town blacksmith, took off his overcoat and spread it over her. Then he gathered her into his arms and started off to town, all the others following silently. At that time no one knew who she was.

V

I had seen everything, had seen the oval in the snow, like a miniature race-track, where the dogs had run, had seen how the men were mystified, had seen the white bare young-looking shoulders, had heard the whispered comments of the men.

The men were simply mystified. They took the body to the undertaker's, and when the blacksmith, the hunter, the marshal and several others had got inside they closed the door. If father had been there perhaps he could have got in, but we boys couldn't.

I went with my brother to distribute the rest of his papers and when we got home it was my brother who told the story.

I kept silent and went to bed early. It may have been I was not satisfied with the way he told it.

Later, in the town, I must have heard other fragments of the old woman's story. She was recognized the next day and there was an investigation.

The husband and son were found somewhere and brought to town and there was an attempt to connect them with the woman's death, but it did not work. They had perfect enough alibis.

However, the town was against them. They had to get out. Where they went I never heard.

I remember only the picture there in the forest, the men standing about, the naked girlish-looking figure, face down in the snow, the tracks made by the running dogs and the clear cold Winter sky above. White fragments of clouds were drifting across the sky. They went racing across the little open space among the trees.

The scene in the forest had become for me, without my knowing it, the foundation for the real story I am now trying to tell. The fragments, you see, had to be picked up slowly, long afterwards.

Things happened. When I was a young man I worked on the farm of a German. The hired-girl was afraid of her employer. The farmer's wife hated her.

I saw things at that place. Once later, I had a half-uncanny, mystical sort of adventure with dogs in a forest on a clear, moonlit Winter night. When I was a schoolboy, and on a Summer day, I went with a boy friend out along a creek some miles from town and came to the house where the old woman had lived. No one had lived in the house since her death. The doors were broken from the hinges, the window lights were all broken. As the boy and I stood in the road outside, two dogs, just roving farm dogs no doubt, came running around the corner of the house. The dogs were tall, gaunt fellows and came down to the fence and glared through at us, standing in the road.

The whole thing, the story of the old woman's death, was to me as I grew older like music heard from far off. The notes had to be picked up slowly one at a time. Something had to be understood.

The woman who died was one destined to feed animal life. Anyway, that is all she ever did. She was feeding animal life before she was born, as a child, as a young woman working on the farm of the German, after she married, when she grew old and when she died. She fed animal life in cows, in chickens, in pigs, in horses, in dogs, in men. Her daughter had died in childhood and with her one son she had no articulate relations. On the night when she died she was hurrying homeward, bearing on her body food for animal life.

She died in the clearing in the woods and even after her death continued feeding animal life.

You see it is likely that, when my brother told the story, that night when we got home and my mother and sister sat listening, I did not think he got the point. He was too young and so was I. A thing so complete has its own beauty.

I shall not try to emphasize the point. I am only explaining why I was dissatisfied then and have been ever since. I speak of that only that you may understand why I have been impelled to try to tell the simple story over again.

The District School

by CLARENCE DARROW, 1857–1938. One of the most eminent lawyers of his day, Darrow was born in Kinsman, Ohio. He was admitted to the bar in 1878 and from 1888 onward he practiced his profession in Chicago. He was defense counsel in several widely publicized trials, namely, the Loeb-Leopold case of 1924, the Scopes case at Dayton, Tennessee, in 1925, and the Scottsboro Negro case of 1932. After 1927 he retired from regular law practice to devote himself chiefly to lecturing and writing. His autobiography, The Story of My Life, appeared in 1932. Perhaps the most charming piece of writing to come from Darrow's pen was Farmington (1904), an account of life in a small Ohio town which is both fiction and autobiography. It should be compared with William Dean Howells' A Boy's Town. "The District School" is the fifth chapter of Farmington.

THE first school that I remember was not in the little town near which we lived, but about half a mile away in the opposite direction. Our house must have stood just outside the limits of the little village; at any rate, I was sent to the country school. Every morning we children were given a dinner-pail packed full of pie and cake, and now and then a piece of bread and butter (which I always let the other children eat), and were sent off to school. As we passed along the road we were joined by other little boys and girls, and by the time we reached the building our party contained nearly all the children on the road travelling in the direction from which we came. We were a boisterous, thoughtless crowd,—that is, the boys; the girls were quieter and more reserved, which we called "proud."

Almost as soon as the snow was off the ground in the spring, we boys took off our shoes (or, rather, boots) and went barefooted to the school. It was hard enough for us to wait until our parents said the ground was warm enough for us to take off our boots; we felt so light and free, and could run so fast barefooted, that we always begged our mother to let us leave them off at the very earliest chance. The chief disadvantage was that we often stubbed out toes. This was sometimes serious, when we were running fast and would bring them full tilt against a stone. Most of the time we managed to have one or more toes tied up in rags; and we found much pleasure in comparing our wounds, to see whose were the worst, or which were getting well the fastest. The next most serious trouble connected with going barefoot was the necessity for washing our feet every night before we went to bed. This seemed a grievous hardship; sometimes we would forget it, when we could, and I remember now and then being called up out of bed after

I thought I had safely escaped and seemed to be sound asleep, and when my feet were clean enough without being washed.

It seemed to us children that our mother was unreasonably particular about this matter of washing our feet before we went to bed. She always required it when we had been barefoot through the day, even though it had been raining and we had wiped our feet in the grass. Still the trouble of washing our feet was partly made up by our not being obliged to put on or take off our stockings and our boots. This was a great relief, especially in the morning; for this part of our toilet took longer than all the rest, and when the time came around to go barefoot we had only to jump into a few clothes and start away.

In the summer-time it took a long while for us children to travel the short half-mile to the district school. No matter how early we left home, it was nearly always past the hour of nine when we reached the door. For there were birds in the trees and stones in the road, and no child ever knew any pain except his own. There were little fishes in the creek over which we slid in winter and through which we waded in the summer-time; then there were chipmunks on the fences and woodchucks in the fields, and no boy could ever go straight to school, or straight back home after the day was done. The procession of barefoot urchins laughed and joked, and fought, and ran, and bragged, and gave no thought to study or to books until the bell was rung and they were safely seated in the room. Then we watched and waited eagerly for recess; and after that, still more anxiously for the hour of noon, which was always the best time by far of all the day, not alone because of the pie and cake and apples and cheese which the more prudent and obedient of us saved until this time, but also because of the games, in which we had enough boys to go around.

In these games the girls did not join to any great extent; in fact, girls seemed of little use to the urchins who claimed everything as their own. In the school they were seated by themselves on one side of the room, and sometimes when we failed to study as we should we were made to go and sit with them. This was when we were very young. As we grew older, this form of punishment seemed less and less severe, until some other was substituted in its stead. Most of the boys were really rather bashful with the girls,—those who bragged the loudest and fought the readiest somehow never knew just what to say when they were near. We preferred rather to sit and look at them, and wonder how they could be so neat and clean and well "fixed up." I remember when quite a small boy how I used to look over toward their side of the room, especially at a little girl with golden hair that was always hanging in long curls about her head; and it seemed to me that nothing could ever be quite so beautiful as this curly head; which may explain the fact that all my life nothing has seemed quite so beguiling as golden hair,—unless it were black, or brown, or some other kind.

To the boys, school had its chief value, in fact its only value, in its games and sports. Of course, our parents and teachers were always urging us to work. In their efforts to make us study, they resorted to every sort of means—headmarks, presents, praise, flattery, Christmas cards, staying in at recess, staying after school, corporal punishment, all sorts of persuasion, threats, and even main force—to accomplish this result. No like rewards or punishments were required to make us play; which fact, it seems to me, should have shown our teachers and parents that play, exercise, activity, and change are the law of life, especially the life of a little child; and that study, as we knew it, was unnatural and wrong. Still, nothing of this sort ever dawned upon their minds.

I cannot remember much real kindness between the children of the school; while we had our special chums, we never seemed to care for them, except that boys did not like to be alone. There were few things a boy could do alone, excepting tasks, which of course we avoided if we could. On our way to and from the school, or while together at recess and noon, while we played the ordinary games a very small matter brought on a quarrel, and we always seemed to be watching for a chance to fight. In the matter of our quarrels and fights we showed the greatest impartiality, as boys do in almost all affairs of life.

While our books were filled with noble precepts, we never seemed to remember them when we got out of doors, or even to think that they had any application to our lives. In this respect the boy and the grown-up man seem wonderfully alike.

But really, school was not all play. Our teachers and parents tried their best to make us learn,—that is, to make us learn the lessons in the books. The outside lessons we always seemed to get without their help, —in fact, in spite of their best endeavors to prevent our knowing what they meant.

The fact that our teachers tried so hard to make us learn was no doubt one of the chief reasons why we looked on them as our natural enemies. We seldom had the same teacher for two terms of school, and we always wondered whether the new one would be worse or better than the old. We started in prepared to find her worse; and the first kind words we ever had for our teacher were spoken after she was gone and we compared her with the new one in her place. Our teachers seemed to treat us pretty well for the first few days. They were then very kind and sweet; they hardly ever brought switches to the school until the second week, but we were always sure that they would be called into service early in the term. No old-time teacher would have dreamed that she could get through a term of school without a whip, any more than a judge would believe that society could get along without a jail. The methods that were used to make us learn, and the things we were taught, seem very absurd as I look back upon them now; and still, I presume, they were not different from the means employed today.

Most of us boys could learn arithmetic fairly well,—in this, indeed, we always beat the girls. Still, some parts of arithmetic were harder than the rest. I remember that I mastered the multiplication-table up to "twelve times twelve," backwards and forwards and every other way, at a very early age, and I fancy that this knowledge has clung to me through life; but I cannot forget the many weary hours I spent trying to learn the tables of weights and measures, and how much vexation of spirit I endured before my task was done. However, after weary weeks and months I learned them so well that I could say them with the greatest ease. This was many, many years ago; since that time I have found my place in the world of active life, but I cannot now remember that even once have I had occasion to know or care about the difference between "troy weight" and "apothecaries' weight," if, in fact, there was any difference at all. And one day, last week I think it was, for the first time in all these endless years I wished to know how many square rods made an acre, and I tried to call back the table that I learned so long ago at school; but as to this my mind was an utter blank, and all that I could do was to see the little girl with the golden locks sitting at her desk—and, by the way, I wonder where she is today. But I took a dictionary from the shelf, and there I found it plain and straight, and I made no effort to keep it in my mind, knowing that if perchance in the uncertain years that may be yet to come I shall need to know again, I will find it there in the dictionary safe and sound.

And all those examples that I learned to cipher out! I am sure I know more today than the flaxen-haired barefoot boy who used to sit at his little desk at school and only drop his nibbled slate-pencil to drive the flies away from his long bare legs, but I could not do those sums today even if one of my old-time teachers should come back from her long-forgotten grave and threaten to keep me in for the rest of my life unless I got the answer right.

And then the geography! How hard they tried to make us learn this book, and how many recesses were denied us because we were not sure just which river in Siberia was the longest! Of course we knew nothing about Siberia, or whether the rivers ran water or blood; but we were forced to know which was the largest and just how long it was. And so all over the great round world we travelled, to find cities, towns, rivers, mountain ranges, peninsulas, oceans, and bays. How important it all was! I remember that one of the ways they took to make us learn this book was to have us sing geography in a chorus of little voices. I can recall today how one of those old tunes began, but I remember little beyond the start. The song was about the capitals of all the States, and it began, "State of Maine, Augusta, is on the Kennebec River," and so on through the whole thirty-three or four, or whatever the number was when I was a little child. Well, many, many years have passed away since then, and I have wandered far and wide from my old-time country home. There are few places in the United States that I have not seen, in my quest for activity and change. I have even stood on some of the highest peaks of the Alps, and looked down upon its quiet valleys and its lovely lakes; but I have never yet been to Augusta on the Kennebec River in the State of Maine, and it begins to look as if I never should. Still, if Fortune ever takes me there, I shall be very glad that I learned when yet a child at school that Augusta was the capital of Maine and on the Kennebec River. So, too, I have never been to Siberia, and, not being a Russian, I presume that I shall never go. And in fact, wherever I have wandered on the earth I have had to learn my geography all over new again.

But, really, grammar made me more trouble than any other study. Somehow I never could learn grammar, and it always made me angry when I tried. My parents and teachers told me that I could never write or speak unless I learned grammar, and so I tried and tried, but even now I can hardly tell an adverb from an adjective, and I do not know that I care. When a little boy, I used to think that if I really had anything to tell I could make myself understood; and I think so still. The longer I live the surer I am that the chief trouble of writers and speakers is the lack of interesting thoughts, and not of proper words. Certainly grammar was a hideous nightmare to me when a child at school. Of all the parts of speech the verb was the most impossible to get. I remember now how difficult it was to conjugate the verb "to love," which the books seemed always to put first. How I stumbled and blundered as I tried to learn that verb! I might possibly have mastered the present tense, but when it came to all the different moods and various tenses it was a hopeless task. I am much older now, but somehow that verb has never grown easier with the fleeting years. The past-perfect tense has always been well-nigh impossible to learn. I never could tell when it left off, or whether it ever left off or not. Neither have I been able to keep it separate from the present, or, for that matter, from the future. A few years after the district school, I went for a brief time to the Academy on the hill, where I studied Latin; and I remember that this same verb was there, with all the old complications and many that were new, to greet me when I came. To be sure, it had been changed to

"Amo, Amas, Amat," but it was the old verb just the same, and its various moods and tenses caused me the same trouble that I had experienced as a little child. My worry over this word has made me wonder whether this verb, in all its moods and tenses, was not one of the many causes of the downfall of the Roman Empire, of which we used to hear so much. At any rate, I long since ceased trying to get it straight or keep it straight; indeed, I am quite sure that it was designed only to tangle and ensnare.

Young Poet in Davenport

by FLOYD DELL, 1887—   . *There is no better account of the artistic and intellectual life of the smaller cities of the Middle West about 1900 than that contained in the novels and autobiography of Floyd Dell. Born in Barry, Illinois, of mixed Pennsylvania-Dutch and Irish stock, Dell attended high school at Quincy, Illinois, and worked as a reporter in Davenport, Iowa. At Davenport, too, he became acquainted with such writers as George Cram Cook, Arthur Davison Ficke, and Susan Glaspell. In the fall of 1908 Dell went to Chicago and until 1913 served as associate literary editor and then as literary editor of the Chicago Evening Post. Subsequently Dell did journalistic work in New York and was a member of the staff of the Masses and the Liberator. He is the author of a dozen novels, the best known of which are Moon-Calf (1920), The Briary-Bush (1921), Janet March (1923), and Diana Stair (1932), his own favorite; volumes of verse and plays; a biography of Upton Sinclair (1927); and Homecoming—an Autobiography (1933). Since 1935 he has done editorial work and special reports for the WPA. The pages describing Dell's attempt to educate himself by reading and to experiment with poetry comprise a section of his autobiography Homecoming.*

WE LIVED in one side of a double house on West Sixth street. Davenport was one of three towns which altogether had a population of about a hundred thousand people. Across the river, with Rock Island and its Government Arsenal in between, was the city of Rock Island, and beside it Moline with its great plow-factories. One of my brothers had a harness-maker's job at the Arsenal; my other brother and sister less distinguished jobs—but still, jobs; and my father had hopes.

Davenport had a large German population, some of it with the traditions of the exiles of '49; and a considerable Jewish population; both of these facts were to be of some importance as affecting my happiness. The town had the bravado of an old Mississippi river-port, and the liberal "cosmopolitan" atmosphere of a place that is in touch with European influences. It had its nose not too closely pressed against the grindstone of "practical" fact. It had an intelligentsia, who knew books and ideas. It had even some live authors, a famous one, and some who might one day be famous. Supposing, as a young person is prone to do, that all really famous people have been dead a long time, I naturally took for granted that "Octave Thanet" was so, and was greatly astonished and rather incredulous when told she was actually alive. However, at that time the only American authors who existed for me were Frank Norris and Mark Twain; and Frank Norris had died last year, while Mark Twain was only a boyhood memory. Fiction did not interest me much.

But I retained from Frank Norris's "Octopus" a picture of a girl that was to haunt me always—a sturdy, earth-strong girl, with hair as yellow as the ripe wheat, serene, calm-browed, happy-hearted. I was in love with her image in my mind.

And now I was reading poetry. Back in Quincy a footnote in Prescott's "Conquest of Peru" had sent me to Southey's "Thalaba"; I had read all of Southey, and admired it all. But Byron now swept Southey out of existence. Keats came next, a never-to-be-forgotten delight. I read, in a five-and-ten-cent store, standing on one foot and then the other, the "Rubaiyat," and carried home in dazed wonder that casket of enchantments. Browning's poems became mine at the same price; my library was growing. I was reading English and some other poetry at the rate of one great poet a week; I read and knew vastly by heart Wordsworth, Shelley, Walt Whitman, Kipling, Wilde, the Rossettis, Tennyson, Wilfred Scawen Blunt, Herrick, Milton, Heine, Swinburne, John Donne, Marvell, Drayton, Shakespeare's Sonnets; some Persian and Chinese poetry of which I made my own rhymed versions; among living Americans I was enthusiastic about Bliss Carman and William Vaughn Moody; then came a magnificent discovery that for a long time no one in Davenport would share—A. E. Housman's "Shropshire Lad," bought with a dollar that was being saved to buy shoes with; and with an appetite geared to that pitch, the world has seemed, ever since, in this respect, a poor, barren starveling place, which cannot produce more than two or three great poets in a century.

In the intervals of reading poetry, I made poetry. I didn't especially intend to make it, and I certainly never knew what it was going to be about in advance. I could feel a poem coming on; and I was able to sympathize with the behavior of a cat who feels that she is going to have kittens and searches restlessly about for a good place to have them. I knew just how the cat felt; and I probably had the same glazed look in my eye as I wandered off into the night to have a poem. Night and solitude were best; interruption in the process was frightfully painful. So, late at night, I walked across the bridge that crossed from Davenport to the Government Island. Policemen would pass at intervals, swinging their clubs, pairs of late lovers would emerge slowly from the darkness into the glare of an arc-light. I went past them, walking rapidly, head bent down. Where the bridge came to an end, a stone walk began that skirted the Island toward Moline, where at intervals the darkness was suddenly burst open by the crimson flare of a blasting furnace. I paused at the parapet, looking at the lights reflected in the river. Lines would begin to emerge entire from my mind. I would say them over, holding on to them with my memory, listening to the rhythm. *I dare not look into your eyes—For fear I should see there— The naked soul behind the guise—That earth-born spirits wear.* I turned homeward. *Lest gazing on immortal love—I should go mad, like him—Who saw Her bathing in a grove—The Huntress white and slim.* I whispered the lines over and over, walking faster, overtaking the policeman. The late lovers stepped from my path impatiently. Behind me the furnace flares lighted the sky at lurid intervals. My solitary tramp sounded noisily on the bridge. I emerged from the fantastic shadowy tangle of girders upon the streets of Davenport. Bathed in an enchantment of beauty, I walked swiftly along the homeward streets, whispering aloud the words that eased my heart.

At home, the light was burning. I hoped that my mother had had sense enough to go to bed. But no, there she was, coming downstairs wrapped in her old brown shawl, to make sure that her boy was safe. "Mother, you haven't been waiting up for me?" "No, I just wasn't sleepy." While she hovered about, I would get the poem written down on paper. And then, awakened from my trance, I looked at it, and wondered: "But what the devil is this poem about?" My mother, lingering, asked, "Have you written something new?" "Oh, just a poem." Its literal meaning was not obscure, but to whom was it addressed? Not to Margaret. Not to any girl I knew. Yet it had meant something to me. "Will you read it to me?" Mothers are like that. They want to be proud of their sons; they want to believe in them; and so—if it gives her any satisfaction—

> I dare not look into your eyes,
>   For fear I should see there
> The naked soul, behind the guise
>   That earth-born spirits wear.
>
> Lest, gazing on immortal love,
>   I should go mad, like him
> Who found Her bathing in a grove,
>   The Huntress white and slim.

413

"That's all. It's a short poem. The Huntress is Diana, of course." "I think it's very pretty," my mother replied. She looked about, saw nothing to do, and went back up the stairs. And I, looking at the lines, reflected: "It doesn't make any difference what a poem is about, anyway, if it sounds all right."

I liked Davenport. It was, or so it seemed to me, different from its sister towns across the river, Rock Island and Moline. Rock Island was merely commonplace and uninteresting. Moline seemed like a nightmare—the inconceivably hideous product of unrestricted commercial enterprise; its center was occupied by the vast, bare, smoke-begrimed structures of the greatest plow-factory on earth; a little fringe of desultory shops, insulted and apparently pushed aside by incessantly switching trains of freight-cars, gave way to a drab and monotonous area of cheap and hastily-constructed workingmen's dwellings, each house exactly like the rest, street after street and mile after mile—while afar, set almost inaccessibly upon the hills like the castles of robber barons, could be discerned the houses of Moline's leisure class. The town of Davenport was like neither of these towns. It had a kindlier aspect. Its long tree-shaded streets, its great parks, its public buildings, even its shops and homes, seemed to have a kind of dignity and serenity, as though it were understood that in this town life was meant to be enjoyed.

I had heard that there were many Socialists in Davenport, and that they had their meetings in Turner Hall. So, one afternoon, not long after we came to town, I had tried to find them. I went to Turner Hall in quest of information. It was an imposing building, with four entrances, one of them the lobby of the German Theatre. The man in the box-office knew the price of seats for the German play to be given there that evening, but he didn't know anything about where the Socialists met. So I tried the next entrance, and found myself suddenly in a gymnasium, where a bloomered class of young frauleins were at that moment engaged in turning handsprings. The director plainly regarded me as a rash intruder, and refused to give me any information about anything. So I backed out, apologizing. The third entrance revealed a flight of steps. I went up. At the first landing I came upon someone who seemed to be the janitor; but he did not understand English very well, so I explored for myself. There were many lodge-halls at the top of the first flight of stairs, with no sign to indicate that any of them was a Socialist meeting-place. I went on from door to door, entering and looking about. I did not know exactly what I was looking for—perhaps a red banner; but I found nothing distinctly Socialist in any of the little rooms. Nevertheless, I continued to look, and having exhausted the possibilities of that floor, I went on to the next. On the top floor, I broke in upon an assembly of German matrons. They seemed angry and suspicious, and I went downstairs in great embarrassment. But I had not given up. There was still another entrance. It opened upon a saloon. The busy bartender admitted that he had heard of the Socialists, and in a reflective interval in the serving of drinks he seemed to remember that they met on Fridays—in just which hall he couldn't say.

So on the next Friday evening I stood again in front of the building. Flocks of people came and went, in and out. There was something discouragingly commonplace about these people, something which made it difficult for me to imagine them as Socialists. But I followed some of them up the winding stairway, and watched them enter one or another of the little halls. I thought of knocking and inquiring at each doorway in turn. The number of doors, however large, was still finite, and in time I should come to the right one. But the appearance of the people that I saw within the rooms discouraged me. I could not face their stolid, unimaginative stares forty times. I went slowly downstairs, and again took up my position by the door. I was too hopeless now to ask anyone for information; I waited, as if I were expecting someone to come up and hail me. Perhaps my inward feeling was that the Socialists should recognize me as one of them. But no one came up and greeted me.

At last I went home. But the next Friday evening I went again, this time without much confidence, and hung about the doorway, till the crowd thinned and ceased and the street was deserted.

The next summer, having in the meantime not succeeded in discovering any Socialists in Davenport, I saw in the paper a notice of a Socialist lecture to be given at a church a few blocks from my home, and I went there. It was a Negro church. The congregation was there, and the pastor, and ice-cream and cake were in readiness for a sociable aftermath. But Michael Kennedy, the Socialist candidate for something, did not show up to deliver his lecture. Everybody waited and waited. I had taken my place in one of the front pews. I was the only white person there. Finally the pastor came to me and asked me if I were a Socialist. "Why, yes," I said. "It doesn't look as if Mr. Kennedy was going to get here," said the pastor; "and I was wondering if you would give us a little speech on Socialism." "Well, all right," I said. "Will you just tell me your name, sir, and I'll introduce you." So I went up into the pulpit, and delivered a lecture upon the materialist conception of history, the class-struggle, and the program of Socialism. My lecture was very enthusiastically applauded, and afterward I joined the congregation in eating ice-cream and cake.

One evening, at the public library, I saw a man I would have liked to know. He was talking to somebody, and he had a beautiful voice, and a keenly intelligent mind; he was, though indefinitely older than I, young-looking, with a slender figure, and a sensitive, dark, foreign-looking face. I thought of him as a poet, someone it would be delightful to know. I stared at him intently, and then became embarrassed. I went out of the library, and paused on the steps. The man came out, smiled at me in which seemed a faintly satiric way, sniffed eagerly at the evening breeze, and spoke to me. He said: "What a beautiful night!" And I, who had been wishing I could talk to this man, said nothing whatever in reply. I wanted his friendship too much to believe that it was possible for me to have it. The man added, with a gesture: "See— the moon!" And as if that gesture, or the words, or the singularly beautiful tune of the man's voice, had called it into being, I became aware of the great white moon over the roofs—aware too of the breeze with its odors of cool dampness—aware of the poignant wonder of night. I was ashamed at the thought that I might have revealed this rush of feeling to what might be hostile eyes. The man made a little signal of farewell, and started to walk away. Then I was sorry I hadn't talked to him. I wanted to rush after him; but I couldn't. And upon some evening afterward, a poem came into my mind:

> As each one passed I scanned his face,
> And each, methought, scanned mine;
> Each looked on each a little space,
> Then passed, and made no sign.

> And every cold glance answered Nay!
> Would no one understand?
> None brush the cobweb bars away,
> Stand forth and clasp my hand?

> But as into each face I peered,
> My glance was cold as theirs,
> That they whose scornful laugh I feared
> Might pass me unawares.

As a poet, I was happy with a strange happiness that was made out of pain. Night, the moon, the shadows of the trees, the wind with its strange scents, all the beauty that tortured me, became strangely comforting when they turned into words in my mind. Through streets that were not the streets I knew by day, down light-and-shadow-enchanted ways, I wandered by night, making my poems. I entered for a long golden hour an enchanted land where there was neither desire nor fear, only the solace of magic words. I grew indifferent to the outer world. It seemed less real to me than this realm of dreams into which I was transported in an instant.

And I was not lonely in that realm, for I was companioned by a shadow, soft and vague—a mere hint or whisper, so unobtrusive it was, of a being almost without sex as it was almost without existence, yet faintly breathing the perfume of girlhood—a delicate and perfect comradeship.

Midway of that enchanted ground
There is a lazy well-sweep found,
And dreaming waters, at whose brink
On summer noons we stop to drink.
Out underneath the listless boughs,
Down in the grass the shadows drowse,
And all the indolent slow hours,
No breezes come to wake the flowers,
Or cast a ripple in the lake,
To writhe, a ghostly water-snake.
And there for you and me is peace,
Where passions fade, ambitions cease;
For all the loves and hates that toss
The helpless soul, come out across
The far-off purple hills that lie
Aswoon beneath that sapphire sky.

But meanwhile, there was the world of reality that I had to live in. I felt that I ought to be at work earning money to help the family. My destiny was to be a factory hand. I had no illusions of being able to rise from the ranks. I would remain a factory-hand, and an ill-paid one. I saw myself falling in love with some girl at a factory; getting married some day, having children, and living in a little house that was like all the others up and down the block. Some workingmen had gardens in their back yards; my brother Harry had a nice little garden within the narrow confines of our back yard here. If I had a garden, it would be the worst garden on the block where I lived. It would be the worst, because I would be thinking about poetry, instead of about potatoes. And if I thought about poetry at my factory job, I would get fired. It wasn't a cheerful prospect.

I was walking through the streets as I thought of these things one day, and I stopped in front of a window to look at the crimson and gold wings of a dead butterfly pinned to a card, with the words, "We can't all be butterflies." No, I reflected, not even butterflies can! For those wings, which people thought merely pretty, were part of the serious business of life to that butterfly. He must wing his way to the nectar-cup for his dinner, and seek his mate with them; and when that is finished, he cannot drink any more nectar, for his thorax contracts (or so I had read). Life is through with him, and he dies.

417

They know thee not, who deem thy hues
The splendid appanage of pride,
As on some idle pleasure-cruise
Thou seemest royally to guide
With summer's soft and languorous tide
Down crimson-bannered avenues. . . .

I walked away, framing the words into rhythmic sequence.

Yet is that fancy dear to me!
It is not good to look around
And see no single creature free
From these chains wherewith I am bound.
I still believe that thou hast found
Release from laws men think to be
Relentless, from the dreary round
Of . . .

Of what? The phrase eluded me. I looked at the workingmen's houses
about me, thinking of the life lived within them. That was the fate of
others, why should it not be my fate, too? Why should I ask something better—something like the fancied life of the butterfly? Yet I
did. . . .

And if in bitterness and scorn
I walk the ways my fathers trod,
Thou, flashing through the perfumed morn,
Shalt be my plea to God!

Someone talked to me about going to business college. I thought it
over, and decided that I would rather end in the poorhouse than go to
business college and work in an office.

Haircut

by RING LARDNER, 1885–1933. *Ringgold Wilmer Lardner exem-
plifies the writer who came to the creation of short stories through the
medium of the newspaper sports page. Born in Niles, Michigan, Lardner was
educated in the local schools and at the Armour Institute of Technology,
Chicago. In 1905 he entered newspaper work in South Bend, Indiana, and
later worked on newspapers in Chicago, St. Louis, and Boston; after 1919 his
work was widely syndicated. His early short stories, in which baseball and*

pugilism were common themes, appeared in such volumes as You Know Me, Al (1916), Gullible's Travels (1917), and Treat 'Em Rough (1918). His more mature work was published in How to Write Short Stories (1924) and The Love Nest and Other Stories (1926); his stories were collected in 1929 under the title of Round Up. Lardner has been frequently praised for his successful use of the American idiom, especially the speech of the half-educated. He was not only a humorist but a satirist with caustic undertones, as demonstrated in the following selection.

I GOT another barber that comes over from Carterville and helps me out Saturdays, but the rest of the time I can get along all right alone. You can see for yourself that this ain't no New York City and besides that, the most of the boys works all day and don't have no leisure to drop in here and get themselves prettied up.

You're a newcomer, ain't you? I thought I hadn't seen you round before. I hope you like it good enough to stay. As I say, we ain't no New York City or Chicago, but we have pretty good times. Not as good, though, since Jim Kendall got killed. When he was alive, him and Hod Meyers used to keep this town in an uproar. I bet they was more laughin' done here than any town its size in America.

Jim was comical, and Hod was pretty near a match for him. Since Jim's gone, Hod tries to hold his end up just the same as ever, but it's tough goin' when you ain't got nobody to kind of work with.

They used to be plenty fun in here Saturdays. This place is jam-packed Saturdays, from four o'clock on. Jim and Hod would show up right after their supper, round six o'clock. Jim would set himself down in that big chair, nearest the blue spittoon. Whoever had been settin' in that chair, why they'd get up when Jim come in and give it to him.

You'd of thought it was a reserved seat like they have sometimes in a theayter. Hod would generally always stand or walk up and down, or some Saturdays, of course, he'd be settin' in this chair part of the time, gettin' a haircut.

Well, Jim would set there a w'ile without openin' his mouth only to spit, and then finally he'd say to me, "Whitey,"—my right name, that is, my right first name, is Dick, but everybody round here calls me Whitey—Jim would say, "Whitey, your nose looks like a rosebud tonight. You must of been drinkin' some of your aw de cologne."

So I'd say, "No, Jim, but you look like you'd been drinkin' somethin' of that kind or somethin' worse."

Jim would have to laugh at that, but then he'd speak up and say, "No, I ain't had nothin' to drink, but that ain't sayin' I wouldn't like somethin'. I wouldn't even mind if it was wood alcohol."

Then Hod Meyers would say, "Neither would your wife." That

419

would set everybody to laughin' because Jim and his wife wasn't on very good terms. She'd of divorced him only they wasn't no chance to get alimony and she didn't have no way to take care of herself and the kids. She couldn't never understand Jim. He *was* kind of rough, but a good fella at heart.

Him and Hod had all kinds of sport with Milt Sheppard. I don't suppose you've seen Milt. Well, he's got an Adam's apple that looks more like a mushmelon. So I'd be shavin' Milt and when I'd start to shave down here on his neck, Hod would holler, "Hey, Whitey, wait a minute! Before you cut into it, let's make up a pool and see who can guess closest to the number of seeds."

And Jim would say, "If Milt hadn't of been so hoggish, he'd of ordered a half a cantaloupe instead of a whole one and it might not of stuck in his throat."

All the boys would roar at this and Milt himself would force a smile, though the joke was on him. Jim certainly was a card!

There's his shavin' mug, settin' on the shelf, right next to Charley Vail's. "Charles M. Vail." That's the druggist. He comes in regular for his shave, three times a week. And Jim's is the cup next to Charley's. "James H. Kendall." Jim won't need no shavin' mug no more, but I'll leave it there just the same for old time's sake. Jim certainly was a character!

Years ago, Jim used to travel for a canned goods concern over in Carterville. They sold canned goods. Jim had the whole northern half of the State and was on the road five days out of every week. He'd drop in here Saturdays and tell his experiences for that week. It was rich.

I guess he paid more attention to playin' jokes than makin' sales. Finally the concern let him out and he come right home here and told everybody he'd been fired instead of sayin' he'd resigned like most fellas would of.

It was a Saturday and the shop was full and Jim got up out of that chair and says, "Gentlemen, I got an important announcement to make. I been fired from my job."

Well, they asked him if he was in earnest and he said he was and nobody could think of nothin' to say till Jim finally broke the ice himself. He says, "I been sellin' canned goods and now I'm canned goods myself."

You see, the concern he'd been workin' for was a factory that made canned goods. Over in Carterville. And now Jim said he was canned himself. He was certainly a card!

Jim had a great trick that he used to play w'ile he was travelin'. For instance, he'd be ridin' on a train and they'd come to some little town like, well, like, we'll say, like Benton. Jim would look out the train window and read the signs on the stores.

For instance, they'd be a sign, "Henry Smith, Dry Goods." Well, Jim would write down the name and the name of the town and when he got to wherever he was goin' he'd mail back a postal card to Henry Smith at Benton and not sign no name to it, but he'd write on the card, well, somethin' like "Ask your wife about that book agent that spent the afternoon last week," or "Ask your Missus who kept her from gettin' lonesome the last time you was in Carterville." And he'd sign the card, "A Friend."

Of course, he never knew what really come of none of these jokes, but he could picture what *probably* happened and that was enough.

Jim didn't work very steady after he lost his position with the Carterville people. What he did earn, doin' odd jobs round town, why he spent pretty near all of it on gin and his family might of starved if the stores hadn't of carried them along. Jim's wife tried her hand at dressmakin', but they ain't nobody goin' to get rich makin' dresses in this town.

As I say, she'd of divorced Jim, only she seen that she couldn't support herself and the kids and she was always hopin' that some day Jim would cut out his habits and give her more than two or three dollars a week.

They was a time when she would go to whoever he was workin' for and ask them to give her his wages, but after she done this once or twice, he beat her to it by borrowin' most of his pay in advance. He told it all round town, how he had outfoxed his Missus. He certainly was a caution!

But he wasn't satisfied with just outwittin' her. He was sore the way she had acted, tryin' to grab off his pay. And he made up his mind he'd get even. Well, he waited till Evans's Circus was advertised to come to town. Then he told his wife and two kiddies that he was goin' to take them to the circus. The day of the circus, he told them he would get the tickets and meet them outside the entrance to the tent.

Well, he didn't have no intentions of bein' there or buyin' tickets or nothin'. He got full of gin and laid round Wright's poolroom all day. His wife and the kids waited and waited and of course he didn't show up. His wife didn't have a dime with her, or nowhere else, I guess. So she finally had to tell the kids it was all off and they cried like they wasn't never goin' to stop.

Well, it seems, w'ile they was cryin', Doc Stair came along and he asked what was the matter, but Mrs. Kendall was stubborn and wouldn't tell him, but the kids told him and he insisted on takin' them and their mother in the show. Jim found this out afterwards and it was one reason why he had it in for Doc Stair.

Doc Stair come here about a year and a half ago. He's a mighty handsome young fella and his clothes always look like he has them made to order. He goes to Detroit two or three times a year and w'ile he's there he must have a tailor take his measure and then make him a suit to order. They cost pretty near twice as much, but they fit a whole lot better than if you just bought them in a store.

For a w'ile everybody was wonderin' why a young doctor like Doc Stair should come to a town like this where we already got old Doc Gamble and Doc Foote that's both been here for years and all the practice in town was always divided between the two of them.

Then they was a story got round that Doc Stair's gal had throwed him over, a gal up in the Northern Peninsula somewheres, and the reason he come here was to hide himself away and forget it. He said himself that he thought they wasn't nothin' like general practice in a place like ours to fit a man to be a good all round doctor. And that's why he'd come.

Anyways, it wasn't long before he was makin' enough to live on, though they tell me that he never dunned nobody for what they owed him, and the folks here certainly has got the owin' habit, even in my business. If I had all that was comin' to me for just shaves alone, I could go to Carterville and put up at the Mercer for a week and see a different picture every night. For instance, they's old George Purdy—but I guess I shouldn't ought to be gossipin'.

Well, last year, our coroner died, died of the flu. Ken Beatty, that was his name. He was the coroner. So they had to choose another man to be coroner in his place and they picked Doc Stair. He laughed at first and said he didn't want it, but they made him take it. It ain't no job that anybody would fight for and what a man makes out of it in a year would just about buy seeds for their garden. Doc's the kind, though, that can't say no to nothin' if you keep at him long enough.

But I was goin' to tell you about a poor boy we got here in town— Paul Dickson. He fell out of a tree when he was about ten years old. Lit on his head and it done somethin' to him and he ain't never been right. No harm in him, but just silly. Jim Kendall used to call him cuckoo; that's a name Jim had for anybody that was off their head, only he called people's head their bean. That was another of his gags, callin' head bean and callin' crazy people cuckoo. Only poor Paul ain't crazy, but just silly.

You can imagine that Jim used to have all kinds of fun with Paul. He'd send him to the White Front Garage for a left-handed monkey wrench. Of course they ain't no such a thing as a left-handed monkey wrench.

And once we had a kind of a fair here and they was a baseball game between the fats and the leans and before the game started Jim called Paul over and sent him way down to Schrader's hardware store to get a key for the pitcher's box.

They wasn't nothin' in the way of gags that Jim couldn't think up, when he put his mind to it.

Poor Paul was always kind of suspicious of people, maybe on account how Jim had kept foolin' him. Paul wouldn't have much to do with anybody only his own mother and Doc Stair and a girl here in town named Julie Gregg. That is, she ain't a girl no more, but pretty near thirty or over.

When Doc first come to town, Paul seemed to feel like here was a real friend and he hung round Doc's office most of the w'ile; the only time he wasn't there was when he'd go home to eat or sleep or when he seen Julie Gregg doin' her shoppin'.

When he looked out Doc's window and seen her, he'd run downstairs and join her and tag along with her to the different stores. The poor boy was crazy about Julie and she always treated him mighty nice and made him feel like he was welcome, though of course it wasn't nothin' but pity on her side.

Doc done all he could to improve Paul's mind and he told me once that he really thought the boy was gettin' better, that they was times when he was as bright and sensible as anybody else.

But I was goin' to tell you about Julie Gregg. Old Man Gregg was in the lumber business, but got to drinkin' and lost the most of his money and when he died, he didn't leave nothin' but the house and just enough insurance for the girl to skimp along on.

Her mother was a kind of a half invalid and didn't hardly ever leave the house. Julie wanted to sell the place and move somewheres else after the old man died, but the mother said she was born here and would die here. It was tough on Julie, as the young people round this town—well, she's too good for them.

She's been away to school and Chicago and New York and different places and they ain't no subject she can't talk on, where you take the rest of the young folks here and you mention anything to them outside of Gloria Swanson or Tommy Meighan and they think you're delirious. Did you see Gloria in Wages of Virtue? You missed somethin'!

Well, Doc Stair hadn't been here more than a week when he come in one day to get shaved and I recognized who he was as he had been pointed out to me, so I told him about my old lady. She's been ailin' for a couple years and either Doc Gamble or Doc Foote, neither one, seemed to be helpin' her. So he said he would come out and see her, but if she was able to get out herself, it would be better to bring her to his office where he could make a completer examination.

So I took her to his office and w'ile I was waitin' for her in the reception room, in come Julie Gregg. When somebody comes in Doc Stair's office, they's a bell that rings in his inside office so as he can tell they's somebody to see him.

So he left my old lady inside and come out to the front office and that's the first time him and Julie met and I guess it was what they call love at first sight. But it wasn't fifty-fifty. This young fella was the slickest lookin' fella she'd ever seen in this town and she went wild over him. To him she was just a young lady that wanted to see the doctor.

She'd came on about the same business I had. Her mother had been doctorin' for years with Doc Gamble and Doc Foote and without no results. So she'd heard they was a new doc in town and decided to give him a try. He promised to call and see her mother that same day.

I said a minute ago that it was love at first sight on her part. I'm not only judgin' by how she acted afterwards but how she looked at him that first day in his office. I ain't no mind reader, but it was wrote all over her face that she was gone.

Now Jim Kendall, besides bein' a jokesmith and a pretty good drinker, well, Jim was quite a lady-killer. I guess he run pretty wild durin' the time he was on the road for them Carterville people, and besides that, he'd had a couple little affairs of the heart right here in town. As I say, his wife could of divorced him, only she couldn't.

But Jim was like the majority of men, and women, too, I guess. He wanted what he couldn't get. He wanted Julie Gregg and worked his head off tryin' to land her. Only he'd of said bean instead of head.

Well, Jim's habits and his jokes didn't appeal to Julie and of course he was a married man, so he didn't have no more chance than, well, than a rabbit. That's an expression of Jim's himself. When somebody didn't have no chance to get elected or somethin', Jim would always say they didn't have no more chance than a rabbit.

He didn't make no bones about how he felt. Right in here, more than once, in front of the whole crowd, he said he was stuck on Julie and anybody that could get her for him was welcome to his house and his wife and kids included. But she wouldn't have nothin' to do with him; wouldn't even speak to him on the street. He finally seen he wasn't gettin' nowheres with his usual line so he decided to try the rough stuff. He went right up to her house one evenin' and when she opened the door he forced his way in and grabbed her. But she broke loose and before he could stop her, she run in the next room and locked the door and phoned to Joe Barnes. Joe's the marshal. Jim could hear who she was phonin' to and he beat it before Joe got there.

Joe was an old friend of Julie's pa. Joe went to Jim the next day and told him what would happen if he ever done it again.

I don't know how the news of this little affair leaked out. Chances is that Joe Barnes told his wife and she told somebody else's wife and they told their husband. Anyways, it did leak out and Hod Meyers had the nerve to kid Jim about it, right here in this shop. Jim didn't deny nothin' and kind of laughed it off and said for us all to wait; that lots of people had tried to make a monkey out of him, but he always got even.

Meanw'ile everybody in town was wise to Julie's bein' wild mad over the Doc. I don't suppose she had any idear how her face changed when him and her was together; of course she couldn't of, or she'd of kept away from him. And she didn't know that we was all noticin' how many times she made excuses to go up to his office or pass it on the other side of the street and look up in his window to see if he was there. I felt sorry for her and so did most other people.

Hod Meyers kept rubbin' it into Jim about how the Doc had cut him out. Jim didn't pay no attention to the kiddin' and you could see he was plannin' one of his jokes.

One trick Jim had was the knack of changin' his voice. He could make you think he was a girl talkin' and he could mimic any man's voice. To show you how good he was along this line, I'll tell you the joke he played on me once.

You know, in most towns of any size, when a man is dead and needs a shave, why the barber that shaves him soaks him five dollars for the job; that is, he don't soak *him*, but whoever ordered the shave. I just charge three dollars because personally I don't mind much shavin' a dead person. They lay a whole lot stiller than live customers. The only thing is that you don't feel like talkin' to them and you get kind of lonesome.

Well, about the coldest day we ever had here, two years ago last winter, the phone rung at the house w'ile I was home to dinner and I answered the phone and it was a woman's voice and she said she was Mrs. John Scott and her husband was dead and would I come out and shave him.

Old John had always been a good customer of mine. But they live seven miles out in the country, on the Streeter road. Still I didn't see how I could say no.

So I said I would be there, but would have to come in a jitney and it might cost three or four dollars besides the price of the shave. So she,

425

or the voice, it said that was all right, so I got Frank Abbott to drive me out to the place and when I got there, who should open the door but old John himself! He wasn't no more dead than, well, than a rabbit.

It didn't take no private detective to figure out who had played me this little joke. Nobody could of thought it up but Jim Kendall. He certainly was a card!

I tell you this incident just to show you how he could disguise his voice and make you believe it was somebody else talkin'. I'd of swore it was Mrs. Scott had called me. Anyways, some woman.

Well, Jim waited till he had Doc Stair's voice down pat; then he went after revenge.

He called Julie up on a night when he knew Doc was over in Carterville. She never questioned but what it was Doc's voice. Jim said he must see her that night; he couldn't wait no longer to tell her somethin'. She was all excited and told him to come to the house. But he said he was expectin' an important long distance call and wouldn't she please forget her manners for once and come to his office. He said they couldn't nothin' hurt her and nobody would see her and he just *must* talk to her a little w'ile. Well, poor Julie fell for it.

Doc always keeps a night light in his office, so it looked to Julie like they was somebody there.

Meanw'ile Jim Kendall had went to Wright's poolroom, where they was a whole gang amusin' themselves. The most of them had drank plenty of gin, and they was a rough bunch even when sober. They was always strong for Jim's jokes and when he told them to come with him and see some fun they give up their card games and pool games and followed along.

Doc's office is on the second floor. Right outside his door they's a flight of stairs leadin' to the floor above. Jim and his gang hid in the dark behind these stairs.

Well, Julie come up to Doc's door and rung the bell and they was nothin' doin'. She rung it again and she rung it seven or eight times. Then she tried the door and found it locked. Then Jim made some kind of a noise and she heard it and waited a minute, and then she says, "Is that you, Ralph?" Ralph is the Doc's first name.

They was no answer and it must of came to her all of a sudden that she'd been bunked. She pretty near fell downstairs and the whole gang after her. They chased her all the way home, hollerin', "Is that you, Ralph?" and "Oh, Ralphie, dear, is that you?" Jim says he couldn't holler it himself, as he was laughin' too hard.

Poor Julie! She didn't show up here on Main Street for a long, long time afterward.

And of course Jim and his gang told everybody in town, everybody but Doc Stair. They was scared to tell him, and he might of never knowed only for Paul Dickson. The poor cuckoo, as Jim called him, he was here in the shop one night when Jim was still gloatin' yet over what he'd done to Julie. And Paul took in as much of it as he could understand and he run to Doc with the story.

It's a cinch Doc went up in the air and swore he'd make Jim suffer. But it was a kind of a delicate thing, because if it got out that he had beat Jim up, Julie was bound to hear of it and then she'd know that Doc knew and of course knowin' that he knew would make it worse for her than ever. He was goin' to do somethin', but it took a lot of figurin'.

Well, it was a couple days later when Jim was here in the shop again, and so was the cuckoo. Jim was goin' duck-shootin' the next day and had came in lookin' for Hod Meyers to go with him. I happened to know that Hod had went over to Carterville and wouldn't be home till the end of the week. So Jim said he hated to go alone and he guessed he would call it off. Then poor Paul spoke up and said if Jim would take him he would go along. Jim thought a w'ile and then he said, well, he guessed a half-wit was better than nothin'.

I suppose he was plottin' to get Paul out in the boat and play some joke on him, like pushin' him in the water. Anyways, he said Paul could go. He asked him had he ever shot a duck and Paul said no, he'd never even had a gun in his hands. So Jim said he could set in the boat and watch him and if he behaved himself, he might lend him his gun for a couple of shots. They made a date to meet in the mornin' and that's the last I seen of Jim alive.

Next mornin', I hadn't been open more than ten minutes when Doc Stair come in. He looked kind of nervous. He asked me had I seen Paul Dickson. I said no, but I knew where he was, out duck-shootin' with Jim Kendall. So Doc says that's what he had heard, and he couldn't understand it because Paul had told him he wouldn't never have no more to do with Jim as long as he lived.

He said Paul had told him about the joke Jim had played on Julie. He said Paul had asked him what he thought of the joke and the Doc had told him that anybody that would do a thing like that ought not to be let live.

I said it had been a kind of a raw thing, but Jim just couldn't resist no kind of a joke, no matter how raw. I said I thought he was all right at heart, but just bubblin' over with mischief. Doc turned and walked out.

At noon he got a phone call from old John Scott. The lake where Jim and Paul had went shootin' is on John's place. Paul had came run-

427

nin' up to the house a few minutes before and said they'd been an accident. Jim had shot a few ducks and then give the gun to Paul and told him to try his luck. Paul hadn't never handled a gun and he was nervous. He was shakin' so hard that he couldn't control the gun. He let fire and Jim sunk back in the boat, dead.

Doc Stair, bein' the coroner, jumped in Frank Abbott's flivver and rushed out to Scott's farm. Paul and old John was down on the shore of the lake. Paul had rowed the boat to shore, but they'd left the body in it, waitin' for Doc to come.

Doc examined the body and said they might as well fetch it back to town. They was no use leavin' it there or callin' a jury, as it was a plain case of accidental shootin'.

Personally I wouldn't never leave a person shoot a gun in the same boat I was in unless I was sure they knew somethin' about guns. Jim was a sucker to leave a new beginner have his gun, let alone a half-wit. It probably served Jim right, what he got. But still we miss him round here. He certainly was a card!

Comb it wet or dry?

An Iowa Childhood

by EDNA FERBER, 1887–   . *Edna Ferber was born in Kalamazoo, Michigan, and was educated in the public schools of Appleton, Wisconsin. After a period of journalistic work when she was a member of the staff of Appleton and Milwaukee newspapers she turned her attention to fiction and has since written a long series of stories. Perhaps her most successful novels are Gigolo (1922), So Big (1924), Show Boat (1926), Cimarron (1929), and Come and Get It (1935), the last a story of the Wisconsin lumbering areas. In 1939 she published her autobiography, A Peculiar Treasure, with vivid sketches of her life in Appleton and Ottumwa, Iowa. She has also collaborated successfully with George S. Kaufman in such plays as "The Royal Family," "Dinner at Eight," and "Stage Door." Her novel Great Son was a selection of the Literary Guild in 1945.*

MY FATHER had decided that Chicago was not, after all, the ideal spot on which to lay the foundations of our future fortunes. A year had gone by during which we had stayed on in the house on Calumet Avenue. During that year my father was off for days at a time looking for a business location. He realized that he might much better have stayed on in Kalamazoo, but it was too late to think of that now. Perhaps he had discovered that the steps toward becoming a second Marshall Field or Carson Pirie Scott & Company were not so simple. He had, after all, been a small-town man always. Some miracle of mischance led him to a small Iowa coal-mining town distinguished by the Indian name of Ottumwa. The word is said to mean Place of Perseverance. Whatever Ottumwa means in the Indian language, it meant only bad luck for the Ferbers. My father had been told that there was absolutely no general store in the town. Ottumwa clamored, apparently, for Ferber's Bazaar. He inspected the place (he must have been blindfolded) and returned with glowing stories of this Iowa town in a farming and coal-mining district. The fact that it boasted more than sixteen thousand population without a decent shop for china, toys, notions and all sorts of household goods should have been significant enough to serve as a warning.

My mother was anguished. She had left Kalamazoo happy at the thought of again becoming a Chicagoan. Now she was to live in an Iowa coal-mining town apparently for the rest of her days. Heavy-hearted with misgivings she gathered up her household goods and her two children, left Chicago and her people behind her, and came to Ottumwa. As soon as she had a good look at the sordid, clay-and-gully Iowa town, she knew. There it lay flanked by the muddy Des Moines River; unpaved, bigoted, anti-Semitic, undernourished. Julia Ferber's days of youth and peace and happiness were over.

Those next seven years—from 1890 to 1897—must be held accountable for anything in me that is hostile toward the world in which I live. Child though I was, the brutality and ignorance of that little town penetrated to my consciousness, perhaps through casual talk as I heard it between my young parents; certainly as it was visited upon me.

I have since visited the town once, some ten years ago, and I found it a tree-shaded, sightly, modern American town of its size; clean, progressive. I had planned to stay overnight in the new and comfortable hotel. Memory was too strong. At eight that evening I drove through the starlit night back to Des Moines, past the rich black-loam farmlands of Iowa, past the substantial square-built fine farm homes, certainly the most modern and even luxurious farmhouses in the world. It was a purple velvet spring night; the air was rich with the smells of freshly turned earth and the first flowers; the highway ran its flawless length, mile on mile; the sky was lavish with brilliants.

For the first time in my life, out of the deep well of repression where they had so long festered, I dragged those seven years of my bitter little girlhood and looked at them. And the cool clean Iowa air cleansed them, and I saw them then, not as bitter corroding years, but as astringent strengthening years; years whose adversity had given me and mine a solid foundation of stamina, determination and a profound love of justice.

My mother kept a sort of skeleton diary through the years, and the scant line-a-day covering the Ottumwa years forms a human document, bare as it is, containing all the elements of courage, vitality, humor, sordid tragedy, high tragedy. Through it all, I may add, the Ferber family went to the theater. Bitter Iowa winters, burning Iowa summers; death, business crises, illness—the Ferber family went to the theater when any form of theater was to be had in the boundaries of that then-benighted little town.

We moved into a new eight-room house on Wapello Street at the foot of a steep hill. The town ran from almost perpendicular hill streets to the flats near the Des Moines River. In the wintertime it was thrilling to be able to coast, gaining rocketlike velocity, down the length of Wapello or Marian street hill. It was before the day of automobiles, there was little danger of being run down as you whizzed past street intersections. An occasional team, plop-plopping along in the snow, pulled up at the hill street crossings. In the summer Wapello hill was almost as exciting because you could count on the runaways. There were runaway horses every few days and, as we lived at the foot of the hill, they usually wound up with a grand flourish and splintering of wood and screaming of occupants practically in our laps. Faulty brakes, steep hill and frightened horse combined to bring about this state of affairs. The best runaway I remember was a heavily laden hay wagon whose driver, helpless, sat perched atop his precarious load. I still can see the unwieldy mass careening wildly down the hill like a vast drunken fat woman. The usually phlegmatic farm horses, teased by the overladen wagon nipping at their heels, had taken fright, had galloped frantically down the steep slope, the mass had overturned, and the farmer lay unconscious, his head bleeding, his arm dislocated at the shoulder and broken. It was midmorning. There were no men about. I remember the doctor, hastily summoned, looking about him in his shirt sleeves for likely help in this emergency.

"Which one of you ladies will pull this man's arm with all your strength while I set it?"

Julia Ferber came forward. "I will." And she pulled with all her strength while the sweat poured down the doctor's face and that of the groaning farmer.

My sister Fannie and I were left increasingly alone as my mother realized that there was more to my father's business than opening a store, stocking it and waiting for customers. With instinctive common sense, though she knew nothing of business, she felt that something was amiss, and she set about finding out what this might be. She was still too young, too newly married, and too life-loving to admit that the whole structure was wrong. She got into the way of going to the store early after midday and staying there through the afternoon. There was the hired girl to look after my sister and myself, and we lived the normal outdoor life of small-town children.

The American maid-of-all-work, known then as the hired girl, was an institution in the middle-class life of that day and until the emigration restrictions largely stopped her. She should have a rich, colorful and important book all to herself. The American hired girl was, in that day, a farm girl, daughter of foreign-born parents; or she was an immigrant newly landed; perhaps at most of five years' standing in this country. She was any one of a half-dozen nationalities: Irish, German, Swedish, Bohemian, Hungarian, Polish. Poverty, famine, persecution, ambition, a spirit of adventure—any one of these may have been the force which catapulted her across the ocean and into the melting pot. She brought into the Eastern and Midwestern middle-class American household a wealth of European ways, manners, customs in speech, cooking, religion, festivals, morals, clothing. If Hungarian, she brought the household such dishes as goulash and strudel; if Irish, stew and shortbread; if Bohemian, noodle-kraut; if Swedish, meat balls and flaky pastry; if Austrian, wienerschnitzel and the best of coffee. She brought her native peasant costume overseas in her funny corded trunk and could be coaxed to don it for the entertainment of the children of the household. To them, too, she brought old-world folk tales, dances, myths, songs. She was warmhearted, simple, honest, and had to be taught to brush her teeth. Her hair, tightly braided, was wound around her head or skewered into an eye-straining knot. She rose at five-thirty to start the kitchen fire; she rose at four on Mondays to do the family wash. Numbers of her you will see queening it now in American so-called society. She loved to dance, she loved to sing, she loved to work. She might be uncouth or graceful, sullen or sunny, neat or slovenly, but she was the American hired girl of the '50s, '60s, '70s, '80s, and '90s, and as such she influenced the manners, morals and lives of millions of American-born children. I always have thought that English children brought up by English maids, French children cared for by French maids, and so on through the countries of Europe, have missed a lot of variety and fun.

Of the Ottumwa hired girls the first I remembered is Sophy. Sophy was swarthy, rather heavily mustached, a superb cook and definitely "touched." Her mental maladjustment was, however, confined to one narrow theme. She thought all men were in love with her. I don't know whether she was Polish or Hungarian. She was somewhere in her forties, very plain. She spoke with an accent, and she was always rushing in, after her days off, with an account of the passionate advances of some strange male encountered in her girlish perambulations. These stories were considered very amusing as told among the married couples of my parents' acquaintance. My sister and I listened, awe-struck, while she regaled us with accounts of her amorous adventures.

"I vass walking on the street and pretty soon I know somebody vass following after me, so I hurry but he catch up wiss me, he is tall and handsome wiss black mustache and black eyes and curly hair. And he says, 'So! You are de vooman I am seeking.'" This last word became sikking in her accent. "'You must come wit me, my beauty, or I will keel you.'" In those simple and rather cruel days this story was re-peated with the accent complete, and greeted by shrieks of mirth. No one seemed to realize that here was a middle-aged virgin in the throes of a mild sex mania. She was devoted to us children and we loved her, but it was not our childish love she wanted.

After Sophy there was Sarah, a dear Welsh girl. Sometimes I used to go to early Mass with her. During my childhood I often went to early Mass when the household maid happened to be Catholic. I liked the drama of it; the color, the rich robes, the procession, the choir boys' fresh young voices; the sweetish prick of incense. Once or twice I went with Sarah to the little cottage where her parents lived, near the mines, and my first trip down into the deep black shaft of a coal mine was made with Sarah and her father. We stumbled through the eery galleries where the men were at work, their tiny cap lamps casting weird shadows. I remember being shocked to learn that people worked in the earth like grubs. I felt sorry for them, and when we came up into the open air again I was relieved. I somehow had felt doomed never to see daylight again.

More and more of my mother's time was spent at the store, though she did little but watch and learn. It was as though scales and scales were falling from her eyes and she were seeing the hard world as it was for the first time. On Saturdays she was there until nine or ten o'clock waiting for her husband, for Saturdays and Saturday nights were the busy times. The farmers and their wives would come in to sell their produce and put in supplies; and the miners would spend their pay. The coal mines lay very near the town. The miners were, for the most part, Welshmen, brought over from the black pits of Cardiff. I would see them coming home from work in the evening, their eyes grotesquely rimmed with black, their trade caps, with the little miner's lamp, on their heads, their tin lunch pails in their tired hands. A lean gaunt lot with few enough quarters and half-dollars to exchange for goods at Ferber's Bazaar.

The town swirled down Main Street on Saturday night. On Saturday afternoon my sister and I went to a matinee if there happened to be a stock company in temporary residence. On Saturday night I was allowed to sit in a tiny chair in a corner and survey the crowds shuffling by. This I insisted on doing. I don't know why a child of five or thereabouts should have enjoyed this diversion, but I did, and I do to this day. My notion of bliss would be to sit in an armchair at the corner of Broadway and 42nd, or State and Madison, or any other busy intersection in America, and watch the town go by. The passer-by does not notice you or care about you; they, the people, are intent on getting somewhere, their faces are open to the reader; they betray themselves by their walk, their voices, their hands, clenched or inert; their feet, their clothes, their eyes.

Well, there I sat at my ease, an intent and obnoxious little student of the human race, fascinated, God knows why, as I saw this cross section of America go shuffling by in a little Iowa town. At about nine o'clock my sister and I would be sent home, either with the hired girl who had come for us, or hand in hand alone through the dark streets and into the empty house. Perhaps that's why I don't understand what women mean when they say that they are timid about being alone on the street at night. All my life I've walked at night. It is my favorite tramping time.

If it was not too late we were allowed to read at night. Our reading was undirected, haphazard. By the dining-room kerosene lamp we read and read and read. We read the Horatio Alger books in which the newsboy helped the white-headed gentleman with the gold-headed cane across perilous Lexington Avenue, and was promptly adopted by the old gentleman (who later turned out to have been his long-lost grandfather all the time). By the time I was nine I had read all of Dickens, but I also adored the Five Little Pepper books, the St. Nicholas Magazine, all of Louisa Alcott, and the bound copies of Harper's Bazaar; Hans Brinker and the Silver Skates; the novels of The Duchess (the Kathleen Norris of her day); Thelma; Between Two Worlds; The First Violin. Good and bad, adult or infantile, I read all the books in the house, all the books in the store stock, all the books in the very inadequate little public library, for this was before the day of Andrew Carnegie's omnipresent Greek temple. I remember that when Fannie and I were simultaneously stricken with measles, and lay in separate rooms, she in the spare bedroom, I in our everyday bed, my mother sat in the hall between the two rooms so that we both might hear plainly as she read aloud from A Texas Steer, a gusty tale which we relished enormously. Of the stand-bys in the household bookcase there was one book of which I never tired. It was known familiarly as the Green Book, because of the color of its worn binding. Its official name

433

was The World of Wit and Humor. I read it to tatters. I still have it, its worn pages held together now by skillful binding, its leaves yellow and dog-eared, but its cover still the old original bilious cloth of the Green Book. Between those boards I was introduced to Bret Harte and George Eliot, Samuel Lover and William Allen Butler, author of the immortal Flora M'Flimsey of Madison Square. There I read of Samuel Warren's Tittlebat Titmouse; Oliver Wendell Holmes' Ballad of the Oysterman; there were Artemus Ward, Charles Lever, Mark Twain. Jokes, poems, Mrs. Caudle's Curtain Lectures—the Green Book was a mine of riches, and is to this day. Curiously enough, a friend of my mother subscribed to Puck and the English humorous magazine, Punch. These she saved for me, and I spent an occasional Saturday afternoon curled up, ecstatically happy, with a pile of these papers. In Puck there was one series I particularly loved. It depicted its characters as very plump, round-cheeked pop-eyed creatures, in type a good deal like the Betty Boop cartoons, but infinitely more human and varied.

Of my few agreeable memories of Ottumwa perhaps the pleasantest is that of Sallie Ainley, one of my mother's friends. She was English-born and lived with her father, for whom she kept house, in a cottage by the river on the other side of the bridge that spanned the Des Moines. Ainley père was a miller, and the mill was just next the house. I adored visiting the mill. I never shall forget the kindness of the miller, his beard and face white with flour; or of his daughter Sallie, who put up with Fannie and me for whole Saturdays, while my mother was busy in the store. We watched the grinding of the grain in the mill, we were fed strange delightful dishes, we picked apples from the tree in the yard, we read all the books and magazines on the Ainley shelves. I can't imagine how they came to be residents of Ottumwa. How good, how kind they were, this father and daughter.

If all this sounds stuffy I hasten to say that it wasn't. Ottumwa of that day was a tough town. There were seven murders in it one year, and no convictions. This annoyed certain of the citizenry. They decided to take steps. Consequently, one day as I was rounding the corner on Main Street I saw people running and I was aware of a strange and blood-curdling sound, not human. It was like the sound made by animals as I remembered them in Chicago's Lincoln Park Zoo at their mealtime. I quickened my steps and cleared the corner just in time to see an odd bundle jerking its way in mid-air up the electric light pole. It had legs and arms that waved like those of an insect, then they ceased to wave, the thing straightened itself and became decorous and limp, its head dropping as though in contrition. The animal sounds from the crowd below swelled, then ceased. Suddenly they melted

434

away, seeming to flow up and down the streets in all directions. I heard the clang of the police patrol wagon.

Whatever there was to see I saw. Yearly there were held Methodist camp meetings in a great tent. People "got religion," they came down the aisle clapping their hands and shouting, rolling their eyes, shrieking and sobbing in an hysteria of induced emotion. They would drop to the floor at the foot of the platform. I was astonished to learn that these frenzies were occasioned by religious fervor. I had thought of religion as something dignified, solemn and a little sad.

Somehow or other I attended Chautauquas, revival meetings, political rallies, political parades, ten-twenty-and-thirties, the circus. We always went to the circus at night because my parents could not very well get away in the daytime. I pitied my small friends who were obliged to be content with the afternoon performance. I thought it must be very dull to see this strange world by daylight exposed beneath a blazing sun. Under the gas flares it was mysterious, romantic. Spangles glittered, color blazed, there was more menace in the snarls and growls of the wild animals. Then, too, there was the added thrill of being up so late. When we stumbled out after the performance, drunk with sound and color and dazzling sights, the smaller tents already had been whisked away like an Arabian Nights dream; hoarse men were shouting to one another and charging about with poles and weird canvas bundles. One heard the thick rich sound of heavy circus wheels on the roadway, like no other sound in the world. It stirred something in me, vague and terrible—something that went back, back, perhaps, to Egyptian days and the heavy wheels of chariots.

The political parades were fine things. The marchers carried torch flares and wore colored hatbands and ribbons fastened crosswise from shoulder to waist, and there were huge signs and painted banners on poles held high in the air. I was in the dense crowd that heard Bryan's Cross of Gold speech. He spoke at the Opera House; the throng waiting for the door to be opened was unmanageable. It was then I came by my lifelong horror of close-packed crowds. The doors were opened, the eager hundreds surged forward, I lost my father's hand, I felt myself suffocating, being trampled, I screamed at the top of a none-too-dulcet voice, a man picked me up out of the welter of trampling feet and crushing knees and swung me up to his shoulder, where I sat perched above the heads of the mob and from which vantage point I calmly listened to the impassioned Mr. Bryan in his historic speech, not a word of which I can recall, for some hidden reason.

I saw Coxey's Army, a pitiful tatterdemalion crew, floating down the muddy Des Moines River on flat boats and rafts, hungry, penniless, desperate, on their way to demand food and work of a government which, at that time, had not even dreamed of Relief, of Social Security, of Old Age Pensions, of PWA Projects. The Panic of 1893 had struck America a violent blow, and the whole country was writhing in terror and misery.

It is not for me to say whether all this was good or bad for me. Probably bad and good. Certainly it made for an interesting childhood. Perhaps it is just as well that I never have had a child. I am afraid I should have wanted to bring him or her up in this way—fending for itself, moving from place to place, seeing all that there is to see. I hear mothers and fathers debating whether or not to allow their offspring to see Snow White and the Seven Dwarfs. They discuss its possible psychological and physical effects on little Junior or Sister. I know they're modern and right and wise and oh, how glad I am that I was not thus sheltered in my childhood. Always to be cared for and serene seems to me to be much like living in a climate where it is always summer. Never to know the bitter nip of winter's cold, and to brace oneself against it and fight it; never to long for the coming of spring and then to witness, in ecstasy, the marvel of the first pale lemon-green haze; not to know the voluptuous luxury of rare hot summer sun on basking flesh. No. Summer's only fun if winter is remembered.

Going to school, playing with Ora Burney and Maude Hayward and the Trost boys, I had plenty of normal childish pleasure. But there in Ottumwa it was smirched with constant and cruel persecution. Through the seven years during which we lived in Ottumwa I know that I never went out on the street without being subjected to some form of devilment. It was a fine school for a certain sort of fortitude, but it gave me a strong dash of bitterness at an early age, together with a bewildered puzzlement at what was known as the Christian world. Certainly I wasn't wise enough or old enough at five, six, seven, eight, nine, ten, to philosophize about this. But these people seemed to me to be barbarians.

On Saturdays, and on unusually busy days when my father could not take the time to come home to the noon dinner, it became my duty to take his midday meal down to him, very carefully packed in a large basket; soup, meat, vegetables, dessert. This must be carried with the utmost care so as not to spill or slop. No one thought of having a sandwich and a cup of coffee in the middle of the day, with a hot dinner to be eaten at leisure in the peace of the evening.

This little trip from the house on Wapello Street to the store on Main Street amounted to running the gantlet. I didn't so much mind the Morey girl. She sat in front of her house perched on the white gatepost, waiting, a child about my age, with long red curls, a freckled face, very light green eyes. She swung her long legs, idly. At sight of me her listlessness fled.

"Hello, sheeny!" Then variations on this. This, one learned to receive equably. Besides, the natural retort to her baiting was to shout, airily, "Red Head! Wets the bed!"

But as I approached the Main Street corner there sat a row of vultures perched on the iron railing at the side of Sargent's drugstore. These were not children, they were men. Perhaps to me, a small child, they seemed older than they were, but their ages must have ranged from eighteen to thirty. There they sat, perched on the black iron rail, their heels hooked behind the lower rung. They talked almost not at all. The semicircle of spit rings grew richer and richer on the sidewalk in front of them. Vacant-eyed, they stared and spat and sat humped and round-shouldered, doing nothing, thinking nothing, being nothing. Suddenly their lackluster eyes brightened, they shifted, they licked their lips a little and spat with more relish. From afar they had glimpsed their victim, a plump little girl in a clean starched gingham frock, her black curls confined by a ribbon bow.

Every fiber of me shrieked to run the other way. My eyes felt hot and wide. My face became scarlet. I must walk carefully so as not to spill the good hot dinner. Now then. Now.

"Sheeny! Has du gesak de Isaac! De Moses! De Levi! Heh, sheeny, what you got!" Good Old Testament names. They doubtless heard them in their Sunday worship, but did not make the connection, quite. Then they brought their hands, palms up, above the level of their shoulders and wagged them back and forth, "Oy-yoy, sheeny! Run! Go on, run!"

I didn't run. I glared. I walked by with as much elegance and aloofness as was compatible with a necessity to balance a basket of noodle soup, pot roast, potatoes, vegetable, and pudding.

Of course it was nothing more than a couple of thousand years of bigotry raising its hideous head again to spit on a defenseless and shrinking morsel of humanity. Yet it all must have left a deep scar on a sensitive child. It was unreasoning and widespread in the town. My parents were subject to it. The four or five respectable Jewish families of the town knew it well. They were intelligent men and women, American born and bred, for the most part. It probably gave me a ghastly inferiority, and out of that inferiority doubtless was born inside me a fierce resolution, absurd and childish, such as, "You wait! I'll show you! I'll be rich and famous and you'll wish you could speak to me."

Well, I did become rich and famous, and have lived to see entire nations behaving precisely like the idle frustrated bums perched on the drugstore railing. Of course Ottumwa wasn't a benighted town because it was cruel to its Jewish citizens. It was cruel to its Jewish citizens because it was a benighted town. Business was bad, the town was poor, its people were frightened, resentful and stupid. There was, for a place of its size and locality, an unusually large rough element. As naturally as could be these searched for a minority on whom to vent their dissatisfaction with the world. And there we were, and there I was, the scapegoat of the ages. Yet, though I had a tough time of it in Ottumwa and a fine time of it in New York, I am certain that those Ottumwa years were more enriching, more valuable than all the fun and luxury of the New York years.

New England awoke, horrified and ashamed, after its orgy of witch-burning. Ottumwa must feel some embarrassment at the recollection of its earlier ignorance and brutality. A Nazi-infested world may one day hide its face at the sight of what it has wrought in its inhuman frenzy.

There was no Jewish place of worship in Ottumwa. The five or six Jewish families certainly could not afford the upkeep of a temple. I knew practically nothing of the Jewish people, their history, religion. On the two important holy days of the year—Rosh Hashana, the Jewish New Year; and Yom Kippur, the Day of Atonement—they hired a public hall for services. Sometimes they were able to bring to town a student rabbi who had, as yet, no regular congregation. Usually one of the substantial older men who knew something of the Hebrew language of the Bible, having been taught it in his youth, conducted the service. On Yom Kippur, a long day of fasting and prayer, it was an exhausting thing to stand from morning to sunset in the improvised pulpit. The amateur rabbi would be relieved for an hour by another member of the little improvised congregation. Mr. Emanuel Adler, a familiar figure to me as he sat in his comfortable home talking with my parents, a quaint long-stemmed pipe between his lips, a little black skullcap atop his baldish head as protection against drafts, now would don the rabbinical skullcap, a good deal like that of a Catholic priest. He would open on the high reading stand the Bible and the Book of Prayers containing the service for the Day of Yom Kippur; and suddenly he was transformed from a plump middle-aged German-born Jew with sad kindly eyes and a snuffy gray-brown mustache to a holy man from whose lips came words of wisdom and of comfort and of hope.

The store always was closed on Rosh Hashana and Yom Kippur. Mother put on her best dress. If there were any Jewish visitors in the town at that time they were invited to the services and to dinner at some hospitable house afterward. In our household the guests were likely to be a couple of traveling salesmen caught in the town on that holy day. Jewish families came from smaller near-by towns—Marshalltown, Albia, Keokuk.

I can't account for the fact that I didn't resent being a Jew. Perhaps it was because I liked the way my own family lived, talked, conducted its household and its business better than I did the lives of my friends. I admired immensely my grandparents, my parents, my uncles and aunt. Perhaps it was a vague something handed down to me from no one knows where. Perhaps it was something not very admirable—the actress in me. I think, truthfully, that I rather liked dramatizing myself, feeling myself different and set apart. I probably liked to think of myself as persecuted by enemies who were (in my opinion) my inferiors. This is a protective philosophy often employed. Mine never had been a religious family. The Chicago Neumann family sometimes went to the temple at Thirty-third and Indiana, but I don't remember that my parents ever went there while in Chicago. In our own household there was no celebration of the informal home ceremonies so often observed in Jewish families. The Passover, with its Sedar service, was marked in our house only by the appearance of the matzos or unleavened bread, symbolic of the hardships of the Jews in the wilderness. I devoured pounds of the crisp crumbling matzos with hunks of fresh butter and streams of honey, leaving a trail of crumbs all over the house, and thought very little, I am afraid, of the tragic significance of the food I was eating or of that weary heartsick band led by Moses out of Egypt to escape the Hitler of that day, one Pharaoh; or of how they baked and ate their unsalted unleavened bread because it was all they had, there in the wilderness. I still have matzoth (matzos, we always called them) in my house during the Passover, and just as thoughtlessly. Now they come as delicate crisp circlets, but they seem to me much less delicious than the harder, tougher squares of my childhood munching. Ours were not Jewish ways. My father and mother and sister Fan and I exchanged many friendly little calls with the pleasant Jewish families of the town—the Almeyers, the Adlers, Feists, Silvers, Lyons, living in comfortable well-furnished houses, conducting their affairs with intelligence and decorum, educating their children. They saw a little too much of one another. There was a good deal of visiting back and forth, evenings. At nine there would be served wine or lemonade and cake, a moment which I eagerly awaited. The Ferber specialty was a hickory-nut cake, very rich, baked in a loaf, for which I was permitted to crack the nuts and extract the meats. This was accomplished with a flat-iron between my knees and a hammer in my hand. The nuts went into the cake and into me fifty-fifty. Once baked, it was prudently kept under lock and key in the cupboard of the sitting-room desk, rather than in the free territory of the pantry.

My mother, more modern than most in thought and conduct, had numbers of staunch friends among the non-Jewish townspeople, and these enormously enjoyed her high spirits, her vitality, her shrewd and often caustic comment. She, too, was an omnivorous reader, so that when life proved too much for her she was able to escape into the reader's Nirvana. Certainly she was the real head of the family, its born leader; unconsciously she was undergoing a preliminary training which was to stand her in good stead when she needed it.

It is interesting (to me) to note that all this time I never wrote a line outside my school work and never felt the slightest urge toward original composition. But the piece-speaking went on like a house afire. I recited whenever I could. In school we had recitations every Friday afternoon, and a grand burst of entertainment at the end of each term and on that world-rocking occasion, the Last Day of School, in June. I was by this time a confirmed show-off and a chronic reciter. At the slightest chance I galloped to the front of the room and began my recitation, with gestures. My bliss was complete on those days when we went from room to room giving our programs as visiting artists before an entire class of helpless listeners. To a frustrated actress like myself it is significant now to read a phrase that recurs again and again in that hastily scribbled line-a-day kept by Julia Ferber. Edna recited, it says. No comment, no criticism. Edna recited.

During the Ottumwa period my sister and I used to be taken to Chicago once a year, in the summer, to visit Grandma and Grandpa Neumann. By this time money was scarce, and we—my mother and the two of us—sat up all night in the coach. Children of six were allowed to ride free. I was bundled up in a shawl for a supposed nap, and told to make myself very small. There I lay, trembling and sweating, until the conductor had passed on his ticket-collecting trip. He always looked exactly the same, though perhaps he wasn't. Perhaps he only followed the pattern of the Midwest American train conductor —grizzled, spectacled, brownish spots on the backs of his hands; an Elks and a Masonic emblem; service stripes on his sleeve; a worn, patient and rather benevolent face, strangely unembittered by the pettiness, bad manners and vagaries of the American traveling public.

He would cast a doubting eye on the plump mound under the shawl. "Looks like a big girl to me, ma'am."

"She's big for her age."

Which I undeniably was.

Always I watched and waited with enormous anticipation for the first glimpse of the Mississippi River. I can't explain why it held such fascination for me. Perhaps I had been impressed by what I had learned of it in school—three thousand miles long, tributaries, floods, currents, Mark Twain. For an hour before it was time to cross the great bridge that spanned the stream my face was pressed against the car window. With my own eyes I had seen its ruthless power reflected in the wild antics of our Des Moines River, its tributary. Every year, in the spring, we heard stories of the Mississippi's wild career, how it went berserk and destroyed farms and lives with a single lash of its yellow tail, or gobbled up whole towns in one dreadful yawning of its gigantic jaws. It was always a living thing to me. A monster. When we actually sighted it I eagerly knelt up at the window and watched it out of sight —its broad turbulent bosom, its swift current, its eddies, its vast width, like a mighty lake rather than a river.

The lowlands of Ottumwa, and especially the low-lying Main Street which embraced the chief business section of the town, frequently were flooded. I am here rather embarrassed to admit that I was quite old enough to have known better—such was the terror of the rivers in that part of the country—before I realized that the long laden trains of boxcars and flatcars that crept and puffed so slowly and cautiously along the track by the side of the Des Moines River were not 'fraid trains, but freight trains.

It was because of these floods that I knew how rivers behaved. I saw bridges as they swayed, cracked, then, with screams of despair, were swept downstream in the flood. I saw houses tossing like toys in midstream, while sheep, cows, pianos, rocking chairs, bedsteads floated and bobbed by. People sat marooned on rooftops as their houses took to the nautical life.

In the beginning chapters of the novel Show Boat there is a description of the Mississippi at floodtime. I found I did not need to consult books or ask old-timers to relate their river experiences. I just took my childhood memories of the Mississippi and the Des Moines at floodtime out of the back of my head where they had been neatly stored for so many years and pinned them down on paper.

It is a method every writer can use and one which all experienced writers do use. Sometimes (this may be scientifically disputed, but I believe it nevertheless) the memory goes back, back, beyond one's actual lifetime experience, into the unknown past. Most writers must have had the odd sensation of writing a line, a paragraph, a page about something of which they have had no actual knowledge or experience. Somehow, inexplicably, they know. It writes itself. Of course the everyday storehouse method is merely a matter of having a good memory and a camera eye, with the mental films all neatly filed away for future development when needed. That is why, no matter what happens, good or bad, to a professional writer, he may count it as just so much velvet. Into the attic it goes. This can better be illustrated, perhaps, by describing a shabby old yellow trunk kept in the storeroom of the Ferber household in my childhood. When you lifted the rickety lid there was wafted to you the mingled odor of mothballs, lavender, faint perfumery, dyes, and the ghostly emanation peculiar to castoff garments. Inside, the trunk foamed with every shade and variety of material. There were odds and ends and scraps and bolts and yards of silk, satin, passementerie, beads, ruchings, insertion, velvet, lace, ribbon, feathers, flower trimmings, bits of felt, muslin. When my mother needed trimming for a dress or a hat for herself or for my sister Fannie and myself she merely dived into the old trunk, fished around in the whirlpool of stuffs, and came up with just the oddment or elegancy she needed.

Vikings Use Their Heads

by SKULDA V. BANÉR, ?   . Miss Banér grew up and attended school in Ironwood, Michigan. Subsequently she was a rural school teacher in North Dakota, a photographer, a dressmaker, a radio announcer, the editor of a milk company house organ, and a department store advertising writer. She has contributed to magazines and was recently awarded a University of Minnesota Fellowship in Regional Writing. Latchstring Out, published in 1944, is a charming and whimsical account of life in a northern Michigan mining town which places special emphasis on the polyglot population. Miss Banér's father, the Gustaf of Latchstring Out, was J. G. R. Banér, a Swedish journalist and poet who edited a newspaper and ran a store in the iron country. A biography of this gifted but eccentric man is now being written by his daughter. The account of the phrenological reading is a particularly colorful chapter in Latchstring Out.

OTHER-NYMAN's saloon was on the corner. It was the exact center-point between my grandmother's on Vaughn and my father's store on Suffolk. It was kitty-corner from Fay's. It was her arena, into which she brought her lions.

I approached it now, my grandmother's too far behind me, though it was only a half-block, for me to turn tail and run back too. Besides, I was a Viking. Vikings didn't run. I stalked up to the corner, swinging my arms and making my heels sound very bold on the rusty wood walk. I looked straight and up in front of me, the way my father did when he was thinking. My ears boomed with the nearing pressure of Fay and her mob.

"Swede kid, Swede kid, Swede kid!" Fay stepped forward like a Brynhildr from her chorus of Valkyries.

It wasn't heroism that kept my feet from flight. It was the discretion that is the better part of valor. I knew that the six or eight òr hundred who were Fay's henchmen could easily outrun me and ring me in before I could reach that harbor of my father's red granite stoop, an endless half-block down Suffolk. I thought to conciliate. My mouth opened, but there was no voice in it. Nor were there any words in my head. I walked with wound-up precision, squared off mechanically toward Suffolk, put one foot down before the other as if a metronome timed them. The glow of light from my father's store would have given me courage except that Fay was dancing at my elbow and a half-block was a half-block. Her mob fell into procession behind me. They made the thunder of cannon wheels on the warped, uncertain boards.

"Yah, yah, yah, *svenska pojka!*" Fay yelled into my ear. Our tag-tailing *rumpedra* trailed the chant along with it. "*Kyssmejröva, kyss-mejröva!*"

Fay was a Cousin Jinny and she didn't know what it meant. But there were those in the procession who did. They took it up gleefully, greedy over the morsel they'd have been spanked for mouthing even in a whisper at home. "*Kyssmejröva, kyssmejröva!*"

Their singsong went louder and louder, because I cheated them out of the fun of chasing me. Just as I reached my father's stoop, Ashland Mine finished the maneuver of balking them, with the bellow of its eight-thirty curfew. The whistle soared upward like a snowball flung at a star, then heavily rolled down again, fattening as it rolled.

I turned, secure with my father's latch in my hand. "You little children better run home," I said, lofty with the disdain of the reprieved. "Swan Hult will come. And he will put you in jail if he finds you in the street after curfew."

Fay marshaled her forces for a last stand. "Wait, you kids! Listen to her say *day-before-today!* Listen to how funny the little Swede kid says day-before-today! Say it, *svenska pojka!*"

I had said it to her once, in all innocence. *Yesterday* was something complicated out of all reason. So I had called upon the resources of the two languages I knew, the one well and the other yet a bit sketchily. "*In-går!*" I had said. I knew better than to say it again. I turned my back deliberately, instead, and closed the door of my father's store elegantly behind me.

I heard ladies back in my father's office. I knew what that meant. There never were ladies in my father's office except when somebody special came from Sweden like Dala Mor, or when Mr. Calvin brought in a new teacher to have her head read.

It was Mr. Calvin. Everybody called him Superintendent Mr. Calvin. There were a lot of superintendents in Iron Valley. But only Mr. Calvin had a Mister in his name, too. That was to show that he wasn't just a boss of the mines. He was boss of the schools, the little-children's school where you played with pieces of paper, and the middle school where Frieda went, and the big school 'way up the other way from town. That made him boss of all the teachers, too. That made him a very big boss.

Mr. Calvin didn't see me. He was looking at the yellow-haired teacher with the curls. So I said, "Good day, Mr. Calvin," the way my father said was polite.

Mr. Calvin stayed looking at the yellow-haired teacher. "Well, well, well, if it isn't my little girl," he said.

The yellow-haired teacher's face started to get pink around the ears.

I could see my father wanted to get back into that chair the teacher was sitting in. I walked right up to the desk.

"She's got to take off her hat. My father can't read heads through hats," I said firmly.

Mr. Calvin backed up. He started to feel for his fingertips. "To be sure, to be sure! You can't very well read the bumps unless you can feel the bumps? Can you, J. G. R.?"

"Is that why it's called Bumpology? Because it's all about bumps?" the teacher in the chair said, pulling out two gleaming hatpins to arm's length.

"I know nothing whatever about Bumpology," my father said, as if he were telling somebody that no, he didn't sell potato-sausage in his candy store. "The science of Phrenology deals only with the areas of the head and the character traits they govern."

"Like this fellow here." Mr. Calvin reached up and lifted down the Phrenology head from where it stood, naked in its beardless baldness, between the towering and hairy plaster-of-Paris busts of Homer and Plato. "Wouldn't you like to hold him, Miss Rogers?"

Pink around the ears, Miss Rogers drew back. "No, no, no, goodness, no! It makes me nervous, he looks so—so sort of dead. And all those scratchings on his head!"

I glanced at my father, waiting. "He's not dead," I said crisply. "He never was alive. He's just stuff. He was gold all over when he came from New York. My father painted him white, so Homer and Plato shouldn't mind standing with him. And those aren't scratchings. They're Philoprogenitiveness and Causality-and-Comparison."

Miss Rogers, with my father's chair big around her, turned to me. "Goodness! Wherever did you get all those big words?"

I looked right back at her. "My father told me. And I always listen to Mr. Calvin's teachers. And, anyway, it's all in a book, with the numbers in it."

"Shall we begin?" said my father.

Miss Rogers began to pat at her rat. "I'm terribly, terribly nervous—"

"It won't hurt you at all," Mr. Calvin said, coming up. He laughed in a sort of way and touched her shoulder. "And, besides, I'm here to protect you."

I reached over and took the Phrenology head away and put it between Homer and Plato again.

"What would you say she is, J. G. R.?" Mr. Calvin said, not even noticing. "Mental, wouldn't you? The oval face? The pointed chin? The wide forehead?"

My father stood there. "Vital, I should say," he said after a while. "Possibly a little on the Vital-Motive side."

Miss Rogers touched her kiss curls in back and showed her teeth. "Is that nice, Mr. J. G. R.?" she asked. "Vital?"

I stepped forward. "It means fat," I said. "When you get old, you'll be fat."

Miss Rogers sat back quickly and Mr. Calvin looked straight at me over her head.

My father started to tell her what he could see on the top of her head that wasn't done up with too much hair. "Reverence," he said. "It seems to be quite normal."

"Where is that?" Miss Rogers asked, tilting back her head like a bird on a branch.

"On top," I said. "Where the rat isn't."

I could feel my father looking at me. I started to push the Remington-Invisible back and forth so the bell would sound.

All the other things came out, too: Stick-to-Itiveness, Veneration, Benevolence, Combativeness—and yes, she had the one with the longest name of all, that I could hardly say, Philoprogenitiveness. I stopped ringing the bell so I could hear if my father was going to get into the back of her head where the things that weren't so nice were. I turned and looked at Mr. Calvin standing there looking like Emma when everybody said her pie was good.

Miss Rogers fluttered. "Goodness, is that all? And it was so interesting, Mr. J. G. R."

"Aren't there some more things?" Mr. Calvin urged. "Such a short delineation!"

I looked at my father. "Destructiveness," I prompted.

Mr. Calvin made a laugh. "Miss Rogers? Goodness, no! Our little Miss Rogers, here, wouldn't so much as hurt a fly! Would you, Miss Rogers?"

Out of the corner of my eye I saw the *Stumpa* my father was looking at me. I stared right past it to Miss Rogers and Mr. Calvin. "It's what makes her ears stick out," I said.

Miss Rogers's both hands went up to her ears. Mr. Calvin made a laugh again, but it wasn't in his face as he looked across at me. And my father's *Stumpa!* came aloud.

But I waited to finish before I heard it. "Tell her about Amativeness?"

Miss Rogers's face got red.

"We must be careful and never use words when we don't know what they mean. Mustn't we, child?" Mr. Calvin said across to me.

I looked straight back at him. It wouldn't be until next year that he was my superintendent of schools. Maybe by that time he would have learned not to bring in yellow-haired teachers with curls to have my father feel heads for. "I know how to spell it," I said flatly. "Capital A-m-a-t-i-v-e-n-e-s-s. And I know where it is. In the back of her head where she's got the curls pinned on false."

The other lady, who had sat in the corner and not said anything, came up. With her hat off, her hair looked like a plain brown sausage laid on her head, and she was shorter and rounder and had a high net collar that pushed her chin into nearly two. She went right past my father without saying anything about having her head read. She stopped in front of me and she wasn't very much taller.

"I have the kindergarten," she said. "I suppose you're 'way up in the first grade? That's why I never saw you?"

It was good, knowing that surely if she had seen me she would remember. I warmed. "First grade is for little kids," I said. "When I decide to go to school, I guess I'll be starting high school. So I can help Gustaf with all the Latin flowers he will have when we have a house with a yard."

"A very worthy idea," she said. "And you must drop in and let me know when you start. Just ask for Miss Borden."

She wasn't laughing. Not even behind her face, the way Beata did sometimes when I forgot myself and told her things.

"The trouble is," Miss Borden said, "there's only one way of getting up to high school. And that's by starting in the first grade. It doesn't seem quite right. But there it is."

The fact didn't shock me. "Even when I can do my numbers up to the five-times? And I can read out of books?" I remembered about Fay and the galling *in-går*. "Swede books, too."

"No!" said Miss Borden, in a way that denied nothing except her own incredulous power to grasp. "Not really?"

My chest started to pouter out and I looked straight into her respectful brown eyes. I felt stirrings inside that I had never felt before when there was a lady around, a small fledgling of the pride with which I heard Rosén, maybe, or Mr. Werner from Stockholm, say my father had taught me Upsala Swedish.

"Write it, too, I can," I burnished confession into boasting. "American and Swedish, both. And sing, too. And say my father's poems. And even Mr. Tegnér's."

"You can?" Miss Borden marveled, satisfyingly.

Mr. Calvin got lonesome over there, forgotten. "J. G. R., here, has the idea that if one language is good, two are better!" he said. "And books? Goodness, the books! And imagine finding Homer and Plato off here behind the counters of a candy store? And Goath. By the way, where is Goath tonight?"

I glanced briefly over Miss Borden's maroon-wool shoulder. "Göthe," I corrected, knowing my father never would. "And it's not Göthe, anyway. It's Schiller. He's over there with his ruffles around his neck and his hair in a pug. Over by the Norrköping snuff."

I returned to awed Miss Borden. "Do you hear what my mother is singing, out back in the kitchen? Would you like to hear it better?"

"I certainly would!" Miss Borden said, resting her rear against the corner of the desk. "Don't tell me you know it? All of it?"

I didn't answer her. I just showed her, through two verses. "It's about the butterfly that wings over Haga," I explained, getting my wind. "Haga is where the princes live, at Stockholm. It's old and it's got an echo temple and copper tents where the soldier-watch stayed. And this man Bellman, long, long time ago, wrote about it and the naiads that lift up their golden horns and blow water all over Solna Tower. Or something."

"Not really!"

"Bellman wrote it," I said. "Karl Michael Bellman. To his lute. To sing for the king."

"No!" said Miss Borden.

She started to pin her hat back on.

"But your head?" Mr. Calvin remembered. "Aren't you going to have your head read, too?"

She kept on wheedling in the hatpins. "I think not. I think I know where everything is. My ears stick out, too. And I've curls pinned over my Amativeness in the back."

I went nearer to her and looked across the desk at my father, who had got himself lost in some galley sheets. "But you can tell her, is she Mental, Gustaf? She is, isn't she?"

My father looked up. And Miss Borden looked down at me, from where she had hooked her eyes to the inside brim of her hat.

"Is there a Vital-Vital?" she asked, and the little laugh she made gave her the borning of a third chin. "Because I don't even have to wait till I'm old to get fat. Coming, Edith?"

I had no time to urge about the Mental or the reading in front of Miss Borden's head. The store door closed with a bang. I peered around the corner of the office. "It's Magnus!" I announced wondering. "Magnus, walking loud like that."

Magnus came back to us, heavy-footed as if he hadn't always before walked like one walking on the thick mat of pine needles in a Helsinglands forest. "The mine," he said, talking right through Mr. Calvin and Miss Rogers. "Another cave-in."

My father laid down the print sheets and looked up. "Where?"

"E-Shaft. Just a little while ago."

"Bad?" my father asked.

"They don't know for sure. But I got a list of the men they think are down there." Magnus unfolded the paper out of his pocket.

"Bertha's father?" I cut in sharply. "Esther's father? *Basen?*"

Magnus glanced briefly from the list. "They were just off shift."

He started to read. "Hantala. Remember, the brother who just came from Finland last winter? Colosimo. The one who lives out Gile way. Five or six children. Struchynski. Just brought his parents over from Poland. Dahlstrand. Just married last fall, remember, Gustaf? His wife's expecting. Swensen. He should have taken that trip back to his old home in Christiana!"

"Ida's uncle?" I prodded, not breathing.

"They think he was in another section of the mine."

My father snapped a rubber band around the rolled-up galleys.

"Were they—" Mr. Calvin glanced at me. "Killed?" he finished in a whisper meant to pass lightly over my head.

"Too early to say," Magnus said, without looking up from his list. "Haniuk. Carlstedt. Hagelin. Calligaro."

Miss Rogers put her hands on her face. Her eyes were wide like a baby's, going all around us. "How dreadful! How terribly dreadful! Why do people go down and work in mines? Why don't they stay up on top where things like that can't happen to them?"

448

Magnus stood with his feet apart. He didn't even get red around the ears, the way he usually did when he talked to ladies. "Because that's where the iron is, under the ground. And if nobody went down to get it, there'd be none for railroad tracks and kitchen stoves, and plows to work the land with."

Miss Rogers got pink, and started to inspect her gloves.

Mr. Calvin came up. "You must know, my dear child," he said, "that that is all these men have learned how to do, chop out the iron and send it up from the mines. They did it in the old country, and their fathers did and their grandfathers. It is all they know how to do."

Magnus stood there like something that had grown up into the sun and browned there. Beside him, Mr. Calvin looked soft and moist and pale like something come out from under the ferns.

"There is a pride," Magnus said, "in doing the work that your father did well, as well as your father did it. And passing it on to your sons, to do as well. Whether it is cutting diamonds or drilling iron or cutting the straightest black furrow with your plow."

"Oh, yes, yes, of course," Mr. Calvin said quickly. "But if they were educated men—"

"*Basen* is educated!" I cut in, watching Magnus's face and my father's. "Except he doesn't speak American so very good. He went to a big school in Sweden. And Dora's father. He knows almost as many Latin flowers as my father and Dreer's flower book. And they work in the mine!"

"They work in the mine because they have to," Magnus said, almost as tall as the ceiling, almost as tall as my father. "But they also work in the mine because they know it best, and therefore it is what they want to do."

"Besides," I supplemented, "you get killed on farms, too. Mr. Swan did, when the bull got mad and ripped him almost wide open and his insides all came out. That's as bad as being all covered with the mud! And sometimes a plow hits a rock and comes up and knocks your teeth out. It did with Mr. Nystrom."

Miss Rogers shuddered.

"Education," said Mr. Calvin sadly. "Education, that is the answer. The only answer."

My father came quietly around the swivel-chair with Miss Rogers, still looking at her glove-tips, in it. "It would help," he said. "If you could educate the stomach not to need what the earth grows, and iron to lie ready for smelting in layers on the ground."

I looked at Mr. Calvin's hands, fingertipping themselves with small perpetual movements as if they were restless for never having enough to do. Superintendent Rose, who was boss of the mines, had hands like that, too, soft and white and restless. Anders hadn't, nor Charlie nor Ferdinand nor Elof. Nor Mr. Hantala, who would be locked down by the weight of bronzed earth, down there at E-Shaft. Not Simonska's Mr. Simon, either. His hadn't been red with ore. They had been pored with oil and earth from his farm and its tools.

"If your name is Mr. Rose and you talk American good, you stay on top and boss and never get hurt," I said, thinking. "And if your name is Mr. Hantala and you don't know American good, then you get killed in the mine."

The two ladies got up out of their chairs. Mr. Calvin could see my father was waiting, and Magnus, so he started everybody toward where the office left off and the store began.

Miss Borden stopped beside me. "We always talk American in school," she said.

I looked up at her almost-three chins. I put my hand into the hand she held out for me.

"So I think I have changed my mind," I told her from under the weight of the decision. "I shan't wait for high school. You can be expecting me in first grade almost any day now."

THE CITY

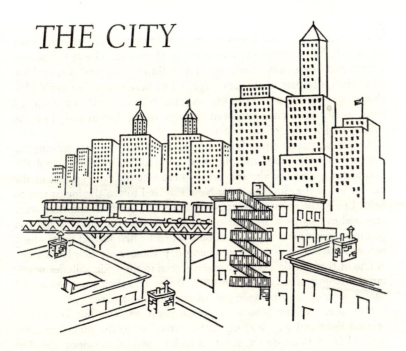

Old St. Louis

by JESSIE BENTON FREMONT, 1824–1902. *The daughter of Senator Thomas Hart Benton of Missouri, Jessie Benton was born on her maternal grandfather's estate near Lexington, Virginia. After a girlhood spent there, at Washington, and at St. Louis, she married John Charles Fremont in 1841. The first few years of her married life Mrs. Fremont spent at her father's home, her husband being absent on various trips of exploration. In Washington she studied under Senator Benton's surveillance, translated State Department papers from the Spanish, and served as hostess in place of her ailing mother. Later she helped Fremont with his official reports of his journeys. In 1849 she went via Panama to San Francisco but later returned to Washington when Fremont became the first senator from California. When her husband became the Republican candidate for president in 1856 Mrs. Fremont by her charm and diplomacy attracted many votes to his standard. In later years she drew upon her varied experiences for numerous articles and books including Souvenirs of My Time (1887), and Far West Sketches (1890). The remainder of her life she spent largely in San Francisco and on a California ranch. Mrs. Fremont is the subject of a recent biographical novel by Irving Stone entitled Immortal Wife. The account of life in Creole St. Louis is the tenth chapter of Souvenirs of My Time.*

Coming back to Saint Louis always in springtime, even after the mild winters of Washington the contrast was charming. The Potomac was a wide and beautifully blue river, but it did nothing, and was nothing more than a feature in the landscape, while here the tawny swift Mississippi was stirring with busy life, and the little city itself, was animated from its thronged river-bank out through to the Indian camps on the rolling prairie back of the town.

And it was such an embowered fragrant place in that season; the thickets of wild plum and the wild crab-apples which covered the prairie embalmed the air, and everywhere was the honey-scent of the locust. What the elm is to some New England towns the locust was to Saint Louis; the narrow streets were bordered by them and they were repeated everywhere. My father had an affection for this tree and had planted a great many about his house when he first settled there—long before he was married. In my young day these were fine large trees. A line of them made a delicate green screen to the wide galleries which ran the length of the house, on both stories, and their long clusters of vanilla-scented blooms made part of our home-memories. . . .

Not only did the blossoming town seem *en fête*, but everybody seemed light and gay, and my father, freed from the official and exacting life of Washington, reverted to his cheerful out-door life. The long gallery of the parlor-floor was his place when at home, even if light rains were falling. He never breathed in-door air when he could be, head uncovered, in a bath of sunshine. His "settee" and a table, and "a colony of chairs" for others, made his favorite settlement, where the early light breakfast of coffee and bread and fruit was taken—by any number who might chance to come. I *never* heard the word "*trouble*" applied to household arrangements. For all we knew, everything grew ready to be served.

The day begins early in warm climates, and from early morning on, there was a coming and going of varied but all welcome friends. There came governing citizens to talk of political affairs. Much had to be only personal information in those days before railways and telegraphs, and when the plans of an administration were only talked over confidentially with its friends. The father of Mrs. Grant was one of my father's old friends and political allies of that time. General Grant honored himself by the honor and thoughtful attention he always gave to this venerable man who was a conspicuous figure in the Presidential receptions. After I had made my respects to the President and Mrs. Grant, one or the other would be sure to say, "Now step back here and talk to Mr. Dent"—who always kept me sitting by him on his sofa, talking of my father and telling of the great contests they had gone through together; and when his memory failed calling me only "Mrs. Benton," but always lighting up with pleased remembrances.

There, too, came officers of the army. My father was their comprehending friend. Himself an old officer, and for twenty years Chairman of the Senate Military Committee, he was their sure and intelligent friend. With both knowledge and good will, such a position can be made of the utmost advantage to the service, as well as of personal advantage to officers. The certainty of sympathy and proper official aid never failed those who came to him. He was practically the Secretary of War in all those years, for he was a fixture while a Secretary is only a political accident, and in the War and Navy Departments usually quite ignorant of the personal as well as of the special requirements of service. Through such ignorance much injustice can be done, but in all my long knowledge of Washington, I have known of but one Secretary who found actual pleasure in giving pain to officers and in thwarting all personal feelings, even family feelings.

The French neighbors enjoyed coming for their chat, and invariably brought some fine fruit or flower for Madame, who fully appreciated both the kindly feeling and the fine skilful cultivation.

There too came many priests who were soldiers in their missionary work, and had as stirring adventures to relate as the trappers and hunters who knew they were always welcome to my father.

And often, gliding past into my mother's rooms, would come the good Sister Elizabeth on active duty for her hospital—going away with a basket of useful things and many a solid piece of money from those on the gallery, with a *"permettez ma soeur"* and a warm *"Bon jour, ma soeur"* from every one.

Two friends of my father's were specially interesting to me. One a Spanish officer *and gentleman*, in the fullest meaning, who had served under Wellington in Spain; the other who was already a captain in the French army when Waterloo broke it up. Col. Garnier was much the elder. He had accepted his exile and its resulting poverty and sufferings with silent dignity. My father had a good knowledge of Spanish, but he always tried to add improvement to all his knowledge, and Col. Garnier and himself had a Spanish talking-lesson daily. He taught us our Spanish also. My father thought we ought to know the language of our near neighbor, Mexico, with whom closer relations must come. I was a great favorite with Col. Garnier. Some fancied resemblance to a little sister, won for me his kindest voice and the name of "Rosita." Usually he took the early coffee with my father, and if Judge Lawless joined them as he often did, then their talk was sure to fall on the Peninsular

453

war. A sign would send me in for the maps and the box of pins—beeswax heads for the Spanish troops, red wax for the English, and for the French, black.

Never was that discussion ended. Not only day after day, but summer after summer, did those three move those pins that put the troops in differing positions, and proved "what might have been"; but never did either of the three convince the other. For hours they would be at it; generally the heat of discussion would be stopped by my mother's sending out an iced watermelon or a great basket of fruit which was a signal they understood. *Her* feeling was English—without discussion. My father's mother used to say to us, "Your mother is English; and she has the English genius for home comfort."

This grandmother was one of our returning pleasures in going back to Saint Louis where she had lived chiefly after my father's going there. She was more English than my mother in nearness to the mother-country, but she had a singularly large unprejudiced view of things, and had outlived every personal interest except in my father and a few of her grandchildren. Both her father and husband were English—both scholarly men and misfits in a new country. My Grandfather Benton's library in Greek, Latin, French, Spanish and English, had been his joy while he lived and made the atmosphere in which my father grew up—guided by his mother and his father's close friend, a clergyman, like himself an Oxford man, who put my father at his Greek Testament when he was but eight; at which age my grandfather's death left him the eldest son in a family of seven children.

My father has told me of the awe and singular feeling of loss of youth that fell on him when, after his father's death and a long illness which came on his mother, he was taken in to see her.

She was about thirty; a very tall slender woman with blue eyes that never lost their steady clearness. And, as all the Hart family, she had splendid long, thick, waving, auburn-brown hair. In her six weeks' illness this had changed to a silvery white—which, with her white and thinned face, so alarmed my father that he ran into a grove near by when he came out, and "had to war with himself to accept that shadow as his mother." Nearly all her children died young; of rapid consumption, as their father had died; and the silent grief with which my grandmother bore her eighty-three years of life invested her with a dignity none intruded on. She had her wing in my father's house, and her own old servants who knew her ways. A fall on the ice and a badly-set leg crippled her and caused keen suffering from rheumatisms for the last years of her life, but her powerful clear inquiring mind made books a great solace.

Our Virginia grandmother, with her unbroken domestic life, her

454

active health and child's heart for simple pleasures, was just the opposite to my Grandmother Benton, who could not tolerate our sewing. "It is not good for your chest," she would say; and "you should never waste your time, doing what an uneducated person can do better for you." One of her few pleasures was to have her hair brushed. This remained thick and long; so long that the thick plait reached nearly to the knee. When coiled around her head it filled the crown of the "mob-cap," as the widow's cap of that day was called, leaving only space for the band of black crape back of the narrow crimped ruffles. It was a pleasure to her and a privilege to me to let down and brush and smooth out this beautiful hair, and to hear her talk. Her extensive reading made all countries familiar to her. She made on me, even as a young child, the effect of being *above* other people. And though she died when I was but thirteen I have kept the realization of a lofty and great soul. I know that my father and his nearest friends very often referred questions to her and deferred to her calm wisdom and unprejudiced perceptions.

In Washington all our lessons were had at home but my father did the important part of appointing studies and preparing us for our teachers, making broad and lucid what they might have left as "parroting," as he expressed it. Here in Saint Louis we were let to go to school; chiefly for the practice in French among other children.

It makes me smile to look back at that word "school" which had not the first idea of studies, of punctuality, or discipline attached to it as I knew it. The going there each morning was as good as playing truant. *Never* could it happen that children of any position left the house alone, or even together. We were big girls of eight and ten and every one knew us, and the distance was only a short mile between houses and grounds of friends; but to go without a maid was never dreamed of. We should have greatly preferred our French nurse, Madeleine, but she was not sufficiently important for such duty. Our mother's maid, "aunt" Sara, was. She had been trained from her youth up for her post—as was the Southern custom—and understood "manners." Erect, silent, holding a hand of each, she drilled us in manners as we went along. When we passed the small house of M'âme Desirée where she in *very* negligée loose gown patted her muslins on the sunny gallery, we had to stop if she spoke to us.

M'âme Desirée was the clear-starcher and fine-muslin genius of Saint Louis; too fat now, but still a most handsome quadroon who had a gay word for every passer-by. M'âme Saraah was a crony of hers, and when she would give us the good day and praise our neatness and good condition (as all due to M'âme Saraah!) we had to wait and listen politely: "You can't hurry her, because she is a poor working woman and it would hurt her feelings"—aunt Sara had never heard the words, but her conviction was that "Time was made for slaves," and not for little young ladies.

Then the garden doors of many pleasant enclosures would be open and the various Madame Augustes or Madame Caddys would be out in the fresh of the morning and the ladies themselves—also in most easy negligée—going about their grounds. If they saw us we would be called in and *cette bonne Sara* asked after Madame and praised for her *petites*. And with deliberation (time no object), some pretty fruit would be chosen for us and we would recommence our walk to stop again and again; for, "Madame Auguste is a lady and you can't hurry her"—in fact, there was no hurry anywhere.

When we did reach the school we were consigned to Madame Savary who did not teach, but who looked after us; a small vivacious Swiss-French-woman with a mania for making preserves and doing fine sewing. Monsieur Savary was capable of far more than was required of him. I think he had put away his pride and resigned himself to what he could, not what he would, do. He was a spare tall man with flat black hair and gold spectacles and always wore a short-waisted very long and full-skirted frock coat of gray, with collar and cuffs of black velvet, a sort of uniform for teachers which you often see in old-fashioned French illustrations. He was quiet, gentle and forbearing, and had need to be so as there were about thirty girls, from six to sixteen—of course not a fraction of a boy in a French school—and not one with any intentions of study or habit of discipline; good-natured enough, but trying. They may have learned something. *We* were there only for easy handling of familiar French; and except some spelling, and reading aloud in *Telemachus,* I do not recall anything of lessons. But I won honors in whipping ruffles and hemming handkerchiefs for Madame Savary, and what was really important was when we, the younger ones, were permitted to help her make preserves. If a quantity of strawberries or currants were sent to her all hands turned in to prepare them. For the object my father had in view, it was more useful than reading from a book and vastly better for health than sitting still on a bench; for we adjourned, we young ones I mean, to the inevitable gallery, or the garden which was on the bluff overlooking the river. By one o'clock aunt Sara had come for us to go home and as this was our dinner hour we made no delays.

In French schools Thursday is the holiday. Saturday and Sunday, they think, make too much holiday together. But to us Americans the Sunday was not a holiday in their sense, where after mass all their children were taken around among their elder relations and it was a family fête-day.

We did not go on Saturdays to school. That day our mother had us

456

get our Sunday-school lessons with her—telling us many interesting things and making them, as all our home lessons were, a real pleasure and improvement. Our Sunday dresses were decided on and each thing reviewed and put in order that no delay might come. All our dolls and toys and weekday story-books were put away until Monday; and then we had as wild a play as big grounds and good health and early youth could give. In this our French nurse Madeleine was a great factor; she was so gay and knew such beautiful songs and danced such queer dances in her pretty carved sabots that we doted on her.

Her family had come away from France, from near Bordeaux, because of the cholera. French people do not like to leave their country, the women especially, and these were well-to-do farming people. But the horror of cholera was on them and they came to New Orleans. There they found the climate would not let them work in the fields and they would have to buy slaves. So they came on up the river to the free State of Illinois, and bought a fine farm just across from Saint Louis. There, as the old man said, his own large family, girls and boys—could all work and his and their delight in the rich earth and easy ploughing was great. He had great pride in his vegetables and melons, and my father was capable of doing away with indefinite melons—both the great red watermelons and the delicate little cantelopes which the French cultivate so well. Whenever La Mère had a specially fine melon she brought it to my father; and always we heard over again, and sorrowed with her afresh for the parting from their farm in France. One sister was in service with us, and another, Annette, was nurse in the family of my father's niece. These young ones were satisfied with the change; more than satisfied when they exchanged field and farm labor for the ease of life as nurses and the pleasure of wearing their Sunday clothes every day.

Sometimes, in a summer's day you feel, before you see why, a chill in the air. Something has changed; and though the day looks the same its sweetness is gone. So, in the summer I was about eight, this bright careless Saint Louis life seemed to chill over. At first we were only told we were not to go to school. Then, we were to play only with each other in our own grounds and no more little friends visited us or we them. The friends who came to my father on the long gallery were as many as ever, but they and he himself no longer had any pleasant leisure, but were quick and busy in coming and going, and all looked grave. The tears were all the time on Madeleine's face and constantly she was on her knees telling her beads and praying and sobbing. We saw many, many funerals passing. Our house was on a sloping hill, and we saw to all sides of the square. Then, soon, drays with several coffins piled on jolted fast along the rough street, or a wagon-load of empty coffins would cross another street. Madeleine would run in from the gallery hiding her eyes: "Ah, *Mon Dieu*, it is all funerals on every side— *C'est le cholera.*"

It was the cholera; among a people excitable and ignorant of its treatment, who gave up to it as a fatality if they could not fly from it.

In this condition of universal alarm, when nearly all who could, fled from the town, even clergymen deserting their churches, my father thought it right for him to stay and give the encouragement and example of his presence. With his courage and sense of duty this was easy, but it must have been hard to him to risk my mother and all of us children. The Catholic clergy were true to their post; and among the Protestant clergymen who remained was a young man who became loved and honored there, the Rev. Mr. Potts. He became very intimate with my parents during this cholera time, and later, married a niece of my father's.

I was too young to know details, but I know how the Peninsular war was laid aside for good work from both officers among the sufferers. All were busy, and all needed, for a panic had set in and nothing is so cruel as fear. Our poor gentle Mr. Savary died—alone. Gay M'âme Desirée nursed others like a hero but was herself a victim. Our Madeleine became almost entirely blind—nervous paralysis of the eyelid from the terrified shrinking of the eye from constant passing coffins. Otherwise the disease did not touch one of our family and spared our nearest friends. Our house was a "diet-kitchen"; good soups, preparations of rice, and well-filtered and purified water, it became the occupation of the house to keep ready.

All the water was brought in large barrels from the river and poured bucket by bucket, into great jars of red earthenware, some of them five feet high. These jars had their own large cool room paved with glazed red brick and level with the street. The jars of drinking water and for cooking were clarified of the mud of the river by alum and blanched almonds, and then filtered. So much was needed now that even we children were useful in this sort of work. In that cool dark room the melons used to be kept, but there were no melons or fruit now—we ate only rice and mutton and such simple things.

The sad summer ended as all things must end, bad or good. *Tout passe.* When all seemed safe, suddenly my mother was taken down with cholera, and the nurse who had become blinded by one shock recovered her sight from this other. It was a bad illness, but with that one brush of the dark angel's wing our home stood as before.

458

The Dandy

by THOMAS PEIRCE, 1786–1850. *One of the first western satiric poets, Peirce was born in Chester County, Pennsylvania, and as a result of being left fatherless at the age of five was obliged to support himself from early childhood. He did farm work and became adept at the making of harnesses and saddles. For a time he was enrolled in a Quaker boarding school to study mathematics. In 1813 he went to Cincinnati and engaged in the mercantile business with his father-in-law. He studied medicine and won a diploma but remained a merchant until his death. In 1821 he contributed to the Western Spy and Literary Cadet a series of satirical odes called "Horace in Cincinnati"; these were collected and published in 1822 by George W. Harrison. Peirce later contributed to various Cincinnati periodicals, including the Cincinnati Chronicle and John P. Foote's Literary Gazette. "The Dandy" is reprinted from William T. Coggeshall's Poets and Poetry of the West (Columbus, 1860).*

BEHOLD a pale, thin-visaged wight,
Some five feet, more or less, in height;
   Which, as it frisks and dances,
Presents a body that, at most,
Is less substantial than a ghost,
   As pictured in romances!

A head of hair, as wild and big
As any reverend bishop's wig;
   And on the top inserted
(Or front, or side—as runs the whim)
A something with an inch of brim,
   And crown like cone inverted.

Around its neck a stiff cravat;
Another tightly drawn o'er that,
   And over these, a dozen
Enormous ruffles on his breast;
And close below a tiny vest,
   For gaudy colors chosen.

And over all, a trim surtout
Scanty in length, and tight to boot
   And (what is now no wonder)
Rigg'd out with capes full half a score;
And five small buttons down before,
   Just half an inch asunder.

With trowsers welted down each side,
And spreading out almost as wide
　　As petticoats at bottom;
A small dumb watch some cent'ries old,
With twenty keys and seals of gold—
　　No matter how he got 'em.

To dangle at a lady's side,
Whene'er she takes a walk or ride,
　　A thing extremely handy:—
These constitute—as fashions run
In eighteen hundred twenty-one—
　　A *Cincinnati Dandy*.

Major Amberson's Town

by BOOTH TARKINGTON, 1869—　. *The dean of the Hoosier school of writers, Newton Booth Tarkington was born in Indianapolis. He was educated at Phillips Exeter Academy, Purdue University, and Princeton University, where he showed his versatility by painting and singing as well as writing. In 1902–3 he was a member of the Indiana House of Representatives but most of his life has been devoted to the writing of fiction. After a long struggle to gain the attention of publishers Tarkington won popular favor with two novels, The Gentleman from Indiana (1899) and Monsieur Beaucaire (1900). Some forty books have since appeared, as well as more than a dozen plays. Tarkington's output includes the well-known Penrod stories such as Penrod (1914); a trilogy of novels depicting life in a large and growing middlewestern city, presumably Indianapolis, The Magnificent Ambersons (1918), The Turmoil (1915), and The Midlander (1924); and probably his best story, Alice Adams (1921), which was awarded the Pulitzer prize. Tarkington's great gift for accurate observation and social satire is revealed in the opening chapter of The Magnificent Ambersons. Much of his later work, however, is spoiled by feeble plots and by his willingness to cater to the box office.*

MAJOR AMBERSON had "made a fortune" in 1873, when other people were losing fortunes, and the magnificence of the Ambersons began then. Magnificence, like the size of a fortune, is always comparative, as even Magnificent Lorenzo may now perceive, if he happened to haunt New York in 1916; and the Ambersons were magnificent in their day and place. Their splendour lasted throughout all the years that saw their Midland town spread and darken into a city, but reached its topmost during the period when every prosperous family with children kept a Newfoundland dog.

In that town, in those days, all the women who wore silk or velvet knew all the other women who wore silk or velvet, and when there was a new purchase of sealskin, sick people were got to windows to see it go by. Trotters were out, in the winter afternoons, racing light sleighs on National Avenue and Tennessee Street; everybody recognized both the trotters and the drivers; and again knew them as well on summer evenings, when slim buggies whizzed by in renewals of the snow-time rivalry. For that matter, everybody knew everybody else's family horse-and-carriage, could identify such a silhouette half a mile down the street, and thereby was sure who was going to market, or to a reception, or coming home from office or store to noon dinner or evening supper.

During the earlier years of this period, elegance of personal appearance was believed to rest more upon the texture of garments than upon their shaping. A silk dress needed no remodelling when it was a year or so old; it remained distinguished by merely remaining silk. Old men and governors wore broadcloth; "full dress" was broadcloth with "doeskin" trousers; and there were seen men of all ages to whom a hat meant only that rigid, tall silk thing known to impudence as a "stovepipe." In town and country these men would wear no other hat, and, without self-consciousness, they went rowing in such hats.

Shifting fashions of shape replaced aristocracy of texture: dressmakers, shoemakers, hatmakers, and tailors, increasing in cunning and in power, found means to make new clothes old. The long contagion of the "Derby" hat arrived: one season the crown of this hat would be a bucket; the next it would be a spoon. Every house still kept its bootjack, but high-topped boots gave way to shoes and "congress gaiters"; and these were played through fashions that shaped them now with toes like box-ends and now with toes like the prows of racing shells.

Trousers with a crease were considered plebeian; the crease proved that the garment had lain upon a shelf, and hence was "ready-made"; these betraying trousers were called "hand-me-downs," in allusion to the shelf. In the early 'eighties, while bangs and bustles were having their way with women, that variation of dandy known as the "dude" was invented: he wore trousers as tight as stockings, dagger-pointed shoes, a spoon "Derby," a single-breasted coat called a "Chesterfield," with short flaring skirts, a torturing cylindrical collar, laundered to a polish and three inches high, while his other neckgear might be a heavy, puffed cravat or a tiny bow fit for a doll's braids. With evening dress

461

he wore a tan overcoat so short that his black coat-tails hung visible, five inches below the overcoat; but after a season or two he lengthened his overcoat till it touched his heels, and he passed out of his tight trousers into trousers like great bags. Then, presently, he was seen no more, though the word that had been coined for him remained in the vocabularies of the impertinent.

It was a hairier day than this. Beards were to the wearers' fancy, and things as strange as the Kaiserliche boar-tusk moustache were commonplace. "Side-burns" found nourishment upon childlike profiles; great Dundreary whiskers blew like tippets over young shoulders; moustaches were trained as lambrequins over forgotten mouths; and it was possible for a Senator of the United States to wear a mist of white whisker upon his throat only, not a newspaper in the land finding the ornament distinguished enough to warrant a lampoon. Surely no more is needed to prove that so short a time ago we were living in another age!

. . . At the beginning of the Ambersons' great period most of the houses of the Midland town were of a pleasant architecture. They lacked style, but also pretentiousness, and whatever does not pretend at all has style enough. They stood in commodious yards, well shaded by left-over forest trees, elm and walnut and beech, with here and there a line of tall sycamores where the land had been made by filling bayous from the creek. The house of a "prominent resident," facing Military Square, or National Avenue, or Tennessee Street, was built of brick upon a stone foundation, or of wood upon a brick foundation. Usually it had a "front porch" and a "back porch"; often a "side porch," too. There was a "front hall"; there was a "side hall"; and sometimes a "back hall." From the "front hall" opened three rooms: the "parlour," the "sitting room," and the "library"; and the library could show warrant to its title—for some reason these people bought books. Commonly, the family sat more in the library than in the "sitting room," while callers, when they came formally, were kept to the "parlour," a place of formidable polish and discomfort. The upholstery of the library furniture was a little shabby; but the hostile chairs and sofa of the "parlour" always looked new. For all the wear and tear they got they should have lasted a thousand years.

Upstairs were the bedrooms; "Mother-and-father's room" the largest; a smaller room for one or two sons, another for one or two daughters; each of these rooms containing a double bed, a "washstand," a "bureau," a wardrobe, a little table, a rocking-chair, and often a chair or two that had been lightly damaged down-stairs, but not enough to justify either the expense of repair or decisive abandonment in the attic. And there was always a "spare-room," for visitors (where the sewing-machine usually was kept), and during the 'seventies there developed an appreciation of the necessity for a bathroom. Therefore the architects placed bathrooms in the new houses, and the older houses tore out a cupboard or two, set up a boiler beside the kitchen stove, and sought a new godliness, each with its own bathroom. The great American plumber joke, that many-branched evergreen, was planted at this time.

At the rear of the house, upstairs, was a bleak little chamber, called "the girl's room," and in the stable there was another bedroom, adjoining the hayloft, and called "the hired man's room." House and stable cost seven or eight thousand dollars to build, and people with that much money to invest in such comforts were classified as the Rich. They paid the inhabitant of "the girl's room" two dollars a week, and, in the latter part of this period, two dollars and a half, and finally three dollars a week. She was Irish, ordinarily, or German, or it might be Scandinavian, but never native to the land unless she happened to be a person of colour. The man or youth who lived in the stable had like wages, and sometimes he, too, was lately a steerage voyager, but much oftener he was coloured.

After sunrise, on pleasant mornings, the alleys behind the stables were gay; laughter and shouting went up and down their dusty lengths, with a lively accompaniment of curry-combs knocking against back fences and stable walls, for the darkies loved to curry their horses in the alley. Darkies always prefer to gossip in shouts instead of whispers; and they feel that profanity, unless it be vociferous, is almost worthless. Horrible phrases were caught by early rising children and carried to older people for definition, sometimes at inopportune moments; while less investigative children would often merely repeat the phrases in some subsequent flurry of agitation, and yet bring about consequences so emphatic as to be recalled with ease in middle life.

. . . They have passed, those darky hired men of the Midland town; and the introspective horses they curried and brushed and whacked and amiably cursed—those good old horses switch their tails at flies no more. For all their seeming permanence they might as well have been buffaloes—or the buffalo laprobes that grew bald in patches and used to slide from the careless drivers' knees and hang unconcerned, half way to the ground. The stables have been transformed into other likenesses, or swept away, like the woodsheds where were kept the stove-wood and kindling that the "girl" and the "hired-man" always quarrelled over: who should fetch it. Horse and stable and woodshed, and the whole tribe of the "hired-man," all are gone. They went quickly, yet so silently that we whom they served have not yet really noticed that they are vanished.

So with other vanishings. There were the little bunty streetcars on the long, single track that went its troubled way among the cobblestones. At the rear door of the car there was no platform, but a step where passengers clung in wet clumps when the weather was bad and the car crowded. The patrons—if not too absent-minded—put their fares into a slot; and no conductor paced the heaving floor, but the driver would rap remindingly with his elbow upon the glass of the door to his little open platform if the nickels and the passengers did not appear to coincide in number. A lone mule drew the car, and sometimes drew it off the track, when the passengers would get out and push it on again. They really owed it courtesies like this, for the car was genially accommodating: a lady could whistle to it from an upstairs window, and the car would halt at once and wait for her while she shut the window, put on her hat and cloak, went downstairs, found an umbrella, told the "girl" what to have for dinner, and came forth from the house.

The previous passengers made little objection to such gallantry on the part of the car: they were wont to expect as much for themselves on like occasion. In good weather the mule pulled the car a mile in a little less than twenty minutes, unless the stops were too long; but when the trolley-car came, doing its mile in five minutes and better, it would wait for nobody. Nor could its passengers have endured such a thing, because the faster they were carried the less time they had to spare! In the days before deathly contrivances hustled them through their lives, and when they had no telephones—another ancient vacancy profoundly responsible for leisure—they had time for everything: time to think, to talk, time to read, time to wait for a lady!

They even had time to dance "square dances," quadrilles, and "lancers"; they also danced the "racquette," and schottisches and polkas, and such whims as the "Portland Fancy." They pushed back the sliding doors between the "parlour" and the "sitting room," tacked down crash over the carpets, hired a few palms in green tubs, stationed three or four Italian musicians under the stairway in the "front hall"—and had great nights!

But these people were gayest on New Year's Day; they made it a true festival—something no longer known. The women gathered to "assist" the hostesses who kept "Open House"; and the carefree men, dandified and perfumed, went about in sleighs, or in carriages and ponderous "hacks," going from Open House to Open House, leaving fantastic cards in fancy baskets as they entered each doorway, and emerging a little later, more carefree than ever, if the punch had been to their liking. It always was, and, as the afternoon wore on, pedestrians saw great gesturing and waving of skin-tight lemon gloves, while ruinous

464

fragments of song were dropped behind as the carriages rolled up and down the streets.

"Keeping Open House" was a merry custom; it has gone, like the all-day picnic in the woods, and like that prettiest of all vanished customs, the serenade. When a lively girl visited the town she did not long go unserenaded, though a visitor was not indeed needed to excuse a serenade. Of a summer night, young men would bring an orchestra under a pretty girl's window—or, it might be, her father's, or that of an ailing maiden aunt—and flute, harp, fiddle, 'cello, cornet, and bass viol would presently release to the dulcet stars such melodies as sing through "You'll Remember Me," "I Dreamt That I Dwelt in Marble Halls," "Silver Threads Among the Gold," "Kathleen Mavourneen," or "The Soldier's Farewell."

They had other music to offer, too, for these were the happy days of "Olivette" and "The Mascotte" and "The Chimes of Normandy" and "Girofle-Girofla" and "Fra Diavola." Better than that, these were the days of "Pinafore" and "The Pirates of Penzance" and of "Patience." This last was needed in the Midland town, as elsewhere, for the "aesthetic movement" had reached thus far from London, and terrible things were being done to honest old furniture. Maidens sawed what-nots in two, and gilded the remains. They took the rockers from rocking-chairs and gilded the inadequate legs; they gilded the easels that supported the crayon portraits of their deceased uncles. In the new spirit of art they sold old clocks for new, and threw wax flowers and wax fruit, and the protecting glass domes, out upon the trash-heap. They filled vases with peacock feathers, or cat-tails, or sumach, or sunflowers, and set the vases upon mantelpieces and marble-topped tables. They embroidered daisies (which they called "marguerites") and sunflowers and sumach and cat-tails and owls and peacock feathers upon plush screens and upon heavy cushions, then strewed these cushions upon floors where fathers fell over them in the dark. In the teeth of sinful oratory, the daughters went on embroidering; they embroidered daisies and sunflowers and sumach and cat-tails and owls and peacock feathers upon "throws" which they had the courage to drape upon horsehair sofas; they painted owls and daisies and sunflowers and sumach and cat-tails and peacock feathers upon tambourines. They hung Chinese umbrellas of paper to the chandeliers; they nailed paper fans to the walls. They "studied" painting on china, these girls; they sang Tosti's new songs; they sometimes still practiced the old, genteel habit of lady-fainting, and were most charming of all when they drove forth, three or four in a basket phaeton, on a spring morning.

Croquet and the mildest archery ever known were the sports of people

465

still young and active enough for so much exertion; middle-age played euchre. There was a theatre, next door to the Amberson Hotel, and when Edwin Booth came for a night, everybody who could afford to buy a ticket was there, and all the "hacks" in town were hired. "The Black Crook" also filled the theatre, but the audience then was almost entirely of men who looked uneasy as they left for home when the final curtain fell upon the shocking girls dressed as fairies. But the theatre did not often do so well; the people of the town were still too thrifty.

They were thrifty because they were the sons or grandsons of the "early settlers," who had opened the wilderness and had reached it from the East and the South with wagons and axes and guns, but with no money at all. The pioneers were thrifty or they would have perished: they had to store away food for the winter, or goods to trade for food, and they often feared they had not stored enough—they left traces of that fear in their sons and grandsons. In the minds of most of these, indeed, their thrift was next to their religion: to save, even for the sake of saving, was their earliest lesson and discipline. No matter how prosperous they were, they could not spend money either upon "art," or upon mere luxury and entertainment, without a sense of sin.

Against so homespun a background the magnificence of the Ambersons was as conspicuous as a brass band at a funeral. Major Amberson bought two hundred acres of land at the end of National Avenue; and through this tract he built broad streets and cross-streets; paved them with cedar block, and curbed them with stone. He set up fountains, here and there, where the streets intersected, and at symmetrical intervals placed cast-iron statues, painted white, with their titles clear upon the pedestals: Minerva, Mercury, Hercules, Venus, Gladiator, Emperor Augustus, Fisher Boy, Stag-hound, Mastiff, Greyhound, Fawn, Antelope, Wounded Doe, and Wounded Lion. Most of the forest trees had been left to flourish still, and, at some distance, or by moonlight, the place was in truth beautiful; but the ardent citizen, loving to see his city grow, wanted neither distance nor moonlight. He had not seen Versailles, but, standing before the Fountain of Neptune in Amberson Addition, at bright noon, and quoting the favourite comparison of the local newspapers, he declared Versailles outdone. All this Art showed a profit from the start, for the lots sold well and there was something like a rush to build in the new Addition. Its main thoroughfare, an oblique continuation of National Avenue, was called Amberson Boulevard, and here, at the juncture of the new Boulevard and the Avenue, Major Amberson reserved four acres for himself, and built his new house—the Amberson Mansion, of course.

This house was the pride of the town. Faced with stone as far back as the dining-room windows, it was a house of arches and turrets and girdling stone porches: it had the first porte-cochere seen in that town. There was a central "front hall" with a great black walnut stairway, and open to a green glass skylight called the "dome," three stories above the ground floor. A ballroom occupied most of the third story; and at one end of it was a carved walnut gallery for the musicians. Citizens told strangers that the cost of all this black walnut and wood-carving was sixty thousand dollars. "Sixty thousand dollars for the wood-work *alone!* Yes, sir, and hardwood floors all over the house! Turkish rugs and no carpets at all, except a Brussels carpet in the front parlour—I hear they call it the 'reception-room.' Hot and cold water upstairs and down, and stationary washstands in every last bedroom in the place. Their sideboard's built right into the house and goes all the way across one end of the dining room. It isn't walnut, it's solid mahogany! Not veneering—solid mahogany! Well, sir, I presume the President of the United States would be tickled to swap the White House for the Amberson Mansion, if the Major'd give him the chance —but by the Almighty Dollar, you bet your sweet life the Major wouldn't!"

Chicago

by CARL SANDBURG. *Sandburg shares Whitman's democracy, optimism, and belief in a flexible poetic medium. No one has done more than he to make poetry out of the life of ordinary people. His famous poem "Chicago" is not only a tribute to the greatest city of the Middle West but also an illustration of the poet's selection of material.*

HOG Butcher for the World,
Tool Maker, Stacker of Wheat,
Player with Railroads and the Nation's Freight Handler;
Stormy, husky, brawling,
City of the Big Shoulders:

They tell me you are wicked, and I believe them; for I have seen your
    painted women under the gas lamps luring the farm boys.
And they tell me you are crooked, and I answer: Yes, it is true I have
    seen the gunman kill and go free to kill again.

And they tell me you are brutal, and my reply is: On the faces of
women and children I have seen the marks of wanton hunger.
And having answered so I turn once more to those who sneer at this
my city, and I give them back the sneer and say to them:
Come and show me another city with lifted head singing so proud to
be alive and coarse and strong and cunning.
Flinging magnetic curses amid the toil of piling job on job, here is a
tall bold slugger set vivid against the little soft cities;
Fierce as a dog with tongue lapping for action, cunning as a savage
pitted against the wilderness,
    Bareheaded,
    Shovelling,
    Wrecking,
    Planning,
    Building, breaking, rebuilding,
Under the smoke, dust all over his mouth, laughing with white teeth,
Under the terrible burden of destiny laughing as a young man laughs,
Laughing even as an ignorant fighter laughs who has never lost a battle,
Bragging and laughing that under his wrist is the pulse, and under his
ribs the heart of the people,
    Laughing!
Laughing the stormy, husky, brawling laughter of Youth, half-naked,
sweating, proud to be Hog Butcher, Tool Maker, Stacker of
Wheat, Player with Railroads and Freight Handler to the Nation.

Effie Whittlesy

by GEORGE ADE, 1866–1944. *A conspicuous member of the Hoosier
group of writers, Ade was born in Kentland, Indiana, and was educated at
Purdue University, B.A., 1887. He at once entered journalism and after three
years on a paper at Lafayette, Indiana, he joined the staff of the Chicago
Record. Here from 1890 to 1900 he wrote his famous "stories of the streets
and of the town," and amassed the fund of experience which later resulted
in his unique fables. Such books as Fables in Slang (1900), More Fables
(1900), and The Girl Proposition (1902) brought him a wide reputation;
and he was also admired as the creator of such big-city characters as Artie,
Doc Horne, and Pink Marsh. Ade continued to produce his fables with their
excessive capitalization, current slang, and satiric morals for some years, but
gradually he turned his energy into the writing of popular drama. Among his*

best known successes were "The Sultan of Sulu" (1902) and "The College Widow" (1904). In his later years Ade tried his hand at scenario writing but gradually became less productive and spent much of his time at his Indiana farm. Critics were slow to realize the value of his work as a record of metropolitan life and speech about 1900, but Ade is now generally recognized as an original and gifted observer. "Effie Whittlesy" originally appeared on the editorial page of the Chicago Record.

M<small>RS</small>. W<small>ALLACE</small> was in a good humor.

She assisted her husband to remove his overcoat and put her warm palms against his red and wind-beaten cheeks.

"I have good news," said she.

"Another bargain sale?"

"Pshaw, no. A new girl, and I really believe she's a jewel. She isn't young or good looking, and when I asked her if she wanted any nights off she said she wouldn't go out after dark for anything in the world. What do you think of that?"

"That's too good to be true."

"No, it isn't. Wait till you see her. She came here from the intelligence office about 2 o'clock and I put her to work at once. You wouldn't know that kitchen. She has it as clean as a pin."

"What nationality?"

"None—or I mean she's from the country. She's as green as she can be, but she's a good soul, and I know we can trust her."

"Well, I hope so. If she is all that you say, why, for goodness' sake give her any pay she wants—put lace curtains in her room and subscribe for all the story papers on the market."

"Bless you, I don't believe she'd read them. Every time I've looked into the kitchen she's been working like a Trojan and singing 'Beulah Land.'"

"Oh, she sings, does she? I knew there'd be something wrong with her."

"You won't mind that. We can keep the doors closed."

The dinner table was set in tempting cleanliness. Bradley Wallace, aged 8, sat at the left of his father, and Mrs. Wallace, at the right, surveyed the arrangements of glass and silver and gave a nod of approval. Then she touched the bell and in a moment the new servant entered.

She was a tall woman who had said her last farewell to girlhood. She had a nose of honest largeness and an honest spread of freckles, and yet her face was not unattractive. It suggested good nature and homely candor. The cap and apron were of snowy white. She was modest, but not flurried.

469

Then a very strange thing happened.

Mr. Wallace turned to look at the new girl and his eyes enlarged. He gazed at her as if fascinated either by cap or freckles. An expression of wonderment came to his face and he said: "Well, by George!"

The girl had come very near the table when she took the first overt glance at him. Why did the tureen sway in her hands? She smiled in a frightened way and hurriedly set the tureen on the table.

Mr. Wallace was not long undecided, but during that moment of hesitancy he remembered many things. He had been reared in the democracy of a small community and the democratic spirit came uppermost.

"This isn't Effie Whittlesy?" said he.

"For the land's sake!" she exclaimed, backing away, and this was a virtual confession.

"You don't know me."

"Well, if it ain't Ed Wallace!"

Would that words were ample to tell how Mrs. Wallace settled back in her chair, gaping first at her husband and then at the new girl, stunned with surprise and vainly trying to understand what it all meant.

She saw Mr. Wallace reach awkwardly across the table and shake hands with the new girl and then she found voice to gasp: "Of all things!"

Mr. Wallace was painfully embarrassed. He was wavering between his formal duty as an employer and his natural regard for an old friend. Anyway, it occurred to him that an explanation would be timely.

"This is Effie Whittlesy from Brainerd," said he. "I used to go to school with her. She's been at our house often. I haven't seen her for— I didn't know you were in Chicago."

"Well, Ed Wallace, you could knock me down with a feather," said Effie, who still stood in a flustered attitude a few paces back from the table. "I had no more idee when I heard the name Wallace that it'd be you, though knowin', of course, you was up here. Wallace is such a common name I never give it a second thought. But the minute I saw you, law! I knew who it was well enough."

"I thought you were still at Brainerd," said Mr. Wallace, after a pause.

"I left there a year ago November, and came to visit Mort's people. Mort has a real nice place with the street-car company and is doin' well. I didn't want to be no burden on him, so I started out on my own hook, seein' that there was no use of going back to Brainerd to slave for $2 a week. I had a good place with Mr. Sanders, the railroad man on the north side, but I left because they wanted me to serve liquor.

I'd about as soon handle a toad as a bottle of beer. Liquor was the ruination of Jesse. He's gone to the dogs, and been off with a circus somewhere for two years."

"The family's all broken up, eh?" asked Mr. Wallace.

"Gone to the four winds since mother died. Of course, you know that Lora married Huntford Thomas and is livin' on the old Murphy place. They're doin' so well."

"Yes? That's good," said Mr. Wallace.

Was this an old settlers' reunion or a quiet family dinner? The soup had been waiting.

Mrs. Wallace came into the breach.

"That will be all for the present, Effie," said she. Effie gave a startled "Oh!" and vanished into the kitchen.

"What does this mean?" asked Mrs. Wallace, turning to her husband. "Bradley, behave!" This last was addressed to the 8-year-old, who had followed the example of his father and was snickering violently.

"It means," said Mr. Wallace, "that we were children together, made mud pies in the same puddle and sat next to each other in the old schoolhouse at Brainerd. The Whittlesy family was as poor as a church mouse, but they were all sociable—and freckled. Effie's a good girl."

"Effie? Effie? And she called you Ed!"

"My dear, you don't understand. We lived together in a small town where people don't stand on their dignity. She never called me anything but Ed, and everybody called her Effie. I can't put on any airs with her, because, to tell the truth, she knows me too well. She's seen me licked in school and has been at our house, almost like one of the family, when mother was sick and we needed an extra girl. If my memory served me right I took her to more than one school exhibition. I'm in no position to lord it over her and I wouldn't do it anyway. She's a good-hearted girl and I wouldn't want her to go back to Brainerd and say that she met me up here and I was too 'stuck up' to remember old times."

"You took her to school exhibitions?" asked Mrs. Wallace, with a gasp and an elevation of her eyebrows.

"Fifteen years ago, my dear—in Brainerd. I told you you wouldn't understand. You're not jealous, are you?" and he gave a side-wink at his son, who once more giggled.

"Jealous! I'm only thinking how pleasant it will be when we give a dinner party to have her come in and address you as 'Ed.'"

Mr. Wallace laughed as if he enjoyed the prospect, which led his wife to remark: "I really don't believe you'd care."

"Well, are we going to have any dinner?" he asked.

The soup had become cold and Effie brought in the next course.

"Do you get the Brainerd papers?" she asked, when encouraged by an amiable smile from Mr. Wallace.

"Every week. I'll give you some of the late ones," and he had to bite his lips to keep from laughing, seeing that his wife was really in a worried state of mind.

"Something must be done."

Such was the edict issued by Mrs. Wallace. She said she had a sufficient regard for Effie, but she didn't propose to have every meal converted into a social session, with the servant girl playing the star part.

"Never worry, my dear," said Mr. Wallace, "I'll arrange that. Leave it to me."

Effie was "doing up" the dishes when Mr. Wallace lounged up to the kitchen doorway and began his diplomatic campaign.

His wife, seated in the front room, heard the prolonged purr of conversation. Ed and Effie were going over the family histories of Brainerd and recalling incidents that may have related to mud pies or school exhibitions. Somehow Mrs. Wallace did not feel entirely at ease, and yet she didn't want to go any nearer the conversation. It would have pleased her husband too well.

This is how Ed came to the point. Mrs. Wallace should have heard this part of it.

"Effie, why don't you go down and visit Lora for a month? She'd be glad to see you."

"I know, Ed, but I can't hardly afford—"

"Pshaw! I can get you a ticket to Brainerd tomorrow, and it won't cost you anything down there."

"But what'll your wife do? I know she ain't got any other help to look to."

"To tell you the truth, Effie, you're an old friend of mine, and I don't like to see you here in my house except as a visitor. You know Chicago's different from Brainerd."

"Ed Wallace, don't be foolish. I'd as soon work for you as any one, and a good deal sooner."

"I know, but I wouldn't like to see my wife giving orders to an old friend, as you are. You understand, don't you?"

"I don't know. I'll quit if you say so."

"Tut! tut! I'll get you that ticket and you can start for Brainerd tomorrow. Promise me, now."

"I'll go, and tickled enough, if that's the way you look at it."

"And if you come back I can get you a dozen places to work."

Next evening Effie departed by carriage, although protesting against the luxury.

"Ed Wallace," said she, pausing in the hallway, "they never will believe me when I tell it in Brainerd."

"Give them my best regards, and tell them I am the same as ever."

"I'll do that. Good-by. Good-by."

Mrs. Wallace, watching from the window, saw Effie disappear into the carriage. "Thank goodness," said she.

"Yes," said Mr. Wallace, dryly, "I've invited her to call when she comes back."

"To call—here? What shall I do?"

"Don't you know what to do when she comes?"

"Oh, of course I do. I didn't mean what I said."

"That's right. I knew you'd take a sensible view of the thing—even if you never did live in Brainerd."

A Fable in Slang

by GEORGE ADE. *Ade won much of his fame by adapting an old literary form to modern purposes. "A Fable in Slang," reprinted below, illustrates his terse and simple style as well as his use of typographical devices.*

A New York man went to visit a Cousin in the Far West.

The name of the Town was Fostoria, Ohio.

When he came into Town he had his Watch-Chain on the outside of his Coat, and his Pink Spats were the first ever seen in Fostoria.

"Have you a Manicure Parlor in this Beastly Hole?" asked the New York Man, as they walked up from the Train.

"What's that?" asked the Cousin, stepping on his own Feet.

"Great Heavens!" exclaimed the New York Man, and was silent for several Moments.

At Dinner he called for Artichokes, and when told that there were none, he said, "Oh, very well," in a Tone of Chastened Resignation.

After Dinner he took the Family into the Parlor, and told the Members how much they would Enjoy going to Weber and Fields'. Seeing a Book on the Table, he sauntered up to It and said, "Ah, one of Dick Davis' Things." Later in the Evening he visited the only Club House in Town. The Local Editor of the Evening Paper was playing Pin-Pool with the Superintendent of the Trolley Line. When the New York Man came into the Room, they began to Tremble and fell down on their Shots.

The Manager of the Hub and Spoke Factory then asked the New York Man to have a Drink. The New York Man wondered if a Small Bottle was already cold. They said Yes, but it was a Lie. The Boy had to go out for it.

He found One that had been in the Window of the Turf Exchange since the Grand Opening, the Year after Natural Gas was discovered. The New York Man drank it, remarking that it was hardly as Dry as he usually got it at Martin's.

The Club Members looked at Him and said Nothing. They thought he meant Bradley-Martin's.

Next Day the New York Man was Interviewed by the Local Editor. He said the West had a Great Future. In the Evening he attended the Annual Dinner of the Bicycle Club, and went Home early because the Man sitting next to him put Ice in his Claret.

In due time he returned to New York, and Fostoria took off its White Shirt.

Some Weeks after that, the Cousin of the New York Man had an Opportunity to visit the Metropolis. He rode on an Extra Ticket with a Stockman who was shipping three Car-load of Horses, and got a Free Ticket for every Car-load.

When the Cousin arrived at New York he went to the address, and found the New York Man at Dinner.

There was a Sheaf of Celery on the Table.

Opposite the New York Man sat a Chiropodist who drank.

At his right was a Large Woman in a Flowered Wrapper—she had been Weeping.

At his left was a Snake-Charmer from Huber's Museum.

The New York Man asked the Cousin to wait Outside, and then explained that he was stopping there Temporarily. That Evening they went to Proctor's, and stood during the Performance.

Moral: *A New York Man never begins to Cut Ice until he is west of Rahway.*

474

The Auctioneer's Wife

by BEN HECHT, 1894– . *Born in New York City, Hecht attended high school there but entered journalism in Chicago. From 1914 to 1923 he was on the staff of the Chicago Daily News. From 1923 to 1925 he published and edited the Chicago Literary Times, a flamboyant and sophisticated literary weekly. Since then he has devoted his time to writing articles, plays, and fiction. His 1001 Afternoons in Chicago (1923) consists of deft and often ironic reportorial sketches originally contributed to the Chicago Daily News. Among his novels are Erik Dorn (1921), Gargoyles (1922), and A Jew in Love (1930). With Charles MacArthur he has written such plays as The Front Page (1928), and Twentieth Century (1933). "The Auctioneer's Wife" is one of the vignettes of metropolitan life which originally appeared in the Chicago Daily News.*

An AUCTIONEER must have a compelling manner. He must be gabby and stentorian, witheringly sarcastic and plaintively cajoling. He must be able to detect the faintest symptoms of avarice and desire in the blink of an eyelid, in the tilt of a head. Behind his sing-song of patter as he knocks down a piece of useless bric-a-brac he must be able to remain cool, remain calculating, remain like a hawk prepared to pounce upon his prey. Passion for him must be no more than a mask; anger, sorrow, despair, ecstasy no more than the devices of salesmanship.

But more than all this, an auctioneer must know the magic password into the heart of the professional or amateur collector. He must know the glittering phrases that are the keys to their hobbies. The words that bring a gleam to the eye of the Oriental rug collector. The words that fire the china collector. The stamp collector. The period furniture collector. The tapestry enthusiast. The first edition fan. And so on.

"Ladies and gentlemen, I desire your expert attention for a moment. I have here a curious little thing of exquisite workmanship said to be from the famous collection of Count Valentino of Florence. This delicately molded, beautifully painted candelabra has illuminated the feasts of the old Florentines, twinkled amid the gay, courtly rioting of a time that is no more. Before the bidding for this priceless souvenir is opened I desire, ladies and gentlemen, to state briefly—"

Nathan Ludlow is an auctioneer who knows all the things an auctioneer must know. His eye is piercing. His tongue can roll and rattle for twelve hours at a stretch. His voice is the voice of the tempter, myriad-toned and irresistible.

It was evening. An auspicious evening. It was the evening of Mr.

475

Ludlow's divorce. And Mr. Ludlow sat in his room at the Morrison Hotel, a decanter of juniper juice at his elbow. And while he sat he talked. The subjects varied. There were tales of Ming vases and Satsuma bargains, of porcelains and rugs. And finally Mr. Ludlow arrived at the subject of audiences. And from this subject he progressed with the aid of the juniper juice to the subject of wives. And from the subject of wives he stepped casually into the sad story of his life.

"I'll tell you," said Mr. Ludlow. "Tonight I'm a free man. Judge Pam gave me, or gave her, rather, the divorce. I guess he did well. Maybe she was entitled to it. Desertion and cruelty were the charges. But they don't mean anything. The chief complaint she had against me was that I was an auctioneer."

Mr. Ludlow sighed and ran his long, artist's fingers over his eagle features and brushed back a Byronic lock of hair from his forehead.

"It was four years ago we met," he resumed, "in the Wabash Avenue place. I noticed her when the bidding on a rocking chair started. A pretty girl. And as is often the case among women who attend auctions —a bug, a fan, a fish. You know, the kind that stiffen up when they get excited. The kind that hang on your words and breathe hard while you cut loose with the patter, and lose their heads when you swing into the going-going-gone finale.

"Well, she didn't get the rocking chair. But she was game and came back on a Chinese rug. I began to notice her considerably. My words seemed to have an unusual effect on her. Then I could see that she was not only the kind of fish that lose their heads at auctions, but the terrible kind that believe everything the auctioneer says. You know, they believe that the Oriental rugs really came from the harem of the caliph and that the antique bed really was the one in which DuBarry slept and that the Elizabethan tablecloth really was an Elizabethan tablecloth. They are kind of goofily romantic and they fall hard for everything and they spend their last penny on a lot of truck, you know. Not bad stuff and probably a good deal more useful and lasting than the originals would have been."

Mr. Ludlow smiled a bit apologetically. "I'm not confessing anything you don't know, I hope," he said. "Well, to go on about the missus. I knew I had her from that first day. I wasn't vitally interested, but when she returned six days in succession it got kind of flattering. And the way she looked at me and listened to me when I pulled my stuff— say, I could have knocked down a bouquet of paper roses for the original wreath worn by Venus, I felt so good. That's how I began to think that she was an inspiration to me and how I figured that if I could have

476

somebody like her around I'd soon have them all pocketed as auction-eers.

"I forget just how it was we met, but we did. And I swear, the way she flattered me would have been enough to turn the head of a guy ten times smarter than me and forty times as old. So we got married. That's skipping a lot. But, you know, what's it all amount to, the courting and the things you say and do before you get married? So we got married and then the fun started.

"At first I could hardly believe what the drift of it was. But I hope to die if she wasn't sincere in her ideas about me as an auctioneer. I didn't get it, as I say, and that's where I made my big mistake. I let her come to the auctions and told her not to bid. But when I'd start my patter on some useless piece of 5- and 10-cent store bric-a-brac and give it an identity and hint at Count Rudolph's collection and so on, she was off like a two-year-old down a morning track.

"I didn't know how to fix it or how to head her out of it. For a month I didn't have the heart to disillusion her. I let her buy. Damn it, I never saw such an absolute boob as she was. She'd pick out the most worthless junk I was knocking down and go mad over it and buy it with my good money. It got so that I realized I was slipping. I'd get a promise from her that she wouldn't come into the auction, but I never could be sure. And if I felt like cutting loose on some piece of junk and knocking it down with a lot of flourishes I knew sure as fate that the missus would be there and that she would be the fish that caught fire first and most and that I'd be selling the thing to myself.

"Well, after the first two months of my married life I realized that I'd have to talk turkey to the missus. She was costing me my last nickel at these auctions and the better auctioneer I was the more money I lost, on account of her being so susceptible to my line of stuff. It sounds funny, but it's a fact. So I told her. I made a clean breast. I told her what a liar I was and how all the stuff I pulled from the auction stand was the bunk and how she was a boob for falling for it. And so on and so on. Say, I sold myself to her as the world's greatest, all around, low down, hideous liar that ever walked in shoe leather. And that's how it started. This divorce today is kind of an anti-climax. We ain't had much to do with each other ever since that confession."

Mr. Ludlow stared sorrowfully into the remains of a glass of juniper juice.

"I'll never marry again," he moaned. "I ain't the kind that makes a good husband. A good husband is a man who is just an ordinary liar. And me? Well, I'm an auctioneer."

Mr. Dooley on Home Life

by FINLEY PETER DUNNE, 1867–1936. *The creator of the famous Mr. Dooley, Irish saloon-keeper and oracle of Archey Road, Dunne was
born and grew up in that section of Chicago which supplied the atmosphere
for so many of his later sketches. After a public-school education he became
a newspaper reporter and worked for various Chicago papers. Early in 1893
Martin Dooley was introduced to the readers of the Chicago Post, and somewhat later his interlocutor and audience, Hennessy. Thereafter Mr. Dooley
became an established feature of American newspapers. At first Dunne used
his character simply to poke fun at local happenings, with special reference
to the Chicago Irish, but later his sketches took on wider significance and
Mr. Dooley began to express opinions about American politics and im-
perialism, the Spanish-American War, and "Teddy Rosenfelt." Throughout
his work Dunne was careful to preserve the original character of Mr. Dooley,
a shrewd, satiric, but uneducated saloon-keeper. The Dooley sketches were
collected in ten or more volumes, such as Mr. Dooley in Peace and War
(1898), Mr. Dooley's Philosophy (1900), and Dissertations by Mr. Dooley
(1906). "Mr. Dooley on Home Life" is taken from Mr. Dooley on Making
a Will and Other Necessary Evils (1919).*

Th' newspa-apers ar-re a gr-reat blessing," said Mr. Dooley. "I don't
know what I'd do without thim. If it wasn't f'r thim I'd have no society
fit to assocyate with—on'y people like ye'ersilf an' Hogan. But th'
pa-apers opens up life to me an' gives me a speakin' acquaintance with
th' whole wurruld. If th' King iv England happens to take a dhrop
too much an' fall an' skin his elbow, I have it as quick as I wud th' news
iv a bad break be th' head iv th' Hinnissy dynasty. I know more about
th' Impror iv Chiny thin me father knew about th' people in th' next
parish. An' if there's wan thing I want to write to th' iditor iv th' pa-
aper an' thank him about an' sign th' letter 'Pro Bono Publico' it is th'
peek he gives us ivry wanst in a while into th' homes iv th' arrystocracy
iv our own neighborhood. Ye go by wan iv these magnificent brick
mansions, ye see th' automobill dash up, ye see th' jook step out an'
run up th' stairs, ye see th' head hired man in knee breeches open th'
dure an' ye think to ye'ersilf: 'I bet ye thim people ar-re onhappy.'
Ivrything must be cold an' cheerless within, there's so much room. Ye
think iv th' gr-reat cap iv industhree settin' in a marble hall surrounded
be gr-rand piannies, plush chairs, onyx cuspydors an' all th' ividences
iv wealth an' refinement that money an' art can supply. He's so far
away fr'm th' rest iv th' fam'ly that whin he wants to talk to thim he
has to whistle f'r th' butler to take th' message. Ivrybody is polite an'
oncomfortable. If a man has a jook f'r a son-in-law ye don't think he

478

can iver cut loose an' be himsilf. There can't be anny freedom in such surroundings. Th' week passes without a youbedam'd. Ivrything is like it is in a novel. It's: 'Jook, have another saucerful iv tea.' 'Will ye'er grace jine me in a tub iv champagne.' 'Can I throuble ye'er grace to pass th' ketchup.' Ye wondher why th' millyonaire isn't down at th' corner saloon ivry night thryin' to pick a fight with th' bartinder. Ye feel sorry f'r th' rich in their resthricted lives.

"But ye're wrong, Hinnissy, ye're wrong. Th' life iv th' rich is far more home-like thin ye think. There's much more fam'ly feelin' thin ye imagine. Takin' thim all in all an' I don't think ye need to pity thim. A longshoreman doesn't have to walk so far to take a kick at his son-in-law, but thin look at th' amount iv furniture a millyonaire has to throw at anny mimber iv th' fam'ly that don't agree with him. A fam'ly man down on th' dhrainage canal that is thryin' to discipline his relations is limited in ammynition. Afther he's used four chairs, th' plates, a vinegar bottle, th' baby an' a glass case iv artyficyal flowers, he has to rethreat to th' kitchen an' defind it again a younger an' more injanyous man. But th' aged millyonaire has a thousand little objecks iv art that he can hurl, an' if he misses with th' Venus de Midicy, he can flatten th' jook out with a ginooyine Rembrandt. No sir, ye needn't pity th' rich. They have their own nachral injyemints iv life an' they ought to be happy.

"I was readin' about it in th' pa-aper an' it made me long f'r a little loose change more thin annything I've seen in manny a day. It seems that wan iv our most prom'nent capytalists, Mulligan J. Billhooley, had give his daughter in marredge to a Fr-rinch jook. This sign iv a foreign arrystocracy come to America to live with his wife's parents, an' properly so, as Mulligan J. Billhooley did not dare to thrust large sums iv money to th' mails. Th' nobleman made himsilf at home at wanst. There's very little diff'rence between th' arrystocracies iv anny counthries. They're all alike. Blood will tell, an' th' nobility iv th' wurruld are always aisy with each other whether their title dates back to Agincourt or South Bend.

"Th' jook was noble be birth, his fam'ly havin' done no wurruk since th' middle iv th' foorteenth cinchry. Th' Billhooley escutcheon was splashed be a few years that th' old arrystocrat had put in as a stone mason, but that's something we won't talk about. At th' prisint moment no fam'ly has a betther ratin' in Bradsthreet's peerage thin th' Billhooley's. Th' jook's nobility was older but Billhooley's was longer an' more aisily neegotyable at th' meat market.

"Well, sir, th' inthercoorse iv these two gr-reat noblemen was charmin', parfectly aisy an' simple, like a reunion in a Bohaymian fam'ly out at th' yards. I'll give ye an exthract fr'm th' divoorce news

479

about thim: 'Whin they set down to th' table wan night f'r supper, th' duchess happened to pass th' reemark that th' jook was overthrained in th' matther iv dhrink. His grace was nachrally indignant an' slammed her in th' eye. This aggytated Misther Billhooley to such an extint that he uppercut th' jook to th' pint iv jaw, sendin' him through a bank iv pa'ms. Th' jook hurled a small jooled clock at th' proud old man an' th' engagement become gin'ral. Th' jook was holdin' his own well in th' fam'ly council, havin' ar-rmed himsilf with a small marble statue called "Prayer" whin an old retainer iv th' fam'ly, Sam Johnson be name, who had been with th' Billhooley's fr'm his arliest childhood excipt whin he was with th' Pullman Comp'ny, took a hand in th' discussion. This vin'rable dipindant, angered at th' assault on his beloved masther, charged into th' room, felled his grace with a bottle an' was stampin' on his head whin th' polis come in. It is said th' throuble has caused an esthrangement in th' fam'ly. Th' jook has accipted a position on th' vodyville stage where he will do a monologue on th' fam'ly secrets, an' his father-in-law announces that he will be prisint on th' openin' night an' carry along a hatful iv bricks.'

"That's what I call fam'ly life. There's what that there beautiful writer, Laura Jaen, wud call a note iv sweet domisticity about it. Ye needn't throuble ye'er head about th' rich. Don't think iv thryin' to improve their home-lives. It isn't up to ye to organize a comity an' thry an' teach fam'ly fights to th' millyonaires on Mitchigan avnoo. If ye broke into th' stateliest stone home ye might find thim shootin' th' dishes at each other. We don't often hear iv their rale home life because th' neighbors don't complain. Most iv th' time all we know about how they live is an inventhry iv th' furniture. But now an' thin we get a glimpse like this to show that American home life is still uncorrupted be gr-reat wealth an' that th' noblest in our land will lick their son-in-laws if they thry to borrow money fr'm thim."

"Well," said Mr. Hennessy, "it's a shame these rich American girls shud marry these foreign noblemen."

"It's th' on'y chanst they've got," said Mr. Dooley. "A young American business man isn't goin' to sell his heart f'r goold an' thin prob'bly on'y get it in small installments in a pay envelope on Saturdah night. He sizes th' matther up in his simple way an' says he to himsilf: 'I wud hate to have to wurruk f'r me wife th' rest iv me life. I want this old gintleman's money, but th' on'y way f'r me to get it is in th' marts iv thrade. Annyhow, I'll have a betther chanst at it outside the fam'ly thin in,' he says. An' there ye ar-re."

Young Architect in Chicago

by FRANK LLOYD WRIGHT, 1869–   . *The most distinguished American architect of the twentieth century, Wright was born in Richland Center, Wisconsin, and was a student of civil engineering at the University of Wisconsin from 1884 to 1888. He began his architectural practice in Chicago in 1893. Among his more famous buildings are the Oak Park Unity Temple near Chicago, his own Wisconsin residence of "Taliesin," the Millard House at Pasadena, and the Imperial Hotel at Tokyo, Japan, constructed in 1916. For a number of years he has headed an architectural school and cultural fellowship at Taliesin. Wright is the author of many articles and books on architecture. From An Autobiography—Frank Lloyd Wright, which appeared in 1932 and was subsequently revised and expanded, the selection entitled "Young Architect in Chicago" is taken.*

CHICAGO. Wells Street Station: Six o'clock in late Spring, 1887. Drizzling. Sputtering white arc-light in the station and in the streets, dazzling and ugly. I had never seen electric lights before.

Crowds. Impersonal, intent on seeing nothing.

Somehow I didn't like to ask anyone anything. Followed the crowd.

Drifted south to the Wells Street Bridge over the Chicago River. The mysterious dark of the river with dim masts, hulks, and funnels hung with lights half-smothered in gloom—reflected in the black beneath. I stopped to see, holding myself close to the iron rail to avoid the blind hurrying by.

I wondered where Chicago was—if it was near. Suddenly the clanging of a bell. The crowd began to run. I wondered why: found myself alone and realized why in time to get off but stayed on as the bridge swung out with me into the channel and a tug, puffing clouds of steam, came pushing along below, pulling at an enormous iron grain boat, towing it slowly along through the gap.

Stood there studying the river-sights in the drizzling rain until the bridge followed after and closed to open the street again. Later, I never crossed the river without being charmed by somber beauty.

Wondered where to go for the night. But again if I thought to ask anyone, there was only the brutal, hurrying crowd, trying hard not to see.

Drifted south.

This must be Chicago now. So cold, black, blue-white and wet. The horrid blue-white glare of arc-lights was over everything.

Shivering. Hungry. Went into an eating place near Randolph Street and parted with seventy cents, ten per cent of my entire capital.

As I ate, I was sure of one thing, never would I go near Uncle Jenkin Lloyd Jones nor ask his help nor use his name.

Got into the street again to find it colder, raining harder.

Drifted south and turned left, shivering now in front of the Chicago Opera House on Washington Street, the flood of hard city lights made the unseeing faces of the crowd in the drizzle, livid, ghastly. Under a great canopy that made a shelter from the rain were enormous posters—"Sieba"—Extravaganza by David Henderson, Grand Corps de Ballet. And there the dancers were, life size almost, out on the sidewalk, holding color in the glare.

The doors were just open and a dollar let me go in where it was dry and warm to wait nearly an hour for the show to begin. During that waiting . . . went back to the home by the lake—to see the mother and Jennie and Maginel . . . wondered what they would feel when they knew I had gone for good . . . never to come back? But they were all coming to me in Chicago. There must be clean, quiet "home" places in Chicago near the lake, maybe. I wondered if they were anxious about me, hardly realizing I wouldn't be missed until tomorrow night. Saw Mother's sad eyes and pale face as she sat quietly—waiting. She seemed now always waiting and—a pang of homesickness already! But the orchestra filed out from under the stage.

Tuning up began, always exciting.

Then the florid overture.

I knew it wasn't good music—good music was not so sentimental (my father's term of contempt)—but I was glad to hear it.

The Henderson Extravaganzas in those days were duly extravagant. This one took the roof off an unsophisticated mind.

Went out after all was over, drifting with the crowd to Wabash Avenue. Cottage-Grove Avenue cable cars were running there. My first sight of the cable car. So, curious, I got on the grip-car beside the gripman and tried to figure it all out, going south in the process until the car stopped and "all out!" That car was going to the barn.

Got on the one coming out headed north now. Not sleepy nor tired. Half resentful because compelled to read the signs pressing on the eyes everywhere. They claimed your eyes for this, that, and everything beside. They lined the car above the windows. They lined the way, pushing, crowding and playing all manner of tricks on the desired eye.

Tried to stop looking at them. Compelled to look again. Kept on reading until reading got to be torture.

There were glaring signs on the glass shop-fronts against the lights inside, sharp signs in the glare of the sputtering arc-lamps outside.

HURRAH signs. STOP signs. COME ON IN signs. HELLO signs set out before the blazing windows on the sidewalks. Flat fences lettered both sides, man-high, were hanging out across above the sidewalks and lit by electric lamps.

Coming from extravaganza here was the beginning of phantasmagoria.

Supersensitive eyes were fixed by harsh dissonance and recovered themselves: reasoned and fought for freedom. Compelled again—until the procession of saloons, food shops, barber shops, eating houses, saloons, restaurants, groceries, laundries—and saloons, saloons, tailors, dry goods, candy shops, bakeries and saloons, became chaos in a wilderness of Italian, German, Irish, Polak, Greek, English, Swedish, French, Chinese and Spanish names in letters that began to come off, and get about, interlace and stick and climb and swing again.

Demoralization of the eye began: names obliterating everything. Names and what they would do for you or with you or to you for your money. Shutting your eyes didn't end it, for then you heard them louder than you saw them. They would begin to mix with absurd effect and you need take nothing to get the effect of another extravaganza. Letters this time. Another ballet, of A. B. C. D. E. F. G., L. M. N. O. P., X. Y. and Z the premier danseuse, intervening in fantastic dances.

It would have been a mercy not to have known the alphabet. One pays a heavy toll for the joys of being "eye-minded."

Got to bed at the Brigg's House north on Randolph Street, wrapped a sheet around myself—it seemed awfully like a winding sheet as I caught sight of it in the mirror—and slept.

A human item—insignificant but big with interior faith and a great hope. In what? Not yet could I have told you.

Asleep in Chicago.

A Chicago murderously actual.

Next day I began on Chicago.

My hand in my pocket after breakfast, I could feel sure of three silver dollars and a dime.

Took the city directory and made a list of architects, choosing names I had heard in Conover's office or that sounded interesting. All names, and missed the names of all names important to me. The name of the architect of my uncle's new church, "All Souls," I knew by heart—J. L. Silsbee, Lakeside Building, Clark Street, Chicago. But I wasn't going there. Tramped through street after street now seeing Chicago above the sign-belt.

483

And where was the architecture of the great city—The "Eternal City of the West"?

Where was it? Behind these shameless signs?

A vacant block would come by. Then the enormous billboards planted there stood up grandly, had it all their own way, obliterating everything in nothing. That was better.

Chicago! Immense gridiron of noisy streets. Dirty . . . Heavy traffic crossing both ways at once, managing somehow: Torrential noise.

A stupid thing, that gridiron: cross-currents of horses, trucks, street cars, grinding on hard rails, mingling with streams of human beings in seeming confusion and clamor. But habit was in the movement making it expert, and so safe enough. Dreary—dim—smoked. Smoked dim and smoking.

A wide, desolate, vacant strip ran along the water front over which the Illinois Central trains incessantly puffed and ground, cutting the city off from the lake.

Terrible, this grinding and piling up of blind forces. If there was logic here who could grasp it?

To stop and think in the midst of this would be to give way to terror. The gray, soiled river with its mists of steam and smoke, was the only beauty. That smelled to heaven.

Young engineer looking for work? Sam Treat looked me over. "University man, eh!" The kindly intellectual face under a mass of gray hair smiled. "Sorry."

Caught a glimpse of a busy drafting room full of men as I came out.

Well!—there was Beers, Clay and Dutton. More tramping through brutal crowds that never seemed to see anything. Mr. Clay came out and looked me over—a twinkle of kindly humor in his black eyes. I have remembered that *he* seemed to see *me* and was amused. Why? Was it the longish hair again, or what? Took pity on me, maybe, for he asked me to call again in a few weeks if I found nothing. In a few weeks! And I had just three dollars and ten cents!

Over now, to S. S. Beman in the Pullman Building way south on Michigan Avenue.

College "tooth-picks" made in vain if made for walking. Souvenir of sophomore vanity on right little toe raising Cain now. Perspiring freely. Found Mr. Beman "not in!" Foreman looked me over. I. K. Pond?

"University man? What college, Ann Arbor?"

"No, University of Wisconsin."

"No, nobody wanted at present, later perhaps—in a few months."

In a few months!

The famous Pullman Building had come into view. It looked funny —as if made to excite curiosity. Had passed the Palmer House, on the way down, that famous Chicago Pallazzo. It seemed curious to me: seemed like an ugly old, old man whose wrinkles were all in the wrong place owing to a misspent life. As I went on my way to W. W. Boyington's office I passed the Chicago Board of Trade at the foot of La Salle Street. Boyington had done it. This?—thin-chested, hard-faced, chamfered monstrosity? I turned aside from Boyington's office then and there.

Chicago architecture! Where was it? Not the Exposition Building, a rank, much-domed yellow shed on the lake front. No, nor the rank and file along the streets. The rank and file all pretty much alike, industriously varied but with no variety. All the same thought or lack of it. Were all American cities like this one, so casual, so monotonous in their savage, outrageous attempts at variety? All competing for the same thing in the same way? Another senseless competition never to be won?

So thinking, I got on toward Major Jenney's office. Mundie came out. He was President of the Chicago Architectural Club as I knew. "Ah, University man. Engineer?" "Yes." Had I any drawings? No? First time I had been asked for any drawings. "Why don't you come around to the Club meeting Saturday night? You might hear of something there. Bring some of your drawings along with you," he added.

Strange! I had not thought to bring any drawings with me. But some were in the bag, still checked at the Station. Mundie with his sunken eyes in an impassive frozen face was a little kindly warmth in the official atmosphere of the Chicago architect's office.

Too late to go to any more offices now. Got my bag to the Brigg's House not knowing where else to go, hungry. Asked for a cheaper room. Clerk sympathetic,—one for seventy-five cents, almost as good. For supper, what twenty cents would buy at the bakery. I had found Kohlsatt's bakery-lunch. Tempting pastry piled high in plain sight, all that I had been denied or allowed to eat only occasionally, and things beside, I had never even dreamed of. A hungry orphan turned loose in a bake shop? Lucky I had little money.

To bed, dog-tired, not at all discouraged. On the whole everyone had been rather kind. Must be someone who needed me. Tomorrow, maybe.

Two days gone from home, Mother knew now! The thought of her was anguish. I turned away from it to action and repeated the performance of the day before in other offices, this time taking my drawings. Mundie was out. At five other offices, no success.

No lunch.

No supper.

During the day ten cents invested in bananas.

That night, a weird dream. Up in a balloon. Mother below frantically holding to the rope, dragged along the ground, calling Jennie and Maginel to help . . . all dragged along. I shouted down to hitch the end of the rope to something, anything, and make it fast. But it tore out of their helpless hands and I shot up and up and up—until I awoke with a sense of having been lifted miles to the strange ground of another world.

Awakened rudely to the fourth day. Got started again, pavement-sore, gaunt. Something had to happen today. Tired again, three more offices. Same result.

There was still Silsbee's office. He was building my uncle's "All Souls Church," but he needn't know who I was. After noon I went there. Liked the atmosphere of the office best. Liked Silsbee's sketches on the wall. Liked instantly the fine looking, cultured fellow with a fine pompadour and beard, who quietly came forward with a friendly smile.

Cecil Corwin.

"Hello!" he said as though he knew me. He looked the artist-musician. He had come through the gate in the outer office railing humming something from the "Messiah."

I smiled and said, "Do you sing?" He smiled too, looking at my haircut, or lack of it. "Yes . . . try to . . . Do you play?" "Yes . . . try to."

And I had found a kindred spirit.

He sat down by me in the outer office. His sleeves were rolled above the elbow. His arms were thickly covered with coarse hair, but I noticed how he daintily crooked his little finger as he lifted his pencil. He had an air of gentleness and refinement. I told him my trials.

"You are a minister's son?"

"Yes, how did you know?"

"Didn't know, something about you. I am one myself. The 'Old Man' (moving his head in the direction of Silsbee's private office) is one too. And there are two more here already, Wilcox and Kennard. If you come in here, there would be five of us."

We laughed.

"Well . . . could I by any chance come in?" I said anxiously. He looked me over. "I believe we could get along," he said. "Let me see your drawings."

486

He looked carefully at the sketches. "You made these just to please yourself?"

"Yes."

"You've got a good touch. Wait a minute." He took them and went in through a door marked "Private." Presently he appeared at the door with a tall, dark-faced, aristocratic-looking man, gold eye-glasses, with long gold chain, hanging from his nose. He stood in the door looking carelessly at me with a frown. It was Silsbee. "All right," he said, "take him on. Tracer's wages—$8.oo."

And he turned and shut the door after him.

"Not much, but better than nothing," said Cecil. I agreed.

How far from my expectations, "$8.oo." With my "experience" I should be able to earn three times as much. But no one thought much of my "experience." Cecil saw the disappointment following elation. "Had your lunch? No? Come with me." We went downstairs a block away to Kinsley's. Cecil insisted on a good portion of browned corned-beef-hash for me, and coffee.

"Thank you, no coffee. I don't drink it."

"Well then,"—amused—"milk?" And ever since, when feeling hungry, nothing has tasted so good to me as browned corned-beef-hash.

"Got any money left?" he said abruptly.

"Oh, yes!"

"How much?"

"Twenty cents."

"Had anything to eat yesterday?"

This was getting rather too personal so I didn't answer.

"Come home with me tonight and we'll concertize with my new grand-piano."

It was Saturday. I was not to report for work until Monday morning.

So I got my bag from the Brigg's House and went home with Cecil. A nice home. Met his benevolent preacher father, a Congregational missionary. His mother had died some years ago but his sister, Marquita, looked after the father and her bachelor brother. She was "musical" too.

After a "musical" evening together, we went up to the room that was for me. Cecil found how anxious I was about things back home, gave me paper, pen and ink to write. I did.

And then: "Would you lend me ten dollars to send my Mother? I'll pay you back two dollars a week."

He said nothing, took a ten-dollar bill from his pocket and laid it on the table. I put it in the envelope and we took it to the nearest box to post it.

A load went off my heart.

I had a job.

But better still, I had a friend, and no mean one in any sense, as anyone could see.

Now I could go and see my uncle's new Church. Cecil himself had been looking after the building of it. I asked him about it.

"Would you like to see 'The Church,'" he said, with curious emphasis on "Church." "We'll go down to Oakwood Boulevard and Langley Avenue after dinner and have a look at it."

We went. Why the curious emphasis? I knew now. It was in no way like a Church, more like a "Queen Anne" dwelling. We used to say they were Queen Anne front and Mary Ann behind. And this was. But it was interesting to me. Again not beautiful—but . . . curious.

Taking advantage of the unexpected visit, Cecil went about looking after some details in the nearly completed building. I went along Oakwood Boulevard to look it over in perspective. Was standing back, looking over from across the street when a hand from behind took me firmly by the collar and a hearty voice like a blow, "Well, young man! So here you are."

I had recognized the voice instantly, Uncle Jenkin Lloyd Jones! I was in for it.

"I've been expecting you, young fellow. Your mother wrote—distracted. I'll telegraph you're found."

"No!—Please." I said, "I wrote last night telling her I had a job and I sent her some money". . .

A job? "Where have you found a job?"

"Silsbee's office."

"Silsbee's? Of course. That was mighty good of him. Told him who you were I suppose?"

"No!" I said, "I didn't!" He looked suspicious. But got the point quickly. "All right," he said. Then Cecil came up and greeted him. "Where did you get hold of my young nephew?" said Uncle Jenkin.

"He's your nephew? I didn't know it." Cecil said in astonishment. That proved the case.

"Well,—where are you going to stay now?" asked the maternal uncle. I didn't know. "You're coming to stay near here where I can keep an eye on you. Tonight you must come and stay with us."

"No!" said Cecil, "he's going to stay with me tonight."

"All right then, Monday night."

Isn't the opening to "the way" usually as simple? Here the chance end of a sequence that like the end of twine in a skein of indefinite length, would unwind in characteristic events as time went on.

Not at all as I had expected! It seldom is as much or at all as we expect it to be. But Cecil was already more in himself than I could have imagined. His culture similar to mine, yet he was different. And so much more developed in it than I.

I began to go to school to Cecil.

We were soon together everywhere.

Silsbee was doing Edgewater at the time, the latest attempt at "high-class" subdivision and doing it entirely for J. L. Cochran, a real-estate genius in his line.

Silsbee could draw with amazing ease. He drew with soft, deep black lead pencil strokes and he would make remarkable free-hand sketches of that type of dwelling peculiarly his own at the time. His superior talent in design had made him respected in Chicago. His work was a picturesque combination of gable, turret and hip with broad porches quietly domestic and gracefully picturesque. A contrast to the awkward stupidities and brutalities of the period, elsewhere. He would come out to the draughting room as though we, the draughts-men, did not exist, stand talking a moment with Cecil, one lank leg turning one foot over sidewise, the picture of indifference or scorn as he stood on the other. He was grudging of words and shy of patience. All awed by him.

Not so Cecil.

The office system was a bad one. Silsbee got a ground-plan and made his pretty sketch, getting some charming picturesque effect he had in his mind. Then the sketch would come out into the draughting room to be fixed up into a building, keeping the floor-plan near the sketch if possible. The sketches fascinated me. "My God, Cecil, how that man can draw!"

"He can. He's a kind of genius, but something is the matter with him. He doesn't seem to take any of it or himself half seriously. The picture interests him. The rest bores him. You'll see. He is an architectural genius spoiled by way of the aristocrat. A fine education and family in Syracuse, but too contemptuous of everything."

And I did see. I saw Silsbee was just making pictures. And not very close to what was real in the building—that I could soon see, myself.

But I adored Silsbee just the same. He had style. His work had it too, in spite of slipshod methods. There was something finely tragic in his somber mien; authority in the boom of his enormous voice pitched low in his long throat with its big "Adam's apple." I learned a good deal about a house from Silsbee by way of Cecil.

Monday night I had gone to Uncle Jenkin to spend a few days at the parsonage. Interesting people came there to dine. Dr. Thomas, Rabbi Hirsh, Jane Addams, Mangasarian and others. I enjoyed listening.

A letter had come from Mother. She wrote regularly every week. She seemed glad after all that I was at work. Told me to stay close to Uncle Jenkin. He was a good man beset by the countless trials of his position but would help me all he could. And I was not to worry about her.

She had sold Father's library and a few hundred dollars had come to her from her brothers, her small share in Grandfather's farm. If I got along and needed her she would sell the Madison place and come down and make a home for me. There were the usual anxieties about diet, warm underwear, companions.

"I would have you," she wrote, "a man of sense as well as sensibility. You will find Goodness and Truth everywhere you go. If you have to choose, choose Truth. For that is closest to Earth. Keep close to Earth, my boy: in that lies strength. Simplicity of heart is just as necessary for an architect as for a farmer or a minister if the architect is going to build great buildings." And she would put this faith of hers in many different forms as she wrote on different subjects, until I knew just what to expect from her.

Precinct Captain

by JAMES T. FARRELL, 1904–   . *No writer has done so much to picture the social and economic life of lower-class Chicago as James Farrell. A native of Chicago, he attended the University of Chicago for three years and also worked as a clerk, filling-station attendant, and reporter. He was awarded a Guggenheim fellowship for creative writing in 1936. Most of his novels deal with Irish tenement families and the perils of youth in unsavory surroundings. The various volumes about Studs Lonigan were published as a unit in 1937. Among his other books are such novels as A World I Never Made (1936), No Star Is Lost (1938), and Father and Son (1940). His short fiction was collected in 1937 as The Collected Short Stories of James T. Farrell. His Marxist approach to literature is clearly visible in his volume of criticism, A Note on Literary Criticism (1936). "Precinct Captain" appears in the volume Can All This Grandeur Perish? (1937).*

490

O'MALLEY was a stocky man in his forties, with a solid, brick-like face, thinning reddish hair and narrow blue eyes. He had an air about him. He walked, he talked, he sat, he stood, he gesticulated with an air of authority. He was always playing his role in public, the role of a man who had been in the political game for twenty years. The fruits of his public service were a job as deputy sheriff in the county building and the title of precinct captain in his neighborhood near South Shore Drive and Seventy-first Street.

The primary fight put O'Malley on the spot. In the previous election, he had gone around and told all his people to vote for Kline for Governor. He had said that Kline was as fine a man as they would ever find in public life in the whole state of Illinois. He told them that Kline had a fine record. He said that it showed you what a fine country America was when it would elect a Jew. Many of his voters were Irish, and he told them that the Irish and the Jews had to stick together. Look what happened to the Irish in the old country. And look what happened to the Jews in, where was it, Jerusalem? Anyway, look what happened to them. He had thus argued that the Irish had to vote for Kline for Governor because he was a fine man, because he had a fine record, because he was a good Democrat, because the Party and the organization were behind him, and because it was a fine thing for the Irish and the Jews to stick together. If the Irish voted for a Jew, the Jews would return the compliment by voting for a mick. And to Jewish voters in his precinct he had said that they had to come out and stand by a man of their own race and repay him for his public service rendered to them, and to all of the people.

Now, O'Malley was in the hole. All those whom he had lined up to vote for Kline had now to be lined up to cast their ballots for Anderson against Kline. It was a hot primary fight, and the organization needed every vote it could garner in the entire county because Kline was certain to roll up a large downstate plurality. O'Malley was working night and day, ringing doorbells, rapping on doors, trying to compose letters to his voters, handing out cards and cigars, hiring one gang of kids and young men to put Anderson literature into mailboxes and another group to take Kline literature out of the same mailboxes.

Easter Sunday came two days before the primary election. He was still busy, with more people to see, more cards to dispose of, more Kline literature to be destroyed, more Anderson literature to be distributed. The organization was fighting for big spoils, and the machine was built up of such rank-and-file corporals as himself. They had to do the producing. If they didn't, the machine was sunk and they were sunk with it. In every ward the Kline people were putting together an organization. If they won, they could have their own ward committee-men, their own precinct captains, and then, where would O'Malley be? He had to hop to it, and he was doing the hopping. He went to an early Mass on Easter Sunday, received Holy Communion, and then, after a quick breakfast, he was out working. He had to see a printer and arrange for the printing of more cards and for the mimeographing of a letter for distribution to the voters on Tuesday morning. He had sat up almost all of Saturday night composing this letter. It told the Democratic voters of the precinct that their friend and neighbor was Patrick J. Connolly. He had served them long and well. He had guarded the public interest as if it were his own property. He had never turned a deaf ear to their needs and their appeals. And now Patrick J. Connolly needed them as they had needed him. He needed their votes so that he could be returned as ward committeeman, in which capacity he would continue to serve them as he had done in the past. O'Malley was pleased with this letter of his. It convinced him that the big-shots down in the City Hall weren't the only fellows who knew a trick or two. None of them could have written a better letter, a letter that would win more votes than his would. But it had been hard work. He had gone to con-fession, and after midnight he could not eat, drink, even take a sip of water. He had done the job, though. After arranging with the printer, he had his rounds to make. The ballot was so long, and he had to give instructions to the people on how to vote, what names to skip on it, what men to vote for. It was a tough job, and no matter how long he spent explaining the ballot, he still could not be sure that the idea had been put across. And some of his voters were so damn dumb! They might vote for Anderson, but not for Connolly. They might give a vote to some of the traitors on the ticket who had waited until their names were printed on the organization's list on the ballot before they had changed and come out for Kline. Ah, yes, his job was all grief during an election fight.

About four o'clock, tired and weary, he got around to the Doyles. The Doyles were nice people, and he was glad he had met them. He knew that Mr. Doyle must have once been a well-to-do man. He acted and talked like a gentleman. Now he was having hard times and the breaks had gone against him. And the boy, he was all right, too, a fine chap. They were poor because of hard times, and too proud to go on relief. He was going to try and see what he could do for them by way of getting a job for Doyle if he could manage it. The Doyles were the kind of people you called the worthy poor.

He walked in on them in their one-room furnished apartment over a store. The apartment gave the sense of overcrowding, and the furni-ture was old and scratched. It seemed almost to breathe out a feeling of its own unliveableness. O'Malley smiled and handed a box of candy to Mrs. Doyle, a fat, beefy-armed, bovine woman. He pulled out cigars for Doyle, a tall, thin, graying man whose blue trousers were frayed at the pocket and their narrow, worn cuffs were out of style. He also handed two cigars to the son.

"Well, Mildred, here's the best precinct captain in Chicago," Doyle said as Mrs. Doyle was dusting off the best chair for O'Malley.

"No, just the most worn out," O'Malley said.

"You poor man, you must be so tired. Here, let me make you a cup of coffee," Mrs. Doyle said.

"Please don't, Mrs. Doyle. I only got a minute. There's still a long list of people I got to see," he said.

"You work so hard. It'll be a shame if everybody doesn't turn out and vote for you," she said.

"You don't think they will?" he asked, his brows beetling in worry.

"Certainly they will," Doyle quickly said.

"Don't be giving me heart failure, Mrs. Doyle. After all, a man of my advanced age can't take too much," O'Malley said, smiling grimly.

"It looks good, huh, O'Malley?" said the twenty-five-year-old son, a rather emaciated, characterless young chap with badly decayed teeth.

"I think I got it pretty much set. Now, how have you folks got the people managed in this building?"

"Skipper, you needn't worry about this building. Say, it's in your vest pocket," Doyle said.

"That's the way I like to hear you talk," O'Malley said, smiling and lighting a cigar while Doyle and his son puffed on theirs.

"Mr. O'Malley, are you sure you wouldn't take a cup of coffee? It'll only take me a minute to make it for you," Mrs. Doyle said maternally.

"No, thanks. Now, about this fellow across the hall, the Polack?"

"I'm getting up at six in the morning to see him. He's hard to catch," Mrs. Doyle said.

"Be sure to do it. We got to get every vote we can. We got a fight on our hands this time."

"You'll win. Everybody else in the building is going to vote Anderson. And you know, Mr. O'Malley, there was somebody around putting folders for Kline in the mailboxes."

"There was?" he exclaimed, glancing angrily at Mrs. Doyle. "Say, I'll bet he was one of these birds with a fishhook for a nose."

"But wait until you hear the rest of the story. I spoke to him. He asked me who I was for. I said, why I was for Kline. But now wait a minute until I tell you all of the story, Mr. O'Malley, I said that I was for Kline and so was everybody else in the building. I said that I had talked to them for Kline. So he put his folders in the mailboxes, and I

493

asked him for more. He gave me some. I said, 'Oh Mister, give me a lot more. I want to give these to all of my friends in the neighborhood.' So I got a great big pile of Kline literature. And right after I saw that he was gone, I took the stuff out of the boxes and threw the whole she-bang into the garbage can," Mrs. Doyle said.

"Good for you! Good for you, Mrs. Doyle! If all people were like you folks here, I'll tell you, my job would be a good deal easier than it is and I wouldn't be getting early gray hairs from worry."

"Say, what the hell, Skipper! Don't have such a low opinion of your-self. You're the best precinct captain in Chicago," Doyle said in-gratiatingly.

"I only wish I was," O'Malley said with almost histrionic dejection.

"Why, of course you are, Mr. O'Malley," Mrs. Doyle said.

"Sure, but let me tell you something. Roosevelt's the best precinct captain we got."

"My, but isn't he a wonderful man!" Mrs. Doyle exclaimed.

"He's a real bird, all right, fine man. He's done a lot for the people and the country," Doyle said.

"Best president we had since Woodrow Wilson," young Doyle said.

"You're damn tootin', he is! Damn tootin'! And he's the best precinct captain we got. But I ain't worried none about putting him over in my precinct in the fall. What I'm worried about is the primary election this Tuesday. Now, are you sure you got everybody in the building all set?"

"Oh, yes, of course. There isn't one Kline person in the whole build-ing," Mrs. Doyle said.

"Here's the way I handle them. I say that, of course, now, Kline is a fine man. He's governor. A fine man. Sure. But so is Anderson. Anderson is a fine man, and he is the one we got to put over. Kline has that Oriental strain in him that's in his blood. He's not one of us, and he doesn't understand our problems."

"Say, Mr. Doyle, you ought to have my job. You're a smart man. That's the ticket, and I'm going to use that line myself. Say, I wish everybody in my precinct was like you. And you got mostly Irish in this building, haven't you?"

"Yes, Irish and Catholic."

"Of course, there is the Polish man across the way, and Mrs. Hirsch. I don't like her. She's too dirty, and, say, she would talk a leg off you. Now the other day—"

"Who's she for?" O'Malley interrupted.

"Why, Anderson, of course."

"Well, tell her to stay that way. And don't forget to nail the Po-lack," O'Malley said.

"Of course, I will," Mrs. Doyle said.

"You know, folks, I can't understand an Irishman who would vote for Kline after what he has done to us. It was us who put him in, and then he is a turncoat. Why, four years ago I went around and told everybody to vote for him. Why, I got out a bigger vote for Kline in this precinct than I ever got out for anybody except Roosevelt. The Irish didn't go against him because he's a Jew. And what does he do? He turns on us," O'Malley said, his words and tone giving expression to a puzzled wounded feeling.

"He gave us the can, didn't he? But he ain't got a chance, has he?" the son said.

"Not a chance of a snowball in hell if all the others around the city get out the vote the way I'll do it. Now, take that big apartment building down the street here in the next block. There must be a hundred voters in that buildin'. Well, I got every Democratic vote in the joint," O'Malley proudly said.

"Good for you," Mrs. Doyle said.

"The woman who works in the renting office there, I spoke to her and lined her up. So when some dame comes around for Kline, why, this woman, she says to the Kline dame, she says the tenants in the buildin' have just gotten sick and tired of everybody and his brother comin' around about votin' and puttin' cards in the boxes. She says to the Kline dame that she can't let anybody else go around botherin' and annoyin' her tenants, because if she does, a lot of them will move out on her. So this Kline dame she is dumb. You know, she ain't never been in politics and thinks she can come in and lick somebody like myself who has been in the political game all my life. She's dumb, see! She asks the woman, are her tenants for Kline. The woman says of course they are, sure, because everybody is. She takes the Kline literature from this dumb dame and throws it all in the ash-can, just the same as you did, Mrs. Doyle."

"That was clever," Doyle said.

"You ought to meet that woman. She's a fine woman," said O'Malley.

"Well, she helped. And on this game, every little bit helps," the son said profoundly.

"You're a smart young fellow. Every little bit, every vote does count. Every one. And to think of how many votes I swung to Kline four years ago. For him to go and turn his back on the organization and the people that made him, bitin' the hand that fed him. Well, don't worry! I'm cookin' the goose for him in my precinct. We don't waste our time with traitors to us when we're the fellow that made them somebody," O'Malley said vindictively.

"Mr. O'Malley, I'm just so certain that Anderson will get the nomination," Mrs. Doyle said.

"So am I. But we can't take any chances. Every vote counts. Now, are you sure you got every voter in this here buildin'?"

"It's in the bag," the son said.

"Yes, we guarantee it," Doyle said.

"All of the people have promised me already, except that man across the hall, the Polish one. I'm getting up in the morning to make sure of him," Mrs. Doyle said.

"That's the way I like to hear you talk. And if we win, I won't forget how helpful you've been to me," O'Malley said.

"We're doing everything we can," Mrs. Doyle said.

"That's the ticket," O'Malley said.

"And, Mr. O'Malley, what about election day?" Doyle nervously asked.

"Here, I brought these sample ballots," O'Malley said, arising and pulling out long pink-sheeted ballots, one of which he spread out upon the narrow dining-room table. "Now, I got this all marked up just right." The family gathered around him. He became official, and almost coldly professional. His tone of voice changed. "You can all study this after I go, and I'm gonna leave some of these here for you to show to the people in the buildin' and to get them to study it. Now watch me carefully. See, you start here with Anderson's name at the top of the ticket. Now you go straight down until you get to Hogan for sheriff. You skip him. Any man that would turn on his friends the way Hogan did, he doesn't deserve a vote. Coming out yesterday and sayin' he was for Kline like he did on us. Be sure to skip Hogan, and tell your friends in the buildin' here to. And then you go straight down the list, Kaczmarski, Moran, Cogan, Connell, and then, here you skip Schulman for county clerk. See, I got it here, and there's no X after Schulman's name. He is another one who turned his coat and betrayed his friends and the organization. And now here, don't forget, Connolly. See, right here! Tell all your people, absolutely, to mark an X after Connolly's name. See it, for ward committeeman. When you mention Connolly, you say: 'Your ward committeeman.' You see, what good is it going to do us if we get in the top of the ticket but don't get our own man, our own friend and neighbor, in for ward committeeman? So, don't forget it. Above all else, we got to get Connolly in," O'Malley said.

"Of course," Mrs. Doyle said with assurance.

"Now it should all be clear. See how they are marked with an X, and then, I got rings around the names of those you skip, like Hogan. You won't forget this and go votin' for the men I got ringed, will you?"

496

"Holy Moses, no!" Doyle said.

"You can study this sample ballot carefully after I go. And you know, you can take these into the booths with you when you vote, in order to see how to vote. We just got the rulin' on that, and it's O.K. to take sample ballots into the booth."

"We'll study it, Skipper, and show the neighbors what to do," Doyle said.

"If you're sure you can do that, you'll save me a lot of valuable time," said O'Malley.

"Of course we can. And we're glad to do it. You poor man, you must be so tired," said Mrs. Doyle.

"Well, I've been doing this for twenty years. I'm used to it, but, golly, a man does get tired toward the end of a hot primary fight," O'Malley said.

"And what about election day, Mr. O'Malley?" Mrs. Doyle asked.

"I've just been demonstratin' it to you, and I thought you all said you got the dope straight?" O'Malley asked, his expression changing.

"Yes, we understand that. But what I meant is, what time should we come to vote and, you know, Mr. O'Malley, you said something about your wanting us working around the polls, because you said we were so helpful to you," Mrs. Doyle tactfully said.

"Sure, you come around at six, and I'll get you fixed up."

"We'll be there," said Doyle.

"Then, if we win, as I fully expect to, well, as I just said, I don't forget them that sticks with me. If I did, I wouldn't be worthy of the name of O'Malley."

"Oh, we know it. And Mr. O'Malley, you look so tired, haven't you the time for a cup of coffee?" said Mrs. Doyle.

"Gee, no, I spent more time talkin' than I meant to. I'm so busy. I got to get these cards distributed," he said, taking out a stack of Connolly cards and giving some to Mrs. Doyle.

"You better leave a little more than that. I can distribute them," Mrs. Doyle said.

"Ah, that's the way to hear you talk," O'Malley said, handing her additional cards.

Leaving more cigars, he went out, followed by profuse farewells from all of the Doyles.

II

"He's such a nice man," said Mrs. Doyle.

"He's a sketch," the son said.

"We don't care what he is, as long as he gets us a job," said Doyle.

"I wonder? Maybe it would have been better for us if we had gone

497

for Anderson, but let Arty here be a Kline man. Then we might have gotten somewhere either way," Mrs. Doyle said.

"Catch me voting for a Jew," the son said.

"Listen Arty, we don't care what in the name of Jesus Christ he is, if he gives us a job. God, we want to get a job for one of us, or we can't go on! We can't be such choosers," said Doyle.

"Here, he brought this candy, and it's filling. If you watch it, Papa, so the sweets don't get in your teeth, and you do the same, Arty, it's filling," said Mrs. Doyle.

"I can't eat chocolates, not with these molars I got," the son said, as his father took a chocolate and chewed it carefully.

"I'm glad he didn't take the coffee. We hardly have any canned milk left," Mrs. Doyle said.

"Yes, we'll vote for Kline, Anderson, or the Devil himself for a job," Doyle said.

"That's why I talked like I did, about the people here. You know, some of them won't talk to me if I say Anderson. They're Republicans. But we might as well let him think that we're doing everything in our power," Mrs. Doyle said, eating a chocolate.

"Yes, and we'll give him our votes. Golly, I hope that we put Anderson over," Doyle said, grabbing a caramel.

"We got to! If we don't, we won't be anywheres," said Mrs. Doyle while the son enviously watched his parents eating the candy, his tongue playing around in his decayed teeth.

"Damn it, I meant to pray for Anderson's success this morning at Mass, and I forgot to," Doyle said.

"You would! You're just like an absent-minded professor," said Mrs. Doyle.

"Couldn't help it. I meant to. And I can still pray until Tuesday," said Doyle.

"Well, I think the Lord will provide for us by electing Anderson so you can get a job," Mrs. Doyle said, dividing the last two pieces of candy with her husband.

"And after election, Tuesday, we can get a swell meal. We'll have five dollars each. And, Ma, I think that we can spare ourselves a movie. Shirley Temple will be at the show that night," Doyle said.

"But, Pa, we'll have to watch that money. You know, the agent told us last month that he was giving us our last chance. If we got evicted, we got to have a little something, or where will we sleep?" said Mrs. Doyle.

"Goddamn it, Anderson has got to get in," said Doyle, pacing the floor nervously.

The Mills

by JOSEPH HUSBAND, 1885–1938. *Husband was a native of Rochester, New York. He spent much of his life writing about industry and economics, and Chicago was his residence for some years. Among his books are
A Year in a Coal Mine (1911), America at Work (1915), and The Story
of the Pullman Car (1917). Husband was one of the first Americans to see
the color, the beauty, and the poetry in modern industrial life. "The Mills,"
a vivid account of the Minneapolis flour mills at St. Anthony Falls, is the
ninth chapter of America at Work.*

FROM the car-windows, as the train crosses the arched stone bridge,
you can see the mills piled high above the south bank of the river.
Vast and dingy, the broken roofline notches high against the blue Minnesota sky. Like the battlements of some feudal castle, the stone and
brick walls tower upward, here and there the square shaft of a grain-
storage tank rising turret-like above the roofs. At the foot of the cliff,
although the mills seem to rise abruptly from the very edge of the
water, the river courses in bent and broken streams, diverted and
trained in the harness of industry; through a hundred mill-races in thick
black torrents; a white blue shimmer over the apron-dam across the
river.

Gathering strength in every mile of its course, the great river, rising
in the silent waters of Itasca to pour a torrent twenty-five hundred
miles away into the Gulf of Mexico, pauses here for a brief minute to
stroke into life the mighty turbines of the flour-mills. Above the dams
that hold the river in check, the water, deep and silent, floods back between wide banks; below the tail-races of the mills it spurts noisily in a
shallow bed, far down between high bluffs of weathered stone. But at
the falls the mills, silent and apparently devoid of life or activity, mark
the measure of its flow. And from that ceaseless flowing energy comes
the power to grind the grain for a nation's bread.

Like a shelf against a wall the railroad tracks cling to the cliff. Above
the clanking of freight cars and the mutter of the river, a vibrant murmur of myriad muffled wheels fills the shadow of the mills. Beside the
tracks thin streaks of wheat gleam yellow on the grimy ballast. Here
two great floods are meeting! From the flat reaches of the Dakotas,
from the wheat lands of Minnesota and the rolling fields of Montana,
from Manitoba, Saskatchewan, and the banks of the Athabaska, the tide
of grain is at the flood. Unceasing, mightier by far than the "father of
waters," one hundred thousand freight cars, fat and heavy with their
rich lading, are emptying the season's harvest. And from the shipping

platforms fifteen million barrels of flour go out each year into the markets of the world.

The freight cars are unloading. From the wide doors the scoops are pushing a stream of yellow grain. Like liquid it pours over the car-sills and down between the steel grills beside the tracks. Never has the touch of human hands defiled it. Born of the soil, it has been reaped and winnowed by the clean blades of wood and steel; never in the long process which will transform it into flour, will the touch of man's hand stain its perfect purity.

From bins below the tracks, endless conveyors were already gathering the grain in a long flow upward, up above the mill-roofs, far up to the tops of giant elevators, there to fall, a vast measured treasure, into the storage tanks beneath. With the assistant head miller, I climbed slowly to the top. The windows were misted with the dust of harvest, and even at that great height there was a fine powder of ivory flour on the floor and ledges. He pushed up a window. In the warm afternoon sunlight the mill-roofs lay below me. Far down beyond, the river, blue and sparkling, swirled in soft eddies about the dams and forebays. Beyond, the city stretched away to the rolling green of the low hills. And above was the blue of a cloudless sky.

Here, almost two hundred and fifty years ago, the captive Hennepin dedicated to his patron, St. Anthony of Padua, these falls where for so many years, in a cavern beneath, had dwelt that Great Unk-te-hee who created both man and earth. Gone is the guileful father of the Recollets; gone are the Sioux, whose tepees clustered about the cataract; gone even is that sheer leap of the river forty feet, where now the low slant of the apron-dam smooths the water in its descent. The ranges of the buffalo are rich with golden grain. It pours through the grills beside the elevators. From the skein of mazing tracks the wail of a freight engine shrills loud and clamorous.

A conveyor was lifting grain from one of the tanks; on an endless belt it passed through a long high-swung gallery from the elevators to the mill. We followed to watch its progress. At the far end of the gallery the crawling belt with its steady rivulet of grain entered the top floor of the mill and disappeared in a ponderous machine. Above the roar of belts and wheels the miller called to me. His hand was filled with stones and nails and little flakes of wood, a heterogeneous mass of refuse. Here the grain was cleaned, all foreign impurities removed. Across the low ceiling, up and down, slanting at every angle, the "legs," long boxlike tubes through which the flour is carried from floor to floor, cluttered the great room. Down the center a battery of strange objects, bristling with rings of pipes like spokes in a row of rimless wheels, fluttered with unseen life. They looked like a misshapen organ, and I half expected to hear the notes of some strange music echo from the pipes. The dust-collectors.

On the floor below, the maze of the legs grew more bewildering. Here the purifiers were ranged in mighty companies, and the fine white smoke of flour tinged the air. Like soft snow it dusted my shoulders. The miller pushed back a slide in one of the machines; within, a reel of silk was slowly turning, and through its fine meshes the flour sifted continuously. He scooped up a handful and held it out to me. It seemed fine and white, but the grinding and purifying were only half completed.

Every machine was in quiet motion. But the mill seemed deserted. On the vast floors a few men wandered in and out among the machines. In the mellow half-light and the comparative stillness, unaided, almost unattended, these stolid workers of wood and steel performed their laborious functions. In the apparent confusion of a perfect system, all natural order seemed reversed: up a floor or two through the twisting legs, the flour flowed to the next machine, then back again, and again up to a higher floor. It was incomprehensible. The scheme was lost in the multiplicity of operations.

The monotony of the murmuring machines was suddenly broken. Wearied of only the silent turning of hidden wheels, a roomful of huge barrel-like creatures suspended between roof and floor had burst suddenly into impassioned life. Reeling and swaying like drunken dancers, the bolters vibrated with angry tumult. In their allotted places they dizzily shook their dusty sides, flinging madly about in a rotary motion.

The days of the big mill-stones have vanished; corrugated steel-rolls have usurped their places. In aisles, the roller-mills filled the floor, like stocky pianos in a salesroom. Between the fine teeth of the long steel rolls the clean grain flaked to flour. Here a series crushed the outer husk of the wheat berry; and still others there were, each grinding finer and finer, endlessly. And between these grindings came the processes I had seen above, scouring, bolting, separating, and purifying.

Beyond the open doors of the shipping platforms long lines of freight cars were waiting, half filled with sacks and barrels of flour. Here at last was life and activity. In white caps and uniforms the millers were packing the finished product. Between high-piled sacks, trucks trundled noisily. The floor was white with flour. On slow-moving belts the filled sacks passed out from beneath machines which filled and weighed the contents to the fraction of an ounce. With long looping stitches the sewers fastened the tops.

Beside the door two huge mill-stones lay half buried in the earth.

With the wandering father of the Recollets, they were already but memories of a mighty past. Behind the city the sun had set in a strong, clear, yellow light. Up in the mill-windows, electric lights were twinkling. The night run had begun. Ceaselessly, day and night, forever, to grind corn for a nation's bread.

The Chute

by ALBERT HALPER, 1904— . *Halper is one of the younger school of proletarian novelists. Born in Chicago, he attended Northwestern University and since 1929 has devoted himself to creative writing. In 1934 he was awarded a Guggenheim fellowship. His novels include* Union Square (1933), The Foundry (1934), The Chute (1937), *and* Sons of the Fathers (1940). *He has also contributed stories and sketches to various periodicals.*

Crowds of boys and girls were coming from the Elevated at Laflin Street, choking the stairs. The air was cold and they shivered as they ran. All were hurrying toward the entrance of a huge white building, where a clock, to everybody's dismay, pointed to eight twenty-five. Crossing the street, Paul joined the crowd, holding his sandwiches tight. At the entrance he came upon a great crush of young workers pushing and milling to get inside before the eight-thirty bell rang, because if they punched their cards late, even by a minute, a black mark would be placed against their names, also a half-hour's time would be docked from their pay. Pushing and milling desperately to gain entrance, everybody attempted to thrust his fellow aside. Each morning this last-minute stampede was repeated, and in the course of the struggle lunches were crushed and more than one coat button popped to the sky. As the black hands of the clock clicked to eight twenty-eight, the girl employees in the rear held their lunches aloft for safety, begging: "Please—please!" Big Tom Reilly, the house detective, whose post was in the lobby, forced his way to the door. As he came from the inside, however, his big bulk was immediately shoved back by the tide. He struggled forth again, his face purplish, glaring at the mob. "What are you, cattle?" he shouted—and was pushed back again. With a loud *wush*, like the suction of dampish air, the last of the employees flew by him, to scurry to their floors.

Paul stood near the entrance, holding his breath at the scene. The knowledge that he was doomed to take part in such a struggle daily gave him a sickening sensation at the pit of the stomach. And the words of the house detective, *What are you, cattle?* had a numbing effect upon his mind.

"What's *your* name?" Reilly demanded brusquely, seeing him standing there. "Well, make up your mind—out or in!"

Paul came inside, showing the notice he had received from the employment department to report for work. He was directed bluntly by the detective: "The second door to the right, you know where it is!"

In the employment department his birth certificate was scanned, his application sheet taken from the files, and a time-card was made out for him. Then one of the clerks, a young girl, telling him to follow her, led the way out into the lobby toward the elevators. "You're to report to Department 2," she informed him, as they were speeding up past the floors. "That's the men's furnishings department, up on the fifth floor."

Then the gate swung open and Paul followed the girl out of the car. His mouth had become dry but his palms felt wet.

They came out upon a huge floor of merchandise, where aisle after aisle of stock, row after row of shelves, came suddenly into view. Following the girl in silence, Paul stared at the great stores. As they walked by, he could smell the odors of mail-order clothing—corduroy work pants, freshly made overalls, chambray work shirts, and other goods. The stuff was stacked in great piles as high as the water-sprinklers near the ceiling and gave the impression of big mounds of furs. It was the first time Paul had ever been inside a great mercantile institution, and walking past the aisles of stock he felt he was entering the bowels of a new world.

Half-way down the aisle, near the washrooms, the young girl stopped to instruct Paul how to punch his time at the clocks. He inserted his time-card, pulled the lever, and a loud *ping* resulted, a startling report. Then he followed the girl forward, cap in hand, sandwiches under his arm. When they had taken a dozen paces, Paul heard a rumbling—a mysterious sound. "The conveyor belts," the girl told him, cutting down a side aisle and leading the way along the south wall. They passed an office, then a wire-enclosed section where a dozen girls were inserting boys' shirts and rompers into paper bags. At a sewing machine near the girls sat a woman in her early thirties, her blond head bent, doing alterations on men's suits. And behind her, his old face lost amid the steam issuing from his presser, stood the department's fifteen-dollar-a-week tailor, muttering to himself.

Then they came toward the left, where a long row of big windows stretched the full length of the wall; and suddenly, seen through the glass, a panoramic camera shot of the city came into full view. Under a gray sky the roofs of the West Side rooming houses sprawled out like rubble, with their grubbiness stretching for miles. Sagging back porches, broken-down chimneys, and rutted alleyways met Paul's gaze. And in the foreground the tracks of the Metropolitan Elevated, curving like a sinuous reptile, fattened on the blocks. Paul stared out the windows, rooted, until the girl said: "This way, please"—and he followed her on.

Then they turned down another aisle, and suddenly the first sign of life at this end of the floor raised its head. "Bugs" Goldstein, the institution's champion whirlwind order-picker, picking the department's new pin-checked shirts with the snappy Hollywood turned-down style collar, was going on all twelve cylinders, dashing in and out of the aisles. Trying to set a new world's record, he was sure burning up the pace. The sound of rolling machinery grew nearer—again the conveyor belts. Then Paul and the girl came out upon a clearing and here the frantic life of the floor burst into full view—order-pickers were flashing in and out of aisles, girls were wrapping at tables like mad, and two checkers were calling out errors. At a small desk a young boy sat telephoning, trying to make himself understood. Above the noise of the floor his clear boyish voice—"Gibson speaking!"—could be heard.

The girl led Paul up to the floor manager of the department, whose desk was near the wall. Mangan was busy poring over the weekly payroll report. A tall, lean, bitter-faced, red-headed fellow in his middle thirties, he was nursing a hang-over and cracking his brains over the row of figures before his eyes. The girl timidly brought Paul forward, addressing the floor manager's bent head. "Here's the new order-picker," she reported, but Mangan failed to look up. "Here's the new—" she repeated, but Mangan, grunting, said: "All right, all right." The girl moistened her lips but, having delivered the new order-picker to his destination, said nothing and turned on her heel, leaving Paul all alone. Paul stared at the floor, cap in hand. The floor, made of cement, stared stubbornly back at him.

Finally Mangan looked up, raising bloodshot eyes. During the past three seasons he had seen scores of boys arrive and depart and he was sick and tired of breaking them in. "The main thing," he said thickly, "is to keep on your toes." Pause. "I take it," he added, "that you have a pair of wiry feet?"

"Well, n-no—well, yes," Paul answered, not knowing if he were being made sport of or not.

"Good. To begin with, I might as well inform you that you're here to concentrate on accuracy and speed. This is a mail-order house and if you don't know what that means, I'll tell you—speed, speed. Customers send in their money and orders and we have to ship the goods out fast. Twenty-four-hour service, that's our motto, and we have to live up to it, no matter what it costs."

And he found himself going into the same old snappy routine he gave to every new nervous boy coming for the first time on the floor. "In other words," he continued thickly, "this is a place where you have to be on your toes! Gibson, show this new boy around, tell him all the details of the floor!" And passing the buck to his eighteen-year-old assistant, the floor manager lowered his eyes again, to wrestle anew with his splitting headache and the department's weekly payroll report.

With a trembling heart, Paul put his coat, cap, and lunch away, then followed his new guide around. Eugene Gibson led the way forward, to give the new boy a few pointers about the floor. "The main thing," he said conscientiously, "is to pick the orders accurately and pick them fast." And he called attention to the aisle numbers and the little brass tags above the shelves. Paul listened attentively, trying to get things straight. It all sounded very simple but it was complicated because the department had thousands of shelves and tags. As young Gibson was explaining, he led Paul along the north windows, where half a dozen wrapping girls were working under the stern supervision of Big Stella, a big broad-shouldered Slav with fierce black hair and big pasty-looking hands. All the girls looked Paul's way. "Huh, he won't last long!" Big Stella grunted. Then: "You've got to work faster than that, Mary Pulacki, if we're going to make those nine-o'clock orders on time, so quit looking at the aisles!" And little Mary Pulacki, bowing her sweet meek head, worked harder than ever, for she had been gazing at her hero, Johnny Mutsek, who, picking Big Six work shirts and trying to go as hard as his hated rival Bugs Goldstein, was calling on his calves to stand under the strain.

Paul was led past the men's suits, past the trousers stock, then out upon a cleared space near the east wall where the big receiving tables stood. Overcoats, raincoats, bundles of corduroy work pants and stacks of hats were piled up, waiting to be put into stock. And near by were trucks of work shirts and caps, waiting to be emptied and checked off. The man in charge, Big Bill Dorpat, a gigantic Hollander, was working his head off, bending down inside of trucks and hauling the goods out. With his small green eyes glinting, he was checking off bundle after bundle of work pants, panting: ". . . eight dozen, nine dozen . . . ten . . . God in heaven! . . ." scratching down on the receiving tickets the various amounts. Rearing up, he called: "Stueken, forward!" and a sleepy-looking youth, clutching a detective magazine, stuck his blond dome out of an aisle. "You!" yelled Big Bill. "If Mr. Sidell catches you!" And Fritz Stueken, looking scared, came out of the aisle at once. Stueken was Big Bill's assistant, a serial addict, and the big Hollander began to bawl the lad out.

"That's the receiving department," Eugene Gibson explained to Paul as they were passing. "That's where all incoming goods are checked off."

Then they neared a glass-and-wood-enclosed paneled office and at that instant a voice was raised inside, bawling an employee out. "Here it's Wednesday already and you haven't counted the overall stock! I'll have to have those sheets by noon, or I'll have to get somebody else!"

There was a silence, short and painful, then a meek voice replied. "But—but Mr. Sidell and Mr. Mangan told me to count the men's clothing stock first . . ." The words were uttered timidly, they could hardly be heard.

"Never mind what Mr. Sidell and Mr. Mangan tell you, you do what *I* say!"

"Yes, sir," came the second voice meekly, and a moment later the door swung open and a young boy, white of face, emerged. He was a little fellow, consumptive-looking, skinny, and scared around the eyes. As he emerged, holding some long stock sheets, two phones in the office behind him began ringing full blast.

"That's Mr. Myerson's office; he's the buyer," Eugene whispered. "And that was Jimmy Kirby he bawled out." They could see the little stock-inventory boy, looking sick and beginning to go into a fit of coughing, turn tiredly into a dim aisle.

The time was five minutes to nine, and young Gibson led Paul through the hat and cap stock. When they emerged, they were near the wrapping tables by the north windows again where a little kid with a wiry jaw, working with energy, was lining up some trucks. "That's Killer Howard," Eugene said to Paul. "He's called the Killer because he gets rid of the time-orders, which have to go down to the shipping room every half-hour." The Killer, working furiously, was carrying orders from the wrapping tables and putting them into the trucks. A thatch of black hair stood upright from his forehead and below this thatch his white bitter face was intent upon his work. As Eugene and Paul emerged from the aisles, there came the sudden deafening ringing of bells. With an oath, Killer Howard strained forward, throwing his weight against the first truck to start it off. The ringing, too, aroused Big Stella, who, shouting, stepped from behind her wrapping table to assist the Killer, crying: "Down, throw the stuff down!" With a squeal from the wheels, the first loaded truck shot forward, the Killer rolling it frantically over the hard floor. Behind Eugene, Paul stopped in his tracks, staring at the frenzied boy. When the Killer reached the end of the aisle, Paul saw him start unloading the truck. The Killer's arms flailed the air unmercifully while Paul, astonished, looked on. The packages were disappearing into a big black cavity, a hole which was centered in what appeared to be an upright black boiler standing upon its end. Standing rooted, Paul looked at the hollow-shaped object, noting the black sheen of its sides. The huge cylinder, measuring about twenty-five feet in circumference, was bolt-studded, reaching from the ceiling and driven through the floor. There it stood, huge and sinister, its mouth open, while Killer Howard worked. Suddenly Big Stella reared her head again like a stallion, shouting above the bells. "The nine-o'clock orders, the nine-o'clock orders!" From his desk at the extreme end of the floor Mangan lifted his glance, a half-bored look in his eyes. As the furious ringing of the bells continued, Killer Howard stuck his head inside the hole, shaking his fist. "Shut up, shut up!" he cried, then went back to the tables for another load. Truly the department was a madhouse and Paul stood hypnotized by the scene. Watching the Killer roll the second hand truck back loaded, he saw the boy's shirt sticking to his back. The Killer's eyes, shiny and nasty, made him look like a rat. Paul stood staring at the huge cylinder, wondering what it was. There it stood, its iron mouth wide open, demanding to be fed. There it stood, a monster, insatiable, its gullet yawning for more goods.

"Wh-what is it?" Paul whispered, staring in half-awe at that black hole.

"That's the chute," answered Eugene grimly. "That's what gets all of us nuts."

Fiesta in St. Paul

by GRACE FLANDRAU, 18?— . *Grace Hodgson was born in St. Paul and was educated in the public schools of that city and in a girls' school in Paris. In 1909 she married W. Blair Flandrau. Mrs. Flandrau has been occupied much of her life with writing and travel, but for a time she and her husband ran a coffee plantation in Mexico. She is the author of short stories and novels, including Being Respectable (1923), Indeed This Flesh (1934), and Under the Sun (1936). "Fiesta in St. Paul," which originally appeared in the Yale Review for September 1943, shows the spirit of one racial group in a northern city.*

THE celebration in honor of Mexico's Independence Day was to take place in the city's public picnic grounds. We arrived an hour or so after the exercises were supposed to begin, but nothing, of course, had started. In front of the fine new brick pavilion were one or two delivery trucks got up as floats and draped with Mexican and American colors. They were to have been in a parade, which, owing partly to threatened rain, partly to the fact that the paraders couldn't possibly assemble on time, didn't come off. A number of people, all Mexicans and mostly in native costume, had, however, arrived at the pavilion, and it was odd to see them there. An American city on the upper Mississippi does not seem quite the background for Mexicans—especially these full-blooded Mexican Indians who, for the most part, make up St. Paul's Mexican population.

Inside the pavilion, the noise was already satisfactorily loud. The huge, stone-floored hall re-echoed deafeningly to the shrieks of the children, the loud music of a juke box, and the boom of a drum left standing on a bench and pounded unceasingly by a small boy.

Below the platform—alluded to in the program as "*el Altar Patrio*" —were rows of chairs, still empty. There was only a young Indian woman, suckling a three-year-old boy dressed in the uniform of a naval officer, his white navy cap pushed back from his fat face as he fed.

On a bench near the door a group of very dark, very neatly dressed men were sitting. In spite of their American clothes, they might have been any of the Indians who used to come down from their high villages to work on our Mexican plantation in the coffee-picking season.

"Do you know," I asked one of them, chiefly to hear again the clipped Mexican Spanish, "when the program will begin?"

He rose and politely removed his sky-blue felt hat. "Well—who knows, Senora?" His small, studying eyes, liquid-bright and set deep behind high cheekbones, were fastened intently on my face. And he had the alert, upright carriage of those Totonaco Indians in our state of Vera Cruz who carry such incredible loads for such incredible distances over the mountain trails. But he was darker in color; his features were very small; his head, thatched with stiff black hair, was very flat behind.

"May I ask," I said, "from what part of Mexico you come?"

"From Guanajuato, Senora." He gave me a soft, quick smile. "But not from Guanajuato itself. My earth—*mi tierra*—is more beyond, in the hills."

There has always been a good sound to those words, "my earth." And I've often wondered how these people, who are so much a part and product of their earth, can endure the separation. But one remembers, too, those villages in the hills: the remoteness, the poverty, the slow tempo, the utter monotony, eventlessness, stagnation—for all that the romanticists have written to the contrary.

"Do you like it better here, Senor?"

"Well—" he considered carefully, "flowers. Over there are always flowers. Very beautiful. Also fruits—" his pace accelerated—"every class of fruits. One fruit finishes, another begins. Also, no snow and ice. And always flowers." He lingered on the pleasant syllables, *flo-res.* "But here the work is better. In the beet fields it is good for work."

One of his companions who had not taken his eyes off our faces, now stepped forward and inquired in a loud tone, "Franceeschmeet?"

"I beg your pardon?"

"Mees—" slowly, then all in a breath—"Franceeschmeet? Office of Eemeegration? You know?"

No, I did not know Miss Frances Smith. He bowed and stepping back, resumed his intense scrutiny of our persons. He was different in type from Number One, and had that biblical profile—big hooked nose, big lips and teeth—that is characteristic of certain Indian races.

Number One now had something to say. Might it be, he had been asking himself, that the Senora had lived in Mexico?

I said I had, and also in the hills. Beyond Jalapa. "We had plantations of coffee."

"Ah—coffee." As he took this information inside himself to reflect upon it carefully, Number Two came up with another inspiration.

"El Paso, Texas? Meestairereebraoun? You know?"

Unfortunately, I knew neither El Paso nor Mr. R. E. Brown. The smile vanished from his face, and it was plain that he regarded this as not only a melancholy but also a somewhat suspicious circumstance.

Unwilling, however, to close on so negative a note, he suddenly stated: "My Mama"—he pointed to the floor—"here in this same city lives my Mama. Also my sisters. Two." He held up two fingers. "And there you behold them."

Not far off stood the sisters, very dark, very stout, dressed in black with red roses in their hair, and, under the thick paint and powder, their skins showed a faintly bluish tinge. Identical, in every detail, with the young girls who used to walk round and round the park in Jalapa when the moon was shining and the band played bullfight tunes.

They returned our glances with shy and, I thought, expectant curiosity, waiting for him to give them the signal to approach. He did not give it. And I knew that if this were Mexico, he would be riding the donkey, and they trudging dutifully behind in the dust.

The conversation having come to a standstill, we parted with many bows. A refreshment tent had been set up outside under the trees, and we joined the small crowd that was gathering about it. The menu included tamales, and the two varieties of flat corn-cakes—dressed with sauces in which red pepper and garlic annihilate all other flavors —known as *enchiladas* and *tacos*. We chose *tacos*.

But the young girl who was serving shook her head. "I feel it very much, but the *tacos* have not yet arrived."

"*Enchiladas*, then?"

"As little, disgracefully, has the sauce for these come."

"Will it be long?"

"Who knows?" And her smile, notwithstanding many bright gold teeth flecked with carmine lipstick, was rather lovely.

"Excuse me, please," a voice spoke, startlingly, in my ear, "is this not the Senora who owns the rich, the large, the magnificent *fincas* of coffee in Mexico?"

It was a twinkling, skull-like face covered with fine wrinkles that traced a pattern of sly, amiable insignificance. I replied that I thought it was the *agraristas*, now, who owned the plantation—anyhow, not I. And that it had never been especially rich or magnificent.

But this he would not accept. "No, no, very large, very rich, that is certain." Then, unfolding the program, a large sheet of paper in the red and green Mexican colors, he pointed to various items with a dark forefinger narrow as a claw. Patriotic Poem, recited by *el Senor* Refugio Gil. "Myself," he said. Patriotic Poem, recited by the youth, Alessandro Gil. "My son." *Las Chiapanecas*, danced by a group of boys and girls. "My children," he declared with a modest smile.

A truck, in the meantime, had drawn up, and out of the back descended a small man, closely buttoned into an immaculate blue serge suit and carrying a walking stick. Immense steaming kettles were handed down to him, and he dragged them to the tent without once letting go of his cane or removing his pearl-gray derby hat. Following the kettles, out came a stout, pock-marked matron and two young girls in evening dress. Then the head of a small shaggy dog. The dog barked, leaped nimbly to the ground, and scampered off with the air of one accustomed to fiestas.

The *tacos* had come, but no sauce; so we decided not to wait. Through loud-speakers outside the pavilion, records of Mexican songs blared gaily and raucously in the twilight. We left Senor Gil at work with all ten fingers and formidable teeth upon a small mountain of tamales, and went back to the pavilion.

Crowds were pouring in. All the seats were taken, and the floor space was a surging mass of men, women, and especially children.

510

Young men in the uniform of the United States Army, old men in slouch hats and fierce mustachios, crowded about the bar. Young girls strolled in pairs, cracking their gum. And the small naval officer slept soundly, stretched across the laps of his parents.

The non-Mexicans present were few. They were, chiefly, the City Councilmen invited as special guests; the orchestra—and an odd one at that; an unpleasing young man in fancy Western costume, down on the program as "*el Senor* Bert (Sunshine) Kahn," a singer of cowboy songs; and ourselves.

With no diminution of the uproar in the hall, the program got under way. The orchestra leader stepped forward. She was an elderly lady, in spectacles, girlish evening dress, and false curls that nodded coquettishly under one ear. Except for two unconvincing young men, the musicians were female and not young. The banjo-player was a tired blonde in white satin; the pianist a crippled person with a bunch of red roses nodding on top of her pompadour. Why the orchestra should have had to be American I don't know, except that it probably cost more—even this one—and was, therefore, more worthy of so distinguished an occasion.

A dark gentleman in a pink satin blouse stepped to the microphone; a chorus of dark, very plain little children came on the stage. Then to the rousing accompaniment of the orchestra—the schoolmarmish leader alternately playing the violin and conducting with her bow, her foot, her bare shoulders, and her false curls—the Mexican and American national hymns were sung by all.

The reading of the Mexican Act of Independence, in Spanish, and the speeches, in English, of the City Councilmen, were only an incomprehensible booming in the loudspeaker. But when Senor Gil began his recitation, fright diminished his voice to a point where the instrument could pick it up. The poem, however, was a long one, and in the middle of it Senor Gil faltered, stopped, stood with a smile of pure agony rending his face. It was touch and go for a moment; then, alas, memory revived, and he went on for another fifty verses.

More recitations followed. Then came the dances, *jarabes, jotas, zapateadas.* They were danced mostly by children, but the gestures, the music, the costumes, and especially the drumming of feet on the boards were startlingly familiar.

In the old days on our plantation, when the picking season was over and the last of the sacks of coffee had been tied on the mules, and the last of the long caravans had started on its three or four days' journey over the mountain to the nearest railway, the coffee warehouse would be empty and free for more frivolous uses. Often then, on a Saturday, our plantation people would give a dance. All afternoon the rockets would go up, inviting the neighbors to the ball; and the sound of these rockets exploding languidly, without fire or color in the lovely stillness of that remote place, was sad, somehow, and futile— like a pistol fired at nothing.

Far and near, however, they would be heard and heeded. And, as night fell, lights would twinkle along all the jungle-covered slopes and through the groves of coffee. Sometimes it would be a young blood alone on horseback, his gun and knife in his belt, his machete at his side. Oftener it would be a family of Indians, on foot, or with a burro among them. Classic and unchanging their outlines in the dusk—the big hat, the loose white pyjama suit of the man; the woman's head swathed and nun-like, her full ruffled skirts swinging as she walked. The *rebozo* would bind the baby to her back; the children would march sturdily beside her.

Vendors of food came, and of drink; gamblers with their monte tables; the orchestra with harp and the stringed instruments locally called *jaranas*. Torches flared in the darkness under the warehouse porch. And all night there would come to us, distantly, the rhythmic pounding of feet on the wooden floor, stomping out the *zapateadas*.

The dawn is red-gold and sudden in those latitudes, the morning air wonderfully sweet and pure. But this beauty was in no way compatible with the procession that staggered across the patio to our house. The survivors of the dance could not bring themselves to leave without saluting the *patrones;* or the orchestra without offering us a serenade. And, gaily, drunkenly, excruciatingly out of tune, it would play under our window something that could almost be identified as "After the Ball."

Tonight on this Minnesota picnic ground were the same dark, naïve faces, the same feeling of zest, amenity, and good manners that did not in the least preclude the ever-present hint of sleeping violence. And just as on the plantation there had seldom been a ball without its stabbing or shooting, so this St. Paul fiesta produced at least one minor knifing.

"You like, Senora? The fiesta is beautiful, truly?" It would be Senor Gil, his face thrust suddenly into mine. And each time he came back, he would smell increasingly of strong drink. "Poetry, music, the dance! In a word, *el ideal.* Ah!" Then, turning, he would totter off through the dense crowd, in the direction of the bar.

The heat now, the smells, the noise; the children racing about, crowding past you, dripping ice-cream pies down your neck; the stone floor sticky with crackerjack, dampened by the indiscretions of the very young; the state of suffocation and general frenzy—whatever they had to do with the ideal, at least indicated a fiesta that was a complete success.

It had also reached its climax. Her Majesty the Queen was to be crowned by His Honor the Mayor of the city. His Honor arrived on the dot, but, needless to say, Her Majesty did not. During the interminable wait, a space was cleared and the audience danced. A rather large contingent of Syrians had turned up from their adjacent quarter, and there were a number of Negroes. Also, the lady standing next to me stated that she was an American Indian, half Sioux and half Potawatami. And when at last the pretty Mexican girl arrived, she was crowned Queen by an Irish Mayor in a State that boasts the biggest —or is it second biggest?—Scandinavian city in the world.

So it all seemed very American and heart-warming, the times being what they are. And the presence, too, of the Mexican boys in the uniform of the United States Army gave an authentic accent to this small pageant of international good will.

Outside, my new acquaintances waited to say good-bye. There was the man who knew Franceeschmeet; there was Senor Gil, smelling to high heaven of assorted liquors; and there was the little, very dark Indian from "more beyond" Guanajuato, whose studying look now gave way to one of sudden illumination.

"Your husband, Senora,"—he nodded towards the friend who was with me—"he is the Governor of the State, truly?" But he took it quite well when he learned that he was neither my husband nor the Governor of Minnesota.

And then, with expressions of mutual regret, we said good-bye. The night had already taken their dark faces into itself, but the flash of their white teeth was very friendly under the lights.

F.O.B. Detroit

by WESSEL SMITTER, 1894–   . *A graduate of the University of Michigan, B.A., 1922, Smitter is the author of both short stories and novels dealing with modern industrial life and picturing the impact of the factory on the worker. As a result of several years in Detroit he published his novel* F.O.B. Detroit (1938). *The story with the same title is taken from Harper's Magazine, October 1938.*

Russ and I were waiting in the crowded employment office at the Holt automobile factory when one of the clerks came out with a piece of paper.

"Any of you fellows here ever run a manipulator?" he asked.

Not a man answered.

"What's a manipulator?" Russ whispered.

"A kind of derrick," I said. "Used for handling hunks of hot steel."

"Let's grab it," he said.

"Wait a minute—" I warned him. "You don't know what you're getting into."

"If it's a machine," he said, "I can run it." Russ is a big fellow and confident.

The clerk looked the men over. He noticed Russ.

"Anybody here," he said, "that's had experience running electric cranes?"

"That manipulator job—" said Russ, "I'll take it. I'd like this man here to swamp for me."

"Ever run one?" the clerk asked.

"No, but I've run donkey engines and loaders. I'm a good learner. It won't take me long to get what I don't know."

The fellow scratched his head.

"All right," he said. "We'll give you a try. Where's your helper?"

"Right here." And he pointed to me.

I had a job. It all happened so quick I didn't know whether to be glad or not.

We went up and filled out our cards.

"What's the matter?" said Russ. "You look disgusted. You think I stuck my foot into something, don't you?"

"Not your foot," I said. "Your neck. You got any sort of idea the kind of job you grabbed off for us?"

"No. You?"

"No. All I know—I've seen it a couple of times on my way through the drop forge. They use it handling big steel. It's so complicated they have to get a factory man every time it breaks down."

"Swell," he said. "We're going to have fun. We're going to learn something."

"But that outfit's complicated," I said. "More gears and levers than you ever saw. Got an iron claw that picks up ten-ton billets of steel and sticks 'em into the furnaces. Pulls 'em out when they get hot and holds 'em under steam hammers as high as a two-storey building. I'd be scared to climb up on it. Suppose the thing got out of control. Then what?"

514

"They give a man a chance to learn, don't they? They don't expect him to get up there and run it the first day, do they?"

"Oh, sure. They let you learn. Even if you could run it, they wouldn't let you, the first day."

"O-keh," he said. "That's all that matters."

Early the next morning I was in the drop forge, near the time clock, waiting for Russ. The night shift was still on and the heavy production machinery was running full blast. Rows of furnaces were shooting out flames and smoke round the door; hammers and presses were pounding out front axles, gear blanks, and such. The floor of the building covered five or six acres and the ground trembled and shook.

Over in a far corner of the building the top of the manipulator loomed up through the smoke like a battleship's turret, the big boom, or arm, sticking out like a ship's gun.

Russ came in and we went up to the machine. It was as big as a locomotive, and higher—mounted on a carriage that ran over steel rails, wide apart, laid in the concrete floor. On the carriage were other rails that ran crosswise and the superstructure ran on these so that the machine could run in four directions. From the upper part of the machine a big arm, or boom, projected that turned with the superstructure. The arm could be raised or lowered, shortened or made longer, turned or pivoted in any direction and on the end there was a claw with two curved iron fingers big enough to go round a bass drum. Steel ladders ran up the sides of the machine, and from where we stood we could see the tops of two rows of brass control levers. I think the machine weighed sixty tons.

"That's her," I said. "Still want to run it?"

"Oh, sure," he said. "She's a honey. I think we're gonna get along swell. There's room here, room to work."

At the end of the long floor were piles of cold steel, all sizes and shapes. Along one side were the furnaces, some of them under slow heat, grumbling and purring. On the other side were the heavy presses and hammers reaching up into the smoky heights of the building. Overhead, forty or fifty feet above the floor, a traveling bridge crane rumbled back and forth, carrying bundles of steel in cable slings to the production machines. The operator stuck his head out of the steel cage as he rode past and looked us over.

A timekeep gave us our cards and our badges and told us where to punch in and then let out a yell for Johnson, our straw boss. Johnson came up and he was short and the skin on his face was like leather. He had no eyebrows and he looked at us a minute with smoke-colored eyes and said:

515

"Gotcha cards?"

"Yeh."

"Gotcha badges?"

"Yeh."

"Follow me."

The three of us walked over to the floor where the machine stood and here Johnson had a little desk on high legs, but no stool. A lot of blueprints were stuck in a wall cabinet and he pulled out one and began looking at it. Russ had started walking off toward the machine when Johnson said:

"Hey! Stick around here, will you?"

He studied the blueprints again and I motioned to Russ to take it easy and wait and we stood there watching the men drifting in. And then the bell rang and a couple of fellows started oiling the machines; the steam was turned on in the hammers and the big pistons began warming up—sliding up and down in long easy strokes, not quite touching the anvils below. Some little colored lights over the furnaces changed from green to orange and then to red; the flames backfired a couple of times and then settled down to a steady roar.

Johnson raised up again, and called for one of the fellows working on the machine to come over. The man wasn't dressed like a Holt worker. He had on a good suit with a pair of coveralls over it and a temporary badge.

"Barney, here," said Johnson, "is from the factory. He'll break you fellas in. Ride around with him," he said to Russ. "Keep your eyes open and don't be afraid to ask questions. I don't expect you'll try to handle no jobs the first coupla weeks."

"And this man," he said, pointing to me, "will take Hank's place. Introjuice 'em togedda and let Hank show him the work."

"O-keh," said Barney. "And what's the schedule?"

"Load five and six. I'll mark some steel pretty soon. An 'en we'll pull number three and work it up under number one hammer."

The three of us went to the machine. I got introduced to Hank.

After a while Barney finished his oiling, threw in the master switch on the wall, and then he and Russ climbed up on the rig and they rolled down the wide tracks to the end of the bay. In a minute or two they came back, electric horn blowing, and in the big claw sticking out ahead of the rig there was a billet of cold steel that weighed maybe four or five tons. They stopped in front of number five furnace; Barney maneuvered into position; aimed for the door and gave Hank a signal. Hank cut off the air, pressed a button, and the heavy door of the furnace slid up toward the ceiling. Barney's hands fairly played a tune on the levers. The long arm reached in with its load—the claw opened

516

and the steel was laid on the furnace floor. The arm retracted and as Hank pressed another button that closed the door, the flames curled and twisted round the steel.

"Always cut off the air befo' opening the furnace," said Hank. "If you was to forget—the flames might shoot out and singe the hair off yo' buddy. I sho' don't like this job. Half the time I'm trying to remember if I forgot to do something I should—the rest of the time I'm worried les' I did something I shouldn't. I'll be mighty glad when you gets this job learnt and I can go back to the foundry. There I knock sand out of molds. Don't have to rack my brains about nothin'."

There wasn't much to his job—opening and closing the doors; watching to see that the track was kept clear; cutting out the switch in emergencies, and a few things like that.

Barney and Russ loaded the furnaces and then they rolled up to number one and got ready to do some forging. The biggest steam hammer in the factory was there—a pair of shears that had a bite of a thousand tons. What they did to the big billets was likely to give you an idea that steel is about as tough and hard as new cheese, which is all wrong, even when it's been in the fire a long time and is up to white heat.

Barney pulled the hot billet of steel out of the furnace, got a firm hold, and swung the boom round in front of the hammer. There were experts on the job now. Johnson, who directed the work and made all signals; the hammer man, who controlled the force of the giant blows; and Barney, who ran the manipulator. His job was to get the steel up on the anvil; to turn it and tip it—to hold it in position while the hammer got in its work.

Johnson signaled to get the steel up on the anvil. The hammer got into motion. Not striking, yet—but getting ready. Warming up for the signal. That up-and-down motion of the hammer between the smooth slides, that oily flow of movement, gave you an idea of what steam could do: of the power that was held in reserve behind the long piston, of the kind of blows that would come when Johnson gave the signal and the hammer man came down hard on the throttle.

The hammer stopped, poised to strike, and the job was all Barney's. The white-hot billet had to be just so on the anvil—had to be just right for the hammer. A slight turn—a little to the right—a little back maybe. Slight movements, these were, that had to be done quickly. No time to fool, no time to waste, because the steel was all the time losing heat. Five tons of hot steel is something alive, something vicious, waiting for a chance to strike you if you lose control.

Barney was clever, all right. He knew the job, knew the machine, knew the signals. And the last was not the least part of the business.

Johnson made them all with his right thumb; mysterious little jerks and twitches—jabs over his shoulder—past his ear—downward. The brass levers snapped back and forth, switches flashed, circuit breakers popped out and slammed back into place, rheostats smoked. I wondered what Russ was thinking about standing up there next to Barney. Plenty, I guessed.

The steel was battered and pounded, was dropped to the floor, turned over. The iron claw grabbed a new hold and slammed it back on the anvil for more. The hammer crashed down in full strokes. Fire sprayed out in a circular shower and rained to the floor. The ground shook. Not light shakes—heavy and deep—transmitted through a foundation of solid concrete, sixty feet down.

They were unable to finish the work in one heat and the steel was put back into the furnace. Afterward, Russ and Barney came down for a drink. Their shirts were soaked.

"How's she going?" I asked Russ.

"Fine and dandy," he said.

"Be a long two weeks for you," I said. "Riding around up there, doing nothing."

"Don't worry," he said. "In a week I'll be runnin' the thing. See if I won't."

The bell rang and we stopped for lunch, and while eating, Russ asked Barney a lot of questions about the job and the rig. About backlash and overloads, dynamic brakes and magnetic clutches. Barney answered the questions, but not with any great show of enthusiasm. He was a traveling mechanic for the company that made the machine and he'd been round quite a bit and he was full of talk about the towns he'd been in. When Russ asked a question he answered short and then swung the talk to girls he'd met in Pittsburgh or Fort Worth.

He was telling about a girl in Cincinnati who never warmed up right unless she was riding round on a steamboat with a band playing, when Russ interrupted again.

"If one of the rheostats burned out," he asked, "how would you go about to fix it?"

"Now listen," said Barney, "it's lunch time. It's time off. They're not paying you now for asking questions. Let's wait till the bell rings."

"I know, but if you don't mind—"

"All you have to learn is how to punch those levers. If the rheostat breaks down they'll get the electricians to fix it. If you get drunk and bust up the rig—like the other fellow did—they'll send for me."

"I savvy. But just the same I want to know."

"All right then. You've got two weeks to learn. You don't need two weeks. In two days I could turn the job over to you—if I wanted to.

You're the kind that learns quick. But what's the use? Make the thing look easy and they'll figure anybody can run it. Then how you gonna hold 'em up for a raise?"

"I hadn't thought about that."

"Well, now's the time to be thinking about it. Look at the job you'll be handling! Look at the responsibility! Ruin one of these blocks and it's five hundred bucks. Wreck the machine, and it's thousands. Kill a guy—and you're washed up. They've taken the seat off the rig so you can't sit. They won't let you smoke a cigarette to steady your nerves. And what do you get? Five bucks. Five lousy bucks. They's sweepers here in this outfit gets more'n that."

"The time to think about all those things," said Russ, "is later. Right now I'm trying to get the job learnt."

The bell rang and we went back to work.

At the end of the week Russ took over the controls. Barney rode on the machine a couple of days doing nothing; hung about on the floor a couple more, and then left for Cleveland. By the end of the third week Russ was pretty good—good enough to coast along on the job and take it easy if he'd wanted to. But that wasn't his idea. He kept learning.

We'd moved into the same boardinghouse and one night, up in the room while fiddling with his guitar but not really playing, he got an idea.

"Listen," he said, "a pianist doesn't stop to look for the keys when he's playing. What's to hinder a man learning to run that rig the same way? Learning to work the levers without looking at them? There's only a dozen."

"What's your idea?" I said. "Take a little nap now and then?"

"No. Keep my eyes on the steel. On Johnson. Wouldn't have to stop to look for the controls, for positions."

"Could be done, I guess. Only thing is . . ."

"Sure it could be done."

"Only thing is there's a slight difference between playing a piano and running that rig. When the pianist hits the wrong key there's a sour note but no one gets hurt. You hit the wrong control—you may accidentally drop a hunk of steel on somebody's head."

What I said didn't discourage him. The idea stuck. He hauled a couple of two-by-fours up in the room and rigged up a contraption with two rows of sticks the size and shape of the levers. They were spaced accurately and, like the controls on the rig, could be moved back and forth into various positions. Blindfolded, he practiced night after night. That was all right with me, except that I lost some sleep. But

519

when he started practicing on the rig itself, I watched my step and gave him plenty of clearance, with him looking off into space and paying no attention to what lever he struck.

It wasn't long before the white-collars up front began taking notice of what was going on on the floor. You'd see one of them hurrying along down the aisle as though he was late to a circus, and then he'd see Russ up there on the rig handling steel as though it was cordwood, and he'd slow down; come to a stop near a pillar and clean forget what he'd been in such a hurry about. And then one day they changed the routing of the gangs of tourists that came through the factory and had them all bother us. If it happened that Russ was handling a piece of steel under the big hammer—they saw something. It gave them something to remember and tell the brother Masons about in Sioux Center or Oshkosh.

One time Herman, who ran the overhead crane and chewed tobacco, spat down from his cage and hit the claw on the machine. Russ was carrying a piece of cold steel. He stopped the rig, lowered the boom, and got Herman's shirt from the cabinet and wiped off the rig.

That night, at the clock, they had some words. Not much—but sharp. It left bad feelings in both.

A day or two later Herman started being careless with his loads—swinging in close as he went over the rig. Russ got up on his ear.

"Tell your man up there," he said to Herman's helper, "if he does that I'll reach up there and pull him down to the floor."

"Take it easy," I said. "No use getting him sore at you. There's some big jobs coming up. You're going to need his help."

What we called a big job was anything over ten tons, which was the limit capacity of the rig. Anything over, Russ couldn't handle alone and Herman helped. A sling was wrapped round the steel and Herman let down his hook and tied on to it, easing some of the strain off the rig. Co-operation between the two had to be smooth; it was no job for a couple of soreheads to work on together.

The bell rang and Herman came down for lunch. Russ went up to him and made himself plain.

"Listen here," he said, "throw another load of steel over my head— and you and I are going to tangle. One of us is going to the hospital. Understand?"

Herman never opened his mouth. It had some effect on him. For a few days he kept his loads in the clear, and then he began swinging them in close again. Not close enough so that Russ could get down to business and do something about it, but still close enough to make him uncomfortable. He spoke to Johnson about it.

"I t'ot you tol' him," said Johnson. "He tol' me you was givin' him orders what to do. He don't need two bosses."

"I did tell him," said Russ. "Now I'm telling you. If he drops something—hits me—don't try to tell 'em up there it was an accident. See? Because Bennie, here, will be there to prove what I said."

"What's a matta—" said Johnson, "you getting nervous or somethin'? For eight years he's been slinging steel ova guys' hets. He's neva hit nobody yet."

A couple of days later Johnson lined out a job for us that looked tough right from the start. It was a piece of steel half as big as a Holt car and marked "experimental." It was a die job and was the lower block of a set of dies that together would weigh thirty tons. They were to be used for stamping out from a single piece of metal the whole top and a part of the sides of the two-door car body.

Getting it into the furnace was a job for both rigs. Easing it off the floor, Herman helped and took most of the strain; Russ steadied. The eight steel lines coming down from the drums on Herman's rig were as stiff as iron rods with the tension. Herman had most of the load; Russ had the responsibility. Herman could raise and lower and move the load in four directions; Russ had control over every motion that a man has in his shoulder, elbow, and wrist. It was nice teamwork. Smooth and steady the load was raised from the floor and moved up the bay to number one furnace. And then came the ticklish job of getting the steel through the door without wrecking the furnace. Herman got into position—cut off his power, and went dead. "All yours," Johnson signaled to Russ. He eased her in, his hands stroking the levers. Herman still had a dead-gravity load. Russ pushed her gently, easing her in; there wasn't one inch to spare. The front end of the steel touched the floor of the furnace. Herman dropped off and Russ gave her a clean push through the door. He pulled out.

It was nice work, but the hard part—the work under the hammer— was still to come. Johnson spoke to Russ. "Betta check your rig over right afta dinner. I want everything to go extra smooth—see? Once I sta't flattenin' her out you'll never get her back through that door. We gotta do it all in one heat and there's plenty of forge work on that baby before she sta'ts freezing."

Anything that wasn't red-hot to Johnson was cold. A piece of steel that didn't lick the grease off the floor wasn't even warm to the touch.

"I never let a job down yet," said Russ. "Guess I won't this one. Better talk to Herman."

"Herman's doing all right, ain't he?"

"So far," said Russ.

All the forenoon the steel soaked in the furnace. It took up a lot of heat even before starting to turn red, and after that a lot more. We had lunch and then Russ and I worked on the machine. I swiped while he oiled and checked over cam-shafts and gears. His big, gentle hands slid over the journals; the way he felt of the bearings was like a caress. "We'll sling her up there," he said. "We'll twist her tail any old way the Swede says. We'll make her behave."

About two-thirty Johnson said he was ready. We took the hooks off Herman's crane and rigged a sling. The big hammer was cut in on the high-pressure steam and began warming up. Johnson cleared space for action and gave Russ right-of-way on the floor. Russ put on his green goggles, sloshed water on the front of his shirt, and climbed up on the rig. We were ready to start.

A cold piece of steel is one thing; a hot piece of steel is something else. Cold steel is like a wild animal that is dead; hot steel is like one that is alive and dangerous—there is energy in it. Energy to make the breath stick in your throat—to scorch the inside of your lungs if you breathe through your mouth. Yet you have to work close or you lose control.

Russ dragged the steel halfway out of the furnace and clasped on. We wrapped the sling around and, even with long irons, the job was too hot to be fun. Herman picked up his share of the load and they swung her across the floor to the hammer. A minute later they had her up on the iron and the anvil took Herman's load. Russ had it all.

Johnson's signals were fast: "Left turn—a little—lower the front end a hair—a bit more—too much—o-keh—hold her."

The hammer rapped out ten or fifteen blows. Fire sprayed; the ground trembled and an empty milk bottle that someone had left on a switch-box crashed to the floor. One end, the upper side, was beveled off, fairly smooth.

A new position. "Shove her up," Johnson signaled. Herman picked up the load for a minute; Russ pushed her over; once again there were signals. Russ's eyes were on Johnson; his hands on the levers were a sight that was beautiful to see. His shirt was steaming and the red light from the steel was on his face.

Once more the hammer—the upper right side was beveled. Once more a quick change; the hammer again—the left side was finished. Then Johnson signaled: "Pull her off—reverse end positions."

"Judast priest!" I said, "that's gonna make the job tough."

A string of visitors came in and lined up to watch. The guide started his spiel and began telling the crowd all about steel, the number of kinds used in making a car, the cost of the rig.

We lowered off to the floor, switched ends and shifted Herman's

522

rigging while Johnson snapped some measurements with long-handled calipers and the scalers cleaned off the anvil.

"Pick her up!" Johnson signaled. And it was then Herman started his monkey business. He lit into his load with a snap. Russ lost his bite and was helpless.

"What's a madda!" Johnson bellowed. "Can't you fellas come up togedda? Take it easy!"

Herman couldn't have heard what he said. Russ kept his mouth shut and worked out a new hold. The job was harder for him, now; he had the end that was beveled. There were no corners—no rough surfaces to bite into.

"Easy now," Johnson signaled. "Bring her up—"

This time they got her off the floor—were starting to raise her—when Herman jerked. Once more Russ lost his hold. He was beginning to get angry. He motioned for Johnson to come up but Johnson ignored him.

"Get it up there!" he signaled. "Stop horsin' around—she's gettin' cold!" That time they both jerked. She slipped out of Herman's sling and rolled to the floor.

Russ slid down the ladder and went up to Johnson.

"Pull him off," he said. "Give me the floor. I can't work with that fellow—he's trying to queer me."

"You're crazy," said Johnson. "You can't handle 'er."

"I'll handle her," said Russ. "Get him out-a here. I'll shorten my boom—get leverage."

"And burn yourself up."

"What-a you care? We're losing our heat. She's getting cold."

"O-keh," said Johnson. "She's yours—you asked for it."

He waved Herman off the floor.

Russ passed me.

"Keep everybody off the track behind me," he snapped. "I'm gonna move—shoot in and grab—back out for air. Throw me a spray when I come past." He swung up.

There was action without waiting for signals from Johnson. Russ shortened his boom a full quarter. The steel lay on its side. He bit into it—slammed it over—backed away—came from another angle and turned it again. He was after a good hold and got it. He shortened the boom another foot. He could have spit on the steel.

"What's 'e tryin' to do," said Johnson, "get 'er up in his lap?"

Russ began raising the load. Slowly, it came up from the floor. The gears growled; the motors groaned with resentment. Circuit breakers popped out with the sound of explosions and were sent back with a flash. Switches snapped and gave off little corkscrews of blue smoke. The machine responded against a gigantic resistance but you felt that it was not the electrical current that turned the wheels and raised the steel—it was the strength, the speed, and the expert control of those powerful hands on the levers.

He got it up on the anvil and the fancy work started. Johnson stepped in again and for once his signals were clear. There was no sling to worry about now—no clumsy helper. Russ crouched low behind the controls. The heat must have been fierce, and when the heavy blows fell he was in the red rain of hot iron.

The guide stood in line with his gang—forgot his spiel and looked on. The scalers, better able to appreciate what they saw, stopped work and looked as hard as the others. Three times he got the steel in position; three times the hammer battered and pounded. Then he balanced the steel on the anvil, unclamped, and shot back for a breath of cool air.

The paint on the forward end of the machine was beginning to blister. The oil on the open gears smoked and the steel ladder was hot to the touch.

I handed him a clean pair of goggles and one of the scalers threw up some gloves.

"It won't get you nowhere," I hollered, "if you burn yourself up."

"Don't worry," he said. "This time we'll finish her off."

He rolled in again. Johnson signaled. There was a high spot near the center to work down.

This time it was even more difficult to hold. It was beveled all the way round. He got it, but the first light blow of the hammer loosened it up. It was a struggle again to get the right hold and all the time the steel was up there on the anvil. He turned and tilted and once or twice it threatened to get away and slide to the floor. But he got it, and the hammer did its last work.

"O-keh—" Johnson signaled. "All done."

The crowd broke out and applauded.

As I've said, Herman, the fellow who ran the overhead crane, chewed tobacco. You'd see him up there near the ceiling coasting along in his iron cage with his head sticking out, a cud in his cheek the size of a duck egg, and every once in a while sending a long, thin squirt down to the floor. He hardly ever hit anybody and almost never hit Russ's rig, but Russ was worried. At night after work he'd go round the machine, looking it over.

"What's that?" he'd say. "Looks mighty suspicious to me."

"Aw, get out," I'd say. "It's a little iron rust or some water."

From day to day he worked himself up about it something fierce and nothing I said made any difference. And then one day he sent in a long complaint to the safety department, and a couple of days later a general order came through: no more tobacco chewing by crane operators while on duty. Herman was sore as a boil. He knew who was to blame.

Herman took it out on Russ by starting to swing in his loads. All that afternoon he kept swinging closer and once, when Johnson wasn't on the floor, he pulled one straight over the rig. Russ got up on his ear, and that night, after Herman climbed down from the crane, Russ warned him again.

"I'm telling you once more," he said. "Keep your loads in the clear. Swing another load over my head and I'll reach up there and pull you and your cage down to the floor so quick you won't know what's happened."

"Boosh-wah," said Herman. "Tell it to the safety committee, why doncha?"

I had a chance to talk to Herman at the tool crib.

"Better take it serious," I said. "When he gets his hands on them levers—he'll do anything—he ain't human."

"That's all right," he said. "Me—I'm hot-headed too. If he wants to start something—I'm for it."

The next day it happened. It was about three in the afternoon. Johnson was up at the desk talking to Riley. Russ had a piece of cold stuff and was getting in position to load number three. I had the air off and was raising the door when Herman came down the bay with a stack of front axle blanks, three or four tons of them. The load came down the bay in a straight line for Russ. I figured Herman was going to throw a little scare into Russ—figured he'd come up close and then swing his load to the other side of the bay. But he didn't. He came straight on— the load swinging a little at the end of the long cables. He was close— getting closer—without cutting speed. Thirty feet—twenty—coming straight over. But no. Russ dropped his load to the floor and shot backward. He stopped, raised his boom like a snake getting ready to strike, and stood his ground. Herman came straight into it. Russ shot out his boom, the iron claw open for business, smashed into Herman's load, and the front axle blanks clattered and rained to the floor. The racket was something terrific. Iron chips flew in every direction; dust rose thick from the floor; scalers and hammer men scattered. I ducked for a pillar.

The fight was on. Herman rolled back and pulled his hooks up—got into position. Now they were empty—ready to hit. Russ drew in his boom. The big claw snapped open—aimed at the cage—came at Herman. But Herman struck first—dropped his hooks like a swinging plummet in a long curve. It was a good shot. He got a grappling hold on the undercarriage of the rig. He drew tight. A couple of pulls and he'd turn the rig over. But Russ was too quick. He slashed his boom round against the steel cables and wiped himself clear. Snarling steel rope filled the air. In a wild swing Herman's hooks struck the top of a furnace. Bricks rained to the floor. Somewhere a steam line let go. Noise was terrific.

Herman shot back and rolled in his line—came in again, maneuvering for a direct overhead drop, trying to keep Russ on the defensive. But Russ went at him. He shot out his boom—full length—straight for the cage. Herman kicked back—not a second too soon. Another two feet and Russ would have had him down on the floor. Herman dropped the hooks; Russ struck as they fell and sent them spinning, and they crashed against the big hammer. But they were open and on the rebound they hit the undercarriage of the rig—closed up and held. Herman gave her the juice—all he had. His lines tightened. Once more Russ tried to slash himself clear—struck out. It was no good. The steel lines tightened still more. Russ swung his boom—raised and lowered—trying to cut through. Fire leaped from the cables as steel sheared on steel. No use. The rig—one side—began to raise from the floor. He'd go over! To save himself he aimed his boom for the crane—shot out to full length—clamped onto the bridge. It held. Herman was powerless to move him. The two machines were deadlocked to a standstill.

It was then I thought about throwing out the master switches like I'm supposed to do in emergencies. Both switches were up there on the wall pillar and I cut Herman out first, and when I did, Russ settled back to the floor.

And then I got busy. Fellows were running all around, looking up, still not sure whether the building would come down or not. Scalers with brick dust on their clothes began showing up on the floor looking scared.

I went up to a couple.

"Listen," I said. "You fellows. I don't care who you're for. But if one gets fired—they both go. We gotta make them think it was an accident. I'll do the talking."

I had to do some powerful lying. But what could I do? There was Johnson and he had the two men down on the floor, and there was Riley and a whole bunch of others and they wanted to know everything. And after I got started, there was no way of changing my story —no place to stop; and I got in deeper and deeper; and I told them that the two machines had just accidentally come together, and that in trying to untangle they had got scrambled up something awful. Russ was still fighting mad, but looking at him you might have thought that he was just scared, and I was afraid that he would lay into Herman right there while I was talking, though a fist-fight, I guess, would have been pretty tame after the way they had been going at it. And there were the two machines, still standing there with death grips on each other, in what you might call a compromising position—axle blanks and broken bricks scattered all over the floor and smoke pouring from the hole in the furnace. If Johnson or Riley had had a lick of sense in their heads they wouldn't have had to ask any question, but what it came down to, I guess, is what I told Russ. They just couldn't imagine that there would ever be two fellows so dumb and hot-headed that they would try to run off a fight with a bridge crane and a manipulator.

The pow-wow ended up with me getting it in the neck from Johnson.

"When you saw what was happening," he said, "why'n-cha do sumpt'ing? Why'n-cha t'row out the switch right away, 'stead of standin' there with your hands in your pockets?"

One day in May, when times were bad in Detroit, Johnson called Russ and me over and gave us a couple of slips.

"Take these," he said, "and go up to the transfer department and see if ya can get yaself a couple new jobs. I can't use ya no more."

"What's the matter?" said Russ.

"It's nottin' the matta," said Johnson. "It's just what I'm tellin' ya— I can't use ya no more."

"Why not?"

" 'Cause I can't. We got a new way figured out for making dies. We ain't gonna forge 'em no more."

Johnson was fooling round with some blueprints—filing some away —throwing some in the can.

"Who's gonna run the rig?" asked Russ.

"Nobody."

"What's gonna happen to it?"

"They'll feed it to the open-hearths. Melt it up and make some new Holts. In a couple days you'll see it standin' out there in the bone-yard. The big hammer goes too. No more poundin' and bangin'. It ain't civilized to make dies like that."

"Ain't civilized? How are you gonna make dies if you don't forge them?"

"We're gonna type 'em."

"Type them?"

"That's what I said."

"It sounds crazy."

"Might be it sounds crazy to you."

Johnson went on with his work.

"But why junk the rig?"

"It's obsolete, I tol' ya. Odda companies use old-fashion tools. We can't afford to."

"Then why not sell it?"

"Because the Holt Motor Company ain't in the second-hand business."

Johnson put on his coat.

"Betta get going," he said. "They'll be closin' up." Then he left.

I had to wash up and when I got back to the floor Russ was fooling with the rig. He had a piece of rag in his hand—too small to do any good—and pretended to be swiping.

"Don't wait for me," he said. "I'll be along later."

But I didn't go and while waiting for him I went over some old clothes in my locker, throwing some away, saving others; and while doing this, I watched him, and what he was doing was sort of saying farewell to the rig. His big hands curved over the brasses, his fingers touching and feeling—the tips of his fingers sensing the feel of the metal that was still warm from the heat of the day's work. Along the smooth shafts his hands slid, gentle and yet strong in their motions, firm and gentle, flowing along the warm steel. He climbed to the controls and let his hands flow over the levers—levers that his hands knew so well; touching each one—sliding his hands along the smooth metal—feeling them—understanding them with the tips of his fingers. And then down again, reaching a hand intimately into a nest of warm gears, leaning the while against the base of the machine, one hand exploring and touching, the other hand pressed against the bare, unpainted steel.

"Come on," I said. "Let's beat it. They'll be closed up before we get there if we don't get a move on."

He came out of it then, and we left.

528

MIDDLE-
WESTERNERS

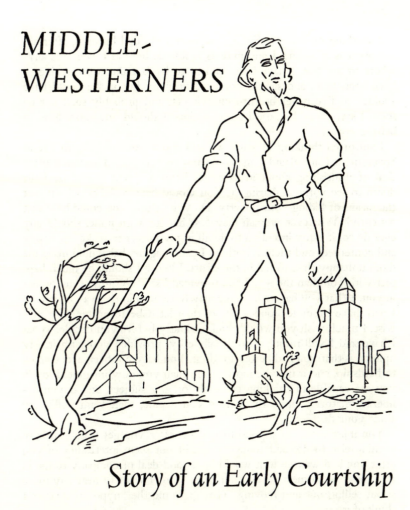

Story of an Early Courtship

by ABRAHAM LINCOLN. *Lincoln's speeches and state papers have long been recognized as models of English prose. Less well known are his familiar letters, especially those written before he became a national celebrity. This epistolary story of a courtship is taken from Carl Sandburg's Abraham Lincoln: The Prairie Years (1926).*

I

MISS MARY S. OWENS.   Springfield, May 7, 1837.

FRIEND MARY: I have commenced two letters to send you before this, both of which displeased me before I got half done, and so I tore them up. The first I thought was not serious enough, and the second was on the other extreme. I shall send this, turn out as it may.

529

This thing of living in Springfield is rather a dull business, after all; at least it is so to me. I am quite as lonesome here as I ever was anywhere in my life. I have been spoken to by but one woman since I have been here, and should not have been by her if she could have avoided it. I've never been to church yet, and probably shall not be soon. I stay away because I am conscious I should not know how to behave myself.

I am often thinking of what we said about your coming to live at Springfield. I am afraid you would not be satisfied. There is a great deal of flourishing about in carriages here, which it would be your doom to see without sharing it. You would have to be poor, without the means of hiding your poverty. Do you believe you could bear that patiently? Whatever woman may cast her lot with mine, should any ever do so, it is my intention to do all in my power to make her happy and contented; and there is nothing I can imagine that would make me more unhappy than to fail in the effort. I know I should be much happier with you than the way I am, provided I saw no signs of discontent in you. What you have said to me may have been in the way of jest, or I may have misunderstood it. If so, then let it be forgotten; if otherwise, I much wish you would think seriously before you decide. What I have said I will most positively abide by, provided you wish it. My opinion is that you had better not do it. You have not been accustomed to hardship, and it may be more severe than you now imagine. I know you are capable of thinking correctly on any subject, and if you deliberate maturely upon this before you decide, then I am willing to abide your decision.

You must write me a good long letter after you get this. You have nothing else to do, and though it might not seem interesting to you after you had written it, it would be a good deal of company to me in this "busy wilderness." Tell your sister I don't want to hear any more about selling out and moving. That gives me the "hypo" whenever I think of it.

Yours, etc.,
LINCOLN.

II

Springfield, August 16, 1837.

FRIEND MARY: You will no doubt think it rather strange that I should write you a letter on the same day on which we parted, and I can only account for it by supposing that seeing you lately makes me think of you more than usual; while at our late meeting we had but few expressions of thoughts. You must know that I cannot see you or think of you with entire indifference; and yet it may be that you are mis-

530

taken in regard to what my real feelings toward you are. If I knew you were not, I should not trouble you with this letter. Perhaps any other man would know enough without further information; but I consider it my peculiar right to plead ignorance, and your bounden duty to allow the plea. I want in all cases to do right, and most particularly so in all cases with women. I want at this particular time, more than anything else, to do right with you; and if I knew it would be doing right, as I rather suspect it would, to let you alone, I would do it. And for the purpose of making the matter as plain as possible, I now say that you can now drop the subject, dismiss your thoughts (if you ever had any) from me forever, and leave this letter unanswered, without calling forth one accusing murmur from me. And I will even go further, and say that if it will add anything to your comfort or peace of mind to do so, it is my sincere wish that you should. Do not understand by this that I wish to cut your acquaintance. I mean no such thing. What I do wish is that our further acquaintance shall depend upon yourself. If such further acquaintance would contribute nothing to your happiness, I am sure it would not to mine. If you feel yourself in any degree bound to me, I am now willing to release you, provided you wish it; while, on the other hand, I am willing and even anxious to bind you faster, if I can be convinced that it will, in any considerable degree, add to your happiness. This, indeed, is the whole question with me. Nothing would make me more miserable than to believe you miserable—nothing more happy than to know you were so.

In what I have now said, I think I cannot be misunderstood, and to make myself understood is the only object of this letter.

If it suits you best to not answer this, farewell. A long life and a merry one attend you. But if you conclude to write back, speak as plainly as I do. There can be neither harm nor danger in saying to me anything you think, just in the manner you think it.

My respects to your sister.

Your friend,
LINCOLN.

III

Springfield, April 1, 1838.

DEAR MADAM:—*

Without apologizing for being egotistical, I shall make the history of so much of my life as has elapsed since I saw you the subject of this letter. And, by the way, I now discover that, in order to give a full and intelligible account of the things I have done and suffered since I saw you, I shall necessarily have to relate some that happened before.

* Mrs. O. H. Browning.

It was, then, in the autumn of 1836 that a married lady of my acquaintance and who was a great friend of mine, being about to pay a
visit to her father and other relatives residing in Kentucky, proposed
to me that on her return she would bring a sister of hers with her on
condition that I would engage to become her brother-in-law with all
convenient despatch. I, of course, accepted the proposal, for you
know I could not have done otherwise, had I really been averse to it;
but privately, between you and me, I was most confoundedly well
pleased with the project. I had seen the said sister some three years before, thought her intelligent and agreeable, and saw no good objection
to plodding life through hand in hand with her. Time passed on, the
lady took her journey sure enough. This stomached me a little; for it
appeared to me that her coming so readily showed that she was a
trifle too willing; but, on reflection, it occurred to me that she might
have been prevailed on by her married sister to come, without anything concerning me ever having been mentioned to her; and so I concluded that, if no other objection presented itself, I would consent to
waive this. All this occurred to me on hearing of her arrival in the
neighborhood; for, be it remembered, I had not yet seen her, except
about three years previous, as above mentioned. In a few days we had
an interview; and, although I had seen her before, she did not look as
my imagination had pictured her. I knew she was over-size, but she
now appeared a fair match for Falstaff. I knew she was called an "old
maid," and I felt no doubt of the truth of at least half of the appellation; but now, when I beheld her, I could not for my life avoid thinking of my mother; and this, not from withered features, for her skin
was too full of fat to permit of its contracting into wrinkles, but from
her want of teeth, weather-beaten appearance in general, and from a
kind of notion that ran in my head that nothing could have commenced at the size of infancy and reached her present bulk in less than
thirty-five or forty years; and, in short, I was not at all pleased with
her. But what could I do? I had told her sister I would take her for
better or for worse; and I made a point of honor and conscience in all
things to stick to my word, especially if others had been induced to
act on it, which in this case I had no doubt they had; for I was now
fairly convinced that no other man on earth would have her, and
hence the conclusion that they were bent on holding me to my bargain.
"Well," thought I, "I have said it, and, be the consequences what they
may, it shall not be my fault if I fail to do it." At once I determined
to consider her my wife; and, this done, all my powers of discovery
were put to work in search of perfections in her which might be fairly
set off against her defects. I tried to imagine her handsome, which, but
for her unfortunate corpulency, was actually true. Exclusive of this,

no woman that I have ever seen has a finer face. I also tried to convince myself that the mind was much more to be valued than the person; and in this she was not inferior, as I could discover, to any with whom I had been acquainted.

Shortly after this, without coming to any positive understanding with her, I set out for Vandalia, when and where you first saw me. During my stay there I had letters from her which did not change my opinion of either her intellect or intention, but on the contrary confirmed it in both.

All this while, although I was fixed, "firm as the surge-repelling rock," in my resolution, I found I was continually repenting the rashness which had led me to make it. Through life I have been in no bondage, either real or imaginary, from the thraldom of which I so much desired to be free. After my return home I saw nothing to change my opinions of her in any particular. She was the same, and so was I. I now spent my time in planning how I might get along through life after my contemplated change of circumstances should have taken place, and how I might procrastinate the evil day for a time, which I really dreaded as much, perhaps more, than an Irishman does the halter.

After all my suffering upon this deeply interesting subject, here I am, wholly, unexpectedly, completely, out of the "scrape"; and now I want to know if you can guess how I got out of it—out, clear, in every sense of the term; no violation of word, honor, or conscience. I don't believe you can guess, and so I might as well tell you at once. As the lawyer says, it was done in the manner following, to-wit: After I had delayed the matter as long as I thought I could in honor do (which, by the way, had brought me round into the last fall), I concluded I might as well bring it to a consummation without further delay; and so I mustered my resolution, and made the proposal to her direct; but, shocking to relate, she answered, No. At first I supposed she did it through an affectation of modesty, which I thought but ill became her under the peculiar circumstances of her case; but on my renewal of the charge, I found she repelled it with greater firmness than before. I tried it again and again, but with the same success, or rather with the same want of success.

I finally was forced to give it up; at which I very unexpectedly found myself mortified almost beyond endurance. I was mortified, it seemed to me, in a hundred different ways. My vanity was deeply wounded by the reflection that I had been too stupid to discover her intentions, and at the same time never doubting that I understood them perfectly; and also that she, whom I had taught myself to believe nobody else would have, had actually rejected me with all my fancied greatness. And, to cap the whole, I then for the first time began to

533

suspect that I was really a little in love with her. But let it all go. I'll try and outlive it. Others have been made fools of by the girls; but this can never with truth be said of me. I most emphatically, in this instance, made a fool of myself. I have now come to the conclusion never again to think of marrying, and for this reason: I can never be satisfied with any one who would be blockhead enough to have me.

When you receive this, write me a long yarn about something to amuse me. Give my respects to Mr. Browning.

Your sincere friend,

A. LINCOLN.

Abraham Lincoln Walks at Midnight

by VACHEL LINDSAY. *Lindsay was born and died at Springfield, Illinois, in the heart of the Lincoln country and for many years now the shrine of the Great Emancipator. He paid more than one tribute in verse to Lincoln but nowhere wrote more eloquently nor more sincerely than in "Abraham Lincoln Walks at Midnight."*

It is portentous, and a thing of state
That here at midnight, in our little town
A mourning figure walks, and will not rest,
Near the old court-house pacing up and down,

Or by his homestead, or in shadowed yards
He lingers where his children used to play,
Or through the market, on the well-worn stones
He stalks until the dawn-stars burn away.

A bronzed, lank man! His suit of ancient black,
A famous high top-hat and plain worn shawl
Make him the quaint great figure that men love,
The prairie-lawyer, master of us all.

He cannot sleep upon his hillside now.
He is among us:—as in times before!
And we who toss and lie awake for long
Breathe deep, and start, to see him pass the door.

His head is bowed. He thinks of men and kings.
Yea, when the sick world cries, how can he sleep?
Too many peasants fight, they know not why,
Too many homesteads in black terror weep.

The sins of all the war-lords burn his heart.
He sees the dreadnaughts scouring every main.
He carries on his shawl-wrapped shoulders now
The bitterness, the folly and the pain.

He cannot rest until a spirit-dawn
Shall come;—the shining hope of Europe free:
A league of sober folk, the Workers' Earth,
Bringing long peace to Cornland, Alp and Sea.

It breaks his heart that kings must murder still,
That all his hours of travail here for men
Seem yet in vain. And who will bring white peace
That he may sleep upon his hill again?

Lucinda Matlock

by EDGAR LEE MASTERS, 1869–   . *The author of the most influential single volume of verse published in America in the twentieth century, Masters was born in Kansas but spent most of his boyhood in the Spoon
and Sangamon river country of Illinois. At Lewistown Masters went to school,
got his first experience in journalism, and studied law. For many years he was
a practicing attorney in Chicago but he never lost his early interest in literature and creative writing. Masters' earliest published books were poetic
dramas and verse in the traditional forms, all relatively unsuccessful. Then
he began to contribute ironic sketches of small-town characters to William
Marion Reedy's Mirror in St. Louis, and eventually these sketches formed the
nucleus of the famous Spoon River Anthology (1915). Although he has since
been prolific as a writer of verse, fiction, and biography, he is best known as
the author of the Spoon River epitaphs. His later work includes the Domesday
Book (1920), Skeeters Kirby (1923), an account of an Illinois boyhood, an
important biography of Vachel Lindsay (1935), and The Sangamon (1942).
"Lucinda Matlock," a portrait of the poet's grandmother, and "Fiddler Jones"
are two of the poems in the anthology.*

I WENT to the dances at Chandlerville,
And played snap-out at Winchester.
One time we changed partners,
Driving home in the moonlight of middle June,
And then I found Davis.
We were married and lived together for seventy years,
Enjoying, working, raising the twelve children,
Eight of whom we lost
Ere I had reached the age of sixty.
I spun, I wove, I kept the house, I nursed the sick,
I made the garden, and for holiday
Rambled over the fields where sang the larks,
And by Spoon River gathering many a shell,
And many a flower and medicinal weed—
Shouting to the wooded hills, singing to the green valleys.
At ninety-six I had lived enough, that is all,
And passed to a sweet repose.
What is this I hear of sorrow and weariness,
Anger, discontent and drooping hopes?
Degenerate sons and daughters,
Life is too strong for you—
It takes life to love Life.

Fiddler Jones

by EDGAR LEE MASTERS

THE earth keeps some vibration going
There in your heart, and that is you.
And if the people find you can fiddle,
Why, fiddle you must, for all your life.
What do you see, a harvest of clover?
Or a meadow to walk through to the river?
The wind's in the corn; you rub your hands
For beeves hereafter ready for market;
Or else you hear the rustle of skirts
Like the girls when dancing at Little Grove.

To Cooney Potter a pillar of dust
Or whirling leaves meant ruinous drouth;
They looked to me like Red-Head Sammy
Stepping it off, to "Toor-a-Loor."
How could I till my forty acres
Not to speak of getting more,
With a medley of horns, bassoons and piccolos
Stirred in my brain by crows and robins
And the creak of a wind-mill—only these?
And I never started to plow in my life
That some one did not stop in the road
And take me away to a dance or picnic.
I ended up with forty acres;
I ended up with a broken fiddle—
And a broken laugh, and a thousand memories,
And not a single regret.

A Plain Man

by EDGAR WATSON HOWE, 1853–1937. *Born in Treaty, Indiana,
Howe had little formal education but learned much about life and literature
through the medium of the printing office. As a boy he accompanied his
family in its westward migration by way of Missouri to Kansas, where he
entered newspaper work. From 1877 to 1911 he was editor and proprietor of
the Atchison Daily Globe, a small-town paper which he made nationally
famous, and thereafter he published E. W. Howe's Monthly (1911–37).
His important position in the development of realistic fiction in America is
due to his novel The Story of a Country Town, which he published privately
in 1883. This grim story of a western prairie community quickly won him
fame. Of his later books only his autobiography, Plain People (1929), seems
significant, although he was long celebrated for his frank and aphoristic
journalism. "A Plain Man" is the opening chapter of his autobiography.*

I COME of a long line of plain people, my immediate ancestor being
Henry Howe, and his father an Englishman who married a Pennsylvania Dutch woman. In reading biography I have observed that while
the writer's ancestors are frequently poor, they have usually been
distinguished in some way, but I cannot recall a distinguished man or
woman related to me. Indeed, in my youth, Howe seemed an uncom-

mon name. A certain Lord Howe early attracted my attention, but I got no comfort from him, as I found in the revolutionary war he fought my countrymen.

Quite recently, while in New Zealand, I met a London man who had visited Pennsylvania long before, and who believed the Pennsylvania Dutch the best people mankind has produced. This compliment for my grandmother greatly pleased me, for though I had long known my grandfather sprang from a notable race, I have been prejudiced against the English, because of unpleasant things they say about us.

I know the addresses of none of my relatives, except a brother who lives next door, and of his children and my own. In visiting homes, I frequently see old pictures, silver or furniture coming down from ancestors. I have nothing of this kind. The only relic I have of my father is an old spectacle case. I have no picture of my mother, nor anything touched by her hands. I do not believe she ever had a picture taken.

Whether my father was born in Pennsylvania or Ohio I do not know certainly, but recall that he had brothers in Ohio, and am rather of the opinion that he originated there. Pennsylvania confuses me somewhat in thinking of his early history, because I occasionally heard him talk Dutch, to amuse his neighbors, who regarded any other language than English as a curiosity. I often heard father say his mother was "the better horse" of his parents, as she ruled the family; a statement which attracted my attention, as I had heard Englishmen are dominant husbands.

His people were farmers, and he engaged in that calling all his life, except that he added school teaching, and later Methodist preaching, as ornaments. I heard little about his relatives in Ohio, beyond a brother Samuel, who late in life concluded to quit tobacco. Soon after he became very ill, and the doctor said that as Uncle Samuel hadn't long to live, he might as well solace his last days with his old bad habit, whereupon my Uncle Samuel began chewing again, and soon recovered his health. I think father told this story as an apology for his own use of tobacco.

We also heard of a sister Susan, who became a clerk in one of the departments in Washington. It was one of our family boasts that she was an expert in her line, but I do not recall what it was, and we may have exaggerated her skill. She had sons who engaged in the development of an addition to the city, but we later heard they "broke up," a misfortune attending a good many of the men of our family. I recall another relative who, in a distant place, was reputed to be a coachman wearing gorgeous livery, but while we were proud of his distinction, we did not boast as much about him as of Aunt Susan. We wondered a good deal that she worked outside her home, as there was no such type where we lived; all the women we knew were what is now called "old-fashioned," and devoted to their homes and men folks, from necessity or pleasure. We knew one husband a little submissive, but his meekness was resented frequently by the other men, who said they would "like to wring her neck," when speaking of his wife, or told what they would do should necessity compel them to deal with her. Lately I met an elderly widow and daughter who spoke so submissively of "Father" that somehow I was reminded of my own boyhood. If at meal time there was a larger number than the table would accommodate, the boys and men ate, and the women and girls waited on them. This custom, tainted with inheritance as far back as Indiana, Ohio, and possibly Pennsylvania, may have influenced me unfairly later when called upon to consider the New Woman.

I do not know the year, but early in life my father moved to Indiana, where he married a woman named Roby. At her death, which seems to have occurred six or seven years later, he married my mother, who brought up two children by his first marriage. I know in a dim sort of way that he lived in a heavily timbered section of Indiana in 1853, where I was born on the third of May of that year. Many years ago I met an elderly man from that section who told me more about it than I had known before. The man said my father was very religious, and at the head of what was called a "Holiness Association," memory of which continued in the vicinity a long time, for no such shouters are known now. But the leader did no shouting himself; he merely inspired it, as an eloquent speaker is rewarded with applause. My informant further said a village called Treaty was later built on the site of our farm, and that it might as well never have been built, as Treaty is now almost no town at all. My informant believed father's first wife was a widow with one child, but I had always regarded this girl as my half sister. She was an uncomfortable incident in my life, as we cordially disliked each other.

I have never been to Treaty since I left it when three years old, in a covered wagon headed West, and have always understood some of our neighbors, including my mother's father and his family, followed us. Of this journey I remember nothing, although I learned something about it later from the talk of my elders. My recollection begins in Harrison county, Missouri, where the travelers found land to suit them. Whether this was wild, and free to anyone, or whether they paid a low price for it, I do not know. They all selected prairie farms, although in the distance could be seen timber land, from which they later hauled their wood. The settlement was called Fairview, and is so known to this day. I have heard my father say that the work of clearing his Indiana farm of heavy trees made him prematurely old, and all

539

the neighbor men talked of the Indiana woods as of a nightmare. I frequently read statements that pioneers should be given credit for hardships in opening up the West. I have always lived in the West, and the many pioneers I have known seemed to feel they were better off than they had been before.

Many years ago I met an old Methodist preacher I had known in Fairview. He told me some gossip about my family that rather disturbed me, and I believe he told it for that purpose; that my father's second marriage occurred within a few months after the death of his first wife, which I have heard him mention as though there had been some criticism among the neighbors, his explanation being that with two little children on his hands, there was nothing else for him to do. When he talked in this strain, my mother said nothing.

Not far from the house we built in Missouri was a combined church and school, in a corner of our field, and I have always understood that my father not only built it, but preached without charge for his services. He was the only pastor the church ever had while I lived in its vicinity. In addition, he frequently rode about on horseback to preach and pray in the homes of the more distant neighbors. I often accompanied him on these journeys, which usually began Saturday night, but we were always home early Monday to begin the week's work.

I visited a good many families in the course of these journeys, but do not recall many of them distinctly, except that as a rule they lived in one-room houses built of logs. On one side was a fireplace, in which they cooked. On the opposite side of the one big room were three four-poster beds, and under each one a trundle-bed for the children. The beds had no springs, but were "corded" with ropes. When the beds began to sag, it was one of the chores of the men and boys to tighten the ropes, and place fresh straw in the mattresses. Feather beds were common in the better families, the feathers being obtained from geese, ducks, and sometimes chickens. I distinctly recall the women occasionally renovating the feathers in the beds, by steaming.

The women cooked in the fireplaces by means of hanging pots, and in what they called "spiders," great skillets with legs. The skillets had iron tops, and live coals were placed on these, to assist in the cooking. At bed time father and I were compelled to undress in the presence of the family, and my first recollection of politeness is of parents and children steadily gazing into the fireplace while we were exposed.

In addition to his circuit riding, every summer father held camp meetings, where collected people from a large territory. I always went with him when he selected the sites, and helped clean up the brush for the platforms and benches, and the covered wagons and tents in which the people lived five or six days.

540

The first wickedness I ever heard of came with attendance on these camp meetings, for on their edges collected strange men who sold keg beer and whiskey in bottles, and their patrons engaged in rough language and fighting. In our immediate neighborhood all were at least afraid of the church, but here I found a good many who were not. Being curious and active, I went everywhere, and heard men ridicule the services for which we were assembled.

All the other children joined the church early, but I never did, nor was I invited to. This seems remarkable, but it is my recollection; I was always so much of an unbeliever in the religion of my father and his neighbors that they let me alone. I recall that my brother Jim, after joining the church, was moaning in bed the night it happened, because of his sins, and I mocked him. He soon lost his temper, and we engaged in a fight. Fortunately my father was out of the house, and only mother caught us at it. On hearing the cause of the disturbance, she joined me in laughing about it. Jim soon forgot his anger, and laughed with us. Many years afterwards he used to say that if he went to the bad place, I would be responsible, as he once started right, and that I made such fun of him that he again became a sinner.

My mother was Elizabeth Irwin, and, so far as I am able to recall, members of her family were not religious. Her father was Charles Irwin, a quiet man who made shingles, and his wife doctor for all our neighbors, with backwoods experience her only diploma. Except my mother, who was weakly, their children were all large men and women, and disposed to good looks. Father was a smaller man than the Irwins, and may have been disposed to envy their finer stature, for he always said they were shiftless.

From going about with him, I had very intimate knowledge of the people attending his religious services, and some of them acted in a way that seemed queer to me. These I mocked in private, greatly to the amusement of my brothers and sisters, and other children with whom we came in contact. I recall giving a performance of this kind on one occasion, my brothers having agreed to do my evening chores as reward for the impiety. Suddenly my mother appeared, and as I loved her, and wasn't afraid, I continued. I recall to this day that she laughed good-naturedly at my imitations of characters she knew as well as I did. Afterwards, when I engaged in mocking our neighbors, some of the children would run to call mother, if father was not at home. But she frequently warned me not to let father catch me, which he did once, and her warning was well timed, for he gave me a whipping.

That was a day of child whipping, and in strong contrast with the indulgence of to-day. Whether the old plan was better than the new I am not able to make up my mind. I learn, and come to conclusions, slowly; when I reach my final days I shall say of a great many other things: "I do not know which is best." If the old Fairview men could come back now, and see present changed conditions as to children and women, I often wonder what they would say. Probably they would be as helpless as the men are now.

A vivid recollection of my childhood is of fathers and mothers leading their children off, the children screaming: "I'll be good! I'll be good!" One night, when we were moving from Indiana to Missouri, a big boy named Joe Adams resisted his father when he attempted to whip him. Man and boy were almost equally matched, as they struggled and fought, the boy screaming he was too old to be whipped, and had repeatedly given warning he would not submit to it again. The most pitiful picture in my memory is of the boy's mother hysterically crying, and not daring to interfere. One man tried to end the fight by assisting in subduing the boy, but Bill Scott pushed him back and stopped the fight, telling the father he should be ashamed of himself.

There was a good deal of excitement about the affair several days, Mr. Adams saying he would conquer his son if it was the last act of his life. The boy left camp that night, but next day we heard he was with the men and boys who were driving loose stock in the rear. Joe Adams was not a bad boy, and food was sent him by the women. He didn't appear in camp for a week, but came in timidly one night at the end of that time. He first stopped and talked with the women and children at the wagon farthest from his own, where his parents sat, the father surly and the mother in tears. Joe slowly advanced from wagon to wagon toward his mother, and finally stood beside her as she sat in an old hickory-bottomed chair they had brought along. She put her arms around him and sobbed so hysterically all could hear. The father said nothing, and was motionless, looking at the ground; which may have been due to Bill Scott, who had approached, and was standing almost within reach of the boy. Finally the father arose and walked out into the dark, crying, as we all were. The mother tidied Joe up a little, and then went into the family wagon and brought out some special delicacy she had been saving for him. That night Joe slept in his usual place, and we heard no more of the affair. Bill Scott was a professional farm hand, and it was said he would never amount to anything else; but he was the most popular member of the party, and the most capable. He helped the tired women with a gentleness and politeness I sincerely admired, since I had never seen anything of the kind before, and his sympathies were always with the children when they were imposed on. All the men were a little afraid of him in an argument or in wrestling.

My father ceased whipping me only after I went to work for myself, at about the age of thirteen, but I have observed that I have been whipped steadily since when deserving it, by the frowns and grumblings of the neighbors. The old Arabs said the whip was sent from heaven for our good; certainly we never escape it.

My father was a cross, dissatisfied man, and often whipped me, but conscience-whipping was worse: I was saved from ruin not by a switch laid on by an angry, unreasonable father, but by conscience-whipping. Let those I have wronged know I have been punished. I believe in sinners brought to repentance by worldly experience that sin does not pay; our best people are sinners with sufficient experience to realize that a sinner is, first of all, a fool.

I was brought up in my own father's family like a bound-boy, for if he ever had affection for me, I never knew it. He drove me to work early, and kept me steadily at it. One of my recollections is of his saying that I had been an expense to him until I was seven years old. I think I was naturally a lazy boy, and now confess his driving me to work was a benefit. Early in life I so thoroughly acquired the habit of industry that I have never recovered from it: to this day I work rapidly. Almost every afternoon, now that I am old, I work in the field for exercise with my brother, an industrious man. Frequently he says to me:

"Don't work so fast! You will hurt yourself."

I learned the habit to quickly complete my daily tasks, that I might have time to play. I could not have been of much assistance on the farm from the age of seven, when I was put to work, until eleven, when we moved to town, but I had my regular hours, as the others had. We threshed wheat by placing it in circular piles, and driving horses over it. My work was to drive the horses. We cut wheat with old-fashioned cradles, and I carried jugs of water to the cradlers. I stripped sorghum in the field, helped when the juice was pressed out, and later in boiling to turn it into molasses. I husked the down-row at corn-picking time. Another of my regular duties was to help mother make tallow candles, using a tin mold holding six. I have seen houses lighted at night with a rag burning in a saucer of grease, but we always used candles. Another of my duties was to grate corn meal for mush. Probably I did this only in the fall when the ears were young and tender, but at this distance it seems to me I did it every day. We had what we called a "long killing" of hogs in the fall, and a "short killing" in the spring, and I helped in these operations. When the lard was rendered out in a great kettle, what we called "cracklings" were left, and the children ate them with relish. "Cracklings" were the first luxury I knew. I do not believe I ever heard of Christmas while in the country, and we had few luxuries except a taffy made from sorghum molasses.

543

Sometimes we were permitted to parch corn, grind it in a coffee mill, and eat it with cream.

It always seemed to me father was unnecessarily harsh with all of us. Once I had a toothache; possibly one of the more stubborn of my first set. He knocked it out with a cold chisel and hammer. It was an efficient way, but nearly killed me, and he whipped me for crying. The whippings were not brutal, but painful and humiliating, and I scarcely escaped a day. My Aunt Sarah, who was at our house a good deal, and whom I sincerely loved, used to say that when I was whipped, I dropped to the ground at the first stroke, and screamed as though losing my life. This caused father to let up somewhat, and Aunt Sarah used to laugh at my way of protecting myself, from which I imagined she did not think I was very severely punished. My half brother Jim was stubborn, and would not cry, which only resulted in the switch being laid on harder.

I am disposed to believe that in managing me father did what he considered his duty. He was brought up, no doubt, as he brought me up, and knew no other way. I am grateful that I have found life less harsh than his had been. He seemed to be a natural backwoodsman, and usually left a community when it became civilized.

He was a singer, and used the talent in his religious services. I think he really had an unusually agreeable voice. There is a famous Italian baritone named Amato. I have his records for the Victrola, and frequently play them, for the voices of the two men were actually much alike, although one was world-famous, and the other an uncultured backwoodsman. He could write music, and arranged duets in which my childish treble fitted well with his mature voice. I am sure he took me with him on his trips because of my ability to assist him in his songs, for my company did not seem to please him at any other time.

Shadows of men and women come and go in my memory, but I am able to recall distinctly only a few of our neighbors at Fairview. I specially love the memory of George Meek and his family, who lived nearest us. I was frequently permitted to go to their house, after I had completed my tasks, and most of the enjoyment I knew while on the farm I have them to thank for, although my mother's brother, Joe Irwin, and my half brother Jim, both older than I, were kind to me.

The first special friend I ever had was one of the Meek boys, but it was so long ago, and there were so many of the Meeks, that I do not recall whether it was Henry, Pascal or Abram. I have not seen him in more than sixty years: if he had wife or children, I do not know it, I am so completely separated from my youth.

I must have been a very little boy when Mary Meek died, and my grief was profound, as we both attended the first Fairview school.

Somehow I recall that her body was moved in the graveyard and I was present; I recall the dripping coffin almost slipping back as it was removed from the grave, and some men getting under it: that was an early terror of my life, and I cannot forget it. Of all the other people and incidents at Fairview, there is something unpleasant to recall, but of George Meek and members of his family I have only pleasant recollections.

Not long ago I read the biography of Henry Wallace, whose son became Secretary of Agriculture. I was greatly impressed, because Henry Wallace's family was as religious as ours, and lived in a rural section; I think in New England. But the neighbors and parents were kind, and they lived comfortably, pleasantly, usefully and intelligently. I believe we might have so lived at Fairview, for all seemed intelligent enough: I do not recall a fool in the neighborhood. But there was some dominating influence that was wrong. I have often regretted George Meek did not control in all Fairview as he did in his own household.

Another neighbor I recall distinctly was named Veazey Price, famous because he had no children. Large families of children were the rule when I was young, and so Veazey Price and Aunt Mahala, his wife, who had none, attracted our wonder. After moving to town I knew a man who had only one child, but a married couple with no children at all was unknown to me until many years later. It is common enough in these days, but I never hear of such a case even now without wondering how it happened.

During the winter there was school in the church, but the only teacher I recall distinctly was a man named Hayworth, who did not belong in our neighborhood. I very dimly remember another, a young woman, and that she taught in a log schoolhouse before the church was built. My Uncle Nate, only eight months older than myself, always came by our house in the morning, and we went to school together. At noon we exchanged special things from our dinner baskets. Once he brought a kind of pie of which I was fond, and I traded him something for a bite of it. Without my knowing it he had placed his finger under the pie, to mark the size of the bite, which he had decided was to be small. With a view of taking more than he intended, I grabbed quickly, and bit his finger. He yelled dismally, and we were both whipped by Hayworth. The last time I saw Nate he was still carrying the scar, and showed it to me.

He was about twenty-five at the time, and I thought him a very creditable young man. The farmers were having one of their regular revolts when I visited him, and Nate was one of their spokesmen. I recall fierce arguments I had with him, in which he triumphed, for he was an excellent talker, and I was surprised at his fund of information:

probably most of it manufactured for the speaking tours in which he was then engaged. I do not know whether he is now living or dead. . . .

One of my impressions is that I never learned anything at school, which I quit for good at an early age. I never studied grammar at all, and common fractions so discouraged me I could not get the faintest glimmer of their meaning. Somehow I learned to read at home before being sent to school: I suppose I wondered what the books about the house were for, and, being lonely, slowly and in stumbling fashion found out, in time adding ability to read letters. When father went to the nearest post office, he returned with mail for half the neighborhood, and I was sent to deliver it. I remember that on these trips geese hissed at me in houseyards, and that I dreaded them as much as cross dogs. If those to whom I delivered letters could not read them, I gave assistance, causing much astonishment. There was so much in the letters about gloomy woods, and toil and hard times that I formed a poor opinion of the country the Fairview people had come from: only recently I passed through Indiana rapidly on a railroad train, and was astonished to find it so beautiful.

My education actually began when I went to work in a printing office, at about the age of eleven. A typesetter cannot avoid learning to spell correctly. If I made too many errors in my proof galleys, I was whipped for them, and, desiring to avoid the whippings, learned to spell as correctly as I could. Likewise I learned the construction of sentences. From that day to this I have been educated as a natural process, without particularly desiring it: I do not remember that I ever had an ambition for a great education. All the best men I have known have been educated, but many of them have attended primary schools only briefly, and college not at all.

Such education as I have was acquired in sentences found here and there in reading; in suggestions from conversation. Both print and conversation are pretty generally uninteresting, even trifling, but every day one encounters wise sayings. I piece these together, and retain them: I have never read a dull book because it has been highly recommended as educational. If a book does not interest me, it can do me no good; I do not believe in the man who wrote it. I am willing to read anything well written; a book need not agree with my own conclusions to interest me: every writer frequently exposes brass when trying to show gold. I do not wish to retain an unsound opinion; only opinions that will stand the test of opposition. Nor do I wish to encounter arguments on my side of the case; I have already supplied them. If anyone can demonstrate I am on the wrong road, he has obliged me.

We had books in our house at Fairview, but I remember none of them save the blue-back McGuffey school readers, and "Watson's

Commentaries," an exposition of the Bible. I presume father greatly admired this author, since he gave me his name. Where the "Edgar" came from I do not know, but have been satisfied with it: it seems to me Edgar is a better name than either Edward or Edwin, if one is to go through life known as "Ed." Quite recently I went back to Fairview to visit the old farm. The house in which we lived then stood in the middle of a pasture, and had been abandoned long before. In going through it I found on a shelf in the pantry a piece of *The Christian Advocate*, yellow with age, and pasted to one of the boards. Probably it had been placed there by my mother, as I recall no other publication we received; our literature was made up of *The Christian Advocate*, religious books and McGuffey's readers.

Ours was a remote section, and I have wondered since there was so little game, outside of prairie chickens, so numerous that every morning at certain seasons we could hear their drumming on the prairie. One Sunday morning, after a heavy fall of snow, we awoke to find a tree near the house full of prairie chickens. Father hastily fired both barrels of a shotgun into the tree, and killed eleven. It was a long joke in the neighborhood that a preacher fired a gun on Sunday, but father rather enjoyed it, having killed so many, though he said that in his excitement he forgot the sacredness of the day. The tree was called a silver maple, and we children believed that when it was old enough to bear, the fruit would be silver dollars.

Old Lee, a renter on our farm, made long trips looking for deer, but I never heard of his finding any. My brother Jim and I were once sent on a journey, with team and wagon, to sell a beef hide. On our return we suddenly encountered a great flock of wild turkeys. It took us two weeks to induce father to permit us to look for them. He gave us a double-barreled rifle for the purpose, a gun of a type I have never seen since: one barrel above the other, and we had one load each, and no more. The upper barrel was considered the better, and somehow I traded Jim out of this. After a weary walk of hours, we came into the vicinity where we had seen the turkeys. Then we crawled a long distance, and looked into the place where the game had been. I think I was never more surprised in my life than when I found no turkeys there. On our way home we concluded to fire our bullets at a mark, and Jim got his hand under the lower hammer while sighting, and hurt himself. He was always so good a boy, and so sincere a friend, that I let him fire my upper barrel if he would quit crying.

There were many quail in the neighborhood, and Old Lee, our renter, was able to catch them, on damp days, with a net. One Sunday I went with him on such an expedition, and my share of the catch was twenty. My sister Sarah Jane "told on" me, and for the impiety I was not allowed to eat any of the quail, though other members of the family did. In addition, I received a whipping. I think of Old Lee now as the first unusual man I ever knew: without knowing why, I liked to be with him. He was poor, and somewhat shiftless, but generally said to be "as sharp as tacks," and of amiable disposition.

Father was easily the leading man of his neighborhood, and never lacked prosperity. He owned a good deal of wild land, and his farming operations were quite extensive. The only five-hundred-dollar bill I ever saw is a recollection from that remote day, and he had it. In thinking of the old days in my life, I always conclude we had plenty to wear and eat, and that my father was a good provider, although he grumbled a good deal about it. One of our staple articles of food we called "thickened milk," which I heard of quite recently for the first time in sixty years, in connection with the statement from an old lady that it would be good for me now.

Father's brother Joseph once came to our house on a visit, when I was called "a good chunk of a boy." The Missouri county in which we lived adjoined Iowa, and my Uncle Joseph came from that state. He looked almost exactly like father, except that he was better dressed, and gentler in manner. He told of his children, and the incidents suggested that theirs was a more contented family than ours. I recall that after he went away, father grumbled about the debasing luxury in which Uncle Joseph and his family evidently lived. When Uncle Joseph returned home, I sent his son some childish possession I was fond of, and he never replied in any way. He wrote me recently, acknowledging eighty-one years, but said nothing about my gift. I find myself still a little resentful.

I never saw any other member of my father's family except an Uncle Jacob, who came from Illinois on a visit. Uncle Jacob looked like father, too, and was also gentler. I have always loved this early memory of Uncle Joseph and Uncle Jacob, because they looked like my father, and had a gentleness I believe their brother might have practiced to his advantage.

While living on the Fairview farm I do not recall a purely social gathering. Occasionally the children "stayed all night" with each other, and, if they misbehaved, were whipped and sent home to learn better manners, it being generally admitted it was the duty as well as privilege of a householder to correct all children under his roof. Once a play was given in the church by the young men: an actor was carried in to represent a murdered man, and an oration delivered over his body, but there was so much indignation that thereafter the occasional spelling and singing schools were given up. I recall but one occasion when father and mother visited a neighbor's house in the evening, and I was whipped on their return, Sarah Jane having "told on me." My offense was connected with parching field corn; we had not heard of the popping kind. I doubt if there is in the world to-day a neighborhood as melancholy as ours was about the time of the beginning of the Civil War.

I note that in my old age I do not like salads, so widely recommended for health. I did not know them in my youth; I was brought up on meat, gravy, bread, potatoes, milk, butter and pie, with green corn, water-melons, and wild blackberries and plums in season. Occasionally we made trips to the woods for nuts. There were no bearing fruit trees on our farm when I lived there, although occasionally father made long journeys to older settlements, and returned with apples. Gardens were not common in my youth; I do not believe we had one on the farm, nor when we moved to town.

I often wonder when I first heard of a bathroom; I did not actually live in a house with one until I had a family of my own. In the country we were taught to wash our faces and hands, but I do not recall the Saturday night bath in the kitchen which so amuses modern town people. In Fairview we had the same sanitary arrangements we had when moving from Indiana to Missouri, in covered wagons. I speak elsewhere of coming of a long line of plain people. Probably I was plainer in early youth than most of my readers.

"Tradin' Joe"

by JAMES WHITCOMB RILEY, 1849–1916. *Famous for his Hoosier dialect verse and often called "the poet laureate of democracy," Riley was born in Greenfield, Indiana. Disinclined to follow his father's legal profession, Riley lived a wandering life for some years as itinerant sign-painter, entertainer, and assistant to patent-medicine shows. This experience taught him much about the psychology, tastes, and idiom of his audience. He contributed his first dialect verse to the Indianapolis Journal under the pseudonym of Benjamin F. Johnson of Boone, and some of this poetry was collected in The Old Swimmin' Hole and 'Leven More Poems (1883). As his fame increased he published more books, he appeared on the lecture platform with Eugene Field and Bill Nye, and in 1915 his birthday was declared an official holiday in Indiana. Riley is best known for his dialect verse, such as "Tradin' Joe," "When the Frost Is on the Punkin," "The Old Swimmin' Hole," and "Little Orphant Annie." That he did not need to resort to the vulgate is proved by such poems as "A Life-Lesson" and "Bereaved."*

549

I'M one o' these cur'ous kind o' chaps
You think you know when you don't, perhaps!
I hain't no fool—ner I don't p'tend
To be so smart I could rickommend
Myself fer a *congerssman*, my friend!—
But I'm kind o' betwixt-and-between, you know,—
One o' these fellers 'at folks calls "slow."
And I'll say jest here I'm kind o' queer
Regardin' things 'at I *see* and *hear*,—
Fer I'm *thick* o' hearin' *sometimes*, and
It's hard to git me to understand;
But other times it hain't, you bet!
Fer I don't sleep with both eyes shet!

I've swapped a power in stock, and so
The neighbers calls me "Tradin' Joe"—
And I'm goin' to tell you 'bout a trade,—
And one o' the best I ever made:

Folks has gone so fur's to say
'At I'm well fixed, in a *worldly* way,
And *bein'* so, and a *widower*,
It's not su'prisin', as you'll infer,
I'm purty handy among the sect—
Widders especially, rickollect!
And I won't deny that along o' late
I've hankered a heap fer the married state—
But some way o' 'nother the longer we wait
The harder it is to discover a mate.

Marshall Thomas,—a friend o' mine,
Doin' some in the tradin' line,
But a'most too *young* to know it all—
On'y at *picnics* er some *ball!*—
Says to me, in a banterin' way,
As we was a-loadin' stock one day,—
"You're a-huntin' a wife, and I want you to see
My girl's mother, at Kankakee!—
She hain't over forty—good-lookin' and spry,
And jest the woman to fill your eye!
And I'm a-goin' there Sund'y,—and now," says he,
"I want to take you along with *me;*
And you marry *her*, and," he says, "by 'shaw!

You'll hev me fer yer son-in-law!"
I studied a while, and says I, "Well, I'll
First have to see ef she suits my style;
And ef she does, you kin bet your life
Your mother-in-law will be my wife!"

Well, Sund'y come; and I fixed up some—
Putt on a collar—I did, by gum!—
Got down my "plug," and my satin vest—
(You wouldn't know me to see me dressed!—
But any one knows ef you got the clothes
You kin go in the crowd wher' the best of 'em goes!)
And I greeced my boots, and combed my hair
Keerfully over the bald place there;
And Marshall Thomas and me that day
Eat our dinners with Widder Gray
And her girl Han'!***

    Well, jest a glance
O' the widder's smilin' countenance,
A-cuttin' up chicken and big pot-pies,
Would make a man hungry in Paradise!
And passin' p'serves and jelly and cake
'At would make an *angel's* appetite *ache!*—
Pourin' out coffee as yaller as gold—
Twic't as much as the cup could hold—
La! it was rich!—And then she'd say,
"Take some o' *this!*" in her coaxin' way,
Tell ef I'd been a hoss I'd 'a' *foundered*, shore,
And jest dropped dead on her white-oak floor!

Well, the way I talked would 'a' done you good,
Ef you'd 'a' been there to 'a' understood;
Tel I noticed Hanner and Marshall, they
Was a-noticin' me in a cur'ous way;
So I says to myse'f, says I, "Now, Joe,
The best thing fer you is to jest go slow!"
And I simmered down, and let them do
The bulk o' the talkin' the evening through.

And Marshall was still in a talkative gait
When he left, that evening—tolable late.
"How do you like her?" he says to me;
Says I, "She suits, to a 't-y-*Tee*'!"

And then I ast how matters stood
With him in the *opposite* neighberhood?
"Bully!" he says; "I ruther guess
I'll finally git her to say the 'yes.'
I named it to her to-night, and she
Kind o' smiled, and said, *'She'd see'*—
And that's a purty good sign!" says he:
"Yes," says I, "you're ahead o' *me!*"
And then he laughed, and said, "*Go in!*"
And patted me on the shoulder ag'in.

Well, ever sense then I've been ridin' a good
Deal through the Kankakee neighberhood;
And I make it convenient sometimes to stop
And hitch a few minutes, and kind o' drop
In at the widder's, and talk o' the crop
And one thing o' 'nother. And week afore last
The notion struck me, as I drove past,
I'd stop at the place and state my case—
Might as well do it at first as last!

I felt first-rate; so I hitched at the gate,
And went up to the house; and, strange to relate,
Marshall Thomas had dropped in, *too.*—
"Glad to see you, sir, how do you do?"
He says, says he! Well—it *sounded queer;*
And when Han' told me to take a cheer,
Marshall got up and putt out o' the room—
And motioned his hand fer the *widder* to come.
I didn't say nothin' fer quite a spell,
But thinks I to myse'f, "There's a dog in the well!"
And Han' *she* smiled so cur'ous at me—
Says I, "What's up?" And she says, says she,
"Marshall's been at me to marry ag'in,
And I told him 'no,' jest as you come in."
Well, somepin' o' 'nother in that girl's voice
Says to me, "Joseph, here's your choice!"
And another minute her guileless breast
Was lovin'ly throbbin' ag'in my vest!—
And then I kissed her, and heerd a smack
Come like a' echo a-flutterin' back,
And we looked around, and in full view
Marshall was kissin' the widder, too!
Well, we all of us laughed, in our glad su'prise,

Tel the tears come *a-streamin'* out of our eyes!
And when Marsh said " 'Twas the squarest trade
That ever me and him had made,"
We both shuck hands, 'y jucks! and swore
We'd stick together ferevermore.
And old 'Squire Chipman tuck us the trip:
And Marshall and me's in pardnership!

Mr. and Mrs. Babbitt

by SINCLAIR LEWIS. *Lewis' novels are famous for their meticulous realism and their recording of daily routine. There is no better example than the opening pages of* Babbitt *with its introduction of a businessman and his family in their home on Floral Heights, a section of Zenith.*

I

THE towers of Zenith aspired above the morning mist; austere towers of steel and cement and limestone, sturdy as cliffs and delicate as silver rods. They were neither citadels nor churches, but frankly and beautifully office-buildings.

The mist took pity on the fretted structures of earlier generations: the Post Office with its shingle-tortured mansard, the red brick minarets of hulking old houses, factories with stingy and sooted windows, wooden tenements colored like mud. The city was full of such grotesqueries, but the clean towers were thrusting them from the business center, and on the farther hills were shining new houses, homes—they seemed—for laughter and tranquillity.

Over a concrete bridge fled a limousine of long sleek hood and noiseless engine. These people in evening clothes were returning from an all-night rehearsal of a Little Theater play, an artistic adventure considerably illuminated by champagne. Below the bridge curved a railroad, a maze of green and crimson lights. The New York Flyer boomed past, and twenty lines of polished steel leaped into the glare.

In one of the skyscrapers the wires of the Associated Press were closing down. The telegraph operators wearily raised their celluloid eye-shades after a night of talking with Paris and Peking. Through the building crawled the scrubwomen, yawning, their old shoes slapping. The dawn mist spun away. Cues of men with lunch-boxes clumped toward the immensity of new factories, sheets of glass and hollow tile, glittering shops where five thousand men worked beneath one roof, pouring out the honest wares that would be sold up the Euphrates and across the veldt. The whistles rolled out in greeting a chorus cheerful as the April dawn; the song of labor in a city built—it seemed—for giants.

II

There was nothing of the giant in the aspect of the man who was beginning to awaken on the sleeping-porch of a Dutch Colonial house in that residential district of Zenith known as Floral Heights.

His name was George F. Babbitt. He was forty-six years old now, in April, 1920, and he made nothing in particular, neither butter nor shoes nor poetry, but he was nimble in the calling of selling houses for more than people could afford to pay.

His large head was pink, his brown hair thin and dry. His face was babyish in slumber, despite his wrinkles and the red spectacle-dents on the slopes of his nose. He was not fat but he was exceedingly well fed; his cheeks were pads, and the unroughened hand which lay helpless upon the khaki-colored blanket was slightly puffy. He seemed prosperous, extremely married and unromantic; and altogether unromantic appeared this sleeping-porch, which looked on one sizable elm, two respectable grass-plots, a cement driveway, and a corrugated iron garage. Yet Babbitt was again dreaming of the fairy child, a dream more romantic than scarlet pagodas by a silver sea.

For years the fairy child had come to him. Where others saw but Georgie Babbitt, she discerned gallant youth. She waited for him, in the darkness beyond mysterious groves. When at last he could slip away from the crowded house he darted to her. His wife, his clamoring friends, sought to follow, but he escaped, the girl fleet beside him, and they crouched together on a shadowy hillside. She was so slim, so white, so eager! She cried that he was gay and valiant, that she would wait for him, that they would sail—

Rumble and bang of the milk-truck.

Babbitt moaned, turned over, struggled back toward his dream. He could see only her face now, beyond misty waters. The furnace-man slammed the basement door. A dog barked in the next yard. As Babbitt sank blissfully into a dim warm tide, the paper-carrier went by whistling, and the rolled-up *Advocate* thumped the front door. Babbitt roused, his stomach constricted with alarm. As he relaxed, he was pierced by the familiar and irritating rattle of some one cranking a Ford: snap-ah-ah, snap-ah-ah, snap-ah-ah. Himself a pious motorist, Babbitt cranked with the unseen driver, with him waited through taut hours for the roar of the starting engine, with him agonized as the roar ceased and again began the infernal patient snap-ah-ah—a round, flat sound, a shivering cold-morning sound, a sound infuriating and inescapable. Not till the rising voice of the motor told him that the Ford was moving was he released from the panting tension. He glanced once at his favorite tree, elm twigs against the gold patina of sky, and fumbled for sleep as for a drug. He who had been a boy very credulous of life was no longer greatly interested in the possible and improbable adventures of each new day.

He escaped from reality till the alarm-clock rang, at seven-twenty.

III

It was the best of nationally advertised and quantitatively produced alarm-clocks, with all modern attachments, including cathedral chime, intermittent alarm, and a phosphorescent dial. Babbitt was proud of being awakened by such a rich device. Socially it was almost as creditable as buying expensive cord tires.

He sulkily admitted now that there was no more escape, but he lay and detested the grind of the real-estate business, and disliked his family, and disliked himself for disliking them. The evening before, he had played poker at Vergil Gunch's till midnight, and after such holidays he was irritable before breakfast. It may have been the tremendous home-brewed beer of the prohibition-era and the cigars to which that beer enticed him; it may have been resentment of return from this fine, bold man-world to a restricted region of wives and stenographers, and of suggestions not to smoke so much.

From the bedroom beside the sleeping-porch, his wife's detestably cheerful "Time to get up, Georgie boy," and the itchy sound, the brisk and scratchy sound, of combing hairs out of a stiff brush.

He grunted; he dragged his thick legs, in faded baby-blue pajamas, from under the khaki blanket; he sat on the edge of the cot, running his fingers through his wild hair, while his plump feet mechanically felt for his slippers. He looked regretfully at the blanket—forever a suggestion to him of freedom and heroism. He had bought it for a camping trip which had never come off. It symbolized gorgeous loafing, gorgeous cursing, virile flannel shirts.

He creaked to his feet, groaning at the waves of pain which passed behind his eyeballs. Though he waited for their scorching recurrence, he looked blurrily out at the yard. It delighted him, as always; it was the neat yard of a successful business man of Zenith, that is, it was perfection, and made him also perfect. He regarded the corrugated iron garage. For the three-hundred-and-sixty-fifth time in a year he reflected, "No class to that tin shack. Have to build me a frame garage. But by golly it's the only thing on the place that isn't up-to-date!" While he stared he thought of a community garage for his acreage development, Glen Oriole. He stopped puffing and jiggling. His arms were akimbo. His petulant, sleep-swollen face was set in harder lines. He suddenly seemed capable, an official, a man to contrive, to direct, to get things done.

On the vigor of his idea he was carried down the hard, clean, unused-looking hall into the bathroom.

Though the house was not large it had, like all houses on Floral Heights, an altogether royal bathroom of porcelain and glazed tile and metal sleek as silver. The towel-rack was a rod of clear glass set in nickel. The tub was long enough for a Prussian Guard, and above the set bowl was a sensational exhibit of tooth-brush holder, shaving-brush holder, soap-dish, sponge-dish, and medicine-cabinet, so glittering and so ingenious that they resembled an electrical instrument-board. But the Babbitt whose god was Modern Appliances was not pleased. The air of the bathroom was thick with the smell of a heathen toothpaste. "Verona been at it again! 'Stead of sticking to Lilidol, like I've re-peat-ed-ly asked her, she's gone and gotten some confounded stinkum stuff that makes you sick!"

The bath-mat was wrinkled and the floor was wet. (His daughter Verona eccentrically took baths in the morning, now and then.) He slipped on the mat, and slid against the tub. He said "Damn!" Furiously he snatched up his tube of shaving-cream, furiously he lathered, with a belligerent slapping of the unctuous brush, furiously he raked his plump cheeks with a safety-razor. It pulled. The blade was dull. He said, "Damn—oh—oh—damn it!"

He hunted through the medicine-cabinet for a packet of new razor-blades (reflecting, as invariably, "Be cheaper to buy one of these dinguses and strop your own blades"), and when he discovered the packet, behind the round box of bicarbonate of soda, he thought ill of his wife for putting it there and very well of himself for not saying "Damn." But he did say it, immediately afterward, when with wet and soap-slippery fingers he tried to remove the horrible little envelope and crisp clinging oiled paper from the new blade.

Then there was the problem, oft-pondered, never solved, of what to do with the old blade, which might imperil the fingers of his young. As usual, he tossed it on top of the medicine-cabinet, with a mental note that some day he must remove the fifty or sixty other blades that were also temporarily piled up there. He finished his shaving in a growing testiness increased by his spinning headache and by the emptiness in his stomach. When he was done, his round face smooth and streamy and his eyes stinging from soapy water, he reached for a towel. The family towels were wet, wet and clammy and vile, all of them wet, he found, as he blindly snatched them—his own face-towel, his wife's, Verona's, Ted's, Tinka's, and the lone bath-towel with the huge welt of initial. Then George F. Babbitt did a dismaying thing. He wiped his face on the guest-towel! It was a pansy-embroidered trifle which always hung there to indicate that the Babbitts were in the best Floral Heights society. No one had ever used it. No guest had ever dared to. Guests secretively took a corner of the nearest regular towel.

He was raging, "By golly, here they go and use up all the towels, every doggone one of 'em, and they use 'em and get 'em all wet and sopping, and never put out a dry one for me—of course, I'm the goat! —and then I want one and— I'm the only person in the doggone house that's got the slightest doggone bit of consideration for other people and thoughtfulness and consider there may be others that may want to use the doggone bathroom after me and consider—"

He was pitching the chill abominations into the bath-tub, pleased by the vindictiveness of that desolate flapping sound; and in the midst his wife serenely trotted in, observed serenely, "Why Georgie dear, what are you doing? Are you going to wash out the towels? Why, you needn't wash out the towels. Oh, Georgie, you didn't go and use the guest-towel, did you?"

It is not recorded that he was able to answer.

For the first time in weeks he was sufficiently roused by his wife to look at her.

IV

Myra Babbitt—Mrs. George F. Babbitt—was definitely mature. She had creases from the corners of her mouth to the bottom of her chin, and her plump neck bagged. But the thing that marked her as having passed the line was that she no longer had reticences before her husband, and no longer worried about not having reticences. She was in a petticoat now, and corsets which bulged, and unaware of being seen in bulgy corsets. She had become so dully habituated to married life that in her full matronliness she was as sexless as an anemic nun. She was a good woman, a kind woman, a diligent woman, but no one, save perhaps Tinka her ten-year-old, was at all interested in her or entirely aware that she was alive.

After a rather thorough discussion of all the domestic and social aspects of towels she apologized to Babbitt for his having an alcoholic headache; and he recovered enough to endure the search for a B.V.D.

undershirt which had, he pointed out, malevolently been concealed among his clean pajamas.

He was fairly amiable in the conference on the brown suit.

"What do you think, Myra?" He pawed at the clothes hunched on a chair in their bedroom, while she moved about mysteriously adjusting and patting her petticoat and, to his jaundiced eye, never seeming to get on with her dressing. "How about it? Shall I wear the brown suit another day?"

"Well, it looks awfully nice on you."

"I know, but gosh, it needs pressing."

"That's so. Perhaps it does."

"It certainly could stand being pressed, all right."

"Yes, perhaps it wouldn't hurt it to be pressed."

"But gee, the coat doesn't need pressing. No sense in having the whole darn suit pressed, when the coat doesn't need it."

"That's so."

"But the pants certainly need it, all right. Look at them—look at those wrinkles—the pants certainly do need pressing."

"That's so. Oh, Georgie, why couldn't you wear the brown coat with the blue trousers we were wondering what we'd do with them?"

"Good Lord! Did you ever in all my life know me to wear the coat of one suit and the pants of another? What do you think I am? A busted bookkeeper?"

"Well, why don't you put on the dark gray suit to-day, and stop in at the tailor and leave the brown trousers?"

"Well, they certainly need— Now where the devil is that gray suit? Oh, yes, here we are."

He was able to get through the other crises of dressing with comparative resoluteness and calm.

His first adornment was the sleeveless dimity B.V.D. undershirt, in which he resembled a small boy humorlessly wearing a cheesecloth tabard at a civic pageant. He never put on B.V.D.'s without thanking the God of Progress that he didn't wear tight, long, old-fashioned undergarments, like his father-in-law and partner, Henry Thompson. His second embellishment was combing and slicking back his hair. It gave him a tremendous forehead, arching up two inches beyond the former hair-line. But most wonder-working of all was the donning of his spectacles.

There is character in spectacles—the pretentious tortoise-shell, the meek pince-nez of the school teacher, the twisted silver-framed glasses of the old villager. Babbitt's spectacles had huge, circular, frameless lenses of the very best glass; the ear-pieces were thin bars of gold. In them he was the modern business man; one who gave orders to clerks and drove a car and played occasional golf and was scholarly in regard to Salesmanship. His head suddenly appeared not babyish but weighty, and you noted his heavy, blunt nose, his straight mouth and thick, long upper lip, his chin overfleshy but strong; with respect you beheld him put on the rest of his uniform as a Solid Citizen.

The gray suit was well cut, well made, and completely undistinguished. It was a standard suit. White piping on the V of the vest added a flavor of law and learning. His shoes were black laced boots, good boots, honest boots, standard boots, extraordinarily uninteresting boots. The only frivolity was in his purple knitted scarf. With considerable comment on the matter to Mrs. Babbitt (who, acrobatically fastening the back of her blouse to her skirt with a safety-pin, did not hear a word he said), he chose between the purple scarf and a tapestry effect with stringless brown harps among blown palms, and into it he thrust a snake-head pin with opal eyes.

A sensational event was changing from the brown suit to the gray the contents of his pockets. He was earnest about these objects. They were of eternal importance, like baseball or the Republican Party. They included a fountain pen and a silver pencil (always lacking a supply of new leads) which belonged in the righthand upper vest pocket. Without them he would have felt naked. On his watch-chain were a gold penknife, silver cigar-cutter, seven keys (the use of two of which he had forgotten), and incidentally a good watch. Depending from the chain was a large, yellowish elk's-tooth—proclamation of his membership in the Benevolent and Protective Order of Elks. Most significant of all was his loose-leaf pocket note-book, that modern and efficient note-book which contained the addresses of people whom he had forgotten, prudent memoranda of postal money-orders which had reached their destinations months ago, stamps which had lost their mucilage, clippings of verses by T. Cholmondeley Frink and of the newspaper editorials from which Babbitt got his opinions and his polysyllables, notes to be sure and do things which he did not intend to do, and one curious inscription—D.S.S.D.M.Y.P.D.F.

But he had no cigarette-case. No one had ever happened to give him one, so he hadn't the habit, and people who carried cigarette-cases he regarded as effeminate.

Last, he stuck in his lapel the Boosters' Club button. With the conciseness of great art the button displayed two words: "Boosters—Pep!" It made Babbitt feel loyal and important. It associated him with Good Fellows, with men who were nice and human, and important in business circles. It was his V.C., his Legion of Honor ribbon, his Phi Beta Kappa key.

With the subtleties of dressing ran other complex worries. "I feel

559

kind of punk this morning," he said. "I think I had too much dinner last evening. You oughtn't to serve those heavy banana fritters."

"But you asked me to have some."

"I know, but— I tell you, when a fellow gets past forty he has to look after his digestion. There's a lot of fellows that don't take proper care of themselves. I tell you at forty a man's a fool or his doctor—I mean, his own doctor. Folks don't give enough attention to this matter of dieting. Now I think— Course a man ought to have a good meal after the day's work, but it would be a good thing for both of us if we took lighter lunches."

"But Georgie, here at home I always do have a light lunch."

"Mean to imply I make a hog of myself, eating down-town? Yes, sure! You'd have a swell time if you had to eat the truck that new steward hands out to us at the Athletic Club! But I certainly do feel out of sorts, this morning. Funny, got a pain down here on the left side—but no, that wouldn't be appendicitis, would it? Last night, when I was driving over to Verg Gunch's, I felt a pain in my stomach, too. Right here it was—kind of a sharp shooting pain. I— Where'd that dime go to? Why don't you serve more prunes at breakfast? Of course I eat an apple every evening—an apple a day keeps the doctor away—but still, you ought to have more prunes, and not all these fancy doodads."

"The last time I had prunes you didn't eat them."

"Well, I didn't feel like eating 'em, I suppose. Matter of fact, I think I did eat some of 'em. Anyway— I tell you it's mighty important to— I was saying to Verg Gunch, just last evening, most people don't take sufficient care of their diges—"

"Shall we have the Gunches for our dinner, next week?"

"Why sure; you bet."

"Now see here, George: I want you to put on your nice dinner-jacket that evening."

"Rats! The rest of 'em won't want to dress."

"Of course they will. You remember when you didn't dress for the Littlefields' supper-party, and all the rest did, and how embarrassed you were."

"Embarrassed, hell! I wasn't embarrassed. Everybody knows I can put on as expensive a Tux. as anybody else, and I should worry if I don't happen to have it on sometimes. All a darn nuisance, anyway. All right for a woman, that stays around the house all the time, but when a fellow's worked like the dickens all day, he doesn't want to go and hustle his head off getting into the soup-and-fish for a lot of folks that he's seen in just reg'lar ordinary clothes that same day."

"You know you enjoy being seen in one. The other evening you admitted you were glad I'd insisted on your dressing. You said you

560

felt a lot better for it. And oh, Georgie, I do wish you wouldn't say 'Tux.' It's 'dinner-jacket.' "

"Rats, what's the odds?"

"Well, it's what all the nice folks say. Suppose Lucile McKelvey heard you calling it a 'Tux.' "

"Well, that's all right now! Lucile McKelvey can't pull anything on me! Her folks are common as mud, even if her husband and her dad are millionaires! I suppose you're trying to rub in *your* exalted social position! Well, let me tell you that your revered paternal ancestor, Henry T., doesn't even call it a 'Tux.'! He calls it a 'bobtail jacket for a ringtail monkey,' and you couldn't get him into one unless you chloroformed him!"

"Now don't be horrid, George."

"Well, I don't want to be horrid, but Lord! you're getting as fussy as Verona. Ever since she got out of college she's been too rambunctious to live with—doesn't know what she wants—well, I know what she wants!—all she wants is to marry a millionaire, and live in Europe, and hold some preacher's hand, and simultaneously at the same time stay right here in Zenith and be some blooming kind of a socialist agitator or boss charity-worker or some damn thing! Lord, and Ted is just as bad! He wants to go to college, and he doesn't want to go to college. Only one of the three that knows her own mind is Tinka. Simply can't understand how I ever came to have a pair of shilly-shallying children like Rone and Ted. I may not be any Rockefeller or James J. Shakespeare, but I certainly do know my own mind, and I do keep right on plugging along in the office and— Do you know the latest? Far as I can figure out, Ted's new bee is he'd like to be a movie actor and— And here I've told him a hundred times, if he'll go to college and law-school and make good, I'll set him up in business and— Verona just exactly as bad. Doesn't know what she wants. Well, well, come on! Aren't you ready yet? The girl rang the bell three minutes ago."

V

Before he followed his wife, Babbitt stood at the westernmost window of their room. This residential settlement, Floral Heights, was on a rise; and though the center of the city was three miles away—Zenith had between three and four hundred thousand inhabitants now—he could see the top of the Second National Tower, an Indiana limestone building of thirty-five stories.

Its shining walls rose against April sky to a simple cornice like a streak of white fire. Integrity was in the tower, and decision. It bore its strength lightly as a tall soldier. As Babbitt stared, the nervousness was soothed from his face, his slack chin lifted in reverence. All he articulated was "That's one lovely sight!" but he was inspired by the rhythm of the city; his love of it renewed. He beheld the tower as a temple-spire of the religion of business, a faith passionate, exalted, surpassing common men; and as he clumped down to breakfast he whistled the ballad "Oh, by gee, by gosh, by jingo" as though it were a hymn melancholy and noble.

Modern Gothic

by VINCENT SHEEAN, 1899– . *James Vincent Sheean was born in Christian County, Illinois, and was educated at the University of Chicago— an experience which he described vividly in "Modern Gothic." Going at once into journalism he became a distinguished foreign correspondent in Africa and Europe. He is the author of the celebrated* Personal History *(1935), from which the account of his education is taken, and of such novels as* Sanfelice *(1936),* Not Peace but a Sword *(1939), and* Bird of the Wilderness *(1941).*

THE armistice came when I was eighteen. What it meant to the war generation I can only imagine from the stories they tell; to me it meant that we in the University of Chicago, that mountain range of twentieth-century Gothic near the shores of Lake Michigan, went out of uniform and into civilian clothes.

The world has changed so much that it seems downright indecent to tell the truth: I was sorry when the war ended. I fumed with disappointment on the night of the false armistice—the celebrated night when the American newspapers reported the end of the war some days before it happened. We were all patriots then. We knew nothing about that horror and degradation which our elders who had been through the war were to put before us so unremittingly for the next fifteen years. There were millions of us, young Americans between the ages of fifteen or sixteen and eighteen or nineteen, who cursed freely all through the middle weeks of November. We felt cheated. We had been put into uniform with the definite promise that we were to be trained as officers and sent to France. In my case, as in many others, this meant growing up in a hurry, sharing the terrors and excitements of a life so various, free and exalted that it was worth even such hardships as studying trigonometry. So we went into uniform and marched about the place from class to class like students in a military academy; listened to learned professors lecturing about something called "War Aims"; lived in "barracks"; did rifle drill. The rifles were dummies, and the "barracks" were only the old dormitories rechristened, but such details made little difference. We played at being soldiers for a few months with tremendous seriousness, and then the glorious uproar to which we had been preparing our approach suddenly died down. Our part of the war had been a prelude to something that did not take place.

And when demobilization came at last the prospect of returning to the regular life of the University had become repellent to me. I had nobody to persuade but my mother, who was still too thankful for the Armistice to make many objections. Consequently I went job hunting and spent three months as secretary to a millionaire builder and real estate operator in the Chicago financial district. It was there, hanging out a window above the crevasse of LaSalle Street, that I watched the Black Hawk Division come home. Waving flags and the thump of a military march were enough to stir me to any extravagance; we all shouted and waved and winked back the hysterical tears. Those were patriotic days.

My employer was an odious little man who had quarreled with his wife and disinherited his son because the latter wanted to go on the stage. He was a brilliant entrepreneur, the little man: he used to point with pride to the ceilings of the skyscraper in which he had his office, saying, "That ceiling is a good six inches shallower than the law allows. You can always arrange things if you know how. I got eight extra storeys into this building by that little detail." When I inquired if the building was likely to fall down he sniffed contemptuously. "Buildings don't fall down," he said. The building did start to fall down some years later, was condemned and demolished. By an unfortunate accident, its builder was not buried under the ruins.

He sent me on one occasion to collect rents from the impoverished tenants of a village he owned in Indiana. It was a horrible experience from which I escaped as quickly as I could, but the thought of it came back to me for years. The tenants of the wretched little Indiana town worked in a coal mine belonging to my employer when they worked at all, but they had not worked for many months. They lived in houses belonging to him (if you could call such hovels houses) and bought their food from stores belonging to him. I was to collect what I could of the back rent owed on the disgraceful shacks in which they were obliged to live. I was a failure at the job, for the sight of the life into which children were there being born disorganized whatever efficiency I possessed as a secretary. That day in the little mining town was my

563

introduction to capitalism at work, and it filled me, even then, with disgust. I blamed the busy little entrepreneur as well as the system of which he was a part, and it was not long before the idea of continuing to work for him became insupportable. "Business" (if this was business) bored, irked and revolted me, and I determined to do whatever I could to avoid being involved in it again.

In the spring of 1919, therefore, I went back to the University and stayed on throughout the summer to make up for lost time. My education up to then had been a sorry failure. I had never made any headway with science, mathematics or the classical languages. Of the first two I remembered nothing; of the second I remembered just one Greek sentence, *enteuthen exelaunei* ("and the next day he marched onward")—this not because it had any stirring significance for me, but because it marked the welcome end of nearly every chapter in the Anabasis.

I had derived, it was true, considerable pleasure of a low order from some other academic pursuits in my first two years of college. I had come to the University knowing some Italian, German, and French (particularly French), and could easily make a better showing in these subjects than my contemporaries. My favourite trick had been to register for courses in which I was unlikely to encounter anything I did not already know. Such conduct was lazy and dishonest, but you could make out a good case for the theory that young people were all lazy and dishonest when they could be. Certainly what the undergraduates called "snaps" (i. e., courses easy to get through without undue effort) were always crowded in my day at the University. The football players, the social lights, the pretty co-eds, and all the other students who regarded study as an inconvenient detail in college life, rushed to inscribe themselves for "snap" courses. I was in a more advantageous position than some of my fellows for wasting time, since more courses were "snaps" for me. I could go to a series of lectures on Victorian Prose, for example, and be confident of hearing nothing new; similarly, in French, with the novels of Victor Hugo or the plays of Molière. I had read altogether too much in the two languages, thanks to a bookish childhood. There was thus a group of studies open to me at the University in which I could, without working or learning, impress my instructors sufficiently to make a good record.

More than two years of my three and a half at the University of Chicago had already been wasted in this way. It was a kind of confidence game of which the victim was, of course, myself. I did well enough in the subjects I already knew to make up for my failures in the subjects I did not know and was too lazy to study. I was too undisciplined, too indolent, and too dishonest to force myself to learn

what did not interest me. And it was not until that summer of 1919 that
I began to realize the silliness of such an approach to what ought to be
one of the great experiences of a life. The University of Chicago in
summer was invaded by hordes of earnest men and women from the
smaller colleges and schools of the Middle West, working towards
their master's or their doctor's degree. These thin, spectacled myrmi-
dons, humpbacked from carrying armfuls of books up and down
academic steps for many years, filled the cool gray corridors and
covered the green lawns I had always thought reserved for pretty girls
and long-legged youths. The summer school, I discovered, was an
altogether different affair from the ordinary academic year. If you
tried to talk to a summer student during a lecture, a cold glance through
glittering spectacles was the only reply. The brilliant hot sun of a
Chicago July threw into merciless relief all the unloveliness of these
dank visitors from the provincial colleges of Indiana, Wisconsin,
Illinois, Iowa, and Minnesota. Their presence was somehow unbecom-
ing, both to their surroundings and to the general fitness of things.
I resented them for two or three weeks, and on the few occasions when
I saw my vacationing friends, the undergraduates who had finished
their college year in June, we were exceedingly witty about the looks,
manners, lives, and minds of the pitiable summer students. There were
probably not a half a dozen of these bookworms, we calculated, who
could dance the fox trot decently.

But as the summer study advanced I became more and more uncomfortable about them. They were not beautiful, but neither were
they ignorant. They were always putting me to shame, somehow or
other. I was not to remember much about most of the studies of that
summer; only one was vivid in retrospect. It was a fairly advanced
course in French—the poetry of Victor Hugo, all of it, including every
pitiless line of *La Légende des Siècles*. The instructor was a visiting
bigwig from one of the Eastern universities, a Frenchman with a
German name. He used to conduct the course in an informal fashion,
lecturing some of the time, reading occasionally, and starting discussions whenever the spirit moved him. It was assumed that students
in such a course as this would be mature and educated enough to know
something besides the actual subject matter itself. Comparisons were
always popping up, were constantly invited. Most of the students—
there may have been twelve or fifteen, men and women—were well
past thirty, and probably all of them taught French literature somewhere or other. In that company, through July and August, I first
began to be ashamed of my evil ways, and no amount of smug scorn
for the bookworms could disguise the fact.

"Vous trouverez ici sans doute que Hugo a beaucoup emprunté à

Chateaubriand; n'est-ce pas, Mademoiselle?" the professor would inquire innocently, smiling across his desk at an eager spinster from Indiana. And then off she would go, talking about Hugo and Chateaubriand in a French accent that would have been incomprehensible to either of those gentlemen—but talking, just the same, with information and intelligence. The professor would argue with her; others would join in; and it appalled me that I could not even follow their battle from afar. I had never read a word of Chateaubriand; my interest in Christianity was almost nonexistent; I had no real idea why it had ever seemed intellectually important to Victor Hugo or to anybody else. And I looked at the summer students in amazement. Their excitement over such subjects actually brought colour to their wan faces; they could smile, make jokes, go through all the movements of living organisms when their attention was aroused.

My salvation was that the instructor was a Frenchman. If he had been an American or an Englishman he would have seen at once that my glibness in French was a sheer accident, and that I actually understood nothing of the turmoil through which Victor Hugo had lived and written. But, being French, the professor had a natural prejudice in favor of hearing his language pronounced correctly. In spite of all their knowledge and interest, most of the students in this course had abominable accents; it seemed to be a rule among American school teachers. I had learned French so young that all the laziness in the world could never rob me of a fairly good pronunciation. Consequently, when I had occasion to read some of Victor Hugo's detested verses aloud, the professor would lean back in his chair with satisfaction. This, combined with a prudent silence when the discussions were out of my depth, gave the good man the idea that I really knew something of the subject, and I finished the course with an unjustifiably handsome record.

But something important happened to me during the summer of 1919, thanks chiefly to the Hugo poems. I had been realizing with increasing clarity, week after week, the superficial character of my own mind. I was nineteen, and I knew nothing. The fact that I could speak a sort of French had nothing to do with me; what credit there might be for that should have gone to the devout and kindly Irish priest who had tutored me in it for years. Of the actual meaning of French literature I knew far less than the scrubbiest high-school teacher from Iowa. The struggles of men's minds—whether of contemporary minds or of those like Chateaubriand's and Hugo's, long gone to dust—meant nothing to me at all. I had existed without realizing that it seriously mattered to anybody what men believed, or under what form of government, in what structure of society, they lived. The summer's study gave me no love for the poetry of Victor Hugo: on the contrary, the mere thought of *La Légende des Siècles* made me feel slightly uneasy for years to come. But I did derive from it some idea of what the process of literature could be—some hint of the stormy sincerity in which minds like Hugo's sought for the truth. The suggestion, however dim, was sufficient reward for the boredom of reading what then seemed to me an intolerable quantity of pompous, overstuffed verse.

My ideas of what I might get out of the University thereafter submitted to rearrangement. Words could no longer suffice: I understood Hugo's words well enough, the upholstery of his mind, but it was the mind itself that escaped me. If a mind of Hugo's quality was incomprehensible, how could I expect to know anything about the rarer minds that did (even then) seem to me most worth the effort of comprehension: Molière, Racine, Shakespeare? And, even in a world I found tiresome beyond my powers of resistance, the world of the "Victorian Prose Writers," what could I hope to understand by words alone? It was clear, after the Hugo experience, that literature involved something at once more complex and more ordinary, more closely related to the whole life of mankind, than the science of stringing words together in desirable sequences, however fascinating the contemplation of such patterns might seem to a bookish and word-conscious nature.

Nothing could be learned about literature by studying literature: that was what it came to. Courses in literature seldom took on the vitality of that special Hugo course with its special participants. In general, they were either arranged to suit average students with no interest in the subject, or specialists with an interest so minute that it was (in my view) equivalent to no interest at all. I had no desire to count the feminine endings in the lines of the Canterbury Tales. What I wanted to know—in so far as I really wanted to know anything about them—was why the Canterbury Tales were written; what mysterious springs existed in the mind and heart of a man named Geoffrey Chaucer to bring forth such a particular stream of articulated language; what the world was like for which he wrote, in which he lived, and what was his particular struggle with it. Professors did sometimes try to convey this sort of information; but it was obvious that they had obtained it elsewhere and were passing it on in capsule form. Where had they obtained it?

History, perhaps, was the answer; philosophy might be part of it.

That autumn, when the regular academic year began, I switched from the faculties of English literature and Romance languages to those of history and philosophy. And perhaps if this had been the arrangement two years before I might not have wasted quite so much time.

I am not suggesting that I became a model of industry and scholarship promptly at nine o'clock on the morning of registration day in October, 1919. I still frittered away a good three quarters or four fifths of my time, still registered for an occasional course of lectures that could be treated cavalierly as a "snap" (History of Venetian Art, for instance). But at least I was not behaving altogether as if the University were a country club. Both in history and in philosophy I learned something—not much, but something. There was a course in Plato that conveyed meaning to me; another, on the German idealists, I found as exciting as a romantic novel. But perhaps the most interesting of all—the one to be recalled most often in subsequent life—was a term of lectures and reading on the Decline of the Ottoman Empire.

This—an "advanced," and therefore a rather small, class—was in charge of an inspired teacher. I never knew what made the difference between a good and a bad teacher, but I did know that Ferdinand Schevill was a superlatively good one. He was a German, short and rather formidable in appearance, with eyeglasses and a neatly trimmed Vandyke beard. His university was Heidelberg or Bonn, I believe, and yet he had none of that pedantry which is supposed to be the vice of German scholarship. When he led us through the immense and complicated story of the decay that fell upon Suleiman's empire after the seventeenth century he did not try to treat it microscopically as an isolated phenomenon. He talked about the Arabs, the Turks, the Balkan peoples, as if they were alive; and they soon began to come to life for me. Schevill's system was to allow his students to read at will through the whole literature of the subject, and therefrom to choose, halfway through the course, a particular aspect for further reading and a final paper. I began to read everything I could find about the Asiatic empire of the Turks. Almost from the first day that side of the Bosphorus seemed to me of greater interest than this. I extended my researches to the files of newspapers and magazines, and when it came time to choose, I took for my term paper the history of the Wahabite movement.

An odder choice for a nineteen-year-old undergraduate at the University of Chicago would be hard to imagine. Ibn es-Sa'ud was then almost unknown to the Western world, and the literature on the Wahabi was scarce indeed. I read everything I could find in English, French, or German, and performed the best piece of honest work I had ever done. For a few weeks, while I was reading in the library, I nearly persuaded myself that I was living in Arabia, and sometimes the vast cloaks and camel turbans of the Bedawin seemed more real than the swishing skirts of the co-eds going by. Later on I obtained permission to go down into the stacks of that huge library—steel stacks with glass floors running among them, layer upon layer. The world's knowledge lay there like a sunken continent swimming in subaqueous light, and through its fields I ranged more or less at will. My interest in Islam, such as it was, began that year, and what I learned in Schevill's course was never wholly forgotten. If other teachers had been like him, other subjects as vivid to me as the disintegration of Turkey became, I might have learned more in my long sojourn under the sham-Gothic towers.

Mary White

by WILLIAM ALLEN WHITE, 1868–1944. *William Allen White demonstrated that it was not necessary to go to New York to become a nationally famous journalist. As editor of The Emporia Gazette for almost fifty years he expressed the views of the Kansas farmer, businessman, and housewife with such cogency and clearness that the nation was glad to listen. White was born in Emporia and educated at the University of Kansas. In 1895 he became proprietor of The Emporia Gazette, but even a full-time newspaper job did not prevent him from engaging in other kinds of writing. His short stories were collected in The Real Issue and Other Stories (1896) and In Our Town (1906); among his novels are A Certain Rich Man (1909) and In the Heart of a Fool (1918). In later years he wrote biographies of Woodrow Wilson (1924) and Calvin Coolidge (1938), and he collected some of his thoughts on the role of the Middle West in The Changing West (1939). For a number of years he was a member of the editorial board of the Book-of-the-Month Club. The tribute to his daughter originally appeared in The Emporia Gazette, May 17, 1921.*

THE Associated Press reports carrying the news of Mary White's death declared that it came as the result of a fall from a horse. How she would have hooted at that! She never fell from a horse in her life. Horses have fallen on her and with her—"I'm always trying to hold 'em in my lap," she used to say. But she was proud of few things, and one was that she could ride anything that had four legs and hair. Her death resulted not from a fall, but from a blow on the head which fractured her skull, and the blow came from the limb of an overhanging tree on the parking.

The last hour of her life was typical of its happiness. She came home from a day's work at school, topped off by a hard grind with the copy on the High School Annual, and felt that a ride would refresh her. She climbed into her khakis, chattering to her mother about the work she was doing, and hurried to get her horse and be out on the dirt roads for the country air and the radiant green fields of the spring. As she rode through the town on an easy gallop, she kept waving at passersby. She knew everyone in town. For a decade the little figure with the long pigtail and the red hair ribbon has been familiar on the streets of Emporia, and she got in the way of speaking to those who nodded at her. She passed the Kerrs, walking the horse, in front of the Normal Library, and waved at them; passed another friend a few hundred feet further on, and waved at her. The horse was walking and as she turned into North Merchant street she took off her cowboy hat, and the horse swung into a lope. She passed the Tripletts and waved her cowboy hat at them, still moving gaily north on Merchant street. A Gazette carrier passed—a High School boy friend—and she waved at him, but with her bridle hand; the horse veered quickly, plunged into the parking where the low-hanging limb faced her, and, while she still looked back waving, the blow came. But she did not fall from the horse; she slipped off, dazed a bit, staggered and fell in a faint. She never quite recovered consciousness.

But she did not fall from the horse, neither was she riding fast. A year or so ago she used to go like the wind. But that habit was broken, and she used the horse to get into the open to get fresh, hard exercise, and to work off a certain surplus energy that welled up in her and needed a physical outlet. That need has been in her heart for years. It was back of the impulse that kept the dauntless, little brown-clad figure on the streets and country roads of this community and built into a strong, muscular body what had been a frail and sickly frame during the first years of her life. But the riding gave her more than a body. It released a gay and hardy soul. She was the happiest thing in the world. And she was happy because she was enlarging her horizon. She came to know all sorts and conditions of men; Charley O'Brien, the traffic cop, was one of her best friends. W. L. Holtz, the Latin teacher, was another, Tom O'Connor, farmer-politician, and Rev. J. H. J. Rice, preacher and police judge, and Frank Beach, music master, were her special friends, and all the girls, black and white, above the track and below the track, in Pepville and Stringtown, were among her acquaintances. And she brought home riotous stories of her adventures. She loved to rollick; persiflage was her natural expression at home. Her humor was a continual bubble of joy. She seemed to think in the hyperbole and metaphor. She was mischievous without malice, as full of faults as an old shoe. No angel was Mary White, but an easy girl to live with, for she never nursed a grouch five minutes in her life.

With all her eagerness for the out-of-doors, she loved books. On her table when she left her room were a book by Conrad, one by Galsworthy, "Creative Chemistry" by E. E. Slosson, and a Kipling book. She read Mark Twain, Dickens and Kipling before she was 10—all of their writings. Wells and Arnold Bennett particularly amused and diverted her. She was entered as a student in Wellesley in 1922; was assistant editor of the High School Annual this year, and in line for election to the editorship of the Annual next year. She was a member of the executive committee of the High School Y.W.C.A.

Within the last two years she had begun to be moved by an ambition to draw. She began as most children do by scribbling in her school books, funny pictures. She bought cartoon magazines and took a course—rather casually, naturally, for she was, after all, a child, with no strong purposes—and this year she tasted the first fruits of success by having her pictures accepted by the High School Annual. But the thrill of delight she got when Mr. Ecord, of the Normal Annual, asked her to do the cartooning for that book this spring, was too beautiful for words. She fell to her work with all her enthusiastic heart. Her drawings were accepted, and her pride—always repressed by a lively sense of the ridiculousness of the figure she was cutting—was a really gorgeous thing to see. No successful artist ever drank a deeper draught of satisfaction than she took from the little fame her work was getting among her schoolfellows. In her glory, she almost forgot her horse—but never her car.

For she used the car as a jitney bus. It was her social life. She never had a "party" in all her nearly seventeen years—wouldn't have one; but she never drove a block in the car in her life that she didn't begin to fill the car with pick-ups! Everybody rode with Mary White—white and black, old and young, rich and poor, men and women. She liked nothing better than to fill the car full of long-legged High School boys and an occasional girl, and parade the town. She never had a "date," nor went to a dance, except once with her brother, Bill, and the "boy proposition" didn't interest her—yet. But young people—great, spring-breaking, varnish-cracking, fender-bending, door-sagging car-loads of "kids"—gave her great pleasure. Her zests were keen. But the most fun she ever had in her life was acting as chairman of the committee that got up the big turkey dinner for the poor folks at the county home; scores of pies, gallons of slaw; jam, cakes, preserves, oranges and a wilderness of turkey were loaded in the car and taken to the county home. And, being of a practical turn of mind, she risked her own Christmas dinner by staying to see that the poor folks actually got it all. Not that she was a cynic; she just disliked to tempt folks. While there she found a blind colored uncle, very old, who could do nothing but make rag rugs, and she rustled up from her school friends

571

rags enough to keep him busy for a season. The last engagement she tried to make was to take the guests at the county home out for a car ride. And the last endeavor of her life was to try to get a rest room for colored girls in the High School. She found one girl reading in the toilet, because there was no better place for a colored girl to loaf, and it inflamed her sense of injustice and she became a nagging harpy to those who she thought could remedy the evil. The poor she had always with her, and was glad of it. She hungered and thirsted for righteousness; and was the most impious creature in the world. She joined the Congregational Church without consulting her parents; not particularly for her soul's good. She never had a thrill of piety in her life, and would have hooted at a "testimony." But even as a little child she felt the church was an agency for helping people to more of life's abundance, and she wanted to help. She never wanted help for herself. Clothes meant little to her. It was a fight to get a new rig on her; but eventually a harder fight to get it off. She never wore a jewel and had no ring but her High School class ring, and never asked for anything but a wrist watch. She refused to have her hair up; though she was nearly 17. "Mother," she protested, "you don't know how much I get by with in my braided pigtails that I could not, with my hair up." Above every other passion of her life was her passion not to grow up, to be a child. The tom-boy in her, which was big, seemed to loathe to be put away forever in skirts. She was a Peter Pan, who refused to grow up.

Her funeral yesterday at the Congregational Church was as she would have wished it; no singing, no flowers save the big bunch of red roses from her Brother Bill's Harvard classmen—Heavens, how proud that would have made her! and the red roses from the Gazette force—in vases at her head and feet. A short prayer, Paul's beautiful essay on "Love" from the Thirteenth Chapter of First Corinthians, some remarks about her democratic spirit by her friend, John H. J. Rice, pastor and police judge, which she would have deprecated if she could, a prayer sent down for her by her friend, Carl Nau, and opening the service the slow, poignant movement from Beethoven's Moonlight Sonata, which she loved, and closing the service a cutting from the joyously melancholy first movement of Tschaikowski's Pathetic Symphony, which she liked to hear in certain moods on the phonograph; then the Lord's Prayer by her friends in the High School.

That was all.

For her pallbearers only her friends were chosen; her Latin teacher, W. L. Holtz; her High School principal, Rice Brown; her doctor, Frank Foncannon; her friend, W. W. Finney; her pal at the Gazette office, Walter Hughes; and her brother Bill. It would have made her smile to know that her friend, Charley O'Brien, the traffic cop, had been transferred from Sixth and Commercial to the corner near the church to direct her friends who came to bid her goodbye.

A rift in the clouds in a gray day threw a shaft of sunlight upon her coffin as her nervous, energetic little body sank to its last sleep. But the soul of her, the glowing, gorgeous, fervent soul of her, surely was flaming in eager joy upon some other dawn.

The Mayos at Work

by HELEN CLAPESATTLE, 1908— . *Miss Clapesattle was born in Fort Wayne, Indiana, and was graduated from Oberlin College in 1934. In 1937 she received her M.A. degree in history from the University of Minnesota. Since then she has been assistant editor and editor for the University of Minnesota Press. In 1941 she published* The Doctors Mayo *(a condensed version of which was published in the Atlantic Monthly), a book which not only traces the achievements of William Worrall Mayo and his two famous sons at Rochester, Minnesota, but is also substantially a history of American medicine during much of the nineteenth and twentieth centuries. The excerpt included here shows the personality as well as the scientific accomplishments of the well-known surgeons.*

THERE was as much to be heard as seen in a Mayo clinic, for the brothers accompanied their operations with a running clinical commentary, reviewing the case history and the diagnosis, describing the conditions they found, and explaining what they did and why. In these talks they ranged through the whole of medical science, literature, and history, giving freely the convictions born of their wide reading and experience and, according to one listener, bringing out "points in surgical anatomy and physiology in a way so plain and forceful that one marvels at the barrenness of textbook literature on such matters."

At the operating table they illustrated with unforgettable object lessons the principles of differential diagnosis, antemortem pathology, and early surgery that filled their formal papers. No man could attend Dr. Will's clinics very often without witnessing such a demonstration as this: The history, read by the assistant while the anesthetic was given, was a classic one of "stomach trouble"—years of treatment for indigestion without relief—yet when incision brought the stomach into view it looked perfectly normal.

"You have heard the history, gentlemen, but you see this stomach.

In my opinion there is nothing wrong with it; the trouble is somewhere else. If I am right in a few minutes you will notice a spasm of the pylorus." Shortly a spasm of the pyloric muscles was evident to all.

"That does net tell us where the trouble is, but it is not in the stomach. I will see if it is in the appendix." And he pulled into view a badly diseased appendix.

Then as he proceeded to remove the appendix and close the abdomen he told them of his own experience. Thinking that the pylorospasm in connection with a history of stomach pain meant something functionally wrong with the stomach, he had performed gastroenterostomy in several cases with no relief of symptoms, but when he reoperated and took out a bad appendix or gallbladder the symptoms vanished. He had learned the lesson, but he was still undoing many a gastroenterostomy some other surgeon had lately done for stomach trouble that was not in the stomach. The next day the men might watch him undo just such a gastroenterostomy, or they might see him operate on a "dyspeptic" who had a normal stomach but a gallbladder full of stones.

Such lessons went home as they would in no amount of public speaking without demonstration, so that soon a paper on stomach or gallbladder disease at any medical meeting was likely to call forth a flock of stories beginning "The first time I understood . . . was when I saw Dr. Will Mayo in his clinic . . ." Dr. Ernest Hall of British Columbia did not exaggerate when he wrote:

"We are enjoying at the Mayos' clinic the third revelation within the history of the present generation of surgeons. Thirty years ago Birmingham dispelled the fallacy of pelvic cellulitis, and in its place gave us a new pathology of pus tubes. Twenty years ago America put inflammation of the bowels out of business, and gave us the interesting appendix to juggle with; and today catarrh of the stomach and chronic dyspepsia, through the genius of Dr. Will Mayo, are fast becoming matters of history, and in their place he is giving us a pathology of organic stomach, liver, and duodenal disease as definite and accurate as that which we possess of the lower abdomen. What Lawson Tait was to the pelvis, Will Mayo is to the upper abdomen."

Dr. Charlie was working in too many fields to have yet attained such an outstanding position in any one, but he was fast rising to the fore in thyroid surgery, and visitors noted it. Dr. Andrew Smith of Portland, Oregon, vice-president of the American Medical Association, reported to the Surgeons Club one day that Dr. C. H. Mayo had that morning "dissected and shelled out two cysts of the thyroid with such ease that it seemed very simple. The cysts seemed to *roll out*," in great contrast, said Dr. Smith, to a similar case he had seen elsewhere not long before, in which the patient had almost bled to death. Dr. Will saw what was coming and once remarked to Dr. William D. Haggard, professor of surgery at Vanderbilt University in Nashville, "Charlie is going to be the Kocher of America."

As a clinical speaker Dr. Charlie was surely unique. He "kept his audience in a bubble of anticipation. During the morning's work of anything from ten to fifteen major cases he might discuss the number of nails and match-heads, the weight of charcoal and gunpowder which could be made from the constituents of the human body; he might philosophize about the gallbladder of the pocket gopher, the pineal eye of the tuatara lizard, the galls on his oak trees, the tuberculous lesions of turkey's livers, or a hundred other odd subjects, and between these divagations introduce sound clinical teaching drawn from the accumulated wisdom of his vast experience. Those who listened . . . fascinated by his extraordinary discourse never knew what curious information his wide reading and shrewd observation would bring to light."

Both brothers had a gift for putting things so they stuck in the hearer's mind and he went away quoting the "maxims" of the Mayos. Dr. Charlie's forte was description through homely analogy. "Don't remove the parathyroid. It looks like a piece of fat, somewhat harder, and is about the size of a lima bean," he would say. Or, "When the hatchet-sharp edge of the liver is gone, you had better take out the gallbladder." Those who heard that had seen the normal liver many times, but they had never seen its edge as hatchet-sharp until Dr. Charlie saw it for them.

Dr. Will's gift was for an almost epigrammatic conciseness. "Don't monkey with the ovary; either remove it or leave it alone." "In obstruction a silent belly is a septic belly. The bowels are paralyzed and the case is inoperable." "Forty per cent of 'gastric' ulcers are in the duodenum." "Draw your conclusions before your experience is large. . . . Those of large experience are wary of conclusions." "Always report the postmortem findings; for if there is a lesson to be taught it is right that it should travel as far as possible."

Grateful as they were for the instruction, many visitors wondered how the surgeons stood the strain of giving it. A verbatim report of either brother's daily clinical talk runs to fifteen or twenty printed pages, and all the while they talked they were "working placidly yet rapidly . . . cutting, sewing, ligating, and performing all the manipulations of surgical technique."

The Mayos were not brilliant surgeons in the sense in which that term had been applied in earlier years; they did not dazzle their audience with a display of speed, daring, and flourish. But surgeons no longer asked to be thrilled by a spectacular performance. The principles of Halsted were coming into their own, and sureness, soundness, and thoroughness were now more generally respected than brilliance. Of these saner qualities the Mayos had a large share, with the added polish and mastery of technique they had acquired with long practice.

One day an onlooker asked Dr. Will how he had done the operation he had just finished. After thinking a few seconds Dr. Will replied, "Well, I hardly know myself until I go home and look it up in Binnie." Dr. J. Fairbairn Binnie, a Scotsman who had transferred his practice from Aberdeen to Kansas City, had just published a manual of surgery in which the technique of operation after operation was described precisely as the author had seen it done in one of the Mayos' clinics. So the audience that morning greeted Dr. Will's remark with delight, thinking it a sally at Binnie, who was in the group. But it may not have been so. Like all skilled craftsmen, the Mayos had mastered their techniques till they could use them almost without thinking, leaving their minds free for the more important questions of which to use and when.

Their surgery was, in the words of one who studied it, "the essence of the techniques of all masters of surgery, enriched with the original ideas of the Mayo brothers." They did not claim to be original very often; they were more concerned that they should know and practice the very best methods available, no matter who had discovered them. To repeat Dr. Will's fine figure of speech, they were gathering good ideas from every source, tying them into practical bundles for which they provided the string, and demonstrating the use of the bundle to all who wished to learn it. Those functions they rightly considered about as important for the advance of surgery and the better care of the sick as the function of discovery itself.

Both men were perfectly frank about their role, constantly telling visitors where they had picked up this good thing or that. Sometimes it was from their father, often from Joseph Price, Ochsner, Murphy, or Halsted. "I used to do this differently, but Moynihan showed me his method when he was here and it was better, so I use it now," Dr. Will would say. And Dr. Charlie, "The first time I tried this operation I got stuck at this point, but Dr. George Monk of Boston was here and he told me what to do."

Many of their listeners, more used to the kind of man who "invented" some good method or instrument he had seen used in Europe, were humbled by the Mayos' simple honesty. When they spoke to the brothers about it or complimented them on their constant efforts to keep on learning from other surgeons, the answer was merely an echo from the Old Doctor: "No man is big enough to be independent of others." Or Dr. Charlie would cite the European surgeon who was doing several hundred abdominal operations a year but who never bothered to see or read what others were doing, so that he was proud of a mortality of sixteen per cent when others had reduced it to three.

Dr. Will and Dr. Charlie pretended to infallibility no more than they did to originality. In some American clinics the morning schedule would list several "abdominal operations," a vagueness that permitted the surgeon to make sure of his diagnosis while the assistant was reading the case history. The Mayos always listed a specific diagnosis, or if they had been unable to reach one they admitted it with "Explore stomach, duodenum, and gallbladder." If their diagnosis proved wrong they called for a rereading of the history and in the presence of their visitors, and sometimes with their aid, tried to discover what had led them astray.

Some surgeons, notably John B. Murphy, saved the difficult operations for doing in private, but every visitor was welcome to see any operation the Mayos did and learn from the hard luck as well as the good. Often the master was most fully revealed when things went wrong. Among Dr. W. J. Mayo's outstanding characteristics as a surgeon, next to his remarkable judgment as to how far he could go in an operation—when to go in and when to get out—was his imperturbability in a crisis.

One day he was removing a tumor of the kidney. As an upheaval of the ocean floor might render useless the navigator's charts, so the huge growth had pushed all the familiar surgical landmarks out of place and attached itself to the adjoining body parts. As Dr. Will lifted it to the surface, the largest vein in the body was ruptured; blood welled forth in a horrifying flow that would have ended life in a few minutes.

With one flash of his finger Dr. Mayo found and plugged the rent, entirely by his trained sense of touch, for the blood shut everything else from sight.

Then he said quietly to the tense watchers, "Gentlemen, I have torn the *vena cava* and it will be necessary to make another incision to repair the vein."

He stitched up the tear, made sure it was tight, and then went calmly on with the task of cutting the growth away from the tissues to which it was attached. Suddenly the tumor came loose, making a long tear in the bowel. Dr. Mayo continued talking: "This, gentlemen, is a much more serious accident than the injury to the vein. I have torn a long rent in the duodenum and if it is not made intact, the contents will leak out and the patient will live but a few days." Then slowly and carefully he sutured the torn bowel before he went on to complete the work on the kidney.

The operation took three and a half hours. At the end the spectators were exhausted by the strain and stared in awe at the outwardly unperturbed man who had carried the responsibility.

Either accident would have meant death in the hands of the average surgeon, so the men naturally watched the postoperative course of the case with great interest. There were no complications, no signs of shock, and the patient progressed smoothly to a complete recovery.

Asked one time to compare the two Mayos as surgeons, Dr. Haggard replied, "Dr. Will is a wonderful surgeon; Dr. Charlie is a surgical wonder." The amazing characteristics in Dr. Charlie were his versatility and ingenuity. Other surgeons could not get over the ease with which he turned from removing a thyroid in one case to taking out a prostate or a varicose vein in the next, always with admirable skill. To him was due the range of surgery at Rochester, which made it possible for one man to say, "If you stay here long enough you can see every operation known to surgery."

His ingenuity in devising operative procedures for the unusual case became a byword in the profession. The fellows of the American Surgical Association met in Rochester one year, and wanting to see Dr. Charlie's peculiar talent in action, they asked Dr. Will to select some difficult case that Charlie had not examined and let them see what he did with it. As Dr. Will told the story:

"I chose the case of a woman who had been operated on seven times before coming here, and whose condition was apparently hopeless of surgical repair, and had the Fellows examine her. They all agreed that it was a case hopeless of relief, and so the whole crowd was prepared to see Charlie floored. The patient was placed before him, and when he looked at the ghastly postoperative results he whistled. Then, without apparent effort, he outlined an entirely new plan of operative treatment, which was successful, and the crowd of doctors was simply dazed."

The Bitter Drink .

by JOHN DOS PASSOS, 1896–   . A native of Chicago, Dos Passos was educated at Harvard, B.A., 1916, and served as an ambulance driver in France in World War I. A period of travel followed after which Dos Passos settled down to the work of a writer. He has written verse, essays, and plays but he is known chiefly for his fiction. Three Soldiers (1921) was the first *important American novel to deal realistically with World War I. It was followed by four significant novels treating various aspects of the American scene: Manhattan Transfer (1925), The 42nd Parallel (1930), Nineteen Nineteen (1931), and The Big Money (1936). Much of his recent work has taken the form of expository and descriptive prose, for example, The Ground We Stand On (1941), but in 1943 he published another novel, Number One. Three of Dos Passos' earlier novels have recently been reprinted as a trilogy under the title of U.S.A. (1938). "The Bitter Drink," with its caustic sketch of the society into which the economist Thorstein Veblen was born, is taken from that volume.*

Veblen,

a greyfaced shambling man lolling resentful at his desk with his cheek on his hand, in a low sarcastic mumble of intricate phrases subtly paying out the logical inescapable rope of matteroffact for a society to hang itself by,

dissecting out the century with a scalpel so keen, so comical, so exact that the professors and students ninetenths of the time didn't know it was there, and the magnates and the respected windbags and the applauded loudspeakers never knew it was there.

Veblen

asked too many questions, suffered from a constitutional inability to say yes.

Socrates asked questions, drank down the bitter drink one night when the first cock crowed,

but Veblen

drank it in little sips through a long life in the stuffiness of classrooms, the dust of libraries, the staleness of cheap flats such as a poor instructor can afford. He fought the boyg all right, pedantry, routine, time-servers at office desks, trustees, collegepresidents, the plump flunkies of the ruling businessmen, all the good jobs for yesmen, never enough money, every broadening hope thwarted. Veblen drank the bitter drink all right.

The Veblens were a family of freeholding farmers.

The freeholders of the narrow Norwegian valleys were a stubborn hardworking people, farmers, dairymen, fishermen, rooted in their fathers' stony fields, in their old timbered farmsteads with carved gables they took their names from, in the upland pastures where they grazed the stock in summer.

During the early nineteenth century the towns grew; Norway filled up with landless men, storekeepers, sheriffs, moneylenders, bailiffs, notaries in black with stiff collars and briefcases full of foreclosures under their arms. Industries were coming in. The townsmen were beginning to get profits out of the country and to finagle the farmers out of the freedom of their narrow farms.

The meanspirited submitted as tenants, daylaborers; but the strong men went out of the country

as their fathers had gone out of the country centuries before when Harald the Fairhaired and St. Olaf hacked to pieces the liberties of the northern men, who had been each man lord of his own creek, to make Christians and serfs of them,

only in the old days it was Iceland, Greenland, Vineland the northmen had sailed west to; now it was America.

Both Thorstein Veblen's father's people and his mother's people had lost their farmsteads and with them the names that denoted them free men.

Thomas Anderson for a while tried to make his living as a traveling carpenter and cabinetmaker, but in 1847 he and his wife, Kari Thorsteinsdatter, crossed in a whalingship from Bremen and went out to join friends in the Scandihoovian colonies round Milwaukee.

Next year his brother Haldor joined him.

They were hard workers; in another year they had saved up money to preempt a claim on 160 acres of uncleared land in Sheboygan County, Wisconsin; when they'd gotten that land part cleared they sold it and moved to an all-Norway colony in Manitowoc County, near Cato and a place named Valders after the valley they had all come from in the old country;

there in the house Thomas Anderson built with his own tools, the sixth of twelve children, Thorstein Veblen was born.

When Thorstein was eight years old, Thomas Anderson moved west again into the blacksoil prairies of Minnesota that the Sioux and the buffalo had only been driven off from a few years before. In the deed to the new farm Thomas Anderson took back the old farmstead name of Veblen.

He was a solid farmer, builder, a clever carpenter, the first man to import merino sheep and a mechanical reaper and binder; he was a man of standing in the group of Norway people farming the edge of the prairie, who kept their dialects, the manner of life of their narrow Norway valleys, their Lutheran pastors, their homemade clothes and cheese and bread, their suspicion and stubborn dislike of townsmen's ways.

The townspeople were Yankees mostly, smart to make two dollars grow where a dollar grew before, storekeepers, middlemen, speculators, moneylenders, with long heads for politics and mortgages; they despised the Scandihoovian dirtfarmers they lived off, whose daughters did their wives' kitchenwork.

The Norway people believed as the fathers had believed that there were only two callings for an honest man, farming or preaching.

Thorstein grew up a hulking lad with a reputation for laziness and wit. He hated the irk of everrepeated backbreaking chores round the farm. Reading he was happy. Carpentering he liked or running farm-machinery. The Lutheran pastors who came to the house noticed that this supple mind slid easily round the corners of their theology. It was hard to get farmwork out of him, he had a stinging tongue and was famous for the funny names he called people; his father decided to make a preacher out of him.

When he was seventeen he was sent for out of the field where he was working. His bag was already packed. The horses were hitched up. He was being sent to Carleton Academy in Northfield, to prepare for Carleton College.

As there were several young Veblens to be educated their father built them a house on a lot near the campus. Their food and clothes were sent to them from the farm. Cash money was something they never saw.

Thorstein spoke English with an accent. He had a constitutional inability to say yes. His mind was formed on the Norse sagas and on the matteroffact sense of his father's farming and the exact needs of carpenterwork and threshingmachines.

He could never take much interest in the theology, sociology, economics of Carleton College where they were busy trimming down the jagged dogmas of the old New England bibletaught traders to make stencils to hang on the walls of commissionmerchants' offices.

Veblen's collegeyears were the years when Darwin's assertions of growth and becoming were breaking the set molds of the Noah's Ark world,

when Ibsen's women were tearing down the portieres of the Victorian parlors,

and Marx's mighty machine was rigging the countinghouse's own logic to destroy the countinghouse.

When Veblen went home to the farm he talked about these things with his father, following him up and down at his plowing, starting an argument while they were waiting for a new load for the wheat-thresher. Thomas Anderson had seen Norway and America; he had the squarebuilt mind of a carpenter and builder, and an understanding of tools and the treasured elaborated builtupseasonbyseason knowledge of a careful farmer,

a tough whetstone for the sharpening steel of young Thorstein's wits.

At Carleton College young Veblen was considered a brilliant unsound eccentric; nobody could understand why a boy of such attainments wouldn't settle down to the business of the day, which was to buttress property and profits with anything usable in the debris of Christian ethics and eighteenthcentury economics that cluttered the minds of collegeprofessors, and to reinforce the sacred, already shaky edifice with the new strong girderwork of science Herbert Spencer was throwing up for the benefit of the bosses.

People complained they never knew whether Veblen was joking or serious.

In 1880 Thorstein Veblen started to try to make his living by teaching. A year in an academy at Madison, Wisconsin, wasn't much of a success. Next year he and his brother Andrew started graduate work at Johns Hopkins. Johns Hopkins didn't suit, but boarding in an old Baltimore house with some ruined gentlewomen gave him a disdaining glimpse of an etiquette moth-eaten now but handed down through the lavish leisure of the slaveowning planters' mansions straight from the merry England of the landlord cavaliers.

(The valleyfarmers had always been scornful of outlanders' ways.)

He was more at home at Yale where in Noah Porter he found a New England roundhead granite against which his Norway granite rang in clear dissent. He took his Ph.D. there. But there was still some question as to what department of the academic world he could best make a living in.

He read Kant and wrote prize essays. But he couldn't get a job. Try as he could he couldn't get his mouth round the essential yes.

He went back to Minnesota with a certain intolerant knowledge of the amenities of the higher learning. To his slight Norwegian accent he'd added the broad a.

At home he loafed about the farm and tinkered with inventions of new machinery and read and talked theology and philosophy with his father. In the Scandihoovian colonies the price of wheat and the belief in God and St. Olaf were going down together. The farmers of the Northwest were starting their long losing fight against the parasite businessmen who were sucking them dry. There was a mortgage on the farm, interest on debts to pay, always fertilizer, new machines to buy to speed production to pump in a halfcentury the wealth out of the soil laid down in a million years of buffalo-grass. His brothers kept grumbling about this sardonic loafer who wouldn't earn his keep.

Back home he met again his college sweetheart, Ellen Rolfe, the niece of the president of Carleton College, a girl who had railroad-magnates and money in the family. People in Northfield were shocked when it came out that she was going to marry the drawling pernickety bookish badlydressed young Norwegian ne'erdowell.

Her family hatched a plan to get him a job as economist for the Santa Fe Railroad but at the wrong moment Ellen Rolfe's uncle lost control of the line. The young couple went to live at Stacyville where they did everything but earn a living. They read Latin and Greek and botanized in the woods and along the fences and in the roadside scrub. They boated on the river and Veblen started his translation of the *Laxdaelasaga*. They read *Looking Backwards* and articles by Henry George. They looked at their world from the outside.

In '91 Veblen got together some money to go to Cornell to do postgraduate work. He turned up there in the office of the head of the economics department wearing a coonskin cap and grey corduroy trousers and said in his low sarcastic drawl, "I am Thorstein Veblen,"

but it was not until several years later, after he was established at the new University of Chicago that had grown up next to the World's Fair, and had published *The Theory of the Leisure Class*, put on the map by Howells' famous review, that the world of the higher learning knew who Thorstein Veblen was.

Even in Chicago as the brilliant young economist he lived pioneer-fashion. (The valleyfarmers had always been scornful of outlanders' ways.) He kept his books in packingcases laid on their sides along the walls. His only extravagances were the Russian cigarettes he smoked and the red sash he sometimes sported. He was a man without small-talk. When he lectured he put his cheek on his hand and mumbled out his long spiral sentences, reiterative like the eddas. His language was a mixture of mechanics' terms, scientific latinity, slang and Roget's Thesaurus. The other profs couldn't imagine why the girls fell for him so.

The girls fell for him so that Ellen Rolfe kept leaving him. He'd take summer trips abroad without his wife. There was a scandal about a girl on an ocean liner.

Tongues wagged so (Veblen was a man who never explained, who never could get his tongue around the essential yes; the valleyfarmers had always been scornful of the outlanders' ways, and their opinions) that his wife left him and went off to live alone on a timberclaim in Idaho and the president asked for his resignation.

Veblen went out to Idaho to get Ellen Rolfe to go with him to California when he succeeded in getting a job at a better salary at Leland Stanford, but in Palo Alto it was the same story as in Chicago. He suffered from woman trouble and the constitutional inability to say yes and an unnatural tendency to feel with the workingclass instead of with the profittakers. There were the same complaints that his courses were not constructive or attractive to big money bequests and didn't help his students to butter their bread, make Phi Beta Kappa, pick plums off the hierarchies of the academic grove. His wife left him for good. He wrote to a friend: "The president doesn't approve of my domestic arrangements; nor do I."

Talking about it he once said, "What is one to do if the woman moves in on you?"

He went back up to the shack in the Idaho woods.

Friends tried to get him an appointment to make studies in Crete, a chair at the University of Pekin, but always the boyg, routine, businessmen's flunkeys in all the university offices . . . for the questioner the bitter drink.

His friend Davenport got him an appointment at the University of Missouri. At Columbia he lived like a hermit in the basement of the Davenports' house, helped with the work round the place, carpentered himself a table and chairs. He was already a bitter elderly man with a grey face covered with a net of fine wrinkles, a vandyke beard and yellow teeth. Few students could follow his courses. The college authorities were often surprised and somewhat chagrined that when visitors came from Europe it was always Veblen they wanted to meet.

These were the years he did most of his writing, trying out his ideas on his students, writing slowly at night in violet ink with a pen of his own designing. Whenever he published a book he had to put up a guarantee with the publishers. In *The Theory of Business Enterprise, The Instinct of Workmanship, The Vested Interests and the Common Man,*

he established a new diagram of a society dominated by monopoly capital,

etched in irony

the sabotage of production by business,

the sabotage of life by blind need for money profits,

pointed out the alternatives: a warlike society strangled by the bureaucracies of the monopolies forced by the law of diminishing returns to grind down more and more the common man for profits,

or a new matteroffact commonsense society dominated by the needs of the men and women who did the work and the incredibly vast possibilities for peace and plenty offered by the progress of technology.

These were the years of Debs's speeches, growing laborunions, the I.W.W. talk about industrial democracy: these years Veblen still held to the hope that the workingclass would take over the machine of production before monopoly had pushed the western nations down into the dark again.

War cut across all that: under the cover of the bunting of Woodrow Wilson's phrases the monopolies cracked down. American democracy was crushed.

The War at least offered Veblen an opportunity to break out of the airless greenhouse of academic life. He was offered a job with the Food Administration, he sent the Navy Department a device for catching submarines by trailing lengths of stout bindingwire. (Meanwhile the government found his books somewhat confusing. The postoffice was forbidding the mails to *Imperial Germany and the Industrial Revolution* while propaganda agencies were sending it out to make people hate the Huns. Educators were denouncing *The Nature of Peace* while Washington experts were clipping phrases out of it to add to the Wilsonian smokescreen.)

For the Food Administration Thorstein Veblen wrote two reports: in one he advocated granting the demands of the I.W.W. as a wartime measure and conciliating the workingclass instead of beating up and jailing all the honest leaders; in the other he pointed out that the Food Administration was a businessman's racket and was not aiming for the most efficient organization of the country as a producing machine. He suggested that, in the interests of the efficient prosecution of the war, the government step into the place of the middleman and furnish necessities to the farmers direct in return for raw material;

but cutting out business was not at all the Administration's idea of making the world safe for democracy,

so Veblen had to resign from the Food Administration.

He signed the protests against the trial of the hundred and one wobblies in Chicago.

After the armistice he went to New York. In spite of all the oppression of the war years, the air was freshening. In Russia the great storm of revolt had broken, seemed to be sweeping west, in the strong gusts from the new world in the east the warsodden multitudes began to see again. At Versailles allies and enemies, magnates, generals,

585

flunkey politicians were slamming the shutters against the storm, against the new, against hope. It was suddenly clear for a second in the thundering glare what war was about, what peace was about.

In America, in Europe, the old men won. The bankers in their offices took a deep breath, the bediamonded old ladies of the leisure class went back to clipping their coupons in the refined quiet of their safe-deposit vaults.

the last puffs of the ozone of revolt went stale
in the whisper of speakeasy arguments.

Veblen wrote for the *Dial*,
lectured at the New School for Social Research.

He still had a hope that the engineers, the technicians, the nonprofiteers whose hands were on the switchboard might take up the fight where the workingclass had failed. He helped form the Technical Alliance. His last hope was the British general strike.

Was there no group of men bold enough to take charge of the magnificent machine before the pigeyed speculators and the yesmen at office desks irrevocably ruined it

and with it the hopes of four hundred years?

No one went to Veblen's lectures at the New School. With every article he wrote in the *Dial* the circulation dropped.

Harding's normalcy, the new era was beginning;
even Veblen made a small killing on the stockmarket.

He was an old man and lonely.

His second wife had gone to a sanitarium suffering from delusions of persecution.

There seemed no place for a masterless man.

Veblen went back out to Palo Alto
to live in his shack in the tawny hills and observe from outside the last grabbing urges of the profit system taking on, as he put it, the systemized delusions of dementia praecox.

There he finished his translation of the *Laxdaelasaga*.

He was an old man. He was much alone. He let the woodrats take what they wanted from his larder. A skunk that hung round the shack was so tame he'd rub up against Veblen's leg like a cat.

He told a friend he'd sometimes hear in the stillness about him the voices of his boyhood talking Norwegian as clear as on the farm in Minnesota where he was raised. His friends found him harder than ever to talk to, harder than ever to interest in anything. He was running down. The last sips of the bitter drink.

He died on August 3, 1929.

Among his papers a penciled note was found:

It is also my wish, in case of death, to be cremated if it can be conveniently done, as expeditiously and inexpensively as may be, without ritual or ceremony of any kind; that my ashes be thrown loose into the sea or into some sizable stream running into the sea; that no tombstone, slab, epitaph, effigy, tablet, inscription or monument of any name or nature, be set up to my memory or name in any place or at any time; that no obituary, memorial, portrait or biography of me, nor any letters written to or by me be printed or published, or in any way reproduced, copied or circulated;

but his memorial remains

riveted into the language:

the sharp clear prism of his mind.

Tin Lizzie

by JOHN DOS PASSOS. *Dos Passos is famous for such technical devices in his novels as the newsreel, the camera eye, and compact biographical sketches of significant men sandwiched in between the chapters of his plot. One of the most vivid of his thumbnail biographies is "Tin Lizzie," a sketch of Henry Ford, in* The Big Money.

M R. FORD *the automobileer,*" the featurewriter wrote in 1900,

"*Mr. Ford the automobileer began by giving his steed three or four sharp jerks with the lever at the righthand side of the seat; that is, he pulled the lever up and down sharply in order, as he said, to mix air with gasoline and drive the charge into the exploding cylinder. . . . Mr. Ford slipped a small electric switch handle and there followed a puff, puff, puff. . . . The puffing of the machine assumed a higher key. She was flying along about eight miles an hour. The ruts in the road were deep, but the machine certainly went with a dreamlike smoothness. There was none of the bumping common even to a streetcar. . . . By this time the boulevard had been reached, and the automobileer, letting a lever fall a little, let her out. Whiz! She picked up speed with infinite rapidity. As she ran on there was a clattering behind, the new noise of the automobile.*

For twenty years or more,

ever since he'd left his father's farm when he was sixteen to get a job in a Detroit machineshop, Henry Ford had been nuts about machinery. First it was watches, then he designed a steamtractor, then he built a horseless carriage with an engine adapted from the Otto gasengine he'd read about in *The World of Science*, then a mechanical buggy with a onecylinder fourcycle motor, that would run forward but not back;

at last, in ninetyeight, he felt he was far enough along to risk throwing up his job with the Detroit Edison Company, where he'd worked his way up from night fireman to chief engineer, to put all his time into working on a new gasoline engine,

(in the late eighties he'd met Edison at a meeting of electriclight employees in Atlantic City. He'd gone up to Edison after Edison had delivered an address and asked him if he thought gasoline was practical as a motor fuel. Edison had said yes. If Edison said it, it was true. Edison was the great admiration of Henry Ford's life);

and in driving his mechanical buggy, sitting there at the lever jauntily dressed in a tightbuttoned jacket and a high collar and a derby hat, back and forth over the level illpaved streets of Detroit,

scaring the big brewery horses and the skinny trotting horses and the sleekrumped pacers with the motor's loud explosions,

looking for men scatterbrained enough to invest money in a factory for building automobiles.

He was the eldest son of an Irish immigrant who during the Civil War had married the daughter of a prosperous Pennsylvania Dutch farmer and settled down to farming near Dearborn in Wayne County, Michigan;

like plenty of other Americans, young Henry grew up hating the endless sogging through the mud about the chores, the hauling and pitching manure, the kerosene lamps to clean, the irk and sweat and solitude of the farm.

He was a slender, active youngster, a good skater, clever with his hands; what he liked was to tend the machinery and let the others do the heavy work. His mother had told him not to drink, smoke, gamble or go into debt, and he never did.

When he was in his early twenties his father tried to get him back from Detroit, where he was working as mechanic and repairman for the Drydock Engine Company that built engines for steamboats, by giving him forty acres of land.

Young Henry built himself an uptodate square white dwellinghouse with a false mansard roof and married and settled down on the farm,

but he let the hired men do the farming;

588

he bought himself a buzzsaw and rented a stationary engine and cut the timber off the woodlots.

He was a thrifty young man who never drank or smoked or gambled or coveted his neighbor's wife, but he couldn't stand living on the farm.

He moved to Detroit, and in the brick barn behind his house tinkered for years in his spare time with a mechanical buggy that would be light enough to run over the clayey wagonroads of Wayne County, Michigan.

By 1900 he had a practicable car to promote.

He was forty years old before the Ford Motor Company was started and production began to move.

Speed was the first thing the early automobile manufacturers went after. Races advertised the makes of cars.

Henry Ford himself hung up several records at the track at Grosse Pointe and on the ice on Lake St. Clair. In his 999 he did the mile in thirtynine and fourfifths seconds.

But it had always been his custom to hire others to do the heavy work. The speed he was busy with was speed in production, the records were records in efficient output. He hired Barney Oldfield, a stunt bicyclerider from Salt Lake City, to do the racing for him.

Henry Ford had ideas about other things than the designing of motors, carburetors, magnetos, jigs and fixtures, punches and dies; he had ideas about sales,

that the big money was in economical quantity production, quick turnover, cheap interchangeable easilyreplaced standardized parts;

it wasn't until 1909, after years of arguing with his partners, that Ford put out the first Model T.

Henry Ford was right.

That season he sold more than ten thousand tin lizzies, ten years later he was selling almost a million a year.

In these years the Taylor Plan was stirring up plantmanagers and manufacturers all over the country. Efficiency was the word. The same ingenuity that went into improving the performance of a machine could go into improving the performance of the workmen producing the machine.

In 1913 they established the assemblyline at Ford's. That season the profits were something like twentyfive million dollars, but they had trouble in keeping the men on the job, machinists didn't seem to like it at Ford's.

Henry Ford had ideas about other things than production.

He was the largest automobile manufacturer in the world; he paid high wages; maybe if the steady workers thought they were getting a cut (a very small cut) in the profits, it would give trained men an inducement to stick to their jobs,

wellpaid workers might save enough money to buy a tin lizzie; the first day Ford's announced that cleancut properlymarried American workers who wanted jobs had a chance to make five bucks a day (of course it turned out that there were strings to it; always there were strings to it)

such an enormous crowd waited outside the Highland Park plant

all through the zero January night

that there was a riot when the gates were opened; cops broke heads, jobhunters threw bricks; property, Henry Ford's own property, was destroyed. The company dicks had to turn on the firehose to beat back the crowd.

The American Plan; automotive prosperity seeping down from above; it turned out there were strings to it.

But that five dollars a day

paid to good, clean American workmen

who didn't drink or smoke cigarettes or read or think,

and who didn't commit adultery

and whose wives didn't take in boarders,

made America once more the Yukon of the sweated workers of the world;

made all the tin lizzies and the automotive age, and incidentally,

made Henry Ford the automobileer, the admirer of Edison, the birdlover,

the great American of his time.

But Henry Ford had ideas about other things besides assemblylines and the livinghabits of his employees. He was full of ideas. Instead of going to the city to make his fortune, here was a country boy who'd made his fortune by bringing the city out to the farm. The precepts he'd learned out of McGuffey's Reader, his mother's prejudices and preconceptions, he had preserved clean and unworn as freshprinted bills in the safe in a bank.

He wanted people to know about his ideas, so he bought the *Dearborn Independent* and started a campaign against cigarettesmoking.

When war broke out in Europe, he had ideas about that too. (Suspicion of armymen and soldiering were part of the midwest farm tradition, like thrift, stickativeness, temperance and sharp practice in money matters.) Any intelligent American mechanic could see that if the Europeans hadn't been a lot of ignorant underpaid foreigners who drank, smoked, were loose about women and wasteful in their methods of production, the war could never have happened.

When Rosika Schwimmer broke through the stockade of secretaries and servicemen who surrounded Henry Ford and suggested to him that he could stop the war,

he said sure they'd hire a ship and go over and get the boys out of the trenches by Christmas.

He hired a steamboat, the *Oscar II*, and filled it up with pacifists and socialworkers,

to go over to explain to the princelings of Europe

that what they were doing was vicious and silly.

It wasn't his fault that Poor Richard's commonsense no longer rules the world and that most of the pacifists were nuts,

goofy with headlines.

When William Jennings Bryan went over to Hoboken to see him off, somebody handed William Jennings Bryan a squirrel in a cage; William Jennings Bryan made a speech with the squirrel under his arm. Henry Ford threw American Beauty roses to the crowd. The band played *I Didn't Raise My Boy to Be a Soldier*. Practical jokers let loose more squirrels. An eloping couple was married by a platoon of ministers in the saloon, and Mr. Zero, the flophouse humanitarian, who reached the dock too late to sail,

dove into the North River and swam after the boat.

The *Oscar II* was described as a floating Chautauqua; Henry Ford said it felt like a middlewestern village, but by the time they reached Christiansand in Norway, the reporters had kidded him so that he had gotten cold feet and gone to bed. The world was too crazy outside of Wayne County, Michigan. Mrs. Ford and the management sent an Episcopal dean after him who brought him home under wraps,

and the pacifists had to speechify without him.

Two years later Ford's was manufacturing munitions, Eagle boats; Henry Ford was planning oneman tanks, and oneman submarines like the one tried out in the Revolutionary War. He announced to the press that he'd turn over his war profits to the government,

but there's no record that he ever did.

One thing he brought back from his trip
was the Protocols of the Elders of Zion.
He started a campaign to enlighten the world in the *Dearborn Inde-*

pendent; the Jews were why the world wasn't like Wayne County, Michigan, in the old horse and buggy days;

the Jews had started the war, Bolshevism, Darwinism, Marxism, Nietzsche, short skirts and lipstick. They were behind Wall Street and the international bankers, and the whiteslave traffic and the movies and the Supreme Court and ragtime and the illegal liquor business.

Henry Ford denounced the Jews and ran for senator and sued the *Chicago Tribune* for libel,

and was the laughingstock of the kept metropolitan press;

but when the metropolitan bankers tried to horn in on his business he thoroughly outsmarted them.

In 1918 he had borrowed on notes to buy out his minority stockholders for the picayune sum of seventyfive million dollars.

In February, 1920, he needed cash to pay off some of these notes that were coming due. A banker is supposed to have called on him and offered him every facility if the bankers' representative could be made a member of the board of directors. Henry Ford handed the banker his hat,

and went about raising the money in his own way:

he shipped every car and part he had in his plant to his dealers and demanded immediate cash payment. Let the other fellow do the borrowing had always been a cardinal principle. He shut down production and canceled all orders from the supplyfirms. Many dealers were ruined, many supplyfirms failed, but when he reopened his plant,

he owned it absolutely,

the way a man owns an unmortgaged farm with the taxes paid up.

In 1922 there started the Ford boom for President (high wages, waterpower, industry scattered to the small towns) that was skilfully pricked behind the scenes

by another crackerbarrel philosopher,

Calvin Coolidge;

but in 1922 Henry Ford sold one million three hundred and thirtytwo thousand two hundred and nine tin lizzies; he was the richest man in the world.

Good roads had followed the narrow ruts made in the mud by the Model T. The great automotive boom was on. At Ford's production was improving all the time; less waste, more spotters, strawbosses, stoolpigeons (fifteen minutes for lunch, three minutes to go to the toilet, the Taylorized speedup everywhere, reach under, adjust washer, screw down bolt, shove in cotterpin, reachunder adjustwasher, screwdown bolt, reachunderadjustscrewdownreachunderadjust until every ounce

592

of life was sucked off into production and at night the workmen went home grey shaking husks).

Ford owned every detail of the process from the ore in the hills until the car rolled off the end of the assemblyline under its own power, the plants were rationalized to the last tenthousandth of an inch as measured by the Johansen scale;

in 1926 the production cycle was reduced to eightyone hours from the ore in the mine to the finished salable car proceeding under its own power,

but the Model T was obsolete.

New Era prosperity and the American Plan
(there were strings to it, always there were strings to it)
had killed Tin Lizzie.
Ford's was just one of many automobile plants.
When the stockmarket bubble burst,
Mr. Ford the crackerbarrel philosopher said jubilantly,
"I told you so.
Serves you right for gambling and getting in debt.
The country is sound."
But when the country on cracked shoes, in frayed trousers, belts tightened over hollow bellies,
idle hands cracked and chapped with the cold of that coldest March day of 1932,
started marching from Detroit to Dearborn, asking for work and the American Plan, all they could think of at Ford's was machineguns.
The country was sound, but they mowed the marchers down.
They shot four of them dead.

Henry Ford as an old man
is a passionate antiquarian,
(lives besieged on his father's farm embedded in an estate of thousands of millionaire acres, protected by an army of servicemen, secretaries, secret agents, dicks under orders of an English exprizefighter,
always afraid of the feet in broken shoes on the roads, afraid the gangs will kidnap his grandchildren,
that a crank will shoot him,
that Change and the idle hands out of work will break through the gates and the high fences;
protected by a private army against
the new America of starved children and hollow bellies and cracked shoes stamping on souplines,

that has swallowed up the old thrifty farmlands
of Wayne County, Michigan,
as if they had never been).
Henry Ford as an old man
is a passionate antiquarian.

He rebuilt his father's farmhouse and put it back exactly in the state
he remembered it in as a boy. He built a village of museums for buggies,
sleighs, coaches, old plows, waterwheels, obsolete models of motorcars.
He scoured the country for fiddlers to play old-fashioned squaredances.

Even old taverns he bought and put back into their original shape,
as well as Thomas Edison's early laboratories.

When he bought the Wayside Inn near Sudbury, Massachusetts, he
had the new highway where the newmodel cars roared and slithered
and hissed oilily past (*the new noise of the automobile*),
moved away from the door,
put back the old bad road,
so that everything might be
the way it used to be,
in the days of horses and buggies.

INTERPRETATIONS

Progress in the Northwest

by **WILLIAM D. GALLAGHER, 1808–94.** *The son of an Irish refugee, Gallagher was born in Philadelphia but spent his youth with his widowed mother on a farm near Mount Pleasant in southern Ohio. After attending elementary school and a Lancasterian seminary he entered journalism and was connected with newspapers and magazines in Xenia, Ohio, in Cincinnati, Columbus, and Louisville. The most important of the periodicals which he himself edited were the Cincinnati Mirror and the Hesperian. In later years he served as private secretary to two secretaries of the treasury, Thomas Corwin and Salmon P. Chase, he was appointed by Lincoln as special collector of the customs and commercial agent for the West, and he was surveyor of the customs and pension agent at Louisville. In addition to his periodical* work Gallagher wrote prolifically in many fields, articles, verse, fiction. His three volumes of Erato, two in 1835 and one in 1837, and his Miami Woods, A Golden Wedding and Other Poems (1881), contain most of his verse. In 1841 he edited the first anthology of western verse, Selections from the Poetical Literature of the West, in which he included (and quite rightly) fourteen of his own poems. He was second only to James Hall and Timothy Flint in his championing of western literary culture. The discussion of progress in the Middle West is taken from a speech which Gallagher delivered in Cincinnati on April 8, 1850.

On the North-American Continent, scooped out by the hand of Omnipotence with wonderful adaptation to the wants of man, and the purposes of his existence, lies the most stupendous and favored Inland Valley upon which the sun shines. Having for its eastern edge the Allegheny and the Cumberland Mountains, and for its western the Rocky Mountains and the Black Hills, for its northern rim the summitlands between Lake Winnipeg and the headwaters of the Mississippi River, and for its southern the Guadalupe Mountains and the Gulf of Mexico, it extends in one direction over twenty-four parallels of longitude, and in the other embraces eighteen degrees of latitude. Within it are all the varieties of temperate climate, and all the geological and topographical features that are essential to fit it for the residence of man. It produces in perfection all the fruits and vegetables that are most valued by civilized communities for wholesome and nutritive properties, and all the grains that are so associated with the history of mankind, as to have received the name of 'the staff of life.' Its rivers are the most wonderful known to Christendom, and its lakes are so large, and commercially so important, as to have been designated 'inland seas.' Its mineral wealth is beyond computation; the richness of its soil is inexhaustible; and its general adaptation to the purposes of agriculture, commerce, and manufactures, is unsurpassed, perhaps unequaled, by that of any other part of the earth.

Geographically, it is difficult to conceive of anything better than the position of this great valley, whose plains stretch west from the base of the Allegheny Mountains to the Mississippi River, with an almost uniform pitch in that direction, and east from the base of the Rocky Mountains to the same water, with an almost uniform pitch in this direction, the two natural divisions meeting in that great trough, and finding on its edges their lowest common level. Into the immense channel on this level, pour, generally in an east and southeast direction, the waters from the hither slopes of the Rocky Mountains, and the drainage from the western half of the great valley: into it also pour, generally in a west and southwest direction, the waters from the hither slopes of the

Alleghenies, and the drainage of the eastern half of the valley: showing that not only have the two natural divisions of this Great Basin Plain an eastern and a western declivity, but that both divisions have also a common pitch to the south, which at the same time carries their surplus waters into the Gulf of Mexico, exposes their fertile bosoms to the warm and generating beams of the sun, and secures to them an unfailing prevalence of gentle and salubrious winds.

The western of these two natural divisions of the great valley under view, is for the most part a desert land, and much of it must for a long course of years remain so. Some of it, also, is totally unfitted for the abode of man, and will forever continue an uninhabited waste. But the uniformly cultivable character of the eastern division, is one of the most remarkable features of this region. This division is watered as is no other known country, and divided into uplands and lowlands, hill-ranges and intervening valleys, heavily-timbered tracts and naked prairies, which alternate over much of its surface in a manner the most favorable to the productive interests of life. Upland and lowland, prairie and forest, alike have a soil of great fertility, the capacity of which to produce, under good tillage, is inexhaustible.

In this division of the great valley, natural and artificial causes have induced a subdivision, the more important part of which is called the NORTH-WEST. The region thus known has an almost uniform southwestern exposure, and embraces nearly the whole of the valley north of thirty-six degrees thirty minutes, stretching from the western slopes of the Alleghenies to the Mississippi River, and beyond that great natural line ascending the western division first to the eighteenth parallel of longitude west from Washington, then to the nineteenth parallel, and finally (in Minnesota) to the twentieth. This region, as now organized and civilly divided, embraces the States of Kentucky, Ohio, Indiana, Illinois, Missouri, Michigan, Iowa, and Wisconsin, with Minnesota Territory, the aggregate superficial area of which is 478,349 square miles—to which I add a small strip of Western Virginia and Western Pennsylvania lying immediately upon the Ohio River, and on its two forming tributaries chiefly near their point of confluence, and obtain, in round numbers, the grand territor[i]al extent of 500,000 square miles, or three hundred and twenty millions of acres: a territorial superficies greater than the entire extent of the Original Thirteen States of the Union.

This is the great field of observation, that is now spread before me. And ere surveying it, with a view to my ultimate purpose, it is necessary to go back to some specific period, as a starting point from which to trace its progress. We are now just at the middle of a hundred years. The meridian line of the nineteenth century is over our heads. Fifty years is but a short time in the history of great nations: and fifty years ago the oldest State of this region, was admitted into the Union.* To the beginning of this century, then, let us turn, for a moment, and see what there was in the region under view, at that time, to invite the presence of civilized man. At Pittsburgh, at Marietta, at Cincinnati, at the Falls of the Ohio, on the Muskingum, the Kentucky, the Wabash, the Upper Mississippi, and the Illinois Rivers, and scattered about at a few other points, were small villages, composed in part of hardy adventurers, soldiers, and traders, in a small degree of men of education and ambition, who had sought the region that they might grow up with it to wealth and distinction, and to some extent of religious missionaries and their converts from among the aboriginal tribes. There were none of the refinements of life here, and but few of its comforts. The whole population of the State of Kentucky was then 220,955 persons, that of what is now the State of Ohio was 45,365, and that of Indiana 4,875. And this was about all: 271,195 persons, scattered over an area of 500,-000 square miles—making an average of one person to a fraction less than two square miles. On the Ohio River were a few barges and keel-boats, and now and then one or two of this description of craft would ascend the Upper Mississippi to St. Louis; but the waters of the Illinois, the Wabash, and other streams, and those also of the Lakes, were still swept by the birchen bark of the Indian. Ten years later, Kentucky had a population of 406,511 persons, Ohio of 230,760, Indiana of 24,520, Missouri of 20,845, Illinois of 12,282, and Michigan of 4,762: making an ag[g]regate of 699,680, or one person on the average to about every three quarters of a mile square.

The tide of emigration had now fairly *set* in this direction. Little communities were pitching their tents and building their cabins on most of the better streams. The settler's ax resounded through the depths of the wilderness in all directions, and the blue smoke curled above the tops of the tall trees, at once advising newcomers of the presence of a habitation, and giving the watchful savage note of a place where he might strike at those who were encroaching on his old heritage. The Indians were now receding fast before the whites—going reluctantly, but every year further and further, their dark forms disappearing in the recesses of the wilderness, as the dusky shadows of a dark and unblest age, recede and disappear before the light of a high, christian civilization. And all this continued—and in another period of ten years, the population of the region had swelled to 1,423,622.

A new agent of civilization and settlement was now introduced. The keel of the steamboat had been plowing the waters of the West for three or four years. This description of navigation was no longer a

* Editor's Note. Kentucky was actually admitted in 1792.

598

mere experiment. Speaking relatively to what was then attempted, it had succeeded; and every time the escape of steam or the splash of the paddles woke the echoes of the still solitary shores, a requiem sounded for the departing Indian, and a song of gladness went up for the arrival of his adventurous successor. The genius of Fulton was, in the hands of these adventurers, the Lamp of Alad[d]in: it opened to them freely the doors of the Great West, frightened away their enemies, and displayed to their enraptured gaze, the many and glittering charms of this beautiful land. And still the paddles dashed the waters—and still the piercing shriek of the escapepipe woke the deep echoes—and still the child of the forest receded further and further—and still rolled on the stream of emigration, through the gaps of the Cumberland, over the hights [*sic*] of the Alleghenies, down into the rich valley through which coursed the calm waters of the Ohio. And another period of ten years passed—the third decade in the half century—and the population was become 2,298,390.

By this time, over nearly the whole broad bosom of the region which I have mapped out, were scattered the habitations of men, and introduced the institutions of christian, civilized life. In the interiors of its different sections, the wigwams of the savage had given place to the cabins of the newcomers, and the farmhouses of the first settlers. On the small streams, which everywhere sent up their glad voices, giving to the deep solitude a tongue that was eloquent, the hand of enterprise had taken the willing waters, and borne them to the clattering wheels of the manufactory, where they labored and yet sported, and, like virtue, were overruled and yet free. On the broad lakes, on the mighty rivers, the arm of Steam—

> That fleshless arm, whose pulses leap
> With floods of living fire,—

was propelling the gigantic hull, freighted with hundreds of human beings, coming from afar to cultivate the land, to fabricate its crude products, to engage in trade and commerce, to 'multiply and replenish the earth.' On the great natural highways, populous cities had taken the place of the primeval groves, and the schoolhouse, the church, the depots of commerce, and the elegant mansion, invited the on-coming multitudes to seek in and around them new and better homes. And the years of the fourth decade were told, and the population had swelled to 4,131,370 souls.

Still went on the work. The seat of a commerce of hundreds of millions per year, was this now populous region. The marts of its trade were filled with the surplus products of its soil, which were borne away in thousands of vessels, to feed the hungry in less-favored lands.

599

Its flocks were feeding on unnumbered hills, and in countless fields its crops sprang up, and ripened, and bowed before the sickle. That subtle Power, which by water had brought its myriads of people to its generous bosom, and borne its rich products away in exchange for what its own soil did not yield, scorned longer to be confined to the rivers and the lakes, and their comparatively slow-moving keels. Spring upon the dry land, and seeking the iron tracks which science and labor had laid on the leveled earth, he clutched the loaded car with his invisible fingers, and bore it from point to point, for hundreds of miles, with an ease and velocity before unknown—

The beatings of his mighty heart

still sounding through the storm or the calm, and giving the only note of his approach, as he rushed through forest and field, over streams and marshes, and around the bases of many hills, with his gigantic burden. Nor was this enough. For commerce it might have been, and for bodily transit from place to place, but not for thought. And next flashed upon human genius the still more subtle essence of the electric spark; and hither came its whispering wires, stretching from hill to hill and from state to state, crossing mountains, leaping ravines, spanning rivers, and bearing to the depths of this far Interior, in the twinkling of an eye, the message spoken a thousand miles away, on the outer rim of the vast Continent. And the human tide has still rolled on and on—and the remoter forests of this region have been pierced and subdued, till the solitudes that, at the period from which this retrospect started, heard only the eternal chime of the Falls of St. Anthony, and the wild voices of the dark Chippeways, are filling with the homes of civilized man, and becoming vocal with prayers and hymns of thanksgiving to God. And the fifth decade has gone by, and *seven millions* now number the population of this region, which a half century ago, as was shown, contained less than 300,000 souls!

Only two prominent facts remain to be mentioned, as entering into and assisting this wonderful progress. One of them is that blessed boon, the Ordinance of 1787, which sprang from the profound regard of the Fathers of the Republic for the Rights of Man, and forever closed the doors of all that part of the region under view, which lies north of the Ohio and east of the Mississippi rivers, against the entrance of human slavery; the other is the evidence which the settlement of this region has afforded, that it lies in just that geographical belt of the globe, to which the natural sagacity of man leads him, when he is departing from an old and seeking a new home. These two facts, I shall consider together. The circumstances that connected them, indeed, render them almost inseparable.

600

Making a Home

by LOGAN ESAREY, 1873–1942. *Born in Branchville, Indiana, Esarey was educated at the University of Indiana, B.A., 1905, Ph.D., 1913. His life was devoted to the teaching and study of history. After serving as school superintendent and high-school principal in various Indiana communities Esarey became professor of history at his alma mater and from 1915 to 1928 was editor of the Indiana Magazine of History. His two-volume A History of Indiana appeared in 1915–18. His charming little book The Indiana Home, published posthumously in 1943, was edited from Esarey's classroom notes and lectures by R. C. Buley. It is a richly concrete picture of homesteading in the primeval woods of the Middle West. "Making a Home" is the second chapter of this volume.*

THERE were at the time, 1816, about twelve thousand homes in the state [Indiana], yet a passenger in an airplane ten thousand feet high might not have noticed a single house outside the towns. The region was perhaps as beautiful a forest as the world has ever known. Year after year forest fires had burned away the leaves and underbrush until only the large trees remained, their limbs intermingling and shutting out the sky. Armies on horseback had traveled through it without pretense of cutting a road. Flowers in season grew everywhere. In the open glades were meadows of wild grass and the hill country from New Albany to Greencastle was covered with wild pea vines, acceptable to horses and cattle as our clover. Streams of water rambled here and yonder, apparently content to remain in the deep shades. When the sky was clear the sunlight trickled through here and there; in storm the great trees groaned and bent before the wind, and the rain dripped from the wet leaves for hours after the cloud had passed. The opened-eyed movers were on the alert, for they were now in Indiana. Occasionally there was a cabin in a clearing and friendly settlers came out to chat with the movers and invite them to spend the night.

They received all kinds of advice. "The soil is purty thin up on the headwaters," they were told at Franklin and Connersville. "Don't go up thar unless you can live on crab apples." "Some fine land up on the Muscatatuck," they were told at Madison, "but don't go up into the hickory land on the flats." At Vernon they were told there were fine locations on Flat Rock but it was a long way from the river. At Salem, "Good deep sile up around Vallonia and Brownstown on Driftwood, but it takes a mighty sight of choppin' in them thar woods. If yer want good rollin' land and fine springs go over toward Bono, Palestine or above. They say that limestone land produces somethin' amazin'."

601

At Petersburg they were told to "stick to the hills" although the oldest settlers over by Maysville and Liverpool declared they "couldn't mind ever seein' or hearin' of anybuddy ailin' or dyin' in that region." At Paoli and Bloomington they were told there was wonderful soil over on Big Shiney but not to go up into the big flat woods. At Indianapolis they were told the squatters up in Boone County had moss on their legs clean above their knees and that all the bullfrogs had died with the shakes above Noblesville. At Vincennes and Carlisle they were warned to be "keerful of speckelaters up and around Tare Holt." So the gossip continued and after every fresh report the little family of movers went into a huddle. The best land was always just a little farther on.

There was no agreement on what was the best site for a home. In some counties as many as one thousand people settled in a single year. Of course all could not have first choice even if each knew exactly what he wanted and all wanted alike. Two families came into the state soon after 1800. One settled near a big spring. There were some small patches of level land, nice sloping hillsides, a clear gravel bedded stream and, at the time, plenty of game. It was a good home for a good family. The land is still owned in the family and is worth perhaps five dollars an acre and was never worth more. The other family selected a beautiful level tract of rich land, worth now two hundred dollars per acre. Both families have prospered about equally. Many avoided the springs because they thought the dreadful disease, milk sickness, lurked in the spring branches. Some avoided the low lands because jack-o'-lanterns or will-o'-the-wisps hovered over the wet meadows and wherever the jack-o'-lantern wandered there were the fevers. Whole sections had to be avoided because the deadly nightshade grew there and would kill all the stock and perhaps the children. The limestone soil would "perduce" but it was heavy and sticky. The light or dark sandy loam where the beech, sugar or spicewood grew was better. Many, no doubt, bought land "jinin' " (adjoining) an old friend or relative. Others with visions of wealth located on the large streams whence they could load their flatboats for New Orleans. No explanation will fit all selections. Soil, water, vegetation, drainage, roads, neighbors, hunting, "lay" of land—each had its influence and rarely did two people agree on which was most important. Brothers disagreed and settled miles apart; children, when grown up, moved on to different locations; and many families, after a season, packed up and moved farther on.

In many cases the man came alone in the spring, cleared a small field and, while the crop was growing, built a house. Then in the following winter or spring he moved his family to the new home; quite as often he came in the fall and built a house, brought his family in winter or spring and began clearing land for his spring planting.

In any case the first work was a camp to live in until some kind of a house could be built. The "half-faced" camp was common. It was made of poles, usually with three walls, and covered with poles and brush. A bed or beds were made of leaves and grass and woven coverlets or skins were used for covering. A fireplace for warmth and cooking was made outside, usually in front of the open side of the camp. An oven could be made in the hillside with walls of clay or small stones from the creek bed. The common cooking utensils were a spider or three-legged skillet in which to fry meat, and a larger skillet with a lid, in which corn pone could be made. Venison steaks, squirrel and other fresh meats were usually broiled or roasted on spits or sticks. Often in fair weather the outside cooking was continued after the house was finished. Little work was wasted on the camp, if health was good, for the first rush was to "get something growin'." If the settlers were in a hurry, and nearly all were the first years, the brush was cleared away and piled in a row at the edge of the field to serve as a fence, after which the corn, potatoes and garden seeds were planted. The new soil was loose and could be plowed or dug up between the rows while the seeds were coming up. Meanwhile the large trees had to be deadened or girdled. This consisted of chopping a notch through the bark and sap entirely around the tree. If a hickory, oak, beech, sugar or poplar the tree would die in a few days; the leaves would wilt and thus allow the sunshine to reach the growing crop.

As soon as the crop was planted, if all went well, the settler proceeded to cut about twenty logs, each about one foot in diameter and perhaps twenty feet long, and an equal number ten, twelve or fifteen feet long. These were for sides and ends of the house. Then came three or four, each shorter than the one below, to form the gables. Each log was notched at the end so the corners would not build up faster than the walls. If the logs were straight and carefully notched each log would rest on the one beneath so neatly that they formed a solid wall. Smaller poles were laid on the top logs to serve as rafters. If two rooms were desired, cross logs could be fitted in at the middle. At side or end three or four logs could be cut to form a door perhaps three feet wide and five feet high. At the other end a hole was made three or four logs high and whatever width was desired for a fireplace. A chimney was built up from the fireplace, formed of a framework of small poles or split sticks a couple of inches square and filled in with clay. The fireplace was lined with stone and then all was heated slowly until it was glazed and fireproof. Some time before winter came, the spaces between the logs were filled with clay and small pieces of split wood.

603

This was called "chinking." If good clay could be had it made the house snug and warm. The roof was made of clapboards split with a frow from nice straight-grained oak. Each clapboard was about four feet long, six inches wide and an inch thick. These were laid on overlapping and held in place by weight poles. A door was made of split pieces of wood similar to the clapboards and hung on wooden or leather (buckskin) hinges. Finally the floor was made, the first one probably of six or eight inches of clay well packed down and then covered with white sand. Later when a foot adz or broad axe could be had a puncheon floor could be put in and windows added. It took a good workman to build such a house that would keep out wind, rain and snow. Not a nail was used and few of the first settlers had more than an axe and a frow to work with.

By driving a post in the floor and laying poles to the walls a bed was soon made in one corner and in another corner beside the fireplace a table was made. Three-legged stools had to serve for chairs until time could be found to make better ones from hickory poles with woven bark seats and backs. Wooden bowls were burned out, especially if a large sound knot could be found. Years later these utensils would give way to metal or earthenware pots and pans.

Some time before winter a small house was built over the spring. This in time grew into a house for the storage of vegetables, meats, milk and fruits, serving the pioneers as an icehouse or refrigerator. A pool of water was provided just large enough for gourd or bucket and not large enough to permit the water to become warm in summer or freeze in winter. Later perhaps a smokehouse would be set up in which to smoke and hang the hams and sidemeat.

As soon as possible an ash-hopper would have been built. First a log, some two feet in diameter, was split. Half of it was hollowed out into a trough, with one end left open. In this clapboards were placed upright forming a large funnel shaped hopper. As fast as burned, ashes were placed in it, before they were wet, until it was full. Then water was poured in until it stood on the top. When this water leached through, it ran out the open end of the trough into something prepared to hold it. Next it was necessary to get an iron "kittle" to boil the dark lye water and mix it with a proper amount of bear or hog grease to form soft soap. Most probably a kettle could be borrowed somewhere in the neighborhood by walking five or ten miles. It would weigh thirty to sixty pounds and have to be carried home. People could of course make out without soap, but the sweat and grime from the black logs let loose much easier with a small piece of soft soap; and wash day with hard spring water and no soap was not appreciated. However, the small children could never see any use for it.

The soap and lye were also necessary to change the deer hide into buckskin. Thongs of buckskin were always handy when there were no nails or screws and perhaps no augur. The family might all get along "barefooted" until frost came, but it would certainly soon come and then shoepacks and moccasins would be necessary. It would be several years until there would be a tannery near where folks could have the deer hides tanned or trade them for leather, and they might not live to see ready-made shoes for sale in the country stores. Moreover, pioneer work was hard on clothing and more than one suit of buckskin would be worn out before the spinning wheel could be made and flax and wool grown and spun for linsey-woolsey. Most likely first settlers would not live to buy a ready-made suit of clothes or dress.

The planting season was the most important of the whole year. The settler had to raise his "grub." What he didn't raise or kill he did without. He might borrow from or "swap" with a neighbor but there was no grocery. The first season settlers had to depend largely on themselves. Friendly families along the road might give them a few seeds and tell them something of farming in the new home, but most of it was a great experiment. Corn and potatoes were necessary and fortunately anyone could raise them. Cornbread, meat and potatoes would do, but they got to be common, three times a day through the long winter and spring. The garden belonged to the women and on it depended the table, the one great attraction of pioneer life. Long, hard work in the outdoors developed enormous appetites for men, women, children and dogs.

The first warm days in March a brush pile was burned and in the mingled soil and ashes the cabbage, tobacco and pepper seeds were sown. The tender plants were covered to protect them from frost. As soon as all danger of frost was over and "the sign got in the head" they were transplanted or "set out" in the garden. There were early Winnigstadt cabbages for summer use and big "Drumheads" for fall and winter. (A pot of "biled" cabbage with a chunk of fat meat for "seasonin'" is mighty "fillin'" when everybody is "dog tired" and "hog hungry." Besides, for every drop of "Dutch" blood in your veins, there must be made a gallon of sauerkraut.) Equally "pushin'" were the lettuce and radishes. By the middle of April a row or two of each would be in the ground. After the first year a bed of potato onions would be planted in the fall and covered with straw or fodder to prevent heaving out of the ground. These sturdy fellows came early and led in time all the garden truck. If the appetite was too strong, greens and wild onions could be found and nobody turned up his nose at a ham bone "biled" in sour dock or polk. Some early "bunch" or "pole" beans and perhaps some garlic made up the summer garden. All these with new potatoes, peas and roastin' ears were supposed to be on the table by harvest time—many of them earlier. Folks had to wait until wheat could be threshed and flour ground before the big juicy berry cobblers could be added to this early summer menu.

With the corn planted and the early vegetables coming on, gardeners turned to the winter vegetables. Far the most important were the potatoes and beans. After the potatoes were grown they could be left in the ground until after the hot weather, then dug and piled in a cool place and with the approach of winter "holed ·up." As soon as the corn was up three or four inches high the field-beans could be planted—one or two "cutshorts" or "navys" besides each hill of corn. If these were planted too early they would climb all over the corn and pull the stalks down, ruining the corn. The beans grew rank and a few short rows would produce a bushel or two of hulled beans. Not only that, the "cutshorts" bloomed all fall, and fresh, tender green beans for cooking could be found here long after the garden beans were gone. Bread was the staff of life, all right, but a pot of boiled beans and a hunk of hog had restoring grace after a long hunt in winter or a day of hard chopping in the "new ground." The farmer didn't like to be bothered with the beans in his corn but there just had to be dry beans in the house from January until June to "bile" with the pork. Potatoes gave out in February usually, and nothing was left but the corn pone, pork and beans to make up the bulk of his grub.

Ten or twelve hills of cucumbers had to be planted somewhere. They didn't care where. Give them a start any place and they would cover up everything else with their thrifty vines. No respectable people would eat them for they caused "summer complaint," "chills," "biles," "yaller janders" and maybe cancer and consumption. But the housewife usually sliced three or four of the fat, chubby "cukes" with an equal amount of onions or lettuce and covered it over with vinegar and somehow it disappeared from the table. But their principal use was for "pickling." Some time during the fall if possible the settler made a barrel or tub and filled it with vinegar or brine. Into this the wife placed two or three bushels of the fat young cucumbers and petrified them for winter and spring use. A half or quarter of one of these fossils, so sour they would wrinkle one's face just to look at them, made an excellent relish with corn pone, hominy, beans or fat pork. In the cornfield also the pumpkins were raised. Usually planted, one seed in each corn hill, about the first of June, they would begin to vine about the time the corn was "laid by." They were no trouble to raise and in the absence of orchard fruit "punkin" butter made a good side dish for fresh meat. Cut into thin strips they could be hung in the top of the house to dry and so kept all winter.

If there were any children it was necessary to plant about one hundred hills of popcorn. Some time toward the last of October, the little ears were gathered, strung and hung on the wall to season. On winter evenings it was good sport to sprinkle the grains in the hot "embers" of the fireplace and then catch the fluffy grains as they hopped out.

Sage and red pepper were also needed where there was so much fresh meat to be cooked. In the neighborhood some place a few slips of sage could be obtained. These were set out in the garden and grew into dwarf bushes two feet high. In the fall when the velvety leaves were full they were picked and dried and put away to keep dry. A half dozen leaves crushed fine and sprinkled over the frying meat gave it a flavor which is still relished and the little sage bushes still keep their places in our gardens.

Pepper seeds were planted in a box, usually, and when two inches high transplanted to the garden. One could nearly always borrow a dozen plants from a neighbor. They grew about a foot high and each plant produced ten or twelve red pods the size of hen eggs. When ripe they were picked and laid away like the sage in a dry place. One or two pods in a pot of beans or cabbage would "cut" the grease. Peppers were also considered healthful, especially in the hot summer and fall weather when dysentery, chills and typhoid fever were common. The old folks will remember strings of red peppers hung in graceful folds on the walls.

Finally, about the first of June, a small patch of new ground was prepared and the turnip seed sown. Turnips were best when about the size of duck eggs. The larger ones were hollow or pithy. Most of them were eaten raw in the fall and winter, before apples could be had. Two or three bushels were "holed up" like the potatoes for spring cooking. They were generally boiled with pork. Occasionally a garden would contain a row of parsnips. These were shaped like radishes and grew like radishes, but were "holed up" and cooked in the spring like turnips. A "patch" of watermelons, and they grew almost without attention, in the rich weedless soil of the new country, filled up the circle of farm and garden crops. Occasionally there was a field of hemp and nearly every farmer had his field or "patch" of tobacco and flax, but they were not for food.

The log cabin with its clay chinking, its rude doors and windows and mud and stick chimney, was not a thing of beauty. It remained for the wife to make it into the log cabin of poetry. Walks of flat stones were laid to the spring, to the garden, to the barn and to the road, if one were close. On either side of the walks, beds of flowers were planted. Hollyhocks of all colors, wild roses, marigolds, verbenas, bachelor buttons and whatever else could be borrowed, begged, or traded for among the neighbors, together with plants that could be transplanted from the forest, kept one's eye from the unsightly logs. A trellis of poles supported the honeysuckle (trumpet) vine that transformed the door into a bower. Gourd seeds planted at each corner not only helped to decorate but the fruits were extremely useful. Jonah's gourd was no miracle to the early settler. Almost overnight its vines covered the walls and dozens of long-handled calabashes hung down like huge ear bobs. Scores of these ripened gourds cut in all forms were used as dippers, cups, saucers, glasses, cans, boxes and ornaments. If everything else failed the morning glory came up of its own accord and covered everything with its luxuriant vines. Like all things common and lowly it was not appreciated, but there are few things in the flower world more beautiful than a riot of filmy, velvety red, white and blue morning glories. Under the spell of the flowers the cabin-in-the-clearing changed from an unsightly pile of poles and mud to a dream of beauty.

The work was not done when the crops were grown. These pioneers never lived to see—maybe even hear of—a seed store. So as things ripened seeds had to be gathered and carefully stored away. This was where the little gourds came in handy. Each with its particular "batch" of seed, free from mice and insects, was hung on the wall or fastened to the rafters. Most of the crops matured in one season, but Messrs. Turnip, Parsnip and Cabbage had to be kept green during the winter to produce seed the second year. This again was woman's business. She always tried to gather more seeds than she would need so she could swap with some neighbor for a new variety. Also some neighbor's cabin might burn or a new "mover" might come in, needing help. "Seed swappin' " was a social pastime among pioneer women in February and March, somewhat as bridge is now. While they were "swapping" seeds they also swapped methods of cultivation. Some had "best luck" one way, some another, but all kept eyes on the sun and moon and planted or transplanted when the "sign" was right. The famous proverbs or "sayings" of Franklin come from such talk among the German farmers of Pennsylvania. The descendants of these same "Pennsylvania Dutch" were by far the best farmers in early Indiana.

While gathering seeds for next year's sowing the prudent housewife also laid in a supply of medicinal "yarbs." Mullein, polk-root, calomel, mint or hoarhound could be obtained at any time. But senna, pennyroyal, elder blossoms, and many others had to be gathered in season. The habit or custom persisted, and even today in many homes bunches of these may be seen in the attic carefully put away against the time when colds, sore throat, rheumatism or indigestion put in their unwelcome appearance. Such, in brief, were those first eager years of pioneer life in Indiana.

608

Iowa

by RUTH SUCKOW. *Although Miss Suckow is best known for her tales and novels, she has not confined herself to fiction, and certainly no one is better qualified to interpret the commonwealth of Iowa. This sketch of her native state originally appeared in the* American Mercury, *September 1926.*

I

Iowa is, in a way, the center of the big region called the Middle West. It combines the qualities of half a dozen States; and perhaps that is the reason why it so often seems, and more to its own people than to any others, the most undistinguished place in the world. Its northern corner borders on Minnesota, and is windy and sloughy, with numerous lakes and Scandinavian towns. The beautiful northeastern portion is like an extension of the woods and dells of Wisconsin. The southern part is tinged with the softness, laxness and provincialism of Missouri and Arkansas. Much of the west is flat, windy, harsh, like Kansas, Nebraska or the Dakotas. The central portion is the very heart of the prairie region—smooth, plain, simple, fresh and prosperous. All these differing elements, however, are smoothed down with a touch of gentleness into that lovely, open pastoral quality which is peculiarly Iowan after all.

The culture of the State is composed of elements seemingly as various. The early influx from the South softened the intense fibre of its Puritan inheritance and gave it a certain easy-going quality. This Southern influence lingers now about the Mississippi and in out-of-the-way hill and timber regions where little settlements unbelievably primitive can still be found. The State is dotted all over with communities of Europeans: German, Dutch, Scandinavian, Welsh, Bohemian, Scotch and Irish, and English of fairly recent immigration. But many of these have been so thoroughly assimilated into the life of the State as to be virtually indistinguishable from what we call the native stock. Even their churches are rapidly going under and the few old people who cling to their native languages are relegated to the evening services which no one else wants to attend.

These are all, however, underlying fertilizing elements. "Culture" as it has always been known in Iowa—and it is a term of great repute—has been derived almost wholly from the Eastern States and particularly from New England. New Englanders brought culture to the new State as once they had brought their religion to the new continent. But with an important difference. It was not a primary but a side issue. These people did not come to Iowa to plant this sacred culture in the wilderness. They came to farm and to acquire land. The settlement of Iowa (in spite of all its bands of home missionaries) was frankly material in its nature, as was that of the whole Middle West. Therefore, culture was cherished with devotion, perhaps, but not with confidence. In spite of the number of colleges early dedicated to it, Iowans never have, and do not to this day, quite believe in the possibility of its existence among them in any strong degree. When their forefathers went out to the raw country, it was with the belief that they were leaving culture behind. Thus Iowans have always felt themselves in the nature of intellectual poor relations to the Eastern States. And New Englanders, especially, have never got over a home missionary attitude toward them.

Thus has grown up a timid, fidgety, hesitant state of mind. Iowa has never had the rampant boosterism of Kansas and Minnesota, although Rotary and Kiwanis are now laboring hard. It has always been far too deprecatory and self-doubting for that. It has even railed at its generally healthy climate. Its "well-fixed" ancients have sought climate in the West, and its aspiring young intellectuals culture in the East. Iowans are great travelers. Their foreign colonies in California, Florida, Boston and New York are always among the largest. This comes chiefly from their humility. Some are dissatisfied and come back; but the most that is permitted them to say is: "Well, I guess old Iowa isn't such a bad place after all." Anything more would be a proof of ignorance.

Iowa is proud—fairly proud—of its material prosperity, its land and corn and hogs. But like an old farmer—or rather, like a timid farmer wife—it has taken it for granted that other things are really above it. It has copied its best houses from New England and California, disregarding climatic and topographical conditions in its faith that only something from somewhere else can really be artistic. Until the last very few years it has been accepted almost without question that its young intellectuals must go away—preferably to New York, but at least away!—in order to find something "interesting" to write about. Interest in Iowa's own towns and plain people was a direct blow to "culture."

II

This thing called culture, in Iowa, has always been accepted as a distinctly feminine affair. The men went out here for business. They left all such things to the women. Puritan mothers brought along their cherished ideals of New England culture as they brought family heirlooms and slips for house plants. School teachers, especially in the colleges, taught these ideals with the zeal of devotees. Twenty years ago, every Iowa schoolroom had a picture, enlarged, of its own poet on the wall; and the poets were, of course, Henry Wadsworth Longfellow, John Greenleaf Whittier, James Russell Lowell, Oliver Wendell Holmes and Celia Thaxter. Emerson was above our heads. Whitman, needless to say, was beyond the pale. Such a native genius as Thoreau was far too rugged for genuine cultural esteem. Mark Twain was a rude Westerner. "Huckleberry Finn" and "Tom Sawyer" might be exciting, but they were bad rough books, and the librarian really did not think they should be given out to children. Thus were the best elements of our national culture preserved.

But always, in this noble striving to keep the lamp of culture burning, there was a sad and hopeless feeling that it must be against terrible odds. How could we—so young and crude and raw, so far from the center of refinement in Massachusetts—aspire to do more than keep the little light from flickering out, and perhaps kindle a tiny flame that would show the rich relations we were not wholly benighted? We had our colleges—dozens of them—with their traditions cherished all the more fervently because so new. And they did very well—if we did not have the money to go East to school.

There was good reason for this hopelessness. The whole Middle West was big, breezy and plain. It was miscellaneous. The spare, narrow intensity of New England was out of place on the prairies. Even the type of face (as Sinclair Lewis noted in "Main Street") changed from the thin and bleak to the round and pink. Prosperity came with the second, sometimes even with the first, generation. There was hard work and plain living; but why should there be *spare* living in the midst of acres and acres of great fat cornfields growing out of the richest, most fertile soil on earth? Spare living and transcendental thinking did not go with the Iowa landscape, but with

> . . . the stony fields where clear
> Through the thin trees the skies appear,
> In delicate spare soil and fen,
> And slender landscape and austere.

Really heroic efforts were made to preserve the old ideals. Little delicate children of New Englanders were carefully set apart, guarded in speech and action from the common herd, and destined for Wellesley. Every religious denomination set up two or three colleges. The Colonial Dames and the D. A. R. held off the rabble. One family even papered the walls of a necessary building with quotations from Emerson for the spiritual edification of its children; devotion to the finer things can not be expected to go much farther than that. But it was like holding a little fort against the barbarians. And instead of being

611

sent reinforcements from the central citadel, the poor meek outlanders were sneered upon and neglected.

It might have been a simpler problem had our earlier settlers actually been aborigines. But they were beings from nations that had already reached a degree of civilization. Distance could differentiate, but not completely separate them. Cultural activities had to be suspended for a time while the people made for themselves a secure shelter in this new wilderness. Raw nature was conquered almost within the space of a generation. The material basis was quickly established. It was natural that, freshened and invigorated by change, the other activities should be quickly resumed.

This was where the difficulty came in. For the sheer distance had wrought a difference, just as the loyal torch-bearers had feared. The elements of population were diverse. They could not fit into that New England mold of culture which was the only conceivable mold. It was as if a young sculptor had been given tools carefully preserved for him but designed for a material not his, and told at the same time that it would be a crime against art to devise others; or as if with unused clay all about him and tempting him to design, he had been warned that only that far away somewhere, the nature of which he did not understand, could ever be fit for design at all. There were books, and reading was not a lost art. But there seemed to be no bridging of the gulf between the experience of life and the experience of books. Culture, art, beauty, were fixed in certain places.

This faith was so drilled into the children in various and subtle ways that all our bright young people grew up with the most curious sense of exile. An instance may be taken from "Main Street," for the thing was true of the whole Middle West. At first glance, it would seem incongruous that Carol Kennicott, born in Mankato, Minn., and with an experience of travel ranging from St. Paul to Chicago, should feel herself an exile and a stranger in Gopher Prairie. But nothing could have been more natural. Carol's father, "the learned and the kindly," was a judge from Massachusetts, and Mankato, Sinclair Lewis carefully tells us, was not a prairie town but "green-and-white New England re-born." Had Carol been born in Gopher Prairie itself, of devout New England parents, she would have felt the same. And had she been born in Iowa, her faith would have been disputed by no one, not even by Doc Kennicott himself.

It was an axiom of youth that the home town was "dead." All sorts of changes, from the facetious to the agonizing, were rung upon this theme—and with partial truth. Many young people forced themselves away and doomed themselves to a kind of rootless exile simply to prove themselves socially or intellectually and artistically enterprising, and to escape the stigma attached to "just settling down at home." To say of a bright young man when college was over, "Oh, he's gone back to Cornville and he's living there," was to prove him without ambition. The flocks of talented girls graduated every year from the colleges must go East if they were to live up to the flowery expectations held for them. Boys and girls no sooner got away to college, perhaps eighty miles from home, than they began to regard the home town from a standpoint of detached superiority, with a lightly humorous and patronizing touch. Some of this, of course, was assumed from youthful smartness, but the peculiar thing is that most of it was genuine. Those who went on, seeking something indefinable in far places, some stamp of mystic authority, repudiated the home town with a feeling of bitter alienation.

This sense of exile has colored nearly all the expression of the Middle West, in whatever medium; and for years it kept timorous and reverent Iowa from any expression at all except that of a nervous imitation. It is the spirit of colonialism at its last gasp, and to some extent the counterpart of that pathetic lack of self-dependence and uncertain nostalgia for something fixed and certain of the semi-Europeanized American, which is reflected in so many of the novels of Henry James and Anne Douglas Sedgwick. It is the thing which differentiates the provincial of America from the provincial of Europe. The wandering children of our Middle Western small towns do not own that deep loyalty to the province and the village of their birth sung in old ballads (although they may have tremendous loyalty to European villages!). Instead, they labor for years to obliterate all traces of it. They delve into the remotest branches of their ancestry and announce themselves "from Virginia," or "from California" after their parents have spent a Winter in Los Angeles, South or West of the Fiji Islands—but not the home town. The most noticeable thing about this attitude is not so much its existence, however, as its intense self-consciousness.

III

The thing which gave this sense of exile its peculiarly American quality was the fact of distance without the more complete separation which a great body of water gives. The East was far away, but not too far to be reached. Therefore, the timid Middle Western States could never forget its existence. Its eye might be upon them, even if negligently.

Of all these meek States, Iowa, which is on the fence geographically, politically, religiously and aesthetically, has been the meekest. A trifle more of even Babbitt bumptiousness would have helped it long ago. It was far too deeply imbued with a reverence for Puritan culture to attempt even a youthful swagger. It is, therefore, this very distance which has proved the one saving necessity, rescuing Iowa from the neither-this-nor-thatness of such a State as Ohio.

For, placed inland, far from every coast, Iowa was hopelessly far from Europe. New England looked to England; Iowa looked to New England and the Eastern sea board. New England took culture at second hand; Iowa took it at third hand. And while the whole Middle West had the East as a bug-a-boo, it did not have the hypothetical opinions of that "highly civilized European" which so long made the cultured Easterner shake in his shoes. Here, pure ignorance and pure humility saved Iowa. "He that is down need fear no fall," Bunyan sang. Almost the only claim of Iowa among these United States (aside from a little pride in the matter of corn and hogs) has been for the place of the lowest. But yielding itself thus, not only submissively but with ardor, to the charge of provincialism, it lost colonialism, by far the more insidious disease of the two.

There can be some pretension about a garment worn at second hand. But that worn at third hand gets too thread-bare. Yet there was pioneer blood in Iowa for all its meekness. It could not stay away forever because of lack of the proper clothes. Its first literary efforts, largely poetical, had been naturally the dilution of a dilution. It was perhaps unforgiveable impudence even to contemplate poetry in a country where the lanes were dirt roads, the rills "cricks" and the villages "burgs." These early poetizers used a manner that sat as stiffly upon their material as his Sunday suit upon a farmer. They called it "style." Little real roughnesses which kept creeping in were quickly put out of sight for fear of "the opinion the East would get of us." Our culture must always be dressed up in its third hand garments to meet the eye of the East. At last the garment went to pieces. The awkward, growing young creature could no longer attempt to hide his big hands and feet. The culture of Iowa either had to shut itself up or appear in homemade clothes.

It appeared, but still with the customary note of fear and apology. A gentleman pleaded in the now deceased *Grinnell Review* for an Iowa literature; but for one which would deal, not with the "uncouth characters" of Hamlin Garland, that gave such a bad impression to the East, but with our best people. Herbert Quick wrote his lovable records of pioneer life in "Vandemark's Folly" and "The Hawkeye." But he was careful to link this life to the life of books. "I know this is a raw country," he said in effect. "These are only common folks. But remember that these young people of mine were lovers, just as Lancelot and Guinevere were lovers, and don't entirely despise them." This attitude was not so surprising when you consider that for years Mr.

Quick had been wanting to write these stories and had been told by editors that "Iowa was not literary material." The point, however, is the customary docility and lack of conviction which led him to accept this dictum for so long, and not, like the old Scotchman, feel that he "must do it whatever."

But Mr. Quick kept faith with his material in the end and his achievement is to be respected. Long before, Hamlin Garland with his "uncouth characters" had made the first vital attempt to deal with the raw material of art in a new country. He fell by the wayside. After writing his saga of the Garlands and the McClintocks in "A Son of the Middle Border," we find him in the succeeding volume thanking his readers with lowly amazement for their interest in such commonplace chronicles. "A Daughter of the Middle Border" is the sum total of this whole matter of the mental meekness and uncertainty of the Middle Westerner. It is an intellectual and spiritual tragedy with terribly comic elements. The attitude of Mr. Garland that is revealed with only too much transparency in this book has been the attitude of the Middle West, and of Iowa above all, for many years. Mr. Garland's people moved West and he had to go out into the fields. But he knew that farmer clothes were not the thing for a literary man. He ought to dress up in either a cowboy suit or a silk hat, or perhaps a velvet tam o' shanter. The sad thing is that his native gift was far superior to Mr. Quick's. It was courage rather than ability which failed him.

Later writers have been most uncomfortably aware of the home State and the home town. They have tried to deal with each from a perch of humorous aloofness, attained after an absence of five or six years, introducing characters from the great world with all the fidgety awareness of a youth ashamed of his humble antecedents and trying to pass them off as funny. This cringing attitude is apparent in all the admitted culture of Iowa. It is extremely self-conscious, uncertain now of the old and still more uncertain of the new. The thin grasp of New England has gradually weakened. New York has to a great extent taken its place in the people's awe, but New York is full of Middle Westerners and therefore attainable. The raw vigor of other elements in the life of the State is working into its sacred culture as well. The fog of old timidities still hangs over its intellectual life like a damp cloud; but—tentatively, humbly, with sad disillusionment mingled with a faint hope—a native culture has begun to work its way out.

The foreign element is important here. The prairies more than the cities, it may be, have been a melting-pot, for on them the foreign element has been welded into the life of the place and something that goes far toward being genuine is resulting. Some of the old Germans and Dutch and Norwegians have clung tightly to their ancient customs, but the majority, when they came to this country, definitely left the Old World behind. They looked back with affection, very deep and real, to the "old country," but it was not the "mother country"; and there was an immense difference of viewpoint in this very difference of phrase. These people were coming on a desperate adventure. They had to strike their roots deeply and finally here. It is not the English of the second or third generation in Iowa who look back with awe to England. Strangely enough, it is those who have been longest established on this young continent and proudly call themselves its native stock, who are most worried and timid about the American attitude and unable to accept it naturally. The same thing is true, in its slightly differing way, of our oldest families in Iowa.

To be sure, there have been great cultural lacks and disadvantages in this attitude of the foreign stock. Part of a very precious heritage has been lost. Crudeness has inevitably resulted. But crudeness is after all of less importance than the quality of the metal. And it has had its rough value, like the old method of plunging a boy straight into the water and making him sink or swim in the new element. It has added a certain tough hardiness to the pale remnant of transcendentalism.

The thin little stream of colonialism has almost dried up on the prairies. They are too big for it. Simple space defeats it. Besides, hundreds of ignorant young "foreigners" on the farms have never heard of it. They are so simple as to accept their own country as having its natural claims to a natural place in the world. One after another of the prairie States has begun to find this out, the least cultured first, until at last timid Iowa has dared to lift its eyes even in the presence of the East. Even those old and final strongholds, the colleges, are weakening. Professors, uncomfortably although disdainfully aware of iconoclastic young instructors, retreat farther and farther as they hold their standards against the onslaught of the mob.

The effect of this general break-up of culture has been distinctly and amazingly noticeable during the last three or four years. A terrific rattle of typewriters has broken out. Newspapers are beginning to carry book columns of their own. People dare to send their own unsubstantiated opinions to the liberal and lively book page of the Des Moines *Register*. The group at the State university has at last been accepted as culturally respectable in spite of its native origin. The barriers have come down, to the horror of the old guard, who can really recommend no American contemporaries except Mrs. Wharton. No longer is our literature in the hands of a caste. It is snatched at by everybody—farmer boys, dentists, telegraph editors in small towns, students, undertakers, insurance agents and nobodies. All have a try at it. Every good-sized town has its band of ladies who meet to discuss the literary markets (wearing smocks in one instance as a badge of aesthetic dignity), and who yearn to desert their husbands for a year at Columbia. A gathering of the literary clans is enough to bowl over the observer with the sight of its astounding and delicious diversity. All the elements, old and new, are jumbled up together until it seems impossible to guess what can be fished out of the muddle. But miscellaneous as the thing is, it is at least active, which under the old régime was the very last thing it dared to be.

IV

And this very activity is a sign that a settling process is going on. The old self-deprecation is still on top. It persists among our best people and our ex-patriots. Just a layer below this is the mild idealism of the colleges, very milk-and-watery, into which the faith of the Pilgrims has developed under the impetus of material prosperity. It trusts that all things can be tested upon an ethical basis according to the moral value of their service to humanity, and is touchingly innocent of the cold rigor of aesthetics. Below this, and supporting it, is good prosperous Babbittry that judges life in terms of houses, automobiles and radios, and lets its womenfolk go in for books and frills in the Woman's Club. There is the Main Street element of small town hardness, dreariness and tense material ambition. Still below this, solid and unyielding, is the retired farmer element in the towns: narrow, cautious, steady and thrifty, suspicious of "culture" but faithful to the churches, beginning to travel a little in big automobiles; of varying nationalities, but in the main Anglo-Saxon, Teutonic and Scandinavian; whose womenfolk still apologize if caught spending good time (which might be given to fancy work) over a book. And then there are the working farmers, the folk element and still the very soil and bedrock of our native culture. Raw, book-ignorant, travel-ignorant, stubborn and hard-headed; but in their best aspect hard-working, serious-minded, strong and fresh. They give a saving rudeness, vigor and individuality to the too mild brew which—now that pioneer days are over—would be the spirit of Iowa without them.

Whatever real intrinsic value the culture and art of Iowa can have is founded upon this bedrock. Other elements may influence and vary it, but this is at the bottom of them all. Our varying nationalities meet in this rich soil which has still some of the old pioneer virtue of sturdy freshness—perhaps the only virtue, genuine and clearly distinguishable from all others, which the native culture of this young country has to offer. Certainly, without this underlying strong basis, and if it depended merely upon our best people, what we call culture in Iowa would still be as insipid as cambric tea.

Now that all these diversities have at last come together, they begin to suggest something distinctive. That something is, at its worst, timid, deprecating, wishy-washy, colorless, and idealistic in a mild fruitless way. At its best, it is innocently ingenuous, fresh and sincere, unpretentious, and essentially ample, with a certain quality of pure loveliness—held together and strengthened by the simplicity and severity of its hard-working farmer people.

Nebraska

by WILLA CATHER, 1876–   . *One of the most distinguished modern American novelists, Willa Cather was born in Winchester, Virginia, but as a child was taken to Nebraska and there spent her adolescent years. After being graduated from the University of Nebraska, B.A., 1895, she engaged in teaching and journalism in Pittsburgh and New York City. From 1906 to 1912 she was associate editor of McClure's Magazine, but she resigned to devote all her time to writing. Miss Cather has written verse and essays but she is known primarily as a novelist. Some of her best work is to be found in her early trilogy of Nebraska novels, O Pioneers (1913), The Song of the Lark (1915), and My Antonia (1918). These deal largely with the problems of Swedish and Bohemian immigrants on the Nebraska prairies and suggest the rewards that are inevitable if the farmers show sufficient energy and optimism. A later novel, One of Ours (1922), was awarded the Pulitzer prize, but Miss Cather's most successful novels have been re-creations of Santa Fe and Quebec, respectively Death Comes for the Archbishop (1927) and Shadows on the Rock (1931). Always a careful and charming stylist, she wrote probably her finest prose in her descriptions of the New Mexico scenery. The essay on Nebraska was contributed to a symposium on the forty-eight states and is unique in its perception of the racial and geographical backgrounds of the state.*

THE State of Nebraska is part of the great plain which stretches west of the Missouri River, gradually rising until it reaches the Rocky Mountains. The character of all this country between the river and the mountains is essentially the same throughout its extent: a rolling, alluvial plain, growing gradually more sandy toward the west, until it breaks into the white sand-hills of western Nebraska and Kansas and eastern Colorado. From east to west this plain measures something over five hundred miles; in appearance it resembles the wheat lands of

Russia, which fed the continent of Europe for so many years. Like Little Russia it is watered by slow-flowing, muddy rivers, which run full in the spring, often cutting into the farm lands along their banks; but by midsummer they lie low and shrunken, their current split by glistening white sandbars half overgrown with scrub willows.

The climate, with its extremes of temperature, gives to this plateau the variety which, to the casual eye at least, it lacks. There we have short, bitter winters; windy, flower-laden springs; long, hot summers; triumphant autumns that last until Christmas—a season of perpetual sunlight, blazing blue skies, and frosty nights. In this newest part of the New World autumn is the season of beauty and sentiment, as spring is in the Old World.

Nebraska is a newer State than Kansas. It was a State before there were people in it. Its social history falls easily within a period of sixty years, and the first stable settlements of white men were made within the memory of old folk now living. The earliest of these settlements —Bellevue, Omaha, Brownville, Nebraska City—were founded along the Missouri River, which was at that time a pathway for small steamers. In 1855–1860 these four towns were straggling groups of log houses, hidden away along the wooded river banks.

Before 1860 civilization did no more than nibble at the eastern edge of the State, along the river bluffs. Lincoln, the present capital, was open prairie; and the whole of the great plain to the westward was still a sunny wilderness, where the tall red grass and the buffalo and the Indian hunter were undisturbed. Fremont, with Kit Carson, the famous scout, had gone across Nebraska in 1842, exploring the valley of the Platte. In the days of the Mormon persecution fifteen thousand Mormons camped for two years, 1845–1846, six miles north of Omaha, while their exploring parties went farther west, searching for fertile land outside of government jurisdiction. In 1847 the entire Mormon sect, under the leadership of Brigham Young, went with their wagons through Nebraska and on to that desert beside the salty sea which they have made so fruitful.

In forty-nine and the early fifties, gold hunters, bound for California, crossed the State in thousands, always following the old Indian trail along the Platte Valley. The State was a highway for dreamers and adventurers; men who were in quest of gold or grace, freedom or romance. With all these people the road led out, but never back again.

While Nebraska was a camping-ground for seekers outward bound, the wooden settlements along the Missouri were growing into something permanent. The settlers broke the ground and began to plant the fine orchards which have ever since been the pride of Otoe and Nemaha counties. It was at Brownville that the first telegraph wire was brought across the Missouri River. When I was a child I heard ex-Governor Furness relate how he stood with other pioneers in the log cabin where the Morse instrument had been installed, and how, when it began to click, the men took off their hats as if they were in church. The first message flashed across the river into Nebraska was not a market report, but a line of poetry: "Westward the course of empire takes its way." The Old West was like that.

The first back-and-forth travel through the State was by way of the Overland Mail, a monthly passenger-and-mail-stage service across the plains from Independence to the newly founded colony at Salt Lake—a distance of twelve hundred miles.

When silver ore was discovered in the mountains of Colorado near Cherry Creek—afterward Camp Denver and later the city of Denver —a picturesque form of commerce developed across the great plain of Nebraska: the transporting of food and merchandise from the Missouri to the Colorado mining camps, and on to the Mormon settlement at Salt Lake. One of the largest freighting companies, operating out of Nebraska City, in the six summer months of 1860 carried nearly three million pounds of freight across Nebraska, employing 515 wagons, 5,687 oxen, and 600 drivers.

The freighting began in the early spring, usually about the middle of April, and continued all summer and through the long, warm autumns. The oxen made from ten to twenty miles a day. I have heard the old freighters say that, after embarking on their six-hundred mile trail, they lost count of the days of the week and the days of the month. While they were out in that sea of waving grass, one day was like another; and if one can trust the memory of these old men, all days were glorious. The buffalo trails still ran north and south then; deep, dusty paths the bison wore when, single file, they came north in the spring for the summer grass, and went south again in the autumn. Along these trails were the buffalo "wallows"—shallow depressions where the rain water gathered when it ran off the tough prairie sod. These wallows the big beasts wore deeper and packed hard when they rolled about and bathed in the pools, so that they held water like a cement bottom. The freighters lived on game and shot the buffalo for their hides. The grass was full of quail and prairie chickens, and flocks of wild ducks swam about on the lagoons. These lagoons have long since disappeared, but they were beautiful things in their time; long stretches where the rain water gathered and lay clear on a grassy bottom without mud. From the lagoons the first settlers hauled water to their homesteads, before they had dug their wells. The freighters could recognize the lagoons from afar by the clouds of golden coreopsis which grew up out of the water and waved delicately above its surface. Among the pioneers the coreopsis was known simply as "the lagoon flower."

As the railroads came in, the freighting business died out. Many a freight-driver settled down upon some spot he had come to like on his journeys to and fro, homesteaded it, and wandered no more. The Union Pacific, the first transcontinental railroad, was completed in 1869. The Burlington entered Nebraska in the same year, at Platts-mouth, and began construction westward. It finally reached Denver by an indirect route, and went on extending and ramifying through the State. With the railroads came the home-seeking people from overseas.

When the first courageous settlers came straggling out through the waste with their oxen and covered wagons, they found open range all the way from Lincoln to Denver; a continuous, undulating plateau, covered with long, red, shaggy grass. The prairie was green only where it had been burned off in the spring by the new settlers or by the Indians, and toward autumn even the new grass became a coppery brown. This sod, which had never been broken by the plow, was so tough and strong with the knotted grass roots of many years, that the home-seekers were able to peel it off the earth like peat, cut it up into bricks, and make of it warm, comfortable, durable houses. Some of these sod houses lingered on until the open range was gone, and the whole face of the country had been changed.

Even as late as 1885 the central part of the State, and everything to the westward, was, in the main, raw prairie. The cultivated fields and broken land seemed mere scratches in the brown, running steppe that never stopped until it broke against the foothills of the Rockies. The dugouts and sod farm houses were three or four miles apart, and the only means of communication was the heavy farm wagon, drawn by heavy work horses. The early population of Nebraska was largely transatlantic. The county in which I grew up, in the south-central part of the State, was typical. On Sunday we could drive to a Nor-wegian church and listen to a sermon in that language, or to a Danish or a Swedish church. We could go to the French Catholic settlement in the next county and hear a sermon in French, or into the Bohemian township and hear one in Czech, or we could go to church with the German Lutherans. There were, of course, American congregations also.

There is a Prague in Nebraska as well as in Bohemia. Many of our Czech immigrants were people of a very superior type. The political emigration resulting from the revolutionary disturbances of 1848 was distinctly different from the emigration resulting from economic causes, and brought to the United States brilliant young men both from Germany and Bohemia. In Nebraska our Czech settlements were large and very prosperous. I have walked about the streets of Wilber, the county seat of Saline County, for a whole day without hearing a word of English spoken. In Wilber, in the old days, behind the big, friendly brick saloon—it was not a "saloon," properly speaking, but a beer garden, where the farmers ate their lunch when they came to town—there was a pleasant little theater where the boys and girls were trained to give the masterpieces of Czech drama in the Czech language. "Americanization" has doubtless done away with all this. Our lawmakers have a rooted conviction that a boy can be a better American if he speaks only one language than if he speaks two. I could name a dozen Bohemian towns in Nebraska where one used to be able to go into a bakery and buy better pastry than is to be had anywhere except in the best pastry shops of Prague or Vienna. The American lard pie never corrupted the Czech.

Cultivated, restless young men from Europe made incongruous figures among the hard-handed breakers of the soil. Frederick Amiel's nephew lived for many years and finally died among the Nebraska farmers. Amiel's letters to his kinsman were published in the *Atlantic Monthly* of March, 1921, under the title "Amiel in Nebraska." Camille Saint-Saëns's cousin lived just over the line, in Kansas. Knut Hamsun, the Norwegian writer who was awarded the Nobel Prize for 1920, was a "hired hand" on a Dakota farm to the north of us. Colonies of European people, Slavonic, Germanic, Scandinavian, Latin, spread across our bronze prairies like the daubs of color on a painter's palette. They brought with them something that this neutral new world needed even more than the immigrants needed land.

Unfortunately, their American neighbors were seldom open-minded enough to understand the Europeans, or to profit by their older traditions. Our settlers from New England, cautious and convinced of their own superiority, kept themselves isolated as much as possible from foreign influences. The incomers from the South—from Missouri, Kentucky, the two Virginias—were provincial and utterly without curiosity. They were kind neighbors—lent a hand to help a Swede when he was sick or in trouble. But I am quite sure that Knut Hamsun might have worked a year for any one of our Southern farmers, and his employer would never have discovered that there was anything unusual about the Norwegian. A New England settler might have noticed that his chore-boy had a kind of intelligence, but he would have distrusted and stonily disregarded it. If the daughter of a shiftless West Virginia mountaineer married the nephew of a professor at the University of Upsala, the native family felt disgraced by such an alliance.

Nevertheless, the thrift and intelligence of its preponderant European population have been potent factors in bringing about the present prosperity of the State. The census of 1910 showed that there were then 228,648 foreign-born and native-born Germans living in Nebraska; 103,503 Scandinavians; 50,680 Czechs. The total foreign population of the State was then 900,571 while the entire population was 1,192,214. That is, in round numbers, there were about nine hundred thousand foreign Americans in the State, to three hundred thousand native stock. With such a majority of foreign stock, nine to three, it would be absurd to say that the influence of the European does not cross the boundary of his own acres, and has had nothing to do with shaping the social ideals of the commonwealth.

When I stop at one of the graveyards in my own county, and see on the headstones the names of fine old men I used to know: *"Eric Ericson, born Bergen, Norway . . . died Nebraska," "Anton Pucelik, born Prague, Bohemia . . . died Nebraska,"* I have always the hope that something went into the ground with those pioneers that will one day come out again. Something that will come out not only in sturdy traits of character, but in elasticity of mind, in an honest attitude toward the realities of life, in certain qualities of feeling and imagination. Some years ago a professor at the University of Nebraska happened to tell me about a boy in one of his Greek classes who had a very unusual taste for the classics—intuitions and perceptions in literature. This puzzled him, he said, as the boy's parents had no interest in such things. I knew what the professor did not: that, though this boy had an American name, his grandfather was a Norwegian, a musician of high attainment, a fellow-student and life-long friend of Edvard Grieg. It is in that great cosmopolitan country known as the Middle West that we may hope to see the hard molds of American provincialism broken up; that we may hope to find young talent which will challenge the pale proprieties, the insincere, conventional optimism of our art and thought.

The rapid industrial development of Nebraska, which began in the latter eighties, was arrested in the years 1893–1897 by a succession of crop failures and by the financial depression which spread over the whole country at that time—the depression which produced the People's Party and the Free Silver agitation. These years of trial, as every one now realizes, had a salutary effect upon the new State. They winnowed out the settlers with a purpose from the drifting malcontents who are ever seeking a land where man does not live by the sweat of his brow. The slack farmer moved on. Superfluous banks failed, and money lenders who drove hard bargains with desperate men came to grief. The strongest stock survived, and within ten years those who had weathered the storm came into their reward. What that reward is, you can see for yourself if you motor through the State from Omaha to the

Colorado Line. The country has no secrets; it is as open as an honest human face.

The old, isolated farms have come together. They rub shoulders. The whole State is a farm. Now it is the pasture lands that look little and lonely, crowded in among so much wheat and corn. It is scarcely an exaggeration to say that every farmer owns an automobile. I believe the last estimate showed that there is one motor car for every six inhabitants in Nebraska. The old farm houses are rapidly being replaced by more cheerful dwellings, with bathrooms and hardwood floors, heated by furnaces or hot-water plants. Many of them are lighted by electricity, and every farm house has its telephone. The country towns are clean and well kept. On Saturday night the main street is a long black line of parked motor cars; the farmers have brought their families to town to see the moving picture show. When the school bell rings on Monday morning, crowds of happy looking children, well nourished— for the most part well mannered, too—flock along the shady streets. They wear cheerful, modern clothes, and the girls, like the boys, are elastic and vigorous in their movements. These thousands and thousands of children—in the little towns and in the country schools— these, of course, ten years from now, will be the State.

In this time of prosperity any farmer boy who wishes to study at the State University can do so. A New York lawyer who went out to Lincoln to assist in training the university students for military service in war time exclaimed when he came back: "What splendid young men! I would not have believed that any school in the world could get together so many boys physically fit, and so few unfit."

Of course, there is the other side of the medal, stamped with the ugly crest of materialism, which has set its seal upon all of our most productive commonwealths. Too much prosperity, too many moving picture shows, too much gaudy fiction have colored the taste and manners of so many of these Nebraskans of the future. There, as elsewhere, one finds the frenzy to be showy; farmer boys who wish to be spenders before they are earners, girls who try to look like the heroines of the cinema screen; a coming generation which tries to cheat its aesthetic sense by buying things instead of making anything. There is even danger that that fine institution, the University of Nebraska, may become a gigantic trade school. The men who control its destiny, the regents and the lawmakers, wish their sons and daughters to study machines, mercantile processes, "the principles of business"; everything that has to do with the game of getting on in the world—and nothing else. The classics, the humanities, are having their dark hour. They are in eclipse. Studies that develop taste and enrich personality are not encouraged. But the "Classics" have a way of revenging themselves. One may venture to hope that the children, or the grandchildren, of a generation that goes to a university to select only the most utilitarian subjects in the course of study—among them, salesmanship and dressmaking—will revolt against all the heaped up, machine-made materialism about them. They will go back to the old sources of culture and wisdom—not as a duty, but with burning desire.

In Nebraska, as in so many other States, we must face the fact that the splendid story of the pioneers is finished, and that no new story worthy to take its place has yet begun. The generation that subdued the wild land and broke up the virgin prairie is passing, but it is still there, a group of rugged figures in the background which inspire respect, compel admiration. With these old men and women the attainment of material prosperity was a moral victory, because it was wrung from hard conditions, was the result of a struggle that tested character. They can look out over those broad stretches of fertility and say: "We made this, with our backs and hands." The sons, the generation now in middle life, were reared amid hardships, and it is perhaps natural that they should be very much interested in material comfort, in buying whatever is expensive and ugly. Their fathers came into a wilderness and had to make everything, had to be as ingenious as shipwrecked sailors. The generation now in the driver's seat hates to make anything, wants to live and die in an automobile, scudding past those acres where the old men used to follow the long corn-rows up and down. They want to buy everything ready-made: clothes, food, education, music, pleasure. Will the third generation—the full-blooded, joyous one just coming over the hill—will it be fooled? Will it believe that to live easily is to live happily?

The wave of generous idealism, noble seriousness, which swept over the State of Nebraska in 1917 and 1918, demonstrated how fluid and flexible is any living, growing, expanding society. If such "conversions" do not last, they at least show of what men and women are capable. Surely the materialism and showy extravagance of this hour are a passing phase! They will mean no more in half a century from now than will the "hard times" of twenty-five years ago—which are already forgotten. The population is as clean and full of vigor as the soil; there are no old grudges, no heritages of disease or hate. The belief that snug success and easy money are the real aims of human life has settled down over our prairies, but it has not yet hardened into molds and crusts. The people are warm, mercurial, impressionable, restless, overfond of novelty and change. These are not the qualities which make the dull chapters of history.

Kansas

by CARL BECKER, 1873–1945. *One of the most distinguished of American historians, Dr. Becker was born in Blackhawk County, Iowa, and educated at Cornell College and the University of Wisconsin, B.Litt., 1896, Ph.D., 1907. A long teaching career followed which took him to Pennsylvania State College, Dartmouth, the University of Kansas, the University of Minnesota, and finally in 1917 Cornell University. Dr. Becker has written many articles and books on historical themes, among them The Eve of the Revolution (1918), Modern History (1931), and Every Man His Own Historian (1935). The essay on Kansas, contributed to the volume commemorating the historical work of Frederick Jackson Turner (1910), is a shrewd and informative appraisal of one middlewestern state.*

SOME years ago, in a New England college town, when I informed one of my New England friends that I was preparing to go to Kansas, he replied rather blankly, "Kansas?! Oh." The amenities of casual intercourse demanded a reply, certainly, but from the point of view of my New England friend I suppose there was really nothing more to say; and, in fact, standing there under the peaceful New England elms, Kansas did seem tolerably remote. Some months later I rode out of Kansas City and entered for the first time what I had always pictured as the land of grasshoppers, of arid drought, and barren social experimentation. In the seat just ahead were two young women, girls rather, whom I afterwards saw at the university. As we left the dreary yards behind, and entered the half-open country along the Kansas River, one of the pair, breaking abruptly away from the ceaseless chatter that had hitherto engrossed them both, began looking out of the car window. Her attention seemed fixed, for perhaps a quarter of an hour, upon something in the scene outside—the fields of corn, or it may have been the sunflowers that lined the track; but at last, turning to her companion with the contented sigh of a returning exile, she said, *"Dear old Kansas!"* The expression somehow recalled my New England friend. I wondered vaguely, as I was sure he would have done, why anyone should feel moved to say "Dear old Kansas!" I had supposed that Kansas, even more than Italy, was only a geographical expression. But not so. Not infrequently, since then, I have heard the same expression—not always from emotional young girls. To understand why people say "Dear old Kansas!" is to understand that Kansas is no mere geographical expression, but a "state of mind," a religion, and a philosophy in one.

The difference between the expression of my staid New England friend and that of the enthusiastic young Kansan is perhaps symbolical, in certain respects, of the difference between those who remain at home and those who, in successive generations, venture into the unknown "West"—New England or Kansas—wherever it may be. In the seventeenth century there was doubtless no lack of Englishmen—prelates, for example, in lawn sleeves, comfortably buttressed about by tithes and the Thirty-nine Articles—who might have indicated their point of view quite fully by remarking, "New England? Oh." Whether any New Englander of that day ever went so far as to say "Dear old New England" I do not know. But that the sentiment was there, furnishing fuel for the inner light, is past question. Nowadays the superiority of New England is taken for granted, I believe, by the people who live there; but in the seventeenth century, when its inhabitants were mere frontiersmen, they were given, much as Kansans are said to be now, to boasting—alas! even of the climate. In 1629, Mr. Higginson, a reverend gentleman, informed his friends back in England that "The temper of the air of New England is one special thing that commends this place. Experience doth manifest that there is hardly a more healthful place to be found in the world that agreeth better with our English bodies. Many that have been weak and sickly in old England, by coming hither have been thoroughly healed and grown healthful strong. For here is a most extraordinary clear and dry air that is of a most healing nature to all such as are of a cold, melancholy, phlegmatic, rheumatic temper of body. . . . And therefore I think it a wise course for all cold complexions to come to take physic in New England; for a sup of New England air is better than a whole draft of old England's ale." Now we who live in Kansas know well that its climate is superior to any other in the world, and that it enables one, more readily than any other, to dispense with the use of ale.

There are those who will tell us, and have indeed often told us, with a formidable array of statistics, that Kansas is inhabited only in small part by New Englanders, and that it is therefore fanciful in the extreme to think of it as representing Puritanism transplanted. It is true, the people of Kansas came mainly from "the Middle West"—from Illinois, Indiana, Ohio, Iowa, Kentucky, and Missouri. But for our purpose the fact is of little importance, for it is the ideals of a people rather than the geography they have outgrown that determine their destiny; and in Kansas, as has been well said, "it is the ideas of the Pilgrims, not their descendants, that have had dominion in the young commonwealth." Ideas, sometimes, as well as the star of empire, move westward, and so it happens that Kansas is more Puritan than New England of today. It is akin to New England of early days. It is what New England, old

England itself, once was—the frontier, an ever-changing spot where dwell the courageous who defy fate and conquer circumstance.

For the frontier is more than a matter of location, and Puritanism is itself a kind of frontier. There is an intellectual "West" as well as a territorial "West." Both are heresies, the one as much subject to the scorn of the judicious as the other. Broad classifications of people are easily made and are usually inaccurate; but they are convenient for taking a large view, and it may be worth while to think, for the moment, of two kinds of people—those who like the sheltered life, and those who cannot endure it, those who think the world as they know it is well enough, and those who dream of something better, or, at any rate, something different. From age to age society builds its shelters of various sorts—accumulated traditions, religious creeds, political institutions, and intellectual conceptions, cultivated and well-kept farms, well-built and orderly cities—providing a monotonous and comfortable life that tends always to harden into conventional forms resisting change. With all this the homekeeping and timid are well content. They sit in accustomed corners, disturbed by no fortuitous circumstance. But there are those others who are forever tugging at the leashes of ordered life, eager to venture into the unknown. Forsaking beaten paths, they plunge into the wilderness. They must be always on the frontier of human endeavor, submitting what is old and accepted to conditions that are new and untried. The frontier is thus the seed plot where new forms of life, whether of institutions or types of thought, are germinated, the condition of all progress being in a sense a return to the primitive.

Now, generally speaking, the men who make the world's frontiers, whether in religion or politics, science, or geographical exploration and territorial settlement, have certain essential and distinguishing qualities. They are primarily men of faith. Having faith in themselves, they are individualists. They are idealists because they have faith in the universe, being confident that somehow everything is right at the center of things; they give hostage to the future, are ever inventing God anew, and must be always transforming the world into their ideal of it. They have faith in humanity and in the perfectibility of man, are likely, therefore, to be believers in equality, reformers, intolerant, aiming always to level others up to their own high vantage. These qualities are not only Puritanism transplanted, but Americanism transplanted. In the individualism, the idealism, the belief in equality that prevail in Kansas, we shall therefore see nothing strangely new, but simply a new graft of familiar American traits. But, as Kansas is a community with a peculiar and distinctive experience, there is something peculiar and distinctive about the individualism, the idealism, and the belief in equality of its people. If we can get at this something peculiar and distinctive, it will be possible to understand why the sight of sunflowers growing beside a railroad track may call forth the fervid expression "Dear old Kansas."

Individualism is everywhere characteristic of the frontier, and in America, where the geographical frontier has hitherto played so predominant a part, a peculiarly marked type of individualism is one of the most obvious traits of the people. "To the frontier," Professor Turner has said, "the American intellect owes its striking characteristics. That coarseness and strength combined with acuteness and inquisitiveness; that practical, inventive turn of mind, quick to find expedients; that masterful grasp of material things, lacking in the artistic but powerful to effect great ends; that restless nervous energy; that dominant individualism, working for good and for evil, and withal that buoyancy and exuberance that comes from freedom." On the frontier, where everything is done by the individual and nothing by organized society, initiative, resourcefulness, quick, confident, and sure judgment are the essential qualities for success. But, as the problems of the frontier are rather restricted and definite, those who succeed there have necessarily much the same kind of initiative and resourcefulness, and their judgment will be sure only in respect to the problems that are familiar to all. It thus happens that the type of individualism produced on the frontier and predominant in America has this peculiarity, that, while the sense of freedom is strong, there is nevertheless a certain uniformity in respect to ability, habit, and point of view. The frontier develops strong individuals, but it develops individuals of a particular type, all being after much the same pattern. The individualism of the frontier is one of achievement, not of eccentricity, an individualism of fact rising from a sense of power to overcome obstacles, rather than one of theory growing out of weakness in the face of oppression. It is not because he fears governmental activity, but because he has so often had to dispense with it, that the American is an individualist. Altogether averse from hesitancy, doubt, speculative or introspective tendencies, the frontiersman is a man of faith: of faith, not so much in some external power, as in himself, in his luck, his destiny; faith in the possibility of achieving whatever is necessary or he desires. It is this marked self-reliance that gives to Americans their tremendous power of initiative; but the absence of deep-seated differences gives to them an equally tremendous power of concerted social action.

The confident individualism of those who achieve through endurance is a striking trait of the people of Kansas. There, indeed, the trait has in it an element of exaggeration, arising from the fact that whatever has been achieved in Kansas has been achieved under great difficulties. Kansans have been subjected, not only to the ordinary hardships of the frontier, but to a succession of reverses and disasters that could be survived only by those for whom defeat is worse than death, who cannot fail because they cannot surrender. To the border wars succeeded hot winds, droughts, grasshoppers; and to the disasters of nature succeeded in turn the scourge of man, in the form of "mortgage fiends" and a contracting currency. Until 1895 the whole history of the state was a series of disasters, and always something new, extreme, bizarre, until the name Kansas became a byword, a synonym for the impossible and the ridiculous, inviting laughter, furnishing occasion for jest and hilarity. "In God we trusted, in Kansas we busted" became a favorite motto of emigrants, worn out with the struggle, returning to more hospitable climes; and for many years it expressed well enough the popular opinion of that fated land.

Yet there were some who never gave up. They stuck it out. They endured all that even Kansas could inflict. They kept the faith, and they are to be pardoned perhaps if they therefore feel that henceforth there is laid up for them a crown of glory. Those who remained in Kansas from 1875 to 1895 must have originally possessed staying qualities of no ordinary sort, qualities which the experience of those years could only accentuate. And, as success has at last rewarded their efforts, there has come, too, a certain pride, an exuberance, a feeling of superiority that accompany a victory long delayed and hardly won. The result has been to give a peculiar flavor to the Kansas spirit of individualism. With Kansas history back of him, the true Kansan feels that nothing is *too much* for him. How shall he be afraid of any danger, or hesitate at any obstacle, having succeeded where failure was not only human, but almost honorable? Having conquered Kansas, he knows well that there are no worse worlds to conquer. The Kansas spirit is therefore one that finds something exhilarating in the challenge of an extreme difficulty. "No one," says St. Augustine, "loves what he endures, though he may love to endure." With Kansans it is particularly a point of pride to suffer easily the stings of fortune, and, if they find no pleasure in the stings themselves, the ready endurance of them gives a consciousness of merit that is its own reward. Yet it is with no solemn martyr's air that the true Kansan endures the worst that can happen. His instinct is rather to pass it off as a minor annoyance, furnishing occasion for a pleasantry, for it is the mark of a Kansan to take a reverse as a joke rather than too seriously. Indeed, the endurance of extreme adversity has developed a keen appreciation for that type of humor, everywhere prevalent in the West, which consists in ignoring a difficulty or transforming it into a difficulty of precisely the opposite kind. There is a tradition surviving from the grasshopper time that illustrates the point. It is said that in the midst of that overwhelming disaster, when the pests were six inches deep in the streets, the editor of a certain local paper fined his comment on the situation down to a single line, which appeared among the trivial happenings of the week: "A grasshopper was seen on the courthouse steps this morning." This type of humor, appreciated anywhere west of the Alleghenies, is the type *par excellence* in Kansas. Perhaps it has rained for six weeks in the spring. The wheat is seemingly ruined; no corn has been planted. A farmer, who sees his profits for the year wiped out, looks at the murky sky, sniffs the damp air, and remarks seriously, "Well, it looks like rain. We may save that crop yet." "Yes," his neighbor replies with equal seriousness, "but it will have to come soon, or it won't do any good." When misfortunes beat down upon one in rapid succession, there comes a time when it is useless to strive against them, and in the end they engender a certain detached curiosity in the victim, who finds a mournful pleasure in observing with philosophical resignation the ultimate caprices of fate. Thus Kansans, "coiners of novel phrases to express their defiance of destiny," have employed humor itself as a refuge against misfortune. They have learned not only to endure adversity, but in a very literal sense to laugh at it as well.

I have already said that the type of individualism that is characteristic of America is one of achievement, not of eccentricity. The statement will bear repeating in this connection, for it is truer of Kansas than of most communities, notwithstanding there is a notion abroad that the state is peopled by freaks and eccentrics. It was once popularly supposed in Europe, and perhaps is so yet, that Americans are all eccentric. Now Kansans are eccentric in the same sense that Americans are: they differ somewhat from other Americans, just as Americans are distinguishable from Europeans. But a fundamental characteristic of Kansas individualism is the tendency to conform; it is an individualism of conformity, not of revolt. Having learned to endure to the end, they have learned to conform, for endurance is itself a kind of conformity. It has not infrequently been the subject of wondering comment by foreigners that in America, where everyone is supposed to do as he pleases, there should nevertheless be so little danger from violence and insurrection. Certainly one reason is that, while the conditions of frontier life release the individual from many of the formal restraints of ordered society, they exact a most rigid adherence to lines of conduct inevitably fixed by the stern necessities of life in a primitive community. On the frontier men soon learn to conform to what is regarded as essential, for the penalty of resistance or neglect is extinction: there the law of survival works surely and swiftly. However eccentric frontiersmen may appear to the tenderfoot, among themselves there is little variation from type in any essential matter. In the new community, individualism means the ability of the individual to succeed, not by submitting to some external formal authority, still less by following the bent of an unschooled will, but by recognizing and voluntarily adapting himself to necessary conditions. Kansas, it is true, has produced its eccentrics, but there is a saying here that freaks are raised for export only. In one sense the saying is true enough, for what strikes one particularly is that, on the whole, native Kansans are all so much alike. It is a community of great solidarity, and to the native it is "the Easterner" who appears eccentric.

The conquest of the wilderness in Kansas has thus developed qualities of patience, of calm, stoical, good-humored endurance in the face of natural difficulties, of conformity to what is regarded as necessary. Yet the patience, the calmness, the disposition to conform, is strictly confined to what is regarded as in the natural course. If the Kansan appears stolid, it is only on the surface that he is so. The peculiar conditions of origin and history have infused into the character of the people a certain romantic and sentimental element. Beneath the placid surface there is something fermenting which is best left alone—a latent energy which trivial events or a resounding phrase may unexpectedly release. In a recent commencement address Mr. Henry King said that conditions in early Kansas were *"hair-triggered."* Well, Kansans are themselves hair-triggered; slight pressure, if it be of the right sort, sets them off. "Everyone is on the *qui vive,* alert, vigilant, like a sentinel at an outpost." This trait finds expression in the romantic devotion of the people to the state, in a certain alert sensitiveness to criticism from outside, above all in the contagious enthusiasm with which they will without warning espouse a cause, especially when symbolized by a striking phrase, and carry it to an issue. Insurgency is native in Kansas, and the political history of the state, like its climate, is replete with surprises that have made it "alternately the reproach and the marvel of mankind." But this apparent instability is only the natural complement of the extreme and confident individualism of the people: having succeeded in overcoming so many obstacles that were unavoidable, they do not doubt their ability to destroy quickly those that seem artificially constructed. It thus happens that, while no people endure the reverses of nature with greater fortitude and good humor than the people of Kansas, misfortunes seemingly of man's making arouse in them a veritable passion of resistance; the mere suspicion of injustice, real or fancied exploitation by those who fare sumptuously, the pressure of laws not self-imposed, touch something explosive in their nature that transforms a calm and practical people into excited revolutionists. Grasshoppers elicited only a witticism, but the "mortgage fiends" produced the Populist regime, a kind of religious crusade against the infidel

Money Power. The same spirit was recently exhibited in the "Boss Busters" movement, which in one summer spread over the state like a prairie fire and overthrew an established machine supposed to be in control of the railroads. The "higher law" is still a force in Kansas. The spirit which refused to obey "bogus laws" is still easily stirred. A people which has endured the worst of nature's tyrannies, and cheerfully submits to tyrannies self-imposed, is in no mood to suffer hardships that seem remediable.

Idealism must always prevail on the frontier, for the frontier, whether geographical or intellectual, offers little hope to those who see things as they are. To venture into the wilderness, one must see it, not as it is, but as it will be. The frontier, being the possession of those only who see its future, is the promised land which cannot be entered save by those who have faith. America, having been such a promised land, is therefore inhabited by men of faith: idealism is ingrained in the character of its people. But as the frontier in America has hitherto been geographical and material, American idealism has necessarily a material basis, and Americans have often been mistakenly called materialists. True, they seem mainly interested in material things. Too often they represent values in terms of money: a man is "worth" so much money; a university is a great university, having the largest endowment of any; a fine building is a building that cost a million dollars—better still, ten millions. Value is extensive rather than intensive or intrinsic. America is the best country because it is the biggest, the wealthiest, the most powerful; its people are the best because they are the freest, the most energetic, the *most* educated. But to see a materialistic temper in all this is to mistake the form for the spirit. The American cares for material things because they represent the substance of things hoped for. He cares less for money than for making money: a fortune is valued, not because it represents ease, but because it represents struggle, achievement, progress. The first skyscraper in any town is nothing in itself, but much as an evidence of growth; it is a white stone on the road to the ultimate goal.

Idealism of this sort is an essential ingredient of the Kansas spirit. In few communities is the word *progress* more frequently used, or its meaning less frequently detached from a material basis. It symbolizes the *summum bonum*, having become a kind of dogma. Mistakes are forgiven a man if he is progressive, but to be unprogressive is to be suspect; like Aristotle's nonpolitical animal, the unprogressive is extra-human. This may explain why every Kansan wishes first of all to tell you that he comes from the town of X———, and then that it is the finest town in the state. He does not mean that it is strictly the finest town in the state, as will appear if you take the trouble to inquire a little about the country, its soil, its climate, its rainfall, and about the town itself. For it may chance that he is free to admit that it is hot there, that the soil is inclined to bake when there is no rain, that there is rarely any rain—all of which, however, is nothing to the point, because they are soon to have water by irrigation, which is, after all, much better than rainfall. And then he describes the town, which you have no difficulty in picturing vividly: a single street flanked by nondescript wooden shops; at one end a railroad station, at the other a post office; side streets lined with frame houses, painted or not, as the case may be; a schoolhouse somewhere, and a church with a steeple. It is such a town, to all appearances, as you may see by the hundred anywhere in the West—a dreary place, which, you think, the world would willingly let die. But your man is enthusiastic; he can talk of nothing but the town of X——. The secret of his enthusiasm you at last discover in the inevitable "but it will be a great country some day," and it dawns upon you that, after all, the man does not live in the dreary town of X——, but in the great country of *some day*. Such are Kansans. Like St. Augustine, they have their City of God, the idealized Kansas of some day: it is only necessary to have faith in order to possess it.

I cannot illustrate this aspect of Kansas idealism better than by quoting from Mrs. McCormick's little book of personal experience and observation. Having related the long years of struggle of a typical farmer, she imagines the Goddess of Justice revealing to him a picture of "the land as it shall be" when justice prevails.

"John beheld a great plain four hundred miles long and two hundred miles wide—a great agricultural state covered with farmers tilling the soil and with here and there a city or village. On every farm stood a beautiful house handsomely painted outside and elegantly furnished inside, and equipped with all modern conveniences helpful to housekeeping. Brussels carpets covered the floors, upholstered furniture and pianos ornamented the parlors, and the cheerful dining room had elegant table linen, cut glass, and silverware. Reservoirs carried the water into the houses in the country the same as in the cities. The farmers' wives and daughters, instead of working like slaves without proper utensils or house furnishings, now had everything necessary to lighten work and make home attractive. They had the summer kitchen, the washhouse, houses for drying clothes, arbors, etc. The dooryards consisted of nicely fenced green lawns, wherein not a pig rooted nor mule browsed on the shrubbery nor hen wallowed in the flower beds. Shade trees, hammocks, and rustic chairs were scattered about, and everything bespoke comfort. Great barns sheltered the stock. The farms were fenced and subdivided into fields of waving grain and pastures green."

634

This is what John is supposed to have seen on a summer's day when, at the close of a life of toil, he had just been sold up for debt. What John really saw had perhaps a less feminine coloring; but the picture represents the ideal, if not of an actual Kansas farmer, at least of an actual Kansas woman.

This aspect of American idealism is, however, not peculiar to Kansas: it is more or less characteristic of all western communities. But there is an element in Kansas idealism that marks it off as a state apart. The origin of Kansas must ever be associated with the struggle against slavery. Of this fact Kansans are well aware. Kansas is not a community of which it can be said, "Happy is the people without annals." It is a state with a past. It has a history of which its people are proud, and which they insist, as a matter of course, upon having taught in the public schools. There are old families in Kansas who know their place and keep it—sacred bearers of the traditions of the Kansas Struggle. The Kansas Struggle is for Kansas what the American Revolution is for New England; and, while there is as yet no "Society of the Daughters of the Kansas Struggle," there doubtless will be some day. For the Kansas Struggle is regarded as the crucial point in the achievement of human liberty, very much as Macaulay is said to have regarded the Reform Bill as the end for which all history was only a preparation. For all true Kansans, the border wars of the early years have a perennial interest: they mark the spot where Jones shot Smith, direct the attention of the traveler to the little village of Lecompton, or point with pride to some venerable tree bearing honorable scars dating from the Quantrill raid. Whether John Brown was an assassin or a martyr is a question which only a native can safely venture to answer with confidence. Recently, in a list of questions prepared for the examination of teachers in the schools, there appeared the following: "What was the Andover Band?" It seems that very few teachers knew what the Andover Band was; some thought it was an iron band, and some a band of Indians. The newspapers took it up, and it was found that, aside from some of the old families, ignorance of the Andover Band was quite general. When it transpired that the Andover Band had to do with the Kansas Struggle, the humiliation of the people was profound.

The belief that Kansas was founded for a cause distinguishes it, in the eyes of its inhabitants, as pre-eminently the home of freedom. It lifts the history of the state out of the commonplace of ordinary westward migration, and gives to the temper of the people a certain elevated and martial quality. The people of Iowa or Nebraska are well enough, but their history has never brought them in touch with cosmic processes. The Pilgrims themselves are felt to have been actuated by

635

less noble and altruistic motives. The Pilgrims, says Thayer, "fled from oppression, and sought in the new world 'freedom to worship God.'" But the Kansas emigrants migrated "to meet, to resist, and to destroy oppression, in vindication of their principles. These were self-sacrificing emigrants, the others were self-seeking. Justice, though tardy in its work, will yet load with the highest honors the memory of the Kansas pioneers who gave themselves and all they had to the sacred cause of human rights."

This may smack of prejudice, but it is no heresy in Kansas. The trained and disinterested physiocratic historian will tell us that such statements are unsupported by the documents. The documents show, he will say, that the Kansas emigrants, like other emigrants, came for cheap land and in the hope of bettering their condition; the real motive was economic, as all historic motives are; the Kansas emigrant may have thought he was going to Kansas to resist oppression, but in reality he went to take up a farm. At least, that many emigrants thought they came to resist oppression is indisputable. Their descendants still think so. And, after all, perhaps it is important to distinguish those who seek better farms and know they seek nothing else from those who seek better farms and imagine they are fighting a holy war. When the people of Newtown wished to remove to Connecticut, we are told that they advanced three reasons: first, "their want of accommodation for their cattle"; second, "the fruitfulness and commodiousness of Connecticut"; and finally, "*the strong bent of their spirits to remove thither.*" In explaining human history perhaps something should be conceded to "the strong bent of their spirits." Unquestionably cattle must be accommodated, but a belief, even if founded on error, is a fact that may sometimes change the current of history. At all events, the people of Kansas believe that their ancestors were engaged in a struggle for noble ends, and the belief, whether true or false, has left its impress upon their character. In Kansas the idealism of the geographical frontier has been strongly flavored with the notion that liberty is something more than a by-product of economic processes.

If Kansas idealism is colored by the humanitarian liberalism of the first half of the last century, it has nevertheless been but slightly influenced by the vague, emotional, Jean Paul romanticism of that time. Of all despondent and mystic elements the Kansas spirit is singularly free. There are few Byrons in Kansas, and no Don Juans. There is plenty of light there, but little of the "light that never was on land or sea." Kansas idealism is not a force that expends itself in academic contemplation of the unattainable. It is an idealism that is immensely concrete and practical, requiring always some definite object upon which to expend itself, but, once having such an object, expending itself with a restless, nervous energy that is appalling: whatever the object, it is pursued with the enthusiasm, the profound conviction given only to those who have communed with the absolute. It would seem that preoccupation with the concrete and the practical should develop a keen appreciation of relative values; but in new countries problems of material transformation are so insistent that immediate means acquire the value of ultimate ends. Kansas is a new state, and its inhabitants are so preoccupied with the present, so resolutely detached from the experience of the centuries, that they can compare themselves of today only with themselves of yesterday. The idea embodied in the phrase *Weltgeschichte ist das Weltgericht* has slight significance in a community in which twenty years of rapid material improvement has engendered an unquestioning faith in indefinite progress towards perfectibility. In such a community, past and future appear foreshortened, and the latest new mechanical device brings us an appreciable step nearer the millennium, which seems always to be just over the next hill. By some odd mental alchemy it thus happens that the concrete and the practical have taken on the dignity of the absolute, and the pursuit of a convenience assumes the character of a crusade. Whether it be religion or paving, education or the disposal of garbage, that occupies for the moment the focus of attention, the same stirring activity, the same zeal and emotional glow are enlisted: all alike are legitimate objects of conquest, to be measured in terms of their visual and transferable assets, and won by concerted and organized attack. I recall reading in a local Kansas newspaper some time ago a brief comment on the neighboring village of X—— (in which was located a small college mistakenly called a university) which ran somewhat as follows: "The University of X—— has established a music festival on the same plan as the one at the state university, and with most gratifying results. The first festival was altogether a success. X—— is a fine town, one of the best in the state. It has a fine university, and a fine class of people, who have made it a center of culture. X—— lacks only one thing: it has no sewers." Perhaps there are people who would find the juxtaposition of culture and sewers somewhat bizarre. But to us in Kansas it does not seem so. Culture and sewers are admittedly good things to possess. Well, then, let us pursue them actively and with absolute conviction. Thus may an idealized sewer become an object worthy to stir the moral depths of any right-minded community.

An insistent, practical idealism of this sort, always busily occupied with concrete problems, is likely to prefer ideas cast in formal mold, will be a little at a loss in the midst of flexible play of mind, and look with suspicion upon the emancipated, the critical, and the speculative spirit. It is too sure of itself to be at home with ideas of uncertain pressure. Knowing that it is right, it wishes only to go ahead. Satisfied with certain conventional premises, it hastens on to the obvious conclusion. It thus happens that Americans, for the most part, are complaisantly satisfied with a purely formal interpretation of those resounding words that symbolize for them the ideas upon which their institutions are supposed to rest. In this respect Kansas is truly American. Nowhere is there more loyal devotion to such words as *liberty, democracy, equality, education*. But preoccupation with the concrete fixes the attention upon the word itself, and upon what is traditionally associated with it. Democracy, for example, is traditionally associated with elections, and many of them. Should you maintain that democracy is not necessarily bound up with any particular institution, that it is in the way of being smothered by the complicated blanket ballot, you will not be understood, or, rather, you will be understood only too well as advocating something aristocratic. Democracy is somehow bound up with a concrete thing, and the move for the shorter ballot is therefore undemocratic and un-American. Or, take the word *socialism*. Your avowed socialist is received politely, and allowed to depart silently and without regret. But, if you tell us of the movement for the governmental control of corporate wealth, we grow enthusiastic. The word *socialism* has a bad odor in Kansas, but the thing itself, by some other name, smells sweet enough.

If one is interested in getting the essential features of socialism adopted in Kansas, or in America itself, the name to conjure with is indeed not *socialism*, but *equality*.

In a country like America, where there is such confident faith in the individual, one might naturally expect to find the completest toleration, and no disposition to use the government for the purpose of enforcing uniform conditions: logically, it would seem, so much emphasis on liberty should be incompatible with much emphasis on equality. Yet it is precisely in America, and nowhere in America more than in the West, that liberty and equality always go coupled and inseparable in popular speech; where the sense of liberty is especially strong, there also the devotion to equality is a cardinal doctrine. Throughout our history the West has been a dominant factor in urging the extension of the powers of the national government, and western states have taken the lead in radical legislation of an equalizing character. This apparent inconsistency strikes one as especially pronounced in Kansas. The doctrine of equality is unquestioned there, and that governments exist for the purpose of securing it is the common belief. "A law against it" is the specific for every malady. The welfare of society is thought to be always superior to that of the individual, and yet no one doubts that perfect liberty is the birthright of every man.

Perhaps the truth is that real toleration is a sentiment foreign to the American temper. Toleration is for the skeptical, being the product of much thought or of great indifference, sometimes, to be sure, a mere *modus vivendi* forced upon a heterogeneous society. In America we imagine ourselves liberal-minded because we tolerate what we have ceased to regard as important. We tolerate religions but not irreligion, and diverse political opinion, but not unpolitical opinion, customs, but not the negation of custom. The Puritans fought for toleration—for themselves. But, having won it for themselves, they straightway denied it to others. No small part of American history has been a repetition of the Puritan struggle; it has been a fight, not for toleration as a general principle, but for recognition of a civilization resting upon particular principles: in exterior relations, a struggle for recognition of America by Europe; in interior relations, a struggle for recognition of "the West" by "the East." The principle of toleration is written in our constitutions, but not in our minds, for the motive back of the famous guarantees of individual liberty has been recognition of particular opinion rather than toleration of every opinion. And in the nature of the case it must be so. Those who create frontiers and establish new civilizations have too much faith to be tolerant, and are too thoroughgoing idealists to be indifferent. On the frontier conditions are too hazardous for the speculative and the academic to flourish readily: only those who are right and are sure of it can succeed. Certainly it is characteristic of Americans to know that they are right. Certainly they are conscious of having a mission in the world and of having been faithful to it. They have solved great problems hitherto unsolved, have realized utopias dreamed of but never realized by Europe. They are therefore in the van of civilization, quite sure of the direction, triumphantly leading the march towards the ultimate goal. That everyone should do as he likes is part of the American creed only in a very limited sense. That it is possible to know what is right and that what is right should be recognized and adhered to is the more vital belief.

That *liberty* and *equality* are compatible terms is, at all events, an unquestioned faith in Kansas. The belief in equality, however, is not so much the belief that all men are equal as the conviction that it is the business of society to establish conditions that will make them so. And this notion, so far from being inconsistent with the pronounced individualism that prevails there, is the natural result of it. In Kansas, at least, no one holds to the right of the individual to do as he likes, irrespective of what it is that he likes. Faith in the individual is faith in the particular individual, the true Kansan, who has learned through adversity voluntarily to conform to what is necessary. Human nature, or, at all events, Kansas nature, is essentially good, and if the environment is right all men can measure up to that high level. That the right environment can be created is not doubted. It is not possible for men so aggressive and self-reliant, who have overcome so many obstacles, to doubt their ability to accomplish this also. Having conquered nature, they cheerfully confront the task of transforming human nature. It is precisely because Kansans are such thoroughgoing individualists, so resourceful, so profoundly confident in their own judgments, so emancipated from the past, so accustomed to devising expedients for every new difficulty, that they are unimpressed by the record of the world's failures. They have always thrived on the impossible, and the field of many failures offers a challenge not to be resisted.

To effect these beneficent ends, the people of Kansas turn naturally to the government because they have a very simple and practical idea of what the government is and what it is for. The government, in Kansas, is no abstract concept. It is nothing German, nothing metaphysical. In this frontier community no one has yet thought of the government as a power not ourselves that makes for evil. Kansans think of the government, as they think of everything else, in terms of the concrete. And why, indeed, should they not? Within the memory of man there was no government in Kansas. They, Kansans, made the government themselves for their own purposes. The government is therefore simply certain men employed by themselves to do certain things; it is the sum of the energy, the good judgment, the resourcefulness of the individuals who originally created it, and who periodically renew it. The government is the individual writ large; in it every Kansan sees himself drawn to larger scale. The passion for controlling all things by law is thus not the turning of the hopeless and discouraged individual to some power other and higher than himself for protection; it is only the instinct to use effectively one of the many resources always at his command for achieving desired ends. Of a government hostile to the individual they cannot conceive; such a government is a bogus government, and its laws are bogus laws; to resist and overthrow such a government, all the initiative and resourcefulness is enlisted that is devoted to supporting one regarded as legitimate. There is a higher law than the statute book; the law of the state is no law if it does not represent the will of the individual.

To identify the will of the individual with the will of society in this easy fashion presupposes a certain solidarity in the community: an identity of race, custom, habits, needs; a consensus of opinion in respect to morals and politics. Kansas is such a community. Its people are principally American-born, descended from settlers who came mainly from the Middle West. It is an agricultural state, and the conditions of life are, or have been until recently, much the same for all. "Within these pastoral boundaries," says ex-Senator Ingalls, in his best Kansas manner, "there are no millionaires nor any paupers, except such as have been deprived by age, disease, and calamity of the ability to labor. No great fortunes have been brought to the state, and none have been accumulated by commerce, manufacture, or speculation. No sumptuous mansions nor glittering equipages nor ostentatious display exasperates or allures." And the feeling of solidarity resulting from identity of race and uniformity of custom has been accentuated by the peculiar history of the state. Kansans love each other for the dangers they have passed; a unique experience has created a strong *esprit de corps*—a feeling that, while Kansans are different from others, one Kansan is not only as good as any other, but very like any other. The philosophy of numbers, the doctrine of the majority, is therefore ingrained, and little sympathy is wasted on minorities. Rousseau's notion that minorities are only mistaken finds ready acceptance, and the will of the individual is easily identified with the will of society.

And in a sense the doctrine is true enough, for there is little difference of opinion on fundamental questions. In religion there are many creeds and many churches, but the difference between them is regarded as unimportant. There is, however, a quite absolute dogmatism of morality. Baptism is for those who enjoy it, but the moral life is for all. And what constitutes the moral life is well understood: to be honest and pay your debts; to be friendly and charitable, good-humored but not cynical, slow to take offense, but regarding life as profoundly serious; to respect sentiments and harmless prejudices; to revere the conventional great ideas and traditions; to live a sober life and a virtuous—to these they lay hold without questioning. Likewise in politics. One may be Democrat or Republican, stalwart or square-dealer, insurgent or stand-patter: it is no vital matter. But no one dreams of denying democracy, the will of the people, the greatest good to the greatest number, equal justice and equal opportunity to all. Whether in respect to politics or economics, education or morals, the consensus of opinion is very nearly perfect: it is an opinion that unites in the deification of the average, that centers in the dogmatism of the general level.

It goes without saying that the general level in Kansas is thought to be exceptionally high. Kansans do not regard themselves as mere Westerners, like Iowans or Nebraskans. Having passed through a superior heat, they are Westerners seven times refined. "It is the quality of piety in Kansas," says Mr. E. H. Abbott, "to thank God that you are not as other men are, beer-drinkers, shiftless, habitual lynchers, or even as these Missourians." The pride is natural enough, perhaps, in men whose judgment has been vindicated at last in the face of general skepticism. Having for many years contributed to the gaiety of nations, Kansas has ceased to be the pariah of the states. Kansans have endured Job's comforters too long not to feel a little complaisant when their solemn predictions come to naught. "While envious rivals were jeering, . . . pointing with scorn's slow unmoving finger at the droughts, grasshoppers, hot winds, crop failures, and other calamities of Kansas, the world was suddenly startled and dazzled by her collective display of . . . products at the Centennial at Philadelphia, which received the highest awards." It is inevitable that those who think they have fashioned a cornerstone out of the stone rejected by the builders should regard themselves as superior workmen.

To test others by this high standard is an instinctive procedure. There is an alert attention to the quality of those who enter the state from outside. The crucial question is, are they "our kind of men"? Do they speak "the Kansas language"? Yet the Kansas language is less a form of speech or the expression of particular ideas than a certain personal quality. Some time since a distinguished visitor from the East came to the state to deliver a public address. He was most hospitably received, as all visitors are, whether distinguished or otherwise, and his address—permeated with the idealistic liberalism of a half century ago—was attentively listened to and highly praised. But to no purpose all these fine ideas. The great man was found wanting, for there was discovered, among his other impedimenta, a valet. It was a fatal mischance. The poor valet was more commented upon than the address, more observed than his master. The circumstance stamped the misguided man as clearly not our kind of man. Obviously, no man who carries a valet can speak the Kansas language. Needless to say, there are no valets in Kansas.

The feeling of superiority naturally attaching to a chosen people equally inclines Kansans to dispense readily with the advice or experience of others. They feel that those who have worn the hair shirt cannot be instructed in asceticism by those who wear silk. In discussing the university and its problems with a member of the state legislature, I once hazarded some comparative statistics showing that a number of other states made rather more liberal appropriations for their universities than the state of Kansas did for hers. I thought the comparison might be enlightening, that the man's pride of state might be touched. Not at all. "I know all about that," he replied. "That argument is used by every man who is interested in larger appropriations for any of the state institutions. But it doesn't go with a Kansas legislature. In Kansas, we don't care much what other states are doing. Kansas always leads, but never follows." And, in fact, the disregard of precedent is almost an article of faith; that a thing has been done before is an indication that it is time to improve upon it. History may teach that men cannot be legislated into the kingdom of heaven. Kansans are not ignorant of the fact, but it is no concern of theirs. The experience of history is not for men with a mission and faith to perform it. Let the uncertain and the timid profit by history; those who have at all times the courage of their emotions will make history, not repeat it. Kansans set their own standards, and the state becomes, as it were, an experiment station in the field of social science.

The passion for equality in Kansas is thus the complement of the individualism and the idealism of its people. It has at the basis of it an altruistic motive, aiming not so much to level all men down as to level all men up. The Kansan's sense of individual worth enables him to believe that no one can be better than he is, while his confident idealism encourages him to hope that none need be worse.

The Kansas spirit is the American spirit double distilled. It is a new grafted product of American individualism, American idealism, American intolerance. Kansas is America in microcosm: as America conceives itself in respect to Europe, so Kansas conceives itself in respect to America. Within its borders, Americanism, pure and undefiled, has a new lease of life. It is the mission of this self-selected people to see to it that it does not perish from off the earth. The light on the altar, however neglected elsewhere, must ever be replenished in Kansas. If this is provincialism, it is the provincialism of faith rather than of the province. The devotion to the state is devotion to an ideal, not to a territory, and men can say "Dear old Kansas!" because the name symbolizes for them what the motto of the state so well expresses, *ad astra per aspera.*

Sheep Country

by ARCHER B. GILFILLAN, 1886– . *The son and grandson of ministers, Gilfillan was for a time a theological student himself but later gave up the ministry for the life of a sheepman. Born at White Earth, Minnesota, and educated at the University of Pennsylvania, he homesteaded for a while on the prairies of Harding County, one hundred miles north of the*

Black Hills; later he worked as a sheepherder near Buffalo, South Dakota. In his volume Sheep (1929), of which "Sheep Country" is the second chapter, Gilfillan outlines with shrewdness, perception, and a pleasant sense of humor the tribulations and gratifications of a sheepman.

WHEN the white man with his superior civilization and his superiority complex took this continent from his red brother, he gave back to him certain patches of land here and there, together with an urgent invitation to make his home on these and not elsewhere. At that time the white man did not know that Nature had slipped a joker into the deck in the form of certain hidden oil pools, and by the time he found that out he was in a position where he could afford himself the luxury of a conscience, and so he magnanimously decided to let the tail go with the hide. The reservation system resulted in the damming here and there of the western flood of migration. One such barrier against which the human flood heaped itself was the large Indian reservation on the west bank of the Missouri River midway of the State of South Dakota, containing the historic spot at the mouth of Grand River where Sitting Bull, the greatest of the Sioux, met his destined and still-debated end. North of this reservation the advancing tide swept along the route marked out by the Milwaukee and the Northern Pacific, and south of it traffic had long flowed to the Black Hills. But directly west of it was an eddy, a scantly inhabited region of big cattle outfits, a land which remained, except for the substitution of cattle for buffalo, in the same state in which the ages had left it till as late as the year 1909.

This, at least, is one theory employed to explain the fact that the northwestern corner of South Dakota was an untouched wilderness less than twenty years ago, and in any argument as to the location of the much-discussed Last Frontier this region has at least the right to be considered. But the fact that it was not settled did not mean that it had no history of its own. It lay on the outskirts of the battle that was waged for the possession of the Black Hills. The last of the huge northern herd of buffalo were said to have been slaughtered on its western edge, along the banks of the Little Missouri River. And some sixty miles north along this historic stream is the region made famous for all time by Theodore Roosevelt and the Marquis de Mores, and beautified for all time by Nature in those Bad Lands which are soon to become a national park.

Following the early period of the big outfits, there came the nesters. A cowboy working for one of the big cattle companies would spot some particularly desirable location for a ranch, would file on it, and start to build up a herd of his own. Sometimes when the growth of his bunch of cattle was phenomenally rapid, the big owners perhaps might say of him sorrowfully, as we are wont to do of the departed, "His gain is our loss." Gradually the big outfits were squeezed out or voluntarily abandoned the field, and the nester, now called the old-timer, inherited the land.

Then came a sort of Golden Age, to which every old-timer looks back with reverence and longing. In spite of his name, time really meant very little to him at all. If he did not see a particular bunch of cattle one day, he could see them some other day—or the following week for that matter. He knew all his neighbors from one railroad to the other, a distance of a hundred and fifty miles. The ranches were located so far apart that there was very little range trouble. No man could go to the next ranch and return before mealtime, and so a man ate wherever he happened to be, and hospitality was the rule. Dances that were scheduled for one night only, and all night according to custom, might be prolonged for several days by storms or the impassable condition of such roads as there were. And many a schoolma'am gave proof of the tough fibre of pioneer womanhood by riding horseback forty miles to a dance, and when there taking her only rest during the supper hour.

The peaceful serenity of this existence not only was shattered, but overwhelmed and all but obliterated, by a tidal wave of homesteaders that swept across the prairies from the east, and left in its wake a shack, dugout, or sod shanty on every quarter section. Sometimes the old-timer would try to sweep back the sea with his broom, sometimes he was wiped out of existence, but in many cases the ranch that he built up still remains, an island washed by an alien flood. For the homesteader was of a different breed altogether, and in spite of twenty years of association the two types remain distinct to this day. The homesteader could never comprehend the easy-going ways of the old-timer, and the latter in turn never will be able to understand the psychology of a man who, in answer to a knock, could come to the door of his shack busily masticating a mouthful of his dinner, answer the stranger's questions with regard to the road, and then shut his door and return to his meal without having asked the other if he had eaten.

Although the nesters almost without exception were cattlemen to begin with, there came to be a sprinkling of sheepmen among them. There never was in this region the deadly hatred between the two kinds of stockmen that led to a reign of terror in the region farther west. As cattle fell and sheep rose in price, more and more cattlemen were converted. With the influx of the homesteaders, the cattlemen were still further embarrassed; while the sheepmen, with their personally conducted flocks, were able to adapt themselves to the new conditions more readily. For a time the balance was about even, but now the cattlemen are in the minority, and the print of the Golden Hoof is seen all over the land.

There are several factors which make this region preeminently a stock country. The distance at which it lies from the railroad puts a premium on that form of production which can negotiate the long and difficult journey on its own four legs. The cheapness of the land renders large holdings possible to men of even moderate means. And the peculiarities of the climate make the winter feeding of stock particularly easy.

The grass in the East is apt to be much more luxuriant than that of the West, and it grows all summer long. The farmer of the East may or may not figure on forty cows to the acre, but the cattleman of the West used to figure on forty acres for the support of one cow the year round. Even at that, though, the western stockman's grass was better for all-year feed. The grass of the East grows all summer and freezes green in the fall, and from then on is practically useless for stock purposes until its rejuvenation in the spring. The grass on the prairies of the West has a short growing season. By August the prairies are brown. But that same August sun has cured the grass and made hay of it right where it grew. The stockman gathers enough of this hay for his barn use or as much as he has the help to put up. But the millions of tons of it that he cannot handle his stock contentedly harvest for him during the winter months, when the much objurgated wind has swept the ridges bare. And if there is an open winter, that is, one with little snow, his stock will come through rolling fat and he will be able to save his hay stacks for another year. The combination of summer sun and winter wind provides him with an abundance of hay, and his stock attends to putting it up for him.

Although this region is included in what the old geographies used to call the Great American Desert, it is hard to see how it could ever have deserved that name. There is abundance of grass everywhere, and enough running water to supply the needs of stock. True, the rainfall is somewhat light, as was discovered by the stranger passing through the country who stopped to talk with a homesteader leaning against his shack. In the course of the conversation he asked: "Have you had any rain here lately?" "I don't know," was the languid response, "I have only been here three years."

When we speak of the West as a new country, we usually mean in point of settlement and civilization. But this region is new geologically as well. Here are strange sights never seen east of the Mississippi —mud buttes standing solitary like the solidified cores of mud volcanoes, cut banks with bare perpendicular walls of earth exposed, deep draws like gashes cut in the ground with some giant's knife, and so-called Bad Lands with their weird formation and fantastic coloring. In the East the lines of the landscape are softened and rounded; in the West they are sharp and crude.

Owing to the altitude, the air is so light that hills which are miles away stand out against the sky with knife-like clearness. People who came here from the East are invariably fooled as to distances. They have always associated clearness with nearness, and sometimes they learn the difference to their sorrow. An old-timer told me how, when he came here, he tried out a new rifle on the slopes of Bear Butte and was much disappointed at not seeing the dust fly from it. He learned later that the butte was many miles away. They tell a story of a stranger who set out one morning to walk to a certain butte before breakfast. He walked a mile or two and then met a native who told him that the butte was still several miles away, so he decided to return. They traveled by a slightly different route and came to a small stream, a mere trickle across the sand. As the native stopped to water his horse, he was amazed to see the stranger busily stripping off his clothes. "What are you going to do?" he asked. "I'm going to swim this river," was the dogged response. "Swim it!" ejaculated the native. "Why, you can step across it!" "Well, I don't know," was the cautious answer. "Distances are deceiving in this country, and I'm not taking any chances."

Six miles from the ranch buildings, at the eastern edge of the range over which I herd, rise the white cliffs of the Slim Buttes, a high range of hills starting abruptly from the surrounding plain. Halfway to the top is a small bench, upon which is a spring capable of watering hundreds of cattle. This bench is the site of an old ranch called "The Moonshine," a ranch that goes back to the days of free grass and big outfits. As you stand on a hill above where the log ranch house lay, you find yourself in a natural amphitheatre. Behind you the rock-strewn earth rises almost sheer to the plateau, two hundred feet above you. To the north a great white limestone wall thrusts out into space, its rough sides forming many a niche for an eagle's nest, and its jagged top their favored resting place. To the south a grass-covered, pine-clad shoulder reaches out like another protecting arm, with a giant pine crowning a knoll at its very tip; and below it a sheer upthrust of limestone wall is pierced by a roughly shaped window. Almost at your feet, nestling among the rough hummocks of the bench, is the Moonshine Lake, a bright jewel in a waterless landscape.

As your eyes go farther afield, you note that from the bench the land drops away another hundred feet or so to the plain beneath. Twenty miles to the northwest you see the large rolling outlines of the

Cave Hills, while thirty miles west are the white-cliffed, pine-clad summits of the Short Pine Hills. Beyond them, a mere blue line, are the Long Pine Hills of Montana. As your eye follows the horizon south, it pauses at the Crow Buttes, where the Crow and Sioux Indians once fought a bloody battle, and at the twin peaks, Castle Rock and Square Top, rising in solitary state above many a flat and weary mile of gumbo. And just beyond them, you see on the horizon what looks like a row of rounded blue hummocks. These are the Black Hills, one hundred miles from where you are standing.

But just as one swallow does not make a summer, so one view, however enchanting, does not make an unusual landscape. There are, however, scattered over the face of the country, innumerable sharply rising hills or peaks, called buttes. From the top of any of these the herder may watch his sheep spread out below him peacefully grazing. He may watch the alternate sunlight and shadow chase each other over twenty miles of prairie. A car crawls lazily along a distant road. Out on the horizon a row of jagged peaks reveals a more pretentious range of hills. The sky seems to come down to shoulder height all around. Strange it would be if the all-pervading calm did not bring with it an interior peace.

Revolt against the City

by GRANT WOOD, 1891–1942. *With John Steuart Curry and Thomas Hart Benton, Wood is one of three artists who have done much in the way of transferring middlewestern scenes to canvas. Wood was born on a farm near Anamosa, Iowa, studied at the Chicago Art Institute and in Paris, taught in the public schools of Cedar Rapids, Iowa, from 1919 to 1924, and at the time of his death was professor of graphic and plastic arts at the University of Iowa. His French sojourn undoubtedly helped his technical facility, but upon his return to the United States he rebelled against European influences and strove to utilize middlewestern themes. His essay "Revolt against the City" is a strong plea for artistic regionalism. Among Wood's more famous canvases are "American Gothic," now part of the permanent collection of the Chicago Art Institute; "Stone City," "Arbor Day," and "Dinner for Threshers." Darrell Garwood's biography of the painter (1944) clarifies his faith in the region of his birth.*

648

THE present revolt against the domination exercised over art and letters and over much of our thinking and living by Eastern capitals of finance and politics brings up many considerations that ought to be widely discussed. It is no isolated phenomenon, and it is not to be understood without consideration of its historical, social and artistic backgrounds. And though I am not setting out, in this essay, to trace and elaborate all of these backgrounds and implications, I wish to suggest a few of them in the following pages.

One reason for speaking out at this time lies in the fact that the movement I am discussing has come upon us rather gradually and without much blowing of trumpets, so that many observers are scarcely aware of its existence. It deserves, and I hope it may soon have, a much more thorough consideration than I can give it here.

But if it is not vocal—at least in the sense of issuing pronunciamentos, challenges, and new credos—the revolt is certainly very active. In literature, though by no means new, the exploitation of the "provinces" has increased remarkably; the South, the Middle West, the Southwest have at the moment hosts of interpreters whose Pulitzer-prize works and best sellers direct attention to their chosen regions. In drama, men like Paul Green, Lynn Riggs, and Jack Kirkland have been succeeding in something that a few years ago seemed impossible —actually interesting Broadway in something besides Broadway. In painting there has been a definite swing to a like regionalism; and this has been aided by such factors as the rejection of French domination, a growing consciousness of the art materials in the distinctively rural districts of America, and the system of PWA art work. These developments have correlations in the economic swing toward the country, in the back-to-the-land movement—that social phenomenon which Mr. Ralph Borsodi calls the "flight" from the city.

In short, America has turned introspective. Whether or not one adopts the philosophy of the "America Self-Contained" group, it is certain that the Depression Era has stimulated us to a re-evaluation of our resources in both art and economics, and that this turning of our eyes inward upon ourselves has awakened us to values which were little known before the grand crash of 1929 and which are chiefly non-urban.

Mr. Carl Van Doren has pointed out the interesting fact that America rediscovers herself every thirty years or so. About once in each generation, directed by political or economic or artistic impulses, we have re-evaluated or reinterpreted ourselves. It happened in 1776, of course, and again a generation later with the Louisiana Purchase and

649

subsequent explorations and the beginnings of a national literature. It came again with the expansion of the Jacksonian era in the eighteen-thirties, accompanied by a literary flowering not only in New England but in various frontier regions. It was marked in the period immediately after our Civil War, when Emerson observed that a new map of America had been unrolled before us. In the expansionist period at the turn of the century, shortly after the Spanish War when the United States found herself a full-fledged world power, we had a new discovery of resources and values. And now, with another thirty-year cycle, it comes again. It is always slightly different, always complex in its causes and phenomena; but happily it is always enlightening.

Moreover, these periods of national awakening to our own resources have always been in some degree reactions from foreign relationships. These reactions are obvious even to the casual reader of history and need not be listed here except as to their bearing on the present rediscovery. Economic and political causes have contributed in these days to turn us away from Europe—high tariff walls, repudiation of debts by European nations, the reaction against "entangling alliances" which followed upon President Wilson's effort to bring this country into the League of Nations, and the depression propaganda for "America Self-Contained."

But one does not need to be an isolationist to recognize the good which our artistic and literary secession from Europe has done us. For example, until fifteen years ago it was practically impossible for a painter to be recognized as an artist in America without having behind him the prestige of training either in Paris or Munich, while today the American artist looks upon a trip to Europe much as any tourist looks upon it—not as a means of technical training or a method of winning an art reputation, but as a valid way to get perspective by foreign travel. This is a victory for American art of incalculable value. The long domination of our own art by Europe, and especially by the French, was a deliberately cultivated commercial activity—a business, —and dealers connected with the larger New York galleries played into the hands of the French promoters because they themselves found such a connection profitable.

Music, too, labored under similar difficulties. Singers had to study in Germany or Italy or France; they had to sing in a foreign language, and they even had to adopt German or Italian or French names if they were to succeed in opera. In literature the language relationship made us subject especially to England. The whole of the nineteenth century was one long struggle to throw off that domination—a struggle more or less successful, but complicated in these later years by a continuation of the endless line of lionizing lecture tours of English authors and by the attempt to control our culture by the Rhodes scholarships which have been so widely granted.

This European influence has been felt most strongly in the Eastern States and particularly in the great Eastern seaport cities. René d'Arnencourt, the Austrian artist who took charge of the Mexican art exhibit a few years ago and circulated it throughout the United States, and who probably has a clearer understanding of American art conditions than we do who are closer to them, believes that culturally our Eastern States are still colonies of Europe. The American artist of today, thinks d'Arnencourt, must strive not so much against the French influence, which, after all, is merely incidental, but against the whole colonial influence which is so deepseated in the New England States. The East is nearer to Europe in more than geographical position, and certain it is that the eyes of the seaport cities have long been focussed upon the "mother" countries across the sea. But the colonial spirit is, of course, basically an imitative spirit, and we can have no hope of developing a culture of our own until that subserviency is put in its proper historical place.

Inevitable though it probably was, it seems nevertheless unfortunate that such art appreciation as developed in America in the nineteenth century had to be concentrated in the large cities. For the colonial spirit thereby was given full rein and control. The dominant factor in American social history during the latter part of that century is generally recognized as being the growth of large cities. D. R. Fox, writing an introduction to Arthur M. Schlesinger's "The Growth of the City," observes:

"The United States in the eighties and nineties was trembling between two worlds, one rural and agricultural, the other urban and industrial. In this span of years . . . traditional America gave way to a new America, one more akin to Europe than to its former self, yet retaining an authentic New World quality. . . . The present volume is devoted to describing and appraising the new social force which waxed and throve while driving the pioneer culture before it: the city."

This urban growth, whose tremendous power was so effective upon the whole of American society, served, so far as art was concerned, to tighten the grip of traditional imitativeness, for the cities were far less typically American than the frontier areas whose power they usurped. Not only were they the seats of the colonial spirit, but they were inimical to whatever was new, original and alive in the truly American spirit.

Our Middle West, and indeed the "provinces" in general, have long had much the same attitude toward the East that the coastal cities had toward Europe. Henry James's journey to Paris as a sentimental pilgrim was matched by Hamlin Garland's equally passionate pilgrimage to Boston. It was a phase of the magnetic drawing-power of the Eastern cities that the whole country, almost up to the present time, looked wistfully eastward for culture; and these seaport centers drew unto them most of the writers, musicians and artists who could not go to Europe. And the flight of the "intelligentsia" to Paris was a striking feature of the years immediately after the World War.

The feeling that the East, and perhaps Europe, was the true goal of the seeker after culture was greatly augmented by the literary movement which Mr. Van Doren once dubbed "the revolt against the village." Such books as "Spoon River Anthology" and "Main Street" brought contempt upon the hinterland and strengthened the cityward tendency. H. L. Mencken's urban and European philosophy was exerted in the same direction.

But sweeping changes have come over American culture in the last few years. The Great Depression has taught us many things, and not the least of them is self-reliance. It has thrown down the Tower of Babel erected in the years of a false prosperity; it has sent men and women back to the land; it has caused us to rediscover some of the old frontier virtues. In cutting us off from traditional but more artificial values, it has thrown us back upon certain true and fundamental things which are distinctively ours to use and to exploit.

We still send scholars to Oxford, but it is significant that Paul Engle produced on his scholarship time one of the most American volumes of recent verse. Europe has lost much of its magic. Gertrude Stein comes to us from Paris and is only a seven days' wonder. Ezra Pound's new volume seems all compound of echoes from a lost world. The expatriates do not fit in with the newer America, so greatly changed from the old.

The depression has also weakened the highly commercialized New York theatre; and this fact, together with the wholesome development of little theatres, may bring us at last an American drama. For years our stage has been controlled by grasping New York producers. The young playwright or actor could not succeed unless he went to New York. For commercial reasons, it was impossible to give the drama any regional feeling; it had little that was basic to go on and was consequently dominated by translations or reworkings of French plays and by productions of English drawing-room comedies, often played by imported actors. The advent of the movies changed this condition only by creating another highly urbanized center at Hollywood. But we have now a revolt against this whole system—a revolt in which we have enlisted the community theatres, local playwriting contests, some active regional playwrights, and certain important university theatres.

Music (and perhaps I am getting out of my proper territory here, for I know little of music) seems to be doing less outside of the cities than letters, the theatre, and art. One does note, however, local music festivals, as well as such promotion of community singing as that which Harry Barnhardt has led.

But painting has declared its independence from Europe, and is retreating from the cities to the more American village and country life. Paris is no longer the Mecca of the American artist. The American public, which used to be interested solely in foreign and imitative work, has readily acquired a strong interest in the distinctly indigenous art of its own land; and our buyers of paintings and patrons of art have naturally and honestly fallen in with the movement away from Paris and the American pseudo-Parisians. It all constitutes not so much a revolt against French technique as against the adoption of the French mental attitude and the use of French subject matter. For these elements the new artists would substitute an American way of looking at things, and a utilization of the materials of our own American scene.

This is no mere chauvinism. If it is patriotic, it is so because a feeling for one's own milieu and for the validity of one's own life and its surroundings is patriotic. Certainly I prefer to think of it, not in terms of sentiment at all, but rather as a commonsense utilization for art of native materials—an honest reliance by the artist upon subject matter which he can best interpret because he knows it best.

Because of this new emphasis upon native materials, the artist no longer finds it necessary to migrate even to New York, or to seek any great metropolis. No longer is it necessary for him to suffer the confusing cosmopolitanism, the noise, the too intimate gregariousness of the large city. True, he may travel, he may observe, he may study in various environments, in order to develop his personality and achieve backgrounds and a perspective; but this need be little more than incidental to an educative process that centers in his own home region.

The great central areas of America are coming to be evaluated more and more justly as the years pass. They are not a hinterland for New York; they are not barbaric. Thomas Benton returned to make his home in the Middle West just the other day, saying, according to the newspapers, that he was coming to live again in the only region of the country which is not "provincial." John Cowper Powys, bidding farewell to America recently in one of our great magazines, after a long sojourn in this country, said of the Middle West:

"This is the real America; this is—let us hope!—the America of the future; this is the region of what may, after all, prove to be, in Spenglerian phrase, the cradle of the next great human 'culture.' "

When Christopher Morley was out in Iowa last Fall, he remarked on its freedom, permitting expansion "with space and relaxing conditions for work." Future artists, he wisely observed, "are more likely to come from the remoter areas, farther from the claims and distractions of an accelerating civilization."

So many of the leaders in the arts were born in small towns and on farms that in the comments and conversation of many who have "gone East" there is today a noticeable homesickness for the scenes of their childhood. On a recent visit to New York, after seven continuous years in the Middle West, I found this attitude very striking. Seven years ago my friends had sincerely pitied me for what they called my "exile" in Iowa. They then had a vision of my going back to an uninteresting region where I could have no contact with culture and no association with kindred spirits. But now, upon my return to the East, I found these same friends eager for news and information about the rich funds of creative material which this region holds.

I found, moreover, a determination on the part of some of the Eastern artists to visit the Middle West for the purpose of obtaining such material. I feel that, in general, such a procedure would be as false as the old one of going to Europe for subject matter, or the later fashion of going to New England fishing villages or to Mexican cities or to the mountains of our Southwest for materials. I feel that whatever virtue this new movement has lies in the necessity the painter (and the writer, too) is under, to use material which is really a part of himself. However, many New York artists and writers are more familiar, through strong childhood impressions, with village and country life than with their adopted urban environment; and for them a back-to-the-village movement is entirely feasible and defensible. But a cult or a fad for Midwestern materials is just what must be avoided. Regionalism has already suffered from a kind of cultism which is essentially false.

I think the alarming nature of the depression and the general economic unrest have had much to do in producing this wistful nostalgia for the Midwest to which I have referred. This region has always stood as the great conservative section of the country. Now, during boom times conservatism is a thing to be ridiculed, but under unsettled conditions it becomes a virtue. To the East, which is not in a position to produce its own food, the Middle West today looks a haven of security. This is, of course, the basis for the various projects for the return of urban populations to the land; but it is an economic condition not without implications for art. The talented youths who, in the expansive era of unlimited prosperity, were carried away on waves of enthusiasm for projects of various sorts, wanting nothing so much as to get away from the old things of home, now, when it all collapses, come back solidly to the good earth.

But those of us who have never deserted our own regions for long find them not so much havens of refuge, as continuing friendly, homely environments.

As for my own region—the great farming section of the Middle West—I find it, quite contrary to the prevailing Eastern impression, not a drab country inhabited by peasants, but a various, rich land abounding in painting material. It does not, however, furnish scenes of the picture-postcard type that one too often finds in New Mexico or further West, and sometimes in New England. Its material seems to me to be more sincere and honest, and to gain in depth by having to be hunted for. It is the result of analysis, and therefore is less obscured by "picturesque" surface quality. I find myself becoming rather bored by quaintness. I lose patience with the thinness of things viewed from outside, or from a height. Of course, my feeling for the genuineness of this Iowa scene is doubtless rooted in the fact that I was born here and have lived here most of my life. I shall not quarrel with the painter from New Mexico, from further West, or from quaint New England, if he differs with me; for if he does so honestly, he doubtless has the same basic feeling for his material that I have for mine—he believes in its genuineness. After all, all I contend for is the sincere use of native material by the artist who has command of it.

Central and dominant in our Midwestern scene is the farmer. The depression, with its farm strikes and the heroic attempts of Government to find solutions for agrarian difficulties, has emphasized for us all the fact that the farmer is basic in the economics of the country —and, further, that he is a human being. The farm strikes, strangely enough, caused little disturbance to the people of the Middle West who were not directly concerned in them; but they did cause both surprise and consternation in the East, far away as it is from the source of supplies. Indeed, the farm strikes did much to establish the Midwestern farmer in the Eastern estimation as a man, functioning as an individual capable of thinking and feeling, and not an oaf.

Midwestern farmers are not of peasant stock. There is much variety in their ancestry, of course; but the Iowa farmer as I know him is fully as American as Boston, and has the great advantage of being farther away from European influence. He knows little of life in crowded cities, and would find such intimacies uncomfortable; it is with difficulty that he reconciles himself even to village life. He is on a little unit of his own, where he develops an extraordinary independence. The economics, geography, and psychology of his situation have always accented his comparative isolation. The farmer's reactions must be toward weather, tools, beasts, and plants to a far greater extent than those of city dwellers, and toward other human beings far less: this makes him not an egoist by any means, but (something quite different) a less socialized being than the average American. The term "rugged individualism" has been seized upon as a political catchword, but it suits the farmer's character very well.

Of course, the automobile and the radio have worked some change in the situation; but they have not altered the farmer's essential character in this generation, whatever they may do in the next. More important so far as change is concerned have been recent economic conditions, including the foreclosing of mortgages; and these factors, threatening the farmer's traditional position as a self-supporting individual, threatening even a reduction to a kind of American peasantry, brought on the violent uprisings of the farm strikes and other protests.

The farmer is not articulate. Self-expression through literature and art belong not to the set of relationships with which he is familiar (those with weather, tools, and growing things), but to more socialized systems. He is almost wholly preoccupied with his struggle against the elements, with the fundamental things of life, so that he has no time for Wertherism or for the subtleties of interpretation. Moreover, the farmers that I know (chiefly of New England stock) seem to me to have something of that old Anglo-Saxon reserve which made our ancient forebears to look upon much talk about oneself as a childish weakness. Finally, ridicule by city folks with European ideas of the farmer as a peasant, or, as our American slang has it, a "hick," has caused a further withdrawal—a proud and disdainful answer to misunderstanding criticism.

But the very fact that the farmer is not himself vocal makes him the richest kind of material for the writer and the artist. He needs interpretation. Serious, sympathetic handling of farmer-material offers a great field for the careful worker. The life of the farmer, engaged in a constant conflict with natural forces, is essentially dramatic. The drouth of last Summer provided innumerable episodes of the most gripping human interest. The nomadic movements of cattlemen in Wisconsin, in South Dakota, and in other states, the great dust storms, the floods following drouth, the milk strikes, the violent protests against foreclosures, the struggle against dry-year pests, the sacrifices forced upon once prosperous families—all these elements and many more are colorful, significant, and intensely dramatic.

It is a conflict quite as exciting as that of the fisherman with the sea. I have been interested to find in the little town of Waubeek, near my home, farmer-descendants of the folk of New England fishing villages. Waubeek has not changed or grown much since it was originally settled, because it was missed by the railroads and by the paved highways. The people of this community have kept as family heirlooms some of the old whaling harpoons, anchors, and so on which connect them with the struggle which their ancestors waged with the sea. But their own energies are transferred to another contest, and their crops come not out of the water but out of the land. I feel that the drama and color of the old fishing villages have become hackneyed and relatively unprofitable, while little has been done, in painting at least, with the fine materials that are inherent in farming in the great region of the Mid-American States.

My friend and fellow-townsman Jay Sigmund devotes his leisure hours to the writing of verse celebrating the kind of human beings I have been discussing. He is as much at home in Waubeek—perhaps more so—as in the office of his insurance company. I wish to quote a poem of his in this place.

VISITOR

I knew he held the tang of stack and mow—
    One sensed that he was brother to the soil;
    His palms were stained with signs of stable toil
And calloused by the handles of the plow.

Yet I felt bound to him by many ties:
    I knew the countryside where he was born;
    I'd seen its hillsides green with rows of corn,
And now I saw its meadows in his eyes.

For he had kept deep-rooted in the clay,
    While I had chosen market-place and street;
    I knew the city's bricks would bruise his feet
And send him soon to go his plodding way.

But he had sought me out to grip my hand
    And sit for one short hour by my chair.
    Our talk was of the things that happen where
The souls of men have kinship with the land.

I asked him of the orchard and the grove,
    About the bayou with its reedy shore,
    About the grey one in the village store
Who used to doze beside a ruddy stove.

He told me how the creek had changed its bed,
  And how his acres spread across the hill;
  The hour wore on and he was talking still,
And I was hungry for the things he said.

Then I who long had pitied peasant folk
  And broken faith with field and pasture ground
  Felt dull and leaden-footed in my round,
And strangely like a cart-beast with a yoke!

There is, of course, no ownership in artistic subject matter except that which is validated by the artist's own complete apprehension and understanding of the materials. By virtue of such validation, however, the farm and village matter of a given region would seem peculiarly to belong to its own regional painters. This brings up the whole of the ancient moot question of regionalism in literature and in art.

Occasionally I have been accused of being a flag-waver for my own part of the country. I do believe in the Middle West—in its people and in its art, and in the future of both—and this with no derogation to other sections. I believe in the Middle West in spite of abundant knowledge of its faults. Your true regionalist is not a mere eulogist; he may even be a severe critic. I believe in the regional movement in art and letters (comparatively new in the former though old enough in the latter); but I wish to place no narrow interpretation on such regionalism. There is, or at least there need be, no geography of the art mind or of artistic talent or appreciation. But painting and sculpture do not raise up a public as easily as literature, and not until the break-up caused by the Great Depression has there really been an opportunity to demonstrate the artistic potentialities of what some of our Eastern city friends call "the provinces."

Let me try to state the basic idea of the regional movement. Each section has a personality of its own, in physiography, industry, psychology. Thinking painters and writers who have passed their formative years in these regions, will, by care-taking analysis, work out and interpret in their productions these varying personalities. When the different regions develop characteristics of their own, they will come into competition with each other; and out of this competition a rich American culture will grow. It was in some such manner that Gothic architecture grew out of competition between different French towns as to which could build the largest and finest cathedrals. And indeed the French Government has sponsored a somewhat similar kind of competition ever since Napoleon's time.

The germ of such a system for the United States is to be found in the art work recently conducted under the PWA. This was set up by geographical divisions, and it produced remarkable results in the brief space of time in which it was in operation. I should like to see such encouragement to art work continued and expanded. The Federal Government should establish regional schools for art instruction to specially gifted students in connection with universities or other centers of culture in the various sections.

In suggesting that these schools should be allied with the universities, I do not mean to commit them to pedantic or even strictly academic requirements. But I do believe that the general liberal arts culture is highly desirable in a painter's training. The artist must know more today than he had to know in former years. My own art students, for example, get a general course in natural science—not with any idea of their specializing in biology or physics, but because they need to know what is going on in the modern world. The main thing is to teach students to think, and if they can to feel. Technical expression, though important, is secondary; it will follow in due time, according to the needs of each student. Because of this necessity of training in the liberal arts, the Government art schools should be placed at educational centers.

The annual exhibits of the work of schools of this character would arouse general interest and greatly enlarge our American art public. A local pride would be excited that might rival that which even hard-headed business men feel for home football teams and such enterprises. There is nothing ridiculous about such support; it would be only a by-product of a form of public art education which, when extended over a long period of time, would make us a great art-loving nation.

Mural painting is obviously well adapted to Governmental projects, and it is also highly suitable for regional expression. It enables students to work in groups, to develop original ideas under proper guidance, and to work with a very definite purpose. I am far from commending all the painting that has gone onto walls in the past year or two, for I realize there has not been much success in finding a style well suited to the steel-construction building; but these things will come, and there is sure to be a wonderful development in mural painting within the next few years. In it I hope that art students working with Government aid may play a large part. My students at the State University of Iowa hope to decorate the entire University Theatre, when the building is finished, in true fresco; and there is to be regional competition for the murals and sculpture in three new Iowa postoffices— at Dubuque, Ames, and Independence.

I am willing to go so far as to say that I believe the hope of a native American art lies in the development of regional art centers and the competition between them. It seems the one way to the building up of an honestly art-conscious America.

It should not be forgotten that regional literature also might well be encouraged by Government aid. Such "little" magazines as Iowa's "Midland" (now unfortunately suspended), Nebraska's "Prairie Schooner," Oklahoma's "Space," Montana's "Frontier" might well be subsidized so that they could pay their contributors. A board could be set up which could erect standards and allocate subsidies which would go far toward counteracting the highly commercialized tendencies of the great eastern magazines.

But whatever may be the future course of regional competitions, the fact of the revolt against the city is undeniable. Perhaps but few would concur with Thomas Jefferson's characterization of cities as "ulcers on the body politic"; but, for the moment at least, much of their lure is gone. Is this only a passing phase of abnormal times? Having at heart a deep desire for a widely diffused love for art among our whole people, I can only hope that the next few years may see a growth of non-urban and regional activity in the arts and letters.

Dusk over Wisconsin

by AUGUST DERLETH. *Although better known for his fiction Derleth has also published a considerable amount of poetry, the best of which appears in his Selected Poems (1944). "Dusk over Wisconsin," a nostalgic sketch of the poet's native state, reveals his blending of history and environment.*

Wisconsin is still a young man with names remembered.

He can think of Black Hawk and Red Bird and Yellow Thunder,
and he can think how slowly years turn past things under.

Hearing the long cry of locomotives in the night and motors humming
    in the air,
he can remember how canoes came down his waters,
    and how the rafts, and how the river boats went up and down.
And he can think of ox-carts trailing into valleys from the hills.
Every spring and every summer he can hear the whippoorwills

singing in the early evening, and in this nostalgic sound
he can tell himself again a round
of memories:

    legend-tired Frontenac, wanting knowledge
  of the stream called Father of Waters:
John Jacob Astor and the outposts of his fur empire:
imprisoned Black Hawk sick with longing for his hills and prairies, for
  his dying sons and daughters:
Senator La Follette fighting lumber kings and railroad kings, all
  despoilers of his land with his death-bound fire . . .
Wisconsin is still a young man with centuries remembered.

Carver and Marquette and Joliet
drowsing down his yesterday:
Dewey and La Follette scarcely gone,
Schurz and Garland fingering his dawn.

Still a young man sprawled in the deep grass of a summer afternoon,
remembering how Sacs and Foxes, and how Chippewas fell back, and
  how soon
the forests came to end, dreaming memoried footfalls soft against un-
  quiet earth:
Quebec and New Orleans, and Pere Marquette seeing in a dawn, how
  the Ouisconsin gave birth
to that elder stream, proud Black Hawk fronting General Street on
  the Prairie of the Dog: "I am Black Hawk of the Sacs, surrendering."

    Wisconsin is a young man knowing kinship
  with the whickering hawk above, as on a stair—
but restless, restless, nostrils distended to the change,
  knowing some time night comes where hangs at thickening
  twilight, sharpened air.

Lincoln

by HENRY A. WALLACE, 1888– . *Grandson and son of distin-
guished agricultural writers and economists, Henry Wallace was born in
Adair County, Iowa, and was graduated from Iowa State College, B.S., 1910.
From 1910 to 1929 he was associate editor and editor of Wallaces' Farmer*

and from 1929 to 1933 he edited its successor, Iowa Homestead and Wallaces' Farmer. From 1933 to 1940 Wallace was secretary of agriculture in the cabinet of Franklin D. Roosevelt, and in 1940 was elected vice-president of the United States. He failed to win renomination to his office in 1944, but shortly after President Roosevelt was inaugurated for a fourth term in 1945 he appointed Wallace secretary of commerce. Despite his absorption in national politics Wallace has spoken and written extensively on economic and agricultural topics. His work has been collected under such various titles as New Frontiers (1934), Paths to Plenty (1938), The American Choice (1940), Democracy Reborn (1944). Wallace's writing is notable for conciseness, simplicity, and a vigorous candor. These qualities are especially apparent in the tribute to Lincoln which was delivered at Springfield, Illinois, February 12, 1944.

Uɴᴛɪʟ the end of time men will come here to Springfield to pay tribute to the memory of Abraham Lincoln. He who speaks here should speak from his heart, and briefly.

Every schoolboy, every American and all lovers of freedom everywhere know the Lincoln story. He was born poor, he united a nation torn asunder and he freed men. Lincoln was a man of faith who looked beyond private sorrow and public woe. His name and his deeds will live forever.

Within a few months after Abraham Lincoln became President we were engaged in a terrible war which was not won until a few days before his tragic death. It was not an easy war to win. The opposing armies in the field were strong. Those who gave lip service to the United States but who found fault with everything he said and did were powerful. Influential newspapers continually and severely criticized him. At one time, only a few months before he was renominated for President, he had only one supporter in Congress. This great man who spoke truly when he said, "I have never willingly planted a thorn in any man's bosom," was misrepresented and maligned by swarms of little men. Lincoln, nevertheless, bent his great energies to winning the war and planning for the peace. He was struck down while the people of the United States, North and South, were celebrating the return of peace.

We meet tonight in the midst of another great war. Ten million American fighting men are engaged in work as important as any which has ever been done on this earth. As soon as this war has been won, the soldiers and the workers in war plants will be ready to make peacetime goods. There must be jobs for all willing workers. We have come out of the dark cellars of unemployment and doles, and we must never go back. The people have a right to ask, "Why can we not work and get enough to eat and wear in peace as we have in war?"

The answer is, "We can and we must!" With full employment the people of the United States can have the things they have always wanted—homes, schools, household furnishings and time to spend with their children.

Those who are blinded by fear say that we must go back to the old days—the days of hunger and despair. We must not heed them. They are not of the stature to which Lincoln grew.

The future calls for faith and work—faith and intelligent planning. Peace, goodwill, jobs, health and family security are possible and obtainable, and should become the tools of man's march toward the fuller and richer life. If Lincoln were here today he would concern himself with striving for a better tomorrow.

Shortsighted, fearful people in Lincoln's day said that we could never recover from the wreckage of the Civil War. Lincoln himself looked ahead with hope and confidence. He planned for new frontiers —for the West that was to be. The American enterprise and the American government of 1864 knew that the men who returned to civilian life needed work to do. The jobs that were provided by the building of the West saved us from chaos after the Civil War.

This experience of our grandfathers is a lamp for our feet.

Who does not wish to see swamps drained, harbors deepened, dams built, soil saved, inventions encouraged and new and better goods for use and comfort provided for men everywhere? The man who cannot see, the man who fears and waits, is not of the material of which Lincoln was made. Rather he is like the Copperheads whom Lincoln fought—those who wanted peace at the price of a divided nation. Those who seek a people's peace have the right to see through the eyes of Lincoln, and our duty is continually to work with vigilance always against the national and international carpetbaggers who would starve and enslave the world.

Lincoln said, "Trust the common people." He believed in their common sense and in their ultimate unselfishness. Today, while democracy is menaced abroad and while American Fascists are endeavoring to enslave us here, the words and deeds and inspiration of Lincoln give strength to those who battle in the cause of the people.

So long as there is human need in the United States it is criminal for men to be idle. It is bad business and bad morals to allow believers in scarcity to hold down production while people need goods and men are out of work. The people of America are our most valuable possession. The poorest people of America are our most valuable, untapped market. Men are more important than dollars. Abraham Lincoln believed this. Shortly before he became President he said that he was both for the man and for the dollar, but in case of conflict he was for the man before the dollar. He believed and died believing that the rights of man were more precious than the rights of private property.

Those who fight for us in this war belong to many parties, many creeds and many races. This is a people's war. The peace must be a people's peace. Lincoln would have it so. We shall fight unceasingly against anyone who puts the dollar above the man. We shall win the people's peace.

America Remembers

by PAUL ENGLE, 1908–   . *A native of Cedar Rapids, Iowa, Engle was educated at Coe College, B.A., 1931, and at the University of Iowa, M.A., 1932. From 1936 to 1939 he was a Rhodes scholar at Merton College, Oxford. Subsequently he was appointed lecturer on poetry at the University of Iowa. Engle has published several books of poems, chief of which are American Song (1934), Break the Heart's Anger (1936), and Corn (1939). He has also written one novel, Always the Land (1941). His poetry reveals a mastery of various rhythms and forms together with a warm feeling for the characters, the history, and the countryside of his native Iowa. "America Remembers," which was awarded the Century of Progress Prize offered by Poetry: A Magazine of Verse for a poem to celebrate the achievements of the twentieth century, is taken from American Song.*

HERE by this midland lake, the sand-shored water
That pulses with no sea-tide heart, where the grain
Of a nation pauses on its golden way
To the world's belly, and the long trains plunge—
From the honey-hearted South (*O go down, Moses*),
From the land of the shining mountains, the cloud-high
West where the Indian god and the Indian ghost
Ride down the Montana wind, from the England-feigning
States beating back the Atlantic-traveled
Surf, from the winter-flinging North, the maple
Leaf land—here at the prairie's edge, that
Mocker of oceans in the wide earth, where they raise
These buildings shaped with light to mark my living
Briefly in this place, by the Michigan curve
(*O Dearborn cabins, the heart-cringing cry, the hair*

Ripped from the skull, the child brained on the wall—
Now the blue iris bloom in the spring from the rich earth);
                                   Here I remember the strange
Way I have had in this land, the incredible
Trail I have followed to this sun-bright morning
By the lake bend. I remember the continent
Wheeling to the sun when by day its sounds were calm
Sounds—the wild elk calling in the windy hills,
Song of the spirit-painted arrow, the partridge
Drum on the hollow log, the reverent prayer
Of the lonely Huron paddler to the water;
By night the silence of a land asleep, only
The unimaginable cry of earth
Working its ancient states of being, the crash
Of rain-corroded stone, the delicate shudder
Of leaves, the crumble of root-split sand, the river's
Multitude of muted voices murmuring.
                                   I remember men, callers
To gods in the gusty rain, to the thunder birds,
Chippers of flint, scratchers of soil thinly
(Now has the earth been torn with the anvil-hammered
Plough deeply for our hunger, and the black shaft sunk).
The trail through the hills was moccasin wide and a stone
Twisted it, the rivers were swum. *(What of this*
Concrete trampling the wild arum, the arched bridge?)
The continent lived in its own and eternal way
Dreamless of change.
                                   I remember the sea-defying
Ships that came from the East with the life-fulfilling
Sun, the scooped earth and the blood-crying sword lifted
To heaven, the god pledged, and after, the heel
Print in the sand was a brief thing.
                                   I remember the first-coming men
With the English voices crying the harsh praise
Of a stern and awful god; the rotten fish
In the corn hill, the half-chinked cabin, the secret dead
In the first winter, the women wailing the abandoned
Home over the cold ocean, the little children
Who could not lie in the family burial lot
With their grandfathers, but had to bear a grave
In a new and lonely earth. *(It was a strange thing*
When the first white men took their Christian hearts
Under the pagan land—Did the haunting spirits

Of red braves who had peopled their hills with gods
Shaped in their own image, who could not see
The hallowed bones of their ancestral dead
Crushed by the plough, rise up and drive the pale
Ghosts howling back across the sea to wander
The mountainous winds of the world, with neither
The old home nor the new to shelter them?) And always
The great hand of memory gripping the heart. In the North
The fur-searching French, the Jesuit priest
With no warmth from the skin-splitting cold but the hard flame
Of a close and living God:

                    (*"My Reverend Father,*
The peace of Christ be with you. From Tadoussac
In this barbarous land I write you. Our life
Is a long and slow martyrdom, moose hair
Defiles our food, we wipe our hands on the hairy dogs.
I have baptized one, a scrofulous son of despairing parents,
Dying within the hour. I tell you we carry
Many crosses, our hands bleed, but we do not all die, Thanks be
    to God.")

             I remember Atlantic towns and striding
War, the dwindling army, and the English soul
Plunged seven years in flame and steel and become
The American soul—O strange, strong thing! And over
The land ranged the unique American dream
Of the common man and his right before all men
To shape his own peculiar single self
Tempered in the wild flame of beating out
On the huge anvil of the wilderness
A young and iron nation.

                 Land hunger drove them
West with the arc of the sun on the scant, blazed road
And the Boone way; the Wilderness Road through the Gap
To the Bloody Ground, and the salt licks, forever
Thrusting beyond the Appalachian valleys
The frail and fumbling fingers that would grow
To the brawny-fisted arms of empire. On
Into the prairie where the winds were lost
In the great stretches of the grass, and a man
Might dig into the hard mysterious deeps
Of his own soul and never reach the end
Till the pick shattered on the bedded rock
And the tired hands dropped.

                              Bracing themselves against
The Mississippi banks, they lunged unendingly
Up the Missouri and the Platte till the faint
Indian paths and the day-wide buffalo runs
Were crisscrossed and tramped out by wagon roads:
Oregon trail and the lonely mountain dying,
Santa Fé and the bones of the Spanish dream
That once had run across the land with laughter
And a sun-dark Southern body (*Coronado, sleep*),
The California and the waterless
Death of the desert mother where the sand
Sifted into the heart and the child cried
With swollen tongue, and the delirium
Came early with the morning sun—but beyond was gold
And the red flesh fought and rotted for that yellow
Softness beyond the stinking Humboldt Sink.

These were not heroes with the gods behind them
But humble people, clerks and farmers, merchants,
Soldiers and traders, foreign-speaking men,
Cobblers and carpenters, preachers, even, and tailors,
Many with wives and children, who, had they known
The actual danger, would have been content
To let the wild dream go, and let the West
Be their own familiar fields where sunset
Lingered an hour in twilight before it ran
The Juniata with bare feet and jumped the peaks.
These were simple folk, but chosen to prove again
That when a man and his destiny have met
In the high narrow place where there is room
For only one, man with a shout will rise
And laugh into the eager face of death
To loom an hour against the fires of fate
Somehow divine, but always with his feet
Touching the proud and certain earth.
                                        These were
Family affairs, with the kids, the treasured
Rose cuttings from back East, the horses named, the dog
Wise in the family ways, the longing for home
Where the soil was deep (*O bare New Hampshire fields*) and
   wind
Came a vast way to the little garden:
                        (*Virgin body
Of rich American earth, the silver stroking*

                                                      667

Of the smooth hands of ploughs mated you to those
Men, and the lusty seeds of the new corn struck
Their roots in Missouri River silt where the naked
Dakota squaws danced fertility in you
From the moonlight—are you not weary with long bearing
To so many strangely speaking sires?)

                                I remember
The bayberry candles, frail flicker in the wolf-howling
Night, the hearth swept with the turkey wing;
The council lodges shoved to the stony West
Where the Indian mind was split with the arrow-sharp
Hate, the too-tight-drawn bow snapped, the tribes
Gathered to the last riding, and Reno came.
The Yellowstone, the Platte, the Niobrara
(*Lovely, Greek-sounding name*), the mountain-coiling
Snake, were silvered with the horse-dashed spray. They met
There in the great eye-wearying West: Gall
Whose heart was bitter as his name, Chief Joseph,
Roman Nose, Sitting Bull, Black Kettle,
Proud chiefs, good horsemen, with the iron body and the iron
Will, pious before their own gods in their own way, hard
Fighters with the desperate home-defending courage.
The arrows sang their bitter songs, the feathers
Crimsoned in the stuck breast, the rifles
Shouted with brazen steel voices over the blood-thick
Whoop from the pierced throat, and the Indian women
Knew that the white faces were the Indian doom.
These proudest and most life-passionate men
Of all the American passage through the wide lands
Grubbed out their lives at the potato patch, although
The wind yet had certain words for them, and the chant
Was sung again in the mountain night. When their bones
Were buried with strange white prayers in the new
Government cemeteries on the sandy hills
Of the barren reservation fields where none
Of their kind had slept before (*Being brave men*
They were content to die, but sad not to rest
In the friendly graves of the tribal burying ground
Where the spirits of the place were known, and a man's
Horse was slain above him and his bow
Placed unstrung in his hand), a vital portion
Of the American soul forever passed away.

The cities came and the sun-following men

Struck the Pacific and the force of their traveling
Flung them back over the way they had come.
The North and the South brothers fought to declare
Whether there should be one power in the land or many;
The North won, bitterly, in the mightiest war
The world had seen, and the hurt and suffering parts
Were joined again to a whole, the outflung hands
Knew again the body that held them. And after
The shambling states with the red bandana tied
Loose at the throat and the pants pushed into the boot top
Became a nation and the world knew it.
                                                And all
The pulses of the earth were stirred by the pounding
Heart of America and poured their blood
Over the great sea arteries, finding
Sometimes a country like their own, the Finns
By the Minnesota lakes, the Germans over
The prairie farms of Iowa, the English
In the Berkshire hills and valleys. The Southern folk
Left the gay dances, the vineyards mellowed with sunlight
On the terraced hills, and as Wop and Dago joined
Polack and Bohunk in the towns of steel
Where the great fires burned their guts out—Bethlehem
(*O mockery of the little Christ-found village*), Gary,
Youngstown, the hard, trip-hammer-beaten names.
The ancient features of the type were changed
Under a different sun, in a clearer air
That entered the lungs like wine, the swarthy face
Paled, cheek bones lifted and narrowed, hair
Straightened and faded, and the body moved
With a lighter step, the toes springy, the eyes
Eager as a bird's, and every man
Had a coiled spring in his nerves that drove him
In a restless fury of life.
                        The bloods mingled
Madly, the red flame of the sons of men
Who had rowed Ulysses on the wine-dark sea
Burned in the pale blue eyes of the North, eyes hardened
With centuries of staring from Viking masts
Into the unknown oceans—Leif the Lucky
Once beached their dragon-headed prows on the bare
Coast of this land, the first white man. (*Who knows
What strange, multi-fathered child will come*

Out of the nervous travail of these bloods
To fashion in a new world continent
A newer breed of men?)
                    Money and noise
Came with the clang of steel day long, night long, the nervous
Body that could not sleep, but moaned and mumbled
From dawn to dawn, and would not quiet but screamed
Through the salary-earning day, through the night
Of the dinner-pail pause, shouting to make the useful
Thing, the device of comfort, and always, always
Make more, make more!—O cruel mechanic soul.
(*Great drummer, you have beat so long that barren*
Chant it has become your blood and heart
With a wild hypnosis that will never stop
Till the mad drum break and the dulled brain hear again
The simple sounds of earth.)
                        A new war ranged the world,
And the fatal Horsemen rode, their bloody hoofs
Beating even these Europe-fronting beaches,
And this destiny moved outward to the farthest
Of the man-living lands. But the American
Soul, that should have soared, flapped in the driving wind
That blew with the stench of sweat and oil and the fetid
Fat breath that cried for gold. The rational
Imagination brooding on the stuff of earth,
Lucid science like a living spirit
Shaping the crude ways of light, was held only
As the convenient author of our ease.
Eyes that watched their ships circle the ultimate
Oceans of earth could not see beyond
The diamonds flashing their hands. (*You gave us shoes*
For our feet, shirts for our backs, will you not give us
Power and peace for our hearts?)
                        The ships bring few now.
It is strange to be a land of no more coming, of no
Men turned to the sun-refuge West. In the New England
Villages the dead are a more populous city
Than the living—death has entered into the being
Of these states and will be with them forever
Making them dreamful of time.
                        Where shall they go
Now, the forever westward-wandering people?
They cannot be quiet, they cannot rest, they would not

Be American if they could do that. I tell them: You
Shall fit again the curved felloe, and with the bucket
Swinging under the wagon, the slouch-gaited hound
Following its restless shade patch, plunge
Into that vaster and more savage West,
The unfamiliar country of your heart.
With a new axe you shall build the clay-chinked cabin
On heights where the Sierras are as hills
And the heaven-harrying eagle hurls the wind,
Or in fire-running prairies where the autumn ducks
Shatter cold moonlight on a thousand lakes.
And wear the coonskin cap, jauntily if you will!
But when your fields bear greatly, the nearest neighbor
A hundred miles away confines you, your fences
Cut the horizon, the new house almost roofed,
Look one long evening down the cattle-trampled
Lane to the road where the last East-fleeing wagon's
Dust hangs in the air, and all the golden light
Of the westward-falling sun is a madman's song
As man-compelling as death—pack that night.
Let morning show the new shingles on the roof
Behind you, the hand-worn, finger-softened reins
Loose at the bit.
              Wander that land until your life has shaped
Over the last grave in the unmarked grass
A soul as splendid as your long going-up-and-down
In that land (*O England-forgetting, self-creating heart!*) so you
May shout out of dawn above the last night's fire
Before you swing again with the arc of the sun, a song
That will defy the little interval of man
In this American earth, so his memory in the world
Will last as long as light roams through the hollow
Ways of heaven. And at the weary evening camp, O thrust
Your hands to the waning sun, they will not crisp
But rather will hold the sun between their palms
Till they become eternal as its flame
And a perpetual light unto the face.

Then will be time for you to forge your own
Singular vision of eternity.
You, with behind you the American faith,
Shall find out, more profoundly now than ever
The thoughtful nations of the world have known,
The deep spirituality of man.

O remember
That in the general doom of nations, there
Is but one certain immortality
(*After the wind has ripped the last bright flag*
To bird-mocked tatters of despair, after
The muffled horns of fate have mumbled out
The last low taps, after an alien hand
Has ploughed the barley fields, an alien tongue
Cried in the streets), and that is not the thrust
Of courage against the world, nor the beating down
Of all the barriers of a continent
However bravely—but the searching out
Of the new way that a new country makes,
From all the blind impulses of its life,
A vision of the universal heart
That recreates the living form of man
In the unique and individual way
That is the shape and spirit of that land.
O let your eyes be subtle as a bird's
To glean in the harvest fields of history
The spilled-out grain of truth.
                              And while you front
Your fate between the ocean and the ocean
Let the American quality, the dream
Of a land where men shall work their destiny
Deeply as they will, give you the power
To realize with proud and reverent heart
The strange identity of man as man
And fling it up against the dark of time
Where it may loom forever as the bright
Image of godhead in the simple man
That now has risen from this American earth
And shall but with the bitter end of things
Go back again into the humble earth.
                              Here at the Windy City
Where the long trains whistle by the sun-loud lake
I shall remember these men in my land.

Acknowledgments and Index

DERLETH, AUGUST. "Buck in the Bottoms," reprinted from *Country Growth* by permission of Charles Scribner's Sons; "Dusk over Wisconsin," reprinted from *Selected Poems*, copyright 1938, 1944, by permission of the author. 291, 660

DOS PASSOS, JOHN. "The Bitter Drink" and "Tin Lizzie," reprinted from *The Big Money*, later included in *U.S.A.*, by permission of the author. 578, 587

DRAKE, BENJAMIN. "Putting a Black-Leg on Shore," reprinted from *Tales and Sketches from the Queen City*. 342

DUNNE, FINLEY PETER. "Mr. Dooley on Home Life," reprinted from *Mr. Dooley on Making a Will and Other Necessary Evils* by permission of Charles Scribner's Sons. 478

EGGLESTON, EDWARD. "Spelling Down the Master," reprinted from *The Hoosier Schoolmaster*. 176

ENGLE, PAUL. "America Remembers," reprinted from *American Song*, copyright 1933, 1934, by permission of Doubleday, Doran and Company. . 664

ESAREY, LOGAN. "Making a Home," reprinted from *The Indiana Home* by permission of Mrs. Logan Esarey and the publisher, R. E. Banta, Crawfordsville, Indiana. 601

FARRELL, JAMES T. "Precinct Captain," reprinted from *The Short Stories of James T. Farrell*, copyright 1937, by permission of the Vanguard Press. 490

FERBER, EDNA. "An Iowa Childhood," reprinted from *A Peculiar Treasure* by permission of the author. 428

FIELD, EUGENE. "Christian-County Mosquitoes," reprinted from *Culture's Garland*. 13

FLAGG, EDMUND. "Mamelle Prairie," reprinted from *The Far West*. . . 120

FLANDRAU, GRACE. "Fiesta in St. Paul," reprinted by permission of the editors of the *Yale Review*, copyright Yale University Press. 507

FLINT, TIMOTHY. "Early River Travel," reprinted from *Recollections of the Last Ten Years*. 127

FREMONT, JESSIE BENTON. "Old St. Louis," reprinted from *Souvenirs of My Time*. 451

GALLAGHER, WILLIAM D. "Progress in the Northwest," reprinted from the address *Facts and Conditions of Progress in the North West*. 595

GARLAND, HAMLIN. "Under the Lion's Paw," reprinted from *Main-Travelled Roads*, and "Color in the Wheat," reprinted from *Prairie Songs*, by permission of Isabel Garland Lord. 265, 290

GILFILLAN, ARCHER B. "Sheep Country," reprinted from *Sheep* by permission of Little, Brown and Company and the Atlantic Monthly Press. . . . 643

HALL, BAYNARD RUSH. "Travel in the Woods," reprinted from *The New Purchase*. 132

674

SMITTER, WESSEL. "F.O.B. Detroit," reprinted by permission of the editors of *Harper's Magazine* and Harper and Brothers. 513

SNELLING, WILLIAM JOSEPH. "Payton Skah," reprinted from *Tales of the Northwest* by permission of the University of Minnesota Press. 58

STEVENS, JAMES FLOYD. "The Black Duck Dinner," reprinted by permission of the author and the editors of the *American Mercury*. 18

STEWART, CHARLES D. "Belling a Fox" and "Old Times on the Missouri," reprinted from *Fellow Creatures* by permission of the author. . . 317, 373

SUCKOW, RUTH. "A Start in Life," reprinted from *Carry-Over*, copyright 1924, 1926, 1928, 1931, 1936, by Ruth Suckow, by permission of Farrar and Rinehart; "Iowa," copyright 1926, reprinted by permission of the author's agent, Ellan McIlvaine. 277, 609

TARKINGTON, BOOTH. "Major Amberson's Town," reprinted from *The Magnificent Ambersons*, copyright 1918 by Doubleday, Page and Company, by permission of Brandt and Brandt. 460

TURNER, FREDERICK JACKSON. "The Middle West," reprinted from *The Frontier in American History* by permission of Henry Holt and Company. 3

VAN ETTEN, WINIFRED. "The Judas Goose," reprinted by permission of the author and the editors of the *Atlantic Monthly*. 300

WALLACE, HENRY A. "Lincoln," a speech delivered at Springfield, Illinois, February 12, 1944, reprinted from *Democracy Reborn* by permission of Reynal and Hitchcock. 661

WATERLOO, STANLEY. "Growing Up with the Country," reprinted from *A Man and a Woman*. 262

WETMORE, ALPHONSO. "Biography of Blackbird," reprinted from *Gazetteer of the State of Missouri*. 52

WHITE, STEWART EDWARD. "The Drive," reprinted from *The Blazed Trail*, copyright 1902, 1930, by permission of Doubleday, Doran and Company. 219

WHITE, WILLIAM ALLEN. "Mary White," reprinted from *The Emporia Gazette* by permission of W. L. White. 569

WOOD, GRANT. "Revolt against the City," reprinted by permission of Frank Luther Mott. 648

WRIGHT, FRANK LLOYD. "Young Architect in Chicago," reprinted from *An Autobiography—Frank Lloyd Wright* by permission of Duell, Sloan and Pearce. 481